Chinese–English
Edition 汉英对照本

Editor–in–chief
Li Shaozhi, Tan Xiaohon
主编：李绍芝　谭晓红

Chinese Therapeutic Methods of Acupoints

Hunan Science & Technology Press

中国穴位疗法

湖南科学技术出版社

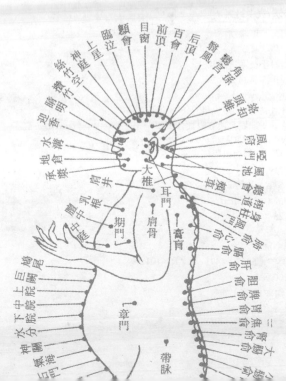

图书在版编目（ＣＩＰ）数据

中国穴位疗法 / 李绍芝，谭晓红编著. —2版. —长沙：湖南科学技术出版社，2005.12
ISBN 7-5357-4471-0

Ⅰ.中... Ⅱ.①李...②谭... Ⅲ.穴位疗法
Ⅳ.R245.9

中国版本图书馆CIP数据核字（2005）第148546号

Chinese Therapeutic Methods of Acupoints

中国穴位疗法（汉英对照本）

主　　编：李绍芝　谭晓红
责任编辑：汪　华　黄一九
出版发行：湖南科学技术出版社
社　　址：长沙市湘雅路 276 号
　　　　　http://www.hnstp.com
邮购联系：本社直销科　0731－4375808
印　　刷：湖南新华印刷集团有限责任公司
　　　　　（印装质量问题请直接与本厂联系）
厂　　址：湖南望城·湖南出版科技园
邮　　编：410219
出版日期：2006 年 1 月第 2 版第 2 次
开　　本：850mm×1168mm　1/32
印　　张：21.25
插　　页：4
字　　数：716 000
书　　号：ISBN 7－5357－4471－0／R·1012
定　　价：38.00 元

李绍芝 男，医学博士，获美国国家针灸、中药证书。2001 年开始任美国得克萨斯州中医学院教授；曾发表论文 54 篇，主编和参编著作 12 本；获湖南省科技成果奖 6 次；曾任湖南中医学院中医诊断实验室主任。1992～1995 年国家教委公派留美访问学者；1998～1999 年任湖南中医学院赴俄罗斯医疗队队长。

Li Shaozhi male, M.D., Ph.D., National Certificates of both Acupuncture and Chinese Herbology, professor of Texas College of Traditional Chinese Medicine since 2001, has had 54 papers and 12 books published, received 6 prizes given by Hunan Government for important scientific and technical achievement, was the director of Research Laboratory of Diagnostics of Hunan College of Traditional Chinese Medicine, studied in the United States as a visiting scholar send by the Chinese Government from 1992 to 1995, worked in Russia at the leader of the medical team sent by Hunan College of Traditional Chinese Medicine form 1998 to 1999.

谭晓红 女，获美国国家针灸、中药证书，中国针灸学会会员，1999 年开始任美国兰辛市 Jamieson 健康医疗中心针灸医师。曾发表学术论文 21 篇，参编著作 4 本，获湖南省科技成果奖 1 次；曾任湖南中医学院附属第一医院针灸科副教授。1998～1999 年为湖南中医学院委派的针灸专家在俄罗斯从事针灸临床工作。

Tan Xiaohong female, M.D., National Certificates of both Acupuncture and Chinese Herbology, member of all-China Acupuncture and Moxibustion, Acupuncturist of Dr. Jamieson Total Health Care Center at Lansing, Michigan since 1999, has published 21 papers and 4 books published, received 1 prize given by Hunan Government for important scientific and technical achievement, was associate professor, Department of Acupuncture, The first Affiliated Hospital of Hunan College of Traditional Chinese Medicine, worked in Russia at the medical specialist sent by Hunan College of Traditional Chinese Medicine form 1998 to 1999.

再版前言

穴位疗法源于中国民间，几千年来为中华民族的繁衍昌盛作出了巨大的贡献，受到了广大民众的厚爱。近来，随着中国传统医学的迅速发展，中外学术交流日益频繁，穴位疗法越来越受到了海外医学界的重视，成为世界医学的一个重要组成部分。为了促进中外学术交流，适应中医学不断发展的需要，我们编写了这本《中国穴位疗法》，忠诚希望能为弘扬民族精华作出应有的一点贡献。

作者积 20 余年教学、临床、科研工作和数年海外学习的经验，遵循理论与实际相结合的原则，精心选择临床行之有效、用之简便的穴位治疗方法。所选之法，多为亲验目睹。本着认真负责的态度，历经数载，几易其稿，而成此册。全书分为三章，第一章简介常用腧穴 400 多个，第二章收编各种穴位治疗方法 20 余种，第三章介绍百余种常见疾病的穴位疗法。力求文字简明扼要，通俗易懂，译文准确流畅，并配大量插图，以达到图文并茂之效果而便于自学。

《中国穴位疗法》自 1998 年第一次出版发行后，深受国内外读者的欢迎。此书出版后不久，作者便移居美国从事针灸、中药临床和教学工作，并以此书作为教材传授学业。现在我们将此书修订再版以满足世界各国读者的需要。

本书能为国内中医院校学生和临床医师学习中医专业英语和穴位治疗方法提供帮助和参考，同时也能成为海外读者学习中医和汉语的良师益友。由于作者的水平有限，错误之处敬请读者批评指正。

作者衷心感谢加拿大 Patrick Quon 先生和澳大利亚 Chris Lack 先生热情为本书的英文部分进行校对工作。

李绍芝

谭晓红

2005 年 9 月 29 日

Forword for reediting the book

Therapeutic method of acupoint originates from China. It has made a great contribution to the thriving and prosperity of the Chinese nation for several thousand years and has been greatly loved by people. In recent years, traditional Chinese medicine has attained a very high level of development and exchange of traditional Chinese medicine has accelerated. Forcign medical scholars have paid more and more attention to it. There is no doubt that therapeutic method of acupoint becomes an important component in world medicine. In order to improve academic ex change in medical science between China and foreign countries and meet with the ever-growing demand for traditional Chinese medicine, we wrote this book with hopes to make a contribution for carry forward the national essence.

The authors, with more than 20 year experience in their teaching, clinic, research and work in foreign countries, chose carefully effective and simple therapeutic methods of acupuncture according to the principle of the integration of theory and practice. Most of the chosen methods have been used or seen by the authors in the clinic. We spent several years to write this book and have revised the manuscript many times in light of conscientious attitude. The book is divided into three chapters. The first chapter introduces channels and collaterals and more than 400 commonly used acupoints including their locations, indications, and methods of needling. The second chapter describes more than 20 different therapeutic methods of acupuncture which are effective, simple, and safe. The third chapter introduces the treatment of more than 100 common diseases with therapeutic methods. The authors have strived to be concise and easy to understand in writing with correct and fluent English. The book is filled with illustrative pictures in order to be studied independently.

ı Chinese Therapeutic Methods of Acupoints has been welcome by the readers in both foreign countries and China since the publication of the first edition in 1998. Shortly after the book was published, the authors moved to United States to teach and practice acupuncture. The book has been used for acupuncture textbook there. It is necessary to reedit the book after 7 years in order to satisfy the demand of the readers in the world.

This book can provide assistance in the study of acupuncture English and therapeutic methods of acupuncture for students and doctors in China. It can also be good teacher and reliable friend for overseas student of traditional Chinese medicine and Chinese. We have tried our best in compiling this book, however, any comment or any suggestion for the further revision of this book would be very appreciated.

The authors are grateful to Mr. Patrick Quon from Canada and Mr. Chris Lack from Australia for their proofreading the English version.

Li Shaozhi
Tan Xiaohong
September 29, 2005

目　　录

第三章　常见病的治疗

Contents

Section 5 The Heart Channel of Hand-Shaoyin and Commonly Used Acupoints

Section 6 The Small Intestine Channel of Hand-Taiyang and Commonly Used Acupoints

Section 7 The Bladder

Contents

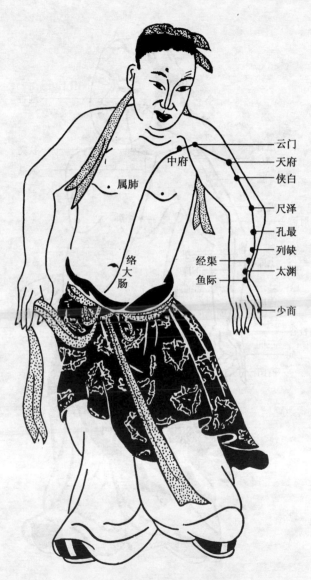

云门
天府
侠白
中府
尺泽
属肺
孔最
列缺
经渠
太渊
络大肠
鱼际
少商

中国古代经络图——手太阴肺经
Ancient Chinese Meridian Picture – The
Lung Meridian of Hand-Taiyin

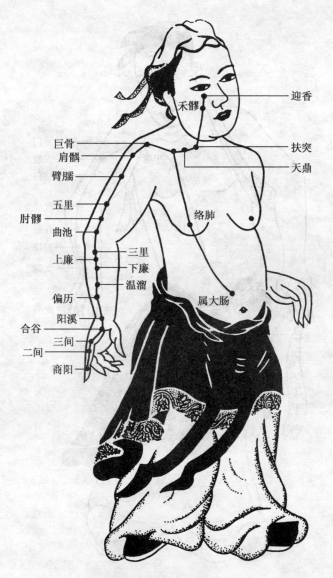

迎香

禾髎

巨骨
肩髃

臂臑

五里

肘髎

曲池

上廉

三里
下廉
温溜

偏历

阳溪

合谷

三间
二间

商阳

扶突
天鼎

络肺

属大肠

中国古代经络图——手阳明大肠经
Ancient Chinese Meridian Picture – The
Large Intestine Meridian of Hand-Yangming

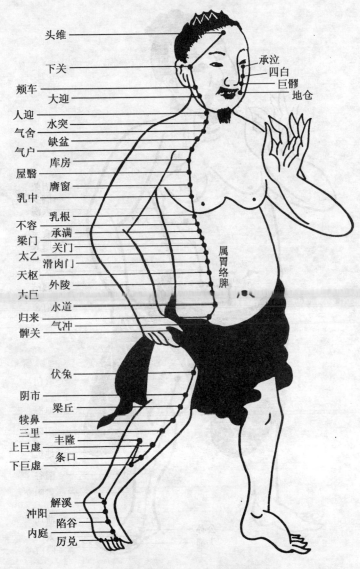

头维

承泣
四白
巨髎
地仓

下关

颊车　大迎

人迎
气舍
气户
屋翳
乳中

水突
缺盆
库房
膺窗
乳根

不容
梁门
太乙
天枢
大巨

承满
关门
滑肉门
外陵
水道
气冲

属胃络脾

归来
髀关

伏兔

阴市
梁丘

犊鼻
三里
上巨虚
下巨虚

丰隆
条口

解溪

冲阳
陷谷
内庭

厉兑

中国古代经络图——足阳明胃经

Ancient Chinese Meridian Picture – The
Stomach Meridian of Foot-Yangming

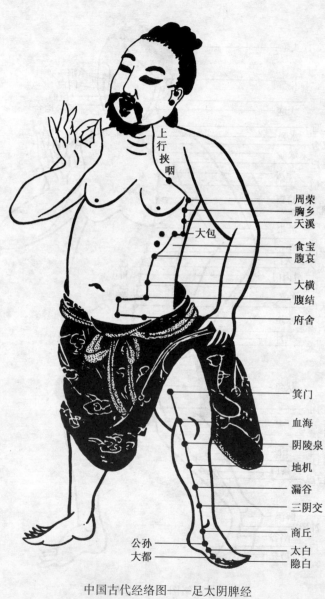

上行挟咽

周荣
胸乡
天溪
大包
食宝
腹哀
大横
腹结
府舍

箕门
血海
阴陵泉
地机
漏谷
三阴交
商丘
公孙
大都
太白
隐白

中国古代经络图——足太阴脾经
Ancient Chinese Meridian Picture – The
Spleen Meridian of Foot-Taiyin

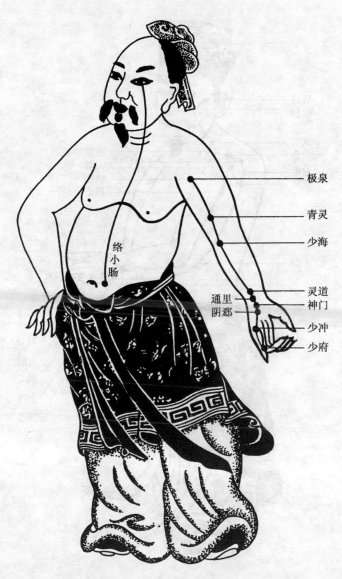

极泉

青灵

少海

络
小肠

灵道
通里
神门
阴郄
少冲
少府

中国古代经络图——手少阴心经
Ancient Chinese Meridian Picture – The
Heart Meridian of Hand-Shaoyin

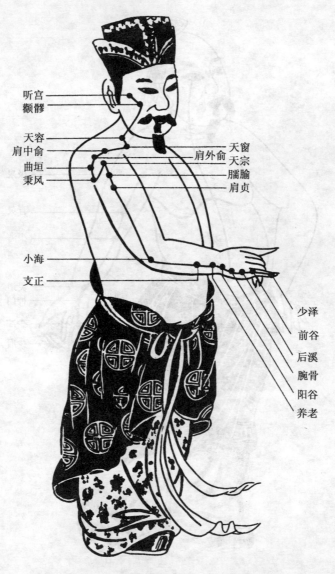

听宫
颧髎

天容
肩中俞
曲垣
秉风

天窗
肩外俞
天宗
臑腧
肩贞

小海
支正

少泽
前谷
后溪
腕骨
阳谷
养老

中国古代经络图——手太阳小肠经
Ancient Chinese Meridian Picture – The
Small Intestine Meridian of Hand-Taiyang

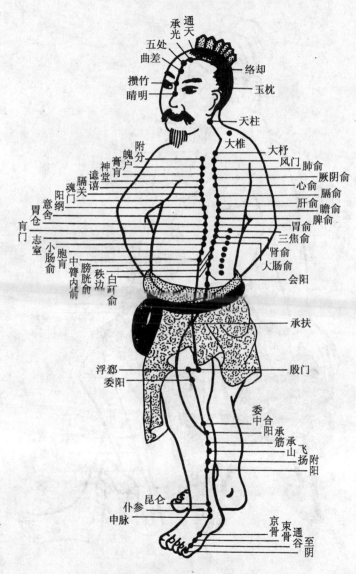

中国古代经络图——足太阳膀胱经

Ancient Chinese Meridian Picture–The

Bladder Meridian of Foot-Taiyang

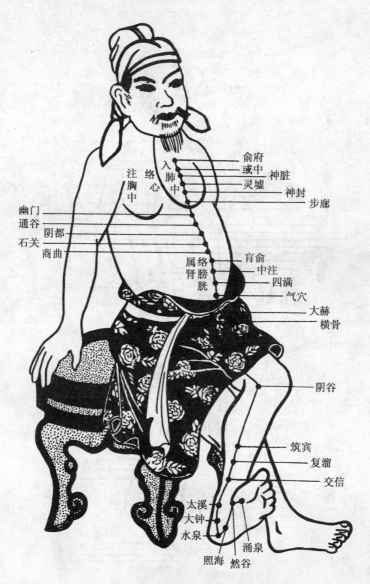

俞府
或中　神脏
灵墟　神封
　　　步廊

注胸中　络心　入肺中

幽门
通谷　阴都
石关　商曲

属肾　络膀胱

肓俞
中注
四满
气穴
大赫
横骨

阴谷

筑宾
复溜
交信

太溪
大钟
水泉
照海　然谷　涌泉

中国古代经络图——足少阴肾经
Ancient Chinese Meridian Picture – The
Kidney Meridian of Foot-Shaoyin

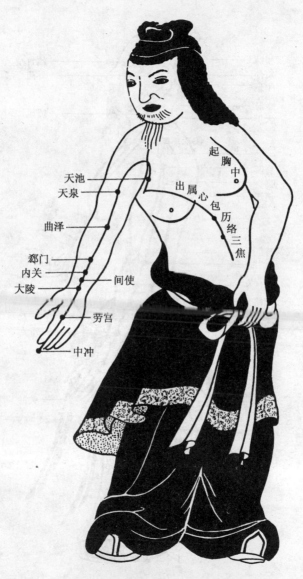

天池
天泉

曲泽

郄门
内关
大陵

间使

劳宫

中冲

起胸中
出属心包
历络三焦

中国古代经络图——手厥阴心包经

Ancient Chinese Meridian Picture – The
Pericardium Meridian of Hand-Jueyin

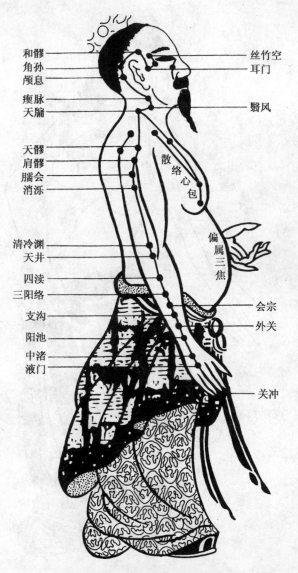

和髎
角孙
颅息
瘈脉
天牖

天髎
肩髎
臑会
消泺

清冷渊
天井

四渎
三阳络

支沟

阳池

中渚
液门

丝竹空
耳门

翳风

散络心包

偏属三焦

会宗

外关

关冲

中国古代经络图——手少阳三焦经
Ancient Chinese Meridian Picture－The
Sanjiao Meridian of Hand-Shaoyang

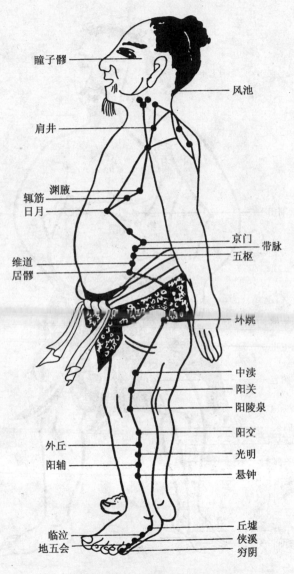

瞳子髎

风池

肩井

渊腋
辄筋
日月

京门　带脉
五枢

维道
居髎

环跳

中渎
阳关
阳陵泉

阳交
光明
悬钟

外丘
阳辅

丘墟
侠溪
窍阴

临泣
地五会

中国古代经络图——足少阳胆经
Ancient Chinese Meridian Picture - The
Gallbladder Meridian of Foot-Shaoyang

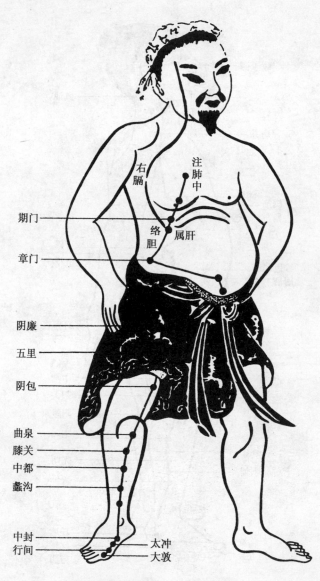

期门

章门

阴廉

五里

阴包

曲泉
膝关
中都
蠡沟

中封
行间

右膈

注肺中

络胆　属肝

太冲
大敦

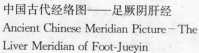

中国古代经络图——足厥阴肝经
Ancient Chinese Meridian Picture－The
Liver Meridian of Foot-Jueyin

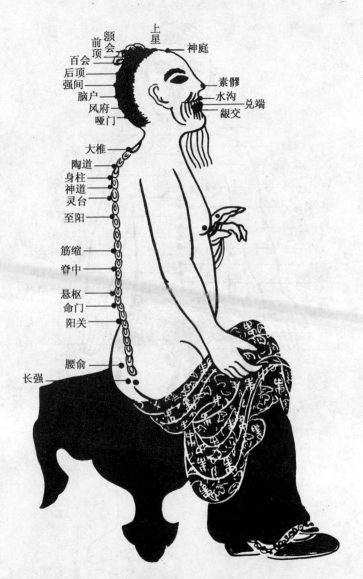

颐会 上星
前顶 神庭
百会
后顶 素髎
强间 水沟
脑户 兑端
风府 龈交
哑门

大椎
陶道
身柱
神道
灵台
至阳

筋缩
脊中

悬枢
命门
阳关

腰俞
长强

中国古代经络图——督脉

Ancient Chinese Meridian Picture－The
Du Meridian

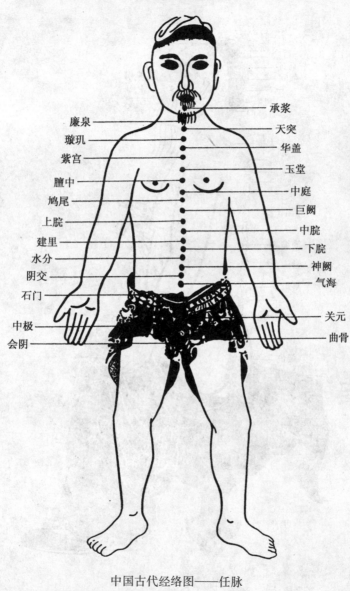

廉泉
璇玑
紫宫
膻中
鸠尾
上脘
建里
水分
阴交
石门
中极
会阴

承浆
天突
华盖
玉堂
中庭
巨阙
中脘
下脘
神阙
气海
关元
曲骨

中国古代经络图——任脉

Ancient Chinese Meridian Picture – The
Ren Meridian

第一章　经络与腧穴

Chapter One　　The Channels，Collaterals and Acupoints

第一节　手太阴肺经及其常用腧穴

Section 1 The Lung Channel of Hand-Taiyin and Commonly Used Acupoints

1．经脉循行

①起于中焦，向下联络大肠；②回过来沿胃上口，③通过横膈；④属肺；⑤从肺与喉咙联系处横行而出；⑥沿上臂内侧桡侧缘下行；⑦至肘中；⑧沿前臂内侧桡侧缘下行；⑨入寸口（太渊穴）；⑩经鱼际；⑪沿鱼际边缘；⑫到达拇指桡侧端；⑬其支脉从列缺分出；经手背到达示指桡侧末端（图1－1）。

1. The Course of the Channel

①The Lung Channel of Hand-Taiyin originates from the Middle Jiao and runs downwards to connect with the large intestine. ②Turning back, it runs along the cardiac orifice. ③ Passing through the diaphragm, ④it enters its pertaining organ, the lung. ⑤ From the portion connecting the trachea with the larynx, it comes out transversely. ⑥Descending along the radial border of the medial aspect of the upper arm, ⑦ it reaches the cubital fossa. ⑧Then it goes continuously downwards along the anterior border of the radial side in the medial aspect of the forearm and⑨enters Cunkou（Taiyuan, LU 9）. ⑩ Passing through Yuji (LU 10), ⑪and going along the border of the thenar eminence, ⑫it ends at the radial side of the tip of the thumb. ⑬Its branch emerges from Lieque (LU 7) and runs along the dorsum of the hand onto the radial side of the tip of the index finger (Fig.1－1).

2．常用经穴主治提要

本经腧穴主治咳嗽、气喘、咳血、胸闷、胸痛、咽喉疼痛等胸、肺部病症以及本经经脉循行部位的病症。

2. Principal Indications of Commonly Used Acupoints of the Meridian

Diseases of the chest and lung such as cough, asthma, hemoptysis, oppressed sensation in the chest, chest pain, and sore throat diseases of the regions along the course of this channel.

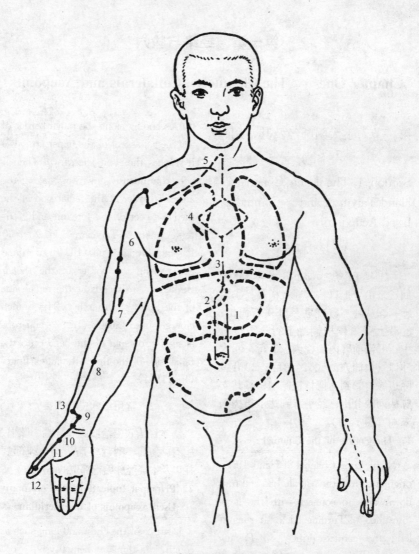

图 1－1　手太阴肺经循行示意图
Fig. 1－1　Running Course of the Lung Channel of Hand-Taiyin

3. 常用腧穴（图 1－2）

3. The Commonly Used Acupoints
（Fig. 1－2）

| 中 府 |

定位 胸前壁外上方，距正中线旁开6寸，第一肋间隙中。

主治 咳嗽，气喘，胸背痛，肺胀满，咽喉肿痛。

操作 向外斜刺或平刺0.5～0.8寸，不可向内斜刺，以免伤肺。可灸。

| **Zhongfu（LU 1）** |

Location: On the lateral and superior side of the chest, six cun lateral to the midline of the chest, at the level of the first intercostal space.

Indications: Cough, asthma, pain in the chest and back, distension and fullness in the chest, sore throat.

Method: Puncture obliquely or subcutaneously 0.5～0.8 cun toward the lateral aspect of the chest. It is forbidden to puncture obliquely toward the interior aspect of the chest, otherwise the lung may be injured. Moxibustion is applicable.

| 云 门 |

定位 胸前壁外上方，前正中线旁开6寸，锁骨外端下缘凹陷中。

主治 咳嗽，气喘，胸痛，肩痛。

操作 向外斜刺0.5～0.8寸。可灸。

| **Yunmen（LU 2）** |

Location: On the lateral and superior side of the chest, superior to the coracoid process of the scapula, in the depression at the infraclavicular fossa, 6 cun lateral to the midline.

Indications: Cough, asthma, pain in the chest, pain in the shoulder.

Method: Puncture obliquely 0.5～0.8 cun towards the lateral aspect of the chest. Moxibustion is applicable.

| 天 府 |

定位 腋前皱襞纹头下3寸，肱二头肌桡侧缘处。

主治 气喘，鼻衄，肩痛。

操作 直刺0.5～1寸。

| **Tianfu（LU 3）** |

Location: On the medial aspect of arm, 3 cun below the end of the axillary fold, on the radial side of the biceps muscle.

Indications: Asthma, nosebleed, pain in the upper arm.

Method: Puncture perpendicularly 0.5～1 cun. Moxibustion is applicable.

| 侠 白 |

定位 腋前皱襞纹头下4寸，肘横纹上5寸。

主治 咳嗽，气喘，烦满，肩痛。

操作 直刺0.5～1寸。可灸。

| **Xiabai（LU 4）** |

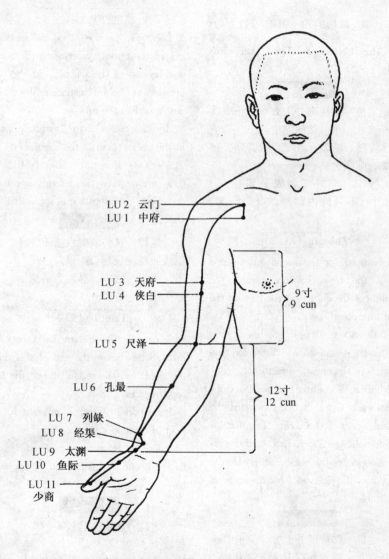

LU 2　云门
LU 1　中府

LU 3　天府
LU 4　侠白

9寸
9 cun

LU 5　尺泽

LU 6　孔最

12寸
12 cun

LU 7　列缺
LU 8　经渠
LU 9　太渊
LU 10　鱼际
LU 11
少商

图 1-2　手太阴肺经穴位图

Fig.1-2 Acupoints of the Lung Channel of Hand-Taiyin

Location: On medial aspect of arm, 4 cun below end of axillary fold, or 5 cun above cubital crease.

Indications: Cough, asthma, dry retching, vexation and fullness, pain in the upper arm.

Method: Puncture perpendicularly 0.5～1 cun. Moxibustion is applicable.

尺　泽

定位　肘横纹中，肱二头肌腱桡侧缘。

主治　咳嗽，咳血，潮热，咽喉肿痛，胸部胀满，肘臂挛痛。

操作　直刺 0.8　1.2 寸，或点刺出血。

Chize（LU 5）

Location: On the cubital crease, in the depression on the radial side of the tendon of the biceps muscle.

Indications: Cough, hemoptysis, hectic fever, sore throat, fullness in the chest, spasmodic pain of the elbow and arm.

Method: Puncture perpendicularly 0.8～1.2 cun, or prick with three-edged needle to cause bleeding. Moxibustion is applicable.

孔　最

定位　前臂掌侧，太渊与尺泽连线的中点，腕横纹上 7 寸处。

主治　咳嗽，气喘，咳血，咽喉肿痛，肘臂挛痛，痔疮。

操作　直刺 0.8～1 寸。可灸。

Kongzui（LU 6）

Location: On the palmar aspect of the forearm, on the line joining Taiyuan (LU 9) and Chize (LU 5), 7 cun above the transverse crease of the wrist.

Indications: Cough, asthma, hemoptysis, sore throat, spasmodic pain in the elbow and arm, and hemorrhoids.

Method: Puncture perpendicularly 0.5～1 cun. Moxibustion is applicable.

列　缺

定位　桡骨茎突上方，腕横纹上 1.5 寸，肱桡肌与拇长展肌腱之间。或者两手虎口交叉，腕关节伸直，一手示指压在另一手的桡骨茎突上，示指尖所达之凹陷处是穴。

主治　头痛，咳嗽，气喘，鼻塞，咽喉肿痛，牙痛，口眼喎斜。

操作　向上斜刺 0.5～0.8 寸。

Lieque（LU 7）

Location Superior to the styloid process of the radius, 1.5 cun above the transverse crease of the wrist, between the brachioradial muscle and the tendon of the long abductor muscle of the thumb. Or when the index fingers and thumbs of both hands are crossed with the wrist joint extended and index finger of one hand placed on the styloid process of the radius of the other, the acupoint is in the depression on the dorsum of the wrist under the tip of the index finger.

Indications: Headache, cough, stuffy nose, sore throat, asthma, toothache, deviation of the mouth and eye.

Method: Puncture 0.5 ~ 0.8 cun obliquely upward. Moxibustion is applicable.

经　渠

定位　前臂掌面桡侧，腕横纹上1寸，桡骨茎突与桡动脉之间的凹陷中。

主治　咳嗽，气喘，胸痛，咽喉肿痛，手腕疼痛。

操作　避开桡动脉，直刺0.3~0.5寸。

Jingqu（LU 8）

Location: On the radial side of the palmar, surface of the forearm, 1 cun above the transverse crease of the wrist, in the depression between the radial artery and the medial aspect of the styloid process of the radius.

Indications: Cough, asthma, pain in the chest, sore throat, pain in the wrist.

Method: Avoiding the radial artery, puncture perpendicularly 0.3~0.5 cun.

太　渊

定位　腕横纹桡侧端，桡动脉桡侧凹陷中。

主治　咳嗽，气喘，咳血，胸

痛，咽喉肿痛，腕臂疼痛，无脉症。

操作　避开桡动脉，直刺0.3~0.5寸。可灸。

Taiyuan（LU 9）

Location: On the radial end of the crease of the wrist, in the depression on the radial side of the radial artery.

Indications: Cough, asthma, hemoptysis, chest pain, sore throat, pain in the wrist and arm, pulselessness.

Method: Avoiding the radial artery, puncture perpendicularly 0.3 ~ 0.5 cun. Moxibustion is applicable.

鱼　际

定位　第1掌骨掌侧中点，赤白肉际处。

主治　咳嗽，咳血，咽喉肿痛，失音，发热。

操作　直刺0.5~0.8寸。可灸。

Yuji（LU 10）

Location: At the midpoint of the palmar side of the first metacarpal bone, at the junction of the red and white skin.

Indications: Cough, hemoptysis, sore throat, aphonia, fever.

Method: Puncture perpendicularly 0.5~0.8 cun. Moxibustion is applicable.

少　商

定位　拇指桡侧指甲角旁约0.1寸。

主治　咳嗽，咽喉肿痛，鼻衄，发热，昏迷，癫狂。

操作 直刺0.1寸或点刺出血。

Shaoshang（LU 11）

Location：On the radial side of the thumb, 0.1 cun posterior to the proximal corner of the nail.

Indications：Cough, sore throat, nosebleed, fever, coma, manic-depressive disorders.

Method：Puncture perpendicularly 0.1 cun, or prick the point to cause bleeding.

第二节 手阳明大肠经及其常用腧穴

Section 2 The Large Intestine Channel of Hand-Yangming and Commonly Used Acupoints

1. 经脉循行

①起于示指末端（商阳穴）；②沿示指挠侧向上，通过第1、第2掌骨之间，向上进入拇长伸肌腱与拇短伸肌腱间的凹陷处；③沿前臂前方；④至肘部外侧；⑤沿上臂外侧前缘；⑥上至肩端；⑦沿肩峰前缘；⑧上至第7颈椎（大椎穴）；⑨再降至缺盆；⑩联络肺脏；⑪通过横膈；⑫属于大肠；⑬缺盆支脉上走颈部；⑭通过面颊；⑮进入下齿龈；⑯回绕至上唇，交叉于人中，左脉向右，右脉向左，分布在鼻孔两侧迎香穴，与足阳明胃经相接（图1-3）。

1. The Course of the Channel

①Starting from the tip of the index finger（Shangyang, LI 1）. ②Running upwards along the radial side of the index finger and passing through the interspace of the first and second metacarpal bones, it dips into the depression between the tendon of m. extensor pollicis longus and brevis. ③Running on along the anterior aspect of the forearm, ④it reaches the lateral side of the elbow. ⑤It continues upwards along the lateral anterior border of the upper arm⑥to the highest point of the shoulder. ⑦Then, along the anterior border of the acromion, ⑧it ascends to the seventh cervical vertebra（Dazhui DU 14）, ⑨then descends to Quepen（ST 12）⑩to connect with the lung. ⑪It goes downwards through the diaphragm ⑫to enter the large intestine, its pertaining organ. ⑬The branch from Quepen（ST 12）runs upwards to the neck, ⑭passes through the cheek ⑮and enters the lower gums. ⑯Then, it curves around the upper lip and crosses at the philtrum. From there, it ends at the opposite side of the naris at Yingxiang（LI 20）, where it connects with the Stomach Meridian of Foot-Yangming（Fig. 1-3）.

2. 常用经穴主治提要

本经腧穴主治头面、五官、咽喉病和发热，以及本经循行部位的其他病症，例如痛证及痿痹。

2. Principal Indications of the Commonly Used Acupoints of the Meridian

Disease of the head, face, five sense organs, throat and fever. Other diseases in the regions along the course of this channel, such as pain and flaccidity in the upper limbs.

3. 常用腧穴（图1-4）

3. The Commonly Used Acupoints (Fig. 1-4)

商　　阳

定位　示指桡侧指甲角旁约0.1寸。

主治　耳聋，牙痛，咽喉肿痛，手指麻木，热病，昏迷。

操作　直刺0.1寸，或点刺出血。可灸。

Shangyong （LI 1）

Location: On the radial side of the index finger, about 0.1 cun posterior to the proximal corner of the nail.

Indications: Deafness, toothache, sore throat, numbness of fingers, febrile diseases, coma.

Method: Puncture perpendicularly 0.1cun, or prick the point to cause bleeding. Moxibustion is applicable.

二　　间

定位　微握拳，示指桡侧掌指关节前凹陷中。

主治　目疾，鼻衄，牙痛，肩背痛，口眼㖞斜。

操作　直刺0.2～0.3寸。可灸。

Erjian （LI 2）

Location: With the fist slightly made, in the depression on the radial side on the index finger, distal to the second metacarpal-phalangeal joint.

Indications: Diseases of the eye, nosebleeding toothache, pain in the shoulder and back, deviation of the mouth and eye.

Method: Puncture perpendicularly 0.2～0.3 cun. Moxibustion is applicable.

三　　间

定位　微握拳，第2掌骨小头桡侧后凹陷中。

主治　目痛，齿痛，咽喉肿痛，身热，腹满，肠鸣。

操作　直刺0.5～0.8寸。可灸。

Sanjian （LI 3）

Location: With the fist slightly made, in the depression of the radial side, proximal to the second metacarpal-phalangeal joint.

Indications: Pain in the eye, toothache, sore throat, fever, fullness in the abdomen, borborygmus.

Method: Puncture perpendicularly 0.5～0.8 cun. Moxibustion is applicable.

合　　谷

定位　手背第1、第2掌骨之间，

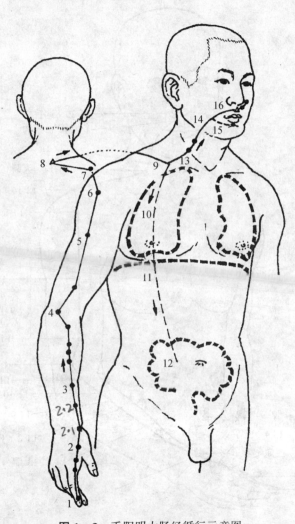

图 1-3 手阳明大肠经循行示意图

Fig. 1-3 Running Course of the Large Intestine Channel of Hand-Yang-ming

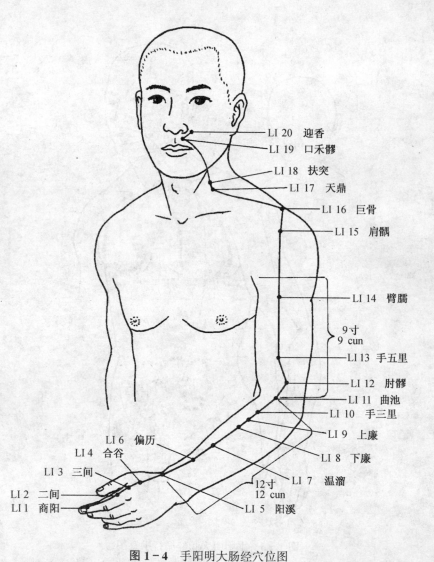

图 1 - 4 　手阳明大肠经穴位图

Fig. 1 - 4   Acupoints of the Large Intestine Channel of Hand-Yangming

第 2 掌骨桡侧缘的中点处。或者以一手的拇指指骨关节横纹，放在另一手的拇指、示指之间的指蹼缘上，屈指当拇指尖尽处取穴。

主治 头痛，目赤肿痛，鼻衄，齿痛，牙关紧闭，口眼㖞斜，耳聋，痄腮，咽喉肿痛，热病，无汗，多汗，腹痛，便秘，经闭，滞产。

操作 直刺 0.5~0.8 寸，可灸。孕妇禁针灸。

Hegu（LI 4）

Location: On the dorsum of the hand, between the first and second metacarpal bones, along the middle of the second metacarpal bone on the radial side. Or, make the patient place the interphalangal crease of the palmar surface of the thumb of one hand on the margin of the web between the thumb and index finger of the other hand. The point is located just beneath the tip of the thumb when the thumb is at flexion.

Indications: Headache, redness, swelling and pain of the eye, epistaxis, toothache, trismus, deviation of the mouth and eye, deafness, mumps, sore throat, fever, anhibrosis, hidrosis, abdominal pain, constipation, amenorrhoea, dystocia.

Method: Puncture perpendicularly 0.5~0.8 cun. Moxibustion is applicable. Acupuncture and moxibustion is contraindicated for pregnant women.

阳 溪

定位 腕背横纹桡侧端，拇指翘起时，在拇短伸肌腱与拇长伸肌腱之间的凹陷中。

主治 头痛，目赤肿痛，耳聋，耳鸣，齿痛，咽喉肿痛，手腕痛。

操作 直刺 0.5~0.8 寸。可灸。

Yangxi（LI 5）

Location: On the radial end of the dorsal crease of the wrist, in the depression between the tendons of m. extensor pollicis longus and brevis when the thumb is titled upward.

Indications: Headache, redness, swelling and pain of the eye, deafness, tinnitus, toothache, sore throat, pain in the wrist.

Method; Puncture perpendicularly 0.5~0.8 cun. Moxibustion is applicable.

偏 历

定位 阳溪穴与曲池穴连线上，阳溪穴上 3 寸处。

主治 目赤，耳鸣，耳聋，鼻衄，咽喉肿痛，手腕乏力疼痛。

操作 直刺或斜刺 0.5~0.8 寸。可灸。

Pianli（LI 6）

Location: On the line joining Yangxi (LI 5) and Quchi（LI 11），3 cun above Yangxi（LI 5）.

Indications: Redness of the eye, tinnitus, deafness, nosebleeding, sore throat, weakness and pain in the wrist, edema.

Method: Puncture perpendicularly or obliquely 0.5～0.8 cun. Moxibustion is applicable.

温　溜

定位　阳溪穴与曲池穴连线上，阳溪穴上 5 寸处。

主治　头痛，面肿，咽喉疼痛，肩背酸痛，肠鸣腹痛。

操作　直刺0.5～1寸。可灸。

Wenliu（LI 7）

Location: On the line joining Yangxi (LI 5) and Quchi (LI 11), 5 cun above Yangxi (LI 5).

Indications: Headache, swelling of the face, sore throat, pain in the back and shoulder, borborygmus and abdominal pain.

Method: Puncture perpendicularly 0.5～1 cun. Moxibustion is applicable.

下　廉

定位　阳溪穴与曲池穴连线上，曲池穴下 4 寸处。

主治　头痛，眩晕，手臂痛，腹胀，肠鸣。

操作　直刺0.5～1寸，可灸。

Xialian（LI 8）

Location: On the line joining Yangxi (LI 5) and Quchi (LI 11), 4 cun below Quchi (LI 11).

Indications: Headache, dizziness,

pain in the arm, fullness in the abdomen, borborygmus.

Method: Puncture perpendicularly 0.5～1 cun. Moxibustion is applicable.

上　廉

定位　阳溪穴与曲池穴连线上，曲池穴下 3 寸处。

主治　头痛，肩背酸痛，半身不遂，手臂麻木，肠鸣腹痛。

操作　直刺0.5～1寸。可灸。

Shanglian（LI 9）

Location: On the line joining Yangxi (LI 5) and Quchi (LI 11), 3 cun below Quchi (LI 11).

Indications: Headache, pain in shoulder and arm, half-body paralysis, numbness in the arm, borborygmus and pain in the abdomen.

Method: Puncture perpendicularly 0.5～1 cun. Moxibustion is applicable.

手　三　里

定位　在阳溪穴与曲池穴连线上，曲池穴下 2 寸处。

主治　牙痛，颊肿，上肢麻木，腹痛肠鸣。

操作　直刺0.8～1.2寸。可灸。

Shousanli（LI 10）

Location: On the line joining Yangxi (LI 5) and Quchi (LI 11), 2 cun below Quchi (LI 11).

Indications: Toothache, swelling in

the cheek, numbness in the arm, pain in the abdomen, borborygmus.

Method: Puncture perpendicularly 0.8~1.2 cun. Moxibustion is applicable.

曲 池

定位 屈肘，成直角，在肘横纹外端与肱骨外上髁连线的中点。

主治 咽喉肿痛，牙痛，目赤痛，呕吐，腹泻，痢疾，水肿，眩晕，半身不遂，手臂肿痛，高血压。

操作 直刺1~1.5寸。可灸。

Quchi (LI 11)

Location: When the elbow is flexed to form a right angle , the point is at the midpoint of the line linking the lateral end of the transverse cubital crease and the lateral epicondyle of the humerus.

Indications: Sore throat, toothache, redness and pain in the eye, vomiting, diarrhea, dysentery, edema, dizziness shelf-body paralysis, swelling and pain of the arm, hypertension.

Method: Puncture perpendicularly 1~1.5 cun. Moxibustion is applicable.

肘 髎

定位 屈肘，曲池穴外上方1寸，肱骨边缘。

主治 肘臂部酸痛、麻木、挛急。

操作 直刺0.5~0.1寸。可灸。

Zhouliao (LI 12)

Location: With the elbow flexed, 1 cun superior and lateral to Quchi (LI 11), on the border of humerus.

Indications: Pain, numbness and contracture of the elbow and arm.

Method: Puncture perpendicularly 0.5~1 cun. Moxibustion is applicable.

手五里

定位 在曲池穴与肩髃穴的连线上，曲池穴上3寸处。

主治 肘臂挛痛，咳血，咳嗽。

操作 避开动脉，直刺0.5~1寸。可灸。

Shouwuli (LI 13)

Location: On the line linking Quchi (LI 11) and Jianyu (LI 15), 3 cun above Quchi (LI 11).

Indications: Pain and contracture of the elbow and arm, hemoptysis, cough.

Method: Avoiding the artery, puncture perpendicularly 0.5~1 cun. Moxibustion is applicable.

臂 臑

定位 曲池穴与肩髃穴连线上，曲池穴上7寸，三角肌止点处。

主治 肩臂痛，颈项拘挛，瘰疬，目疾。

操作 直刺或向上斜刺0.8~1.5寸。可灸。

Binao (LI 14)

Location: On the line linking Quchi

(LI 11) and Jianyu (LI 15), 7 cun above Quchi (LI 11), at the insertion of the deltoid muscle.

Indications: Pain in the shoulder and arm, stiffness of the neck, tuberculous cervical lymphadenitis, eye disorders.

Method: Puncture perpendicularly or obliquely upwards 0.8 ~ 1.5 cun. Moxibustion is applicable.

肩　髃

定位　在肩部，三角肌上，臂外展，或向前平伸时，当肩峰前下方凹陷处。

主治　肩臂挛痛，半身不遂，瘰疬。

操作　直刺或向下斜刺 0.8～1.5 寸。可灸。

Jianyu (LI 15)

Location: On the shoulder, superior to the deltoid muscle, in the depression anterior and inferior to the acromion when the arm is abducted or raised on the level of the shoulder.

Indications: Contracture and pain of the shoulder and arm, hemiplegia, tuberculous cervical lymphadenitis.

Method: Puncture perpendicularly or obliquely downwards 0.8 ~ 1.5 cun. Moxibustion is applicable.

巨　骨

定位　锁骨峰端与肩胛冈之间凹陷中。

主治　肩臂挛痛，瘰疬，瘿气。

操作　直刺或向斜下方刺 0.5～1 寸。可灸。

Jugu (LI 16)

Location: In the depression between the acromial extremity of the clavicle and scapular spine.

Indications: Contractiure and pain of the shoulder and arm, tuberculous cervical lymphadenitis, goiter.

Method: Puncture perpendicularly or obliquely downwards 0.5 ~ 1 cun. Moxibustion is applicable.

天　鼎

定位　扶突直下 1 寸，胸锁乳突肌后缘。

主治　暴喑气梗，咽喉肿痛，瘰疬，瘿气。

操作　直刺 0.5～0.8 寸。可灸。

Tianding (LI 17)

Location: 1 cun below Futu (LI 18), on the posterior border of m. sternocleidomastoideus.

Indications: Sudden aphonia and choking in the chest, sore throat, tuberculous cervical lymphadenitis, goiter.

Method: Puncture perpendicularly 0.5~0.8 cun. Moxibustion is applicable.

扶　突

定位　喉结旁开 3 寸，胸锁乳突肌的胸骨头与锁骨头之间。

主治　咳嗽，气喘，咽喉肿痛，暴

喑，瘰疬，瘿气。

操作 直刺 0.5~0.8 寸。可灸。

Futu （LI 18）

Location：3 cun lateral to Adam's apple, between the sternal head and clavicular head of m. sternocleido-mastoideus.

Indications: Cough, asthma, sore throat, sudden loss of voice, tuberculous cervical lymphadenitis, goiter.

Method: Puncture perpendicularly 0.5~0.8 cun. Moxibustion is applicable.

口 禾 髎

定位 在上唇部，鼻孔外缘直下，与水沟平齐处。

主治 鼻塞，鼻衄，口喎，口噤。

操作 直刺或斜刺 0.3~0.5 寸。

Kouheliao （LI 19）

Location: On the upper lip, directly below the lateral border of the nostril, on the level with Renzhong （DU 26）.

Indications: Nasal congestion, nose-bleeding, deviation of the mouth, clenched jaw.

Method: Puncture perpendicularly or obliquely 0.3~0.5 cun.

迎 香

定位 鼻翼外缘中点，旁开 0.5 寸，当鼻唇沟中。

主治 鼻塞，鼻衄，口喎，面痒，胆道蛔虫。

操作 斜刺或平刺 0.3~0.5 寸。

Yingxiang （LI 20）

Location：0.5 cun lateral to the midpoint of the lateral border of ala nasi, in the nasolabial groove.

Indications: Nasal stuffiness, nose-bleeding, deviation of the mouth, itch of the face, biliary roundworm.

Method: Puncture obliquely or sub-cutaneously 0.3~0.5cun.

第三节 足阳明胃经及其常用腧穴

Section 3 The Stomach Channel of Foot-Yangming and Commonly Used Acupoints

1. 经脉循行

①起于鼻翼两侧，上行至鼻根部；②与旁边足太阳经交会；③向下沿着鼻的外侧；④进入上齿龈；⑤回出环绕口唇；⑥下交颏唇沟；⑦向后沿下颌；⑧至下颌角；⑨上耳前；⑩沿发际；⑪到前额。

⑫面部支脉：从大迎下走人迎，沿喉咙；⑬进入缺盆；⑭向下通过横膈；⑮属于胃，联络脾。

⑯缺盆支脉：经乳头；⑰向下挟脐旁，进入少腹气冲。

⑱胃下口部支脉：沿腹里向下到气冲会合；⑲再由此下行到髀关；⑳直抵伏兔部；㉑下至膝盖；㉒沿胫骨外侧前缘；㉓下经足跗；㉔进入第 2 足趾外端。

㉕胫部支脉：从膝下 3 寸足三里
处分出；㉖进入足中趾外侧。

㉗足跗部支脉：从足背（冲阳）
分出，进入足大趾内侧端，与足太阴
脾经相接（图 1 - 5）。

1. The Course of the Channel

①Originating from the side of the ala nasi and ascending to the root of the nose, ② where it meets the Bladder Channel of Foot-Taiyang. ③ Turning downwards along the lateral side of the nose, ④it enters the upper gum. ⑤Emerging, it winds around the lips ⑥ and descends to meet the mentolabial groove. ⑦ Running backwards along the lower jaw, ⑧it reaches the angle of the mandible. ⑨Then, it ascends in front of the auricle, ⑩ goes along the anterior hairline ⑪and reaches the forehead.

⑫The facial branch starting in front of Daying (ST 5) runs downwards to Renying (ST 9). From there it goes along the throat and ⑬enters the supraclavicular fossa. ⑭ Descending, it passes through the diaphragm, ⑮ enters the stomach, its pertaining organ, and connects with the spleen.

⑯The branch arising in the supraclavicular fossa runs downward⑰ passing through the nipple. It descends by the umbilicus and enters Qichong (ST 30) on the lateral side of the lower abdomen.

⑱The branch from the lower orifice of the stomach descends inside the abdomen and joints the previous portion of the channel at Qichong (ST 30). ⑲ Further running downwards, traversing Biguan (ST 31), ⑳ and further through Futu (ST 32) at the Femur, ㉑it reaches the knee. ㉒From there, it continues downwards along the anterior border of the lateral aspect of the tibia, ㉓passes through the dorsum of the foot, ㉔and reaches the lateral side of the tip of the second toe.

㉕The tibial branch comes out 3 cun below the knee, ㉖and enters the lateral side of the tip of the middle toe.

㉗The branch from the dorsum of the foot rises from Chongyang (ST 42) and ends at the medial side of the tip of the great toe, where it links with the Spleen Channel of Foot-Taiyin (Fig. 1 - 5).

2. 常用经穴主治提要

本经腧穴主治胃肠病，如胃痛，
腹痛，腹胀，肠鸣，腹泻，痢疾，便
秘，头、面、眼、鼻、口病，牙痛，
神志病和经脉循行部位的其他病症。

2. Principal Indications of Commonly Used Acupoints of the Meridian

Gastrointestinal diseases, such as stomachache, abdominal pain or distension, borborygmus, diarrhea, dysen -

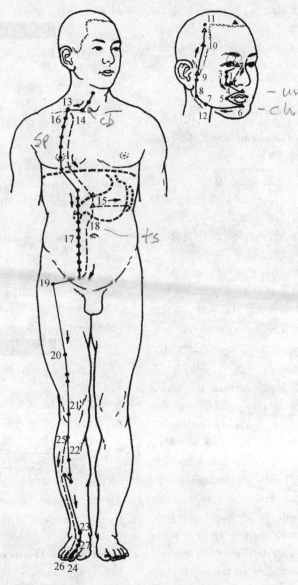

图 1 - 5 足阳明胃经循行示意图

Fig. 1 - 5 Running Course of the Stomach Channel of Foot-Yangming

tery, constipation, diseases of the head, face, eye, nose and mouth, toothache, mental illnesses, diseases in the regions along the course of this channel.

3. 常用腧穴（图 1 - 6，图 1 - 7）

3. The Commonly Used Acupoints (Fig.1 - 6, Fig.1 - 7)

承　泣

定位　目正视，瞳孔直下，眶下缘与眼球之间。

主治　目赤肿痛，眼睑瞤动，口眼㖞斜，流泪，头痛，眩晕。

操作　左手拇指向上轻推眼球，沿眶下缘直刺 0.3～0.7 寸，不宜提插，以防刺破血管引起血肿。禁灸。

Chengqi（ST 1）

Location: With the eyes looking straight forward, the point is directly below the pupil, between the infraorbital ridge and the eyeball.

Indications: Redness, swelling and pain of the eye, flickering of the eye lids, deviation of the mouth and eye, epiphora, headache, dizziness.

Method: Push the eyeball upward slightly with the left thumb and puncture perpendicularly $0.3 \sim 0.7$ cun along the infraorbital ridge. It is forbidden to manipulate the needle with large amplitude in order to avoid injuring the blood vessels and causing hematoma.

Moxibustion is contraindicated.

四　白

定位　目正视，瞳孔直下，眶下孔凹陷处。

主治　目赤痒痛，目翳，眼睑瞤动，口眼㖞斜，面痛。

操作　直刺或斜刺 0.3～0.5 寸。

Sibai（ST 2）

Location: With the eyes looking straight forward, directly below the pupil, the point is in the depression at the infraorbital foramen.

Indications: Redness, painful itching of the eye, corneal opacity, flickering of the eyelids, deviation of the mouth and eye, pain in the face.

Method: Puncture perpendicularly or obliquely $0.3 \sim 0.5$ cun.

巨　髎

定位　目正视，瞳孔直下，平鼻翼下缘处。

主治　口眼㖞斜，眼睑瞤动，鼻衄，牙痛，唇颊肿。

操作　斜刺或平刺 0.3～0.5 寸。

Juliao（ST 3）

Location: With the eyes looking straight forward, directly below the pupil, on the level of the lower border of ala nasi.

Indications: Deviation of the mouth and eye, twitching of the eyelids, nosebleeding, toothache, swelling of the lip and cheek.

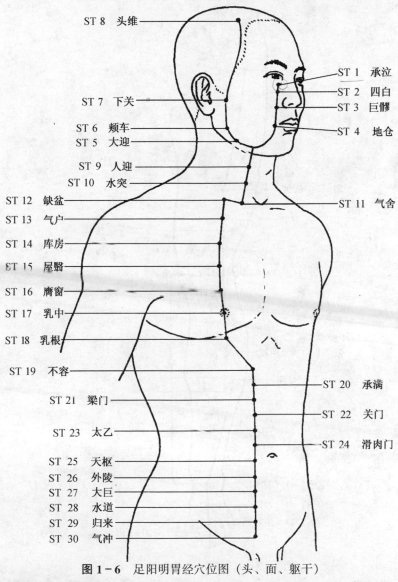

ST 8 头维

ST 1 承泣
ST 2 四白
ST 3 巨髎

ST 7 下关

ST 4 地仓

ST 6 颊车
ST 5 大迎

ST 9 人迎
ST 10 水突

ST 12 缺盆

ST 11 气舍

ST 13 气户

ST 14 库房

ST 15 屋翳

ST 16 膺窗

ST 17 乳中

ST 18 乳根

ST 19 不容

ST 20 承满

ST 21 梁门

ST 22 关门

ST 23 太乙

ST 24 滑肉门

ST 25 天枢
ST 26 外陵
ST 27 大巨
ST 28 水道
ST 29 归来
ST 30 气冲

图 1-6 足阳明胃经穴位图（头、面、躯干）

Fig. 1-6 Acupoints of the Stomach Channel of Foot-Yangming（Head, Face and Truck）

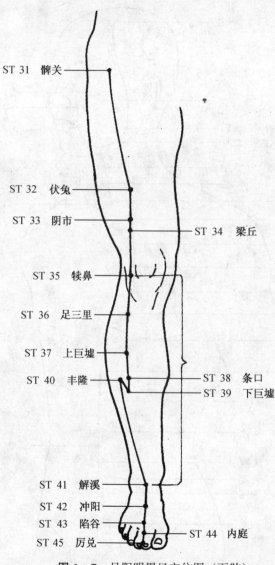

ST 31　髀关

ST 32　伏兔

ST 33　阴市

ST 34　梁丘

ST 35　犊鼻

ST 36　足三里

ST 37　上巨墟

ST 40　丰隆

ST 38　条口

ST 39　下巨墟

ST 41　解溪

ST 42　冲阳

ST 43　陷谷

ST 44　内庭

ST 45　厉兑

图 1-7　足阳明胃经穴位图（下肢）

Fig.1-7　Acupoints of the Stomach Channel of Foot-Yangming（Lower Limb）

Method: Puncture obliquely or subcutaneously 0.3~0.5 cun.

地 仓

定位 口角旁 0.4 寸。巨髎穴直下取之。

主治 口㖞，流涎，眼睑瞤动。

操作 斜刺或平刺 0.5~0.8 寸。可灸。

Dicang (ST 4)

Location: 0.4 cun lateral to the angle of the mouth, directly below Juliao (ST 3).

Indications: Deviation of the mouth, salivation, flickering of the eyelids.

Method: Puncture obliquely or subcutaneously 0.5~0.8 cun. Moxibustion is applicable.

大 迎

定位 下颌角前方，咬肌附着部的前缘，当面动脉搏动处。

主治 口㖞，口噤，颊肿，牙痛。

操作 避开动脉，斜刺或平刺 0.3~0.5 寸。

Daying (ST 5)

Location: Anterior to the angle of the mandible , on the anterior border of the attached portion of the masseter muscle, at the facial artery.

Indications: Deviation of the mouth, trismus, swelling of the cheek, toothache.

Method: Avoiding the artery,

puncture obliquely or subcutaneously 0.3~0.5 cun.

颊 车

定位 下颌角前上方 1 横指凹陷中，咀嚼时咬肌隆起最高点处。

主治 口㖞，牙痛，颊肿，口噤不语。

操作 直刺 0.3~0.5 寸，平刺 0.5~1 寸。

Jiache (ST 6)

Location: In the depression where the masseter muscle is prominent, one finger breadth anterior and superior to the mandibular angle.

Indications: Deviation of the mouth, toothache, swelling of the cheek, trismus.

Method: Puncture perpendicularly 0.3~0.5 cun or subcutaneously 0.5~1 cun.

下 关

定位 颧弓下缘，下颌骨髁状突之前方凹陷中。合口有孔，张口即闭。

主治 口㖞，牙痛，颊肿，口噤不语，耳聋，耳鸣。

操作 直刺 0.3~0.5 寸，平刺 0.5~1 寸。可灸。

Xiaguan (ST 7)

Location: At the lower border of the zygomatic arch, in the depression anterior to the condyloid process of the mandible. This point is located when the mouth is closed.

Indications: Deviation of mouth, toothache, swelling of the cheek, trismus, deafness, tinnitus.

Method: Puncture perpendicularly 0.3 ~ 0.5 cun, or subcutaneously 0.5~ 1 cun. Moxibustion is applicable.

头   维

定位　额角发际直上0.5寸。

主治　头痛，目眩，眼睑瞤动，流泪，口痛。

操作　平刺0.5~1寸。

Touwei（ST 8）

Location: 0.5 cun directly above the hairline at the corner of the forehead.

Indications: Headache, blurred vision, flickering of eyelids, lacrimation, pain of the mouth.

Method: Puncture subcutaneously 0.5~1 cun.

人   迎

定位　喉结旁1.5寸，颈总动脉之后，胸锁乳突肌前缘。

主治　咽喉肿痛，气喘，瘰疬，瘿气，高血压。

操作　避开颈总动脉，直刺0.3~0.8寸。

Renying（ST 9）

Location: 1.5 cun lateral to the Adam's apple, just behind the common carotid artery, on the anterior border of m. sternocleidomastoideus.

Indications: Sore throat, asthma, scrofula, goiter, hypertension.

Method: Avoiding the common carotid artery, puncture perpendicularly 0.3~0.8 cun.

水   突

定位　人迎穴至气舍穴连线中点，当胸锁乳突肌前缘。

主治　咽喉肿痛，咳嗽，气喘。

操作　直刺0.3~0.8寸。可灸。

Shuitu（ST 10）

Location: Midway on the line linking Renying（ST 9）and Qishe（ST 11）, at the anterior border of m. sternocleidomastoideus.

Indications: Sore throat, cough, asthma.

Method: Puncture perpendicularly 0.3~0.8 cun. Moxibustion is applicable.

气   舍

定位　锁骨上缘，胸锁乳突肌的胸骨头与锁骨头之间。

主治　咽喉肿痛，气喘，瘰疬，瘿瘤，颈项强。

操作　直刺0.3~0.5寸。可灸。

Qishe（ST 11）

Location: At the upper border of the medial end of the clavicle, between the sternal head and the clavicular head of m. sternocleidomastoideus.

Indications: Sore throat, asthma, scrofula, goiter, neck rigidity.

Method: Puncture perpendicularly 0.3~0.5 cun. Moxibustion is applicable.

缺　盆

定位　锁骨上窝中央，前正中线旁开4寸。

主治　咳嗽，气喘，咽喉肿痛。

操作　直刺或斜刺0.3~0.5寸。深刺危险。可灸。

Quepen (ST 12)

Location: In the midpoint of the supraclavicular fossa, 4 cun lateral to the anterior midline.

Indications: Cough, asthma, sore throat, scrofula.

Method: Puncture perpendicularly or subcutaneously 0.3 ~ 0.5 cun. Deep puncture is dangerous. Moxibustion is applicable.

气　户

定位　锁骨下缘，前正中线旁开4寸。

主治　咳嗽，气喘，胸胁支满，胸痛。

操作　斜刺或平刺0.5~0.8寸。

Qihu (ST 13)

Location: At the midpoint of the lower border of clavicle, 4 cun lateral to the anterior midline.

Indications: Cough, asthma, fullness in the chest and hypochondrium, pain in the chest.

Method: Puncture obliquely and subcutaneously 0.5 ~ 0.8 cun. Moxibustion is applicable.

库　房

定位　第1肋间，前正中线旁开4寸。

主治　咳嗽，气喘，咳唾脓血，胸胁胀痛。

操作　斜刺或平刺0.5~0.8寸。可灸。

Kufang (ST 14)

Location: In the first intercrostal space, 4 cun lateral to the anterior midline.

Indications: Cough, asthma, purulent sputum mixed with blood, pain and fullness in the chest and hypochondriac region.

Method: Puncture obliquely and subcutaneously 0.5 ~ 0.8 cun. Moxibustion is applicable.

屋　翳

定位　第2肋间隙，前正中线旁开4寸。

主治　咳嗽，气喘，咳唾脓血，胸胁胀痛，乳痈。

操作　斜刺或平刺0.5~0.8寸。可灸。

Wuyi (ST 15)

Location: In the second intercostal space, 4 cun lateral to the anterior midline.

Indications: Cough, asthma, purulent sputum mixed with blood, pain and fullness in the chest and hypochondriac region, acute mastadenitis.

Method: Puncture obliquely and subcutaneously $0.5 \sim 0.8$ cun. Moxibustion is applicable.

膺　窗

定位　第 3 肋间隙, 前正中线旁开 4 寸。

主治　咳嗽, 气喘, 胸胁胀满, 乳痈。

操作　斜刺或平刺 $0.5\sim0.8$ 寸。

Yingchuang（ST 16）

Location: In the third intercostal space, 4 cun lateral to the anterior midline.

Indications: Cough, asthma, pain and fullness in the chest and hypochondriac region, acute mastadenitis.

Method: Puncture perpendicularly or subcutaneously $0.5 \sim 0.8$ cun. Moxibustion is applicable.

乳　中

定位　乳头中央。

主治　本穴不针不灸, 只作定位标志。

Ruzhong（ST 17）

Location: In the center of the nipple.

Indications: Anatomical landmark of locating points.

乳　根

定位　第 5 肋间隙, 乳头直下。

主治　咳嗽, 气喘, 胸痛, 乳痈。

操作　直刺或斜刺 $0.5\sim0.8$ 寸。可灸。

Rugen（ST 18）

Location: In the fifth intercostal space, directly below the nipple.

Indications: Cough, asthma, pain in the chest, mastitis.

Method: Puncture perpendicularly or subcutaneously $0.5 \sim 0.8$ cun. Moxibustion is applicable.

不　容

定位　脐上 6 寸, 前正中线旁开 2 寸。

主治　呕吐, 胃痛, 食欲不振, 腹胀。

操作　直刺 $0.5\sim0.8$ 寸。可灸。

Burong（ST 19）

Location: 6 cun above the umbilicus, 2 cun lateral to the anterior midline.

Indications: Vomiting, stomachache, poor appetite, abdominal distension.

Method: Puncture perpendicularly $0.5\sim0.8$ cun. Moxibustion is applicable.

承　满

定位　脐上 5 寸, 前正中线旁开 2 寸。

主治　胃痛, 吐血, 食欲不振, 腹胀。

操作 直刺 0.8～1 寸。可灸。

Chengman (ST 20)

Location: 5 cun above umbilicus, 2 cun lateral to the anterior midline.

Indications: Stomachache, retching of blood, poor appetite, abdominal distension.

Method: Puncture perpendicularly 0.8～1 cun. Moxibustion is applicable.

梁 门

定位 脐上 4 寸，前正中线旁开 2 寸。

主治 胃痛，呕吐，食欲不振，腹胀，泄泻。

操作 直刺 0.8～1.2 寸。

Liangmen (ST 21)

Location: 4 cun above umbilicus, 2 cun lateral to the anterior midline.

Indications: Stomachache, vomiting, poor appetite, abdominal distension, diarrhea.

Method: Puncture perpendicularly 0.8～1.2 cun. Moxibustion is applicable.

关 门

定位 脐上 3 寸，前正中线旁开 2 寸。

主治 腹胀，腹痛，肠鸣泄泻，水肿。

操作 直刺 0.8～1.2 寸。可灸。

Guanmen (ST 22)

Location: 3 cun above the umbilicus, 2 cun lateral to the anterior midline.

Indications: Abdominal distension, abdominal pain, borborygmus, diarrhea, edema.

Method: Puncture perpendicularly 0.8～1.2 cun. Moxibustion is applicable.

太 乙

定位 脐上 2 寸，前正中线旁开 2 寸。

主治 胃痛，心烦，癫狂。

操作 直刺 0.8～1.2 寸。

Taiyi (ST 23)

Location: 2 cun above the umbilicus, 2 cun lateral to the anterior midline.

Indications: Stomachache, vexation, mania and withdrawal.

Method: Puncture perpendicularly 0.8～1.2 cun. Moxibustion is applicable.

滑 肉 门

定位 脐上 1 寸，前正中线旁开 2 寸。

主治 胃痛，呕吐，癫狂。

操作 直刺 0.8～1.2 寸。可灸。

Huaroumen (ST 24)

Location: 1 cun above the umbilicus, 2 cun lateral to the anterior midline.

Indications: Stomachache, vomiting, mania and withdrawal.

Method: Puncture perpendicularly 0.8~1.2 cun. Moxibustion is applicable.

天　枢

定位　脐旁2寸。

主治　肠鸣腹胀，绕脐痛，便秘，泄泻，癥瘕，痢疾，月经不调。

操作　直刺1~1.5寸。可灸。

Tianshu（ST 25）

Location: 2 cun lateral to the umbilicus

Indications: Abdominal distension, borborygmus, pain around the umbilicus, constipation, diarrhea, abdominal mass, dysentery, irregular menstruation.

Method: Puncture perpendicularly 1~1.5 cun. Moxibustion is applicable.

外　陵

定位　脐下1寸，前正中线旁开2寸。

主治　腹痛，疝气，痛经。

操作　直刺1~1.5寸。可灸。

Wailing（ST 26）

Location: 1 cun below the umbilicus, 2 cun lateral to the anterior midline.

Indications: Abdominal pain, hernia, dysmenorrhea.

Method: Puncture perpendicularly 1~1.5 cun. Moxibustion is applicable.

大　巨

定位　脐下2寸，前正中旁开2寸。

主治　小腹胀满，小便不利，疝气，遗精，早泄。

操作　直刺1~1.5寸。可灸。

Daju（ST 27）

Location: 2 cun below umbilicus, 2 cun lateral to the anterior midline.

Indications: Lower abdominal distension, retention of urine, hernia, seminal emission, premature ejaculation.

Method: Puncture perpendicularly 1~1.5 cun. Moxibustion is applicable.

水　道

定位　脐下3寸，腹正中线旁开2寸。

主治　小腹胀满，小便不利，痛经，不孕，疝气。

操作　直刺1~1.5寸。可灸。

Shuidao（ST 28）

Location: 3 cun below the umbilicus, 2 cun lateral to the anterior midline.

Indications: Lower abdominal distension, retention of urine, dysmenorrhea, sterility, hernia.

Method: Puncture perpendicularly 1~1.5 cun. Moxibustion is applicable.

归 来

定位 脐下4寸，前正中线旁开2寸。

主治 腹痛，疝气，月经不调，白带，阴挺。

操作 直刺1~1.5寸。可灸。

Guilai（ST 29）

Location: 4 cun below the umbilicus, 2 cun lateral to the anterior midline.

Indications: Abdominal pain, hernia, irregular, menstruation, leukorrhagia, prolapse of the uterus.

Method: Puncture perpendicularly 1~1.5 cun. Moxibustion is applicable.

气 冲

定位 脐下5寸，前正中线旁开2寸。

主治 腹痛，肠鸣，疝气，月经不调，不孕，阳痿，阴肿。

操作 直刺0.5~1寸。可灸。

Qichong（ST 30）

Location: 5 cun below the umbilicus, 2 cun lateral to the anterior midline.

Indications: Abdominal pain, borborygmus, hernia, irregular menstruation, sterility, impotence, swelling of the vulva.

Method: Puncture perpendicularly 0.5~1 cun. Moxibustion is applicable.

髀 关

定位 髂前上棘与髌骨外缘连线上，屈股时，平会阴，居缝匠肌外侧凹陷处。

主治 腰腿疼痛，下肢麻痹，挛急。

操作 直刺1~2寸。可灸。

Biguan（ST 31）

Location: On the line linking the anterior superior illiac spine and lateral border of the patella, at the level of the perineum when the thigh is flexed, in the depression lateral to the sartorius muscle.

Indications: Pain in the leg and waist, numbness or contracture of the lower limbs, abdominal pain.

Method: Puncture perpendicularly 1~2 cun. Moxibustion is applicable.

伏 兔

定位 髂前上棘与髌骨连线上，髌骨外上缘上6寸。

主治 腰痛，下肢麻痹、疼痛，疝气。

操作 直刺1~1.5寸。可灸。

Futu（ST 32）

Location: On the line linking the anterior superior iliac spine and lateral border of the patella, 6 cun above the laterosuperior border of the patella.

Indications: Pain in the lumbar region, paralysis and pain of the lower extremities, hernia.

Method: Puncture perpendicularly 1~1.5 cun. Moxibustion is applicable.

阴　市

定位　髂前上棘与髌骨外缘连线上，髌骨外上缘上3寸。

主治　腿膝疼痛麻木，疝气，腹胀疼痛。

操作　直刺1~1.5寸。

Yinshi （ST 33）

Location: On the line linking the anterior superior iliac spine and lateral border of the ilium, 3 cun above the laterosuperior border of the patella.

Indications: Pain and numbness of the knee and leg, hernia, abdominal distension and pain.

Method: Puncture perpendicularly 1~1.5 cun. Moxibustion is applicable.

梁　丘

定位　髂前上棘与髌骨外上缘连线上，髌骨外上缘上2寸。

主治　膝肿痛，下肢不遂，胃痛。

操作　直刺1~1.2寸。可灸。

Liangqiu （ST 34）

Location: On the line linking the anterior superior iliac spine and lateral border of the patella, 2 cun above the laterosuperior border of the patella.

Indications: Swelling and pain of the knee, paralysis of the lower extremities, stomachache.

Method: Puncture perpendicularly

1~1.2 cun. Moxibustion is applicable.

犊　鼻

定位　髌骨下缘，髌韧带外侧凹陷中。

主治　膝痛，下肢麻痹，脚气。

操作　直刺0.5~1.2寸。可灸。

Dubi （ST 35）

Location: At the lower border of the patella, in the depression lateral to the patellar ligament.

Indications: Pain in the knee, paralysis and pain of the lower extremities, beriberi.

Method: Puncture perpendicularly 0.5~1.2 cun. Moxibustion is applicable.

足　三　里

定位　犊鼻穴下3寸，胫骨前嵴外1横指处。

主治　胃痛，呕吐，腹胀，泄泻，痢疾，便秘，肠痈，下肢痹痛，水肿，癫狂，脚气，虚劳羸瘦。

操作　直刺1~2寸。可灸。

Zusanli （ST 36）

Location: 3 cun below Dubi （ST 35）, one finger-breadth from the anterior crest of the tibia.

Indications: Stomachache, vomiting, abdominal distension, diarrhea, dysentery, constipation, acute appendicitis, paralysis and pain of the lower extremities, edema, mental disorder, beriberi, weakness of the whole body.

Method: Puncture perpendicularly 1~2 cun. Moxibustion is applicable.

上 巨 墟

定位　足三里穴下3寸。

主治　肠鸣，腹痛，泄泻，便秘，肠痈，下肢痿痹，脚气。

操作　直刺1~2寸。可灸。

Shangjuxu（ST 37）

Location: 3 cun below Zusanli (ST 36).

Indications: Borborygmus, abdominal pain, diarrhea, constipation, acute appendicitis, muscular atrophy and pain of lower extremities, beriberi.

Method: Puncture perpendicularly 1~2 cun. Moxibustion is applicable.

条 口

定位　上巨墟穴下2寸。

主治　腹痛，下肢痿痹，转筋，跗肿，肩臂痛。

操作　直刺1~1.5寸。可灸。

Tiaokou（ST 38）

Location: 2 cun below Shangjuxu (ST 37).

Indications: Abdominal pain, muscular atrophy and pain of the lower extremities, systremma, swelling of the dorsum and foot, pain in the shoulder and arm.

Method: Puncture perpendicularly 1~1.5 cun Moxibustion is applicable.

下 巨 墟

定位　上巨墟穴下3寸。

主治　小腹痛，泄泻，痢疾，乳痈，下肢痿痹，腰背痛，睾丸痛。

操作　直刺1~1.5寸。可灸。

Xiajuxu（ST 39）

Location: 3 cun below Shangjuxu (ST 37).

Indications: Lower abdominal pain, diarrhea , dysentery, acute mastadenitis, muscular atrophy of the lower extremities, backache, pain in the testicle.

Method: Puncture perpendicularly 1~ 1.5 cun. Moxibustion is applicable.

丰 隆

定位　外踝高点上8寸，条口穴外1寸。

主治　头痛，眩晕，痰咳，便秘，呕吐，水肿，癫狂，下肢痿痹。

操作　直刺1~1.5寸。可灸。

Fenglong（ST 40）

Location: 8 cun superior to the external malleolus, 1 cun lateral to Tiaokou (ST 38).

Indications: Headache, dizziness, phlegm cough constipation, vomiting, edema, mental disorder, muscular atrophy and pain of the lower extremities.

Method: Puncture perpendicularly 1~ 1.5 cun. Moxibustion is applica-

ble.

解　溪

定位　足背踝关节横纹的中央，
踇长伸肌腱与趾长伸肌腱之间的凹
陷中。

主治　头痛，眩晕，癫狂，腹
胀，便秘，下肢痿痹。

操作　直刺 0.5~1 寸。可灸。

Jiexi （ST 41）

Location: On the dorsum of the
foot, at the midpoint of the transverse
crease of the ankle joint, in the depression between the tendons of m. extensor hallucis longus and digitorum
longus.

Indications: Headache, dizziness,
mental disorder, abdominal distension,
constipation, muscular atrophy and
pain of the lower extremities.

Method: Puncture perpendicularly
0.5 ~ 1 cun. Moxibustion is applicable.

冲　阳

定位　位于足背最高点，踇长伸
肌腱和趾长伸肌腱之间，当第 2、第
3 跖骨与楔状骨间凹陷中，足背动脉
搏动处。

主治　口眼喎斜，面肿，牙痛，
癫狂，胃痛，下肢痿软。

操作　避开动脉，直刺 0.3~
0.5 寸。可灸。

Chongyong （ST 42）

Location: At the highest point of the

dorsum of the foot, between the tendons of m. extensor hallucis longus and
digitorum longus, in the depression between the second and third metatarsal
bones and the cuneiform bone, where
the dorsal artery of the foot pulsates.

Indications: Deviation of the mouth
and eye, swelling of the face,
toothache, mental disorder, stomachache, muscular atrophy and weakness of the foot.

Method: Avoid the artery, puncture
perpendicularly 0.3 ~ 0.5 cun. Moxibustion is applicable.

陷　谷

定位　足背第 2、第 3 跖趾关节
后凹陷中。

主治　面浮身肿，目赤肿痛，肠
鸣，腹痛，发热，足背肿痛。

操作　直刺或斜刺 0.3~0.5 寸。
可灸。

Xiangu （ST 43）

Location: In the depression distal to
the junction of the second and third
metatarsal bones.

Indications: Facial and general edema, swelling, redness and pain of the
eye, borborygmus, abdominal pain,
fever, swelling and pain of the dorsum
of the foot.

Method: Puncture perpendicularly or
obliquely 0.3 ~ 0.5 cun. Moxibustion
is applicable.

内 庭

定位 足背第2、第3趾间缝纹端。

主治 牙痛，咽喉肿痛，口喝，鼻衄，胃痛吐酸，腹胀，泄泻，痢疾，便秘，热病，足背肿痛。

操作 直刺或斜刺0.5～0.8寸。可灸。

Neiting (ST 44)

Location: Proximal to the vertical skin crease of the web between the second and third toes.

Indications: Toothache, sore throat, deviation of the mouth, nose-bleeding, stomachache and acid regurgitation, abdominal distension, diarrhea, dysentery, constipation, fever, swelling and pain of the dorsum of the foot.

Method: Puncture perpendicularly or obliquely 0.5～0.8 cun. Moxibustion is applicable.

厉 兑

定位 第2趾外侧趾甲角旁约0.1寸。

主治 鼻衄，牙痛，咽喉肿痛，腹胀，发热，多梦，癫狂。

操作 浅刺0.1寸。可灸。

Lidui (ST 45)

Location: On the lateral side of the second toe, about 0.1 cun posterior to the proximal corner of the nail.

Indications: Nosebleed, toothache, sore throat, abdominal distension, fever, dream-disturbed sleep, mental disorder.

Method: Puncture shallowly 0.1 cun. Moxibustion is applicable.

第四节 足太阴脾经及其常用腧穴

Section 4 The Spleen Channel of Foot-Taiyin and Commonly Used Acupoints

1. 经脉循行

①起于足大趾末端；②沿大趾内侧赤白肉际；③上行至内踝前面；④再上行小腿内侧；⑤沿胫骨后面；⑥交出足厥阴肝经的前面；⑦经膝、股部内侧前缘；⑧进入腹部；⑨属于脾脏，联络胃；⑩通过横膈上行；⑪挟食管旁边；⑫连系舌根，分散于舌下。

⑬胃部支脉：向上通过横膈；⑭流注于心中，与手少阴心经相连接（图1-8）。

1. The Course of the Channel

①It starts from the tip of the big toe. ②Then, it runs along the medial aspect of the big toe at the junction of the red and white skin, ③and ascends to the front of the medial malleolus, ④and further up to the medial aspect of the leg. ⑤It follows the posterior aspect of the tibia⑥and passes through the front of the Liver Channel of Foot-Jueyin. ⑦Going on along the anterior medial aspect of the knee and then the thigh, ⑧ it enters the abdomen, ⑨ reaches the spleen, its pertaining organ, and connects with the stomach. ⑩ From there, it ascends, passing through the diaphragm⑪and running alongside the esophagus. ⑫ When it reaches the root of the tongue, it spreads over its under surface.

⑬ The branch starting from the stomach ascends through the diaphragm⑭ and flows into the heart to connect with the Heart Channel of Hand-Shaoyin (Fig.1 - 8)

2. 常用经穴主治提要

本经腧穴主治脾胃病，如呕吐、胃痛、泄泻、痢疾、便秘，以及妇科和循经部位的其他病症。

2. Principal Indications of Commonly Used Acupoints of the Meridian

Diseases of the spleen and stomach, such as vomiting, stomachache, diarrhea, dysentery, constipation, diseases of gynecopathies and diseases of the regions along the course of this channel.

3. 常用腧穴 (图 1 - 9, 图 1 - 10)

3. The Commonly Used Acupoints (Fig.1 - 9, Fig.1 - 10)

隐　白

定位　踇趾内侧趾甲角旁约0.1寸。

主治　腹胀，便血、尿血，月经过多，崩漏，癫狂，多梦，惊风。

操作　浅刺0.1寸。可灸。

Yinbai (SP 1)

Location: On the medial side of the great toe, about 0.1 cun lateral to the proximal corner of the nail.

Indications: Abdominal distension, bloody stools, hematuria, menorrhagia, metrorrhagia and metrostaxis, mental disorder, dream-disturbed sleep, convulsion.

Method: Puncture shallowly 0.1 cun. Moxibustion is applicable.

大　都

定位　踇趾内侧，第1跖趾关节前缘，赤白肉际处。

主治　腹胀，胃痛，呕吐，泄泻，便秘，热病。

操作　直刺0.3~0.5寸。可灸。

Dadu (SP 2)

Location: On the medial side of the great toe, anterior to the first metatarsophalangeal joint, at the junction of the red and white skin.

Indications: Abdominal distension, stomachache, vomiting, diarrhea, constipation, febrile diseases.

Method: Puncture perpendicularly 0.3~0.5 cun. Moxibustion is applicable.

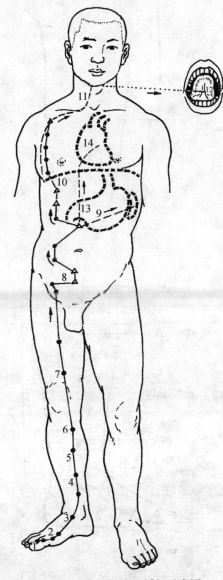

图 1 - 8　足太阴脾经循行示意图

Fig. 1 - 8　Running Course of the Spleen Channel of Foot-Taiyin

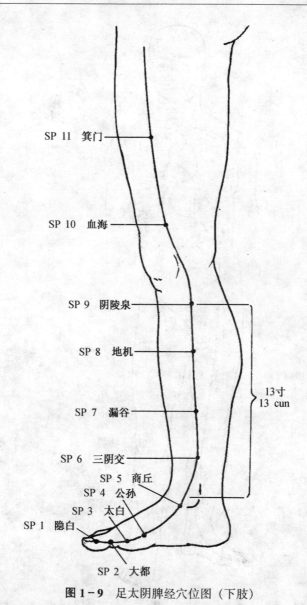

SP 11 箕门

SP 10 血海

SP 9 阴陵泉

SP 8 地机

13寸
13 cun

SP 7 漏谷

SP 6 三阴交

SP 5 商丘

SP 4 公孙

SP 3 太白

SP 1 隐白

SP 2 大都

图 1-9 足太阴脾经穴位图（下肢）

Fig. 1-9 Acupoints of the Spleen Channel of Foot-Taiyin (Lower Limb)

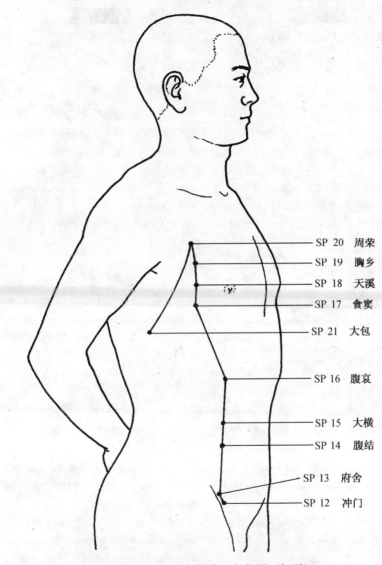

图 1 - 10 足太阴脾经穴位图（躯干）

Fig. 1 - 10 Acupoints of the Spleen Channel of Foot-Taiyin（Truck）.

太　白

定位　第1趾骨小头后缘，赤白肉际处。

主治　胃痛，腹胀，肠鸣，泄泻，便秘，痔瘘，脚气。

操作　直刺0.5～0.8寸。可灸。

Taibai （SP 3）

Location: Posterior to the small head of the first metatarsal bone, at the junction of the red and white skin.

Indications: Stomachache, abdominal distension, borborygmus, diarrhea, constipation, hemorrhoids, beriberi.
Method: Puncture perpendicularly 0.5～0.8 cun. Moxibustion is applicable.

公　孙

定位　足内侧缘，第1跖骨基底部前下方，赤白肉际处。

主治　胃痛，呕吐，腹痛，泄泻，痢疾。

操作　直刺0.6～1.2寸。可灸。

Gongsun （SP 4）

Location: On the medial border of the foot, antero-inferior to the proximal end of the first metatarsal bone, at the junction of the red and white skin.

Indications: Stomachache, vomiting, abdominal pain, diarrhea, dysentery.

Method: Puncture perpendicularly 0.6～1.2 cun. Moxibustion is applicable.

商　丘

定位　内踝前下方凹陷中。

主治　腹胀，泄泻，便秘，黄疸，足踝痛。

操作　直刺0.5～0.8寸。可灸。

Shangqiu （SP 5）

Location: In the depression distal and inferior to the medial malleolus.

Indications: Abdominal distension, diarrhea, constipation, jaundice, pain in the foot and ankle.

Method: Puncture perpendicularly 0.5～0.8 cun. Moxibustion in applicable.

三　阴　交

定位　内踝高点直上3寸，胫骨内侧面后缘。

主治　肠鸣，腹胀，泄泻，月经不调，带下，阴挺，不孕，遗精，阳痿，遗尿，疝气，失眠，下肢痿痹，脚气。

操作　直刺1～1.5寸，可灸。

Sanyinjiao （SP 6）

Location: 3 cun directly above the tip of the medial malleolus, on the posterior border of the medial, aspect of the tibia.

Indications: Borborygmus, abdominal distension, diarrhea, irregular menstruation, morbid leukorrhea, vaginal protrusion, sterility, spermatorrhea, impotence, enuresis, hernia, insomnia, muscular atrophy and pain of the lower extremities, beriberi.

Method: Puncture perpendicularly 1~1.5 cun. Moxibustion is applicable.

漏　谷

定位　三阴交穴上3寸。

主治　腹胀，肠鸣，小便不利，遗精，下肢痿痹。

操作　直刺1~1.5寸。可灸。

Lougu（SP 7）

Location: 3 cun above Sanyinjiao (SP 6).

Indications: Abdominal distension, borborygmus, difficulty in urination, seminal emission, muscular atrophy and pain of the lower extremities.

Method: Puncture perpendicularly 1~1.5 cun, Moxibustion is applicable.

地　机

定位　阴陵泉下3寸。

主治　腹痛，泄泻，小便困难，水肿，遗精，月经不调，痛经。

操作　直刺1~1.5寸。可灸。

Diji（SP 8）

Location: 3 cun below Yinlingquan (SP 9).

Indications: Abdominal pain, diarrhea, difficulty in urination, edema, seminal emission, irregular menstruation, dysmenorrhea.

Method: Puncture perpendicularly 1~1.5 cun. Moxibustion is applica-

ble.

阴　陵　泉

定位　胫骨内侧髁下缘凹陷中。

主治　腹胀，泄泻，水肿，黄疸，小便困难，膝痛。

操作　直刺1~2寸，可灸。

Yinlingquan（SP 9）

Location: In the depression of the lower border of the medial condyle of the tibia.

Indications: Abdominal distension, diarrhea, edema, jaundice, difficulty of urination, pain in the knee.

Method: Puncture perpendicularly 1~2 cun. Moxibustion is applicable.

血　海

定位　髌骨内缘直上2寸。

主治　月经不调，崩漏，经闭，荨麻疹，湿疹。

操作　直刺1~1.5寸。可灸。

Xuehai（SP 10）

Location: 2 cun above the medial border of the patella.

Indications: Irregular menstruation, metrorrhagia and metrostaxis, amenorrhea, urticaria, eczema.

Method: Puncture perpendicularly 1~1.5 cun. Moxibustion is applicable.

箕　门

定位　血海穴与冲门穴的连线上，血海穴直上6寸。

主治　小便不利，遗尿，腹股沟肿痛。

操作　避开动脉，直刺 0.5～1 寸。可灸。

Jimen （SP 11）

Location: On the line linking Xuehai (SP 10) and Chongmen (SP 12), 6 cun directly above Xuehai (SP 10).

Indications: Difficulty in urination, enuresis, swelling and pain.

Method: Avoiding the artery, puncture perpendicularly 0.5 ～ 1 cun. Moxibustion is applicable.

冲　　门

定位　耻骨联合上缘中点旁开 3.5 寸。

主治　腹痛，疝气，崩漏，带下。

操作　避开动脉，直刺 0.5～1 寸。可灸。

Chongmen （SP 12）

Location: 3.5 cun lateral to the midpoint of the upper margin of the pubic symphysis.

Indications: Abdominal pain, hernia, metrorrhagia and metrostaxis, leukorrhagia.

Method: Avoiding the artery, puncture perpendicularly 0.5 ～ 1 cun, Moxibustion is applicable.

府　　舍

定位　冲门穴外上方 0.7 寸，前正中线旁开 4 寸。

主治　腹痛，疝气，积聚。

操作　直刺 1～1.5 寸。可灸。

Fushe （SP 13）

Location: 0.7 cun above Chongmen (SP 12), 4 cun lateral to the front midline.

Indications: Abdominal pain, hernia, mass in the abdomen.

Method: Puncture perpendicularly 1～1.5 cun. Moxibustion is applicable.

腹　　结

定位　府舍穴上 3 寸，大横穴下 1.3 寸。

主治　腹痛，泄泻，疝气。

操作　直刺 1～2 寸。可灸。

Fujie （SP 14）

Location: 3 cun above Fushe (SP 13), 1.3 cun below Daheng (SP 15).

Indications: Abdominal pain, diarrhea, hernia.

Method: Puncture perpendicularly 1～2 cun. Moxibustion is applicable.

大　　横

定位　脐中旁开 4 寸。

主治　泄泻，便秘，腹痛。

操作　直刺 1～2 寸。可灸。

Daheng （SP 15）

Location: 4 cun lateral to the center of the umbilicus.

Indications: Diarrhea, constipation, abdominal pain.

Method: Puncture perpendicularly

1～2 cun. Moxibustion is applicable.

腹　哀

定位　大横穴上3寸，前正中线旁开4寸。

主治　消化不良，腹痛，便秘，痢疾。

操作　直刺1～1.5寸。可灸。

Fuai （SP 16）

Location: 3 cun above Daheng（SP 15），4 cun lateral to the front midline.

Indications: Indigestion, abdominal pain, constipation, dysentery.

Method: Puncture perpendicularly 1～1.5 cun. Moxibustion is applicable.

食　窦

定位　第5肋间隙中，前正中线旁开6寸。

主治　胸胁胀痛，腹胀，水肿。

操作　平刺或斜刺0.5～0.8寸。可灸。

Shidou （SP 17）

Location: In the fifth intercostal space, 6 cun lateral to the front midline.

Indications: Fullness and pain in the chest and hypochondrium, abdominal distension, edema.

Method: Puncture transversely or obliquely 0.5～0.8 cun. Moxibustion is applicable.

天　溪

定位　第4肋间隙中，前正中线旁开6寸。

主治　胸胁疼痛，咳嗽，乳汁不足，乳痈。

操作　平刺或斜刺0.5～0.8寸。可灸。

Tianxi （SP 18）

Location: In the fourth intercostal space, 6 cun lateral to the front midline.

Indications: Pain in the chest and hypochondrium, cough, insufficient lactation, acute mastadenitis.

Method: Puncture transversely or obliquely 0.5～0.8 cun. Moxibustion is applicable.

胸　乡

定位　第3肋间隙中，前正中线旁开6寸。

主治　胸胁胀痛。

操作　平刺或斜刺0.5～0.8寸。可灸。

Xiongxiang （SP 19）

Location: In the third intercostal space, 6 cun lateral to the front midline.

Indications: Fullness and pain in the chest and hypochondrium.

Method: Puncture transversely or obliquely 0.5～0.8 cun. Moxibustion is applicable.

周　荣

定位　第2肋间隙中，前正中线

旁开6寸。

主治 咳嗽，气逆，胸胁胀满。

操作 平刺或斜刺0.5～0.8寸。可灸。

Zhourong（SP 20）

Location: In the second intercostal space, 6 cun lateral to the front midline.

Indications: Cough, Qi counterflow, fullness in the chest and hypochondrium.

Method: Puncture transversely or obliquely $0.5 \sim 0.8$ cun. Moxibustion is applicable.

大　包

定位 腋中线上，第6肋间隙中。

主治 气喘，胸胁痛，全身疼痛，四肢无力。

操作 平刺或斜刺0.5～0.8寸。可灸。

Dabao（SP 21）

Location: In the sixth intercostal space, on the midaxillary line.

Indications: Asthma, pain in the chest and hypochondrium, pain in the whole body, weakness of the extremities.

Method: Puncture transversely or obliquely $0.5 \sim 0.8$ cun. Moxibustion is applicable.

第五节 手少阴心经及其常用腧穴

Section 5 The Heart Channel of Hand-Shaoyin and Commonly Used Acupoints

1. 经脉循行

①起于心中，出属心系（心与其他脏器连系的部位）；②通过横膈，联络小肠；③从"心系"向上的脉；④挟食管上行；⑤连目系（眼球连系于脑的部位）；⑥"心系"直行的脉：上行于肺部，再向下出于腋窝部；⑦沿上臂内侧后缘，行于手太阴肺经和手厥阴心包经的后面；⑧到达肘窝，沿前臂内侧后缘；⑨至掌后豌豆骨部；⑩进入掌内；⑪沿小指内侧至末端，与手太阳小肠经相连接（图1－11）。

1. The Course of the Channel

① It originates from the heart. Emerging, it spreads over the "heart system" (the connection between the heart and connected viscera). ② It passes through the diaphragm to connect with the small intestine. ③ The ascending portion of the channel from the "heart system" ④ runs alongside the esophagus ⑤ to connect with the "eye system", the connection between the eyeball and brain.

⑥ The straight portion of the channel

(from the "heart system") goes upwards to the lung. Then it runs downwards and emerges from the axilla. ⑦ From there it goes along the posterior border of the medial aspect of the upper arm behind the Lung Channel of Hand-Taiyin and the Pericardium Channel of Hand-Jueyin⑧ down to the cubital fossa. From there it descends along the posterior border of the medial aspect of the forearm ⑨ to the pisiform region proximal to the palm⑩ and enters the palm. ⑪Then it follows the medial aspect of the little finger to its tip and links, with the Small Intestine Channel of Hand-Taiyang (Fig.1 - 11).

2. 常用经穴主治提要

本经腧穴主治心、胸、神志病以及经脉循行部位的其他病症。

2. Principal Indications of Commonly Used Acupoints of the Meridian

Diseases in the heart and chest, mental diseases and the regions along the course of this channels.

3. 常用腧穴 (图 1 - 12)

3. The Commonly Used Acupoints (Fig.1 - 12)

极 泉

定位 腋窝正中,腋动脉搏动处。

主治 心痛,咽干烦渴,胁肋疼痛,瘰疬,肩臂疼痛。

操作 避开腋动脉,直刺0.5~1寸。可灸。

Jiquan (HT 1)

Location: In the centre of the axilla, at the pulsating point of the axillary artery.

Indications: Heart pain, dryness of the throat and excessive thirst, pain in the costal region, scrofula, pain in the shoulder and arm.

Method: Avoiding the artery, puncture perpendicularly or obliquely 0.3~0.5 cun. Moxibustion is applicable.

青 灵

定位 少海穴与极泉穴的连线上,少海穴上3寸,肱二头肌的内侧沟中。

主治 头痛,目黄,胁痛,肩臂疼痛。

操作 直刺0.5~1寸。可灸。

Qingling (HT 2)

Location: On the line linking Shaohai (HT 3) and Jiquan (HT 1), 3 cun above Shaohai (HT 3), in the medial groove of the biceps muscle.

Indications: Headache, yellowing of the eyes, pain in the costal region, pain in the shoulder and arm.

Method: Puncture perpendicularly 0.5~1 cun. Moxibustion is applicable.

少　　海

定位　屈肘，当肘横纹内端与肱骨内上髁连线之中点。

主治　心痛，肘臂挛痛，瘰疬，头项痛，腋胁痛。

操作　直刺0.5～1寸。可灸。

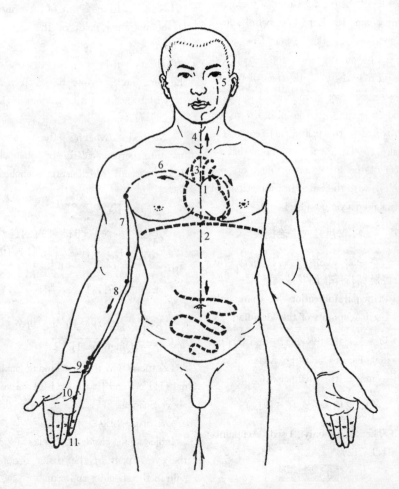

图1-11　手少阴心经循行示意图

Fig.1-11 Running Course of the Heart Channel of Hand-Shaoyin

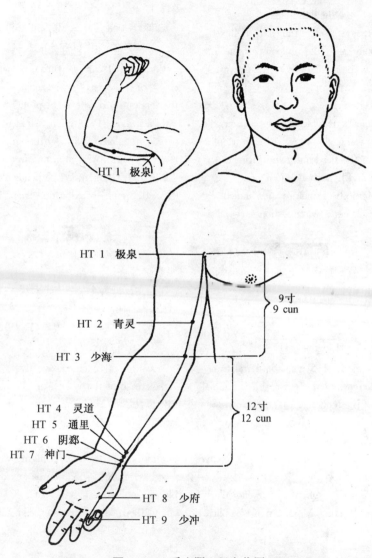

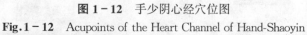

图 1 – 12 手少阴心经穴位图

Fig. 1 – 12 Acupoints of the Heart Channel of Hand-Shaoyin

Shaohai （HT 3）

Location： When the elbow is flexed, the point is at the midpoint of the line linking the medial end of the transverse cubital crease and the medial epicondyle of the humerus.

Indications： Heart pain, spasmodic pain of the elbow and arm, scrofula, pain in the head and nape, pain in the axilla and hypochondriac region.

Method： Puncture perpendicularly 0.5～1 cun. Moxibustion is applicable.

灵　　道

定位　腕横纹上1.5寸，尺侧腕屈肌腱的桡侧。

主治　心痛，暴喑，肘臂挛痛。

操作　直刺0.3～0.5寸。可灸。

Lingdao （HT 4）

Location： 1.5 cun above the transverse crease of the wrist, on the radial side of the tendon of m. flexor carpi ulnaris.

Indications： Heart pain, sudden loss of voice, spasmodic pain of the elbow and arm.

Method： Puncture perpendicularly 0.3～0.5 cun. Moxibustion is applicable.

通　　里

定位　腕横纹上1寸，尺侧腕屈肌腱的桡侧。

主治　心悸，暴喑，舌强不语，

腕臂痛。

操作　直刺0.3～0.5寸。可灸。

Tongli （HT 5）

Location： 1 cun above the transverse crease of the wrist, on the radial side of the tendon of m. flexor carpi ularis.

Indications： Palpitation, sudden loss of voice, aphasia with stiffness of the tongue, pain in the wrist and forearm.

Method： Puncture perpendicularly 0.3～0.5 cun. Moxibustion is applicable.

阴　　郄

定位　腕横纹上0.5寸，尺侧腕屈肌腱的桡侧。

主治　心痛，惊悸，骨蒸盗汗，吐血，衄血，暴喑。

操作　直刺0.3～0.5寸。可灸。

Yinxi （HT 6）

Location： 0.5 cun above the transverse crease of the wrist, on the radial side of the tendon of m. flexor carpi ularis.

Indications： Heart pain, fright palpitation, hectic fever and night sweat, blood ejection, spontaneous external bleeding, sudden loss of voice.

Method： Puncture perpendicularly 0.3～0.5 cun. Moxibustion is applicable.

神　　门

定位　腕横纹尺侧端，尺侧腕屈肌腱的桡侧凹陷中。

主治 心痛，心烦，惊悸，怔忡，健忘，失眠，癫、狂、痫，胸胁痛。

操作 直刺 0.3～0.5 寸。可灸。

Shenmen (HT 7)

Location: At the ulnar end of the transverse crease of the wrist, in the depression on the radial side of the tendon of m. flexor carpi ulnaris.

Indications: Heart pain, vexation, fright palpitation, severe palpitation, amnesia, insomnia, depressive psychosis, mania, epilepsy, pain of the chest and hypochondrium.

Method: Puncture perpendicularly 0.3～0.5 cun. Moxibustion is applicable.

少 府

定位 第 4、第 5 掌骨之间，握拳，当小指端与无名指端之间。

主治 心悸、胸痛，小便不利，阴痒痛，小指挛痛。

操作 直刺 0.3～0.5 寸。可灸。

Shaofu (HT 8)

Location: Between the fourth and fifth metacarpal bones. When a fist is made, the point is between the tips of the little finger and ring finger.

Indications: Palpitation, chest pain, dysuria, pruritus of the external genitalia, spasmodic pain of the little finger.

Method: Puncture perpendicularly 0.3～0.5 cun. Moxibustion is applicable.

少 冲

定位 小指桡侧指甲角旁约 0.1 寸。

主治 心悸，心痛，胸胁痛，热病，昏迷，癫狂。

操作 浅刺 0.1 寸或用三棱针点刺出血。可灸。

Shaochong (HT 9)

Location: On the radial side of the little finger, about 0.1 cun proximal to the corner of the nail.

Indications: Palpitation, heart pain, pain in the chest and hypochondrium, febrile disease, loss of consciousness, depressive psychosis, mania.

Method: Puncture shallowly 0.1 cun or prick the point to cause bleeding with the three-edged needle. Moxibustion is applicable.

第六节 手太阳小肠经及其常用腧穴

Section 6 The Small Intestine Channel of Hand-Taiyang and Commonly Used Acupoints

1. 经脉循行

①起于手小指外侧端；②沿着手背外侧至腕部，出于尺骨茎突；③直上沿前臂外侧后缘，经尺骨鹰嘴与肱

骨内上髁之间；④沿上臂外侧后缘；
⑤出于肩关节；⑥绕行肩胛部；⑦交
会于大椎（督脉）；⑧向下进入缺盆
部；⑨联络心脏；⑩沿食管；⑪通过
横膈；⑫到胃部；⑬属于小肠。

⑭缺盆部支脉：⑮沿着颈部；⑯
上达面颊；⑰至目外眦；⑱转入耳中。

⑲颊部支脉：上行目眶下，抵于
鼻旁，至目内眦，与足太阳膀胱经相
连接（图 1－13）。

1. The Course of the Channel

①Starting from the ulnar side of the
tip of the little finger, ②following the
ulner side of the dorsum of the hand, it
reaches the wrist where it emerges from
the styloid process of the ulna. ③From
there, it ascends along the posterior
border of the lateral aspect of the forearm, passes between the olecranon of
the ulna and the medial epicondyle of
the humerus, and ④ runs along the
posterior border of the lateral aspect of
the upper arm⑤ to the shoulder joint.
⑥Circling around the scapular region,
⑦it meets Dazhui (DU 14) on the superior aspect of the shoulder. ⑧Then,
turning downwards to the supraclavicular fossa, ⑨it connects with the heart.
⑩ From there, it descends along the
esophagus, ⑪ passes through the diaphragm,⑫reaches the stomach, ⑬and
finally enters the small intestine, its
pertaining organ.

⑭The branch from the supraclavicular
fossa⑮ runs along the neck⑯ and ascends to the cheek. ⑰ It reaches the
outer canthus⑱and then enters the ear.
⑲The branch from the cheek runs upwards to the infraorbital region and further to the lateral side of the nose.
Then it reaches the inner canthus to
link with the BladderChannel of Foot-
Taiyang (Fig.1－13).

2. 常用经穴主治提要

本经腧穴主治头、项、耳、目、
咽喉病，热病，神志病及经脉循行部
位的其他病症。

2. Principal Indications of the Commonly Used Acupoints of the Meridican

Diseases of the head, nape, ear,
eye and throat, febrile and mental diseases, and the diseases of the regions a-
long the course of this channel.

3. 常用腧穴（图 1－14）

3. The Commonly Used Acupoints (Fig.1－14)

少　　泽

定位　小指尺侧指甲角旁约
0.1 寸。

主治　头痛，目翳，咽喉肿痛，
乳痈，昏迷，热病。

操作　浅刺 0.1 寸或点刺出血，
可灸。

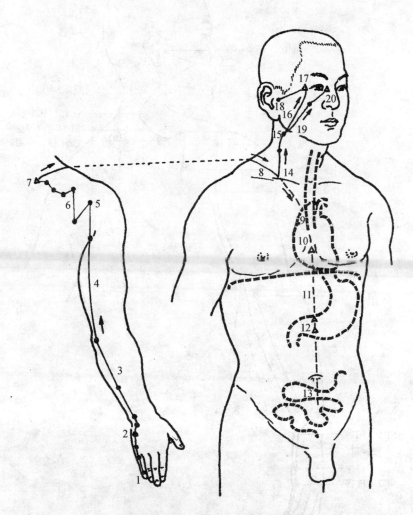

图 1 - 13 手太阳小肠经循行示意图

Fig. 1 - 13 Running Course of the Small Intestine Channel of Hand-Taiyang

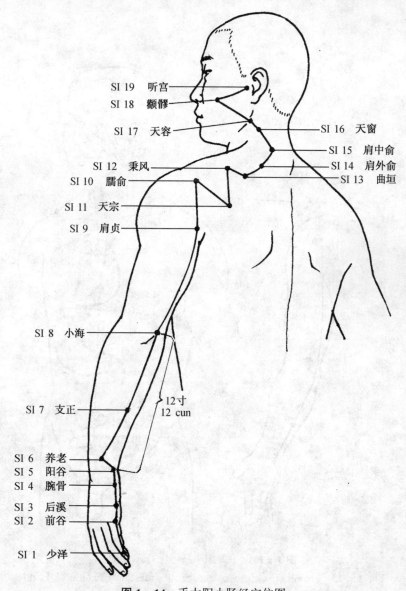

SI 19　听宫
SI 18　颧髎
SI 17　天容
SI 16　天窗
SI 15　肩中俞
SI 12　秉风
SI 14　肩外俞
SI 10　臑俞
SI 13　曲垣
SI 11　天宗
SI 9　肩贞
SI 8　小海
12寸
12 cun
SI 7　支正
SI 6　养老
SI 5　阳谷
SI 4　腕骨
SI 3　后溪
SI 2　前谷
SI 1　少泽

图 1 - 14　手太阳小肠经穴位图

Fig. 1 - 14　Acupoints of the Small Intestine Channel of Hand-Taiyang

Shaoze（SI 1）

Location: On the ulnar side of the little finger, about 0.1 cun proximal to the corner of the nail.

Indications: Headache, corneal opacity, sore throat, acute mastitis, coma, febrile disease.

Method: Puncture shallowly 0.1 cun or prick the point to cause bleeding. Moxibustion is applicable.

前 谷

定位　握拳，第5指掌关节前尺侧，横纹头赤白肉际。

主治　头痛，目痛，耳鸣，咽喉肿痛，乳汁不足，热病。

操作　直刺0.3～0.5寸。

Qiangu（SI 2）

Location: When a fist is made, the point is on the ulnar side, distal to the fifth metacarpophalangeal joint, at the end of the transverse crease and the junction of the red and white skin.

Indications: Headache, pain in the eye, tinnitus, sore throat, insufficient lactation, febrile disease.

Method: Puncture shallowly 0.3～0.5 cun.

后 溪

定位　握拳，第5指掌关节后侧，横纹头赤白肉际处。

主治　头项强痛，目赤，耳聋，咽喉肿痛，腰背痛，癫、狂、痫，疟疾，手指及肘臂挛痛。

操作　直刺0.5～1寸。可灸。

Houxi（SI 3）

Location: When a fist is made, the point is on the ulnar side, proximal to the fifth metacarpophalangeal joint, at the junction of the red and white skin.

Indications: Pain and rigidity of the head and neck, redness of the eye, deafness, sore throat, lumbar pain, backpain, depressive psychosis, mania, epilepsy, malaria, spasmodic pain of the finger, elbow and arm.

Method: Puncture perpendicularly 0.5～1 cun. Moxibustion is applicable.

腕 骨

定位　后溪穴直上，于第5掌骨基底与三角骨之间赤白肉际处。

主治　头项强痛，耳鸣，目翳，黄疸，热病，疟疾，指腕挛痛。

操作　直刺0.3～0.5寸。可灸。

Wangu（SI 4）

Location: Directly proximal to Houxi (SI 3), between the base of the fifth metacarpal bone and the triquetral bone, at the junction of the red and white skin.

Indications: Pain and rigidity of the head and neck, tinnitus, corneal opacity, jaundice, febrile diseases, malaria, pain and contracture of the fingers and wrist.

Method: Puncture perpendicularly

0.3～0.5 cun. Moxibustion is applicable.

阳　谷

定位　腕背横纹尺侧端，尺骨茎突前凹陷中。

主治　头痛，目眩，耳鸣，耳聋，热病，癫、狂、痫，腕痛。

操作　直刺0.3～0.5寸，可灸。

Yanggu（SI 5）

Location: On the ulnar end of the transverse crease of the wrist, in the depression distal to the styloid process of the ulna.

Indications: Headache, dizziness, tinnitus, deafness, febrile diseases, depressive psychosis, mania, epilepsy, pain in the wrist.

Method: Puncture perpendicularly 0.3～0.5 cun. Moxibustion is applicable.

养　老

定位　以掌向胸，在尺骨茎突桡侧缘缝隙处。

主治　目视不明，肩、背、肘、臂酸痛。

操作　直刺或斜刺0.5～0.8寸。可灸。

Yanglao（SI 6）

Location: When the palm faces the chest, the point is in the bony cleft on the radial side of the styloid process of the ulna.

Indications: Blurred vision, pain in

the shoulder, back, elbow and arm.

Method: Puncture perpendicularly or obliquely 0.5～0.8 cun. Moxibustion is applicable.

支　正

定位　阳谷穴与小海穴的连线上，阳谷穴上5寸。

主治　头痛，目眩，热病，癫狂，项强，肘臂酸痛。

操作　直刺或斜刺0.5～0.8寸。可灸。

Zhizheng（SI 7）

Location: On the line linking Yanggu（SI 5）and Xiaohai（SI 8）, 5 cun above Yanggu（SI 5）.

Indications: Headache, dizziness, febrile diseases, depressive psychosis, mania, neck rigidity, pain in the elbow and arm.

Method: Puncture perpendicularly or obliquely 0.5～0.8 cun. Moxibustion is applicable.

小　海

定位　屈肘，当尺骨鹰嘴与肱骨内上髁之间凹陷中。

主治　肘臂疼痛，癫痫。

操作　斜刺0.5～0.8寸。可灸。

Xiaohai（SI 8）

Location: When the elbow is flexed, the point is located in the depression between the olecranon of the ulna and the medial epicondyle of the huemrus.

Indications: Pain in the elbow and

arm, epilepsy.

Method: Puncture obliquely 0.5 ~ 0.8 cun. Moxibustion is applicable.

肩 贞

定位 腋后皱襞上1寸。

主治 肩臂疼痛，瘰疬，耳鸣。

操作 直刺1~1.5寸。可灸。

Jianzhen (SI 9)

Location: 1 cun above the posterior axillary fold.

Indications: Pain in the shoulder and arm, scrofula, tinnitus.

Method: Puncture perpendicularly 1 ~ 1.5 cun. Moxibustion is applicable.

臑 俞

定位 腋后皱襞直上，肩胛骨下缘凹陷中。

主治 肩臂疼痛，瘰疬。

操作 直刺或斜刺0.5~1.5寸。可灸。

Naoshu (SI 10)

Location: Directly above the posterior end of the axillary fold, in the depression on the inferior side of the scapular spine.

Indications: Pain in the shoulder and arm, scrofula.

Method: Puncture perpendicularly or obliquely 1 ~ 1.5 cun. Moxibustion is applicable.

天 宗

定位 肩胛骨岗下窝的中央。

主治 肩胛疼痛，气喘，乳痈。

操作 直刺或斜刺0.5~1寸。可灸。

Tianzong (SI 11)

Location: In the centre of the infraspinous fossa of the scapula.

Indications: Pain in the scapular region, asthma, acute mastitis.

Method: Puncture perpendicularly or obliquely 0.5 ~ 1 cun. Moxibustion is applicable.

秉 风

定位 肩胛骨岗上窝中，天宗穴直上。

主治 肩胛疼痛，上肢麻木疼痛。

操作 直刺或斜刺0.5~1寸。可灸。

Bingfeng (SI 12)

Location: In the centre of the suprascapular fossa, directly above Tianzong (SI 11).

Indications: Pain in the scapular region, pain and numbness of the arm.

Method: Puncture perpendicularly or obliquely 0.5 ~ 1 cun. Moxibustion is applicable.

曲 垣

定位 肩胛骨岗上窝内侧端，在臑俞与第2胸椎棘突连线的中点。

主治 肩胛疼痛。

操作 直刺或斜刺0.5~1寸。

可灸。

Quyuan (SI 13)

Location: At the medial border of the suprascapular fossa, at the midpoint of the line between Naoshu (SI 10) and the spinous process of the second thoracic vertebra.

Indications: Pain in the scapular region.

Method: Puncture perpendicularly or obliquely 0.5～1 cun. Moxibustion is applicable.

肩　外　俞

定位　第1胸椎棘突下旁开3寸。
主治　肩背疼痛，项强。
操作　斜刺0.5～0.8寸。可灸。

Jianwaishu (SI 14)

Location: 3 cun lateral to the lower border of the spinous process of the first thoracic vertebra.

Indications: Pain in the shoulder and back, neck rigidity.

Method: Puncture obliquely 0.5～0.8 cun. Moxibustion is applicable.

肩　中　俞

定位　第7颈椎棘突下旁开2寸。
主治　咳嗽，气喘，肩背疼痛，目视不明。
操作　斜刺0.5～0.8寸。可灸。

Jianzhongshu (SI 15)

Location: 2 cun lateral to the lower border of the spinous process of the sev-

enth cervical vertebra.

Indications: Cough, asthma, pain in the shoulder and back, blurred vision.

Method: Puncture obliquely 0.5～0.8 cun. Moxibustion is applicable.

天　　窗

定位　喉结旁开3.5寸，在胸锁乳突肌后缘。
主治　耳鸣，耳聋，咽喉肿痛，颈项强痛，暴喑。
操作　直刺0.5～1寸。可灸。

Tianchuang (SI 16)

Location: 3.5 cun lateral to the Adam's apple, in the posterior border of m. sternocleidomastoideus.

Indications: Tinnitus, deafness, sore throat, stiffness and pain of the nape, sudden loss of voice.

Method: Puncture perpendicularly 0.5～1 cun. Moxibustion is applicable.

天　　容

定位　下颌角后，胸锁乳突肌前缘。
主治　耳鸣，耳聋，咽喉肿痛，颈项肿痛。
操作　直刺0.5～1寸。可灸。

Tianrong (SI 17)

Location: Posterior to the angle of the mandible, in the depression of the anterior border of m. sternocleidomasdoideus.

Indications: Tinnitus, deafness, sore throat, swelling and pain of the nape.

Method: Puncture perpendicularly $0.5 \sim 1$ cun. Moxibustion is applicable.

颧　髎

定位　目外眦直下，颧骨下缘凹陷中。

主治　口眼㖞斜，眼睑瞤动，齿痛，颊肿。

操作　直刺 $0.3 \sim 0.5$ 寸，或斜刺、平刺 $0.5 \sim 1$ 寸。

Quanliao (SI 18)

Location: Directly below the outer canthus, in the depression on the lower border of zygoma.

Indications: Deviation of the mouth and eye, twitching of the eyelids, toothache, swelling of the cheek.

Method: Puncture perpendicularly $0.3 \sim 0.5$ cun, puncture obliquely or subcutaneously $0.5 \sim 1$ cun.

听　宫

定位　耳屏前，下颌骨髁状突的后缘，张口之凹陷处。

主治　耳鸣，耳聋，聤耳，牙痛，癫、狂、痫。

操作　张口，直刺 $1 \sim 1.5$ 寸。可灸。

Tinggong (SI 19)

Location: Anterior to the tragus and posterior to the condyloid process of the mandible, in the depression formed when the mouth is open.

Indications: Tinnitus, deafness, otorrhea, toothache, depressive psychosis, mania, epilepsy.

Method: Puncture perpendicularly $1 \sim 1.5$ cun when the mouth is open. Moxibustion is applicable.

第七节　足太阳膀胱经及其常用腧穴

Section 7 The Bladder Channel of Foot-Taiyang and Commonly Used Acupoints

1. 经脉循行

①起于目内眦；②上额；③交督脉于巅顶；④巅顶部支脉：从头顶到颞颥部；⑤巅顶部直行的脉：从头顶入里联络于脑；⑥回出分开下行项后；⑦沿肩胛部内侧，挟脊柱；⑧到达腰部；⑨从脊旁肌肉进入体腔；⑩联络肾脏；⑪属于膀胱。⑫腰部的支脉：向下通过臀部，⑬进入腘窝中。⑭后项的支脉：通过肩胛骨内缘直下；⑮经过臀部下行；⑯沿大腿外侧后面；⑰与腰部下来的支脉会合于腘窝中；⑱从此向下，通过腓肠肌；⑲出于外踝的后面；⑳沿着第 5 跖骨粗隆；㉑至小趾外侧端，与足少阴肾经相连接（图 1－15）。

1. The Course of the Channel

① The Bladder Channel of Foot-

Taiyang starts from the inner canthus. ② Ascending to the forehead, ③ it meets the Du Channel at the vertex. ④The branch arising at the vertex runs to the temple. ⑤ The straight portion of the channel enters and communicates with the brain from the vertex. ⑥ It then emerges and bifurcates to descend along the posterior aspect of the neck. ⑦Running downward along the medial aspect of the scapula region and paralled to the vertebral column, ⑧ it reaches the lumbar region ⑨where it enters the body cavity via the paravertebral muscle ⑩to connect with the kidney⑪and join its pertaining organ, the urinary bladder. ⑫ The branch of the lumbar region descends through the gluteal region ⑬and ends in the popliteal fossa. ⑭ The branch from the posterior aspect of the neck runs straight downward along the medial border of the scapula. ⑮ Passing through the gluteal region and going downward⑯along the lateral aspect of the thigh⑰it meets the preceding branch descending from the lumbar region in the popliteal fossa. ⑱ From there, it descends through the gastrocnemius muscle⑲to the posterior aspect of the external malleous. ⑳ Then, running along the tuberosity of the fifth metatarsal bone, ㉑it reaches the lateral side of the tip of the little toe where it links with the Kidney Channel of Foot-Shaoyin (Fig.1－15)。

2. 常用经穴主治提要

本经腧穴主治头、项、目、腰、下肢部病症以及神志病，背部第 1 侧线的背俞穴及第 2 侧线相平的腧穴，主治与其相关的脏腑病症和有关的组织器官病症。

2. Principal Indications of the Commonly Used Acupoints of the Meridian

Diseases of the head, nape, eye, lumbar region and the lower extremities, mental diseases. The Back-Shu Points along the first lateral line and the corresponding points parallel to them on the second lateral line over the back are used to treat diseases of their relevant Zang-fu organs and tissues respectively.

3. 常用腧穴（图 1－16，图 1－17）

3. The Commonly Used Acupoints (Fig.1－16, Fig.1－17)

睛　明

定位　目内眦旁 0.1 寸。

主治　目赤肿痛，流泪，视物不明，眩晕，近视，夜盲，色盲。

操作　嘱患者闭目，医者左手轻推眼球向外侧固定，右手持针缓慢进针，直刺 0.1～1.0 寸，不捻转，不提插。出针后压迫针孔 1～2 分钟，防止出血。禁灸。

Jingming（BL 1）

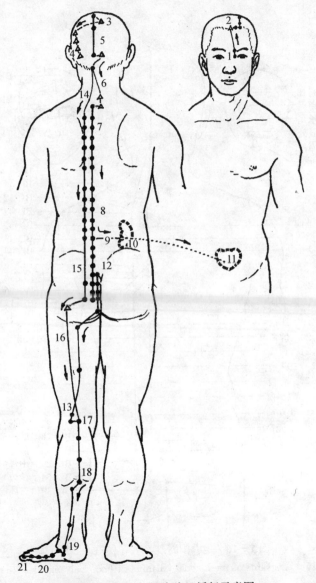

图 1 − 15　足太阳膀胱经循行示意图

Fig.1 − 15　Running Course of the Bladder Channel of Foot-Taiyang

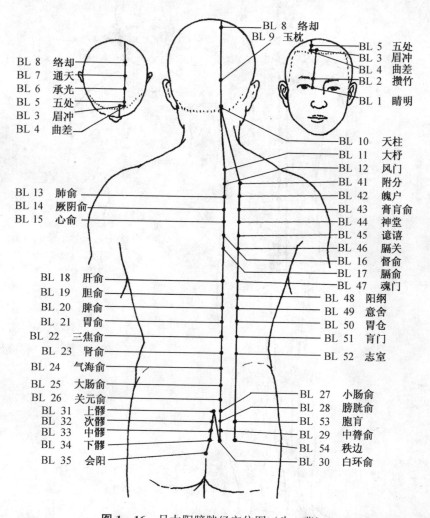

BL 8 络却
BL 9 玉枕

BL 8 络却
BL 7 通天
BL 6 承光
BL 5 五处
BL 3 眉冲
BL 4 曲差

BL 5 五处
BL 3 眉冲
BL 4 曲差
BL 2 攒竹
BL 1 睛明

BL 13 肺俞
BL 14 厥阴俞
BL 15 心俞

BL 10 天柱
BL 11 大杼
BL 12 风门
BL 41 附分
BL 42 魄户
BL 43 膏肓俞
BL 44 神堂
BL 45 譩譆
BL 46 膈关
BL 16 督俞
BL 17 膈俞
BL 47 魂门

BL 18 肝俞
BL 19 胆俞
BL 20 脾俞
BL 21 胃俞
BL 22 三焦俞
BL 23 肾俞
BL 24 气海俞
BL 25 大肠俞
BL 26 关元俞
BL 31 上髎
BL 32 次髎
BL 33 中髎
BL 34 下髎
BL 35 会阳

BL 48 阳纲
BL 49 意舍
BL 50 胃仓
BL 51 肓门
BL 52 志室

BL 27 小肠俞
BL 28 膀胱俞
BL 53 胞肓
BL 29 中膂俞
BL 54 秩边
BL 30 白环俞

图 1 - 16　足太阳膀胱经穴位图（头、背）

Fig. 1 - 16 Acupoints of the Bladder Channel of Foot-Taiyang(Head and Back)

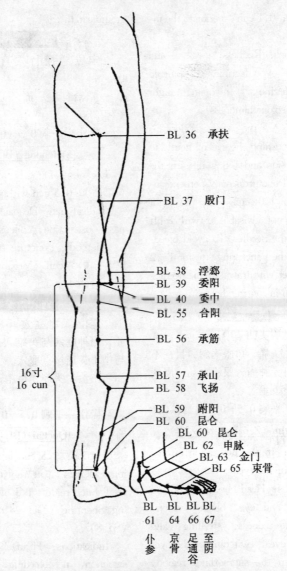

图 1－17 足太阳膀胱经穴位图（下肢）

Fig. 1－17 Acupoints of the Bladder Channel of Foot-Taiyang（Lower Limb）

Location: 0.1 cun superior to the inner canthus.

Indications: Redness, swelling and pain of the eye, lacrimation, blurred vision, dizziness, myopia, night blindness, colour blindness.

Method: Ask the patient to close his eyes when pushing the eyeball gently to the lateral side and fixing it with the left hand. Puncture slowly perpendicularly 0.1 ~ 1.0 cun with the right hand. It is not advisable to twirl or lift and thrust the needle. To avoid bleeding, press the puncturing site for 1~2 minutes after withdrawal of the needle. Moxibustion is contraindicated.

攒　　竹

定位　眉头凹陷中。

主治　头痛，口眼㖞斜，目视不清，流泪目赤肿痛，眼睑瞤动，眉棱骨痛，眼睑下垂。

操作　平刺0.5~0.8寸。禁灸。

Cuanzhu（Zanzhu）（BL 2）

Location: In the depression on the media lend of the eyebrow.

Indications: Headache, deviation of the mouth and eye, blurred vision, lacrimation, redness, swelling and pain in the eyes, twitching of the eyelids, pain in the supraorbital region, blepharoptosis.

Method: Puncture subcutaneously 0.5 ~ 0.8 cun. Moxibustion is con-

traindicated.

眉　　冲

定位　攒竹穴直上，入发际0.5寸。

主治　头痛，眩晕，鼻塞，癫痫。

操作　平刺0.3~0.5寸。禁灸。

Meichong（BL 3）

Location: Directly above Cuanzhu (BL 2), 0.5 cun within the hairline.

Indications: Headache, dizziness, nasal obstruction, epilepsy.

Method: Puncture subcutaneously 0.3 ~ 0.5 cun. Moxibustion is contraindicated.

曲　　差

定位　神庭穴（督脉）旁1.5寸，当神庭穴与头维穴连线的内1/3与中1/3连接点取穴。

主治　头痛，鼻塞，鼻衄，目视不清。

操作　平刺0.5~0.8寸。禁灸。

Quchai（BL 4）

Location: 1.5 cun lateral to Shenting (DU 24), at the junction of the medial and middle 1/3 of the line linking Shenting (DU 24) and Touwei (ST 8).

Indications: Headache, nasal obstruction, nosebleeding, blurred vision.

Method: Puncture subcutaneously 0.5 ~ 0.8 cun. Moxibustion is contraindicated.

五　　处

定位　曲差穴上 0.5 寸，距头部正中线 1.5 寸。

主治　头痛，目眩，癫痫。

操作　平刺 0.5～0.8 寸。禁灸。

Wuchu（BL 5）

Location：0.5 cun above Quchai, 1.5 cun lateral to the anterior midline of the head.

Indications：Headache, dizziness, epilepsy.

Method：Puncture subcutaneously 0.5 ～ 0.8 cun. Moxibustion is contraindicated.

承　　光

定位　五处穴后 1.5 寸。

主治　头痛，目眩，鼻塞，热病。

操作　平刺 0.3～0.5 寸。可灸。

Chengguang（BL 6）

Location：1.5 cun posterior to Wuchu（BL5）.

Indications：Headache, dizziness, nasal obstruction, febrile diseases.

Method：Puncture subcutaneously 0.3～0.5 cun. Moxibustion is applicable.

通　　天

定位　承光穴后 1.5 寸。

主治　头痛，眩晕，鼻塞，鼻衄，鼻渊。

操作　平刺 0.3～0.5 寸。可灸。

Tongtian（BL 7）

Location：1.5 cun posterior to Chengguang（BL 6）.

Indications：Headache, dizziness, nasal obstruction, nosebleeding, deep-source nasal congestion.

Method：Puncture subcutaneously 0.3～0.5 cun. Moxibustion is applicable.

络　　却

定位　通天穴后 1.5 寸。

主治　头晕，目视不明，耳鸣，癫狂。

操作　平刺 0.3～0.5 寸。可灸。

Luoque（BL 8）

Location：1.5 cun posterior to Tongtian（BL 7）.

Indications：Dizziness, blurred vision, tinnitus, epilepsy.

Method：Puncture subcutaneously 0.3～0.5 cun. Moxibustion is applicable.

玉　　枕

定位　后发际正中直上 2.5 寸，旁开 1.3 寸。

主治　头痛，目痛，鼻塞，颈项痛。

操作　平刺 0.3～0.5 寸。可灸。

Yuzhen（BL 9）

Location：2.5 cun above the mid-posterior hairline, 1.3 cun lateral to the midline.

Indications: Headache, pain of the eye, nasal obstruction, neck pain.

Method: Puncture subcutaneously 0.3~0.5 cun. Moxibustion is applicable.

天　　柱

定位　后发际正中直上 0.5 寸，旁开 1.3 寸，当斜方肌外缘凹陷中。

主治　头痛，项强，鼻塞，癫、狂、痫，肩背痛，热病。

操作　直刺或斜刺 0.5~0.8 寸。不可向内上方深刺。可灸。

Tianzhu（BL 10）

Location: 0.5 cun directly above and 1.3 cun lateral to the midpoint of the posterior hairline in the depression on the lateral margin of m. trapezius.

Indications: Headache, neck rigidity, nasal obstruction, depressive psychosis, malaria, epilepsy, pain in the shoulder and back, febrile diseases.

Method: Puncture perpendicularly or obliquely 0.5 ~ 0.8 cun. Moxibustion is applicable.

大　　杼

定位　第 1 胸椎棘突下，旁开 1.5 寸。

主治　咳嗽，发热，项强，肩背痛。

操作　平刺 0.5~0.8 寸。可灸。

Dashu（BL 11）

Location: 1.5 cun lateral to the low-er border of the spinous process of the first thoracic vertebra.

Indications: Cough, fever, neck rigidity, pain in the shoulder and back.

Method: Puncture obliquely 0.5 ~ 0.8 cun. Moxibustion is applicable.

风　　门

定位　第 2 胸椎棘突下，旁开 1.5 寸。

主治　咳嗽，发热，头痛，项强，胸背痛。

操作　平刺 0.5~1 寸。可灸。

Fengmen（BL 12）

Location: 1.5 cun lateral to the low-er border of the spinous process of the second thoracic vertebra.

Indications: Cough, fever, headache, neck rigidity, pain in the chest and back.

Method: Puncture subcutaneously 0.5~1 cun. Moxibustion is applicable.

肺　　俞

定位　第 3 胸椎棘突下，旁开 1.5 寸。

主治　咳嗽，气喘，吐血，骨蒸，潮热，盗汗，鼻塞。

操作　斜刺 0.5~0.8 寸。可灸。

Feishu（BL 13）

Location: 1.5 cun lateral to the low-er border of the spinous process of the third thoracic vertebra.

Indications: Cough, asthma, blood ejection, hectic fever due to yin-deficiency, tidal fever, night sweating, nasal obstruction.

Method: Puncture obliquely 0.5～0.8 cun. Moxibustion is applicable.

厥 阴 俞

定位 第 4 胸椎棘突下，旁开 1.5 寸。

主治 咳嗽，心痛，胸闷，呕吐。

操作 斜刺 0.5～0.8 寸。可灸。

Jueyinshu（BL 14）

Location: 1.5 cun lateral to the lower border of the spinous process of the fourth thoracic vertebra.

Indications: Cough, heart pain, chest oppression, vomiting.

Method: Puncture obliquely 0.5～0.8 cun. Moxibustion is applicable.

心 俞

定位 第 5 胸椎棘突下，旁开 1.5 寸。

主治 心痛，惊悸，咳嗽，吐血，失眠，健忘，盗汗，梦遗，癫痫。

操作 斜刺 0.5～0.8 寸。可灸。

Xinshu（BL 15）

Location: 1.5 cun lateral to the lower border of the spinous process of the fifth thoracic vertebra.

Indications: Heart pain, palpitation, cough, spitting of blood, insomnia, amnesia, night sweating, nocturnal emission, epilepsy.

Method: Puncture obliquely 0.5～0.8 cun. Moxibustion is applicable.

督 俞

定位 第 6 胸椎棘突下，旁开 1.5 寸。

主治 心痛，胸闷，腹痛，寒热，气喘。

操作 斜刺 0.5～1 寸。可灸。

Dushu（BL 16）

Location: 1.5 cun lateral to the lower border of the spinous process of the sixth thoracic vertebra.

Indications: Heart pain, chest oppression, abdominal pain, chill and fever, asthma.

Method: Puncture obliquely 0.5～1 cun. Moxibustion is applicable.

膈 俞

定位 第 7 胸椎棘突下，旁开 1.5 寸。

主治 呕吐，呃逆，气喘，咳嗽，吐血，潮热，盗汗。

操作 斜刺 0.5～0.8 寸。可灸。

Geshu（BL 17）

Location: 1.5 cun lateral to the lower border of the spinous process of the seventh thoracic vertebra.

Indications: Vomiting, hiccup, asthma, cough, hectic fever, night sweating.

Method: Puncture obliquely 0.5～0.8 cun. Moxibustion is applicable.

肝　俞

定位　第 9 胸椎棘突下，旁开 1.5 寸。

主治　黄疸，胁痛，目赤，吐血，目赤，目眩，雀目，癫、狂、痫，背痛。

操作　斜刺 0.5～0.8 寸。可灸。

Ganshu（BL 18）

Location: 1.5 cun lateral to the lower border of the spinous process of the ninth thoracic vertebra.

Indications: Jaundice, pain in the hypochondriac region, spitting of blood, redness of eyes, dizziness, night blindness, depressive psychosis, mania, epilepsy, pain in the back.

Method: Puncture obliquely 0.5～0.8 cun. Moxibustion is applicable.

胆　俞

定位　第 10 胸椎棘突下，旁开 1.5 寸。

主治　黄疸，口苦，胁痛，肺痨，潮热。

操作　斜刺 0.5～0.8 寸。可灸。

Danshu（BL 19）

Location: 1.5 cun lateral to the lower border of the spinous process of the tenth thoracic vertebra.

Indications: Jaundice, bitter taste of the mouth, pain in the hypochondriac region, pulmonary tuberculosis, tidal fever.

Method: Puncture obliquely 0.5～

0.8 cun. Moxibustion is applicable.

脾　俞

定位　第 11 胸椎棘突下，旁开 1.5 寸。

主治　腹胀，黄疸，呕吐，泄泻，痢疾，便血，水肿，背痛。

操作　斜刺 0.5～0.8 寸。可灸。

Pishu（BL 20）

Location: 1.5 cun lateral to the lower border of the spinous process of the eleventh thoracic vertebra.

Indications: Abdominal distension, jaundice, vomiting, diarrhea, dysentery, bloody stools, edema, back pain.

Method: Puncture obliquely 0.5～0.8 cun. Moxibustion is applicable.

胃　俞

定位　第 12 胸椎棘突下，旁开 1.5 寸。

主治　胸胁痛，胃脘痛，呕吐，腹胀，肠鸣。

操作　斜刺 0.5～0.8 寸。可灸。

Weishu（BL 21）

Location: 1.5 cun lateral to the lower border of the spinous process of the twelfth thoracic vertebra.

Indications: Pain in the hypochondriac region, stomachache vomiting, abdominal distension, borborygmus.

Method: Puncture obliquely 0.5～0.8 cun. Moxibustion is applicable.

三 焦 俞

定位　第 1 腰椎棘突下，旁开 1.5 寸。

主治　肠鸣，腹胀，呕吐，腹泻，痢疾，水肿，腰背强痛。

操作　直刺 0.5～1 寸。可灸。

Sanjiaoshu（BL 22）

Location: 1.5 cun lateral to the lower border of the spinous process of the first lumbar vertebra

Indications: Borborygmus, abdominal distension, vomiting, diarrhea, dysentery, edema, pain and stiffness of the lower back.

Method: Puncture perpendicularly 0.5～1 cun. Moxibustion is applicable.

肾 俞

定位　第 2 腰椎棘突下，旁开 1.5 寸。

主治　遗尿，遗精，阳痿，月经不调，白带，水肿，腰痛，耳鸣，耳聋。

操作　直刺 0.5～1 寸。可灸。

Shenshu（BL 23）

Location: 1.5 cun lateral to the lower border of the spinous process of the second lumbar vertebra.

Indications: Enuresis, nocturnal emission, impotence, irregular menstruation, leukorrhagia, edema, lower back pain, tinnitus, deafness.

Method: Puncture perpendicularly 0.5～1 cun. Moxibustion is applicable.

气 海 俞

定位　第 3 腰椎棘突下，旁开 1.5 寸。

主治　肠鸣，腹胀，痔疾，痛经，腰痛。

操作　直刺 0.5～1 寸。可灸。

Qihaishu（BL 24）

Location: 1.5 cun lateral to the lower border of the spinous process of the third lumbar vertebra.

Indications: Borborygmus, abdominal distension, hemorrhoids, menstrual pain, lumbar pain.

Method: Puncture perpendicularly 0.5～1 cun. Moxibustion is applicable.

大 肠 俞

定位　第 4 腰椎棘突下，旁开 1.5 寸。

主治　腹胀，泄泻，便秘，腰痛。

操作　直刺 0.8～1.2 寸。可灸。

Dachangshu（BL 25）

Location: 1.5 cun lateral to the lower border of the spinous process of the fourth lumbar vertebra.

Indications: Abdominal distension, diarrhea, constipation, lower back pain.

Method: Puncture perpendicularly 0.8～1.2 cun. Moxibustion is applicable.

关 元 俞

定位　第5腰椎棘突下，旁开1.5寸。

主治　腹胀，泄泻，小便不利，遗尿，腰痛。

操作　直刺0.8～1.2寸。可灸。

Guanyuanshu（BL 26）

Location：1.5 cun lateral to the lower border of the spinous process of the fifth lumbar vertebra.

Indications：Abdominal distension, diarrhea, dysuria, enuresis, lower back pain.

Method：Puncture perpendicularly 0.8～1.2 cun. Moxibustion is applicable.

小 肠 俞

定位　第1骶椎棘突下，旁开1.5寸。

主治　腹痛，泄泻，痢疾，遗尿，尿血，痔疾，遗精，白带，腰痛。

操作　直刺或斜刺0.8～1.2寸。可灸。

Xiaochangshu（BL 27）

Location：1.5 cun lateral to the lower border of the spinous process of the first sacral vertebra.

Indications：Abdominal pain, diarrhea, dysentery, enuresis, hematuria, hemorrhoid, nocturnal emission, leukorrhagia, lower back pain.

Method：Puncture perpendicularly or obliquely 0.8～1.2 cun. Moxibustion is applicable.

膀 胱 俞

定位　第2骶椎棘突下，旁开1.5寸。

主治　小便不利，遗尿，泄泻，便秘，腰脊强痛。

操作　直刺或斜刺0.8～1.2寸。可灸。

Pangguangshu（BL 28）

Location：1.5 cun lateral to the lower border of the spinous process of the second sacral vertebra.

Indications：Retention of urine, enuresis, diarrhea, constipation, stiffness and pain of the lower back.

Method：Puncture perpendicularly or obliquely 0.8～1.2 cun. Moxibustion is applicable.

中 膂 俞

定位　第3骶椎棘突下，旁开1.5寸。

主治　泄泻，疝气，腰脊强痛。

操作　直刺1～1.5寸。可灸。

Zhonglushu（BL 29）

Location：1.5 cun lateral to the lower border of the spinous process of the third sacral vertebra.

Indications：Diarrhea, hernia, stiffness and pain of the lower back.

Method：Puncture perpendicularly 1～1.5 cun. Moxibustion is applicable.

白 环 俞

定位　第 4 骶椎棘突下，旁开 1.5 寸。

主治　遗尿，疝气，月经不调，白带，遗精，腰骶疼痛。

操作　直刺 1~1.5 寸。可灸。

Baihuanshu（BL 30）

Location：1.5 cun lateral to the lower border of the spinous process of the fourth sacral vertebra.

Indications：Enuresis, hernia, irregular menstruation, leukorrhagia, nocturnal emission, lumbosacral pain.

Method：Puncture perpendicularly 1~1.5 cun. Moxibustion is applicable.

上 髎

定位　第 1 骶后孔中，约当髂后上棘与督脉的中点。

主治　大小便不利，月经不调，白带，阴挺，遗精，阳痿，腰痛。

操作　直刺 1~1.5 寸。可灸。

Shangliao（BL 31）

Location：In the first posterior sacral foramen, which is approximately at the midpoint on the line linking the lower border of the posterior superior iliac spine and the Du Channel.

Indications：Constipation and dysuria, irregular menstruation, leukorrhagia, vaginal protrusion, nocturnal emission, impotence, stiffness and pain of the lower back.

Method：Puncture perpendicularly 1~1.5 cun. Moxibustion is applicable.

次 髎

定位　第 2 骶后孔中，约当髂后上棘下与督脉的中点。

主治　疝气，月经不调，痛经，带下，小便不利，遗精，背痛，下肢痿痹。

操作　直刺 1~1.5 寸。可灸。

Ciliao（BL 32）

Location：In the second posterior sacral foramen, which is approximately at the midpoint on the line linking the lower border of the posterior iliac spine and the Du Channel.

Indications：Hernia, irregular menstruation, dysmenorrhea, leukorrhagia, dysuria, nocturnal emission, back pain, muscular atrophy and pain of the lower extremities.

Method：Puncture perpendicularly 1~1.5 cun. Moxibustion is applicable.

中 髎

定位　第 3 骶后孔中，约当中膂俞与督脉之间。

主治　便秘，泄泻，小便不利，月经不调，带下，腰痛。

操作　直刺 1~1.5 寸。

Zhongliao（BL 33）

Location：In the third posterior sacral foramen, which is approximately at the midpoint on the line linking the lower border of the posterior superior iliac spine and the Du Channel.

Indications: Constipation, diarrhea, dysuria, irregular menstruation, leukorrhagia, back pain.

Method: Puncture perpendicularly 1~1.5 cun. Moxibustion is applicable.

下　　髎

定位　第 4 骶后孔中，约当白环俞与督脉之间。

主治　腹痛，便秘，小便不利，带下，腰痛。

操作　直刺 1~1.5 寸。可灸。

Xialiao（BL 34）

Location: In the fourth posterior sacral foramen, which is approximately at the midpoint on the line linking the lower border of the posterior superior iliac spine and the Du Channel.

Indications: Abdominal pain, constipation, dysuria, leukorrhagia, back pain.

Method: Puncture perpendicularly 1~1.5 cun. Moxibustion is applicable.

会　　阳

定位　尾骨尖旁开 0.5 寸。

主治　泄泻，便血，痔疾，阳痿，带下。

操作　直刺 1~1.5 寸。可灸。

Huiyang（BL 35）

Location: 0.5 cun lateral to the end of the coccyx.

Indications: Diarrhea, bloody stools, hemorrhoids, impotence, morbid leukorrhea.

Method: Puncture perpendicularly 1~1.5 cun. Moxibustion is applicable.

承　　扶

定位　臀横纹中央。

主治　腰骶臀股部疼痛，痔疾，下肢痿痹。

操作　直刺 1~2 寸。可灸。

Chengfu（BL 36）

Location: In the middle of the transverse gluteal fold.

Indications: Pain in the lower back, sacral, gluteal and femoral regions, hemorrhoids, muscular atrophy and pain of the lower extremities.

Method: Puncture perpendicularly 1~2 cun. Moxibustion is applicable.

殷　　门

定位　承扶穴与委中穴连线上，承扶穴下 6 寸。

主治　腰痛，下肢痿痹。

操作　直刺 1~2 寸。

Yinmen（BL 37）

Location: 6 cun below Chengfu（BL 36）, on the line linking Chengfu（BL 36）and Weizhong（BL 40）.

Indications: Back pain, muscular atrophy and pain of the lower extremities.

Method: Puncture perpendicularly 1~2 cun. Moxibustion is applicable.

浮　　郄

定位　委阳穴上 1 寸，在股二头

肌腱内侧。

主治 便秘，股腘部疼痛，麻木。

操作 直刺1~1.5寸。可灸。

Fuxi （BL 38）

Location：1 cun above Weiyang（BL 39），on the medial border of the tendon of m. biceps femoris.

Indications：Constipation，pain in the popliteal fossa and leg，numbness.

Method：Puncture perpendicularly 1~ 1.5 cun. Moxibustion is applicable.

委　阳

定位 腘横纹外端，股二头肌腱内缘。

主治 腹满，小便不利，腰脊强痛，足挛痛。

操作 直刺1~1.5寸。可灸。

Weiyang （BL 39）

Location：At the lateral end of the popliteal transverse crease，on the medial border of the tendon of m. biceps femoris.

Indications：Abdominal fullness，dysuria，stiffness and pain of the lower back，cramp of the leg and foot.

Method：Puncture perpendicularly 1~ 1.5 cun. Moxibustion is applicable.

委　中

定位 腘横纹中央。

主治 腰痛，下肢痿痹，腹痛，吐泻，小便不利，遗尿，丹毒。

操作 直刺1~1.5寸，可灸。

Weizhong （BL 40）

Location：Midpoint of the transverse crease of the popliteal fossa.

Indications：Back pain，muscular atrophy and pain of the lower extremities，abdominal pain，vomiting and diarrhea，dysuria，enuresis，erysipelas.

Method：Puncture perpendicularly 1~ 1.5 cun. Moxibustion is applicable.

附　分

定位 第2胸椎棘突下，旁开3寸。

主治 颈项强痛，肩背拘急，肘臂麻木。

操作 斜刺0.5~0.8寸。可灸。

Fufen （BL 41）

Location：3 cun lateral to the lower border of the spinous process of the second thoracic vertebra.

Indications：Pain and rigidity in the neck，rigidity of the shoulder and back，numbness in the elbow and arm.

Method：Puncture obliquely 0.5~ 0.8 cun. Moxibustion is applicable.

魄　户

定位 第3胸椎棘突下，旁开3寸。

主治 咳嗽，气喘，肺痨，项强，肩背痛。

操作 斜刺0.5~0.8寸。可灸。

Pohu （BL 42）

Location: 3 cun lateral to the lower border of the spinous process of the third thoracic vertebra.

Indications: Cough, asthma, pulmonary tuberculosis, neck rigidity, pain in the shoulder and arm.

Method: Puncture obliquely 0.5 ~ 0.8 cun. Moxibustion is applicable.

膏　肓　俞

定位　第 4 胸椎棘突下，旁开 3 寸。

主治　咳嗽，气喘，肺痨，健忘，遗精。

操作　斜刺 0.5~0.8 寸。可灸。

Gaohuangshu （BL 43）

Location: 3 cun lateral to the lower border of the spinous process of the fourth thoracic vertebra.

Indications: Cough, asthma, pulmonary tuberculosis, amnesia, nocturnal emission.

Method: Puncture obliquely 0.5 ~ 0.8 cun. Moxibustion is applicable.

神　堂

定位　第 5 胸椎棘突下，旁开 3 寸。

主治　咳嗽，气喘，胸闷，脊背强痛。

操作　斜刺 0.5~0.8 寸。可灸。

Shentang （BL 44）

Location: 3 cun lateral to the lower

border of the spinous process of the fifth thoracic vertebra.

Indications: Cough, asthma, stuffy chest, rigidity and pain of the back.

Method: Puncture obliquely 0.5 ~ 0.8 cun. Moxibustion is applicable.

譩　譆

定位　第 6 胸椎棘突下，旁开 3 寸。

主治　咳嗽，气喘，疟疾，热病，肩背痛。

操作　斜刺 0.5~0.8 寸。可灸。

Yixi （BL 45）

Location: 3 cun lateral to the lower border of the spinous process of the sixth thoracic vertebra.

Indications: Cough, asthma, malaria, febrile diseases, pain in the shoulder and back.

Method: Puncture obliquely 0.5 ~ 0.8 cun. Moxibustion is applicable.

膈　关

定位　第 7 胸椎棘突下，旁开 3 寸。

主治　胸闷，嗳气，呕吐，脊背强痛。

操作　斜刺 0.5~0.8 寸。可灸。

Geguan （BL 46）

Location: 3 cun lateral to the lower border of the spinous process of the seventh thoracic vertebra.

Indications: Stuffy chest, belching vomiting, rigidity and pain of the back.

Method: Puncture obliquely 0.5 ~ 0.8 cun. Moxibustion is applicable.

魂 门

定位 第9胸椎棘突下，旁开3寸。

主治 胸胁痛，呕吐，泄泻，背痛。

操作 斜刺0.5~0.8寸。可灸。

Hunmen（BL 47）

Location: 3 cun lateral to the lower border of the spinous process of the ninth thoracic vertebra.

Indications: Pain in the chest and hypochondriac regions, vomiting, diarrhea, back pain.

Method: Puncture obliquely 0.5 ~ 0.8 cun. Moxibustion is applicable.

阳 纲

定位 第10胸椎棘突下，旁开3寸。

主治 肠鸣，腹痛，泄泻，黄疸，消渴。

操作 斜刺0.5~0.8寸，可灸。

Yanggang（BL 48）

Location: 3 cun lateral to the lower border of the spinous process of the tenth thoracic vertebra.

Indications: Borborygmus, abdominal pain, diarrhea, jaundice, wasting-thirst.

Method: Puncture obliquely 0.5 ~ 0.8 cun. Moxibustion is applicable.

意 舍

定位 第11胸椎棘突下，旁开3寸。

主治 腹胀，肠鸣，呕吐，泄泻。

操作 斜刺0.5~0.8寸。可灸。

Yishe（BL 49）

Location: 3 cun lateral to the lower border of the spinous process of the eleventh thoracic vertebra.

Indications: Abdominal distension, borborygmus, vomiting, diarrhea.

Method: Puncture obliquely 0.5 ~ 0.8 cun. Moxibustion is applicable.

胃 仓

定位 第12胸椎棘突下，旁开3寸。

主治 胃脘痛，腹胀，小儿食积，水肿，背脊痛。

操作 斜刺0.5~0.8寸。可灸。

Weicang（BL 50）

Location: 3 cun lateral to the lower border of the spinous process of the twelfth thoracic vertebra.

Indications: Stomachache, abdominal distension, food accumulation in children, edema, back pain.

Method: Puncture obliquely 0.5 ~ 0.8 cun. Moxibustion is applicable.

肓 门

定位 第1腰椎棘突下，旁开3寸。

主治　腹痛，便秘，痞块，乳疾。

操作　斜刺0.5～0.8寸。可灸。

Huangmen（BL 51）

Location: 3 cun lateral to the lower border of the spinous process of the first lumbar vertebra.

Indications: Abdominal pain, constipation, lump glomus, breast diseases.

Method: Puncture obliquely 0.5～0.8 cun. Moxibustion is applicable.

志　室

定位　第2腰椎棘突下，旁开3寸。

主治　遗精，阳痿，小便不利，水肿，腰脊强痛。

操作　斜刺0.5～0.8寸。可灸。

Zhishi（BL 52）

Location: 3 cun lateral to the lower border of the spinous process of the second lumbar vertebra.

Indications: Nocturnal emission, impotence, dysuria, edema, rigidity and pain of the back.

Method: Puncture obliquely 0.5～0.8 cun. Moxibustion is applicable.

胞　肓

定位　第2骶椎棘突下，旁开3寸。

主治　肠鸣，腹胀，便秘，癃闭，腰脊强痛。

操作　直刺1～1.5寸。可灸。

Baohuang（BL 53）

Location: 3 cun lateral to the lower border of the spinous process of the second sacral vertebra.

Indications: Borborygmus, abdominal distension, constipation, dysuria, rigidity and pain of the back.

Method: Puncture perpendicularly 1～1.5 cun. Moxibution is applicable.

秩　边

定位　第4骶椎棘突下，旁开3寸。

主治　小便不利，便秘，痔疾，腰骶痛，下肢痿痹。

操作　直刺1.5～2寸。可灸。

Zhibian（BL 54）

Location: 3 cun lateral to the lower border of the spinous process of the fourth sacral vertebra.

Indications: Dysuria, constipation, hemorrhoids, lower back pain, muscular atrophy and pain of the lower extremities.

Method: Puncture perpendicularly 1.5～2 cun. Moxibustion is applicable.

合　阳

定位　委中穴直下2寸。

主治　腰脊强痛，下肢痿痹，疝气，崩漏。

操作　直刺1～2寸。可灸。

Heyang（BL 55）

Location: 2 cun directly below Weizhong (BL 40).

Indications: Rigidity and pain in the back, muscular atrophy and pain of the lower extremities, hernia, uterine bleeding.

Method: Puncture perpendicularly 1~2 cun. Moxibustion is applicable.

承 筋

定位 合阳穴与承山穴连线的中点。

主治 痔疾，腰腿拘急疼痛。

操作 直刺1~1.5寸。可灸。

Chengjin（BL 56）

Location: At the midpoint of the line linking Heyang（BL 55）and Chengshan（BL 57）.

Indications: Hemorrhoids, rigidity and pain of the back and leg.

Method: Puncture perpendicularly 1~ 1.5 cun. Moxibustion is applicable.

承 山

定位 腓肠肌肌腹下，委中穴与跟腱的连线上，约在委中穴下8寸处。

主治 痔疾，脚气，便秘，腰腿拘急疼痛。

操作 直刺1~2寸。可灸。

Chengshan（BL 57）

Location: Directly below the belly of m. gastrocnemius, on the line linking Weizhong（BL 40）and tendo calcaneus, about 8 cun below Weizhong（BL 40）.

Indications: Hemorrhoids, beriberi, constipation, contracture and pain of the lower back and leg.

Method: Puncture perpendicularly 1~2 cun. Moxibustion is applicable.

飞 扬

定位 昆仑穴直上7寸，承山穴外下方约1寸。

主治 头痛，目眩，鼻衄，腰腿疼痛，痔疾。

操作 直刺1~1.5寸。可灸。

Feiyang（BL 58）

Location: 7 cun directly above kunlun（BL 60），about 1 cun inferior and lateral to Chengsha（BL 57）.

Indications: Headache, dizziness, nosebleeding, pain in the lower back and leg, hemorrhoids.

Method: Puncture perpendicularly 1~ 1.5 cun. Moxibustion is applicable.

跗 阳

定位 昆仑穴直上3寸。

主治 头痛，腰骶疼痛，下肢痿痹，外踝肿痛。

操作 直刺0.8~1.2寸。可灸。

Fuyang（BL 59）

Location: 3 cun directly above Kunlun（BL 60）.

Indications: Headache, pain in the lower back, muscular atrophy and pain of the lower extremities, pain and swelling of the external malleolus.

Method: Puncture perpendicularly 0.8~1.2 cun. Moxibustion is applicable.

昆　仑

定位　外踝高点与跟腱之间凹陷中。

主治　头痛，项强，目眩，鼻衄，癫痫，难产，腰骶疼痛，脚跟肿痛。

操作　直刺 0.5~0.8 寸。可灸。

Kunlun（BL 60）

Location: In the depression between the tip of the external malleolus and tendo calcaneus.

Indications: Headache, neck rigidity, dizziness, nosebleeding, epilepsy, difficult labour, pain in the lumbosacral region, pain of the heel.

Method: Puncture perpendicularly 0.5~0.8 cun. Moxibustion is applicable.

仆　参

定位　昆仑穴直下，赤白肉际处。

主治　下肢痿痹，足跟痛，癫痫。

操作　直刺 0.3~0.5 寸。可灸。

Pucan（BL 61）

Location: Directly below Kunlun（BL 60），at the junction of the red and white skin.

Indications: Muscular atrophy and pain of the lower extremities, pain of the heel, epilepsy.

Method: Puncture perpendicularly 0.3~0.5 cun. Moxibustion is applicable.

申　脉

定位　外踝下缘凹陷中。

主治　头痛，眩晕，癫、狂、痫，腰腿疼痛，目赤痛，失眠。

操作　直刺 0.3~0.5 寸。可灸。

Shenmai（BL 62）

Location: In the depression on the inferior border of the external malleolus.

Indications: Headache, dizziness, manic-depressive disorders, epilepsy, pain in the lower back and leg, redness and pain in the eye, insomnia.

Method: Puncture perpendicularly 0.3~0.5 cun. Moxibustion is applicable.

金　门

定位　申脉穴与京骨穴连线中点，当骰骨外侧凹陷中。

主治　头痛，癫痫，小儿惊风，腰痛，下肢痿痹，外踝痛。

操作　直刺 0.3~0.5 寸。可灸。

Jinmen（BL 63）

Location: At the midpoint of the line linking Shenmai（BL 62）and Jinggu（BL 64），in the depression lateral to the cuboid bone.

Indications: Headache, epilepsy, infantile convulsion, back pain, muscular atrophy and pain of the lower extremities, pain of the external malleolus.

Method: Puncture perpendicularly 0.3~0.5 cun. Moxibustion is applicable.

京 骨

定位 第5跖骨粗隆下，赤白肉际处。

主治 头痛，项强，目翳，癫痫，腰痛。

操作 直刺0.3~0.5寸。可灸。

Jinggu (BL 64)

Location: Below the tuberosity of the fifth metatarsal bone, at the junction of the red and white skin.

Indications: Headache, neck rigidity, corneal opacity, epilepsy, pain in the lower back.

Method: Puncture perpendicularly 0.3 - 0.5 cun. Moxibustion is applicable.

束 骨

定位 第5跖骨小头后方，赤白肉际处。

主治 癫狂，头痛，项强，目眩，腰腿痛。

操作 直刺0.3~0.5寸。可灸。

Shugu (BL 65)

Location: Posterior to the small head of the fifth metatarsal bone, at the junction of the red and white skin.

Indications: Manic-depressive disorders, headache, neck rigidity, dizziness, pain of the lower back and leg.

Method: Puncture perpendicularly 0.3~0.5 cun. Moxibustion is applicable.

足 通 谷

定位 第5跖趾关节前缘，赤白肉际处。

主治 头痛，项强，目眩，鼻衄，癫狂。

操作 直刺0.2~0.3寸。可灸。

Zutonggu (BL 66)

Location: Anterior to the fifth metatarsophalangeal joint, at the junction of the red and white skin.

Indications: Headache, neck rigidity, dizziness, nosebleeding, manic-depressive disorders.

Method: Puncture perpendicularly 0.2~0.3 cun. Moxibustion is applicable.

至 阴

定位 足小趾外侧趾甲角旁约0.1寸。

主治 头痛，目痛，鼻塞，鼻衄，胎位不正，难产。

操作 浅刺0.1寸。可灸。

Zhiyin (BL 67)

Location: On the lateral side of the small toe, about 0.1 cun lateral to the corner of the nail.

Indications: Headache, pain in the eye, nasal obstruction, nosebleeding, malposition of the fetus, difficult labour.

Method: Puncture shallowly 0.1 cun. Moxibustion is applicable.

第八节　足少阴肾经及其常用腧穴

Section 8 The Kidney Channel of Foot-Shaoyin and Commonly Used Acupoints

1．经脉循行

①起于足小趾之下，斜向足心（涌泉）；②出于舟骨粗隆下；③沿内踝后；④进入足跟；⑤再向上行于腿肚内侧；⑥出腘窝的内侧；⑦向上行股内后缘；⑧通过脊柱（长强）属于肾脏；⑨联络膀胱；⑩肾脏部直行的脉：⑪从肾向上通过肝和横膈；⑫进入肺中；⑬沿着喉咙；⑭挟于舌根部。⑮肺部支脉：从肺部出来，联络心脏，流注于胸中，与手厥阴心包经相接（图1－18）。

1．The Course of the Channel

①It starts from the inferior aspect of the small toe and runs obliquely towards the sole (Yongquan KI 1). ②Emerging from the lower aspect of the tuberosity of the navicular bone and ③running behind the medial malleolus, ④it enters the heel. ⑤Then, it as-cends along the medial side of the leg ⑥to the medial side of the popliteal fos-sa. ⑦It goes further upward along the posteromedial aspect of the thigh ⑧towards the vertebral column (Changqiang DU 1), where it enters the kidney, its pertaining organ ⑨and connects with the bladder. ⑩The straight portion of the channel ⑪rem-erges from the kidney. Ascending and passing through the liver and di-aphragm, ⑫it enters the lung, ⑬runs along the throat ⑭and terminates at the root of the tongue. ⑮A branch springs from the lung, joins the heart and runs into the chest to link with the Pericardium Channel of Hand-Jueyin (Fig.1－18).

2．常用经穴主治提要

本经腧穴主治妇科、肺、肾、咽喉疾病及经脉循行部位所出现的病症。

2．Principal Indications of Commonly Used Acupoints of the Meridian

Disorders of gynecology, diseases of the lung, kidney and throat as well as some other symptoms appearing on the pathway of this meridian.

3．常用腧穴（图1－19，图1－20）

3．The Commonly Used Acupoints (Fig.1－19, Fig.1－20)

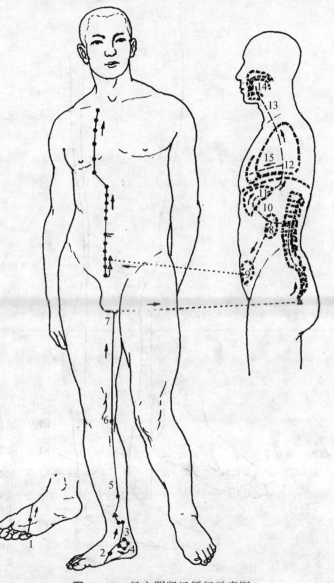

图 1 - 18 足少阴肾经循行示意图

Fig.1 - 18 Running Course of the Kidney Channel of Foot-Shaoyin

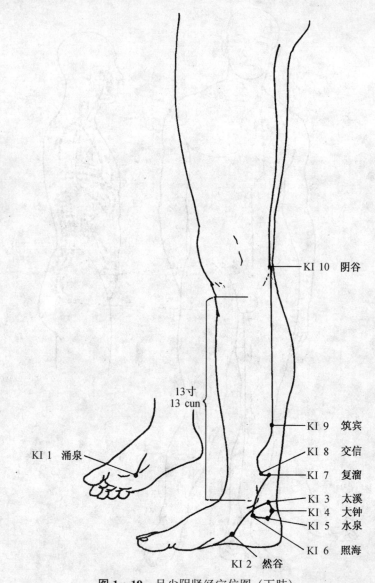

图 1 - 19　足少阴肾经穴位图（下肢）

ig.1 - 19　Acupoints of the Kidney Channel of Foot-Shaoyin（Lower Limb）

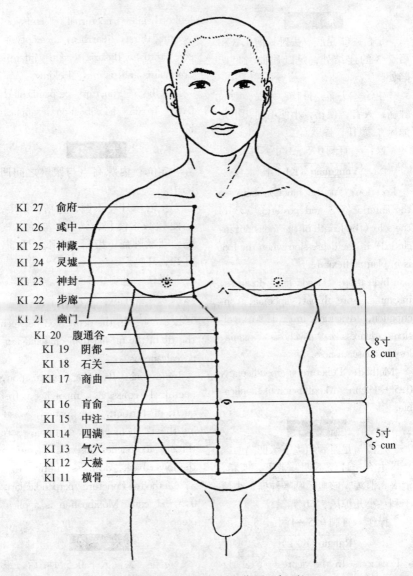

KI 27　俞府
KI 26　彧中
KI 25　神藏
KI 24　灵墟
KI 23　神封
KI 22　步廊
KI 21　幽门
KI 20　腹通谷
KI 19　阴都
KI 18　石关
KI 17　商曲
KI 16　肓俞
KI 15　中注
KI 14　四满
KI 13　气穴
KI 12　大赫
KI 11　横骨

8寸
8 cun

5寸
5 cun

图 1 - 20　足少阴肾经穴位图（躯干）

Fig. 1 - 20　Acupoints of the Kidney Channel of Foot-Shaoyin（Truck）

涌　泉

定位　于足底（去趾）前 1/3 和后 2/3 的连结处，足趾屈曲时呈凹陷处。

主治　头痛，目眩，失眠，咽喉肿痛，失音，便秘，小便不利，小儿惊风，癫狂，昏厥。

操作　直刺 0.5～1 寸。可灸。

Yongquan（KI 1）

Location: At the junction between the anterior 1/3 and posterior 2/3 of the sole (the length of the toe is not included) in the depression when the foot is in plantar flexion.

Indication: Headache, dizziness, insomnia, sore throat, aphonia, constipation, dysuria, infantile convulsion, depressive psychosis, mania, loss of consciousness.

Method: Puncture perpendicularly 0.5～1 cun. Moxibustion is applicable.

然　谷

定位　足舟骨粗隆下缘凹陷中。

主治　月经不调，带下，遗精，消渴，泄泻，咳血，咽喉肿痛，小便不利，小儿惊风，口噤。

操作　直刺 0.5～1 寸。可灸。

Rangu（KI 2）

Location: In the depression on the lower border of the tuberosity of the navicular bone.

Indications: Irregular menstruation, leukorrhagia, nocturnal emission, wasting-thirst, diarrhea, hemoptysis, sore throat, dysuria, acute infantile omphalitis and tetanus, lockjaw.

Method: Puncture perpendicularly 0.5～1 cun. Moxibustion is applicable.

太　溪

定位　内踝高点与跟腱之间凹陷中。

主治　月经不调，遗精，阳痿，小便频数，便秘，消渴，咳血，气喘，咽喉肿痛，齿痛，失眠，腰痛，耳聋，耳鸣。

操作　直刺 0.5～1 寸。可灸。

Taixi（KI 3）

Location: In the depression between the tip of the medial malleolus and tendo calcaneous.

Indications: Irregular menstruation, nocturnal emission, impotence, frequent micturition, constipation, wasting-thirst, hemoptysis, asthma, sore throat, toothache, insomnia, pain in the lower back, deafness, tinnitus.

Method: Puncture perpendicularly 0.5～1 cun. Moxibustion is applicable.

大　钟

定位　太溪穴下 0.5 寸稍后，跟腱内缘。

主治　癃闭，遗尿，便秘，咳血，气喘，痴呆，足跟痛。

操作　直刺 0.3～0.5 寸。可灸。

Dazhong（KI 4）

Location：0.5 cun below and slightly posterior to Taixi（KI 3）on the medial border of the tendo calcaneus.

Indications：Retention of urine, enuresis, constipation, hemoptysis, asthma, dementia, pain of the heel.

Method：Puncture perpendicularly 0.3～0.5 cun. Moxibustion is applicable.

水　泉

定位　太溪穴直下 1 寸。

主治　月经不调，痛经，经闭，阴挺，小便不利。

操作　直刺 0.3～0.5 寸。可灸。

Shuiquan（KI 5）

Location：1 cun directly below Taixi（KI 3）.

Indications：Irregular menstruation, menstrual pain, amenorrhea, prolapse of uterus, dysuria.

Method：Puncture perpendicularly 0.3～0.5 cun. Moxibustion is applicable.

照　海

定位　内踝下缘凹陷中。

主治　月经不调，带下，阴挺，小便频数，癃闭，便秘，咽喉肿痛，癫痫，失眠。

操作　直刺 0.5～1 寸。可灸。

Zhaohai（KI 6）

Location：In the depression of the lower border of the tip of the medial malleolus.

Indications：Irregular menstruation, leukorrhagia, prolapse of the uterus, frequency of micturition, retention of urine, constipation, sore throat, epilepsy, insomnia.

Method：Puncture perpendicularly 0.5～1 cun. Moxibustion is applicable.

复　溜

定位　太溪穴上 2 寸。

主治　水肿，腹胀，泄泻，盗汗，下肢痿痹。

操作　直刺 0.6～1 寸。可灸。

Fuliu（KI 7）

Location: 2 cun above Taixi（KI 3）.

Indications：Edema, abdominal distension, diarrhea, night sweating, muscular atrophy and pain of the lower extremities.

Method：Puncture perpendicularly 0.6～1 cun. Moxibustion is applicable.

交　信

定位　复溜穴前约 0.5 寸。

主治　月经不调，崩漏，阴挺，疝气，泄泻，便秘。

操作　直刺 0.6～1.2 寸。可灸。

Jiaoxin（KI 8）

Location：About 0.5 cun anterior to

Fuliu（KI 7）.

Indications: Irregular menstruation, uterine bleeding, prolapse of the uterus, hernia, diarrhea, constipation.

Method: Puncture perpendicularly 0.6~1.2 cun. Moxibustion is applicable.

筑　　宾

定位　太溪穴上5寸，在太溪与阴谷的连线上。

主治　癫狂，疝气，呕吐，小腿疼痛。

操作　直刺1~1.5寸。

Zhubin（KI 9）

Location: 5 cun above Taixi（KI 3）, on the line linking Taixi（KI 3）and Yingu（KI 10）.

Indications: Manic-depressive disorders, hernia, vomiting, pain in the lower leg.

Method: Puncture perpendicularly 1~ 1.5 cun. Moxibustion is applicable.

阴　　谷

定位　屈膝，腘窝内侧，当半腱肌与半膜肌腱之间。

主治　阳痿，疝气，崩漏，小便不利，膝腘酸痛。

操作　直刺1~1.5寸。可灸。

Yingu（KI 10）

Location: When the knee is flexed, the point is on the medial side of the po-

liteal fossa, between the tendons of m. semitendinosus and semimembra nosus.

Indications: Impotence, hernia, uterine bleeding, dysuria, pain in the knee and popliteal fossa.

Method: Puncture perpendicularly 1~1.5 cun. Moxibution is applicable.

横　　骨

定位　脐下5寸，耻骨联合上际，前正中线旁开0.5寸。

主治　少腹胀满，小便不利，遗尿，阳痿，疝气。

操作　直刺1~1.5寸。可灸。

Henggu（KI 11）

Location: 5 cun below the umbilicus, on the superior border of symphysis pubis, 0.5 cun lateral to the anterior midline.

Indications: Fullness and pain in the lower abdomen, dysuria, enuresis, nocturnal e mission, impotence, hernia.

Method: Puncture perpendicularly 1~ 1.5 cun. Moxibustion is applicable.

大　　赫

定位　脐下4寸，前正中线旁开0.5寸。

主治　遗精，阳痿，阴挺，带下。

操作　直刺1~1.5寸。可灸。

Dahe（KI 12）

Location: 4 cun below the umbilicus, 0.5 cun lateral to the anterior midline.

Indications: Nocturnal emission, impotence, prolapse of the uterus, leukorrhagia.

Method: Puncture perpendicularly 1~1.5 cun. Moxibustion is applicable.

气　穴

定位　脐下 3 寸，前正中线旁开 0.5 寸。

主治　月经不调，带下，小便不利，泄泻。

操作　直刺 1~1.5 寸。可灸。

Qixue（KI 13）

Location: 3 cun below the umbilicus, 0.5 cun lateral to the anterior midline.

Indications: Irregular menstruation, leukorrhagia, dysuria, diarrhea.

Method: Puncture perpendicularly 1~1.5 cun. Moxibustion is applicable.

四　满

定位　脐下 2 寸，前正中线旁开 0.5 寸。

主治　月经不调，带下，遗尿，遗精，疝气，便秘，腹痛，水肿。

操作　直刺 1~1.5 寸。可灸。

Siman（KI 14）

Location: 2 cun below the umbilicus, 0.5 cun lateral to the anterior

midline.

Indications: Irregular menstruation, leukorrhagia, enuresis, nocturnal emission, hernia, constipation, abdominal pain, edema.

Method: Puncture perpendicularly 1~1.5 cun. Moxibustion is applicable.

中　注

定位　脐下 1 寸，前正中线旁开 0.5 寸。

主治　月经不调，腹痛，便秘，泄泻。

操作　直刺 1~1.5 寸。可灸。

Zhongzhu（KI 15）

Location: 1 cun below the umbilicus, 0.5 cun lateral to the anterior midline.

Indications: Irregular menstruation, abdominal pain, constipation, diarrhea.

Method: Puncture perpendicularly 1~1.5 cun. Moxibustion is applicable.

肓　俞

定位　脐旁 0.5 寸。

主治　腹痛，腹胀，呕吐，便秘，泄泻。

操作　直刺 1~1.5 寸。可灸。

Huangshu（KI 16）

Location: 0.5 cun lateral to the umbilicus.

Indications: Abdominal pain, abdominal distension, vomiting, constipation, diarrhea.

Method: Puncture perpendicularly 1~1.5 cun. Moxibustion is applicable.

商　　曲

定位　脐上2寸，前正中线旁开0.5寸。

主治　腹痛，泄泻，便秘。

操作　直刺1~1.5寸。可灸。

Shangqu（KI 17）

Location: 2 cun above the umbilicus, 0.5 cun lateral to the anterior midline.

Indications: Abdominal pain, diarrhea, constipation.

Method: Puncture perpendicularly 1~1.5 cun, Moxibustion is applicable.

石　　关

定位　脐上3寸，前正中线旁开0.5寸。

主治　呕吐，腹痛，便秘，不孕。

操作　直刺1~1.5寸。可灸。

Shiguan（KI 18）

Location: 3 cun above the umbilicus, 0.5 cun lateral to the anterior midline.

Indications: Vomiting, abdominal pain, constipation, infertility.

Method: Puncture perpendicularly 1~1.5 cun. Moxibustion is applicable.

阴　　都

定位　脐上4寸，前正中线旁开0.5寸。

主治　腹痛，腹胀，便秘，不孕。

操作　直刺1~1.5寸。可灸。

Yindu（KI 19）

Location: 4 cun above the umbilicus, 0.5 cun lateral to the anterior midline.

Indications: Abdominal pain, abdominal distension, constipation, infertility.

Method: Puncture perpendicularly 1~1.5 cun. Moxibustion is applicable.

腹　通　谷

定位　脐上5寸，前正中线旁开0.5寸。

主治　腹胀，腹痛，呕吐。

操作　直刺0.5~1寸。可灸。

Futonggu（KI 20）

Location: 4 cun above the umbilicus, 0.5 cun lateral to the anterior midline.

Indications: Abdominal distension, abdominal pain, vomiting.

Method: Puncture perpendicularly 0.5~1 cun. Moxibustion is applicable.

幽　　门

定位　脐上6寸，前正中线旁开0.5寸。

主治 腹痛，腹胀，呕吐，泄泻。

操作 直刺0.5~1寸。可灸。

Youmen (KI 21)

Location: 6 cun above the umbilicus. 0.5 cun lateral to the anterior midline.

Indications: Abdominal pain, abdominal distension, vomiting, diarrhea.

Method: Puncture perpendicularly 0.5 ~ 1 cun. Moxibustion is applicable.

步 廊

定位 第5肋间隙，前正中线旁开2寸。

主治 咳嗽，气喘，胸胁胀满，呕吐。

操作 斜刺或平刺0.5~0.8寸。可灸。

Bulang (KI 22)

Location: In the fifth intercostal space, 2 cun lateral to the anterior midline.

Indications: Cough, asthma, fullness and pain in the chest and hypochondrium, vomiting.

Method: Puncture obliquely or subcutaneously 0.5 ~ 0.8 cun. Moxibustion is applicable.

神 封

定位 第4肋间隙，前正中线旁开2寸。

主治 咳嗽，气喘，腹胁胀满，呕吐，乳痈。

操作 斜刺或平刺0.5~0.8寸。可灸。

Shenfeng (KI 23)

Location: In the fourth intercostal space, 2 cun lateral to the anterior midline.

Indications: Cough, asthma, fullness of the hypochondrium and abdomen, vomiting, acute mastitis.

Method: Puncture obliquely or subcutaneously 0.5 ~ 0.8 cun. Moxibustion is applicable.

灵 墟

定位 第3肋间隙，前正中线旁开2寸。

主治 咳嗽，气喘，胸胁胀满，呕吐，乳痈。

操作 斜刺或平刺0.5~0.8寸。

Lingxu (KI 24)

Location: In the third intercostal space, 2 cun lateral to the anterior midline.

Indications: Cough, asthma, fullness in the chest and hypochondriac region, vomiting, acute mastitis.

Method: Puncture obliquely or subcutaneously 0.5 ~ 0.8 cun. Moxibustion is applicable.

神 藏

定位 第2肋间隙，前正中线旁开2寸。

主治 咳嗽，气喘，胸痛，

呕吐。

操作　斜刺或平刺 0.5～0.8 寸。可灸。

Shencang（KI 25）

Location: In the second intercostal space, 2 cun lateral to the anterior midline.

Indications: Cough, asthma, chest pain, vomiting.

Method: Puncture obliquely or subcutaneously 0.5～0.8 cun. Moxibustion is applicable.

或　　中

定位　第 1 肋间隙，前正中线旁开 2 寸。

主治　咳嗽，气喘，胸胁胀满。

操作　斜刺或平刺 0.5～0.8 寸。可灸。

Yuzhong（KI 26）

Location: In the first intercostal space, 2 cun lateral to the anterior midline.

Indications: Cough asthma, fullness in the chest and hypochondriac region.

Method: Puncture obliquely or subcutaneously 0.5～0.8 cun. Moxibustion is applicable.

俞　　府

定位　锁骨下缘，前正中线旁开 2 寸。

主治　咳嗽，气喘，胸痛，呕吐。

操作　斜刺或平刺 0.5～0.8 寸。

可灸。

Shufu（KI 27）

Location: On the lower border of the clavcle, 2 cun lateral to the anterior midline.

Indications: Cough, asthma, chest pain, vomiting.

Method: Puncture obliquely or subcutaneously 0.5～0.8 cun. Moxibustion is applicable.

第九节　手厥阴心包经及其常用腧穴

Section 9 The Pericardium Channel of Hand-Jueyin and Commonly Used Acupoints

1．经脉循行

①起于胸中，出属心包络；②向下通过横膈；③从胸至腹依次联络上、中，下三焦。

④胸部支脉：沿着胸中，⑤出于胁部，至腋下 3 寸处（天池穴）；⑥上行抵腋窝中；⑦沿上臂内侧，行手太阴经和手少阴经之间；⑧进入肘窝中；⑨向下行于前臂掌长肌腱与桡侧腕屈肌腱之间；⑩进入掌中；⑪沿着中指到指端。

⑫掌中支脉：从劳宫分出，沿着无名指到指端，与手少阳三焦经相连接（图 1－21）。

1．The Course of the Channel

① It starts from the chest . Emerg -

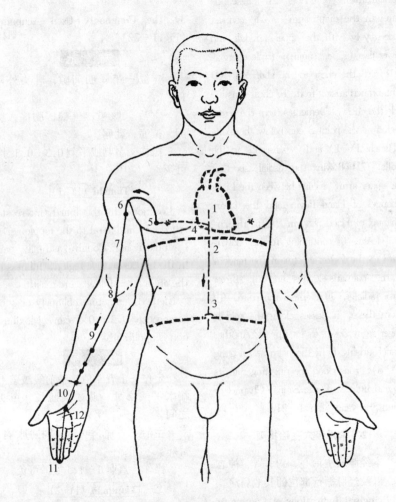

图 1 - 21 手厥阴心包经循行示意图

Fig.1 - 21 Running Course of the Pericardium Channel of Hand-Jueyin

ing, it enters its pertaining organ, the pericardium. ② Then it descends through the diaphragm ③ to connect successively with the upper, middle and lower jiao (i. e. sanjiao, triple energizer) from the chest to the abdomen. ④ The branch arising from the chest runs inside the chest, ⑤emerges from the costal region at the point 3 cun below the axilla (Tianchi PC 1) and ⑥ ascends to the axilla. ⑦ Following the medial aspect of the upper arm, it runs between the Lung Channel of Hand-Taiyin and the Heart Channel of Hand-Shaoyin ⑧ to the cubital fossa, ⑨ continuing further downward to the forearm between the tendons of m. palmaris longus and m. flexor carpi radialis, ⑩ it enters the palm. ⑪ From there, it passes along the middle finger right down to its tip. ⑫Another branch arising from the palm at Laogong (PC 8), runs along the ring finger to its tip and links with the Sanjiao Channel of Hand-Shaoyang (Fig.1－21).

2．常用经穴主治提要

本经腧穴主治心、胸、胃、神志病，以及经脉循行部位的其他病症。

2. Principal Indications of Commonly Used Acupoints of the Meridian

Diseases of the heart, chest and stomach, mental diseases, and diseases at the regions along this channel.

3．常用腧穴（图 1－22）

3. The Commonly Used Acupoints (Fig.1－22)

天　池

定位　第 4 肋间隙，乳头外侧 1 寸。

主治　咳嗽，气喘，胸痛，胸闷，瘰疬，乳痈。

操作　斜刺或平刺 0.3～0.5 寸。可灸。

Tianchi（PC 1）

Location：In the fourth intercostal space, 1 cun lateral to the nipple.

Indications：Cough, asthma, pain in the hypochondriac region, fullness in the chest, scrofula, acute mastitis.

Method：Puncture obliquely or subcutaneously 0.3～0.5 cun. Moxibustion is applicable.

天　泉

定位　上臂掌侧，腋前线皱襞上端水平线 2 寸，肱二头肌长、短头之间。

主治　心痛，咳嗽，胸胁胀痛，臂痛。

操作　直刺 1～1.5 寸。可灸。

Tianquan（PC 2）

Location：On the medial aspect of the arm, 2 cun below the end of the anterior axillary fold. Between the two heads of m. biceps brachii.

Indications：Heart pain, cough,

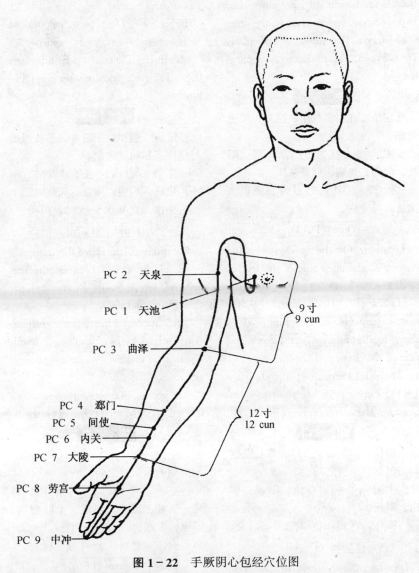

PC 2 天泉

PC 1 天池

9寸
9 cun

PC 3 曲泽

PC 4 郄门
PC 5 间使

12寸
12 cun

PC 6 内关

PC 7 大陵

PC 8 劳宫

PC 9 中冲

图 1 - 22 手厥阴心包经穴位图

Fig. B1 - 22 Acupoints of the Pericardium Channel of Hand-Jueyin

fullness and pain of the chest and hypochondriac region, pain in the arm.

Method: Puncture perpendicularly 1~1.5 cun. Moxibustion is applicable.

曲　泽

定位　在肘横纹中，肱二头肌腱尺侧。

主治　心痛，心悸，胃痛，呕吐，泄泻，热病，肘臂挛痛。

操作　直刺 1~1.5 寸，或点刺出血。可灸。

Quze（PC 3）

Location: On the transverse cubital crease, at the ulnar side of the tendon of m. biceps brachii.

Indications: Heart pain, palpitation, stomachache, vomiting, diarrhea, febrile diseases, contracture and pain of the elbow and arm.

Method: Puncture perpendicularly 1~1.5 cun or prick the point to cause bleeding. Moxibustion is applicable.

郄　门

定位　腕横纹上 5 寸，掌长肌腱与桡侧腕屈肌腱之间。

主治　心痛，心悸，呕血，咳血，癫痫。

操作　直刺 0.8~1.2 寸。可灸。

Ximen（PC 4）

Location: 5 cun above the transverse crease of the wrist, between the tendons of m. palmaris longus and m.

flexor carpi radialis.

Indications: Heart pain, palpitation, hematemesis, hemoptysis, epilepsy.

Method: Puncture perpendicularly 0.8~1.2 cun. Moxibustion is applicable.

间　使

定位　腕横纹上 3 寸，掌长肌腱与桡侧腕屈肌腱之间。

主治　心痛，心悸，胃痛，呕吐，热病，疟疾，癫狂，痫病。

操作　直刺 0.5~1 寸。可灸。

Jianshi（PC5）

Location: 3 cun above the transverse crease of the wrist, between the tendons of m. palmaris longus and m. flexor carpi radialis.

Indications: Heart pain, palpitation, stomachache, vomiting, febrile diseases, malaria, manic-depressive disorders, epilepsy.

Method: Puncture perpendicularly 0.5~1 cun. Moxibustion is applicable.

内　关

定位　腕横纹上 2 寸。掌长肌腱与桡侧腕屈肌腱之间。

主治　心痛，心悸，胸闷，胃痛，呕吐，癫痫，热病，上肢痹痛，偏瘫，失眠，眩晕，头痛。

操作　直刺 0.5~1 寸。可灸。

Neiguan（PC 6）

Location: 2 cun above the transverse crease of the wrist, between the tendons of m. palmaris longus and m. flexor radialis.

Indications: Heart pain, palpitation, oppression in the chest, stomachache, vomiting, epilepsy, febrile diseases, pain in the arm, hemiplegia, insomnia, dizziness, headache.

Method: Puncture perpendicularly 0.5~1 cun. Moxibustion is applicable.

大 陵

定位 腕横纹中央,掌长肌腱与桡侧腕屈肌腱之间。

主治 心痛,心悸,胃痛,呕吐,癫狂,胸胁痛。

操作 直刺0.5~0.8寸。可灸。

Daling（PC 7）

Location: At the midway point of the transverse crease of the wrist. Between the tendons of m. palmaris longus and m. flexor radialis.

Indications: Heart pain, palpitation, stomachache, vomiting, manic-depressive disorders, pain in the chest and hypochondriac region.

Method: Puncture perpendicularly 0.5~0.8 cun. Moxibustion is applicable.

劳 宫

定位 第2、第3掌骨之间,握拳,中指尖下是穴。

主治 心痛,呕吐,癫、狂、痫,口疮,口臭。

操作 直刺0.3~0.5寸。可灸。

Laogong（PC 8）

Location: Between the second and third metacarpal bones. When the fist is clenched, the point is just under the tip of the middle finger.

Indications: Heart pain, vomiting, manic-depressive disorders, epilepsy, aphthous ulcer, foul breath.

Method: Puncture perpendicularly 0.3~0.5 cun. Moxibustion is applicable.

中 冲

定位 中指尖端的中央。

主治 心痛,昏迷,舌强肿痛,热病,小儿夜啼,中暑。

操作 浅刺0.1寸或点刺出血。

Zhongchong（PC 9）

Location: In the centre of the tip of the middle finger.

Indications: Heart pain, coma, pain, swelling and stiffness of the tongue, febrile diseases, child's night crying, summerheat stroke.

Method: Puncture shallowly 0.1 cun or prick the point to cause bleeding.

第十节 手少阳三焦经及其常用腧穴

Section 10 The Sanjiao（Triple Warmer）Channel of Hand-Shaoyang and Commonly Used Acupoints

1．经脉循行

①起于无名指末端（关冲穴）；②向上出于第4、第5掌骨间；③沿着腕背；④出于前臂外侧桡骨和尺骨之间；⑤向上通过肘尖；⑥沿上臂外侧；⑦上达肩部；⑧交出足少阳胆经的后面；⑨向前进入缺盆部；⑩分布于胸中，联络心包；⑪向下通过横膈，从胸至腹，属于上、中、下三焦。⑫胸中的支脉：从胸向上，⑬出于缺盆部；⑭上走项部；⑮沿耳后直上；⑯出于耳部，上行额角上方；⑰再屈而下行至面颊部，到达眼眶下。

⑱耳部支脉：从耳后进入耳中，出走耳前，与前脉交叉于面颊部；⑲到达目外眦，与足少阳胆经相连接（图1-23）。

1. The Course of the Channel

①It starts from the tip of the ring finger (Guanchong, SJ 1). ②It runs upwards between the fourth and fifth metacarpal bones ③along the dorsal aspect of the wrist ④to the lateral aspect of the forearm between the radius and ulna. ⑤ Ascending through the olecranon and ⑥going along the lateral aspect of the upper arm, ⑦it reaches the shoulder region, ⑧ where it goes across and passes behind the Gallbladder Channel of Foot-Shaoyang. ⑨Winding over to the supraclavicular fossa, ⑩it spreads in the chest to connect with the pericardium. ⑪ It then descends through the diaphragm to the abdomen, and joins its pertaining organ, the upper, middle and lower jiao (i. e. Sanjiao). ⑫A branch originates from the chest. Running upwards, ⑬it emerges from the supraclavicular fossa. ⑭From there, it ascends to the neck, ⑮runs along the posterior of the ear, ⑯and further to the corner of the anterior hairline. ⑰ Then it runs downwards to the cheek and terminates in the infraorbital region. ⑱The auricular branch arises from the retroauricular region and enters the ear. Then it emerges in front of the ear, crosses the previous branch at the cheek ⑲and reaches the outer canthus to link with the Gallbladder Channel of Foot-Shaoyang (Fig.1-23).

2．常用经穴主治提要

本经腧穴主治头、耳、目、胸胁、咽喉病，热病以及经脉循行部位的其他病症。

2. Principal Indications of Commonly Used Acupoints of the Meridian

Diseases of the head, ear, chest, hypochondrium and throat, febrile diseases as well as diseases in the regions along this channel.

3．常用腧穴（图1-24）

3. The Commonly Used Acupoints

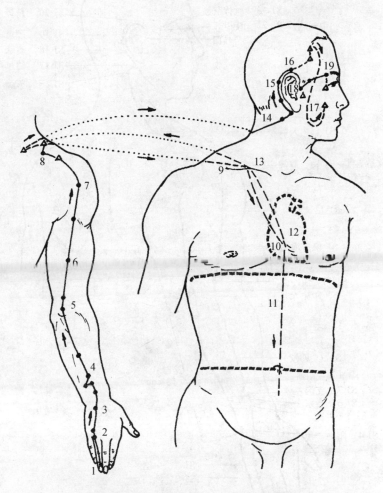

图 1 - 23　手少阳三焦经循行示意图

Fig. 1 - 23　Running Course of the Sanjiao Channel of Hand-Shaoyang

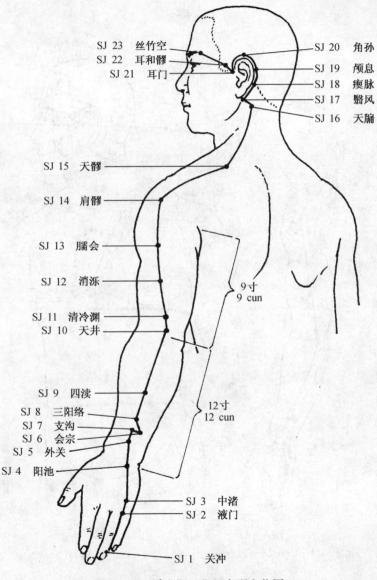

SJ 23　丝竹空
SJ 22　耳和髎
SJ 21　耳门

SJ 20　角孙
SJ 19　颅息
SJ 18　瘈脉
SJ 17　翳风
SJ 16　天牖

SJ 15　天髎

SJ 14　肩髎

SJ 13　臑会

SJ 12　消泺

SJ 11　清冷渊
SJ 10　天井

9寸
9 cun

SJ 9　四渎

SJ 8　三阳络
SJ 7　支沟
SJ 6　会宗
SJ 5　外关

12寸
12 cun

SJ 4　阳池

SJ 3　中渚
SJ 2　液门

SJ 1　关冲

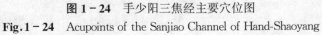

图 1 - 24　手少阳三焦经主要穴位图

Fig. 1 - 24　Acupoints of the Sanjiao Channel of Hand-Shaoyang

（Fig.1－24）

关　冲

定位　第4指尺侧指甲角旁约0.1寸。

主治　头痛，目赤，耳聋，咽喉肿痛，热病，昏厥。

操作　浅刺0.1寸，或点刺出血。可灸。

Guanchong（SJ 1）

Location: On the ulnar aspect of the ring finger, about 0.1 cun lateral to the proximal corner of the nail.

Indications: Headache, redness of the eye, deafness, sore throat, febrile diseases, loss of consciousness.

Method: Puncture shallowly 0.1 cun or prick the point to cause bleeding. Moxibustion is applicable.

液　门

定位　握拳，第4、第5指之间，指掌关节前凹陷中。

主治　头痛，目赤，耳聋，咽喉肿痛，疟疾。

操作　直刺0.3～0.5寸。可灸。

Yemen（SJ 2）

Location: When the fist is clenched, the point is located in the depression anterior to the metacarpophalangeal joint. Between the ring and small fingers.

Indications: Headache, redness of the eye, deafness, sore throat, malaria.

Method: Puncture perpendicularly 0.3～0.5 cun. Moxibustion is applica-ble.

中　渚

定位　握拳，第4、第5掌骨小头后缘之间凹陷中，液门穴后1寸。

主治　头痛，目赤，耳鸣，耳聋，咽喉肿痛，热病，手指不能屈伸。

操作　直刺0.3～0.5寸。可灸。

Zhongzhu（SJ 3）

Location: When the fist is clenched, the point is in the depression between the posterior borders of the small ends of the fourth and fifth metacarpal bones, 1 cun posterior to Yemen（SJ 2）.

Indications: Headache, redness of the eye, tinnitus, deafness, sore throat, febrile diseases, motor impair-ment of the fingers.

Method: Puncture perpendicularly 0.3～0.5 cun. Moxibustion is applica-ble.

阳　池

定位　腕背横纹中，指总伸肌腱尺侧缘凹陷中。

主治　目赤肿痛，耳聋，咽喉肿痛，疟疾，腕痛，消渴。

操作　直刺0.3～0.5寸。可灸。

Yangchi（SJ 4）

Location: On the transverse crease of the dorsum of the wrist, in the depression at the ulnar aspect of the tendon of m. extensor digitorum communis.

Indications: Swelling and pain of the

eye, deafness, sore throat, malaria, pain in the wrist, wasting-thirst.

Method: Puncture perpendicularly 0.3~0.5 cun. Moxibustion is applicable.

外 关

定位 腕背横纹上 2 寸，桡骨与尺骨之间。

主治 热病，头痛，目赤肿痛，耳鸣，耳聋，瘰疬，胁肋痛，上肢痹痛。

操作 直刺 0.5~1 寸。可灸。

Waiguan（SJ 5）

Location: 2 cun above the transverse crease of the dorsum of the wrist, between the radius and ulna.

Indications: Febrile diseases, headache, swelling and pain of the eye, tinnitus, deafness, scrofula, pain in the hypochondrium, pain in the upper extremities.

Method: Puncture perpendicularly 0.5~1 cun. Moxibustion is applicable.

支 沟

定位 腕背横纹上 3 寸，桡骨与尺骨之间。

主治 耳鸣，耳聋，暴喑，瘰疬，胁肋痛，便秘，热病。

操作 直刺 0.8~1.2 寸。可灸。

Zhigou（SJ 6）

Location: 3 cun above the transverse crease of the dorsum of the wrist, between the radius and ulna.

Indications: Tinnitus, deafness, sudden loss of voice, scrofula, pain in the hypochondrium, constipation, febrile diseases.

Method: Puncture perpendicularly 0.8~1.2 cun. Moxibustion is applicable.

会 宗

定位 支沟穴尺侧约 1 寸，于尺骨的桡侧缘取之。

主治 耳聋，癫痫，上肢痹痛。

操作 直刺 0.5~1 寸。可灸。

Huizong（SJ 7）

Location: About 1 cun lateral to the ulnar aspect of Zhigou (SJ 6), on the radial side of the ulna.

Indications: Deafness, epilepsy, pain in the upper extremities.

Method: Puncture perpendicularly 0.5~1 cun. Moxibustion is applicable.

三 阳 络

定位 支沟穴上 1 寸，桡骨与尺骨之间。

主治 耳聋，暴喑，齿痛，上肢痹痛。

操作 直刺 0.8~1.2 寸。可灸。

Sanyangluo（SJ 8）

Location: 1 cun above Zhigou (SJ 6), between the radius and ulna.

Indications: Deafness, sudden loss of voice, toothache, pain in the arm.

Method: Puncture perpendicularly

0.5~1 cun. Moxibustion is applicable.

四　渎

定位　尺骨鹰嘴下 5 寸, 桡骨与尺骨之间。

主治　耳聋, 咽喉肿痛, 暴喑, 齿痛, 上肢痹痛。

操作　直刺 0.5~1 寸。可灸。

Sidu (SJ 9)

Location: 5 cun below the olecranon, between the radius and ulna.

Indications: Deafness, sore throat, sudden loss of voice, toothache, pain in the upper extremities.

Method: Puncture perpendicularly 0.5~1 cun. Moxibustion is applicable.

天　井

定位　屈肘、尺骨鹰嘴上 1 寸许凹陷中。

主治　头痛, 耳聋, 瘰疬, 癫痫。

操作　直刺 0.5~1 寸。可灸。

Tianjing (SJ 10)

Location: In the depression about 1 cun directly above the olecranon with the elbow flexed.

Indications: Headache, deafness, scrofula, epilepsy.

Method: Puncture perpendicularly 0.5~1 cun. Moxibustion is applicable.

清 冷 渊

定位　屈肘, 天井穴上 1 寸。

主治　头痛, 上肢痹痛, 目黄。

操作　直刺 0.8~1.2 寸。可灸。

Qinglengyuan (SJ 11)

Location: 1 cun above Tianjing (SJ 10) with the elbow flexed.

Indications: Headache, pain in the upper extremities, yellowing of the eyes.

Method: Puncture perpendicularly 1~1.5 cun. Moxibustion is applicable.

消　泺

定位　尺骨鹰嘴与肩髎穴连线上, 清冷渊穴上 3 寸。

主治　头痛, 齿痛, 项强, 肩背痛。

操作　直刺 1~1.5 寸。可灸。

Xiaoluo (SJ 12)

Location: 3 cun above Qinglengyuan (SJ 11), on the line joining the olecranon and Jianliao (SJ 14).

Indications: Headache, toothache, stiffness of the nape, pain in the shoulder and arm.

Method: Puncture perpendicularly 1~1.5 cun. Moxibustion is applicable.

臑　会

定位　尺骨鹰嘴与肩髎穴连线上, 肩髎穴下 3 寸, 当三角肌的后缘。

主治　上肢痹痛, 瘿气, 瘰疬。

操作　直刺 1~1.5 寸。可灸。

Naohui (SJ 13)

Location: 3 cun below Jianliao (SJ 14), on the posteroinferior border of m. deltoideus, on the line joining the olecranon and Jianliao (SJ 14).

Indications: Pain in the arm, goiter, scrofula.

Method: Puncture perpendicularly 1~1.5 cun. Moxibustion is applicable.

肩　髎

定位　肩峰后下方，上臂外展，当肩髃穴后寸许的凹陷中。

主治　肩臂挛痛。

操作　直刺1~1.5寸。可灸。

Jianliao (SJ 14)

Location: Posterior and inferior to the acromion, in the depression about 1 cun posterior to Jianyu (LI 15) when the arm is abducted.

Indications: Contracture and pain of the shoulder and arm.

Method: Puncture perpendicularly 1~1.5 cun. Moxibustion is applicable.

天　髎

定位　肩胛骨上角，曲垣穴上1寸。

主治　肩臂痛，颈项强急。

操作　直刺0.5~0.8寸。可灸。

Tianliao (SJ 15)

Location: At the superior angle of the scapula, 1 cun above Quyuan (SI 13).

Indications: Pain in the shoulder and arm, neck rigidity.

Method: Puncture perpendicularly 0.5~0.8 cun. Moxibustion is applicable.

天　牖

定位　乳突后下方，胸锁乳突肌后缘，约平下颌角处。

主治　头痛，目痛，耳聋，瘰疬，项强。

操作　直刺0.5~1寸。可灸。

Tianyou (SJ 16)

Location: Directly below the posterior border of the mastoid process, at the level with the angle of the jaw, On the posterior border of the sternocleidomastoid muscle.

Indications: Headache, pain in the eye, deafness, scrofula, stiff neck.

Method: Puncture perpendicularly 0.5~1 cun. Moxibustion is applicable.

翳　风

定位　乳突前下方，平耳垂后下缘的凹陷中。

主治　暴聋，耳鸣，口眼㖞斜，牙关紧闭，齿痛，颊肿，瘰疬。

操作　直刺0.8~1.2寸。可灸。

Yifeng (SJ 17)

Location: Anteroinferior to the mastoid process, in the depression posterior to the inferior border of the lobule of the ear.

Indications: Sudden deafness, tinnitus, deviation of the mouth and eye, lockjaw, toothache, swelling of the cheek, scrofula.

Method: Puncture perpendicularly 0.8~1.2 cun. Moxibustion is applicable.

瘈　脉

定位　乳突中央，当翳风穴与角孙穴沿耳轮连线的下 1/3 与上 2/3 交界处。

主治　头痛，耳鸣，耳聋，小儿惊风。

操作　平刺 0.3~0.5 寸，或点刺出血。

Chimai (SJ 18)

Location: In the center of the mastoid process, at the junction of the upper 2/3 and lower 1/3 of the line along the helix linking Yifeng (SJ 17) and Jiaosun (SJ 20).

Indications: Headache, tinnitus, deafness, infantile convulsion.

Method: Puncture subcutaneously 0.3 ~ 0.5 cun or prick the point to cause bleeding.

颅　息

定位　耳后，当翳风穴与角孙穴沿耳轮连线的上 1/3 与下 2/3 交界处。

主治　头痛，耳鸣，耳聋，小儿惊风。

操作　平刺 0.3~0.5 寸。可灸。

Luxi (SJ 19)

Location: Behind the ear, at the junction of the upper 1/3 and lower 2/3 of the line along the helix linking Yifeng (SJ 17) and Jiaosun (SJ 20).

Indications: Headache, tinnitus, deafness, infantile convulsion.

Method: Puncture subcutaneously 0.3~0.5 cun. Moxibustion is applicable.

角　孙

定位　当耳尖处的发际。

主治　颊肿，目翳，齿痛，项强。

操作　平刺 0.3~0.5 寸。可灸。

Jiaosun (SJ 20)

Location: Directly above the ear apex. Just on the hair margin.

Indications: Swelling of the cheek, corneal opacity, toothache, rigidity of the neck.

Method: Puncture subcutaneously 0.3~0.5 cun. Moxibustion is applicable.

耳　门

定位　耳屏上切迹前，下颌骨髁状突后缘凹陷中。

主治　耳鸣，耳聋，聤耳，齿痛。

操作　张口，直刺 0.5~1 寸。可灸。

Ermen (SJ 21)

Location: In front of the superior notch of the auricula, in the depression on the posterior border of the mandibular condyloid process.

Indications: Tinnitus, deafness,

otitis media, toothache.

Method: Puncture perpendicularly 0.5~1 cun when the mouth is open. Moxibustion is applicable.

耳　和　髎

定位　鬓发后缘，平耳郭根前，当颞浅动脉后缘。

主治　头痛，耳鸣，牙关紧闭，口㖞。

操作　避开动脉，斜刺或平刺0.3~0.5寸。可灸。

Erheliao（SJ 22）

Location: On the posterior border of the hairline of the temple, at the level with the root of the auricle and superfial temporal artery.

Indications: Headache, tinnitus, lockjaw, deviation of the mouth.

Method: Avoiding the artery, puncture obliquely or subcutaneously 0.3~0.5 cun. Moxibustion is applicable.

丝　竹　空

定位　眉梢处凹陷中。

主治　头痛，目赤疼痛，眼睑瞤动，齿痛，癫、狂、痫。

操作　平刺0.5~1寸。

Sizhukong（SJ 23）

Location: In the depression at the lateral end of the eyebrow.

Indications: Headache, redness and pain of the eye, twitching of the eyelid, toothache, manic-depressive disorders, epilepsy.

Method: Puncture subcutaneously 0.5~1 cun.

第十一节　足少阳胆经及其常用腧穴

Section 11　The Gallbladder Channel of Foot-Shaoyang and Commonly Used Acupoints

1. 经脉循行

①起于目外眦（瞳子髎；②向上到达额角部（颔厌）；③下行至耳后（风池）；④沿着颈部行于手少阳三焦经的前面，至肩上交出手少阳三焦经的后面；⑤向下进入缺盆部。

⑥耳部的支脉：从耳后进入耳中，⑦出走耳前；⑧到目外眦后方。

⑨外眦部的支脉：从目外眦分出，⑩下走大迎；⑪与手少阳三焦经会合于目眶下；⑫下经颊车；⑬至颈部与前入缺盆部的脉相会合；⑭然后向下进入胸中，通过横膈；⑮联络肝脏；⑯属于胆；⑰沿着胁肋部；⑱出于少腹侧的腹股沟动脉部；⑲经过外阴部毛际；⑳横入髋关节部（环跳）。

㉑缺盆部直下的脉；㉒下行腋窝部；㉓沿着侧胸部；㉔经过季胁；㉕向下会合前脉于髋关节部；㉖再向下沿着大腿外侧；㉗出于膝部外侧；㉘向下经腓骨前面；㉙直下到达腓骨下段；㉚再下行到外踝前面，沿着足跗部；㉛进入足第4趾外侧端。

㉜足跗部支脉：从足临泣处分出，沿着第1、2跖骨间，出于足踇趾末端，

穿过趾甲，回到趾甲后的毫毛部，与足厥阴肝经相连接（图 1－25）。

1. The Course of the Channel

① It starts from the outer canthus (Tongziliao, GB 1)，②goes up to the corner of the forehead (Hanyan, GB 4)，③ then curves downwards to the retroauricular region (Fengchi GB 20) ④and runs along the side of the neck in front of the Sanjiao Channel of Hand-Shaoyang to the shoulder. Turning back, it transverses and passes behind the Sanjiao Channel of Hand-Shaoyang ⑤down to the supraclavicular fossa. ⑥The branch arising at the auricle runs from the retroauricular region to enter the ear. ⑦It then emerges and passes the preauricular region　⑧to the posterior aspect of the outer canthus. ⑨The branch arising from the outer canthus ⑩runs downwards to Daying (ST 5) and　⑪meets the Sanjiao Channel of Hand-Shaoyang in the infraorbital region. ⑫Passing through Jiache (ST 6)，⑬it descends to the neck and enters the supraclavicular fossa where it meets the branch which has already reached the place previously. ⑭From there, it further descends into the chest, passes through the diaphragm ⑮to connect with the liver and　⑯enters its pertaining organ, the gallbladder. ⑰Then it runs inside the hypochondriac region，⑱ comes out from the lateral side of the lower abdomen near the femoral artery at the inguinal region. ⑲From there it runs superficially along the margin of the pubic hair　⑳and goes transversely into the hip region (Huantiao, GB 30)．㉑ The straight portion of the channel runs downward from the supraclavicular fossa，㉒passes in front of the axilla　㉓along the lateral aspect of the chest　㉔and through the floating ribs　㉕to the hip region where it meets the previous channel.　㉖Then it descends along the lateral aspect of the thigh　㉗to the lateral side of the knee. ㉘Going further downward along the anterior aspect of the fibula　㉙all the way to its lower end，㉚it reaches the anterior aspect of the external malleolus. It then follows the dorsum of the foot　㉛to the lateral side of the tip of the fourth toe. ㉜The branch of the dorsum of the foot springs from Zulinqi (GB 4)，runs between the first and second metatarsal bones to the distal portion of the great toe, passes through the nail, and terminates at its hairy region, where it links with the Liver Channel of Foot-Jueyin (Fig1－25).

2. 常用经穴主治提要

本经腧穴主治头、目、耳、咽喉病，精神神志病以及经脉循行部位的其他病症。

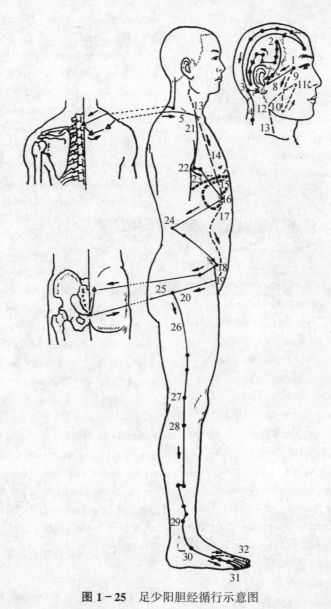

图 1 - 25   足少阳胆经循行示意图

Fig. 1 - 25   Running Course of the Gallbladder Channel of Foot-Shaoyang

2. Principal Indications of Commonly Used Acupoints of the Meridian

Diseases of the head, eye, ear and throat, mental diseases and the diseases in the regions along this channel.

3. 常用腧穴 (图 1−26，图 1−27)

3. The Commonly Used Acupoints
(Fig.1−26, Fig.1−27)

瞳　子　髎

定位　目外眦旁 0.5 寸，眶骨外缘凹陷中。

主治　头痛，目赤痛，目翳，青盲。

操作　平刺 0.3～0.5 寸。

Tongziliao（GB 1）

Location: 0.5 cun lateral to the outer canthus, in the depression on the lateral side of the orbit.

Indications: Headache, redness and pain of the eye, eye screen, optic atrophy.

Method: Puncture subcutaneously 0.3～0.5 cun.

听　会

定位　耳屏间切迹前，下颌骨髁状突的后缘，张口有孔。

主治　耳鸣，耳聋，齿痛，口喎，腮肿。

操作　张口，直刺 0.5～1 寸。可灸。

Tinghui（GB 2）

Location: Anterior to the intertragic notch, at the posterior border of the condyloid process of the mandible. The point is located when the mouth is opened.

Indications: Tinnitus, deafness, toothache, deviation of the mouth, mumps.

Method: Puncture perpendicularly 0.5～1 cun with the patient's mouth opened. Moxibustion is applicable.

上　关

定位　下关穴直上，当颧弓的上缘。

主治　头痛，耳鸣，耳聋，口眼喎斜，齿痛，口噤，慢惊风。

操作　直刺 0.5～1 寸。可灸。

Shangguan（GB 3）

Locations: Directly above Xiaguan (ST 7), at the upper border of the zygomatic arch.

Indications: Headache, tinnitus, deafness, deviation of the mouth and eye, toothache, lockjaw, chronic convulsion.

Method: Puncture perpendicularly 0.5～1 cun. Moxibustion is applicable.

颔　厌

定位　头维穴至曲鬓穴弧形线的上 1/4 与下 3/4 交界处。

主治　偏头痛，目眩，耳鸣，齿痛，癫痫。

操作　平刺 0.5～0.8 寸。可灸。

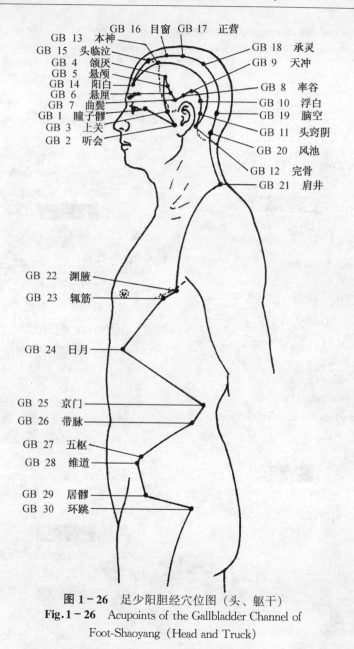

图 1－26 足少阳胆经穴位图（头、躯干）
Fig. 1－26   Acupoints of the Gallbladder Channel of
Foot-Shaoyang（Head and Truck）

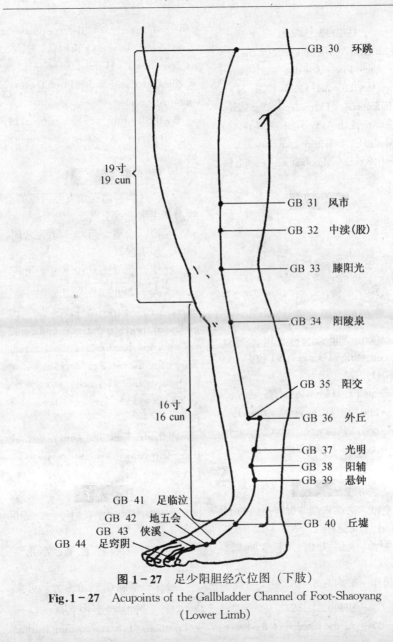

图 1 - 27　足少阳胆经穴位图（下肢）

Fig. 1 - 27　Acupoints of the Gallbladder Channel of Foot-Shaoyang (Lower Limb)

Hanyan （GB 4）

Location：At the junction of the upper 1/4 and lower 3/4 distance between Touwei （ST 8） and Qubin （GB 7）.

Indications：Hemilateral headache, vertigo, tinnitus, toothache, epilepsy.

Method：Puncture subcutaneously 0.5~0.8 cun. Moxibustion is applicable.

悬　颅

定位　头维穴至曲鬓穴弧形线中点。

主治　偏头痛，目赤肿痛，齿痛。

操作　平刺0.5~0.8寸。可灸。

Xuanlu （GB 5）

Location：Midway along the border line connecting Touwei （ST 8） and Qubin （GB 7）.

Indications：Hemilateral headache, redness and pain of the eye, toothache.

Method：Puncture subcutaneously 0.5~0.8 cun. Moxibustion is applicable.

悬　厘

定位　头维穴至曲鬓穴连线的下1/4 和上 3/4 交界处。

主治　偏头痛，目赤肿痛，耳鸣。

操作　平刺0.5~0.8寸。可灸。

Xuanli （GB 6）

Location：At the junction of the lower 1/4 and upper 3/4 distance between Touwei （ST 8） and Qubin （GB 7）.

Indications：Hemilateral headache, swelling, redness and pain of the eye, tinnitus.

Method：Puncture subcutaneously 0.5~0.8 cun. Moxibustion is applicable.

曲　鬓

定位　当耳前鬓角发际后缘的垂线与耳尖水平线交点处。

主治　头痛，齿痛，牙关紧闭，暴喑，颈项强直。

操作　平刺0.5~0.8寸。可灸。

Qubin （GB 7）

Location：At the junction of the vertical line on the posterior border of the anterior temporal hairline and the horizontal line joining the two auricle apexes.

Indications：Headache, toothache, lockjaw, sudden loss of voice, stiffneck.

Method：Puncture subcutaneously 0.5~0.8 cun. Moxibustion is applicable.

率　谷

定位　耳尖直上，入发际1.5寸。

主治　偏头痛，眩晕，小儿急、慢惊风。

操作　平刺0.5~0.8寸。可灸。

Shuaigu （GB 8）

Location：1.5 cun within hairline,

directly above the auricle apex.

Indications: Hemilateral headache, dizziness, acute and chronic convulsion in children.

Method: Puncture subcutaneously 0.5~0.8 cun. Moxibustion is applicable.

天 冲

定位 耳根后缘直上，入发际2寸。

主治 头痛，牙龈肿痛，惊厥。

操作 平刺0.5~0.8寸。可灸。

Tianchong（GB 9）

Location: Above the posterior border of the auricular root, 2 cun within the hairline.

Indications: Headache, swelling and pain in the gums, convulsion.

Method: Puncture subcutaneously 0.5~0.8 cun. Moxibustion is applicable.

浮 白

定位 当耳后乳突的后上方，天冲与完骨弧形连线的中1/3与上1/3交点处。

主治 头痛，耳鸣，耳聋，目痛，瘿气。

操作 平刺0.5~0.8寸。可灸。

Fubai（GB 10）

Location: Superposterior to the mastoid process, at the junction of the middle 1/3 and upper 1/3 curve joining Tianchong（GB 9）and Wangu（GB 12）.

Indications: Headache, tinnitus, deafness, pain in the eye, goiter.

Method: Puncture subcutaneously 0.5~0.8 cun. Moxibustion is applicable.

头 窍 阴

定位 浮白穴直下，乳突根部。

主治 头痛，耳鸣，耳聋。

操作 平刺0.5~0.8寸。可灸。

Touqiaoyin（GB 11）

Location: Directly below Fubai（GB 10）, posterosuperior to the mastoid process.

Indications: Headache, tinnitus, deafness.

Method: Puncture subcutaneously 0.5~0.8 cun. Moxibustion is applicable.

完 骨

定位 乳突后下方凹陷中。

主治 头痛，颈项强痛，齿痛，口㖞，疟疾，癫痫。

操作 斜刺0.5~0.8寸。可灸。

Wangu（GB 12）

Location: In the depression posterior and inferior to the mastoid process.

Indications: Headache, stiffneck, toothache, deviation of the mouth, malaria, epilepsy.

Method: Puncture obliquely 0.5~0.8 cun. Moxibustion is applicable.

本　神

定位　神庭穴旁 3 寸，当神庭穴与头维穴连线的内 2/3 与外 1/3 连接点处。

主治　头痛，目眩，癫痫，小儿惊风。

操作　平刺 0.5～0.8 寸。可灸。

Benshen（GB 13）

Location: 3 cun lateral to Shenting (DU 24), at the junction of the medial 2/3 and lateral 1/3 distance between Shenting (DU 24) and Touwei (ST 8).

Indications: Headache, dizziness, epilepsy, infantile convulsion.

Method: Puncture subcutaneously 0.5～0.8 cun. Moxibustion is applicable.

阳　白

定位　目正视，瞳孔直上，眉上 1 寸。

主治　头痛，目痛，视物模糊，眼睑瞤动。

操作　平刺 0.3～0.5 寸。可灸。

Yangbai（GB 14）

Location: When the patient looks straight forward, the point is directly above the pupil, 1 cun superior to the eyebrow.

Indications: Headache, pain in the eye, blurred vision, twitching of the eyelids.

Method: Puncture subcutaneously 0.3～0.5 cun. Moxibustion is applicable.

头临泣

定位　阳白穴直上，入发际 0.5 寸。

主治　头痛，目眩，流泪，鼻塞，小儿惊风。

操作　平刺 0.3～0.5 寸。可灸。

Toulinqi（GB 15）

Location: Directly above Yangbai (GB 14), 0.5 cun within the hairline.

Indications: Headache, dizziness, epiphora, nasal obstruction, infantile convulsion.

Method: Puncture subcutaneously 0.3～0.5 cun. Moxibustion is applicable.

目　窗

定位　头临泣穴后 1 寸。

主治　头痛，目赤肿痛，青盲，鼻塞，癫痫，面浮肿。

操作　直刺 0.3～0.5 寸。可灸。

Muchuang（GB 16）

Location: 1 cun behind Toulinqi (GB 15).

Indications: Headache, swelling, redness and pain of the eye, optic atrophy, nasal obstruction, epilepsy, edema of the face.

Method: Puncture subcutaneously 0.3～0.5 cun. Moxibustion is applicable.

正　营

定位　目窗穴后 1 寸。

主治　头痛，目眩，齿痛，呕吐，项强。

操作　平刺 0.3～0.5 寸。可灸。

Zhengying（GB 17）

Location：1 cun behind Muchuang (GB 16).

Indications：Headache, dizziness, toothache, vomiting, stiffneck.

Method：Puncture subcutaneously 0.3～0.5 cun. Moxibustion is applicable.

承　灵

定位　正营穴后 1.5 寸。

主治　头痛，眩晕，目痛，鼻塞，鼻衄。

操作　平刺 0.3～0.5 寸。可灸。

Chengling（GB 18）

Location：1.5 cun behind Zhengying (GB 17).

Indications：Headache, dizziness, pain in the eye, nasal obstruction, nosebleeding.

Method：Puncture subcutaneously 0.3～0.5 cun. Moxibustion is applicable.

脑　空

定位　风池穴直上 1.5 寸。

主治　头痛，眩晕，癫、狂、痫，项强。

操作　平刺 0.3～0.5 寸。可灸。

Naokong（GB 19）

Location：1.5 cun directly above Fengchi (GB 20).

Indications：Headache, dizziness, manic-depressive disorders, epilepsy, stiffneck.

Method：Puncture subcutaneously 0.3～0.5 cun. Moxibustion is applicable.

风　池

定位　在胸锁乳突肌与斜方肌之间凹陷中，平风府穴处。

主治　头痛，眩晕，目赤肿痛，鼻渊，鼻衄，耳鸣，颈强，感冒，癫痫，中风，热病，疟疾，瘿气。

操作　针尖微向下，向鼻尖斜刺 0.8～1.2 寸，或平刺透风府。可灸。

Fengchi（GB 20）

Location：In the depression between m. sternocleidomastoideus and m. trapezius, level with Fengfu (DU 16).

Indications：Headache, dizziness, redness, swelling and pain of the eye, rhinorrhea with turbid discharge, nosebleeding, tinnitus, stiffneck, cold, epilepsy, wind stroke, febrile diseases, malaria, goiter.

Method：Puncture obliquely 0.8～1.2 cun towards the nose with the tip of the needle slightly downwards, or subcutaneously through Fengfu. Moxibustion is applicable.

肩　井

定位　大椎穴与肩峰连线的中点。

主治　项强，肩背疼痛，难产，乳汁不下，瘰疬。

操作　直刺0.5～0.8寸。可灸。

Jianjing（GB 21）

Location: At the midpoint of the line joining Dazhui（DU 14）and the acromion.

Indications: Stiffneck, pain in the shoulder and back, difficult labour, insufficient lactation, scrofula.

Method: Puncture perpendicularly 0.5～0.8 cun. Moxibustion is applicable.

渊　腋

定位　举臂，腋中线上，第4肋间隙。

主治　胸满，胁痛，上肢痹痛。

操作　斜刺或平刺0.5～0.8寸。可灸。

Yuanye（GB 22）

Location: With the arm lifted, on the midaxillary line, in the fourth intercostal space.

Indications: Fullness in the chest, pain in the hypochordriac region, pain in the arm.

Method: Puncture obliquely or subcutaneously 0.5～0.8 cun. Moxibustion is applicable.

辄　筋

定位　渊腋穴前1寸，第4肋间隙。

主治　胸满，胁痛，气喘，呕吐，吞酸。

操作　斜刺或平刺0.5～0.8寸。可灸。

Zhejin（GB 23）

Location: 1 cun anterior to Yuanye（GB 22），in the fourth intercostal space.

Indications: Fullness in the chest, pain in the hypochondriac region, asthma, vomiting, acid regurgitation.

Method: Puncture obliquely or subcutaneously 0.5～0.8 cun. Moxibustion is applicable.

日　月

定位　乳头下方，第7肋间隙。

主治　呕吐，吞酸，胁肋疼痛，黄疸。

操作　斜刺或平刺0.5～0.8寸。可灸。

Riyue（GB 24）

Location: Directly below the nipple, in the seventh intercostal space.

Indications: Vomiting, acid swallowing, pain in the hypochondriac region, jaundice.

Method: Puncture obliquely or subcutaneously 0.5～0.8 cun. Moxibustion is applicable.

定位　第 12 肋端。

主治　小便不利，水肿，腰痛，胁痛，腹胀，泄泻。

操作　直刺 0.5～1 寸。可灸。

Jingmen（GB 25）

Location: On the lower border of the free end of the twelfth rib.

Indications: Dysuria, edema, pain in the lower back, pain in the hypochondriac region, abdominal distension, diarrhea.

Method: Puncture perpendicularly 0.5～1 cun. Moxibustion is applicable.

带　脉

定位　第 11 肋端直下平脐处。

主治　腹痛，经闭，月经不调，带下，疝气，腰胁痛。

操作　直刺 1～1.5 寸。可灸。

Daimai（GB 26）

Location: Directly below the free end of the eleventh rib, at the level of the umbilicus.

Indications: Abdominal pain, amenorrhea, irregular menstruation, leukorrhea, hernia, pain in the lower back and hypochondriac region.

Method: Puncture perpendicularly 1～1.5 cun. Moxibustion is applicable.

五　枢

定位　在侧腹，髂前上棘之前 0.5 寸，约平脐下 3 寸处。

主治　腹痛，疝气，带下，便秘，阴挺。

操作　直刺 1～1.5 寸。可灸。

Wushu（GB 27）

Location: On the lateral abdomen, 0.5 cun anterior to the superior illiac spine, 3 cun below the umbilicus.

Indications: Abdominal pain, hernia, leukorrhea, constipation, vaginal protrusion.

Method: Puncture perpendicularly 1～1.5 cun. Moxibustion is applicable.

维　道

定位　五枢穴前下 0.5 寸。

主治　腹痛，疝气，带下，阴挺。

操作　直刺或斜刺 1～1.5 寸。可灸。

Weidao（GB 28）

Location: 0.5 cun anteroinferior to Wushu（GB 27）.

Indications: Abdominal pain, hernia, leukorrhea, vaginal protrusion.

Method: Puncture perpendicularly or obliquely 1～1.5 cun. Moxibustion is applicable.

居　髎

定位　髂前上棘与股骨大转子高点连线的中点。

主治　腰痛，下肢痿痹，疝气。

操作　直刺 1～1.5 寸。可灸。

Juliao（GB 29）

Location: At the midpoint between the anterosuperior iliac spine and the highest point of the greater trochanter.

Indications: Pain in the lower back, muscular atrophy and pain of the lower extremities, hernia.

Method: Puncture perpendicular 1～1.5 cun. Moxibustion is applicable.

环　跳

定位　股骨大转子高点与骶管裂孔连线的外 1/3 与内 2/3 交界处。

主治　下肢痿痹，腰痛。

操作　直刺 2～3 寸。可灸。

Huantiao（GB 30）

Location: At the junction of the lateral 1/3 and medial 2/3 distance between the greater trochanter of the femur and the hiatus of the sacrum.

Indications: Muscular atrophy and pain of the lower extremities, pain in the lower back.

Method: Puncture perpendicularly 2～3 cun. Moxibustion is applicable.

风　市

定位　大腿外侧正中，腘横纹水平线上 7 寸。

主治　下肢痿痹，遍身瘙痒，脚气。

操作　直刺 1～2 寸。可灸。

Fengshi（GB 31）

Location: On the midline of the lateral aspect of the thigh, 7 cun above the transverse popliteal crease.

Indications: Muscular atrophy and pain of the lower extremities, general pruritus, beriberi.

Method: Puncture perpendicularly 1～2 cun. Moxibustion is applicable.

中　渎

定位　风市穴下 2 寸。

主治　下肢痿痹。

操作　直刺 1～2 寸。可灸。

Zhongdu（GB 32）

Location: 2 cun below Fengshi (GB 31).

Indications: Muscular atrophy of the lower extremities.

Method: Puncture perpendicularly 1～2 cun. Moxibustion is applicable.

膝阳关

定位　阳陵泉穴上 3 寸，股骨外上髁上方的凹陷中。

主治　膝腘肿痛挛急，小腿麻木。

操作　直刺 1～1.5 寸。可灸。

Xiyangguan（GB 33）

Location: 3 cun above Yanglingquan (GB 34), in the depression superior to the lateral epicondyle of the femur.

Indications: Swelling, pain and contracture of the knee and popliteal fossa, numbness of the leg.

Method: Puncture perpendicularly 1~1.5 cun. Moxibustion is applicable.

阳 陵 泉

定位 腓骨小头前下方凹陷中。

主治 胁痛,口苦,呕吐,下肢痿痹,脚气,黄疸,小儿惊风。

操作 直刺1~1.5寸。可灸。

Yanglingquan (GB 34)

Location: In the depression anterior and inferior to the small head of the fibula.

Indications: Hypochondriac pain, bitter taste in the mouth, vomiting, atrophy and pain of the lower extremities, beriberi, jaundice, infantile convulsion.

Method: Puncture perpendicularly 1~1.5 cun. Moxibustion is applicable.

阳 交

定位 外踝高点上7寸,腓骨后缘。

主治 胸胁胀满,下肢痿痹,癫狂。

操作 直刺1~1.5寸。可灸。

Yangjiao (GB 35)

Location: 7 cun above the tip of the external malleolus, on the posterior border of the fibula.

Indications: Fullness of the chest and hypochondriac region, muscular at-

rophy and pain of the lower extremities, manic-depressive disorders.

Method: Puncture perpendicularly 1~1.5 cun. Moxibustion is applicable.

外 丘

定位 外踝高点上7寸,腓骨前缘。

主治 胸胁胀满,下肢痿痹,癫狂。

操作 直刺1~1.5寸。可灸。

Waiqiu (GB 36)

Location: 7 cun above the tip of the external malleolus, on the anterior border of the fibula.

Indications: Fullness of the chest and hypochondriac region, muscular atrophy of the lower extremities, manic-depressive disorders.

Method: Puncture perpendicularly 1~1.5 cun. Moxibustion is applicable.

光 明

定位 外踝高点上5寸,腓骨前缘。

主治 目痛,夜盲,下肢痿痹,乳房胀痛。

操作 直刺1~1.5寸。可灸。

Guangming (GB 37)

Location: 5 cun above the tip of the external malleolus, on the anterior border of the fibula.

Indications: Pain in the eye, night

blindness, muscular atrophy and pain of the lower extremities, distension and pain of the breast.

Method: Puncture perpendicularly 1~1.5 cun. Moxibustion is applicable.

阳 辅

定位　外踝高点上4寸，腓骨前缘稍前处。

主治　偏头痛，目外眦痛，瘰疬，脚气，咽喉肿痛，胸胁胀痛，下肢痿痹。

操作　直刺1~1.5寸。可灸。

Yangfu (GB 38)

Location: 4 cun above the tip of the external malleolus slightly anterior to the anterior border of the fibula.

Indications: Hemilateral headache, pain of the outer canthus, scrofula, beriberi, sore throat, distension and pain of the chest and hypochondriac region, muscular atrophy of the lower extremities.

Method: Puncture perpendicularly 1~1.5 cun. Moxibustion is applicable.

悬钟（绝骨）

定位　外踝高点上3寸，腓骨后缘。

主治　项强，胸胁胀满，下肢痿痹，咽喉肿痛，脚气，痔疾。

操作　直刺1~1.5寸。可灸。

Xuanzhong (GB 39)

Location: 3 cun above the tip of the external malleolus, on the posterior of the fibula.

Indications: Stiffneck, distension and pain in the chest and hypochondriac region, muscular atrophy and pain of the lower extremities, sore throat, beriberi, hemorrhoids.

Method: Puncture perpendicularly 1~1.5 cun. Moxibustion is applicable.

丘 墟

定位　外踝前下方，趾长伸肌腱外侧凹陷中。

主治　胸胁胀痛，下肢痿痹，疟疾。

操作　直刺0.5~0.8寸。可灸。

Qiuxu (GB 40)

Location: Anterior and inferior to the external malleolus, in the depression on the lateral side of the tendon of m. extensor digitorum longus.

Indications: Distension and pain in the chest and hypochondriac region, muscular atrophy and pain of the lower extremities, malaria.

Method: Puncture perpendicularly 0.5~0.8 cun. Moxibustion is applicable.

足临泣

定位　在第4、第5跖骨结合部前方，小趾伸肌腱外侧凹陷中。

主治　目赤肿痛，胁肋疼痛，月

经不调，遗溺，乳痈，瘰疬，疟疾，足跗疼痛。

操作 直刺0.3～0.5寸。可灸。

Zulinqi (GB 41)

Location: Anterior to the junction of the fourth and fifth metatarsal bones, in the depression on the lateral side of the tendon of m. extensor digiti minimi of the foot.

Indications: Redness, swelling and pain of the eye, pain in the hypochondriac region, irregular menstruation, enuresis, breast abscess, scrofula, malaria, pain of the dorsum of the foot.

Method: Puncture perpendicularly 0.3～0.5 cun. Moxibustion is applicable.

地 五 会

定位 在第4、第5跖骨之间，当小趾伸肌腱内侧缘处。

主治 头痛，目赤，耳鸣，胁痛，乳痈，足背肿痛。

操作 直刺0.3～0.5寸。可灸

Diwuhui (GB 42)

Location: Between the fourth and fifth metatarsal bones, on the medial side of the tendon of m. extensor of the little toe.

Indications: Headache, redness of the eye, tinnitus, hypochondriac pain, breast abscess, swelling and pain of the dorsum of the foot.

Method: Puncture perpendicularly 0.3～0.5 cun. Moxibustions is applicable.

侠 溪

定位 足背第4、第5趾间缝纹端。

主治 头痛，目眩，耳鸣，耳聋，目赤肿痛，胁肋疼痛，热病，乳痈。

操作 直刺0.3～0.5寸。可灸。

Xiaxi (GB 43)

Location: On the dorsum of the foot, between the fourth and fifth toe, proximal to the margin of the web.

Indications: Headache, dizziness, tinnitus, deafness, swelling, redness and pain of the eye, pain in the hypochondriac region, febrile disease, breast abscess.

Method: Puncture perpendicularly 0.3～0.5 cun. Moxibustion is applicable.

足 窍 阴

定位 第4趾外侧趾甲角旁约0.1寸。

主治 头痛，目赤肿痛，耳聋，咽喉肿痛，热病，失眠，胁痛，咳嗽，月经不调。

操作 浅刺0.1寸，或点刺出血。可灸。

Zuqiaoyin (GB 44)

Location: On the lateral side of the fourth toe, about 0.1 cun lateral to the proximal corner of the nail.

Indications: Headache, redness, swelling and pain of the eye, deafness, sore throat, febrile disease, insomnia, hypochondriac pain, cough, irregular menstruation.

Method: Puncture shallowly 0.1 cun or prick the point to cause bleeding. Moxibustion is applicable.

第十二节　足厥阴肝经及其常用腧穴

Section 12 The Liver Channel of Foot-Jueyin and Commonly Used Acupoints

1. 经脉笔循行

①起于大趾丛毛之际；②沿足跗向上；③经内踝1寸处；④上至内踝8寸，交出于足太阴脾经后方；⑤上行膝内侧；⑥循股内侧；⑦进入阴毛中；⑧过阴部；⑨抵小腹；⑩挟胃，属肝，络胆；⑪上贯膈；⑫布胁肋；⑬循喉咙之后；⑭上入鼻咽；⑮连于"目系"；⑯上出前额；⑰与督脉会合于巅顶。

⑱"目系"的支脉：下行颊里，⑲环绕唇内。

⑳肝部的支脉：从肝分出；㉑过横膈；㉒上注肺（图1－28）。

1. The Course of the Channel

①It starts from the dorsal hair of the great toe. ②Running upward along the dorsum of the foot, ③passing through a point, 1 cun in front of the medial malleolus, ④it ascends to an area 8 cun above the medial malleolus, where it runs across and behind the Spleen Channel of Foot-Taiyin. ⑤ Then it runs further upward to the medial side of the knee ⑥and along the medial side of the thigh ⑦to the pubic hair region, ⑧where it curves around the external genitalia ⑨and goes up to the lower abdomen. ⑩It then runs upward and curves around the stomach to enter the liver, its pertaining organ, and connects with the gallbladder. ⑪From there it continues to ascend, passing through the diaphragm⑫and branching out in the costal and hypochondriac region. ⑬Then it ascends along the posterior aspect of the throat ⑭to the nasopharynx ⑮and connects with the "eye system" (the area where the eyeball links with the brain). ⑯Running further upward, it emerges from the forehead ⑰and meets the DU Channel at the vertex. ⑱The branch arising from the "eye system" descends into the neck ⑲and curves around the inner surface of the lips. ⑳ Another branch arising from the liver ㉑passes through the diaphragm, ㉒ascends into the lung, and connects with the Lung Meridian of Hand-Taiyin (Fig.1 － 28).

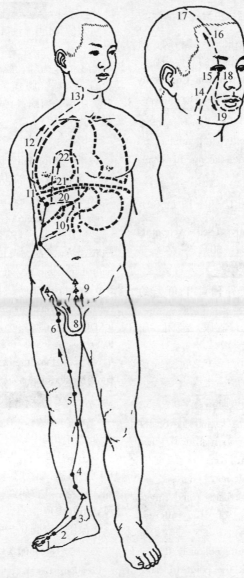

图 1 - 28 足厥阴肝经循行示意图

Fig. 1 - 28 Running Course of the Liver Channel of Foot-Jueyin

2. 常用经穴主治提要

本经腧穴主治肝病、妇科病、前阴病以及经脉循行部位的其他病症。

2. Principal Indications of Commonly Used Acupoints of the Meridian

Diseases of the liver, gynecopathies, diseases of the external genitalia and diseases in the regions along this channel.

3. 常用腧穴（图1-29，图1-30）

3. The Commonly Used Acupoints (Fig.1-29, Fig.1-30)

大　敦

定位　蹈趾外侧趾甲角旁约0.1寸。

主治　疝气，遗尿，经闭，崩漏，阴挺，癫痫。

操作　斜刺0.1～0.2寸，或点刺出血。可灸。

Dadun（LR 1）

Location: On the lateral side of the dorsum of the great toe, about 0.1 cun lateral to the proximal corner of the nail.

Indications: Hernia, enuresis, a-menorrhea, metrorrhagia and met-rostaxis, prolapse of the uterus, epilepsy.

Method: Puncture obliquely 0.1～0.2 cun, or prick the point to cause bleeding. Moxibustion is applicable.

行　间

定位　足背第1、第2趾间缝纹端。

主治　头痛，眩晕，目赤肿痛，夜盲，口喝，胁痛，疝气，小便不利，崩漏，癫痫，月经不调，痛经，带下，中风。

操作　斜刺0.5～0.8寸。可灸。

Xingjian（LR 2）

Location: On the dorsum of the foot between the first and second toes, posterior to the margin of the web.

Indications: Headache, dizziness, redness, swelling and pain of the eye, night blindness, deviation of the mouth, hypochondriac pain, hernia, dysuria, metrorrhagia and metrostaxis, epilepsy, irregular menstruation, dysmenorrhea, leukorrhagia, wind stroke.

Method: Puncture obliquely 0.5～0.8 cun. Moxibustion is applicable.

太　冲

定位　足背，第1、第2跖骨结合部之前凹陷中。

主治　头痛，眩晕，目赤肿痛，口喝，胁痛，遗尿，疝气，崩漏，癫痫，月经不调，痛经，呕吐，小儿惊风，下肢痿痹。

操作　直刺0.5～0.8寸。可灸。

Taichong（LR 3）

Location: On the dorsum of the foot, in the depression anterior to the junction of the first and second metatarsal bones.

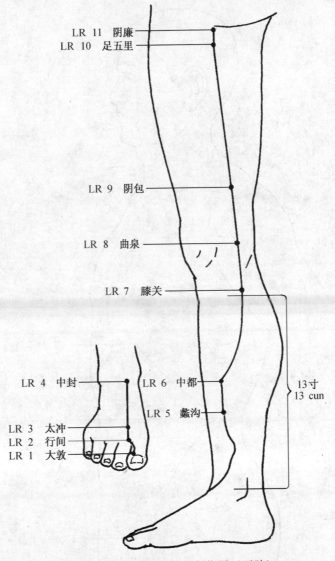

LR 11 阴廉
LR 10 足五里
LR 9 阴包
LR 8 曲泉
LR 7 膝关
LR 4 中封
LR 6 中都
LR 5 蠡沟
LR 3 太冲
LR 2 行间
LR 1 大敦

13寸
13 cun

图 1-29 足厥阴肝经穴位图（下肢）

Fig.1-29 Acupoints of the Liver Channel of Foot-Jueyin (Lower Limb)

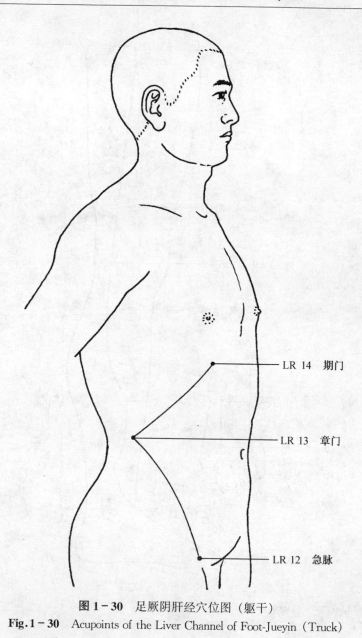

图 1 - 30   足厥阴肝经穴位图（躯干）

Fig. 1 - 30   Acupoints of the Liver Channel of Foot-Jueyin (Truck)

LR 14   期门

LR 13   章门

LR 12   急脉

Indications: Headache, dizziness, redness, swelling and pain of the eye, deviation of the mouth, hypochondriac pain, enuresis, hernia, metrorrhagia and metrostaxis, epilepsy, irregular menstruation, dysmenorrhea, vomiting, infantile convulsion, muscular atrophy and pain of the lower extremities.

Method: Puncture perpendicularly 0.5~0.8 cun. Moxibustion is applicable.

中　封

定位　内踝前1寸，胫骨前肌腱内缘。

主治　疝气，遗精，小便不利，腹痛。

操作　直刺0.5~0.8寸。可灸。

Zhongfeng（LR 4）

Location: 1 cun anterior to the medial malleolus, on the medial side of the tendon of m. tibialis anterior.

Indications: Hernia, nocturnal emission, dysuria, abdominal pain.

Method: Puncture perpendicularly 0.5~0.8 cun. Moxibustion is applicable.

蠡　沟

定位　内踝高点上5寸，胫骨内侧面的中央。

主治　小便不利，遗尿，月经不调，带下，下肢痿痹。

操作　平刺0.5~0.8寸。可灸。

Ligou（LR 5）

Location: 5 cun above the tip of the medial malleolus, around the middle of the medial aspect of the tibia.

Indications: Dysuria, enuresis, irregular menstruation, leukorrhea, muscular atrophy of the lower extremities.

Method: Puncture subcutaneously 0.5~0.8 cun. Moxibustion is applicable.

中　都

定位　内踝高点上7寸，胫骨内侧面的中央。

主治　疝气，崩漏，腹痛，泄泻，恶露不尽。

操作　平刺0.5~0.8寸。可灸。

Zhongdu（LR 6）

Location: 7 cun above the tip of the medial malleolus, around the middle of the medial aspect of the tibia.

Indications: Hernia, metrorrhagia and metrostaxis, abdominal pain, diarrhea, persistent lochia.

Method: Puncture subcutaneously 0.5~0.8 cun. Moxibustion is applicable.

膝　关

定位　阴陵泉穴后1寸。

主治　膝部肿痛。

操作　直刺1~1.5寸。可灸。

Xiguan（LR 7）

Location: 1 cun behind Yinlingquan

(SP 9).

Indications: Swelling and pain of the knee.

Method: Puncture perpendicularly 1~1.5 cun. Moxibustion is applicable.

曲　　泉

定位　屈膝，当膝内侧横纹头上方凹陷中。

主治　腹痛，小便不利，遗精，阴痒，膝痛，月经不调，痛经，带下。

操作　直刺1~1.5寸。可灸。

Ququan（LR 8）

Location: When the knee is flexed, the point is in the depression above the medial end of the transverse popliteal crease.

Indications: Abdominal pain, dysuria, nocturnal emission, pruritus vulvae, pain in the knee, irregular menstruation, dysmenorrhea, leukorrhea.

Method: Puncture perpendicularly 1~1.5 cun. Moxibustion is applicable.

阴　　包

定位　股骨内上髁上4寸，缝匠肌后缘。

主治　腹痛，遗尿，小便不利，月经不调。

操作　直刺1~2寸。可灸。

Yinbao（LR 9）

Location: 4 cun above the medial

epicondyle of the femur, at the posterior border of the m. sartorius.

Indications: Abdominal pain, enuresis, dysuria, irregular menstruation.

Method: Puncture perpendicularly 1~2 cun. Moxibustion is applicable.

足 五 里

定位　曲骨穴旁开2寸，气冲直下3寸。

主治　小腹痛，小便不利，阴挺，睾丸肿痛，嗜卧，瘰疬。

操作　直刺1~2寸。可灸。

Zuwuli（LR 10）

Location: 2 cun lateral to Qugu (RN 2), 3 cun directly below Qichong (ST30).

Indications: Lower abdominal pain, dysuria, prolapse of the uterus, swelling and pain of the testicles, sleepiness, scrofula.

Method: Puncture perpendicularly 1~2 cun. Moxibustion is applicable.

阴　　廉

定位　曲骨穴旁开2寸，气冲直下2寸。

主治　月经不调，带下，小腹痛。

操作　直刺1~2寸。可灸。

Yinlian（LR 11）

Location: 2 cun lateral to Qugu (RN 2), 2 cun directly below Qichong (ST30).

Indications: Irregular menstruation, leukorrhea, lower abdominal pain.

Method: Puncture perpendicularly 1~2 cun. Moxibustion is applicable.

急　脉

定位　在耻骨结节外侧，当气冲外下方腹股沟动脉搏动处，前正中线旁开 2.5 寸。

主治　小腹痛，疝气，阴挺。

操作　避开动脉，直刺 0.5～0.8 寸。可灸。

Jimai（LR 12）

Location: On the lateral side of pubic tubercle, inferolateral to Qichong (ST 30), in the inguinal groove passing by the femoral artery, 2.5 cun lateral to the anterior midline.

Indications: Lower abdominal pain, hernia, prolapse of the uterus.

Method: Avoid the artery, puncture perpendicularly 0.5~0.8 cun. Moxibustion is applicable.

章　门

定位　第 11 肋端。

主治　腹胀，泄泻，胁痛，痞块。

操作　直刺 0.8～1 寸。可灸。

Zhangmen（LR 13）

Location: On the free end of the eleventh rib.

Indications: Abdominal distension, diarrhea, hypochondriac pain, mass in the abdomen.

Method: Puncture perpendicularly 0.8~1 cun. Moxibustion is applicable.

期　门

定位　乳头直下，第 6 肋间隙。

主治　胸胁胀痛，腹胀，呕吐，乳痈。

操作　斜刺或平刺 0.5～0.8 寸。可灸。

Qimen（LR 14）

Location: Directly below the nipple, in the sixth intercostal space.

Indications: Fullness and pain in the chest and hypochondriac region, abdominal distension. vomiting, breast abscess.

Method: Puncture obliquely or subcutaneously 0.5~0.8 cun. Moxibustion is applicable.

第十三节　督脉及其常用腧穴

Section 13　The Du Channel and Commonly Used Acupoints

1. 经脉循行

①起于小腹内，下出会阴部；②向后行于脊柱的内部；③上达项后风府，进入脑内；④上行巅顶；⑤沿前额下行鼻柱（图 1－31）。

1. The Course of the Channel

It arises from the lower abdomen and emerges from the perineum. ②Then it runs posteriorly along the interior of the spinal column③ to Fengfu (Du 16) at the nape, where it enters the brain. ④ It further ascends to the vertex ⑤ and winds along the forehead to the nasal column (Fig. 1 – 31).

2. 常用经穴主治提要

本经腧穴主治神志病，热病，腰骶背、头项及相应的内脏疾病。

2. Principal Indications of Commonly Used Acupoints of the Meridian

Mental diseases, febrile diseases, diseases of the lumbosacral region, back, head, neck and corresponding splanchnopathies.

3. 常用腧穴 （图 1 – 32）

3. The Commonly Used Acupoints (Fig. 1 – 32)

长　强

定位　尾骨尖下 0.5 寸，约当尾骨尖端与肛门的中点。

主治　泄泻，便血，便秘，痔疾，脱肛，癫痫。

操作　紧靠尾骨前面斜刺 0.8～1 寸。可灸。

Changqiang （DU 1）

Location: 0.5 cun below the tip of the coccyx, on the midpoint between the tip of the coccyx and the anus.

Indications: Diarrhea, bloody stools, constipation, hemorrhoids, prolapse of the rectum, epilepsy.

Method: Puncture 0.8 ～ 1 cun obliquely upward in front of the coccyx. Moxibustion is applicable.

腰　俞

定位　当骶管裂孔处。

主治　月经不调，痔疾，腰脊强痛，下肢痿痹，癫痫。

操作　向上斜刺 0.5～1 寸。可灸。

Yaoshu （DU 2）

Location: In the hiatus of the sacrum on the posterior midline.

Indications: Irregular menstruation, hemorrhoids, rigidity and pain of the lower back, muscular atrophy of the lower extremities, epilepsy.

Method: Puncture obliquely upward 0.5～1 cun. Moxibustion is applicable.

腰阳关

定位　第 4 腰椎棘突下，约平髂嵴。

主治　月经不调，遗精，阳痿，腰骶痛，下肢痿痹。

操作　向上斜刺 0.5～1 寸。可灸。

Yaoyangguan （DU 3）

Location: Below the spinous process of the fourth lumbar vertebra, at the level with the crista iliaca.

Indications: Irregular menstruation, nocturnal emission, impotence, pain in the lower back, muscular atrophy and pain of the lower extremities.

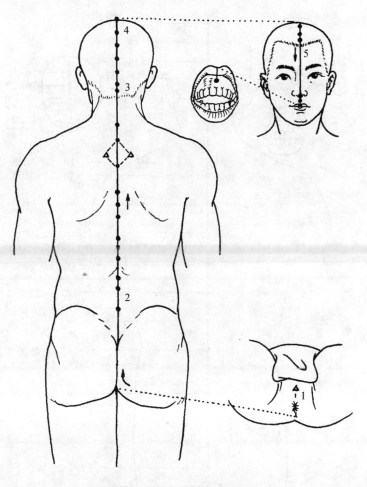

图 1-31 督脉循行示意图

Fig.1-31 Running Course of the Du Channel

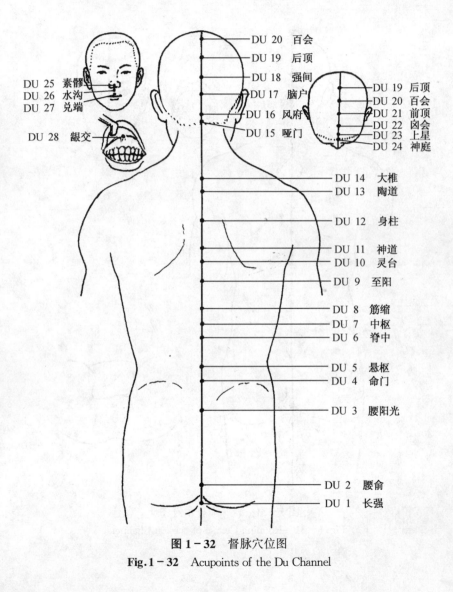

图 1 - 32　督脉穴位图

Fig. 1 - 32　Acupoints of the Du Channel

Method: Puncture obliquely upward 0.5～1 cun. Moxibustion is applicable.

命　门

定位　第2腰椎棘突下。

主治　阳痿，遗精，带下，月经不调，泄泻，腰脊强痛。

操作　向上斜刺0.5～1寸。可灸。

Mingmen（DU 4）

Location: Below the spinous process of the second lumbar vertebra.

Indications: Impotence, nocturnal emission, leukorrhea, irregular menstruation, diarrhea, rigidity and pain of the lower back.

Method: Puncture obliquely upward 0.5～1 cun. Moxibustion is applicable.

悬　枢

定位　第1腰椎棘突下。

主治　泄泻，腹痛，腰脊强痛。

操作　向上斜刺0.5～1寸。可灸。

Xuanshu（DU 5）

Location: Below the spinous process of the first lumbar vertebra.

Indications: Diarrhea, abdominal pain, rigidity and pain of the lower back.

Method: Puncture obliquely upward 0.5～1 cun. Moxibustion is applicable.

脊　中

定位　第11胸椎棘突下。

主治　泄泻，黄疸，痔疾，癫痫，疳积，脱肛。

操作　向上斜刺0.5～1寸。可灸。

Jizhong（DU 6）

Location: Below the spinous process of the eleventh thoracic vertebra.

Indications: Diarrhea, jaundice, hemorrhoids, epilepsy, gan accumulation, prolapse of the rectum.

Method: Puncture obliquely upward 0.5～1 cun. Moxibustion is applicable.

中　枢

定位　第10胸椎棘突下。

主治　黄疸，呕吐，腹满，腰脊强痛。

操作　向上斜刺0.5～1寸。可灸。

Zhongshu（DU 7）

Location: Below the spinous process of the tenth thoracic vertebra.

Indications: Jaundice, vomiting, abdominal distension, rigidity and pain of the back.

Method: Puncture obliquely upward 0.5～1 cun. Moxibustion is applicable.

筋　缩

定位　第9胸椎棘突下。

主治　癫痫，脊强，胃痛。

操作　向上斜刺 0.5～1 寸。
可灸。

Jinsuo (DU 8)

Location: Below the spinous process of the ninth thoracic vertebra.

Indications: Epilepsy, rigidity of the back, stomachache.

Method: Puncture obliquely upward 0.5～1 cun. Moxibustion is applicable.

至　阳

定位　第 7 胸椎棘突下。

主治　黄疸，胸胁胀满，咳喘，腰背痛。

操作　向上斜刺 0.5～1 寸。
可灸。

Zhiyang (DU 9)

Location: Below the spinous process of the seventh thoracic vertebra.

Indications: Jaundice, fullness of the chest and hypochondriac region, cough and asthma, pain in the back.

Method: Puncture obliquely upward 0.5～1 cun. Moxibustion is applicable.

灵　台

定位　第 6 胸椎棘突下。

主治　咳嗽，气喘，脊背强痛。

操作　向上斜刺 0.5～1 寸。
可灸。

Lingtai (DU 10)

Location: Below the spinous process of the sixth thoracic vertebra.

Indications: Cough, asthma, rigidity and pain of the lower back.

Method: Puncture obliquely upward 0.5～1 cun. Moxibustion is applicable.

神　道

定位　第 5 胸椎棘突下。

主治　心悸，健忘，咳嗽，脊背强痛。

操作　向上斜刺 0.5～1 寸。
可灸。

Shendao (DU 11)

Location: Below the spinous process of the fifth thoracic vertebra.

Indications: Palpitation, poor memory, cough, rigidity of the back.

Method: Puncture obliquely upward 0.5～1 cun. Moxibustion is applicable.

身　柱

定位　第 3 胸椎棘突下。

主治　咳嗽，气喘，癫痫，脊背强痛。

操作　向上斜刺 0.5～1 寸。
可灸。

Shenzhu (DU 12)

Location: Below the spinous process of the third thoracic vertebra.

Indications: Cough, asthma, epilepsy, rigidity of the back.

Method: Puncture obliquely upward

0.5～1 cun. Moxibustion is applicable.

陶　道

定位　第1胸椎棘突下。

主治　头痛，疟疾，热病，脊强。

操作　向上斜刺0.5～1寸。可灸。

Taodao（DU 13）

Location: Below the spinous process of the first thoracic vertebra.

Indications: Headache, malaria, febrile diseases, rigidity of the back.

Method: Puncture obliquely upward 0.5～1 cun. Moxibustion is applicable.

大　椎

定位　第7颈椎棘突下。

主治　热病，疟疾，咳嗽，气喘，骨蒸盗汗，癫痫，头痛项强，风疹。

操作　向上斜刺0.5～1寸。可灸。

Dazhui（DU 14）

Location: Below the spinous process of the seventh cervical vertebra.

Indications: Febrile diseases, malaria, cough, asthma, hectic fever due to yin-deficiency accompanied with night sweating, epilepsy, rigidity and pain of the head and neck, urticaria. Moxibustion is applicable.

Method: Puncture obliquely upward

0.5～1.0 cun. Mexibustion is applicable.

哑　门

定位　后发际正中直上0.5寸。

主治　暴喑，舌强不语，癫、狂、痫证，头痛项强。

操作　直刺或向下斜刺0.5～1寸，不可向上斜刺或深刺。

Yamen（DU 15）

Location: 0.5 cun directly above the midpoint of the posterior hairline.

Indications: Sudden loss of voice, stiffness of the tongue, manic-depressive disorder and epilepsy, rigidity and pain of the head and neck.

Method: Puncture perpendicularly or obliquely downward 0.5～1 cun, neither puncturing obliquely upward nor needling deeply.

风　府

定位　后发际正中直上1寸。

主治　头痛，项强，眩晕，咽喉肿痛，失音，癫狂，中风。

操作　直刺或向下斜刺0.5～1寸，不可深刺。可灸。

Fengfu（DU 16）

Location: 1 cun directly above the midpoint of the posterior hairline.

Indications: Headache, neck rigidity, dizziness, sore throat, Sudden loss of voice, epilepsy, wind stroke.

Method: Puncture perpendicularly or obliquely downward 0.5 ～ 1 cun.

Needling deeply is contraindicated. Moxibustion is applicable.

脑　户

定位　风府穴直上1.5寸。

主治　头晕，项强，失音，癫痫。

操作　平刺0.5～0.8寸。可灸。

Naohu（DU 17）

Location：1.5 cun directly above Fengfu（Du16）.

Indications：Dizziness, neck rigidity, loss of voice, epilepsy.

Method：Puncture subcutaneously 0.5～0.8 cun. Moxibustion is applicable.

强　间

定位　脑户穴直上1.5寸。

主治　头痛，目眩，项强，癫狂。

操作　平刺0.5～0.8寸。可灸。

Qiangjian（DU 18）

Location：1.5 cun directly above Naohu（DU 17）.

Indications：Headache, dizziness, neck rigidity, manic-depressive disorder.

Method：Puncture subcutaneously 0.5～0.8 cun. Moxibustion is applicable.

后　顶

定位　强间穴直上1.5寸。

主治　头痛，眩晕，癫、狂、痫证。

操作　平刺0.5～0.8寸。可灸。

Houding（DU 19）

Location：1.5 cun directly above Qiangjian（DU 18）.

Indications：Headache, dizziness, manic-depressive disorder and epilepsy.

Method：Puncture subcutaneously 0.5～0.8 cun. Moxibustion is applicable.

百　会

定位　后发际正中直上7寸。

主治　头痛，眩晕，中风失语，癫狂，脱肛，阴挺，不寐。

操作　平刺0.5～0.8寸。可灸。

Baihui（DU 20）

Location：7 cun directly above the midpoint of the posterior hairline.

Indications：Headache, dizziness, post-apoplectic aphasia, manic-depressive disorder, prolapse of the rectum, vaginal protrusion, insomnia.

Method：Puncture subcutaneously 0.5～0.8 cun. Moxibustion is applicable.

前　顶

定位　百会穴前1.5寸。

主治　头痛，眩晕，鼻渊，癫痫。

操作　平刺0.5～0.8寸。可灸。

Qianding（DU 21）

Location：1.5 cun anterior to Baihui（DU 20）.

Indications: Headache, dizziness, rhinorrhea, epilepsy.

Method: Puncture subcutaneously 0.5~0.8 cun. Moxibustion is applicable.

颟　会

定位　前发际正中直上2寸。

主治　头痛，眩晕，鼻渊，癫痫。

操作　平刺0.5~0.8寸。可灸，婴儿禁刺。

Xinhui (DU 22)

Location: 2 cun directly above the midpoint of the anterior hairline.

Indications: Headache, dizziness, rhinorrhea, epilepsy.

Method: Puncture subcutaneously 0.5~0.8 cun. Moxibustion is applicable. Needling of infants is contraindicated.

上　星

定位　前发际正中直上1寸。

主治　头痛，目痛，鼻渊，鼻衄，癫狂，疟疾，热病。

操作　平刺0.5~1寸。可灸。

Shangxing (DU 23)

Location: 1 cun directly above the midpoint of the anterior hairline.

Indications: Headache, pain of the eye, rhinorrhea, nosebleeding, manic-depressive disorder, malaria, febrile diseases.

Method: Puncture subcutaneously

0.5~1 cun. Moxibustion is applicable.

神　庭

定位　前发际正中直上0.5寸。

主治　头痛，眩晕，失眠，鼻渊，癫痫。

操作　平刺0.5~0.8寸。可灸。

Shenting (DU 24)

Location: 0.5 cun directly above the midpoint of the anterior hairline.

Indications: Headache, dizziness, insomnia, rhinorrhea, epilepsy.

Method: Puncture subcutaneously 0.5~0.8 cun. Moxibustion is applicable.

素　髎

定位　鼻尖正中。

主治　鼻渊，鼻衄，喘息，昏迷，惊厥，新生儿窒息。

操作　向上斜刺0.3~0.5寸。

Suliao (DU 25)

Location: On the tip of the nose.

Indications: Rhinorrhea, nosebleeding, asthma, loss of consciousness, convulsion, asphyxia neonatorum.

Method: Puncture obliquely upward 0.3~0.5 cun.

水　沟

定位　在人中沟上1/3和中1/3交界处。

主治　癫、狂、痫证，小儿惊风，昏迷，口眼㖞斜，腰脊强痛。

操作　向上斜刺 0.3～0.5 寸。可灸。

Shuigou (Renzhong) (DU 26)

Location: At the junction of the superior 1/3 and middle 1/3 of the philtrum.

Indications: Manic-depressive disorders and epilepsy, infantile convulsion, coma, deviation of the mouth and eye, rigidity and pain of the back.

Method: Puncture obliquely upward 0.3～0.5 cun. Moxibustion is applicable.

兑　端

定位　上唇尖端，红唇与皮肤相接处。

主治　癫狂，齿龈肿痛，口㖞，鼻衄。

操作　向上斜刺 0.2～0.3 寸。可灸。

Duiduan (DU 27)

Location: On the median tubercle of the upper lip, at the junction of the skin and upperrlip.

Indications: Manic-depressive disorder, pain and swelling of the gums, deviation of the mouth, nosebleeding.

Method: Puncture obliquely upward 0.2～0.3 cun. Moxibustion is applicable.

龈　交

定位　上唇系带与齿龈连接处。

主治　癫狂，齿龈肿痛，鼻渊。

操作　向上斜刺 0.2～0.3 寸，或点刺出血。

Yinjiao (DU 28)

Location: At the junction of the frenulum of the upper lip and the gum.

Indications: Manic-depressive disorders, pain and swelling of the gums, rhinorrhea.

Method: Puncture obliquely upward 0.2～0.3 cun or prick the point to cause bleeding.

第十四节　任脉及其常用腧穴

Section 14 The Ren Channel and Commonly Used Acupoints

1. 经脉循行

①起于小腹内，下出于会阴部；②向前进入阴毛部；③沿着腹内，向上经过关元等穴；④到达咽喉部；⑤再上行环绕口唇；⑥经过面部；⑦进入目眶下（图 1－33）。

1. The Course of the Channel

①It starts from the inside of the lower abdomen and emerges from the perineum. ②It goes anteriorly to the pubic region and ③ascends along the interior of the abdomen, passing through Guanyuan (RN 4) and the other points ④to the throat. ⑤Ascending further, it curves around the lips, ⑥ passes through the cheek ⑦and enters the infraorbital region (Fig.1－33).

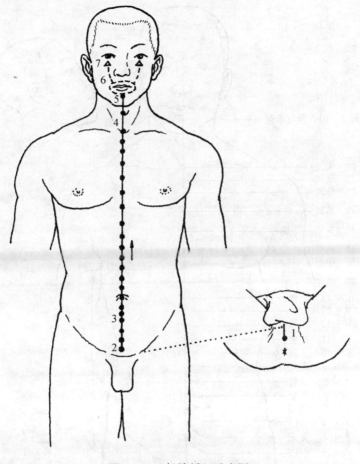

图 1 – 33 任脉循经示意图
Fig. 1 – 33 Running Course of the Ren Channel

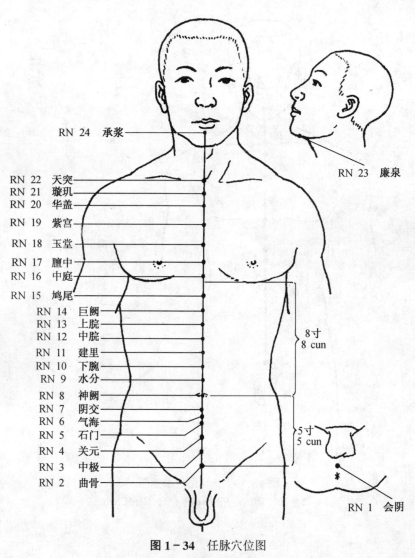

图 1 - 34　任脉穴位图

Fig. 1 - 34　Acupoints of the Ren Channel

2．常用经穴主治提要

本经腧穴主治腹、胸、颈、头面的局部病症及相应的内脏器官疾病，少数腧穴有强壮作用或可治疗神志病。

2．Principal Indications of Commonly Used Acupoints of the Meridian

Local diseases of the abdomen, chest, neck, head and face and diseases of the corresponding internal organs. A few points of this channel have tonifying effects and can be used to treat mental diseases.

3．常用腧穴（图 1－34）

3．The Commonly Used Acupoints (Fig. 1－34)

会　阴

定位　男性在阴囊根部与肛门的中间，女性在大阴唇后联合与肛门的中间。

主治　小便不利，痔疾，遗精，月经不调，癫狂，昏迷。

操作　直刺 0.5～1 寸。可灸。

Huiyin（RN 1）

Location：At the midway of the line between the anus and the scrotum in males, or between the anus and the posterior labial commissure in females.

Indications：Dysuria, hemorrhoids, nocturnal emission, irregular menstruation, manic-depressive disorder, coma.

Method：Puncture perpendicularly 0.5～1 cun. Moxibustion is applicable.

曲　骨

定位　耻骨联合上缘中点。

主治　小便不利，遗尿，遗精，阳痿，月经不调，带下。

操作　直刺 1～1.5 寸。可灸。

Qugu（RN 2）

Location：On the midpoint of the upper border of the symphysis pubis.

Indications：Dysuria, enuresis, nocturnal emission, impotence, irregular menstruation, leukorrhea.

Method：Puncture perpendicularly 1～1.5 cun. Moxibustion is applicable.

中　极

定位　脐下 4 寸。

主治　遗尿，小便不利，疝气，遗精，阳痿，月经不调，崩漏，带下，阴挺，不孕。

操作　直刺 1～1.5 寸。可灸。

Zhongji（RN 3）

Location：4 cun below the umbilicus.

Indications：Enuresis, dysuria, hernia, nocturnal emission, impotence, irregular menstruation, uterine bleeding, leukorrhea, prolapse of the uterus, sterility.

Method：Puncture perpendicularly 1～1.5 cun. Moxibustion is applica-

ble.

关　元

定位　脐下 3 寸。

主治　遗尿，遗精，阳痿，早
泄，小便频数，疝气，带下，不孕，
月经不调，泄泻。

操作　直刺 1～2 寸。可灸。

Guanyuan（RN 4）

Location：3 cun below the umbilicus.

Indications：Enuresis, nocturnal emission, impotence, prospermia, frequency of urination, hernia, leukorrhea, sterility, irregular menstruation, diarrhea.

Method：Puncture perpendicularly 1～2 cun. Moxibustion is applicable.

石　门

定位　脐下 2 寸。

主治　腹痛，水肿，疝气，小便
不利，泄泻，月经不调，带下，
崩漏。

操作　直刺 0.5～1 寸。可灸。

Shimen（RN 5）

Location：2 cun below the umbilicus.

Indications：Abdominal pain, edema, hernia, dysuria, diarrhea, irregular menstruation, leukorrhea, metrorrhagia and metrostaxis.

Method：Puncture perpendicularly 0.5～1 cun. Moxibustion is applicable.

气　海

定位　脐下 1.5 寸。

主治　腹痛，泄泻，便秘，遗
尿，疝气，遗精，月经不调，虚脱。

操作　直刺 1～2 寸。可灸。

Qihai（RN 6）

Location：1.5 cun below the umbilicus.

Indications：Abdominal pain, diarrhea, constipation, enuresis, hernia, nocturnal emission, irregular menstruation, vacuity desertion.

Method：Puncture perpendicularly 1～2 cun. Moxibustion is applicable.

阴　交

定位　脐下 1 寸。

主治　腹痛，水肿，疝气，月经
不调，带下。

操作　直刺 1～2 寸。可灸。

Yinjiao（RN 7）

Location：1 cun below the umbilicus.

Indications：Abdominal pain, edema, hernia, irregular menstruation, leukorrhea.

Method：Puncture perpendicularly 1～2 cun. Moxibustion is applicable.

神　阙

定位　脐的中央。

主治　腹痛，泄泻，脱肛，水
肿，虚脱。

操作　禁针。多用艾炷隔姜、隔

盐或艾条灸。

Shenque（RN 8）

Location: In the centre of the umbilicus.

Indications: Abdominal pain, diarrhea, prolapse of the rectum, edema, vacuity desertion.

Method: Puncture is prohibited. More often, moxibustion with ginger, salt or moxa sticks is used.

水 分

定位 脐上2寸。

主治 水肿，小便不利，腹痛，泄泻，反胃吐食。

操作 直刺1～2寸。可灸。

Shuifen（RN 9）

Location: 1 cun above the umbilicus.

Indications : Edema , dysuria, abdominal pain,

diarrhea, regurgitation of food from the stomach.

Method: Puncture perpendicularly 1～2 cun. Moxibustion is applicable.

下 脘

定位 脐上2寸。

主治 腹痛，腹胀，泄泻，呕吐，食谷不化，痞块。

操作 直刺1～2寸。可灸。

Xiawan（RN 10）

Location: 2 cun above the umbilicus.

Indications: Abdominal pain, distension of the abdomen, diarrhea, vomiting, non-transformation of food, lump glomus.

Method: Puncture perpendicularly 1～2 cun. Moxibustion is applicable.

建 里

定位 脐上3寸。

主治 胃痛，呕吐，食欲不振，腹胀，水肿。

操作 直刺1～2寸。可灸。

Jianli（RN 11）

Location: 3 cun above the umbilicus.

Indications: Stomachache, vomiting, anorexia, abdominal distension, edema.

Method: Puncture perpendicularly 1～2 cun. Moxibustion is applicable.

中 脘

定位 脐上4寸。

主治 胃痛，呕吐，吞酸，腹胀，泄泻，黄疸，癫狂。

操作 直刺1～1.5寸。可灸。

Zhongwan（RN 12）

Location: 4 cun above the umbilicus.

Indications: Stomachache, vomiting, acid regurgitation, abdominal distension, diarrhea, jaundice, epilepsy.

Method: Puncture perpendicularly 1～1.5 cun. Moxibustion is applicable.

上 脘

定位　脐上 5 寸。

主治　胃痛，呕吐，腹胀，癫痫。

操作　直刺 1～1.5 寸。可灸。

Shangwan（RN 13）

Location: 5 cun above the umbilicus.

Indications: Stomachache, vomiting, abdominal distension, epilepsy.

Method: Puncture perpendicularly 1～1.5 cun. Moxibustion is applicable.

巨　阙

定位　脐上 6 寸。

主治　胸痛，心悸，呕吐，吞酸，癫、狂、痫证。

操作　向下斜刺 0.5～1 寸。可灸。

Juque（RN 14）

Location: 6 cun above the umbilicus.

Indications: Pain in the chest, palpitation, vomiting, acid swallowing, manic-depressive disorder and epilepsy.

Method: Puncture obliquely downward 0.5～1 cun. Moxibustion is applicable.

鸠　尾

定位　剑突下，脐上 7 寸。

主治　胸痛，腹胀，癫、狂、痫证。

操作　向下斜刺 0.4～0.6 寸。可灸。

Jiuwei（RN 15）

Location: Below the xiphoid process, 7 cun above the umbilicus.

Indications: Pain in the chest, abdominal distension, manic-depressive disorder and epilepsy.

Method: Puncture obliquely downward 0.4～0.6 cun. Moxibustion is applicable.

中　庭

定位　胸剑联合的中点。

主治　胸胁胀满，心痛，呕吐。

操作　平刺 0.3～0.5 寸。可灸。

Zhongting（RN 16）

Location: At the midpoint of the xiphisternal synchondrosis.

Indications: Fullness of the chest and hypochondriac region, heart pain, vomiting.

Method: Puncture subcutaneously 0.3～0.5 cun. Moxibustion is applicable.

膻　中

定位　前正中线，平第 4 肋间隙。

主治　咳嗽，气喘，胸痛，心悸，乳少，呕吐，噎膈。

操作　平刺 0.3～0.5 寸。可灸。

Tanzhong（RN 17）

Location: On the anterior midline, at the level with the fourth intercostal space.

Indications: Cough, asthma, pain in the chest, palpitation, insufficient lactation, vomiting, dysphagia.

Method: Puncture subcutaneously 0.3~0.5 cun. Moxibustion is applicable.

玉　堂

定位　前正中线，平第 3 肋间隙。

主治　咳嗽，气喘，胸痛，呕吐。

操作　平刺0.3~0.5寸。可灸。

Yutang（RN 18）

Location: On the anterior midline, at the level with the third intercostal space.

Indications: Cough, asthma, pain in the chest, vomiting.

Method: Puncture subcutaneously 0.3~0.5 cun. Moxibustion is applicable.

紫　宫

定位　前正中线，平第 2 肋间隙处。

主治　咳嗽，气喘，胸痛。

操作　平刺0.3~0.5寸。可灸。

Zigong（RN 19）

Location: On the anterior midline, at the level with the second intercostal space.

Indications: Cough asthma, pain in the chest.

Method: Puncture subcutaneously

0.3~0.5 cun. Moxibustion is applicable

华　盖

定位　前正中线，平第 1 肋间隙处。

主治　咳嗽，气喘，胸胁胀痛。

操作　平刺0.3~0.5寸。可灸。

Huagai（RN 20）

Location: On the anterior midline, at the level with the first intercostal space.

Indications: Cough, asthma, fullness and pain in the chest and hypochondriac region.

Method: Puncture subcutaneously 0.3~0.5cun. Moxibustion is applicable.

璇　玑

定位　前正中线，天突穴下 1 寸。

主治　咳嗽，气喘，胸痛，咽喉肿痛。

操作　平刺0.3~0.5寸。可灸。

Xuanji（RN 21）

Location: On the anterior midline, 1 cun below Tiantu (RN 22).

Indications: Cough, asthma, pain in the chest, sore throat.

Method: Puncture subcutaneously 0.3~0.5cun. Moxibustion is applicable.

天　突

定位　胸骨上窝正中。

主治　咳嗽，气喘，胸痛，咽喉
肿痛，暴喑，瘿气，梅核气，噎膈。

操作　先直刺0.2寸，然后将针
尖转向下方。紧靠胸骨后面刺入
0.5～1寸。可灸。

Tiantu（RN 22）

Location: In the centre of the
suprasternal fossa.

Indications: Cough, asthma, pain
in the chest, sore throat, sudden loss
of voice, goiter, plum-pit qi, dysphagia.

Method: First puncture perpendicularly 0.2 cun and then insert the needle
tip downward along the posterior aspect
of the sternum 0.5～1 cun. Moxibustion is applicable.

廉　泉

定位　舌骨体上缘的中点处。

主治　舌下肿痛，舌缓流涎，中
风舌强，暴喑，吞咽困难。

操作　向舌根斜刺0.5～0.8寸。
可灸。

Lianquan（RN 23）

Location: At the midpoint of the upper border of the hyoid bone.

Indications: Swelling and pain of the
subglossal region, salivation with flaccid tongue, stiffness of the tongue due
to wind stroke, sudden loss of voice,
difficulty in swallowing.

Method: Puncture obliquely
0.5～0.8 cun toward the tongue root.

Moxibustion is applicable.

承　浆

定位　颏唇沟的中点。

主治　口㖞，齿龈肿痛，流涎，
暴喑，癫狂。

操作　斜刺0.3～0.5寸。可灸。

Chengjian（RN 24）

Location: In the centre of the mentolabial groove.

Indications: Deviation of the mouth,
swelling and pain of the gums, salivation, sudden loss of voice, manic -de-
pressive disorders.

Method : Puncture obliquely
0.3～0.5 cun. Moxibustion is applicable.

第十五节　经外奇穴

Section 15　Extraordinary Points

1．头面部

1. The Head and Face

四　神　聪

定位　百会穴前后左右各1
寸处。

主治　头痛，眩晕，失眠，健
忘，癫痫。

操作　平刺0.5～0.8寸。可灸。

Sishencong（EX-HN1）

Location: Four points, at the vertex
of the head, 1.0 cun anterior, posteri-
or, and lateral to Baihui (DU 20).

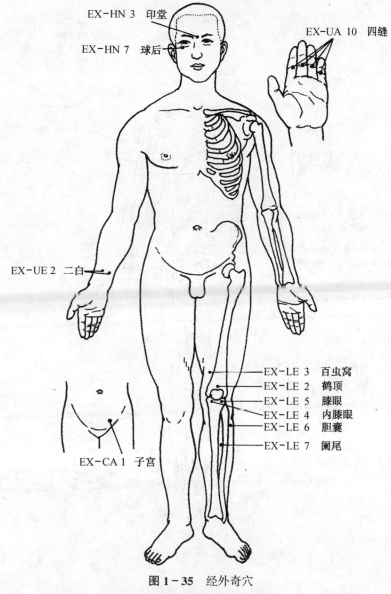

图 1 - 35 经外奇穴

Fig. 1 - 35 Extra ordinary Points

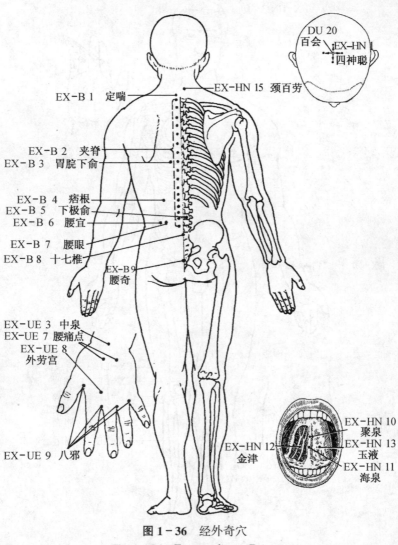

图 1 - 36 　经外奇穴

Fig. 1 - 36   Extra ordinary Points

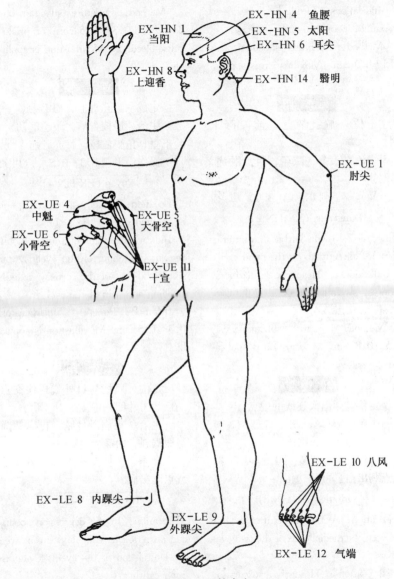

图 1 - 37 经外奇穴

Fig.1 - 37 Extra ordinary Points

Indications: Headache, dizziness, insomnia, poor memory, epilepsy.

Method: Puncture subcutaneously 0.5~0.8 cun. Moxibustion is applicable.

当　阳

定位　瞳孔直上，前发际上1寸。

主治　头痛，眩晕，目赤肿痛，鼻塞。

操作　平刺0.5~0.8寸。可灸。

Dangyang (EX-HN 2)

Location: 1 cun within the anterior hairline, directly above the pupil.

Indications: Headache, dizziness, redness, swelling and pain in the eye, nasal obstruction.

Method: Puncture subcutaneously 0.5~0.8 cun. Moxibustion is applicable.

印　堂

定位　两眉头连线的中点。

主治　头痛，眩晕，鼻衄，鼻渊，小儿惊风，失眠。

操作　向下沿皮刺0.3~0.5寸，或点刺出血。可灸。

Yintang (EX-HN 3)

Location: At the midpoint of the line between the medial ends of the two eyebrows.

Indications: Headache, dizziness, nosebleeding, rhinorrhea, infantile convulsion, insomnia.

Method: Puncture subcutaneously downward 0.3~0.5 cun, or prick to cause bleeding. Moxibustion is applicable.

鱼　腰

定位　瞳孔直上，眉毛中。

主治　眉棱骨痛，眼睑瞤动，眼睑下垂，角膜白斑，目赤肿痛。

操作　平刺0.3~0.5寸。可灸。

Yuyao (EX-HN 4)

Location: Directly above the pupil, at the midpoint of the eyebrow.

Indications: Pain in the supraobital region, twitching of the eyelids, ptosis, cloudiness of the cornea, redness, swelling and pain of the eye.

Method: Puncture subcutaneously 0.3~0.5 cun. Moxibustion is applicable.

太　阳

定位　眉梢与目外眦连线交点，向后约1寸凹陷中。

主治　头痛，目眩，目赤肿痛，口眼㖞斜，面痛。

操作　直刺或平刺0.3~0.4寸，或点刺出血。

Taiyang (EX-HN 5)

Location: In the depression about 1 cun posterior to the midpoint between the lateral end of the eyebrow and the outer canthus.

Indications: Headache, dizziness, redness, swelling and pain of the eye, deviation of the eye and mouth, facial pain.

Method: Puncture perpendicularly or subcutaneously 0.3～0.4 cun, or prick the point to cause bleeding.

耳 尖

定位 在耳郭的上方，当折耳向前，耳郭上方的尖端处。

主治 目赤肿痛，目翳，偏正头痛，咽喉肿痛，麦粒肿。

操作 直刺0.1寸或点刺出血。

Erjian（EX-HN 6）

Location: On the upper portion of the auricle, folding the auricle the point is at the apex.

Indications: Redness, swelling and pain of the eyes, nebula, headache and onesided headache, sore throat, stye.

Method: Puncture perpendicularly 0.1 cun or prick the point to cause bleeding.

球 后

定位 眶下缘外1/4与内3/4交界处。

主治 近视，视神经炎，青光眼，视神经萎缩，视网膜色素变性，玻璃体混浊，内斜视。

操作 将眼球轻压向上方，沿眶下缘缓慢直刺0.3～0.5寸，勿提插捻转。

Qiuhou（EX-HN 7）

Location: At the junction of the lateral 1/4 and medial 3/4 of the infraor-bital margin.

Indications: Myopia, optic neuritis, glaucoma, optic atrophy, pigmentary degeneration of the retina, vitreous opacity, cross-eyed.

Method: Push eyeball upward gently, puncture perpendicularly 0.3～0.5 cun along infraorbital margin slowly without movement of lifting, thrusting, twisting and rotating.

上 迎 香

定位 鼻翼软骨与鼻甲交界处，近鼻唇沟上端处。

主治 头痛，鼻塞，过敏性鼻炎，肥大性鼻炎，萎缩性鼻炎，鼻旁窦炎。

操作 向内上方斜刺0.3～0.5寸。可灸。

Shangyingxiang（EX-HN 8）

Location: At the junction of the alar cartilage and nasal conchae, at the upper end of the nasolabial groove.

Indications: Headache, nasal obstruction, allergic rhinitis, hypertrophic rhinitis, atrophic rhinitis, paranasal sinusitis.

Method: Puncture obliquely upward 0.3～0.5 cun. Moxibustion is applicable.

内 迎 香

定位 在鼻孔内，鼻翼软骨与骨甲交界的黏膜处。

主治 目赤肿痛，鼻疾，咽喉肿

痛，热病，中暑，眩晕。

操作　同三棱针点刺出血。

Neiyingxiang (EX-HN 9)

Location: Within the nostril, at the junction of the alar cartilage and concha.

Indications: Redness, swelling and pain of the eyes, nasal diseases, sore throat, febrile diseases, sunstroke, vertigo.

Method: Prick with a three edged needle to cause bleeding.

聚　　泉

定位　舌背正中缝的中点处。

主治　舌强，舌缓，消渴，哮喘，咳嗽及味觉减退。

操作　直刺 0.1～0.2 寸或点刺出血。

Juquan (EX-HN 10)

Location: At the midpoint of the inferior midline of the tongue.

Indications: stiff tongue, flaccid tongue, diabetes, asthma, cough, hypogeusesthesia.

Method: Puncture perpendicularly 0.1～0.2 cun, or prick to cause bleeding.

海　　泉

定位　舌下系带中点处。

主治　消渴，膈肌痉挛，舌炎。

操作　点刺出血。

Haiquan (EX-HN 11)

Location: At the midpoint of the frenulum of the tongue.

Indications: Diabetes, spasm of the diaphragm, glossitis.

Method: Prick to cause bleeding.

金　　津

定位　舌下系带左侧的静脉上。

主治　舌强，舌肿，咽喉肿痛，消渴，呕吐，泄泻，失语。

操作　点刺出血。

Jinjin (EX-HN 12)

Location: On the vein of the left side of the frenulum of the tongue.

Indications: Stiff tongue, swelling of the tongue, sore throat, diabetes, vomiting, diarrhea, aphasia.

Method: Prick to cause bleeding.

玉　　液

定位　舌下系带右侧静脉上。

主治　舌强，舌肿，消渴，呕吐，腹泻，失语。

操作　点刺出血。

Yuye (EX-HN 13)

Location: On the vein of the right side of the frenulum of the tongue.

Indications: Stiff tongue, swelling of the tongue, sore throat, diabetes, vomiting, diarrhea, aphasia.

Method: Prick to cause bleeding.

翳　　明

定位　在颈部，翳风穴后 1 寸。

主治　近视，远视，夜盲，视神

经萎缩，白内障，耳鸣，眩晕，腮腺炎，头痛，失眠，精神病。

操作　斜刺或平刺 0.5～0.8 寸。可灸。

Yiming（EX-HN 14）

Location: On the nape, 1 cun posterior to Yifeng (SJ 17).

Indications: Near sightedness, hyperopia, night blindness, optic atrophy, cataract, tinnitus, vertigo parotitis, headache, insomnia, mental diseases.

Method: Puncture obliquely or subcutaneously 0.5～0.8 cun. Moxibustion is applicable.

颈　百　劳

定位　在颈部，当大椎直上 2 寸，后正中线旁开 1 寸。

主治　骨蒸潮热，自汗盗汗，瘰疬，咳嗽，气喘，颈项强痛。

操作　直刺 0.5～0.7 寸。可灸。

Jingbailao（EX-HN 15）

Location: On the nape, 2 cun directly above Dazhui（DU 14），1 cun lateral to the posterior midline.

Indications: Hectic fever, spontaneous perspiration, night sweat, scrofula, cough, asthma, stiff pain of the neck.

Method: Puncture perpendicularly 0.5～0.7 cun. Moxibustion is applicable.

2．胸腹部

2．The Chest and Abdomen

子　宫

定位　脐中下 4 寸。中极旁开 3 寸。

主治　子宫脱垂，月经不调，痛经，盆腔炎，妇女不孕，肾盂肾炎，膀胱炎，睾丸炎，阑尾炎。

操作　直刺 0.8～1 寸。可灸。

Zigong（EX-CA 1）

Location: 4 cun below the center of the umbilicus, 3 cun lateral to Zhongji（DU 4）.

Indications: Prolapse of the uterus, irregular menstruation, menorrhalgia, pelvic inflammation, female infertility, pyelonephritis, cystitis, orchitis, appendicitis.

Method: Puncture perpendicularly 0.8～1 cun. Moxibustion is applicable.

3．背部

3．The Back

定　喘

定位　第 7 颈椎棘突下，旁开 0.5 寸。

主治　咳嗽，支气管炎，哮喘，颈项强急，荨麻疹。

操作　直刺 0.5～0.7 寸。可灸。

Dingchuan（EX-B 1）

Location: 0.5 cun lateral to the lower border of the spinous, process of the seventh cervical vertebra.

Indications: Cough, bronchitis, asthma, neck rigidity, urticaria.

Method: Puncture perpendicularly 0.5~0.7 cun. Moxibustion is applicable.

夹　脊

定位　第1胸椎至第5腰椎棘突下两侧，后正中线旁开0.5寸，每侧17穴。

主治　咳嗽，哮喘，痨瘵，神经衰弱，背脊痛，各种慢性疾病。

操作　直刺0.7～1寸，或用梅花针点刺。可灸。

Jiaji (EX-B 2)

Location: 0.5 cun lateral to the lower border of each spinous process from the first thoracic vertebra to the fifth lumbar vetebra. 17 points on each side.

Indication: Cough, asthma, consumptive disease, neurasthenia, pain in the back and spinal column, chronic diseases.

Method: Puncture perpendicularly 0.7~1 cun or prick skin with a 7-star needle. Moxibustion is applicable.

胃脘下俞

定位　第8胸椎棘突下，旁开1.5寸。

主治　糖尿病，胃病，腹痛，呕吐，肋间神经痛。

操作　斜刺0.5～0.8寸。可灸。

Weiwanxiashu (EX-B 3)

Location: 1.5 cun lateral to the lower border of the spinous process of the eighth thoracic vertebra.

Indications: Diabetes, stomach disorders, abdominal pain, vomiting, intercostal neuralgia.

Method: Puncture obliquely 0.5~0.8 cun. Moxibustion is applicable.

痞　根

定位　第1腰椎棘突下，旁开1.5寸。

主治　肝脾肿大，胃炎，肠炎，肾下垂，腰痛。

操作　斜刺0.5～0.7寸。可灸。

Pigen (EX-B 4)

Location: 3.5 cun lateral to the lower border of the spinous process of the first lumbar vertebra.

Indications: Hepatosplenomegaly, gastritis, enteritis, ptosis of the kidney, lower back pain.

Method: Puncture obliquely 0.5~0.7 cun. Moxibustion is applicable.

下　极　俞

定位　后正中线上，第3胸椎棘突下。

主治　腰痛，腹泻，腹痛，小便不利，遗尿，下肢瘫痪。

操作　斜刺0.5～0.7寸。可灸。

Xiajishu (EX-B 5)

Location: Below the lower border of the spinous process of the third lumbar vertebra, on the posterior midline.

Indication: Lower back pain, diarrhea, dysuria, enuresis, paralysis of the lower extremifies.

Method: Puncture obliquely 0.5~0.7 cun. Moxibustion is applicable.

腰　宜

定位　第 4 腰椎棘突下旁开 3 寸。

主治　腰痛，崩漏。

操作　斜刺 0.5~0.7 寸。可灸。

Yaoyi (EX-B 6)

Location: 3 cun lateral to the lower border of the spinous process of the fourth lumbar vertebra.

Indications: Lower back pain, dysfunctional uterine bleding.

Method: Puncture obliquely 0.5~0.7 cun. Moxibustion is applicable.

腰　眼

定位　第 4 腰椎棘突下旁开 3.5 寸凹陷中。

主治　腰部软组织损伤，肾下垂，睾丸炎，尿频，月经失调。

操作　斜刺 0.5~0.7 寸。可灸。

Yaoyan (EX-B 7)

Location: In the depression about 3.5 cun lateral to the lower border of the spinous process of the fourth lumbar vertebra.

Indications: Injury of the soft tissure in the lumbar region, ptosis of the kidney, orchitis, frequent urination, irregular menstruation.

Method: Puncture obliquely 0.5~0.7 cun. Moxibustion is applicable.

十 七 椎

定位　后正中线第 5 腰椎棘突下。

主治　腰骶痛，坐骨神经痛，功能性子宫出血，痛经，肛门疾患，截瘫，尿潴留。

操作　向上斜刺 0.5~1.2 寸。可灸。

Shiqizhui (EX-B 8)

Location: Below the lower border of the spinous process of the fifth lumbar vertebra, on the posterior midline.

Indications: Pain in the lumbosacral portion, sciatica, dysfunctional uterine bleeding, menorrhalgia, diseases of the anus, paraplegia, retention of urine.

Method: Puncture obliquely upward 0.5~1.2 cun. Moxibustion is applicable.

腰　奇

定位　尾骨端直上 2 寸，骶角之间凹陷处。

主治　癫痫，头痛，失眠，

便秘。

操作　向上平刺 0.8～1.2 寸。可灸。

Yaoqi (EX-B 9)

Location: 2 cun directly above the tip of the coccyx, in the depression at the sacral horn.

Indications: Epilepsy, headache, insomnia, constipation.

Method: Puncture subcutaneously upward 0.8～1.2 cun. Moxibustion is applicable.

4. 上肢

4. The Upper Extremities

肘　尖

定位　屈肘，尺骨鹰嘴的尖端。

主治　颈淋巴结核，痈疽，疔疮，肠痈，霍乱。

操作　艾炷灸 7～15 壮。

Zhoujian (EX-UE 1)

Location: On the tip of the ulnar olecranon with the elbow flexed.

Indications: Scrofula, furuncle, carbuncle, appendicitis, cholera morbus.

Method: Moxibustion is applicable with 7～15 moxa cones.

二　白

定位　在前臂掌侧，腕横纹上 4 寸，桡侧腕屈肌腱的两侧，一侧 2 穴。

主治　痔疮，脱肛，前臂神经

痛，胸胁痛。

操作　直刺 0.3～0.7 寸。可灸。

Erbai (EX-UE 2)

Location: On the palmar aspect of the forearm, 4 cun above the transverse crease of the wrist, on both sides of the tendon of the m. flexor carpi radialis, two points on one hand.

Indications: Hemorrhoids, prolapse of the rectum, neuralgia in the forearm, pain in the chest and hypochondrium.

Method: Puncture perpendicularly 0.3～0.7 cun. Moxibustion is applicable.

中　泉

定位　腕背侧横纹中，指总伸肌腱桡侧的凹陷处。

主治　支气管炎，哮喘，目翳，胃痛，胸胁胀痛，腹胀腹痛，掌中热。

操作　直刺 0.2～0.3 寸。可灸。

Zhongquan (EX-UE 3)

Location: On the transverse crease of the wrist on the dorsal aspect, in the depression on the radial side of the tendon of the common extensor muscle of the fingers.

Indications: Bronchitis, asthma, cloudiness of the cornea, stomachache, distension and fullness in the chest and hypochondriac region, distending pain in the abdomen, feverish sensation in the palm of the hand.

Method: Puncture perpendicularly 0.2~0.3 cun. Moxibustion is applicable.

中 魁

定位 中指背侧近端指间关节的中点处。

主治 恶心，呕吐，呃逆，食道痉挛，牙痛，鼻出血，白癜风。

操作 直刺0.2~0.3寸。可灸。

Zhongkui (EX-UE 4)

Location: At the midpoint of the proximal interphalangeal joint of the middle finger on the dorsum.

Indications: Nausea, vomiting, hiccup, esophagospasm, epistaxis, vitiligo.

Method: Puncture perpendicularly 0.2~0.3 cun. Moxibustion is applicable.

大 骨 空

定位 拇指背侧指间关节的中点处。

主治 目痛，目翳，内障，吐泻，衄血。

操作 艾炷灸5~7壮。

Dagukong (DE-UE 5)

Location: At the midpoint of the interphalangeal joint of the thumb on the dorsal aspect.

Indications: Eye pain, cloudiness of the cornea, internal oculopathy, vomiting, diarrhea, epistaxis.

Method: Moxibustion is applicable with 5~7 moxa cones.

小 骨 空

定位 小指背侧近端指间关节中点处。

主治 目赤肿痛，目翳，咽喉肿痛，指间关节痛。

操作 艾炷灸5~7壮。

Xiaogukong (EX-UE 6)

Location: At the midpoint of the proximal interphalangeal joint of the little finger on the dorsal aspect.

Indications: Redness, swelling and pain of the eye, nebula, sore throat, pain in the interphalangeal joints.

Method: Moxibustion is applicable with 5~7 moxa cones.

腰 痛 点

定位 手背2、3掌骨和4、5掌骨之间，腕横纹与掌指关节中点处，一侧2穴。

主治 急性腰扭伤，头痛，小儿急慢惊风，手背红肿疼痛。

操作 由两侧向掌中斜刺0.3~0.5寸。

Yiaotongdian (EX-UE 7)

Location: On the dorsum of the hand, between the second and third and fourth and fifth metacarpals, at the midpoints between the transverse crease of the wrist and metacarpophalangeal joints. 2 points on one hand.

Indications: Acute lumbar sprain, headache, infantile acute or chronic convulsion, redness, swelling and pain of the dorsum of the hand.

Method: Puncture obliquely 0.3~0.5 cun toward the middle of the metacarpus.

外 劳 宫

定位　手背侧 2、3 掌骨之间，掌指关节后 0.5 寸处。

主治　落枕，偏头痛，五指不能屈伸，小儿消化不良，脐风，胃痛，咽喉肿痛，肩臂痛。

操作　直刺或斜刺 0.5~0.7 寸。

Wailaogong (EX-UE 8)

Location: On the dorsum of the hand, between the second and third metacarpals, 0.5 cun posterior to the metacarpophalangeal joint.

Indications: Stiffneck, migraine, motor impairment of the fingers, infantile mal-digestion, tetanus neonatorium, stomachache, sore throat, pain in the shoulder and arm.

Method: Puncture perpendicularly or obliquely 0.5~0.7 cun.

八 邪

定位　手背各指缝中的赤白肉际，左右共 8 穴。

主治　烦热，目痛，毒蛇咬伤，手背肿痛，手指麻木，疼痛。

操作　斜刺 0.3~0.5 寸，或点刺出血。可灸。

Baxie (EX-UE9)

Location: On the dorsum of the hand, at the junction of the red and white skin of the hand webs, both left and right sides, eight in all.

Indications: Excessive heat, pain of the eye, snake-bite, swelling and pain of the dorsum of the hand, numbness and pain of the fingers.

Method: Puncture obliquely 0.3~0.5 cun, or prick to cause bleeding. Moxibustion is applicable.

四 缝

定位　第 2、第 3、第 4、第 5 指掌面，近端指关节横纹中点。

主治　小儿疳积，反胃，呕吐，百日咳。

操作　三棱针点刺，挤出黄白色透明液体。

Sifeng (EX-UE 10)

Location: On the palmar surface, in the midpoint of the transverse crease of the proximal interphalangeal joints of the second, third, fourth and fifth fingers.

Indications: Malnutrition and indigestion syndrome in children, nausea, vomiting, whooping cough.

Method: Prick with a three-edged needle and squeeze out a small amount of yellowish viscous fluid.

十 宣

定位　手十指尖端，距指甲约 0.1 寸。

主治　昏迷，癫痫，癔病，高热，乳蛾，小儿惊厥，中暑。

操作 浅刺 0.1～0.2 寸，或点刺出血。

Shixuan（EX-UE 11）

Location: On the tips of the ten fingers, about 0.1 cun distal to the nails.

Indications: Coma, epilepsy, hysteria, high fever, tonsillitis, infantile convulsion, heat-stroke.

Method: Puncture 0.1 ～ 0.2 cun superficially, or prick to cause bleeding.

5．下肢

5．The Lower Extremities

髋 骨

定位 大腿前面下部，梁丘两旁各 1.5 寸，侧 2 穴。

主治 膝痛，腿痛，下肢瘫痪。

操作 直刺 0.8～1.2 寸。可灸。

Kuangu（EX-LE 1）

Location: On the lower portion of the anterior aspect of the thigh, 1.5 cun lateral and medial to Liangqiu (ST 34), 2 points on one thigh.

Indications: Pain in the knee, thigh and leg, paralysis of the lower extremities.

Method: Puncture perpendicularly 0.8～1.2 cun. Moxibustion is applicable.

鹤 顶

定位 膝上部，髌底的中点上方凹陷处。

主治 膝痛，足胫无力，瘫痪，脚气。

操作 直刺 0.5～0.7 寸。可灸。

Heding（EX-LE 2）

Location: On the upper portion of the knee, in the depression superior to the midpoint of the upper border of the patella.

Indications: Pain in the knee, weakness of the foot and leg, paralysis, beriberi.

Method: Puncture perpendicularly 0.5～0.7 cun. Moxibustion is applicable.

百 虫 窝

定位 屈膝，在大腿内侧，髌底内侧端上 3 寸，即血海上 1 寸。

主治 风疹，湿疹，胃肠寄生虫病，下肢生疮。

操作 直刺 0.8～1.2 寸。可灸。

Baichongwo（EX-LE 3）

Location: On the medial aspect of the thigh, with the knee flexed, 3 cun above the medial end of the upper border of the patella, 1 cun above Xuehai (SP 10).

Indications: Rubella, eczema, gastrointestinal parasitoses, pyogenic infection of the skin on the leg.

Method: Puncture perpendicularly 0.8～1.2 cun. Moxibustion is applicable.

内 膝 眼

定位 屈膝，在髌韧带内侧凹

陷处。

主治   膝关节酸痛，下肢酸软，脚气。

操作   向膝中斜刺0.5~0.7寸。可灸。

Neixiyan (EX-LE 4)

Location: In the depression medial to the patellar ligament with the knee flexed.

Indications: Pain in the knee joint, aching and weakness of the lower extremities, beriberi.

Method: Puncture obliquely 0.5~0.7 cun toward the middle of the knee. Moxibustion is applicable.

膝　　眼

定位   屈膝，髌骨韧带两侧凹陷中。

主治   膝关节酸痛，下肢酸软，脚气。

操作   向膝中斜刺0.5~0.7寸。可灸。

Xiyan (EX-LE 5)

Location: In two depressions on both sides of the patellar ligament with the knee flexed, Neixiyan on the medial side and Waixiyan on the lateral side.

Indications: Pain in the knee joint, aching and weakness of the lower extremities, beriberi.

Method : Puncture obliquely 0.5~0.7 cun toward the middle of the knee. Moxibustion is applicable.

胆　囊　穴

定位   阳陵泉穴下2寸处。

主治   急、慢性胆囊炎，胆石症，胆道蛔虫症，下肢痿痹。

操作   直刺0.8~1.2寸。可灸。

Dannangxue (EX-LE 6)

Location: 2 cun below Yanglingquan (GB 34).

Indications: Acute and chronic cholecystitis, cholelithiasis, biliary ascariasis, flaccidity and numbness of the lower extremities.

Method: Puncture perpendicularly 0.8~1.2 cun. Moxibustion is applicable.

阑　尾　穴

定位   足三里穴下约2寸处。

主治   急、慢性阑尾炎，消化不良。

操作   直刺1.0~1.2寸。可灸。

Lanweixue (EX-LE 7)

Location: About 2 cun below Zusanli (ST 36)

Indications: Acute and chronic appendicitis, indigestion.

Method: Puncture perpendicularly 1.0~1.2 cun. Moxibustion is applicable.

内　踝　尖

定位   在足内侧面，内踝的突起处。

主治   牙痛，扁桃体炎，小腿内

侧痉挛。

操作　浅刺出血，或灸3～5壮。

Neihuaijian（EX-LE8）

Location: On the medial aspect of the foot, at the tip of the medial malleolus.

Indications: Toothache, sore throat, spasm of the medial side of the leg.

Method: Prick to cause bleeding. Moxibustion is applicable with 5 ~ 7 moxa cones.

外　踝　尖

定位　足外侧面，外踝的突起处。

主治　牙痛，扁桃体炎，脚气，足趾拘挛，偏瘫，痛风。

操作　浅刺出血，或灸3～5壮。

Waihuaijian（EX-LE 9）

Location: On the lateral aspect of the foot, at the tip of the external malleolus.

Indications: Toothache, beriberi, spasm of the toes, hemiplegia, gout.

Method: Prick to cause bleeding. Moxibustion is applicable.

八　风

定位　足背各趾缝端凹陷中，左右共8穴。

主治　足跗肿痛，足趾麻木，头痛，毒蛇咬伤，脚气。

操作　直刺0.1～0.3寸。可灸。

Bafeng（EX-LE 10）

Location: On the dorsum of the foot, in the depression of the webs between the toes, on both left and right sides, eight points in all.

Indications: Pain and swelling of the dorsum of the foot, numbness of the toes, headache, snakebite, beriberi.

Method: Puncture perpendicularly 0.1～0.3 cun. Moxibustion is applicable.

独　阴

定位　足第2趾的跖面远侧趾间关节的中点。

主治　月经不调，胞衣不下，心腹痛，胸胁痛，呕吐，吐血，疝气。

操作　直刺0.1～0.2寸。可灸。

Duyin（EX-LE 11）

Location: On the planter aspect of the second toe, at the midpoint of the distal joint.

Indications: Irregular menstruation, retention of the placenta, epigastric pain, pain in the chest and hypochondrium, vomiting, hematemesis, hernia.

Method: Puncture perpendicularly 0.1～0.2 cun, Moxibustion is applicable.

气　端

定位　足10趾尖端，距趾甲游离缘0.1寸，左右共10穴。

主治　中风急救，足趾麻木，脚背红肿疼痛。

操作　直刺 0.1 寸。可灸。

Qiduan（EX-LE 12）

Location：At the tip of the toe, 0.1 cun to the free end of the nail, 10 points on both feet.

Indications：First-aid for apoplexy, numbness of the toes, redness, swelling and pain of the dorsum of the foot.

Method：Puncture perpendicularly 0.1 cun. Moxibustion is applicable.

第十六节　腧穴的定位方法

Section 16　Methods of Locating Acupoints

腧穴定位准确与否，直接影响着治疗效果。为了准确地取穴，必须掌握定位方法。腧穴的定位方法可分为骨度分寸定位法、体表标志定位法、简便取穴法和手指同身寸取穴法。

What is remarkable about the therapeutic results is the accuracy of locations of acupoints. In order to locate acupoints accurately, an acupuncturist must grasp the methods of locating acupoints. The methods of locating acupoints include bonelength measurement, anatomical landmarks, simple measurement and finger measurement.

1. 骨度分寸定位法

骨度分寸定位法古称"骨度法"，即以骨节为主要标志测量周身各部的大小、长短，并依其尺寸，按比例折算成为定穴标准的定位方法。本法已成为腧穴定位的基本原则，现将人体各部常用的骨度分寸以图表说明如下（图 1－38、图－39，表 1－1）。

1. Bone-length Measurement

This, also known as proportional measurement, is a method of locating acupoints in which the bone segments are taken as measurement markers. To measure the width or length of various portions of the body, the measurements are converted proportionately into the acupoint-locating standards. The bone-length measurement has become a basic principle of locating acupoints now. Commonly-used bone-length measurements of various portions of the human body are shown in the following table (Fig.1－38, Fig.1－39, Table 1－1).

2. 体表标志定位法

体表标志定位法是根据人体体表标志而定取穴位的方法。人体体表标志有两种：一是"固定标志"，即不受人体活动影响而固定不移的标志，如五官、指（趾）甲、乳头、肚脐等；二是"活动标志"，即利用关节、肌肉、皮肤等随意活动而出现的孔隙、凹陷、皱纹等作为取穴的标志。如张口于耳屏前方凹陷处取听宫；握拳于掌横纹头取后溪等。

2. Anatomical Landmarks

This method is based on the body

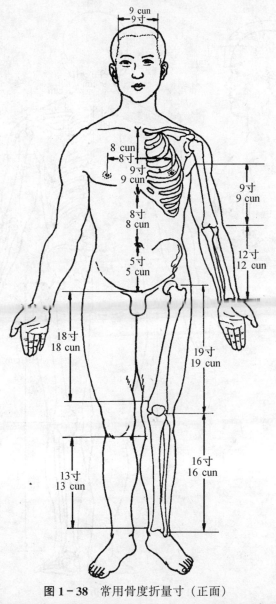

图 1 - 38 常用骨度折量寸（正面）

Fig. 1 - 38 Commonly-Used Bone-length Measurements (Front)

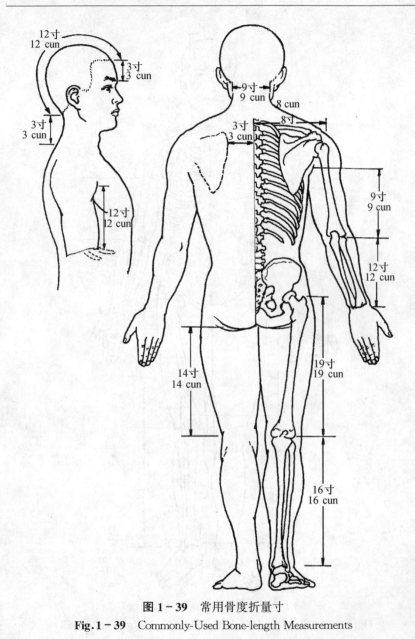

图 1 - 39 常用骨度折量寸

Fig. 1 - 39 Commonly-Used Bone-length Measurements

表 1-1　常用骨度折量寸

部位	起　止　点	折量寸	度量法	说　　明
头面部	前发际正中→后发际正中	12	直寸	用于确定头部经穴的纵向距离
	眉间（印堂）→前发际正中	3	直寸	用于确定前或后发际及其头部经穴的纵向距离
	第 7 颈椎棘突下（大椎）→后发际正中	3	直寸	
	眉间（印堂）→后发际正中→第 7 颈椎棘突下（大椎）	18	直寸	
	前两额发角（头维）之间	9	横寸	用于确定头前部经穴的横向距离
	耳后两乳突（完骨）之间	9	横寸	用于确定头后部经穴的横向距离
胸腹胁部	胸骨上窝（天突）→胸剑联合中点（岐骨）	9	直寸	用于确定胸部任脉穴的纵向距离
	胸剑联合中点（岐骨）→脐中	8	直寸	用于确定上腹部经穴的纵向距离
	脐中→耻骨联合上缘（曲骨）	5	直寸	用于确定下腹部经穴的纵向距离
	两乳之间	8	横寸	用于确定胸腹部经穴的横向距离
	腋窝顶点→第 11 肋游离端（章门）	12	直寸	用于确定胁部经穴的横向距离
背腰部	肩胛骨内缘→后正中线	3	横寸	用于确定背腰部经穴的横向距离
	肩峰缘→后正中线	8	横寸	用于确定肩背部经穴的横向距离
上肢部	腋前、后纹头→肘横纹（平肘尖）	9	直寸	用于确定臂部经穴的纵向距离
	肘横纹（平肘尖）→腕掌（背）侧横纹	12	直寸	用于确定前臂部经穴的纵向距离
下肢部	耻骨联合上缘→股骨内上髁上缘	18	直寸	用于确定下肢内侧足三阴经穴的纵向距离
	胫骨内侧髁下方→内踝尖	13	直寸	
	股骨大转子→腘横纹	19	直寸	用于确定下肢外后侧足三阳经穴的纵向距离（臀沟→腘横纹，相当 14 寸）
	腘横纹→外踝尖	16	直寸	用于确定下肢外后侧足三阳经穴的纵向距离

Table 1 − 1   Bone Proportional Measurement

Position	Origin and end points	Proportion (cun)	Method of measurement	Remarks
Head and face	From the midpoint of the anterior hairline to the midpoint of the posterior hairline	12	Longitudinal measurement	Used for measuring the longitudinal distance of the points of the head
	From Yintang (EX − HN 3) to the midpoint of the anterior hairline	3	Longitudinal measurement	Used for measuring the longitudinal distance of the points on the anterior and posterior hairline and the head
	From the point below the spinous process of the 7th cervical vertebra (Dazhui, DU 14) to the midpoint of the posterior hairline	3	Longitudinal measurement	
	From Yintang (EX − HN 3) to the midpoint of the posterior hairline and then to the point below the spinous process of the 7th cervical vertebra (Dazhui, DU 14)	18	Longitudinal measurement	
	Between the corners of the forehead (Touwei, ST 8)	9	Transverse measurement	Used for measuring the transverse distance of the points on the anterior part of the head
	Between the bilateral mastoid processes	9	Transverse measurement	Used for measuring the transverse distance of the points on the posterior part of the head
Chest, abdomen and hypochondrium	From the suprasternal fossa (Tiantu, RN 22) to the midpoint of the sternoxyphoid symphysis	9	Longitudinal measurement	Used for measuring the longitudinal distance of the points of Ren Meridian (Conception vessel) on the chest
	From the midpoint of the ster-noxyphoid symphysis to the centre of the umbilicus	8	Longitudinal measurement	Used for measuring the longitudinal distance of the points on the upper abdomen

Position	Origin and end points	Proportion (cun)	Method of measurement	Remarks
Chest, abdomen and hypochondrium	From the centre of the umbilicus to the upper border of the pubic symphysis (Qugu, RN 2)	5	Longitudinal measurement	Used for measuring the longitudinal distance of the points on the lower abdomen
	Between the two nipples	8	Transverse measurement	Used for measuring the transverse distance of the points on the chest and abdomen
	From the apex of the axilla to the free end of the 11th rib (Zhangmen, LR 13)	12	Longitudinal measurement	Used for measuring the longitudinal distance of the points on the hypochondrium
Back and low back	From the medial border of the scapula to the posterior midline	3	Transverse measurement	Used for measuring the transverse distance of the points on the back
	From the acromial angle to the posterior midline	8	Transverse measurement	Used for measuring the transverse distance of the points on the shoulder and back
Upper limbs	From the anterior and posterior axillar folds to the cubital crease	9	Longitudinal measurement	Used for measuring the longitudinal distance of the points on the arm
	From the cubital crease to the dorsal crease of the wrist	12	Longitudinal measurement	Used for measuring the longitudinal distance of the points in the forearm
Lower limbs	From the upper border of the pubic symphysis to the upper border of the medial epicondyle of the femur	18	Longitudinal measurement	Used for measuring the longitudinal distance of the points on the three yin meridians of the foot on the medial side of the lower limbs
	From the lower border of the medial epicondyle of the tibia to the tip of the medial malleolus	13	Longitudinal measurement	

Position	Origin and end points	Proportion (cun)	Method of measurement	Remarks
Lower limbs	From the greater trochanter to the popliteal crease	19	Longitudinal measurement	Used for measuring the longitudinal distance of the points on the three yang meridians of the foot on the lateroposterior side of the lower limbs (the distance from the gluteal groove to the popliteal crease is equivalent to 14 cun)
	From the politeal crease to the tip of the lateral malleolus	16	Longitudinal measurement	Used for measuring the longitudinal distance of the points on the three yang meridians of the foot on the latero-posterior side of the lower limds

surface landmarks. The landmarks may be divided into two types. ①fixed landmarks, which are those that do not change with body movement, such as the five sense organs, finger (toe) nails, nipple, umbilicus, etc. ②Movable landmarks refer to spaces, depressions, wrinkles, etc. , that will appear while the joints, muscles, skin and others move voluntarily. For instance, when the mouth is open and a depression anterior to the tragus is formed, Tinggong (SI 19) can be located and when the hand is clenched into a fist and the transverse palmar crease appears, Houxi (SI 3) can be located.

3. 简便取穴法

简便取穴法是临床上一种简便易行的方法。如垂手中指端所到处取风市；两手虎口自然交叉，在示指端到达处取列缺等。

3. Simple Measurement

These are simple methods of point location employed in clinical practice.

For example, Fengshi (G 31) is located at the tip of the middle finger when at attention, or when the index fingers and thumbs of both hands are crossed with the index finger of one hand stretching, Lieque (L 7) is right under the tip of the index finger.

4. 手指同身寸取穴法

手指同身寸取穴法是以患者的手指为标准来定取穴位的方法。临床常用的有以下三种：

（1）中指同身寸：是以患者的中指中节屈曲时内侧两端纹头之间的距离作为 1 寸，用作四肢部取穴的直寸和背部取穴的横寸（图 1－40）。

（2）拇指同身寸：是以患者拇指指关节的横长作为 1 寸，亦适用于四肢部的直寸取穴（图1-41）。

（3）横指同身寸：又名"一夫法"，是令患者将示指、中指、无名指和小指并拢，以中指中节横纹处为准，四指横长作为3寸（图1-42）。

4. Finger Measurement

The length and width of the patient's finger（s）are taken as a standard for point location. The following three methods are commonly used in clinical practice.

（1）Middle finger measurement: When the patient's middle finger is doubled into the palm the distance between the two medial ends of the creases of the interphalangeal joints is taken as one cun. This method is employed for mea-suring the vertical distance to locate the limb points, or for measuring the hori-zontal distance to locate the points on the back（Fig. 1-40）.

（2）Four-finger measurement: The width of the four fingers（index, middle, ring and little）brought close together side by side at the level of the dorsal skin crease of the proximal inter-phalangeal joint of the middle finger is taken as three cun（Fig. 1-41）.

（3）Thumb measurement: The width of the interphalangeal joint of the patient's thumb is taken as one cun. The method is also employed for mea-suring the vertical distance to locate the points on the limbs（Fig. 1-42）

图1-40　中指同身寸
Fig.1-40　Middle Finger Measurement

图1-41　拇指同身寸
Fig.1-41　Thumb Measurement

图1-42　横指同身寸（一夫法）
Fig.1-42　Four-Finger Measurement

第二章　穴位治疗技术

Chapter Two　　The Techniques of Point Treatment

第一节　毫针刺法

Section 1 Acupuncture with the Filiform Needle

1. 针刺前的准备

（1）针具选择

毫针在临床上应用最广。现在使用的毫针多以不锈钢为原料制成。其结构可分为五部分。

1）针尖：针前端的锋锐部分。

2）针体：针尖与针柄之间的部分，又称针身。

3）针根：针体与针柄的连接部分。

4）针柄：针体之后，执针着力的部分。

5）针尾：针柄末端。

用针前应认真检查。针尖不宜过锐，以圆而不钝、形如松针者为佳；针体必须挺直、光滑、坚韧而富有弹性，如有斑驳、锈痕或曲折当弃而不用。针根不能有剥蚀或松动现象，以防折针。此外，还应根据患者的性别、年龄、形体、体质情况以及针刺部位的浅深、厚薄等，选择长短、粗细适宜的针具。

1. Preparations Prior to Acupuncture Treatment

（1）*Selection of the Needle*

The filiform needle is the most commonly used instrument of acpuncture in clinics. Most of the filiform needles used at present are made of stainless steel. A filiform needle may be divided into five parts.

1）Tip: the sharp point of the needle

2）Body: the part between the handle and the tip.

3）Root: the connecting part between the body and the handle.

4）Handle: the part above the body, of which the hand catches hold.

5）Tail: the part at the end of the handle.

The needle should be carefully inspected before use. The needle tip should be round but not dull and should be as sharp as a pine needle. The body must be straight, round, smooth, flexible and resilient. If the body is eroded, rusted or bent, the needle should be discarded. An eroded or loose needle root is not advisable for use because the needle can break easily. In addition, a suitable needle length and thickness should be selected according to the patient's sex, age, body type, and constitution. The depth of needling depends on the thickness of the site where acupuncture is applied.

（2）体位选择

针刺时患者的体位是否合适，对于正确取穴、针刺操作、持久留针以及防止晕针、滞针、弯针、折针等，都具有重要意义。临床常用的体位主要有以下几种。

1）仰卧位：适宜于取头、面、胸、腹部腧穴，以及上肢内侧、下肢前侧及手足等部的腧穴。

2）侧卧位：适宜于头后部和项背部的腧穴。

3）俯卧位：适宜于头后部、后项、腰背部、臀部和下肢后部的腧穴。

4）仰靠坐位：适宜于头前部、面、颈和胸上部的腧穴。

5）俯伏坐位：适宜于头顶、头后部、后项、肩、背部的腧穴。

6）侧伏坐位：适宜于取头部的一侧、面颊及耳前、耳后的腧穴。

临床上对于初诊，精神紧张或年老、体弱病重患者，应当尽量采取卧位，以防患者感到疲劳不适或晕针。

（2）*Selection of the Patient's Posture*

In acupuncture treatment, an appropriate posture for the patient is of importance for correct location of acupoints, manipulation of needles and moxibustion, prolonged retention of needles, and for prevention of fainting, stuck needle, bent needle or broken needle. The most commonly used postures clinically are as follows:

1）Supine posture: Suitable for the points on the head and face, chest and abdominal region, the medial side of the upper limbs, the anterior side of the lower limbs, and the hands and feet.

2）Lateral recumbent: Suitable for the points on the posterior head, neck and back.

3）Prone posture: Suitable for the points on the posterior of the head, neck, back, lumbar and buttock regions, and the posterior part of the lower limbs.

4）Supine sitting posture: Suitable for the points on the forehead, face, neck and the upper portion of the chest.

5）Prone sitting posture: Suitable for the points on the vertex, posterior head, posterior neck, shoulder and back.

6）Lateral sitting posture: Suitable for the points on the lateral side of the head, cheek, and for some points on the preauricular and retroauricular areas.

The lying posture should be adopted as often as possible for a patient who is on the first visit, in a state of nervous tension, who is weak, aged, or seriously ill, in order to prevent the patient from discomfort, fatigue, or fainting from needle insertion.

（3）消毒

消毒工作包括器械消毒、医者手指和施术部位的消毒。

1）器械消毒：可根据具体条件选用下列方法。

高压消毒：将毫针等针具用纱布包扎，放在高压锅内，一般在155.988千帕，120摄氏度高温下持续15分钟以上，即可达到消毒目的。

煮沸消毒：将毫针等应用器械放置清水中，水沸后煮15～20分钟，可达到消毒目的。

药物消毒：将针具放在70%（或75%）乙醇内浸泡30分钟，取出擦干应用。玻璃器具等耐热性较差的物品，可放在1:1000的苯扎溴铵溶液内浸泡1～2小时即可。

2）医者手指消毒：医者须用肥皂水洗擦干净，或用乙醇棉球涂擦后方可施针。

3）施术部位的消毒：被针刺的腧穴部位用75%乙醇棉球擦拭，或先用2.5%碘酊涂擦局部皮肤，稍干后用75%乙醇棉球擦拭即可。当腧穴消毒后，切忌接触污物，以免重新感染。

（3）*Sterilization*

It refers to the sterilization of needles, other instruments, practitioner's fingers and the area on which acupuncture is applied.

1) Sterilization of instruments: The following methods may be chosen according to the concrete conditions.

Autoclave sterilization: Needles and other instruments wrapped with gauze should be sterilized in an autoclave at 1.5 atmosphere pressure and 120°C for more than 15 minutes.

Boiling sterilization: Needles and other instruments are boiled in water for 15～20 minutes.

Medicinal sterilization: Soak the needles in 70% (or 75%) alcohol for 30 minutes. Then take them out and wipe off the liquid from the needles for use. Instrument made of glass and other substances with less heat-resistance should be soaked in bromogeramine solution (1:1000) for 1～2 hours.

2) Disinfection of the practitioner's fingers: Before acupuncture treatment the practitioner's fingers should be cleaned with water and soap or with an alcohol cotton ball.

3) Disinfection of the area where acupuncture is performed: The area on the body surface selected for needling should be cleaned with a 75% alcohol cotton ball or first with a 2.5% tincture of iodine. Then it is removed by a 75% alcohol cotton ball. The disinfected area must not touch soiled articles in order to avoid being polluted again.

2. 进针法

在进行针刺操作时，一般双手协

同紧密配合。常将持针的右手称为刺手，压按穴位辅助进针的左手称为押手。刺手的作用在于持针操作，进针时运用指力于针尖，以便使针快速刺透皮肤，并施行一定手法；押手的作用主要是固定腧穴位置，或使针身有所依附，帮助刺手顺利进针，减少疼痛。临床施术时，刺手（右手）和押手（左手）常配合使用。进针时一边以左手按压或提捏穴位周围皮下组织，一边以右手持针着力刺透皮肤，并协同施行手法。常用进针法有如下两类：

2. Methods about Insertion of the Needle

A doctor generally uses his or her two hands in coordination in the acupuncture operation. The right hand holding the needle is termed as the puncturing hand. The left hand, which assists in insertion by pressing upon the area close to the acupoint, is called the pressing hand. The puncturing hand plays the role of holding and manipulating the needle, allowing finger force to reach the tip of the needle so as to pierce quickly and perform designed manipulations. The pressing hand plays the role of fixing the acupoint location, helping the puncturing hand to facilitate the insertion of the needle by supporting the needle shaft, and minimizing possible pain to the patient during insertion. In clinical operation, the puncturing hand

(right hand) and the pressing hand (left hand) usually work in coordination. During insertion, press or pinch the subcutaneous tissue around the acupoint with the left hand, and at the same time hold and insert the needle through the skin with the right hand. The two hands cooperate in the performance of manipulation. The commonly used methods of insertion of the needle are as follows:

（1）单手进针

单手进针即以右手拇指、示指捏持针柄，中指端紧靠穴位指腹抵住针身下端，当示指运用指力向下按压时，中指随之屈曲将针垂直刺入到所需深度。也可采用中指端在应针腧上揣摩片刻，待患者有酸、麻或舒适感后，再如前法刺入。本法适于0.5～1寸毫针进针。

（1）*Insertion with One Hand*

The needle handle is held with the thumb and index finger of the right hand and the lower portion of the shaft is supported by the tip of the middle finger of the right hand. The needle is inserted into the acupoint to the designed depth by downward pressure of the index finger and the flexing movement of the middle finger. This method may be performed after the acupoint to be punctured is massaged by the tip of the middle finger of the right hand for a few seconds until the patient experiences numbness, soreness or a comfortable feeling. This method is suitable for insertion of a filiform needle 0.5～1 cun long.

（2）双手进针

双手进针即以左右两手配合进针。

1）指切进针法：又称爪切进针法。即以左手拇指或示指的指甲切按在腧穴上，右手持针将针紧靠左手指甲缘刺入皮下。此法适于短针进针。

2）舒张进针法：即左手拇指、示指将所刺腧穴部位的皮肤向两侧撑开，使皮肤绷紧，右手持针从左手拇指、示指间快速刺入。此法适于皮肤松弛部位的进针。

3）提捏进针法：即左手拇指、示指将针刺腧穴部位的皮肤捏起，右手从捏起处的上端将针刺入。此法适于皮肉浅薄部位的进针，如印堂、列缺等。

4）挟持进针法：即左手拇指、示指以乙醇擦拭消毒后，捏住针身下端，或以左手将消毒棉球夹住针身下端露出针尖 0.1～0.2 寸，右手采用执笔式（3 指或 4 指持针法）持针，将针尖对准穴位，双手配合加压，迅速把针刺入皮下直至一定深度。此法适于 3 寸以上长针及肌肉丰厚处的四肢进针。

5）套管进针法：用直径 2～3 毫米（孔径），或大小适中的，长 4～5 厘米消毒后的金属管或玻璃管，代替押手置于应刺的穴位上，选用平柄毫针套于管中、右手示指对准针尾，利用腕力将针弹扣入穴位，然后将套管抽出。此法进针快，易于掌握。

进针的方法虽然有多种，归纳起来无非为速刺与捻转压刺两种形式。速刺即快速进针，其要点是紧挟针身，用腕力迅速叩针入穴内；捻压即运用指力边捻边进，将毫针如旋刀刺压于穴内。以上两种进针形式，可根据穴位所在部位的解剖特点与补泻的不同合理选用。

（2）*Insertion with Both Hands*

The needle is inserted with both hands acting in coordination.

1）Inserting the Needle Aided by the Pressure from the Finger of the Pressing Hand

It is also termed inserting the needle by pressure of the nails. Press the acupoint with the nail of the thumb or the index finger of the left hand. Hold the needle with the right hand and insert it into the acupoint close to the edge of the nail of the left hand. This is suitable for puncturing with short needles.

2）Inserting the Needle with Fingers Stretching the Skin

Stretch the skin where the acupoint is located with the thumb and the index finger of the left hand to cause local tension. Hold the needle with the right hand, and insert it into the skin quickly between the thumb and the index finger of the left hand. This is suitable for inserting the needle into an acupoint around which the skin is loose.

3）Inserting the Needle by Pinching

up the Skin

Pinch up the skin around the acupoint with the thumb and index finger of the left hand. Hold the needle with the right hand and insert it into the upper area of the pinched skin. This is suitable for inserting the needle into an acupoint around which the skin and muscle are thin, such as Yintang (EX 27), Lieque (LU 7), etc.

4) Inserting the Needle by Gripping It

Grip the lower portion of the needle shaft with the thumb and index fingers of the left hand. Be sure the fingers have been swabbed by a sterilized cotton ball first. Or wrap the lower portion of the needle shaft by the sterilized cotton ball with the left hand, exposing the needle tip for $0.1 \sim 0.2$ cun. Hold the needle with the right hand, like holding a pen (holding the needle with three or four fingers), and fix it directly over the acupint. Then quickly insert the needle into the skin to a required depth with the pressure on the needle given by the force from the two hands acting coordinately. This is suitable for puncturing with a 3 cun long needle as well as inserting a needle into the acupoints at the extremities where the muscle is abundant.

5) Inserting the Needle with the Help of the Tube

Select a sterilized metal or glass tube 2 $\sim$ 3 mm in diameter or in proper size and 4 $\sim$ 5 cm in length. The tube plays the role of replacing the pressing hand. Put it on the selected acupoint and place a needle having a flat handle into the tube. Then, direct the index finger of the right hand at the needle tail and quickly press the needle tail with the wrist force to insert the needle into the acupoint. Finally, draw the tube away. This method makes the insertion quick and is easily grasped.

Although there are various methods of insertion of the needle, all of them can be classified into two types i. e. the swift insertion and the insertion with twirling, rotating and pressing the needle. In the swift insertion, the key point in operation is that the needle shaft is tightly held and the needle is quickly inserted into the acupoint with the wrist force. In the insertion with twirling, rotating and pressing manner, the needle is twisted as it is being inserted into the acupoint with pressure. The two types of insertion mentioned above should be selected according to the anatomic feature of the area where the acupoint is located and reinforcing or reducing manipulation required.

3. 针刺的角度和深度

在针刺过程中，掌握正确的针刺角度和深度，是增强针感、提高疗效、防止意外事故发生的重要一环。

（1）针刺的角度

针刺的角度是指进针时针身与皮肤表面所形成的夹角。一般分为以下三种。

1）直刺：针体和皮肤呈 90°角左右垂直刺入。适用于人体大部分的腧穴。

2）斜刺：针体与皮肤呈 45°角左右倾斜刺入。适用于不宜深刺的腧穴，或为避开血管及瘢痕部位而采用的刺法。

3）横刺：又称沿皮刺，或称平刺。将针体皮肤成 15°～25°角，横向刺入。此法适用于皮肉浅薄处的腧穴，亦可用于透穴。

（2）针刺的深度

针刺的深度是指针体刺入体内的深浅而言。不同的病情、不同的部位，对针刺的深浅程度各有不同的要求；不同的体质、不同的形体对针刺感应的强弱也不一样。所以，必须结合具体病情、部位和患者的不同情况等，全面考虑，才能达到治病的目的。

3．Angle and Depth of Insertion

In the process of insertion, angle and depth are especially important in acupuncture. Correct angle and depth help to induce the needling sensation, bring about the desired therapeutic results and guarantee safety.

（1）The angle of insertion refers to one formed by the needle and the skin surface as the needle is inserted. Generally, there are three kinds.

1）Perpendicular: In perpendicular insertion, the needle is inserted perpendicularly, forming a 90° angle with the skin surface. Most points on the body can be punctured in this way.

2）Oblique: The needle is inserted obliquely to form an angle of 45° or so with the skin surface. The method is used for points in which deep insertion is not advisable or used to avoid puncturing blood vessels or scars.

3）Horizontal (also known as subcutaneous or transverse insertion): The needle is inserted transversely to form an angle of 15°～25° with the skin. The method is suitable for points on the thin skin or muscle or for penetrated points.

（2）Depth of needle insertion refers to the depth of the needle body within the skin. Generally, the depth of insertion depends on the pathological condition and the location of points. Patients with different constitutions and body types have different needling sensations, therefore, the depth of insertion must be fully considered according to the concrete condition, location of points and individual patients. Only by doing so can better therapeutic results be obtained.

4. 行针与得气

行针亦名运针，是指将针刺入腧穴后，为了使其得气和调节针感而行施的各种针刺手法。得气亦称针感，是指将针刺入腧穴后产生的经气感应。当针刺得气时，患者会有酸、麻、胀、重的感觉，有时还可能出现凉、热、痒、痛、触电感、蚁行感等；医者则感到针下有沉紧感。

影响得气的因素是多方面的，主要与患者的体质状况、病情轻重，以及取穴和施术手法有关。一般来说，患者经气旺盛、血气充盈者得气迅速，反之得气迟缓，或不得气；取穴准确易得气，反之则不宜得气。施以适当的针刺手法，如长时间留针、循摄即可激发经气，促进气至。

行针手法一般分为基本手法和辅助手法两类：

（1）基本手法

基本手法即针刺的基本动作，常有以下两种。

1）提插法：是将针刺入腧穴的一定深度，使针在穴内进行上、下进退的操作方法。将针从浅层刺入深层为插；由深层退到浅层为提。

2）捻转法：是指将针刺入腧穴的一定深度后，以右手拇指和中指、示指夹住针柄，进行来回旋转捻动的操作方法。

以上两种基本手法，既可单独应用，也可配合应用。临床上可根据患者的身体情况，灵活掌握。

4. Manipulations and Arrival of Qi

Needling manipulation, also known as needling transmission, refers to various manipulations of acupuncture to induce needling sensation after the needle is inserted. The arrival of qi (Deqi, needling sensation) refers to induction of channel qi after the needle is inserted. During the needling sensation, the patient has soreness, numbness, a distention feeling or heaviness around the point. Sometimes, the patient may also experience coldness, warmness, itching, pain, electric-shock feeling, antcrawling feeling, etc. At the same time, the operater may feel tenseness and a dragging sensation around the needle.

There are many factors influencing the arrival of qi. The main ones are related to the constitution of a patient, severity of the illness, location of points and the needling manipulation. Generally speaking, a patient with abundant channel qi, or qi and blood, may have a rapidly developed needling sensation while a man with excessive yin and deficient yang, a slow needling sensation or none. Accurate location of the points may make needling sensation appear quickly, but in case of inaccurate location, it is not easy for needling sensation to come. Proper needling manipulations such as prolonged retaining and pressing the skin along the course of the channel many promote the movement of the channel qi to reach the point.

The manipulation techniques, in general, can be divided into two types: the fundamental ones and the auxiliary ones.

(1) *The fundamental manipulation techniques refer to the basic actions in acupuncture. The two commonly-used techniques are as follows*:

1) Lifting and thrusting: This is a method by which the needle body is perpendicularly lifted and thrust in the point after the needle is inserted to a certain depth. Thrusting means to insert the needle from the superficial layer to the deep layer. On the contrary, lifting, to withdraw the needle from the deep layer to the superficial layer.

2) Twirling or rotating: This refers to the manipulation by which the needle body is twirled or rotated forward and backward continuously after the needle has reached its desired depth. The manipulation is done by the thumb, middle and index fingers of the right hand which hold the needle body.

The two types of fundamental manipulation techniques above may be used either alone or in combination according to the concrete conditions of the patient clinically.

(2) 辅佐手法

辅佐手法即循、弹、刮、摇、飞。

1) 循：以手指随所刺腧穴经脉的顺逆，轻柔地上下循按，是一种催气方法。此法能推动气血，激发经气，使气至病所。

2) 弹：在留针过程中，用手指轻弹针柄，使针体微微振动，以加强得气的感应。

3) 刮：针刺达一定深度后，用右手拇指、示指、中指指甲，由下而上刮动针柄，是一种催气、行气之法。应用刮法可以加强针刺感应的扩散。

4) 摇：针刺达到一定深度后，以手持针柄将针摇动。此法可以行气，使感应向一定方向传导。

5) 飞：针刺达一定深度后，用右手拇指、示指捻动针柄，然后放手，如飞鸟展翅状，可促使经气扩散，增强治疗效果。

(2) *The auxiliary manipulations, i. e. pressing, plucking, scraping, shaking and flying.*

1) Pressing: Slightly press the skin up and down along the course of the channel with the fingers. This is a method of promoting qi by which the circulation of qi and blood is pushed and the channel qi is promoted to reach the diseased part of the body.

2) Plucking: In the process of retaining the needle, pluck the needle handle slightly with the finger causing it to tremble and strengthening the stimu-

lation to obtain qi.

3) Scraping: After the needle is inserted to a certain depth, scrape the handle with the nail of the thumb, index or middle finger of the right hand upward from downward. Scraping is a method of promoting qi. It is used to spread the needling sensation.

4) Shaking: After the needle is inserted to a certain depth, shake the needle with the hand holding the handle. Shaking is a method of conducting the qi flow and the needle sensation in a certain condition.

5) Flying: After the needle is inserted to a certain depth, twirl the needle and depart the thumb and index finger from it. The two fingers separate just like a flying bird spreading its wings. This method can induce the spread of the channel qi and make the therapeutic result better.

5. 补泻手法

虚则补之，实则泻之。能激发身体抵抗力以及增强生理功能的方法称作补法；能祛除病邪以及调和亢进的生理功能的方法称作泻法。常用的补泻手法有以下几种：

（1）提插补泻

当针进到一定深度时，柔和而缓慢地提针，用力而快速地插针，称作补法。相反，用力而快速地提针，柔和而缓慢地插针，称为泻法。

（2）捻转补泻

当针达到一定的深度，轻柔缓慢小幅度捻转是补法；相反，快速有力大幅度捻转是泻法。此外，顺时针方向的捻转为补法，逆时针方向的捻转为泻法。

（3）徐疾补泻

这种方法用于进针和出针。慢进快出是补法，快进慢出是泻法。

（4）开合补泻

这种方法用于出针。出针后迅速按压针孔，以防止气泄出，为补法；出针前，先摇针以扩大其孔，出针后让针孔敞开，以让邪气泄出，为泻法。

（5）呼吸补泻

呼气时进针，吸气时出针为补，吸气时进针，呼气时出针为泻。

（6）迎随补泻

进针时针尖随（顺）着经脉循行的方向而刺为补；针尖迎（逆）着经脉循行的方向而刺为泻。

（7）平补平泻

进针得气后，均匀地提插、捻转即行出针为平补平泻。

5. Tonifying and Reducing Methods

The deficient syndrome should be tonified, while the excessive syndrome should be reduced. The method which is able to invigorate the body resistance and to strengthen the weakened physiological function is called the tonifying method. That which is able to eliminate the pathogenic factors and to harmonize the hyperactive physiological function is called the reducing method. There are several commonly-used tonifying and reducing methods:

(1) *Tonification and reduction by lifting-thrusting the needle*

After the needle is inserted to a given depth, the tonifying method is obtained by lifting the needle gently and slowly while thrusting the needle heavily and rapidly. On the contrary, the reducing method is achieved by lifting the needle forcefully and rapidly, and thrusting the needle gently and slowly.

(2) *Tonification and reduction by twisting the needle*

When the needle is inserted to a certain depth, twisting the needle gently and slowly with a small amplitude is the tonifying method. On the contrary, twisting the needle forcefully and rapidly with a large amplitude is the reducing method. In addition, twisting the needle clockwise is known as the tonifying method, while twisting the needle counter-clockwise is known as the reducing method.

(3) *Tonification and reduction achieved by rapid and slow insertion and withdrawal of the needle*

This kind of method is applied when inserting and withdrawing the needle. Inserting the needle slowly and withdrawing it rapidly are the tonifying method, while inserting the needle rapidly and withdrawing it slowly are the reducing method.

(4) *Tonification and reduction by keeping the hole open or close*

This kind of method is applied in the withdrawal of the needle. When the needle hole is pressed swiftly after the withdrawal of the needle to avoid the discharge of the anti-pathogenic qi. it is known as the tonifying method. When the needle hole is enlarged by shaking the needle in the withdrawal of the needle and is kept open after the withdrawal of the needle to release the pathogenic qi. it is termed the reducing method.

(5) *Tonification and reduction achieved by means of respiration*

The tonification is achieved by inserting the needle when the patient breathes out and withdrawing the needle when the patient breathes in. Reduction is achieved by the opposite way.

(6) *Tonification and reduction achieved by puncturing along or against the direction of the meridian*

When inserting a needle, the tip of the needle poining to the running direction of the course of the meridian is taken as reinforcing. Puncturing with the needle tip against the running direction of the meridian is taken as reducing method. When needling the three yang meridians which run from the hand upward to the head, for example, a manner with the needle tip pointing downward, i.e. against the meridian courses is known as the reducing method. A manner with the needle tip pointing in the opposite direction, i.e. following the running course of the meridians, is known as the reinforcing method.

(7) *Even tonification and reduction*

After the needle is inserted and the needling sensation appears, lift, thrust and rotate the needle evenly. Then withdraw the needle at a moderate speed. This is known as even reinforcing and reducing.

(8) 复式补泻手法

1) 烧山火: 先确定穴位的针刺深度, 分为 3 等份。当进针刺透皮肤后, 在应刺深度的上 1/3 (天部), 重插轻提 9 次; 再将针进入中 1/3 (人部), 依上法重插轻提 9 次; 最后将针进入下1/3 (地部), 又重插轻提 9 次, 然后将针一次退到上 1/3 处 (即从地部一次提到天部), 再如前法操作。自浅层到深层三进一退, 此为 1 度。可反复操作至患者觉针下有温热感为止。出针时快速按闭针孔。也可结合呼多吸少之法, 即在患者呼气时进针, 吸气时出针。

(8) *Comprehensive tonifying and reducing methods*

1) Setting the mountain on fire

First of all, determine the depth of the point to be punctured. Then divide the depth into three equal portions, the superficial, medium and deep. After the needle is inserted slowly beneath the skin, the needle is heavily thrusted and slightly lifted nine times at the upper 1/3 (superficial portion) of the depth. Then the needle is inserted to the middle 1/3 (medium portion) depth and is heavily thrusted and slightly lifted another nine times. Finally, insert the needle to the lower 1/3 (deep portion) depth and thrust and lift nine times. After that, lift the needle up to the upper 1/3 depth (directly from the deep portion to superficial portion), and repeat the process mentioned above. Thrusting thrice according to the superficial, medium and deep portions and lifting once is called one operation. Repeated operations can be conducted for several times until a warm feeling is experienced. Quickly withdraw the needle and press the hole. The operation may also be performed in combination with the technique of tonifying by inserting the needle when the patient breathes out and by withdrawing it when the patient breathes in.

2) 透天凉:将针刺入腧穴应刺深度的下 1/3(地部), 重提轻插 6 次;再退针到中 1/3(人部), 依上法重提轻插 6 次;最后将针退至上1/3(天部), 又重提轻插 6 次, 自深层到浅层三退一进,此为 1 度。可反复操作至患者觉得针下有寒凉感为止。出针时摇大其孔。也可结合呼吸补泻之法,即在患者吸气时进针,呼气时退针、出针。

2) Penetrating-heaven coldness

Insert the needle into the point to the lower third (deep portion) of a required depth. Lift the needle quickly and thrust slowly for six times. After that the needle is lifted to the middle third (medium portion) and given the same performance. Then the needle is further lifted to the upper third (superficial portion) depth and given the same performance too. Lifting the needle thrice according to the deep, medium and superficial sequence and thrusting it once is called one operation. Repeated operations can be conducted several times until a cool feeling is experienced. On withdrawal of the needle, shake it to enlarge the hole. The operation is also performed in combination with the technique of reducing by inserting the needle when the patient breathes in and by withdrawing it when the patient breathes out.

3) 进火补法:操作时,令患者口中呼气,随其呼气用指快速刺法,将针刺入 1 分,一有感应,则用针尖向着有感应的部位连续地急插慢提 3 次,每进 1 分,则按上述方法连续操作 3 次,使热感放散传导。如无热感则令患者做鼻吸口呼的自然呼吸 3 次,或加刮针法使针尖颤动并催其气至。如有热感则缓慢将针拔去急扪闭针穴。

3) Tonifying method by fire

Ask the patient to breathe out with the mouth and during his or her expiration quickly insert the needle 0.1 cun deep aided by the pressure of the fingers of the pressing hand. When the needling sensation has been induced, continuously and rapidly thrust and slowly lift the needle with the needle tip towards the area where the needling sensation is felt by the patient 3 times. Insert the needle deep 0.1 cun by 0.1 cun until the needle tip reaches the designed depth. Repeat this course three times after every insertion for 0.1 cun, making the hot sensation spread. If there is no hot sensation induced, ask the patient to breathe in with the nose and breathe out with the mouth naturally 3 times or scrape the needle handle to make the needle tip tremble so as to promote the arrival of qi. When the hot sensation has been induced in the patient, slowly pull out the needle and immediately press the puncture hole.

4) 进水泻法:由徐疾、呼吸、提插泻法等组合而成的复式手法。操作时,令患者口中吸气,用舒张押手法缓慢不捻转地将针进至地部,待有感应,将针提退 1 分,在 1 分上下的范围内连续慢插急提 3 次,每提退 1 分则按上述方法连续操作 3 次,使凉感放散传导，如无凉感，则令患者做鼻呼口吸的自然呼吸 3 次，或加摇法而催其气至，如有麻凉或触电感觉则将针急速拔出，不扪闭针穴。

4）Reducing method by water

In this method reducing by rapid, slow insertion and withdrawal of the needle, manipulating the needle in co-operation with the patient's respiration, and method by lifting and thrusting the needle are combined. Ask the patient to breathe in with the mouth and when the patient does so, slowly insert the needle into the acupoint to the earth portion (deep portion) with the fingers stretching the skin. Do not twirl or rotate the needle. After the presence of the needling sensation, withdraw the needle 0.1 cun. Then, in a 0.1 cun extent, continuously slowly thrust and rapidly lift the needle 3 times. Withdraw the needle upward another 0.1 cun and repeat this course. After each time of withdrawing the needle 0.1 cun for three times, making the cool feeling spread. If there is no cool sensation induced, ask the patient to breathe out with the nose and breathe in with the mouth naturally 3 times or shake the needle handle to promote the needling sensation. When numbness, coldness, or an electrifying sensation has been induced in the patient, pull out the needle quickly and do not apply pressure over the puncture hole.

6. 留针与出针

留针是指将针刺入腧穴行针施术后，让其在穴内留置一段时间。其目的在于加强针刺的作用和便于再次行针施术。一般病症，可留针 10～20 分钟，但某些特殊病症，可适当延长留针时间，并在留针过程中间歇行针，保持一定的刺激量，以增强疗效。若不得气时，留针还可起到候气的作用。

在行针施术或留针后即可出针。出针时一般以左手拇指、示指按住针孔周围皮肤，右手持针慢慢捻转并提至皮下，然后将针迅速拔出，用消毒干棉球揉按针孔，以防出血。

6. Retaining and Withdrawing the Needle

Retaining the needle means to keep the needle in place after it is inserted into a point. The purpose of retaining the needle is to strengthen the needling sensation and to facilitate the manipulation of the needle. In general, the needle is retained for 10～20 minutes. For some special cases the time for retaining the needle may be appropriately prolonged. Meanwhile, manipulations may be given at intervals to maintain a certain quantum of stimulation to the patient and strengthen the therapeutic effects. For patients with a dull needling sensation, retaining the needle serves as a method to wait for qi to come.

After manipulations or retaining of the needle, it should be withdraw. On withdrawal of the needle, press the skin around the point with the thumb and index finger of the left hand, rotate the needle gently and lift it slowly to the subcutaneous level. Then withdraw it quickly and press the punctured point with an alcohol cotton ball for a while to prevent bleeding.

7. 异常情况的处理

（1）晕针

晕针是由于患者体位不适，精神紧张，体质虚弱，或针刺时手法过重所致。表现为患者突然头晕目眩，恶心欲吐，面色苍白，心慌气短，血压下降，四肢厥冷，汗出，脉象沉细。甚者神志昏迷倒地，唇爪青紫，二便失禁等。

一旦发现上述现象，应立即将针抽出，让患者平卧，或头低足高位，松开衣领、腰带，躺在空气流通处，轻者休息片刻，饮温开水或糖开水即可缓解；重者可掐人中穴，刺内关穴或灸足三里、膻中、气海、百会等穴。如仍不奏效，应采取其他急救措施。

7. Management of Possible Accidents

(1) *Fainting*

The reason for fainting is due to improper position, nervous tension, delicate constitution or too forceful manipulation. The manifestations are sudden dizziness, nausea and vomiting, pallor, palpitation, shortness of breath, drop of blood pressure, cold extremities, sweating, deep and thready pulse. In severe cases, there may be loss of consciousness, falling down to the ground, cyanosis of the lips and claws, incontinence of urine and stool, etc. Once the phenomena mentioned above happen, take the needle out immediately, keep the patient in recumbent position or help the patient lie with the feet elevated. The collar and the waistband should be loosened and the patient should lie in a room with fresh air. For milder cases, advise the patient to take a short rest and drink some warm water or sugar solution. For severe cases, Renzhong (DU 26) may be pressed with the finger-nail. Other alternatives include puncturing Neiguan (PC 6) and apply moxibustion on Zusanli (ST 36), Danzhong (RN 17), Qihai (RN 6), Baihui (DU 20), etc. If the patient does not respond to the above measures, other emergency measures should be taken immediately.

（2）滞针

行针时或留针后，医者感觉针下异常紧涩，不能做捻转和提插动作的现象叫滞针。遇此情况，应根据不同的原因进行处理。

如因局部肌肉痉挛所致者，可嘱患者消除紧张，并延长留针时间，或在所刺腧穴的周围按压或针刺，以缓解局部肌肉紧张而顺利出针。若因单向捻转所致者，须向反方向捻转，将缠绕的肌纤维回释，再行轻度提插，待肌肉松弛后，便可退针。

（2）*Stuck Needle*

This is an abnormal condition in which the needle, after insertion and retaining in place, is difficult or impossible to manipulate. If the needle is stuck, manage it according to its cause. If the stuck needle is due to a local muscle spasm, ask the patient to relax. Leave the needle in place for a while. Then withdraw it by rotating or by massaging the skin near the point or by inserting another needle nearby to relax the state of the muscle spasm. If the stuck needle is caused by excessive rotation in one direction, the condition will be overcome when the needle is twirled in the opposite direction to loosen the bound muscle fibers. Then lift and thrust slightly. After the condition is released, withdraw the needle.

（3）弯针

医者进针手法不熟练，用力过猛；针下碰到坚硬组织；患者针后移了体位；针柄受到外力碰撞及滞针处理不当等，均可造成弯针。如系轻度弯曲，可将针慢慢退出，不能再行捻转；弯曲的角度过大时，可顺着弯曲的方向，将针退出；如果由于体位移动所造成，应先矫正体位，再行退针。

（3）*Bent Needle*

This may result from unskillful manipulation, forceful manipulation, the needle striking hard tissue, a change in the patient's posture, collision of the needle handle with some external force or from improper management of a stuck needle. When the needle is bent slightly, rotating should not be applied. The needle may be removed slowly. If the needle is bent severely, the needle may be withdrawn by following the course of the bend. In case the bent needle is caused by a change in the patient's posture, move him to his original position and then remove the needle.

（4）断针

1）原因和处理：断针临床上较少见，多因针具质量差，针身或针根剥蚀，加之医师操作用力过猛，患者移动体位，或滞针、弯针处理不当，或电针时突然加大电流强度而致断针。一旦发现断针，当嘱患者保持体位，以防断针向肌肉深处陷入，若折针的断端尚出体表，可立即用左手拇指、示指挤压折针周围的皮肤，使断端暴露更多，右手持镊子夹住断端取出。如断端完全陷入肌肉层或体腔内，应手术取出。必要时应在X线投照下定位，再施行手术取出。

2）预防：预防断针的可靠方法，是选择好光滑、质地坚韧、针根牢固的针具，进针时不能将针身全部刺入体内，应当留2～3分在体外，以防万一断针时便于取出。

（4）*Broken Needle*

1）Cause and Management：Occurs occasionally, and may be due to poor quality of needles, corrosion of the needle shaft, violent manipulation, changing of the patient's posture, improper management of stuck or bent needle, or sudden increase of electric current in the electric needling. Once the needle is broken, ask the patient not to change the posture so as to prevent the distal broken fragment of the needle from going deeper into the muscle. If the end of the broken fragment of the needle is above the skin, immediately press the skin around it with the thumb and index finger of the left hand to make the end exposed more, then pull it out with forceps held with the right hand. If the broken fragment end is completely under the skin surface or in an organ in the body, perform the surgical operation to take it out or, if necessary, do the operation under X-ray examination.

2）Prevention：A dependable method of preventing the needle from being broken is to inspect the quality of the needle prior to treatment. Use only smooth and flexible needles with its root fixed. The complete insertion of the whole shaft of the needle into the body is not allowed. The shaft should be left 0.2～0.3 cun above the skin so as to take the fragment of the broken needle out easily if the needle is broken.

（5）血肿

因微量的皮下出血造成局部小块青紫时，一般不必处理，可以自行消退。若局部肿胀疼痛较剧、青紫面积大且影响活动功能时，可先做冷敷止血，然后再做热敷或在局部轻轻揉按，以促进局部瘀血的消散和吸收。

（5）*Hematoma*

A mild hematoma is caused by subcutaneous bleeding. In general, it will disappear by itself. If the local swelling and pain is severe, the hematoma is large and affects the motor functions. First apply a cold compress to the area of the hematoma to stop bleeding. Then apply a warm compress with local pressure or light massage to help disperse and absorb the local stasis of blood.

（6）气胸

在针刺锁骨上窝、胸骨切迹上缘、第 11 胸椎两侧、腋中线第 8 肋间、锁骨中线第 6 肋间以上的腧穴时，有时常因针刺方向、角度和深度不当，刺伤胸膜和肺脏，使空气进入胸腔而造成气胸。此时，患者会突然感到胸闷、胸痛、气短，甚者呼吸困难，出现发绀、出汗、血压下降等休克现象。体检时，患者侧肋间隙变宽，胸部叩诊有过度反响，肺泡呼吸音减弱或消失，甚至气管向健侧移位。X 线胸部透视可进一步确诊。一旦发现气胸，即应采取半卧位休息。轻者可对症处理，如咳嗽者给予镇咳药及抗感染药；严重病例应立即采取抢救措施，如胸腔穿刺抽气、输氧、抗休克等。

(6) *Pneumothorax*

When acupuncture is applied to points above the supraclavicular fossa, suprasternal notch, both sides of the eleventh thoracic vertebra, above the eighth intercostal space on the middle auxillary line and above the sixth intercostal space on the midclavicular line care must be taken. Because of improper direction, angle or depth of the needle, the pleura and lung are sometimes injured and air enters the thoracic cavity to cause a pneumothorax. When the condition takes place, the patient may suddenly feel chest oppression, chest pain, shortness of breath and even dyspnea. Also, there may be symptoms of shock, such as cyanosis, sweating and a drop of blood pressure. On examination, it may be found that the intercostal space of the diseased side becomes wide. A hyperresonance may be got on thoracic percussion. The vesicular respiratory sound becomes weak or disappears. The trachea may even be displaced to the healthy side. Further diagnosis of the condition is confirmed by chest X-ray examination. Once pneumothorax takes place, ask the patient

to rest in a semirecumbent posture. Mild cases can be managed according to their symptoms and signs. If the patient has cough, antitussive and antibiotics or antipholgistics are to be given. For severe cases, emergency measures should be undertaken such as sucking out air by thoracentesis, oxygen inhalation, antishock therapy, etc.

(7) 内脏损伤

1) 原因和临床表现：在心、肝、脾、肾等内脏的体表相应部位腧穴进针过深时，会引起严重后果，特别是肝、脾大，膀胱充盈的患者，尤须注意。

易刺伤心、肝、脾、肾、胆、胃、大肠、小肠、膀胱的常用穴如鸠尾、巨阙、中脘、下脘、气海、石门、关元、中极、天枢、水道、归来、大横、日月、京门、带脉、章门、三焦俞、肾俞、大肠俞、志室等。

刺伤心脏，引起心脏破裂出血，堵塞心包致死；刺伤肝、脾，可引起肝、脾出血，肝区疼痛，有时可向背部放射。如果出血不止，可伴有腹痛，腹肌紧张，腹部压痛、反跳痛；刺伤肾脏可出现腰痛、肾区压痛及叩击痛，并有血尿。出血严重时血压下降以至休克；刺伤胆囊、膀胱、胃、肠时，可有胆汁、尿液、胃、肠内容物外溢，则有腹膜刺激征或急腹症表现等。

(7) *Injury of Internal Organs*

1) Cause and Manifestations

The injury of internal organs may be due to overly deep puncture at the points on the body surface corresponding to the internal organs. Especially, when the patient has hepatomegaly, splenomegaly, or filling of the bladder. The liver, spleen, and bladder are more easily injured by improper puncture. Possible common acupoints relating to injury of the heart, liver, spleen, kidney, gallbladder, stomach, large and small intestines and bladder are Jiuwei (RN 15), Juque (RN 14), Zhongwan (RN 12), Xiawan (RN 10), Qihai (RN 6), Shimen (RN 5), Guanyuan (RN 4), Tianshu (ST 25), Shuidao (ST 28), Guilai (ST 29), Daheng (SP 15), Riyue (GB 24), Jingmen (GB 25), Daimai (GB 26), Zhangmen (LR 13), Dachangshu (BL 25), Zhishi (BL 52).

The manifestations of impairment of the heart by puncture: Symptoms and signs due to bleeding from the heart may be caused and in severe cases, manifestations caused by filling of the pericardium with blood can be seen and even death caused.

Impairment of the liver or spleen by puncture: Hepatalgia due to bleeding of the liver or spleen which sometimes can spread to the back. If the bleeding is not stopped, abdominal pain, tension of the abdominal muscles, abdominal tenderness and rebound pain may be accompanied.

Impairment of the kidney by puncture: Lumbago, tenderness over the kidney region by percussion or pressing, hematuria, or lowering of blood pressure and shock due to large bleeding in severe cases may appear.

Impairment of the gallbladder, bladder, stomach, and intestine due to puncture: signs of peritoneal irritation or even manifestation of acute abdomen may be observed.

2) 处理和预防。处理：轻则注意休息，对症治疗，尚可自愈；重则需手术治疗。

预防：为预防上述事故发生，必须熟知人体解剖结构及脏器在体壁的投影。严格掌握操作规程与进针深度，不可麻痹大意。剑突下心窝附近穴位以1寸为宜，注意选择体位与取穴姿势。如刺鸠尾穴时，要两臂上举以利抬高胸腔内的脏器；脐周以下腹穴位，以1.5寸针为宜。对肝、胆、脾大的患者，严禁深刺期门、日月、章门、梁门等穴；对膀胱尿潴留的患者，严禁深刺上、中、下脘穴及其附近穴位；对肠粘连，肠梗阻患者的腹部穴位如天枢、大横、水道、归来等穴，严禁将针刺透腹壁进入腹腔。

2) Management and prevention

Management: In mild cases, apply expectant treatment and advise the patient to rest allowing the impairment to be cured of its own accord. In severe cases, surgical operation may be needed.

Prevention: Before giving puncture a sound knowledge of human anatomy as well as the projection locations of the internal organs on the corresponding regions of the body surface should be known. Manipulation rules and the puncture depth observed should be strictly. When puncturing points below the xiphoid process and near the epigastric region select needles about 1 cun long and pay attention to the patient's position. On puncturing Jiuwei (RN 15), for example, ask the patient to raise the arms to lift the internal organs in his or her chest. When puncturing points around the umbilicus and points at the lower abdomen, select 1.5 cun long needles. In cases with liver enlargement, gallbladder enlargement, or spleen enlargement, deep insertion is forbidden on puncture at Qimen (LR 14), Riyue (GB 24), Zhangmen (LR 13) and Liangmen (ST 21). In cases with retention of urine, deep insertion is forbidden when puncturing at Qugu (RN 2), Zhongji (RN 3) and Guanyuan (RN 4). In cases with filling of the stomach due to over eating it is forbidden to apply deep puncture at Shangwan (RN 13), Zhongwan (RN 12), Xiawan (RN 10), as well as the points around them. And in cases

with intestinal adhension or intestinal obstruction, it is forbidden to insert the needle through the abdominal wall into the abdominal cavity when puncturing points at the abdomen such as Tianshu (SR 25), Daheng (SP 15,) Shuidao (ST 28) and Guilai (ST 29).

（8）刺伤脑、脊髓

凡在颈项部正中线上的哑门、风府和两旁的风池、天柱等穴进行针刺时，如角度、方向、深度不当，针由颅底枕骨大孔进入颅腔，可伤及延髓、脑桥、小脑及血管，危及生命。在背部正中线督脉，针刺第1腰椎以上棘突间穴位和华佗夹脊穴向棘间方向深刺，皆可刺中脊髓，出现触电样感觉向肢体远端放射。重者可因刺激部位的不同，产生暂时的肢体瘫痪，若属轻症经安静休息，对症治疗，多能逐渐恢复。如有头痛、恶心、呕吐，应注意观察。若进而神志昏迷，就应及时抢救。

为避免针刺意外发生，应严格掌握针刺角度、方向与深度。一旦刺入深部，患者有触电感时，应立即退针，切勿捣刺。

（8）*Injury of the brain and spinal cord*

The bulb pons and cerebellum can be injured when a needle enters the cranial cavity through the great occipital foramen. This condition is usually due to incorrect angle, direction or depth of puncture at the points on the posterior midline of the neck such as Yamen (DU 15) and Fengfu (DU 16), or at points lateral to the midline such as Fengchi (GB 20) and Tianzhu (BL 10). The spinal cord may be injured by deep puncture at the points located between the spinous processes above the first lumbar vertebra or by deep puncture at Jiaji (EX-B 2) with the needling directed towards the interspinal area.

Injury of the brain may cause nausea and vomiting in mild cases and loss of consciousness or even death in severe cases. Take out the needle immediately whenever finding any manifestation of it and pay close attention to the patient's condition. If finding that the patient is in coma, apply emergency treatment immediately.

Injury of the spinal cord may cause an electrifying sensation radiating to the distal ends of the extremities in mild cases and temporary paralysis of the extremities in severe cases. Remove the needle as soon as finding any manifestation of it. Advise the patient to have rest and give some expectant treatment to the patient. Usually, the injury will be cured in its own accord.

In order to prevent injury of the brain and spinal cord the practitioner should carefully control the angle, direction and depth of insertion of the needle when puncturing the points at the areas mentioned above. In cases where electrifying sensations are induced to the patient by puncturing points in these areas never take it as good needling sensation and never apply thrusting lifting manipulation forcefully. Withdraw the needle immediately.

8. 注意事项

(1) 对体质虚弱、初诊患者和精神紧张者，施术手法不宜过强，并尽量选用卧位。

(2) 怀孕 3 个月的妇女，不宜刺小腹腧穴，怀孕 3 个月以上，腹部、腰骶部腧穴也不宜刺。三阴交、合谷、至阴、昆仑等穴，孕妇及月经期经量正常的妇女，在行经期不宜刺。

(3) 不能合作的小儿，针后不留针，囟门未合时，头顶部不宜刺。

(4) 自发性出血疾患及凝血机制较差的患者一般不宜刺。

(5) 胸、肋、背、腰部为重要脏器所在，针刺过深，可刺伤内脏，发生意外，引起不良后果。故施术者一定要熟悉腧穴下的解剖结构，严格把握进针的角度与深度。

(6) 眼眶周围血管丰富的穴位，不可大幅度捻转插，以防出血。

(7) 皮肤有感染、溃疡、瘢痕、肿瘤时，不宜针刺。

8. Precaution

(1) For the patient who is weak, nervous, or at their first visit a recum-

bent posture should be chosen.

(2) It is contraindicated to puncture acupoints on the lower abdomen for pregnant women within the first three months. For those beyond the first three months it is also contraindicated to puncture acupoints on the abdomen and lumbosacral region. Sanyinjiao (SP 6), Hegu (LI 4), Zhiyin (BL 67) and Kunlun (BL 60) should not be punctured in pregnant women and women who have a normal menstrualcycle and are at the menstruation period.

(3) Retention of the needle should not be given to children who may not be in cooperation. Acupoints on the vertex of infants should not be punctured when the fontanel is not closed.

(4) It is contraindicated to apply puncture to patients with spontaneous bleeding or poor blood coagulation mechanisms.

(5) Special attention must be paid in puncturing acupoints on the chest, hypochondrium, back and loin where important viscera are located. Overly deep puncture to acupoints on these areas may injure the coresponding internal viscera leading to accident. An operator must know the anatomy of acupoints well and control the angle and depth of puncture strictly.

(6) In acupoints at the area around the orbital region where the blood vessels are rich the needle should not be rotated, lifted or thrust in a large amplitude so as to prevent bleeding.

(7) Skin with infection, ulcer, scar or tumor should not be punctured.

第二节 灸 法

Section 2 Moxibustion

灸法是利用某种易燃材料和药物, 在身体一定部位的穴位上燃灼、熏熨和贴敷, 借温热的物理效能刺激穴位, 通过经络的传导作用, 达到调整机体生理功能而祛病消疾的一种治疗方法。灸法有温经散寒、行气活血、回阳救逆以及防病健身的功能。因此, 灸法在临床上广泛运用。

Moxibustion is a therapeutic method by burning combustible materials or applying drug compresses or dry-plaster over acupoints on certain regions to produce hot stimulation to the patient. This acts on the acupoints and conducts through the channel so that the equilibrium of bodily physical function is adjusted. Moxibustion functions to warm the meridians and expel cold, circulate qi and activate blood, revive yang for resuscitation, prevent disease and strengthen the body. Therefore, moxibustion is broadly applied in the clinic.

1. 常用灸法

(1) 艾炷灸

艾炷是用艾绒加工特制而成的圆柱形小体（图2-1）。分大、中、小三种（图2-2），大者高1厘米，炷底0.8厘米；中者为大炷一半如枣核；小者如麦粒。每燃完1炷称1壮。艾炷灸有直接灸和间接灸两类。

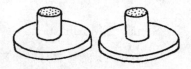

图 2-1　圆柱形艾炷
Fig.2-1　Moxa Cylinder

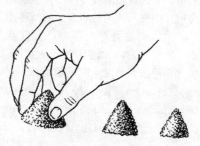

图 2-2　圆锥形艾炷
Fig.2-2　Moxa Cone

1. Commonly Used Moxibustion

(1) *Moxibustion with moxa cones*

Moxa cones are moxa wool formed into small cylinder shapes (Fig.2-1), or small cone shape by the hand. Moxa cones may be small, medium or large in size (Fig. 2 - 2). The large one is 1 cm high with a bottom of 0.8 cm in diameter. The medium one is half of a large one in size like a jubepit. The small one is as big as a grain. One bun-

dle of moxa wool is called a cone (one unit or one zhang). Moxibustion with moxa cones may be divided into two types, direct and indirect moxibustion.

1) 直接灸：是将艾炷直接放在皮肤上施灸的一种方法（图2-3）。根据灸后对皮肤烧灼程度的不同，又分为无瘢痕灸和瘢痕灸两种。

无瘢痕灸：是用大小适宜的艾炷直接放在腧穴上施灸，以局部皮肤红润而不起泡为度，灸后不遗留瘢痕。施灸时，先将施术部位涂以少量凡士林，以增加黏附作用。然后将灸炷置于穴位上，点燃施灸。当艾炷燃剩至2/5或1/4患者感到灼痛时，应更换艾炷再灸。此法适用于慢性虚寒性疾病。

瘢痕灸：是将艾炷直接置于穴位上施灸，以灸至局部皮肤起泡，并令化脓、结痂、留下瘢痕为特点。施灸时可先在穴位上涂敷蒜汁，然后放置艾炷施灸，直至艾炷全部燃尽，艾火自熄，即除去艾灰，再按所需壮数，重新点燃艾炷。灸完1壮，即涂蒜汁1次。在施灸过程中，如患者感到灼痛，医者可在穴位周围用手轻轻拍打，以缓解疼痛。灸后1周左右化脓，形成灸疮，经过45天左右，灸疮可自行痊愈。结痂脱落，留下瘢痕。此法适用于哮喘、肺痨、癫痫等，还有预防中风的作用。

1) Direct moxibustion: A moxa cone placed directly on the skin (Fig.2-3) and ignited is called direct moxibustion.

This type of moxibustion is subdivided into nonscarring moxibustion and scarring moxibustion according to different degrees of burnt skin after moxibustion.

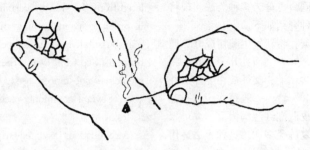

图 2-3　直接灸

Fig. 2-3　Direct Moxibustion

Nonscarring moxibustion: A moxa cone of proper size is placed directly on a point and ignited until the local skin becomes ruddy and non-blistery. There should be no scar formation after moxibustion. Prior to moxibustion, apply a small amount of vaseline to the area around the point in order to increase the adhesion of the moxa cone to the skin. Place a moxa cone on the point and ignite. When 3/5 or 3/4 of the moxa cone is burnt or the patient feels pain remove the cone and repeat. This method is applicable in cold deficiency syndromes.

Scarring moxibustion: Put a moxa cone directly on the point and ignite it. This method is characterized by a local blister, festering and scar on the skin around the point before healing. Prior to moxibustion apply some garlic juice to the point. Then put the moxa cone on the point and ignite until it completely burns out and extinguishes. Remove the ash and repeat this procedure according to the required units of moxa cones. After each unit of moxa cone, apply garlic juice to the point once more. During moxibustion, if the patient feels a burning pain, the practitioner may pat gently on the skin around the point in order to alleviate the pain. Fester appears and post-moxibustion sore is formed a week later after moxibustion. After 45 days or so, the post-moxibustion sore may heal by itself and the scab falls off leaving a scar on the skin. Indications are asthma, pulmonary tuberculosis, epilepsy, etc. This method may be used to prevent apoplexy.

2) 间接灸：间接灸是将艾炷不

直接放在皮肤上而是放在某种材料上，从而防止灼伤皮肤。根据其间隔的物品不同，可分为多种灸法。现将常用的几种介绍如下。

隔姜灸：将新鲜生姜切成0.5厘米厚的片，并在上面扎几个小孔。将姜片置于穴位上，艾炷放在姜片上并点燃（图2-4）。一般每次灸5～20壮至局部皮肤潮红湿润为度，并可根据病情反复施灸多次。这种方法适用于脾胃虚弱引起的病症，如腹泻、腹痛、关节疼痛以及由阳虚引起的病症。

隔蒜灸：将大蒜切成厚0.5厘米的片，并在上面扎几个小孔。将蒜片置于穴位上，将艾炷放在蒜片上并点燃。当患者感觉灼热时，换上1壮并点燃。这种方法适用于瘰疬、结核病、早期的皮肤溃疡、毒虫咬伤等。

隔盐灸：这种方法仅用于肚脐，因此又称为神厥灸。将肚脐填上盐，与皮肤平，在盐上放1艾炷并点燃。这种方法适用于腹痛、呕吐、泄泻、脐周痛、疝痛、慢性痢疾等。此外，隔盐灸还有回阳救逆的功能，如治疗大汗淋漓、四肢厥冷及无脉症。

隔附子灸：临床上常用的有隔中药附片灸和隔附子饼灸两种。操作时，将附片或附子饼针刺数孔放于穴位，上置艾炷点燃灸之。一般5～10壮，以局部温热、皮肤红晕为度。由于附子可逐风驱寒、补肾壮阳，故本法适用于各种阳虚病证，如阳痿、早泄、晨泄、肢厥等。

2) Indirect moxibustion: In indirect moxibustion the ignited moxa cone does not rest on the skin directly but is insulated from the skin by certain materials in order to avoid burning the skin. It may be subdivided into types of moxibustion according to the different medicinal substances used for insulation. Several commonly-used types are as follows:

Moxibustion insulated with ginger: Fresh ginger is cut into a slice about 0.5 cm thick and with several small holes punctured in it. The ginger slice is put on the point selected, then the moxa cone is put and ignited on the ginger slice (Fig. 2 - 4). In general, each treatment needs 5 ～ 10 units of moxa cone until the local skin becomes flush and wet. This type of moxibustion may be repeated many times according to the pathological condition. The method is suitable for diseases caused by deficiency of the spleen and stomach such as diarrhea, abdominal pain, joint pain, as well as diseases caused by yang deficiency.

Moxibustion insulated with garlic: Garlic is cut into a slice about 0.5 cm thick and with several small holes punctured in it. The moxacone is put and ignited on the garlic slice. When the patient feels it scorching the burning moxa cone can be replaced by a new one. This method is suitable for scrofula, tuberculosis, skin ulceration in ear- ly stage, toxic insect bites, etc.

图 2 - 4　隔姜灸

Fig. 2 - 4　Moxibustion Insulated with Ginger

Moxibustion insulated with salt: This method is only used on the umbilicus therefore is also termed Shenque moxibustion (CV 8). The umbilicus is filled with salt to the level of the skin. Then a moxa cone is put and ignited on the top of the salt. The method is suitable for abdominal pain, diarrhea pain around the umbilicus, hernia pain, and chronic dysentery. In addition, moxibustion insulated with salt also has the function to revive yang for resuscitation. For instance, it can be used to treat profuse sweating, extreme chills in the four limbs and pulseless syndrome.

Moxibustion insulated with Monkshood: There are two types commonly used in clinic. One is to place a slice of aconite root between a moxa cone and an acupoint. Another is to place a cake of monkshood between a moxa cone and an acupoint. Cut a slice of monkshood or select a monkshood cake. Then punch numerous holes in it and place it on the acupoint selected. After that, place a moxa cone on it and ignite the cone. The moxibustion continues until there is heat and erythema of the local skin. Generally, 5 ~ 10 cones are burned out on each point selected at one treatment session. As the aconite root has the property to dispel wind and cold and to reinforce kidney-yang. This method is applicable to various syndromes of insufficiency of yang, including importance, premature ejaculation diarrhea at dawn, cold limbs, etc.

（2）艾条灸

艾条灸是将艾条或药条一端点燃在穴位施灸治病的一种方法。常可分为3种。

1）温和灸：将艾条一端点燃，悬于施灸穴位上固定不移，当患者感到皮肤灼痛时移去艾条，至皮肤出现红晕为度。本法能温通经脉，祛除风寒湿邪。

2）回旋灸：将燃着的艾条悬于施灸穴位上，再将艾条回旋移动，使穴位皮肤有温热感。每次10~20分钟，适宜于风湿痛、神经麻痹等病。

3）雀啄灸：将燃着的艾条对准穴位皮肤处，一上一下如雀啄食一样移动。每次5分钟左右。多用于治疗小儿疾病或急救。

（2）*Moxibustion with moxa sticks*

Moxibustion with moxa sticks is a moxibustion method by igniting one end of a moxa stick or a drug stick above an acupoint to treat diseases. It is classified into 3 types.

1) Mild-warming moxibustion: Ignite one of the ends of a moxa stick.

Hold the stick and keep the ignited end above the selected acupoint from a distance without moving. When the patient complains of burning pain on the skin properly lift the ignited end of the moxa stick. Apply the moxibustion until there is erythema of the skin. This method has the property to promote flow of qi by warming the channel and to dispel wind, cold and damp pathogens.

2) Rounding moxibustion: Also termed circling moxibustion. Keep the ignited moxa stick above the selected acupoint at a distance from it. Then, move the moxa stick horizontally around so as to cause a warm sensation on the skin of the acupoint area. Moxibustion lasts 10 ~ 20 minutes for each point. This method is suitable to treat rheumatic pain, nervous paralysis, etc.

3) Sparrow - pecking moxibustion: Hold an ignited moxa stick with its ignited end directed at the acupoint and move it up and down like a sparrow pecking food. In general, moxibustion lasts 5 minutes or so for each point. This method is often used to treat infantile diseases or used as emergency treatment.

（3）温针灸

温针灸（图2-5）是一种针法与灸法相结合的方法。它适用于同时需要留针和温灸的病症。具体操作是：当针刺入穴位并得气后，将少许艾绒

包裹在针柄上,并点燃,以引起穴位周围的热感。这种方法具有温经通络、

行气活血的作用,能治疗寒湿引起的关节酸痛、麻木寒冷以及瘫痪等。

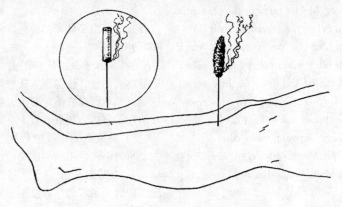

图 2 - 5 温针灸

Fig. 2 - 5 Moxibustion with Warming Needle

（3） *Moxibustion with warming needle*

Moxibustion with warming needle (Fig. 2 - 5) is a method of acupuncture combined with moxibustion. It is used for conditions in which both retention of the needle and moxibustion are needed. After the arrival of the needling sensation with the needle retained in the acupoint, the needle handle is wrapped with moxa wool and ignited to cause a mild heat sensation around the acupoint. This method functions to warm and dredge the meridians, circulate qi and activate blood so as to treat painful joints caused by cold-damp, numbness with cold sensation and paralysis.

（4） 灯火灸

灯火灸（图 2 - 6）是用灯心草蘸植物油,点燃后快速按在穴位上进行焠烫的方法。该法在操作时首先选定穴位做好标记,取灯芯草 4～5 厘米长,将一端浸入油中 1～2 厘米,点火前用卫生纸吸去灯草上浮油,术者右手拇指、示指捏住灯草露出草端 1 厘米左右点燃,对准穴位快速点按,一触即离,此时即出现"叭"的爆碎声,表明施术成功,如未闻爆碎声,可再重复一次,灸后注意局部清洁,防止感染。本法有疏风解表、行气利痰、解郁开胸、开窍熄风的作用。主治流行性腮腺炎、小儿抽搐、昏迷、胃痛、腹痛等症。

（4） *Rush-burning moxibustion*

Rush-burning moxibustion (Fig. 2 - 6) is a moxibustion method performed by pressing a burning oiled rush directly over an acupoint and immediately moving it away. Make a mark at the selected acupoint. Select a segment of rush pith 4~5 cm long and put its one end into vegetable oil 1~2 cm deep. Then, take it out of the oil and dry it slightly with some soft paper. Next, hold the rush with the thumb and index finger of the right hand exposing the oiled end. Quickly press it directly on the acupoint and immediately take the rush away. If a sound like "pa" is heard when the ignited end of the rush touches the skin it indicates the operation was successful. If not, repeat the operation in the same way. Be cautious to keep the local area clean after moxibustion so as to prevent infection. This method may serve to dispel wind for relieving exterior syndrome, to promote flow of qi for dispelling phlegm, to relieve stagnant qi for soothing chest oppression, and to induce resuscitation for calming endogenous wind. It is mainly indicated in Mumps, infantile clonic convulsion, coma, stomachache, abdominal pain, etc.

(5) 天灸

天灸是用对皮肤有刺激性的药物，敷贴于穴位，使之局部充血、起疱的一种治疗方法。常有如下几种：

1）蒜泥灸（图 2－7）：将食用大蒜捣成泥状，取 3～5 克置于穴位上，覆盖塑料膜，再以大于塑料膜的

胶布敷贴固定。敷灸时间为 1～3 小时，以局部皮肤发痒、发红或起疱为度。如敷涌泉穴治疗咳血、衄血；敷合谷穴治疗扁桃体炎；敷鱼际穴治疗咽喉肿痛等。

2）蓖麻子灸：蓖麻子去壳取仁适量捣成泥状，按蒜泥灸法敷贴于穴位上。如敷涌泉穴治疗滞产，敷百会穴治疗子宫垂、脱肛、胃下垂等。

3）吴茱萸灸：取中药吴茱萸适量，研为细末，用醋调成糊膏状，按蒜泥灸法贴敷于穴位上，每日敷 1 次。如敷涌泉穴治疗高血压、口腔溃疡、小儿水肿等。

(5) *Crude herb moxibustion*

Crude herb moxibustion is a therapy by pasting some irritant medicines on the skin at certain acupoints or affected areas to cause local congestion and blistering. Commonly used methods are as follows.

1) Mashed garlic moxibustion (Fig. 2－7): Mash some garlic well. Place 3~5 g of mashed garlic on the skin with a piece of plastic film. Then, cover and fix the plastic film on the skin with a piece of adhesive plaster. Keep the mashed garlic on the acupoint area until there is itching, redness or blisters on the local skin. Usually, keep the garlic on the skin for 1~3 hours. This method can be used in treating many diseases. For instance, hemoptysis and epistaxis are treated by applying mashed

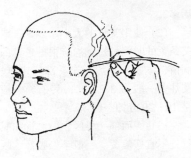

图 2-6 灯火灸

Fig. 2-6 Rush-Burning Moxibustion

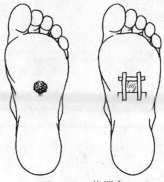

图 2-7 蒜泥灸

Fig. 2-7 Mashed Garlic Moxibustion

garlic moxibustion at Yongquan (KI 1). Tonsilitis is treated by applying it at Hegu (LI 4) and sore throat is treated by applying it at Yuji (LU 10).

2) Castor seed Moxibustion: Take away the shell of a castor seed. Mash the seed and plaster the mashed seed on the selected point in the same way as above. This method can be used in treating the following diseases. For ex-

ample, prolonged labour may be treated by applying this method at Yongquan (KI 1). Prolapse of uterus and anus, gastroptosis may be treated by applying it at Baihui (DU 20).

3) Fructus Evodiae moxibustion: Grind a proper amount of fructus evodiae into powder. Make it into a paste with vinegar. Plaster the paste on the acupoint in the same way as above. This method is performed once a day and can be used in treating the following diseases. Hypertension, canker sores and infantile edema can be treated by performing this method on Yongquan (KI 1).

2. 艾灸补泻

艾灸补泻主要指艾炷的补泻。临床上在应用灸法时，对于邪气偏盛的用泻法，正气虚弱的用补法。施灸时，点燃艾炷后不吹其火，等待它慢慢徐燃自灭，火力微而温和，且时间宜长，壮数较多，施灸完毕后再用手按其施灸穴位，使真气聚而不散者为补。反之，点燃艾炷后以口速吹其火，促使快燃，火力较猛，且快燃快灭，当患者感觉局部热烫时，即迅速更换艾炷再灸，灸治时间较短，壮数较长，施灸完毕后不按其穴，使邪气外散者为泻法。

2. Tonifying and Reducing Methods in Moxibustion Therapy

Tonifying and reducing methods in moxibustion are mainly applicable when using moxa sticks. In clinical application of moxibustion, reducing method is used when a pathogen is dominant and tonifying method is used when the vital-qi is weak. On performing tonifying moxibustion, the moxa stick is ignited and the fire directed at the point selected is not blowed but burns slowly and extinguishes of its own accord. Milder fire should be produced, lasting for a comparatively longer time, with more cones used. The area is pressed with the hand as soon as the moxibustion is over so as to keep the genuine qi inside and prevent it from escaping. In reducing method of moxibustion the fire of the ignited moxa stick is blowed by the mouth to quicken its burning speed and to produce more heat. With quick burning and quick extinction the patient feels local heat and burning. The moxa stick is then quickly replaced with another one. The duration of moxibustion is comparatively short and rather fewer moxa sticks are used. After moxibustion, the applied acupoint is not pressed so as to make the pathogen go out.

3. 施灸注意事项

（1）施灸一般是先上部，后下部；先背部，后腹部；先头部，后四肢；先阳经，后阴经。施灸壮数先少后多。

（2）使用艾炷的大小、多少，或艾条灸的时间长短，均应根据患者的病情、体质、年龄、施灸部位来定。艾炷灸一般为 3～5 壮，艾条灸一般是 10～20 分钟。

（3）颜面部、心区、大血管和肌腱处不宜瘢痕灸。一般孕妇腹部、腰骶部不宜施灸。

（4）对昏迷、肢体麻木不仁及感觉迟钝患者，注意勿灸过量，避免造成烧伤。

（5）施灸后，如皮肤起疱，小者能自行吸收，大者可用消毒针头穿破，放出液体，并敷以消毒纱布固定。

（6）如施用瘢痕灸，在灸疮化脓期间不宜做重体力劳动，并保持局部清洁，以防止感染。如灸疮污染而发炎，可用消炎药膏涂敷。

（7）外感温病、阴虚内热及其他实热证，一般不宜施灸。

3. Precautions of Moxibustion

（1）Moxibustion is generally applied to the upper part of the body first and then to the lower part. Treat the back first, the abdominal region second, the head first and the extremities second, the yang channels first and the yin channels second. First less units are used, then more units.

（2）The volume of moxibustion, including the size of the moxa cones or duration of the moxa stick application should be in parallel to the patients pathological conditions, general constitution, age and the site where moxibustion is applied. Generally, three to five moxa cones are used for each point, or ten to twenty minutes for the application of moxa sticks.

(3) Scarring moxibustion should not be applied to the face, the precardiac region, the vicinity of large blood vessels, and on regions of the muscles and tendons. In general, moxibustion is forbidden on the abdominal region and lumbosacral region of pregnant women.

(4) For patients with coma, numbness of the extremities or dysesthesia excessive moxibustion is not advisable to prevent burning.

(5) Sometimes, a few blisters may result on the skin from moxibustion. Small blisters can heal by themselves. Large blisters should be punctured with a sterilized needle and drained, then dressed with antiseptic gauze.

(6) After scarring moxibustion, the patient should not do heavy physical labour and must keep the local skin clean to avoid infection during suppuration of the post-moxibustion sore. If the post-moxibustion sore is infected apply an antiphlogistic plaster to it.

(7) It is inadvisable to apply moxibustion to febrile disease due to exoge-nous pathogen, interior heat syndrome due to yin deficiency, and excess heat syndrome.

第三节　拔罐疗法

Section 3 Cupping Therapy

拔罐疗法是以杯罐为工具，借助燃烧排除罐内空气，使其吸附于皮肤而造成局部充血现象的一种疗法。本法具有行气活血、消肿止痛、祛除寒湿的作用。常用拔罐工具有竹罐、陶罐和玻璃罐等。

1．火罐的种类（图2-8）

（1）竹罐：用直径3～5厘米的竹子，制成6～8厘米或8～10厘米长的管子，一端留节做底，另一端做罐口，中段略粗，罐口须用砂纸打磨光滑。竹罐轻巧、价廉、不易跌碎，但易燥裂漏气。

（2）陶罐：为陶土烧制而成，罐口光滑、两端较小，中间略向外展，形如腰鼓。特点是吸力大，但易破碎。

（3）玻璃罐：系用玻璃制成，罐口光滑、肚大口小，口边外翻。特点是质地透明，可以观察罐内皮肤的瘀血程度，便于掌握时间，但易破碎。

Cupping is a therapy in which a jar is attached to the skin surface to cause local congestion. The removal of the air from the jar is created by introducing heat in the form of an ignited material in the jar. This method has the function of warming and promoting the free flow of qi and blood in the channels, diminishing swelling and pains, and dispelling cold and dampness. The commonly used cupping material are bamboo, glass, or pottery.

1. Types of Jars　(Fig. 2－8)

(1) Bamboo jar: Cut down a section of bamboo 3～5 cm in diameter and 6～8 cm in length forming a pipe. One end is used as the bottom and the other as the opening. The middle part of the jar is a little thicker. The rim of the jar should be made smooth by a piece of sand paper. The bamboo jar is light, economical and uneasy to break, but easy to crack due to dryness causing air leakage.

(2) Pottery jar: It is made from pottery clay by means of baking. The mouth of the jar is smooth with both ends smaller and the middle part extended slightly. The jar is shaped as a waist drum. The pottery jar is characterized by a big force of suction but easy to break.

(3) Glass cup: The mouth of the cup is smooth and small but the body of the cup is large and the rim of the mouth everted externally. The cup is transparent allowing the congestion of the local skin in the cup to be seen so as to control the time of the treatment. The glass cup is easy to break.

图 2－8　火罐的种类

Fig. 2－8　Types of Jars

2. 适应范围

此法多用于风湿痹痛、急性扭伤、面瘫、半身不遂、感冒、咳嗽、胃痛、腹痛等。

2. Indications

The cupping method is mainly used to treat arthritis due to wind-cold-dampness, acute sprain, facial paralysis, hemiplegia, common cold, cough, stomachache, abdominal pain, etc.

3. 拔罐方法

（1）扣罐的方式

1）投火法：用乙醇棉球或纸片，点燃后投入罐内，立即将罐罩在所取穴位或患病部位的皮肤上。此法宜于火罐横扣，以免纸片掉落皮肤上造成灼伤。

2）闪火法（图2-9）：用镊子夹住已经点燃的乙醇棉球，在罐内壁回旋一下并迅速抽出，立即将罐罩在应拔穴位或患处皮肤上。此法安全多用。

3）贴棉法：将乙醇棉球贴在罐内壁底处，点燃棉球后立即罩在皮肤上。此法乙醇不宜太多，以免滴在皮肤上引起灼伤。

4）架火法：用一圆形硬质橡皮或胶木瓶塞，置于应拔部位皮肤上，其上放95%乙醇棉球一个，点燃后将火罐（最好是玻璃火罐）立即扣上，火罐自然吸附于皮肤上。该法安全牢固。

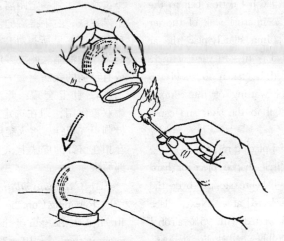

图 2 - 9　闪火法

Fig. 2 - 9　Fire-Twinkling Method

3. Manipulations

（1）*Cup - placing method*

1）Fire-throwing method

Throw an ignited alcohol ball or a piece of ignited paper into a jar and immediately place the mouth of the jar firmly against the skin on the desired location making the jar attach to the skin. This method is applied only when the jar is required to be attached horizontally otherwise the burning material may fall on to and hurt the skin.

2) Fire-twinkling method (Fig. 2 - 9)

Clamp an alcohol cotton ball with forceps. Ignite it and put it into the jar. Then, immediately take it out and place the jar on the selected point or area. This method is frequently applied because it is safe to the patient during the operation.

3) Cotton-attaching method

Attach an alcohol cotton ball to the bottom of the internal wall of the jar and ignite it. Immediately place the jar to the selected point. In this method, caution should be taken to avoid too much alcohol wetting of the cotton, which may fall to the skin and cause burning.

4) Material-placing method

Place a circle-shaped piece of hard rubber or a bakelite stopper over the skin of the selected area. Next, place a cotton ball wetted with 95% alcohol on the hard rubber or bakelite stopper. Then, ignite the ball and immediately place a jar over the skin where the rubber or stopper is on. This method is safe to the patient and makes the jar attach firmly.

（2）罐的用法

1）坐罐：也叫留罐。当罐扣在一定的部位后，留置 10～20 分钟再起掉。此法可一次拔一罐，或在其肌肉丰厚处的局部拔 2～5 罐不等，一般疾病均可采用此法。

2）闪罐：即运用闪火法将罐扣上后立即起下，然后再次闪火扣上又起下，如此反复多次。适宜于局部麻木，或功能减退的虚证。

3）走罐：又称推罐。此法宜于在肌肉丰厚，面积大的部位如背腰、臀、大腿等处进行。即将拔罐部位涂上凡士林，再将罐扣拔在一定部位的皮肤上，右手握好罐子，左手拉罐向下滑移，达到一定距离再将左手紧按下端皮肤，右手推罐向上滑移。如此反复数次，见所过处皮肤红晕即止，起罐擦去油脂。此法多用于脉络阻滞或有窜痛的疾病。

4）针上套罐：此法可起到针、罐双重作用，即在选定穴位或部位，针刺得气留针，将火罐用闪火法迅速套扣在留针的皮肤上，多用来治疗深部顽疾。

（2）*Cup-manipulating method*

1) Retaining Cupping: After a jar is attached to the skin of the selected area retain it there for 10～20 minutes before removing it. With this method, one jar may be employed to the local area with abundant muscle. This method may be applicable to most of the diseases which can be treated with cupping.

2) Successive flash cupping: Make a

jar attach to the skin with fire-twinkling method and immediately remove it. Repeat this course several times. This method is suitable for treating numbness of local skin or deficiency syndrome due to hypofunction.

3）Moving cupping: Also termed pushing cupping. This method is suitable for cupping an area with abundant muscle such as the back, loin, buttock and thigh. Smear vaseline over the selected area and attach a jar. Then, hold the jar with the right hand and draw it with the left hand to slide it downwards for a distance. Then, forcefully press the skin below the jar with the left hand and push it with the right hand to slide it upwards for a distance. Repeat this course several times. After the skin of the local area appears red, take the jar away and wipe the vaseline off. This method is mainly used in treating disorders of obstruction of the channel or wandering pain.

4）Cupping with the needle inside the jar: This method serves as therapy both of acupuncture and cupping. Insert a filiform needle into a selected acupoint to induce needling sensation. Retain the needle there. Then quickly place a jar with the fire twinkling method over the skin where the needle is retained, the needle being inside the jar. This method is mainly used in treating intractable disease in a deep area.

4．起罐法

拔罐后，一般留罐 10 分钟左右，待局部皮肤充血、瘀血呈紫红色时即可起罐。起罐时，先用右手抓住罐身，左手拇指或示指略按压罐口旁的皮肤，使罐内充气，将罐取下。

4．Withdrawing the Cup

Generally, the cup is attached in place for 10 minutes or so. When the local skin becomes congested with violet coloured blood stasis formation, the cup should be withdrawn. On withdrawing the cup, hold the cup with the right hand, press the skin around the rim of the cup with thumb and index finger of the left hand to let air in. Then take the cup away.

5．注意事项

（1）皮肤溃疡、高热抽搐、皮肤过敏、水肿以及孕妇的腹部、腰骶部不宜拔罐。

（2）关节凹凸不平的部位、皮肤过于松弛的部位，均不宜应用。

（3）拔罐后局部呈现红晕或紫绀色，为正常现象。如局部瘀血严重者，不宜在原位再拔。如皮肤出现水疱，小的不需处理；大的可以用针刺破，涂些甲紫药水，覆盖消毒敷料，防止感染。

5．Precautions

（1）It is not advisable to apply cupping to a patient with skin ulcer, high fever or convulsion, skin allergy or edema, and to the abdoninal and sacral regions of pregnant women.

（2）The uneven sites around joints and the areas with very loose skin are not selected for cupping.

（3）After cupping, the local area becomes flushed or bruised. This is a normal condition. If the local blood stasis is severe, further cupping of this area is not advisable. Small blisters occurring on the skin are not necessary to manage. If the blisters are large, puncture them with a sterile needle, apply gentian violet and cover with a sterilized piece of gauze to prevent infection.

第四节　三棱针

Section 4 The Three-edged Needle

三棱针古称锋针，是一种柄粗而圆，针体呈三棱形、针尖锋利的工具。一般用于刺络放血。具有活血消肿、开窍泄热、通经活络的作用。

1．适应范围

三棱针疗法多为放血泻络所用，凡络脉壅滞、血瘀不通、邪气偏盛以及阴阳之气壅遏等病症。也可用于高热、中暑、急性扁桃体炎、咽喉肿痛、眼结膜炎、扭伤、疖肿、淋巴管炎、神经性皮炎等。

The three-edged needle, known as the sharp needle in ancient times, has a thick and round handle, a triangular body and a sharp tip. Generally, it is used in superficial blood vessel pricking to cause bleeding. This method functions to promote the blood circulation to reduce swelling, invoke resuscitation, reduce heat, and to clean and activate the meridians and collaterals.

1. Indications

The three-edged needle is mostly used for blood letting and promoting the smooth flow of qi and blood in the channels. It is used to treat blockage of the channels, blood stasis, pathogenic excess and blockage of both yin-qi and yang-qi. It is also employed in treating high fever, heat stroke, acute tonsilitis, sore throat, conjunctivitis, sprain, furuncle, lymphangitis, neurodermatitis, etc.

2．操作方法

（1）点刺法：此法主要适用于高热、咽喉肿痛、中暑、中风、惊厥、急性扁桃体炎、急性腰扭伤。尤其在医疗条件较差的地区，这种方法很有用处，有时可以收到意外的治疗效果。操作时先用拇指、示指和中指捏紧应刺的部位，右手持三棱针迅速刺入 0.05～0.1 寸后，立即退针，然后用手挤压局部，使之出血，最后用消毒乙醇棉球压按针孔片刻（图 2 - 10）。

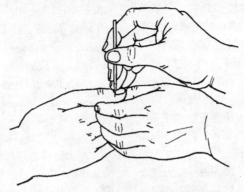

图 2 - 10 点刺法
Fig. 2 - 10 Spot Pricking

2. Manipulation

(1) Spot pricking: This method is mainly used to treat high fever, sore throat, heat stroke, apoplexy, convulsion, acute tonsilitis, and acute lumbar sprain. Especially, where there is poor medical service, this method is usually very useful and sometimes causes miraculous effect in treatment of these diseases. Pinch up the selected area tightly with the thumb, index and middle fingers of the left hand. Hold the three-edged needle with the right hand. Prick swiftly $0.05 \sim 0.1$ cun deep at the selected area and withdraw the needle immediately. Then squeeze and press the local area for blood letting. Finally press over the hole with a sterilized swab. (Fig. 2 - 10).

(2) 散刺法：此法用于痈肿、痹证、丹毒、外伤瘀血疼痛等。围绕红肿周围常规消毒，用三棱针点刺几针或几十针，然后用两手轻轻挤压或用罐吸拔，使恶血出尽，以消肿痛。

(2) Scattering pricking: This method is used to treat carbuncles, arthralgia syndrome, erysipelas and traumatic pain due to stagnant blood. etc. Apply routine sterilization around the reddened swelling. Prick around the lesion several times or several dozen times with a three-edged needle. Then squeeze and press the swelling gently with both hands or cup it to make the decayed blood escape completely. This method may diminish swelling and pain.

（3）挑刺法：本法用于目赤肿
痛、丹毒、痔疮等。医师以左手按压
腧穴或反应点（类似丘疹，一般为
2～4毫米大小，多呈褐色或粉红色、
白色，以手压之褪色）部位的两侧皮
肤，使之固定并减少疼痛。右手横持
针柄，拇指在上，示指、中指、无名
指下露出针尖0.3～0.5厘米，与皮
肤呈15°～30°角，快速将腧穴或反应
点的表皮挑破，再深入皮内将针身倾
斜，并轻轻地提高，挑断部分纤维组
织。挑刺时用腕关节左右摆动力带动
手指运动挑刺，然后局部消毒并覆盖
消毒敷料。

（3）Fibrous-tissue-broken pricking:
This method is used to treat redness,
swelling and pain of the eye,
erysipelas, hemorrhoids. etc. Press
the skin at two sides of the acupoint or
sensitive spot (like a rush, 2～4 mm in
diameter usually with dark-yellow,
green-dark-yellow, reddish, or white
colour which disappears if pressed) with
the left hand to fix the skin. Hold the
needle with right hand, the thumb
above the middle, index and ring fingers, exposing the top of the needle
0.3～0.5 cm. Then quickly prick and
break the skin of the acupoint or treatment spot at an angle of 15° ～ 30°
formed by the needle with the skin surface. Insert the needle deep to the subcutaneous tissue making the shaft of the
needle tilted. Then gently move it upwards to break some of the fibrous tissue. When pricking and breaking, it is
advisable to use the force formed by
left-right movement of the wrist joint
making the finger's movement for
pricking and breaking. After the operation, sterilize the local skin and cover
the area with sterilized dressing.

3．注意事项

施术局部必须严格消毒，以免感
染。手法宜轻、浅、快，出血不宜过
多，避免刺伤深部大血管。体弱、贫
血、孕妇、产妇及有出血性疾病，如
血小板减少、血友病等均不宜使用。
一般1日1次，或隔日1次，或3～7
日挑刺1次，3～5次为1个疗程。

3. Precautions

Strict sterilization must be applied to
the area to be pricked in order to prevent infection. The operation should be
slight, superficial and quick. Bleeding
should not be excessive. Avoid injuring
the deep large arteries. This method
should not be used in patients with
weak constitution, anemia, pregnant
women, parturients and patients with
hemorrhagic diseases, such as throm-
bocytopenia and hemophilia. Generally, this method is carried out once every day or once every other day, or
once every 3～7 days. One therapeutic
course consists of 3～5 times.

第五节 皮肤针

Section 5 Acupuncture with the Skin Needle

皮肤针又称梅花针、七星针。是用7支或更多的小针安装在一个莲蓬头式的针体上，再装上一个长柄制成，是一种浅刺皮肤相应部位治疗疾病的针刺方法。

1. 适应范围

此法适用于高血压、头痛、近视、神经衰弱、胃肠病、斑秃、痛经、关节痛、腰背痛、肤肌麻木，肋间神经痛、面瘫、神经性皮炎等。

Acupuncture with the skin needle is also known as plum-blossom needle, seven-star needle, or cutaneous needle. The skin needle is made up of seven or more sewing needles bound together with their tips at the same level and fixed at one end of a shower nozzle-like substance with a handle. It is a needling method of treatment by taping on the skin of the corresponding area shallowly.

1. Indications

This method is usually used to treat headache, myopia, neurasthenia, gastrointestinal disorder, alopecia areata, dysmenorrhea, arthralgia, pain in the back and loin, numbness of the skin, intercostal neuralgia, facial paralysis,

neurodermatitis, etc.

2. 操作方法

被刺激部位先行皮肤常规消毒，用右手拇指、示指、中指如执鼓槌一样执针柄，运用手腕的弹力似小鸡啄米状将针垂直叩打在皮肤上，并立即提起，此时可引起短促的"哒"声。注意弹刺时一定要平刺，着力要均匀平稳、集中，不能斜刺或拖刺。可分弱、中、强三种不同刺激量。弱刺激以皮肤略有潮红，无明显疼痛为度，适用于体弱、小儿患者和头面部穴位。中刺激叩至皮肤有明显红痕但无出血为度，一般穴位都采用中刺激。强刺激叩至皮肤出血，腰背、肩臀等肌肉丰厚处常用此法。操作时，一处连续叩打5~7次，叩打间距1~2厘米，叩打频率每分钟80次左右。亦可将晶体管电针仪的一对输出导线，其中一根接在皮肤针针组上，另一根接在铜棒上，常用输出峰值电压100~120伏；输入锯齿波频率16~300次/分；电源电压用9伏（直流）干电池；电流小于5毫安，以患者能耐受为宜。操作时，患者手握铜棒，医者持皮肤针如上法进行叩刺。

2. Manipulation

Sterilize the area. Hold the handle of the needle just like holding a drumstick with the thumb, the index and middle fingers of the right hand. Tap quickly and perpendicularly on the skin with a flexible movement of the wrist, like a chicken pecking at rice, causing a short "da" sound. The tapping force should be focused and no oblique or slipping puncture is allowed. The stimulation is of three kinds: weak, medium and strong tapping. Weak tapping is meant pecking the skin until it appears light red without any pain. This is suitable for patients with weak constitution, children and points at the head and face. Medium tapping is meant pecking the skin until it appears obviously red without bleeding which is used in common points. Strong tapping is meant pecking the skin to cause bleeding. This is suitable for points at the lumbar, back, shoulder and hip where muscles are abundant. Generally, in one treatment session $5 \sim 7$ minutes of tapping are done with a frequency of approximately 80 times per minute and an interval space being $1 \sim 2$ cm.

This method may be combined with electro-acupuncture. Connect one of a pair of output leads from a transistor electro-acupuncture unit to the skin needle and the other to a copper stick. Select $100 \sim 120$ volts as the peak voltage of output and $16 \sim 300$ times per minute as the frequency of output of irregular wave. A dry battery with 9 volts and a current below 5 mA (direct current) should be used as the power source. During the operation, the patient is asked to hold the copper stick and the operator holds the skin needle to tap in the same way mentioned above.

3. 刺激部位

（1）常规刺激部位：背部正中线（督脉）及足太阳膀胱经第一侧线（脊正中线旁开 1.5 寸）、第二侧线（脊正中线旁开 3 寸），共 5 条线。常沿此五条线从上至下叩刺。

（2）循经条刺：即在辨证的基础上，确定病变所属经络后，取其相应经脉沿经叩刺。

（3）穴位叩刺：在辨证的基础上，根据穴位的主治特点，选择特定穴进行叩刺。

（4）局部叩刺：即在病变的局部进行条刺、环刺（图 2-11）。

3. Stimulation Area

(1) *The routine area*

The routine area of skin needling includes the posterior median line on the spinal column (namely, the course of the Du Meridian), and the four lines respectively 1.5 cun and 3 cun lateral to the posterior median line on the back (i. e. the branches of the Bladder Meridian). Five lines in total. Tap the five lines from top to bottom.

(2) *The corresponding meridian area*

Based on the differentiation of the

syndromes, take the corresponding meridian course as the stimulating area. Tap on the skin along the corresponding meridian course.

（3）*The corresponding points*

Based on the differentiation of syndromes and chief indications of the acu-points, choose some acupoints as the tapping area.

（4）*The affected area*

Take the diseased area as the tapping area. Usually the line-puncture or circle-puncture is given the area（Fig. 2 – 11）.

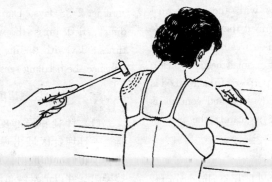

图 2 – 11　局部叩刺示意图

Fig. 2 – 11　Tapping at the Affected Area

4. 注意事项

（1）操作前后严格消毒以防感染。

（2）操作前检查针具，达到针尖平齐无钩。

（3）局部皮肤外伤、溃疡和出血性疾病患者不可用此法叩刺。

4. Precautions

（1）Sterilize strictly before and after operation in order to prevent infection.

（2）Check the needle before the operation. Keep the tips of the needle even and free of any hooks.

（3）Patients with local trauma and ulcers of the skin or with hemorrhagic diseases are not allowed to receive this therapeutic method.

第六节　皮内针

Section 6 Acupuncture with the Intradermal Needle

皮内针又称埋针，是将特制的小型针具刺入皮内，固定并留置一定时间，利用其特殊刺激作用，调整经络脏腑功能来治疗疾病的一种方法。

1．适应范围

本法常用于某些慢性、顽固性疾病，如顽固性头痛、三叉神经痛、牙痛、胃痛、痛经、风湿痛等。亦可用于高血压、哮喘、咳嗽、失眠及其他痛证。

Acupuncture with the intradermal needle, also termed the needle-embedding therapy, is a treatment by inserting and leaving a small needle beneath the skin. The purpose of this method is to give the body long and continuous stimulation for regulating the visceral function.

1．Indications

It is often used to treat chronic or refractory diseases such as headache, trigeminal neuralgia, toothache, stomachache, dysmenorrhea, and rheumatism. It is also used to treat hypertention, asthma, cough, insomnia and some other painful syndromes.

2．操作方法

局部皮肤和针具消毒后，用镊子或血管钳夹住已消毒的皮内针针柄，迅速刺入腧穴内或痛点上，然后再用胶布将皮内针固定。冬天可埋 5～7 天，夏天可埋 2～3 天。在埋针过程中，每日用手指给予加压数次，以加强针感。

2．Manipulation

After sterilization of the local skin and needle apparatus use forceps or clamps to pick up the handle of the sterilized needle. Quickly peck it into the point or painful area and then fix it with adhesive plaster. In winter, it can be embedded for 5 ～ 7 days, while in summer 2～3 days. During the embedding period press the needle several times a day with the fingers in order to enhance the needling sensation.

3．注意事项

（1）针具和局部皮肤应严格消毒。一旦埋针区域出现红、肿、热、痛，应将针立即取出，并在针眼处涂擦碘酊，并以消毒纱布包扎，以防感染扩大。

（2）如果埋针后患者感觉疼痛，应将针取出重埋。

（3）患者伴有皮肤感染禁用埋针治疗。

3．Precautions

（1）The needle apparatus and the local skin should be strictly sterilized. Once the signs of redness, swelling, hotness and pain appear at the area where the needle is embedded, the embedded needle should be immediately taken out. Iodine should be smeared into the hole and sterilized gauze should be used to cover the area to avoid further infection.

(2) If the patient feels pain after the embedment, the embedded needle should be taken out and embedded again.

(3) Patients with infected skin are contraindicated to receive treatment.

第七节 火 针

Section 7 Acupuncture with the Hot Needle

火针是以一种特制的粗针，烧热后刺入穴位以治疗疾病的一种古老方法。具有温经散寒、通经活络的作用。

1. 适用范围

临床常用于治疗风寒湿痹，虚寒痈肿等。亦可用于治疗瘰疬、顽癣、扁平疣、痣等。

Acupuncture with a hot needle is an ancient needling method of treatment. By inserting a thick needle having been warmed into a point, it can serve to warm the meridian, clear and activate the channels and collaterals.

1. Indications

Acupuncture with a hot needle is usually used for arthralgia due to wind-cold-dampness and swelling and pain due to vacuity cold. It can be also used in the treatment of scrofula, neurodermatitis, flat wart, nevus.

2. 操作方法

在选定的穴位或部位上，用 2% 碘酊消毒后，再用 75% 乙醇脱碘，根据患者的适应情况，为减轻疼痛和恐惧，可选用 1% 普鲁卡因（也可加入 0.1% 盐酸肾上腺素以防出血）作为浸润麻醉，2 分钟后即可行针。操作可分深刺和浅刺 2 种。

(1) 深刺：适用于外科疾患，如痈疽、瘰疬、象皮腿等。一般左手用舒张法或挟持法或爪切法固定穴位，右手持针，将针尖和针下端在酒精灯上烧红，对准穴位或一定部位迅速刺入后立即退出，最后用消毒棉球按住针孔（图 2 - 12）。

(2) 浅刺：多用于治疗风湿痛及肌肤冷麻、顽癣等症。操作时右手持针，将针烧红轻轻地在皮肤表面叩刺。间隔 3～6 天治疗 1 次（图 2 - 13）。

2. Manipulation

Sterilize the skin of the selected acupoint or area with 2% iodine and then swab away the iodine with 75% alcohol. Then according to the patient's adaptability, anesthesia with 1% procaine (or add 0.1% adrenalin hydrochloride in order to prevent bleeding) may be given to minimize the patient's pain and terror. Two minutes later the puncture can be carried out. The manipulation of acupuncture with the hot needle may be divided into deep puncture and shallow puncture.

(1) *Deep puncture*: It is suitable to treat external diseases such as carbuncle, cellulitis, scrofula and elephantiasis crus. Fix the acupoint with the left hand, the fingers pressing the acupoint, stretching or pinching the skin. Hold the needle with the right hand. Warm the needle top and the lower portion of the needle shaft by the fire of an alcohol lamp until the colour of these parts of the needle becomes red. Insert the needle accurately into the acupoint or a required area quickly and with draw it immediately. Finally, press the needle hole with a sterilized cotton ball (Fig. 2 - 12).

(2) *Shallow puncture*: It is mainly used in treatment of arthralgia due to wind-dampness, coldness and numbness of the skin, and neurodermatitis. Hold the needle with the right hand and warm the lower portion of the needle on the fire until the colour of this portion becomes red. Then gently tap on the skin surface with the needle. The treatment may be given once per 3 ~ 6 days (Fig. 2 - 13).

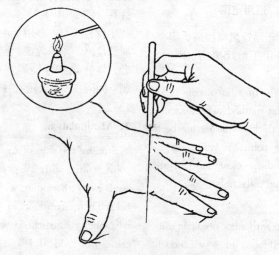

图 2 - 12　火针深刺法示意图

Fig. 2 - 12　Deep Puncture with the Hot Needle

3．注意事项

（1）体弱患者、孕妇和面部禁用火针。

（2）操作时要小心，动作要敏捷，避开血管、肌腱、神经干和内腔器官。

（3）针刺后，局部红肿未消时避免洗浴、抓搔。若针刺较深，可用消毒敷料覆盖针孔，用胶布固定1～2天以防感染。

3．Precautions

（1）The hot needling is contraindicated in patients with a weak constitution, pregnant women and the patient's face.

（2）The operator should be careful. Manipulate the needle swiftly and avoid the blood vessels, muscular tendons nerve trunks and internal organs.

（3）After treatment, the patient should not bathe or scratch the skin until the local redness and swelling have disppeared. If tapping is deep, the needle hole should be covered with a sterilized dressing and the dressing should be fixed with adhesive plaster for one to two days in order to prevent infection.

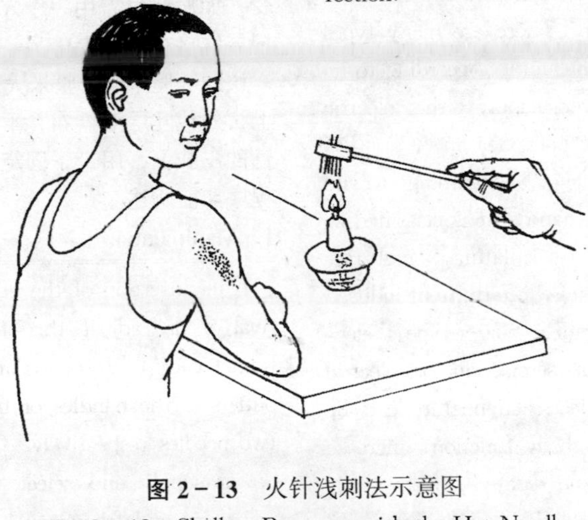

图 2－13 火针浅刺法示意图

Fig.2－13 Shallow Puncture with the Hot Needle

第八节 电 针

Section 8 Electroacupuncture

电针是针刺腧穴得气后，在针上通以微量电流，以针和电的综合刺激作用来治疗疾病的一种方法。电针器械包括毫针和电机两部分。电针机的种类很多，可因电源不同而分为直流和交流电针机。又可根据其构造和性能不同分为低频振荡电针机、高频振荡电针机、感应断续脉冲电针机、蜂鸣式电针机、电子管电针机及半导体电针机等。电针具有调整人体功能，加强镇痛、镇静，促进血液循环，调整肌张力等作用。

Electroacupuncture is a therapy which combines needling and electric stimulation by sending a small amount of electric current to a needle after insertion and arrival of qi to treat diseases. The instrument used in electroacupuncture is composed of two parts: the filiform needle and the electric stimulator. There are many types of electric stimulators. According to its different power supply, the electric stimulator is classfied as an AC or DC electric stimulator. According to its structures and natures it is classified as low-frequency oscillating, high-frequency oscillating, intermittent induced impulse current, buzzer-type, electronic tube or semiconductor electric stimulator. Electroacupuncture can be used to adjust body function, increase the analgesic and sedative effects, promote blood circulation, and adjust muscular tension, etc.

1. 操作方法

针刺得气后，先将电针机的输出电位器调到"零"位，然后分别将两根输出导线连接于两针的针柄或针体上，打开电源，选择所需波型和频率，把输出的电流由小到大逐渐调至患者感觉舒适能耐受的程度，经 1～2 分钟，待人体产生了适应感，可适当加大电流，通电时间一般每次10～20 分钟为宜，亦可根据病情需要适当延长通电时间。当达到预定时间后，先将输出电位器退回到"零"位，然后关闭电源开关，取下导线，最后按照一般起针方法将针取出。

电针的配穴处方与毫针取穴大致相同。一般以两侧肢体 1～3 对穴位为宜。过多会刺激太强，患者难以忍受。如病情只需用一个穴位，可把一根导线接在针柄上，另一根导线接在一块约 2 厘米×3 厘米大小的薄铅板上，外包几层湿纱布，平放在离针稍远的皮肤上，用带子固定，其余操作程序如前所述。

1. Manipulation

After insertion of the needle and arrival of qi, adjust the output potentiometer to "0", then connect the two outlets to the handles or bodies of the two needles respectively. Turn on the power supply and select the required waveform and frequency. Then adjust the output current from small to large until the patient feels comfortable and can tolerate it. If the patient adapts to the situation after 1～2 minutes, the current may be increased properly.

Generally, the time lasts $10 \sim 20$ minutes for each treatment. The time may also be prolonged according to the requirement of the pathological condition. When the required time is up, first adjust the output potentiometer back to "0", then turn off the power supply and disconnect the outlets from the needles. After that, withdraw the needles accordingly.

The way to make the prescription and to select acupoints in electroacupuncture is like that in filiform needle acupuncture. Generally, $1 \sim 3$ pairs of acupoints on both sides are suitable in number. Too many acupoints used of once may induce too strong a stimulation for the patient folerate. If only one acupoint is needed in treatment, one of a pair of leads is connected to the handle of the needle, and the other connected to a thin piece of black about 2 cm × 3 cm in size. This is then wrapped by several layers of wet cloth and laid on the skin somewhat remote to the needle and fixed with a thread. The rest of the operation procedure is as same as mentioned above.

2．波形的选择与适应范围

（1）密波：又称高频。50～100次/秒。能降低神经应激功能，对感觉神经和运动神经产生抑制作用。临床上用来止痛，镇静，缓解肌肉、血管痉挛和针刺麻醉。

（2）疏波：又称低频。2～5次/秒。能引起肌肉收缩，提高肌肉、韧带的张力。临床用于瘫痪和肌肉、关节、韧带、肌腱的劳损等。

（3）疏密波：又称不规则波。是一种疏波和密波交替出现的波形，但以兴奋作用占优势。临床上常用来止痛，治疗扭伤，关节炎，坐骨神经痛和面神经麻痹等。

（4）断续波：是一种有节律地时断时续的波型，断时无脉冲电流输出，续时为密波输出。能提高肌肉组织的兴奋性，临床常用于瘫痪患者。

（5）锯齿波：脉冲波幅变化类似锯齿。可用于刺激膈神经，做人工电动呼吸，抢救呼吸衰竭。还有提高神经肌肉兴奋性，调整经络功能，改善气血循环的作用。

2. Selection and Indications of the Wave Forms

(1) *Dense wave*: Also termed high frequency consists of $50 \sim 100$ pulses per second. It can inhibit sensory nerves and motor nerves through the reduction of irritable nerve stimulation. In clinic it is used to relieve pain, keep calm, and subside spasm of muscle and blood vessels. It is also used in acupuncture anaesthesia.

(2) *Sparse wave*: Also termed low frequency consists of $2 \sim 5$ pulses per second. It can cause the retraction

of muscle and enhance the tension of muscular ligament. In clinic, it is used for paralysis and over exerted lesion of muscle, joint, ligament and tendon.

（3）*Sparse-dense wave*: Also termed irregular wave. A wave-pattern in which sparse wave and dense wave appear alternately with the excitation function in domination. In clinic, it is often used to relieve pain, treat sprain, rheumatism, sciatica and facial paralysis.

（4）*Intermittent wave*: A wave pattern in which a wave appears on and off rythmically. When it is off, there is no output impulse. When it is on dense wave flows out, it stimulates the excitability of muscular tissue and can clinically be used for paralytic patients.

（5）*Sawtooth wave*: The wave pattern looks like a sawtooth. It can stimulate the phrenic nerve and be used as an electric spirophorus to salvage the patient with respiratory failure. It can also enhence the irritability of nerve and muscle, adjust the channel function and improve circulation of qi and blood.

3．注意事项

（1）调节电流量时，应逐渐从小到大，不能突然增强，以防引起肌肉强烈收缩，造成弯针或折针。

（2）电针机最大输出电压在40伏以上者，其最大输出电流应控制在 1毫安内，以免发生触电事故。

（3）心脏病患者，应避免电流回路通过心脏；体质弱、精神紧张者，应注意电流不宜过大，以防晕针。

（4）毫针的针柄如经过温针火烧之后，表面氧化不导电，不宜使用。如使用，输出导线应夹持针体。

3. Precautions

（1）During adjustment of the electric current it should be increased gradually not suddenly in order to prevent intense muscular contraction and result in bent or broken needle.

（2）For the electric stimulator with the maximum output voltage over 40 V, its maximum output current should be limited within 1 mA in order to avoid getting an electric shock.

（3）For patients with heart disease, avoid the electric current passing through the heart. For patients with weak constitution or nervousness, too much electric current is not advisable because it may cause fainting.

（4）After the needle is used in moxibustion with warming needle, the needle handle may be burnt and its surface oxidized resulting in loss of electric conductivity. In this case, it is not advisable to use the needle in the electrotherapy. If used, the needle should be clipped at its body by an outlet clip.

第九节 水 针

Section 9 Hydro-Acupuncture

水针又称穴位注射,是一种针刺与药物相结合的治疗方法。即用注射器将药液注入有关腧穴或阳性反应点,通过针刺与药物的作用,达到治疗疾病的目的。

1. 适应范围

凡针灸所适应的病症,均可采用此法。常用于腰腿痛,关节痛,肌肉麻木,胃肠、肝胆疾患和一些别的慢性病症。

Hydro-acupuncture, also termed point injection, is a therapy combining medicines with acupuncture. That is to say, using a syringe to inject liquid medicine into the acupuncture point or the positive, sensitive spot to treat the disease.

1. Indications

This method can be used in all diseases which are suitable for acupuncture treatment. The Hydro-acupuncture is indicated mostly for pain in the lower back and leg, pain of the joints, numbness of the muscle, gastrointestinal disorders, liver and gallbladder disorders and some other chronic diseases.

2. 操作方法

(1) 根据注射部位的所需注射药量,选用不同类型的注射器及针头。一般多用5号、6号、7号针头。肌肉丰厚处可用9号针头,而耳穴可选用1~2毫升注射器,5号针头。

(2) 根据病情选择有效穴位,一般每次以1~3对穴位为宜。

(3)根据病情用注射器抽入不同的药液。局部皮肤常规消毒,左手固定所选腧穴或阳性反应点,右手持针快速刺入,当达到一定深度时,可产生酸、胀、放散等得气感应,回抽无血,便可注入药液。推注药液时,急性病、体强者宜快;慢性病、体弱者宜缓。

(4) 根据注射的病位、被选择的药液和所患的疾病选择注射剂量和疗程。四肢腰部肌肉丰厚处,每穴或每个阳性反应点可注入药物10~20毫升;头面及耳部等处,一般只注0.3~0.5毫升;抗生素或其他药物,以原药剂量的1/5~2/5为宜。急性病症每日1~2次,慢性病症一般每日或隔日1次,6~8次为1个疗程。

2. Manipulation

(1) Selection of the syringe and syringe needle depends on the location and the amount of solution to be injected. Generally, No.5, No.6 and No.7 needles are usually selected. But if the acupoint is at an area with abundant muscle, No.9 needle may be chosen.

For acupoints on the auricle $1 \sim 2$ mL syringe and No. 5 needle may be used.

(2) Select the effective acupoints according to the patient's condition. Generally, it is suitable to choose $1 \sim 3$ pairs of acupoints once.

(3) Take the syringes and draw the selected liquid medicine according to different diseases. Sterilize the local skin routinely. Fix the selected point or positive sensitive spot with the left hand and then insert the needle into the point quickly with the right hand. When the needle tip reaches a certain depth at which the patient feels the needling sensation of soreness, distention or irradiation, and there is no blood in the syringe after being drawn, push the liquid medicine into the point. For patients with acute diseases and good constitution, it is advisable to push liquid medicine into the point quickly. For those with chronic diseases and weak constitution, slowly.

(4) Select the injection dosage and course of treatment according to the area of injection, chosen medicine and disease. On the four limbs and lumbar regions with abundant and thick muscles, $10 \sim 20$ mL liquid medicine may be injected into each point or each positive sensitive spot. On the head, face and regions of ears, $0.3 \sim 0.5$ mL in general. If antibiotics or others are used, $1/5 \sim 2/5$ of the usual dosage is recommended. For patients with acute diseases $1 \sim 2$ times per day is advisable. For those with chronic diseases one time per day or every other day in general. A course of treatment consists of $6 \sim 8$ times of injection.

3. 注意事项

(1) 治疗前应向患者说明本疗法的治疗特点及其正常反应, 以消除顾虑。

(2) 注意药物的性能、配伍禁忌、副作用和过敏反应。凡能引起过敏反应的药物, 应先做过敏试验。

(3) 切勿将药物注入关节腔内。

(4) 老人、小儿、孕妇和体弱者慎用。

(5) 颈项、胸背部注射时切勿过深, 以免伤及内脏器官在神经干经过的部位, 应注意避免损伤神经。

3. Precautions

(1) Before treatment let the patient know the characteristics and the normal reactions of this therapy in order to dispel his misgivings.

(2) Pay attention to the nature, incompatibilities, side effects and allergic reactions of the medicine to be used. A hypersensitive test should be done before the medicine, which may produce allergic reaction, is used.

(3) Avoid injecting the liquid

medicine into the articular cavities.

（4）It should be used with great care for elderly individuals, children, pregnant women and individuals with weak constitution.

（5）No deep injection is allowed in the nape, chest and back in order to avoid injuring the internal organs. Pay attention to avoid injuring nerve trunks in areas with main nerve trunks passing through.

第十节　耳　　针

Section 10 Ear Acupuncture Therapy

耳针是在耳郭穴位上用针刺或其

他方法进行刺激，以防治疾病的一种方法。此法具有操作简便、适应证广、副作用少、经济有效等特点。

1. 耳郭表面解剖名称（图2－14）

（1）耳郭正面解剖名称

1）耳轮：耳郭外缘卷曲的部分。

2）耳轮结节：耳轮外上方的结节状突起。

3）耳轮脚：耳轮伸到耳甲的部分。

4）对耳轮：与耳轮相对的隆起。

5）对耳轮上脚：对耳轮上部向上的分支。

6）对耳轮下脚：对耳轮上部向下的分支。

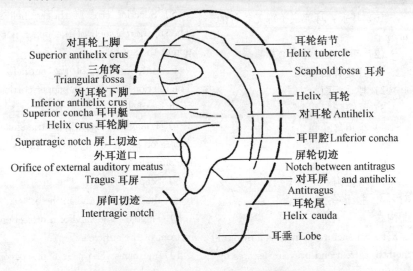

图2－14　耳郭表面解剖名称示意图

Fig. 2－14　Anatomical Nomenclature of the Surface of the Auricle

7）三角窝：对耳轮上、下脚之间构成的凹窝。

8）耳舟：耳轮与对耳轮之间形成的凹沟。

9）耳屏：耳郭前面的瓣状突起。

10）对耳屏：耳垂上部与耳屏相对的隆起。

11）屏上切迹：耳屏与耳轮之间的凹陷。

12）屏间切迹：耳屏与对耳屏之间的凹陷。

13）屏轮切迹：对耳屏与对耳轮之间的凹陷。

14）耳甲艇：耳轮脚以上的耳甲部。

15）耳甲腔：耳轮脚以下的耳甲部。

16）耳垂：耳郭最下部无软骨的部分。

（2）耳郭背面解剖名称

1）耳轮背面。

2）耳垂背面。

3）耳舟隆起。

4）三角窝隆起。

5）耳甲艇隆起。

6）耳甲腔隆起。

7）耳背沟：对耳轮上、下脚及对耳轮主干在耳背呈"Y"字型凹沟。

Ear Acupuncture therapy is a medical method to treat and prevent diseases by stimulating certain points on the auricle with needles or other tools. This method is characterized by easy manipu-lation, wide indications, less side effects, economical treatment and good results, etc.

1. Anatomical Nomenclature of the Surfaces of the Auricle

（1）*Frontal surface*

1）Helix: The portion of the auricular border that bends inward.

2）Tubercle of the helix: The nodular process on the later superior portion of the auricle.

3）Crus of the helix: The portion of the auricle which extends into the auricular concha.

4）Antihelix: The prominence opposite the helix.

5）Superior crus of the antihelix: The superior branch of the upper portion of the antihelix.

6）Inferior crus of the antihelix: The inferior branch of the upper portion of the antihelix.

7）Triangular fossa: The triangular depression between the two branches of the antihelix.

8）Scaphoid fossa: The groove between the helix and the antihelix.

9）Tragus: The valviform projection in front of the auricle.

10）Antitragus: The projection superior to the lobe and contrary to the tragus.

11）Supratragic notch: The depression between the crus of the helix and the tragus.

12）Intertragic notch: The depression between the tragus and the antitragus.

13）Notch between antitragus and antihelix: The depression between the antitragus and antihelix.

14）Superior concha: The concha above the crus of the helix.

15）Inferior concha: The concha below the crus of the helix.

16）Lobe: The lowest portion of the auricle, containing no cartilege.

（2）*Dorsal surface*

1）Dorsal surface of the helix.

2）Dorsal surface of the earlobe.

3）Dorsal eminence of the scaphoid fossa.

4）Dorsal eminence of the triangular fossa.

5）Dorsal eminence of the superior concha.

6）Dorsal eminence of the inferior concha.

7）Groove of the dorsal surface: The groove on the dorsal surface of the auricle resembling a "Y", formed by the antihelix and its two branches.

2．耳穴的分布规律

　　耳郭好像一个倒置的胎儿，头朝下，臀部朝上（图2－15）。身体的每一个部分都有一个相应的穴位或区域

在耳郭的表面。这些穴位或区域既能反映机体的生理、病理情况，也能接受刺激以调整相应部位的功能失调。

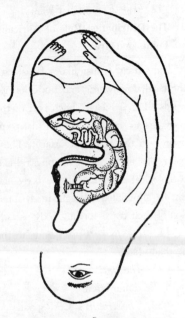

图2－15　耳穴形象分布示意图
Fig.2－15　Regularity of
　　Distribution of Otopoints

（1）耳垂：相当于头面部。
（2）对耳屏：相当于头和脑。
（3）耳屏：相当于咽喉和鼻。
（4）对耳轮体：相当于躯干。
（5）对耳轮上脚：相当于下肢。
（6）对耳轮下脚：相当于臀部。
（7）耳舟：相当于上肢。
（8）三角窝：相当于盆腔和内生殖器。
（9）耳轮脚：相当于膈肌。

10）耳轮脚周围：相当于消化道。

11）耳甲艇：相当于腹腔。

12）耳甲腔：相当于胸腔。

2. The Distribution Rule of Auricular Points and Areas

The auricle is just like a fetus with the head downwards and buttocks upwards (Fig. 2 - 15). Each part of the body has a corresponding auricular point or area on the auricular surface. These points and areas reflect the physical and pathological condition of the body and can be stimulated to regulate dysfunction of their corresponding body parts.

(1) *The lobe*: Corresponds to the head and face.

(2) *The antitragus*: Corresponds to the head and brain.

(3) *The tragus*: Corresponds to the throat and internal nose.

(4) *The body of the antihelix*: Corresponds to the trunk.

(5) *The superior crus of the antihelix*: Corresponds to the lower limbs.

(6) *The inferior crus of the helix*: Corresponds to the buttocks.

(7) *The scaphoid fossa*: Corresponds to the upper limbs.

(8) *The triangular fossa*: Corresponds to the pelvic cavity and the internal genitals.

(9) *The crus of the helix*: Cor-responds to the diaphragm.

(10) *The peripheral crus of the helix*: Corresponds to the digestive tract.

(11) *The superior concha*: Corresponds to the abdominal cavity.

(12) *The inferior concha*: Corresponds to the thoracic cavity.

3. 耳穴定位和主治（图 2 - 16）

耳轮脚和耳轮部

耳中（膈）

定位　耳轮脚处。

主治　呃逆，荨麻疹，皮肤瘙痒症，小儿遗尿，咳血，黄疸。

3. Locations and Indications of Auricular Points (Fig. 2 - 16)

The helix crus and helix

Middle Ear (Diaphragm)

Location: On the helix crus.

Indications: Hiccups, urticaria, cutaneouspruritis, infantile enuresis, hemoptysis, jaundice.

直肠（直肠下段）

定位　近屏上切迹的耳轮处，与大肠穴同一水平。

主治　便秘，腹泻，脱肛，痔疮，里急后重。

Rectum (Lower Rectum)

Location: On the helix close to the notch superior to the tragus, at the level with point Large Intestine.

Indications: Constipation, diarrhea,

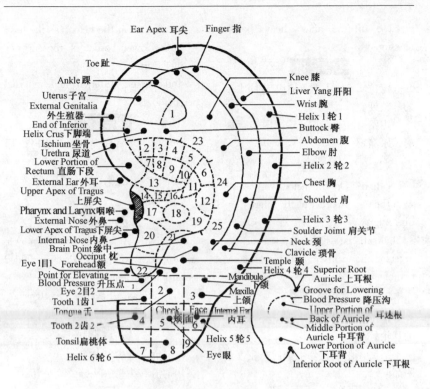

1. Shenmen 神门　　　2. Bladder 膀胱　　　3. Kidney 肾

4. Pancreas 胰　　　　5. Liver 肝　　　　　6. Spleen 脾

7. Large Intestine 大肠　8. Appendix 阑尾　　9. Small Intestine 小肠

10. Duodenum 十二指肠　11. Stomach 胃　　　12. Spleen 脾

13. Septum 膈　　　　14. Mouth 口　　　　15. Esophagus 食管

16. Cardiac Orifice 贲门　17. Trachea 气管　　18. Heart 心

19. Lung 肺　　　　　20. Sanjiao 三焦　　　21. Brain 脑

22. Intertragus 屏间　　23. Sacral Vertebra 骶腰椎

24. Thoracic Vertebra 胸椎　25. Cervical Vertebra 颈椎

图 2 - 16　常用耳穴分布示意图

Fig. 2 - 16　The Commonly Used Otopoints

prolapse of the anus, hemorrhoids, tenesmus.

尿　　道

定位　与对耳轮下脚下缘同水平的耳轮处。

主治　遗尿，尿频，尿急，尿痛，尿潴留。

Urethra

Location: On the helix at the level with the upper border of the inferior antihelix crus.

Indications: Enuresis, frequency, urgency and pain of urination, retention of urine

外生殖器

定位　与对耳轮下脚上缘同水平的耳轮处。

主治　阳痿，外生殖器炎症，会阴部湿疹。

External Genitalia

Location: On the helix, at the level with the upper border of the inferior antihelix crus.

Indications: Impotence, inflammation of external genital organs, eczema of the perineum.

耳　尖　前

定位　与对耳轮上脚下缘同水平的耳轮处。

主治　内、外痔。

Front Ear Apex (Hemorrhoidal Nucleus)

Location: On the helix, at the level with the lower border of the superior antihelix crus.

Indications: Internal and external hemorrhoids.

耳　尖

定位　将耳轮向耳屏对折时，耳郭上尖端处。

主治　发热，高血压，目赤肿痛，麦粒肿。

Ear Apex

Location: At the tip of the auricle and superior to the helix when folded towards the tragus.

Indications: Fever, hypertension, conjunctivitis, hordeolum.

肝　阳

定位　耳轮结节处。

主治　头晕，头痛，高血压。

Liver Yang

Location: At the auricular tubercle.

Indications: Dizziness, headache, hypertension.

轮 1～轮 6

定位　自耳轮结节下缘至耳垂正中下缘分成 5 等份，从上到下 6 点分别为轮 1、轮 2、轮 3、轮 4、轮 5、轮 6。

主治　发热，急性扁桃体炎，高血压。

Helix 1～Helix 6

Location: Region from the lower

border of the auricular tubercle to the midpoint of the lower border of the lobule and is divided into five equal parts. The points making the divisions are respectively helix 1, 2, 3, 4, 5 and 6.

Indications: Fever, acute tonsillitis, hypertension.

耳舟部

指

定位　耳舟顶端。

主治　指部疾患，如手指疼痛、麻木。

The scapha

Finger

Location: At the top of the scapha.

Indications: Disorders of the fingers such as pain and numbness, etc.

风溪（过敏区，荨麻疹点）

定位　指与腕两穴之间。

主治　荨麻疹，皮肤瘙痒症，哮喘，过敏性鼻炎。

Wind Stream (Allergic area, Urticaria Point)

Location: Between Finger and Wrist.

Indications: Urticaria, cutaneous pruritus, asthma, allergic rhinitis.

腕

定位　在平耳轮结节处的耳舟部。

主治　腕部扭伤，肿痛。

Wrist

Location: In the scapha, at the same level with the top of the auricle tubercle.

Indications: Wrist sprain, pain and swelling at the area of the wrist.

肘

定位　在手指穴和锁骨穴之间。

主治　肘痛。

Elbow

Location: Midway between the Finger and the Clavicle.

Indications: Pain in the elbow.

肩

定位　肘与锁骨之间。

主治　肩关节疼痛。

Shoulder

Location: Midway between Elbow and Clavicle.

Indications: Pain in the shoulder joint.

肩 关 节

定位　在肩与锁骨之间。

主治　肩关节疼痛。

Shoulder Joint

Location: Between Shoulder and Clavicle.

Indications: Pain in the shoulder joint.

锁 骨

定位　在轮屏切迹同一水平线的耳舟部。

主治　相应部位疼痛，肩周炎。

Clavicle

Location: In the scapha, at the level with the helixtragic notch.

Indications: Pain at the corresponding area, periarthritis of the shoulder.

对耳轮上脚部

趾

定位　对耳轮上脚的外上角。

主治　足趾疼痛，甲沟炎。

The superior antihelix crus

Toe

Location: Lateral and superior angle of the superior antihelix crus.

Indications: Pain of the toe, paronychia.

跟

定位　对耳轮上脚的内上角。

主治　足跟痛。

Heel

Location: Medial and superior angle of the superior antihelix crus.

Indications: Heel pain.

踝

定位　跟与膝两穴之中部。

主治　踝部疾患，距小腿关节（踝关节）扭伤。

Ankle

Location: Midway between Heel and Knee.

Indications: Diseases at the corresponding part of the body, ankle sprain.

膝

定位　对耳轮上脚的中部。

主治　膝关节肿痛。

Knee

Location: Middle portion of the superior antihelix crus.

Indications: Pain and swelling of the knee joint.

髋

定位　对耳轮上脚的下 1/3 处。

主治　髋关节疼痛，坐骨神经痛。

Hip

Location: At the inferior 1/3 of the superior antihelix crus.

Indications: Pain of the hip joint, sciatica.

对耳轮下脚部

臀

定位　对耳轮下脚的外 1/3 处。

主治　腰骶疼痛，坐骨神经痛。

The inferior antihelix crus

Buttocks

Location: At the lateral 1/3 of the inferior antihelix crus.

Indications: Pain of the lumbosacral region, sciatica.

坐　骨

定位　对耳轮下脚的中 1/3 处。

主治　坐骨神经痛。

Sciatic Nerve (Ischium)

Location: At the middle 1/3 of the inferior antihelix crus.

Indication: Sciatica.

交感 (下脚端)

定位　对耳轮下脚的末端。

主治　心悸，自汗，自主神经功能紊乱，胃肠痉挛，心绞痛，输尿管结石绞痛。

Sympathesis (End of Infrior Antihelix Crus)

Location: The terminus of the inferior antihelix crus.

Indications: Palpitation, spontaneous sweating, functional disorders of the autonomous nervous system, gastrointestinal pain and spasm, angina pectoris, ureteral colic.

对耳轮部

颈　椎

定位　屏轮切迹至对耳轮上下脚分叉处平均分为 5 等份，下 1/5 为颈椎。

主治　落枕，颈椎病。

The antihelix

Cervical Vertebrae

Location: A curved line from the helixtragic notch to the bifurcation of the superior and inferior antihelix crura can be divided into five equal segments. The lower 1/5 of it is Cervical Vertebrae.

Indications: Stiffneck, cervical spondylopathy.

胸　椎

定位　屏轮切迹至对耳轮上下脚分叉处平均分为5等份，中2/5 为胸椎。

主治　胸胁疼痛，乳腺炎，泌乳不足，经前乳房胀痛。

Thoracic Vertebrae

Location: A curved line from the helixtragic notch to the bifurcation of the superior and inferior antihelix crura can be divided into five equal segments. The middle 2/5 of it is Thoracic Vetebrae.

Indications: Pain in the thoracic and hypochondriac regions, mastitis, insufficient lactation, premenstrual mammary distension and pain.

腰 骶 椎

定位　屏轮切迹至对耳轮上下脚分叉处平均分为 5 等份，上 2/5 为腰骶椎。

主治　腰腿痛，腹痛，腹膜炎。

Lumbosacral Vertebrae

Location: A curved line from the helixtragic notch to the bifurcation of the superior and inferior antihelix crura can be divided into five equal segments. The upper 2/5 of it is Lumbosacral Vertebrae.

Indications: Pain of the lower back and leg, abdominal pain, peritonitis.

颈

定位　屏轮切迹偏耳舟侧处。

主治 落枕，颈部肿痛，甲状腺肿大。

Neck

Location: At the notch between antihelix and antitragus, near scapha.

Indications: Stiffneck, swelling and pain of the neck, goiter.

胸

定位 对耳轮上与屏上切迹同水平处。

主治 胸胁痛，乳腺炎，泌乳不足。

Chest

Location: On the antihelix, at the level with supratragic notch.

Indications: Pain in the chest and hypochondriac region, mastitis, insufficient lactation.

腹

定位 对耳轮上与耳轮下脚下缘同水平处。

主治 腹痛，腹胀，腹泻，妇科疾病。

Abdomen

Location: On the antihelix, at the level with the lower border of the inferior antihelix crus.

Indications: Abdominal pain and distension, diarrhea, acute lumbar sprain, women's diseases.

三角窝部

神　　门

定位 对耳轮上、下脚分叉处，三角窝外 1/3 处。

主治 失眠，多梦，疼痛。

The triangular fossa

Shenmen

Location: At the bifurcating point between the superior and inferior antihelix crus and the lateral 1/3 of the triangular fossa.

Indications: Insomnia, dream-disturbed sleep, pain.

盆　　腔

定位 对耳轮上、下脚分叉处内侧稍下方。

主治 盆腔炎，附件炎，月经不调，下腹疼痛，腹胀等。

Pelvic Cavity

Location: Slightly inferior to the medial side of the bifurcating point between the superior and inferior antihelix crus.

Indications: Pelvic inflammation, annexitis, irregular menstruation, pain in the lower abdomen, abdominal distension, etc.

角窝中（喘点、肝炎点）

定位 三角窝中 1/3。
主治 哮喘。

Middle Triangular Fossa (Asthma Point Hepatitis Point)

Location: On the middle 1/3 of the triangular fossa.

Indications: Asthma.

内生殖器（子宫、精宫）

定位　三角窝底之中部凹陷处。

主治　月经不调，痛经，白带过多，功能性子宫出血，遗精，早泄，前列腺炎。

Internal Genitalia (Uterus, Seminal Palace)

Location: In the depression in the midpoint of the bottom of the triangular fossa.

Indications: Irregular menstruation, dysmenorrhea, leukorrhagia, dysfunctional uterine bleeding, nocturnal emission, prospermia, prostatitis.

角窝上（降压点）

定位　三角窝前上方。

主治　高血压。

Superior Triangular Fossa (Blood Pressure Lowering Point)

Location: Anteriosuperior to the triangular fossa.

Indications: Hypertension.

耳屏部

外　耳

定位　屏上切迹近耳轮部。

主治　外耳道炎，中耳炎，耳鸣，眩晕。

The tragus

External Ear

Location: On the supratragic notch close to the helix.

Indications: Inflammation of the external auditory canal, otitis media, tinnitus, dizziness.

外　鼻

定位　耳屏正中。

主治　鼻疖，鼻塞，鼻炎，单纯性肥胖症等。

External Nose

Location: In the center of the tragus.

Indications: Nasal furuncle, nasal obstruction, rhinitis, simple obesity, etc.

屏　尖

定位　耳屏上部隆起的尖端。
主治　发热，疼痛等。

Tragic Apex

Location: At the tip of the upper protuberance on the border of the tragus.

Indications: Fever, pain, etc.

下屏尖（肾上腺）

定位　耳屏下部隆起的尖端。

主治　风湿性关节炎，腮腺炎，下颌淋巴结炎，瘙痒，眩晕，疼痛，听力减退。

Infratragic Apex (Adrenal)

Location: At the tip of the lower protubercle on the border of the tragus.

Indications: Rheumatic arthritis, mumps, mandibular lymphnoditis, pruritus, dizziness, pain, hypoacusis.

咽　喉

定位　耳屏内侧面的上 1/2 处。

主治　声音嘶哑，急、慢性咽炎，扁桃体炎等。

Pharynx-Larynx

Location: Upper half of the medial aspect of the tragus.

Indications: Hoarseness, acute and chronic pharyngitis, tonsillitis, etc.

内　鼻

定位　耳屏内侧面的下 1/2 处。

主治　鼻炎，副鼻窦炎，鼻衄。

Internal Nose

Location: Lower half of the medial aspect of the tragus.

Indications: Rhinitis, paranasal sinusitis, epistaxis.

对耳屏部

对屏尖（平喘）

定位　对耳屏的尖端。

主治　哮喘，支气管炎，咳嗽，腮腺炎，皮肤瘙痒症，附睾炎。

The antitragus

Antitragic Apex (Soothing Asthma)

Location: At the tip of the antitragus.

Indications: Asthma, bronchitis, cough, mumps, cutaneous pruritus, epididymitis.

缘中（脑点）

定位　对屏尖与屏轮切迹之中点。

主治　智能发育不全，遗尿，耳源性眩晕，侏儒症，糖尿病。

Middle Border (Brain)

Location: Midpoint between the antitragic apex and helixtragic notch.

Indications: Oligophrenia, enuresis, auditory vertigo, dwarfism, diabetes.

枕

定位　对耳屏外侧的后上方。

主治　头晕，头痛，失眠，支气管哮喘，癫痫，神经衰弱。

Occiput

Location: At the posterior superior corner of the lateral aspect of the antitragus.

Indications: Dizziness, headache, insomnia, bronchial asthma, epilepsy, neurasthenia.

颞（太阳）

定位　对耳屏外侧的中部。

主治　偏头痛，神经系统疾患，皮肤病，晕厥。

Temple (Taiyang)

Location: At the midpoint of the lateral aspect of the antitragus.

Indications: Migraine, disorders of the nervous system, skin problem, faintness.

睾丸（卵巢）

定位　对耳屏内侧面前下方。

主治　生殖系统疾病。

Testis (Ovary)

Location：Anteroinferior to the medial aspect of the antitragus.

Indications：Disorders of the genital system.

额

定位　对耳屏外侧的前下方。

主治　头痛，头晕，失眠，多梦。

Forehead

Location：At the anterior inferior corner of the lateral aspect of the antitragus.

Indications：Headache, dizziness, insomnia, dreamdisturbed sleep.

脑（皮质下）

定位　对耳屏内侧面。

主治　智能发育不全，失眠多梦，肾虚耳鸣，假性近视，神经衰弱，消化系统疾病。

Brain（Subcortex）

Location：On the medial aspect of the antitragus.

Indications：Oligophrenia, insomnia, dream-disturbed sleep, tinnitus due to kidney deficiency, pseudomyopia, neurosism, digestive diseases.

耳轮周围部

口

定位　外耳道口后上方。

主治　面瘫，口腔炎，胆囊炎，胆石症。

Periphery helix crus

Mouth

Location：Close to the posterior and superior border of the orifice of the external auditory meatus.

Indications：Facial paralysis, stomatitis, cholecystitis, cholelithiasis.

食　管

定位　耳轮脚下方中 2/3 处。

主治　食管炎，食管痉挛。

Esophagus

Location：At the middle 2/3 of the inferior aspect of the helix crus.

Indications：Esophagitis, esophagisms, vomiting.

贲　门

定位　耳轮脚下方处 1/3 处。

主治　贲门痉挛，神经性呕吐，恶心。

Cardiac Orifice

Location：At the lateral 1/3 of the inferior aspect of the helix crus.

Indications：Cardiospasm, nervous vomiting, nausea.

胃

定位　耳轮脚消失处周围。

主治　胃痉挛，胃炎，胃溃疡，失眠，牙痛，消化不良。

Stomach

Location：Around the area where the helix crus terminates.

Indications：Gastrospasm, gastritis, gastric ulcer, insomnia, toothache, indigestion, vomiting, nausea.

十二指肠

定位　耳轮脚上方外 1/3 处。

主治　十二指肠溃疡，幽门痉挛，胆囊炎，胆石症。

Duodenum

Location: At the lateral 1/3 of the superior aspect of the helix crus.

Indications: Duodernal ulcer, pylorospasm, cholecystitis, cholelithiasis.

小　肠

定位　耳轮脚上方中 1/3 处。

主治　消化不良，心悸等。

Small Intestine

Location: At the middle 1/3 of the superior aspect of the helix crus.

Indications: Indigestion, palpitation, etc.

大　肠

定位　耳轮脚上方内 1/3 处。

主治　腹泻，便秘，咳嗽，痤疮。

Large Intestine

Location: At the medial 1/3 of the superior aspect of the helix crus.

Indications: Diarrhea, constipation, cough, acne.

阑　尾

定位　小肠与大肠穴之间。

主治　阑尾炎，腹泻。

Appendix

Location: Between Small Intestine and Large Intestine.

Indications: Appendicitis, diarrhea.

耳甲艇部

肾

定位　对耳轮下脚下缘，小肠穴上方。

主治　泌尿、生殖、妇科疾病，腰痛，耳鸣，失眠，眩晕。

The cymba conchae

Kidney

Location: On the lower border of the inferior antihelix crus, directly above Small Intestine.

Indications: Diseases of the urinary and genital systems, gynecopathy, lumbar pain, tinnitus, insomnia, dizziness.

输　尿　管

定位　肾与膀胱穴之间。

主治　输尿管结石绞痛。

Ureter

Location: Between Kidney and Bladder.

Indications: Colic pain of the ureter calculus.

膀　胱

定位　对耳轮下脚的前下方。

主治　足太阳膀胱经病，腰痛，膀胱炎，尿潴留，后头痛。

Bladder

Location: On the antero-inferior

border of the inferior antihelix crus.

Indications: Diseases of the Bladder Channel of Foot-Taiyang, lower back pain, cystitis, retention of urine, occipital pain.

艇角（前列腺）

定位　耳甲艇内上角。

主治　前列腺炎，尿道炎。

Angle of Cymba Conchae (Prostate)

Location: At the medial superior angle of the cymba conchae.

Indications: Prostatitis, urethritis.

肝

定位　耳甲艇的外下方。

主治　胁痛，眩晕，眼疾，月经不调，痛经。

Liver

Location: On the lateral inferior border of the Cymba conchae.

Indications: Hypochondriac pain, dizziness, diseases of the eye, irregular menstruation, dysmenorrhea.

胰胆（左为胰，右为胆）

定位　在肝、肾两穴之间。

主治　胰腺炎，糖尿病，胆道疾病。

Pancreas and Biliary Tract (Pancreas-left, Biliary Tract-right)

Location: Between Liver and Kidney.

Indications: Pancreatitis, diabetes mellitus, diseases of the biliary tract.

耳甲腔部

心

定位　耳甲腔中心凹陷处。

主治　心悸，失眠，癔症，心绞痛，心律不齐，神经衰弱，口舌生疮。

The cavum conchae

Heart

Location: In the central depression of the cavum conchae.

Indications: Palpitation, insomnia, hysteria, angina pectoris, arrhythmia, neurosism, stomatitis.

肺

定位　耳甲腔中心凹陷处周围。

主治　咳嗽，气喘，胸闷，皮肤瘙痒症，便秘，肥胖症。

Lung

Location: Around the central depression of the cavum conchae.

Indications: Cough, asthma, chest stuffiness, cutaneous pruritus, constipation, obesity.

气　　管

定位　外耳道口与心穴之间。

主治　咳嗽，气喘。

Trachea

Location: Between the orifice of the external auditory meatus and Heart.

Indications: Cough, asthma.

脾

定位　耳甲腔外上方。

主治 腹胀，慢性腹泻，消化不良，月经不调，食欲不振。

Spleen

Location: At the lateral and superior aspect of the cavum conchae.

Indications: Abdominal distension, chronic diarrhea, indigestion, irregular menstruation, anorexia.

屏间（内分泌）

定位 耳甲腔底部，屏间切迹内。

主治 痛经，阳痿，月经不调，更年期综合征，内分泌功能紊乱。

Intertragus（Endocrine）

Location: At the base of the cavum conchae in the intertragic notch.

Indications: Dysmenorrhea, impotence, irregular menstruation, climacteric syndrome, dysfunction of endocrine.

三   焦

定位 耳甲腔底部，屏间切迹上方。

主治 便秘，浮肿，腹胀，手臂外侧疼痛，单纯性肥胖症。

Sanjiao

Location: At the base of the cavum conchae, superior to the intertragic notch.

Indications: Constipation, edema, abdominal distension, pain of the lateral aspect of the hand and arm, simple obesity.

耳垂部

目1

定位 屏间切迹前下方。

主治 青光眼，假性近视。

The ear lobule

Eye1

Location: On the anterior and inferior side of the intertragic notch.

Indications: Glaucoma, Pseudomyopia.

目2

定位 屏间切迹后下方。

主治 屈光不正，假性近视。

Eye 2

Location: On the posterior and inferior aspect of the intertragic notch.

Indications: Ametropia, pseudomyopia.

切迹下（升压点）

定位 屏间切迹直下方。

主治 低血压，虚脱。

Lower Tragic Notch（Elevating Blood Pressure Point）

Location: On the inferior aspect of the intertragic notch.

Indications: Hypotension, collapse.

牙

定位 耳垂正面，从屏间切迹软骨下缘至耳垂下缘画3条等距离水平钱，再在第二水平线上画2条垂直等分线，由前向后，自上而下地把耳垂分为 9 个区，第 1 区为牙。

主治　牙痛，牙周炎，低血压。

Tooth

Location: A grid of nine equal sections is delineated on the frontal surface of the earlobe. Draw three equidistant horizontal lines below the lower border of the cartilege of the notch between the tragus and the antitragus and two equidistant vertical lines. The sections are numbered from anterior to posterior and from top to bottom. Tooth is located in the first section of the earlobe grid.

Indications: Toothache, periodonitits, hypotension.

舌

定位　耳垂正面第 2 区。

主治　舌炎，口腔炎。

Tongue

Location: On the second section of the earlobe grid.

Indications: Glossitis, stomatitis.

颌

定位　耳垂正面第 3 区。

主治　牙痛，颌关节功能紊乱症。

Jaw

Location: On the third section of the earlobe grid.

Indications: Toothache, dysfunction of the temperomandibular joint.

垂　前

定位　耳垂正面第 4 区。

主治　神经衰弱，牙痛。

Anterior Lobe

Location: On the fourth section of the earlobe grid.

Indications: Neurosism, toothache.

眼

定位　耳垂正面第 5 区。

主治　急性结膜炎，电光性眼炎，麦粒肿，假性近视。

Eye

Location: On the fifth section of the earlobe grid.

Indications: Acute conjunctivitis, electric ophthalmitis, stye, psuedomyopia.

内　耳

定位　耳垂正面第 6 区。

主治　内耳眩晕，耳鸣，听力减退。

Internal Ear

Location: On the sixth section of the earlobe grid.

Indications: Meniere's disease, tinnitus, hearing loss.

面　颊

定位　耳垂正面第 5、第 6 区交界线周围。

主治　周围性面瘫，三叉神经痛，痤疮，扁平疣。

Cheek

Location: On the border between the fifth and sixth section of the earlobe grid.

Indications: Peripheral facial paralysis, trigeminal neuralgia, acne, flat wart.

扁 桃 体

定位　耳垂正面第 8 区。
主治　扁桃体炎，咽炎。

Tonsil

Location: On the eighth section of the earlobe grid.

Indications: Tonsilitis, pharyngitis.

耳背部

上 耳 根

定位　耳根最上缘。
主治　鼻衄。

The back auricle

Upper Ear Root

Location: On the upper portion of the ear root.

Indications: Epistaxis.

耳 迷 根

定位　耳背与乳突交界的根部，与耳轮脚对应处。

主治　胆囊炎，胆石症，胆道蛔虫症，鼻塞，心动过速，腹痛，腹泻。

Root of Ear Vagus

Location: On the juncture of the dorsal surface of the auricle and the mastoid process, corresponding to the crus of the helix.

Indications: Cholecystitis, gallstones, biliary ascariasis, nasal obstruction, tachycardia, abdominal pain, diarrhea.

下 耳 根

定位　耳根最下缘。
主治　低血压。

Lower Ear Root

Location: On the lower portion of the ear root.

Indications: Hypotension.

耳背沟（降压沟）

定位　对耳轮上、下脚及对耳轮主干在耳背呈"Y"字型凹沟内。

主治　高血压，皮肤瘙痒症。

Groove of Dorsal Surface (Blood Pressure Lowering Point)

Location: The groove formed by the antihelix and its two branches on the dorsal surface of the auricle.

Indications: Hypertension, cutaneous pruritis.

耳 背 心

定位　在耳背上部。
主治　心悸，失眠，多梦。

Heart of Dorsal Surface

Location: On the upper portion of the dorsal surface of the auricle.

Indications: Palpifation, insomnia, nightmares.

耳 背 脾

定位　耳轮脚消失处耳背部。

主治　胃痛，消化不良，食欲不振。

Spleen of Dorsal Surface

Location: On the dorsal surface of the auricle close to the terminus of the crus of the helix.

Indications: Gastric pain, indigestion, poor appetite.

耳 背 肝

定位　在耳背脾的外侧。

主治　胆囊炎，胆石症，胁痛。

Liver of Dorsal Surface

Location: On the dorsal surface of the auricle lateral to Spleen of Dorsal Surface

Indications: Cholecystitis, gallstone, hypochondriac pain.

耳 背 肺

定位　在耳背脾的内侧。

主治　咳嗽，哮喘，皮肤瘙痒症。

Lung of Dorsal Surface

Location: On the dorsal surface of the auricle medial to Spleen of Dorsal Surface.

Indications: Cough, asthma, cutaneous pruritus.

耳 背 肾

定位　在耳背下部。

主治　头晕，头痛，神经衰弱。

Kidney of Dorsal Surface

Location: On the lower portion of the dorsal surface of the auricle.

Indications: Dizziness, headache, neurosis.

4．耳针的临床应用

（1）选穴原则

1）根据病变部位取穴：选取与病变部位对应的耳穴是耳针取穴的重要原则。例如：选额治疗前额头痛，选眼治疗各种眼病，选大肠治疗各种大肠疾病。每个脏器或组织的各个部分在该脏器或组织在耳郭的对应区内均有对应点，并呈倒置分布。例如：胃区近耳轮脚处代表胃小弯，近十二指肠处代表幽门部。腹区近对耳轮分叉处代表下腹部，近胸区处代表上腹部，中间部分代表中腹部。因此，胃小弯部的溃疡应取与胃小弯对应处，胃幽门部溃疡应取与幽门部对应处，下腹部疼痛应取与下腹部对应处，上腹部疼痛取与上腹部对应处，中腹部疼痛取与中腹部对应处。一般而言，某一穴区内的最敏感反应点就是对应于该穴区脏器或组织的病变部位。所以，可以通过运用耳穴诊断方法探查阳性反应，尤其是压痛，从而明确对应于病变部位的点，为取得疗效奠定基础。

4. Clinical Application of Ear Acupuncture

（1）*Principles for the selection*

of auricular points

1) According to the location of the diseased or affected area of the body.

Choosing auricular points which correspond to the location of the diseased or affected part of the body is an important principle in auricular therapy. For example Forhead is the major point used for treating frontal headache. Eye is used for all eye diseases and large intestine for all problems of the large intestine. Every part of an organ or tissue has a corresponding point on the organ or tissue's corresponding auricular area. The distribution of these corresponding auricular points, like that of the auricular areas, is upside down in relation to the body. For instance, the area of Stomach adjoining the crus of the helix represents the lesser curvature of the stomach. The area of Stomach adjoining Duodenum represents the pylorus. The area of Abdomen adjoining the beginning of the branches of the antihelix represents the lower abdomen. The middle part of Abdomen represents the middle abdomen, and the area of Abdomen adjoining Chest represents the upper abdomen. Accordingly, the auricular point corresponding to the lesser curvature of the stomach is chosen for treating gastric ulcer of the lesser curvature of the stomach. The point corresponding to the pylorus is chosen for treating gastric ulcer of the pylorus. The point corresponding to the lower abdomen is chosen for treating pain in the lower abdomen. The point corresponding to the middle abdomen is used for treating pain in the middle abdomen, etc.

Generally speaking, the most sensitive point on an auricular area usually indicates the precise location of the problem in the corresponding organ or tissue. Consequently, the use of auricular diagnostic methods to locate positive signs, especially tenderness, on the auricle can determine the specific location of a disease or disorder of the body and provide a basis for good therapeutic results.

2) 根据中医理论取穴：耳郭上五脏六腑的十一个穴区具有现代医学和中医学双重含义，其临床运用尤其体现了中医学的特点。这些穴区临床应用甚广，它们不但可以治疗各自脏腑本身的病症，还能分别治疗与其相关组织的病症。为了方便自学，现将脏腑的生理功能及其耳穴主治介绍于下。

心

心主血脉。心区能促进血液循环，可用于治疗冠心病、心律不齐、高血压、脉管炎及雷诺病等。

心藏神。心区能镇静安神，可用于治疗神经衰弱、癔症及自主神经功能紊乱。

心之液为汗。心区能调节汗液分泌，可用于治疗多汗症、自汗或盗汗。

心开窍于舌。心区可用于治疗声音嘶哑、复发性口腔溃疡及舌炎。

心之华在面。心区可用于治疗气血不足导致的面色苍白及心血淤阻导致的面色紫暗。

心经分布于前胸及上肢内侧后缘。心区可用于治疗这些部位的疼痛。

2）According to the Principles of traditional Chinese medicine

The eleven auricular areas corresponding to the five Zang and six Fu organs are especially significant in traditional Chinese medicine. These auricular areas are used extensively in clinical practice, not only to treat disorders of their corresponding Zangfu organs but also to treat the tissues with which the Zangfu organs connect. The physiology of the Zangfu organs and indications of their corresponding auricular areas are described here at length for the benefit of beginners and those in independent study.

Heart

The heart governs the blood and blood vessels, so treating Heart can improve blood circulation. It is used to treat coronary heart disease, arrhythmia, hypertension, angiitis, and Raynaud's disease.

The mind resides in the heart so treating Heart can calm the mind. It is used to treat neurosism, hysteria, and functional disturbance of the autonomic nervous system.

The fluid of the heart is perspiration so treating Heart can regulate secretion of perspiration. It is used to treat hyperhydrosis and spontaneous or night sweating.

The heart opens into the tongue so Heart can be used to treat hoarseness, recurrent ulcer of the mouth, and glossitis.

The heart nourishes the face so Heart can be used to treat pale complexion caused by deficiency of qi and blood or purple complexion caused by blockage of stagnant blood in the heart.

The heart meridian distributes to the prothorax and the lower border of the medial side of the upper limbs so Heart can be used to treat pain in these regions.

肝

肝主疏泄。肝区可用于治疗因肝气郁滞导致的多种病症，包括神经衰弱、癔症等神志病，月经不调，痛经及乳腺囊性增生等妇科病，以及消化不良，腹胀，腹泻等消化系统病症。

肝藏血。肝区有储存血液和调节血量的作用，可用于治疗贫血、便血。

肝之液为泪。肝区能调节泪液分

泌，可用于治疗迎风流泪、目干。

肝开窍于目。肝区可用于治疗目疾，如青光眼、假性近视、结膜炎及电光性眼炎等。

肝主筋。肝区可用于治疗筋病，如面肌抽搐、癫痫、抽搐。

肝经分布于外生殖器、少腹、胸胁及头顶部。肝区可用于治疗这些部位的病症。

Liver

The liver governs the flow of qi in the body so Liver can be used to treat various conditions caused by stagnation of the liver-qi including nervous disorders such as neurosism, hysteria, gynecological problems such as irregular menstruation, dysmenorrhea, hyperplasia of the mammary glands, digestive disorders such as indigestion, abdominal distension, and diarrhea.

The liver stores blood so treating Liver can tonify the blood. It is used to treat anemia and hematochezia.

The fluid of the liver is tears so treating Liver can regulate the secretion of tears. It is used to treat epiphora induced by wind and dryness of the eyes.

The liver opens into the eyes so Liver can be used to treat eye problems such as glaucoma, pseudomyopia, conjunctivitis, and electric opthalmitis.

The liver nourishes the tendons so Liver can be used to treat tendon problems such as facial spasm and epileptic spasm.

The liver is connected internally and externally with the gallbladder so Liver can be used to treat gallbladder problems such as cholecystitis, gall stones, and biliary ascariasis.

The liver meridian distributes to the external genitals, bilateral lower abdomen, hypochondriac region, chest, and top of the head so Liver can be used to treat diseases and disorders of these regions of the body.

脾

脾主运化水谷。脾区能促消化、利水湿，可用于治疗腹泻、腹胀、腹痛、消化不良、儿童厌食、水肿及肥胖。

脾主统血。脾区可用于治疗出血性病症，如功能性子宫出血、月经过多、血小板减少性紫癜及内脏出血。

脾主升清。脾区可用于治疗因中气下陷所致的胃下垂、脱肛或子宫脱垂等病症。

脾之液为唾。脾区能调节唾液分泌，可用于治疗流涎症及因脾气虚所致的口干。

脾开窍于口。脾区可用于治疗复发性口腔溃疡、舌炎及口唇干燥。

脾主肌肉四肢。脾区可用于治疗肌肉萎缩及四肢乏力酸痛等症。

脾与胃相表里。脾区可治疗胃腑病症，如胃痛、胃脘胀满及反酸。

脾经循行于下肢内侧前缘。脾区可用于治疗该部位的疼痛。

Spleen

The spleen dominates transportation and transformation of water and food so treating Spleen can remove dampness and strengthen the digestive function. It is used to treat diarrhea, abdominal distension or pain, indigestion, childhood anorexia, edema, and to stimulate weight loss.

The spleen governs the blood in the meridian so Spleen can be used to treat hemorrhagic problems such as dysfunctional uterine bleeding, hypermenorrhea, thrambocytopenic purpura, and hemorrhage of the internal organs.

The spleen lifts clear-qi so Spleen can be used to treat diseases caused by sinking of the qi in the middle jiao such as gastroptosis and prolapse of the anus or uterus.

The fluid of the spleen is saliva so Spleen can be used to regulate the secretion of saliva. It is used to treat ptyalism and dry mouth caused by deficiency of the spleen-qi.

The spleen opens into the mouth so Spleen can be used to treat recurrent ulcer of the mouth, glossitis, and dryness of the lips.

The spleen nourishes the muscles and limbs so Spleen is used to treat muscular atrophy, weakness and soreness of the limbs.

The spleen is connected internally and externally with the stomach so Spleen can be used to treat gastric problems such as stomachache, epigastric distension, and regurgitation.

The spleen meridian distributes to the anterior border of the medial side of the lower limbs so Spleen can be used to treat pain in these regions.

肺

肺司呼吸。肺区可用于治疗呼吸系统病症，如咳嗽气喘、胸闷及感冒。

肺主通调水道。肺区可用于治疗因水液代谢障碍所致的水肿、尿潴留。

肺主皮毛，司汗孔开阖。肺区可用于治疗皮肤病、自汗及盗汗。

肺开窍于鼻。肺区可用于治疗鼻炎。

肺与大肠相表里。肺区可用于治疗便秘、腹泻、痢疾。

肺经分布于前胸、咽喉及上肢内侧前缘。肺区可用于治疗这些部位的病症。

Lung

The lung governs the breath so treating Lung can regulate breathing. It is used to treat respiratory problems such as cough, asthma, feeling of fullness in the chest, and the common cold.

The Lung regulates drainage of water so Lung can be used to treat dysfunctions of water metabolism such as edema and retention of urine.

The lung nourishers the skin and controls the opening and closing of the pores so Lung can be used to treat skin diseases and spontaneous night sweating.

The lung opens into the nose so Lung can be used to treat rhinitis.

The Lung is connected internally and externally with the large intestine so Lung can be used to treat constipation, diarrhea, and dysentary.

The Lung meridian distributes to the prothorax, throat, and upper border of the medial side of the upper limbs so Lung can be used to treat diseases and disorders of these regions.

肾

肾藏精。肾区能补益精气，可用于治疗多种慢性虚弱性病症，如五更泄、哮喘、慢性支气管炎、腰痛。

肾主生殖。肾区可用于治疗遗精、阳痿、早泄、月经不调、习惯性流产、不育。

肾主水。肾区可用于治疗水肿、尿潴留、腹水及减肥。

肾主骨生髓。肾区可用于治疗颈椎病等骨质退行病变及精神疾病，如智力发育迟钝、老年性痴呆、神经衰弱、自主神经功能紊乱。

肾开窍于耳及前后二阴。肾区可用于治疗耳鸣、听力减退、梅尼埃病、外生殖器及肛门疾病。

肾经循行分布于下肢内侧后缘、胸及咽喉部。肾区可用于治疗慢性咽炎、胸痛及下肢内侧痛。

Kidney

The Kidney stores essence so treating Kidney can tonify the essence. It is used to treat various chronic deficiency diseases such as predawn diarrhea, asthma, chronic bronchitis, and lumbago.

The Kidney governs reproduction so Kidney can be used to treat seminal emission, impotence, premature ejaculation, irregular menstruation, habitual miscarriage, and infertility.

The Kidney regulates water metabolism so Kidney can be used to treat edema, retention of urine, ascites, and to stimulate weight loss.

The Kidney nourishes the bones and produce bone marrow so Kidney can be used to treat degenerative conditions of the bones such as cervical spondylopathy as well as mental problems such as mental retardation, senile dementia, neurosism, and functional disturbance of the autonomic nervous system.

The Kidney opens into the ears, the anterior external genitals, and the anus so Kidney can be used to treat tinnitus, hearing loss, and Meniere's disease, as well as disorders of the external genitals and anus.

The Kidney is connected internally and externally with the urinary bladder so Kidney is usually combined with Urinary Bladder to treat urinary problems such as urinary tract infection, urinary stones, and retention or incontinence of urine.

The kidney meridian distributes to the posterior border of the medial side of the lower limbs, chest, and throat so Kidney can be used to treat chronic pharyngitis and pain in the chest or medial side of the lower limbs.

胆

胆主储存胆汁以助脾胃消化。胆区可用于治疗胆道感染、胆管梗阻、胆囊炎、胆石症、胆道蛔虫症、消化不良、腹胀及呕吐。

胆主决断。胆区可用于治疗犹豫不决、胆怯易惊及失眠、梦魇。

胆经分布于头部颞侧，胁肋及下肢外侧。胆区可用于治疗偏头痛、中耳炎、胁痛及坐骨神经痛。

Gallbladder

The gallbladder stores bile to enable the spleen and stomach to carry out digestion so Gallbladder can be used to treat biliary tract infection, obstruction of the biliary ducts, cholecystitis, gallstones, biliary ascariasis, indigestion, abdominal distension, and vomiting.

The gallbladder governs the power of decision so Gallbladder can be used to treat hesitation and timidity, insomnia, and nightmares.

The gallbladder meridian distributes to the temporal side of the head, the ears, hypochondriac region, and lateral side of the lower limbs so Gallbladder can be used to treat migraine, otitis media, pain in the hypochondriac region, and sciatica.

胃

胃主受纳腐熟水谷。胃区可用于治疗胃炎、胃溃疡、胃痉挛、胃肠功能低下、消化不良及儿童厌食。

胃主降浊。胃区可用于治疗恶心、呕吐、呃逆、嗳气、吞酸。

胃经分布于面，前额、牙齿、咽喉，乳房及下肢外侧前缘部分。胃区可用于治疗面肌抽搐、前头痛、牙痛、咽喉疼痛、乳腺炎及下肢部疼痛。

Stomach

The stomach receives and digests water and food so Stomach can be used to treat gastritis, gastric ulcer, gastric spasm, gastrointestinal dysfunction, indigestion, and childhood anorexia.

The stomach can pull down rebellious qi so Stomach can be used to treat nausea, vomiting, hiccups, belching, and acid regurgitation.

The stomach meridian distributes to the face, forehead, teeth, throat, breasts, and anteriolateral aspect of the lower limbs so Stomach can be used to treat facial spasm, frontal headache, toothache, sore throat, mastitis, and pain in the lower limbs.

小肠

小肠主消化吸收。小肠区可用于治疗消化不良、腹胀、儿童厌食。

小肠和心相表里，小肠可治疗因心火上炎所致的口腔溃疡、舌炎及神志病。

小肠经分布于上肢外侧后缘、肩胛区及颈部。小肠区可用于治疗上肢外下部疼痛、肩周炎及落枕。

Small Intestine

The small intestine governs digestion and absorption so Small Intestine can be used to treat indigestion, abdominal distension, and childhood anorexia.

The small intestine is connected internally and externally with the heart so small Intestine can be used to treat diseases caused by flaring-up of the heart-fire such as ulcerative stomatitis, glossitis, and various mental disorders.

The small intestine meridian distributes to the posterioexternal aspect of the upper limbs, the scapular region, and the back of the neck so small Intestine can be used to treat pain in these regions, stiff neck, and scapulohumeral periarthritis.

大肠

大肠主传导糟粕。大肠区可用于治疗便秘、腹泻、痢疾。

大肠与肺相表里。大肠区可助肺降逆气，用于治疗支气管炎、哮喘、皮肤病。

大肠分布于上肢外侧前缘、肩、牙齿及鼻部。大肠区可用于治疗前臂外侧疼痛、肩周炎、牙痛及鼻部病症。

Large Intestine

The large intestine governs transportation, so Large Intestine can be used to treat constipation, diarrhea, abdominal distension, and dysentary.

The large intestine is connected internally and externally with the lung so treating Large Intestine can help the lung to pull down rebellious qi. It is used to treat bronchitis, asthma, skin diseases, and nasal problems.

The large intestine meridian distributes to the anterioexternal aspect of the upper limbs, shoulders, teeth, and nose so Large Intestine can be used to treat pain in the anterioexternal region of the upper limbs, scapulohumeral periarthritis, toothache, and nasal problems.

膀胱

膀胱主储藏及排泄尿液。膀胱区能促进排尿及利湿，可用于治疗泌尿系感染、尿潴留、泌尿系结石。

膀胱与肾相表里。膀胱区可用于治疗肾气虚所致的夜尿症、尿失禁。

膀胱经分布于枕、项、后背、腰、肛门及下肢后侧。膀胱区可用于治疗枕部疼痛、落枕、后背疼痛、腰痛、痔疮、坐骨神经痛。

Urinary Bladder

The urinary bladder stores and excretes urine so treating Urinary Bladder can promote urination and eliminate dampness. It is used to treat urinary infection, retention of urine, and urinary stones.

The urinary bladder is connected internally and externally with the kidneys so Urinary Bladder can be used to treat nocturnal enuresis and urinary incontinence caused by deficiency of the kidney-qi.

The urinary bladder meridian distributes to the occiput, back of the neck, back, lumbus, anus, and back of the lower limbs so Urinary Bladder can be used to treat pain in the occipital region, stiff neck, backache, lumbago, hemorrhoids, and sciatica.

三焦

上焦如雾，能宣发由中焦上输的水谷精微至周身。三焦区可用于治疗胸闷、胸痛、咳喘。

中焦如沤，能分解消化水谷精微。三焦区可用于治疗腹胀、腹痛、消化不良及食积等消化系统病症。

下焦如渎，能排泄尿液和粪便。三焦区可用于治疗尿潴留、泌尿系感染、便秘、腹泻及痢疾。

三焦经分布于上肢外侧中央、肩及耳。三焦区可用于治疗上肢外侧痛、肩周炎、耳病。

Sanjiao

The Upper Jiao resembles a sprayer sending water and essence produced by the Middle Jiao throughout the entire body so Sanjiao can be used to treat feelings of fullness and pain in the chest, cough, and asthma.

The Middle Jiao resembles a fermentation tank decomposing and digesting food and water so Sanjiao can be used to treat digestive problems such as abdominal distension or pain, indigestion, and retention of food in the stomach.

The Lowerjiao resembles a system of passageways excreting urine and stool so Sanjiao can be used to treat retention of urine, urinary tract infection, constipation, diarrhea, and dysentary.

The Sanjiao meridian distributes to the shoulders, ears, and the middle portion of the external side of the upper limbs so Sanjiao can be used to treat pain in the external aspect of the upper limbs, scapulohumeral periarthritis, and ear problems.

3）根据现代医学理论取穴：依据现代生理、病理、病因学说选取耳穴是耳穴疗法的另一重要取穴原则。例如：交感神经系统有缓解内脏平滑肌痉挛，调节血管舒缩及抑制腺体分泌的作用，因此，交感穴为治疗内脏疼痛，支气管哮喘，雷诺病，多汗症的主穴。大脑皮质有调节神经、消化及心血管系统的功能，因此，皮质下区广泛地用于治疗因这些系统功能障碍所致的病症。内分泌穴和肾上腺穴常一起使用，治疗炎性及过敏性病症。另外，由于枕区和颞区分别对应视觉和听觉中枢，因此，两穴区常分别用于治疗视力和听力障碍。梅尼埃病的主要病理为内耳迷路水肿，因此，内耳和外耳穴被用于治疗本病。

3) According to the principles of modern medicine

Choosing auricular points according to the principles of modern physiology, etiology, and pathology is another important rule in auricular therapy. For example, the sympathetic nervous system functions to relax spasm of the visceral smooth muscles, regulate vasomotion, and inhibit glandular secretion. Therefore, Sympathesis is a major point for the treatment of visceralgia, bronchial asthma, Raynaud's disease, and hyperhydrosis. The cerebral cortex functions to harmonize the digestive, cardiovascular, and nervous systems. Therefore Subcortex is used extensively for treatment of diseases caused by dysfunction of these systems. Endocrine and Adrenal Gland are always used in conjunction for treatment of inflammatory and allergic conditions. Occiput and Temple are used for treatment of auditory and visual disturbances respectively because they correspond to the visual and auditory centers. Internal Ear and External Ear are used to treat Meniere's disease because the major pathogenesis of this condition is labyrinthine hydiops.

4) 根据临床经验取穴：人们在长期的耳穴疗法实践中积累了丰富的经验。临床上，正确运用这些经验对取得满意的疗效有重要作用。例如：耳尖放血有清热、降压、镇静、抗过敏、醒脑、明目等作用。因此，耳尖穴常用于治疗发热、高血压、失眠、过敏性疾病、头痛、健忘、视物昏花等。耳中穴有疏风活血功能，用于治疗荨麻疹、皮肤瘙痒症。耳神门擅长镇静和止痛，用于治疗神志病及各种痛症。

4) According to clinical experience

Practitioners worldwide have accumulated extensive experience during their long-term practice of auricular therapy. The correct application of this knowledge in clinical practice is essential if good therapeutic results are to be attained. For instance, clinical experience has shown that blood-letting puncturing of Apex of Ear functions to dispel heat, lower blood pressure, tranquilize the mind, relieve allergic reactions, restore consciousness, and brighten the eyes. Therefore, Apex of Ear is commonly used to treat fever, hypertension, insomnia, allergies, headache, poor memory, and blurred vision. Center of Ear has been found to function to expel wind and stimulate circulation of the blood, therefore, it is used to treat urticaria and cutaneous pruritis. Ear Shenmen is useful for calming the mind and relieving pain, and so is used for treating mental problems and all kinds of pain.

（2）操作方法

1）寻找反应点：根据疾病需要确定处方之后，在选用的穴位区内寻找反应点。仔细观察、辨认耳郭表皮、皮内和皮下出现的各种病理反应物，即皮肤是否变色，耳郭有无结节、条索、链珠状隆起、凹陷、皱褶、血管变化等阳性反应。亦可用探针、火柴梗、毫针柄按压，找其压痛反应点。也可采用测定耳郭皮肤电阻的方法，寻找低电阻点。这些反应点就是针刺部位。

2）消毒：用2%碘酊和75%乙醇常规消毒。

3）针刺：根据需要选用0.5寸短柄毫针或特定之图钉型揿针。毫针进针时以左手固定耳郭，右手进针。进针深度以穿透软骨而不穿透对侧皮肤为度。揿针刺入耳穴后用胶布固定于皮肤，留针2~3天。多数患者针刺后，局部有疼痛或热胀感；亦有少数患者有酸重乃至特殊之凉、麻、热等感觉沿着经络路线放射传导。一般来说，凡有这些感觉者疗效较好。

4）留针：毫针一般留针20~30分钟，慢性病可留针1~2小时或更长，留针期间可间断行针。

5）出针：出针后用消毒干棉球压迫针孔片刻以防出血，必要时再涂以乙醇或碘酊，以防感染。

（2）*Manipulation*

1）Searching for the sensitive spot: After diagnosis and point prescription are made detect the sensitive spots on the area where the ear points are located. Examine and identify carefully the surface, intracutaneous and subcutaneous pathogenic changes of the auricle, i. e. positive reactions, such as skin color changes, tubercles, striped and chain-like prominences, depressions, folds, vascular changes, etc. A probe such as a match stick or a handle of a filiform needle can also be used to press for detection of the tender spots. In addition, it is recommended to use the method of measuring the electrical resistance for detection of low electrical resistance areas. These sensitive spots are the spots for needling.

2）Sterilization: Auricular points should be swabbed with 2% iodine and 75% alcohol as routine asepsis.

3）Method of needle insertion: According to the requirement of treatment select a short filiform needle, 0.5 cun, or the special thumb-tack needle shaped as a drawing pin. Stabilze the auricle with the left hand. Hold the filiform needle with the right hand and insert it into the point penetrating the cartilage but not penetrating through the ear. If the thumb-tack needle is employed immobilize it in the point with adhesive tape after insertion and retain the needle

for 2~3 days. After needling, most of
the patients feel a sensation of pain,
heat or distension in the local area
where the needle is inserted. A few of
the patients also feel a sensation of soreness, heaviness, numbness, heat or
even a special sensation of cold. These
sensations may radiate along the course
of the channel and collateral. Generally, the patients experiencing these sensations may obtain satisfactory therapeutic results.

4) Retention of needle: Filiform
needle are usually retained for 20~30
minutes but in cases with chronic diseases needles may be retained for 1~2
hours or longer. During retention of
needles manipulate the needles after an
interval.

5) Removal of needles: After the
needle is removed press the puncture
hole with a dry sterilized cotton ball for
a while to avoid bleeding. If necessary,
swab with alcohol or iodine at once to
avoid infection.

（3）疗程

急性病每天针 1～2 次，慢性病
每天 1 次或隔日 1 次，连续治疗 10
天为 1 个疗程。休息 5～7 天后，开
始下一疗程。

（3）*Course of treatment*

Patients with acute diseases are treated once or twice a day. Patients with
chronic diseases are treated once a day

or every other day. 10 days in succes-
ssion constitute a course. After a
course, stop treating for 5~7 days,
then begin another course.

（4）注意事项

1）严格消毒，以防感染。

2）耳郭冻伤和有炎症的部位
禁针。

3）年老体弱患者，针刺前后应
适当休息。有习惯性流产病史的孕
妇，应禁用耳针。

（4）*Precautions*

1) Strict antisepsis is neccessary to
avoid infection.

2) Needling is contraindicated if
frost-bite or in flammation is present on
the auricle.

3) It is necessary for elderly patients
or patients with weak constitution to
take proper rest before and after being
needled. Needling is contraindicated in
pregnant women with a history of habitual abortion.

（5）异常情况的处理

1）晕针：轻度晕针不必起针，
令患者平卧休息，喝点温开水即可。
重度晕针应立即起针，将患者头部放
低，轻刺激下屏尖、皮质下、枕穴后
一般即可逐渐恢复正常。若配合百会
穴，恢复尤快。

2）耳郭感染：局部涂擦 25% 碘
酊，每天 3 次，同时针刺肝、神门等
穴，或用醋调六神丸外敷。一般 1～
3 天后炎症即可控制。

3）耳郭软骨膜炎：将艾条点燃后，对准病灶施灸。热度以患者能忍受为度，每次 15～30 分钟，每日 3 次，直至病灶内液体消散为止。如已化脓，则需要扩创伤口，将脓液全部排出后，再进行灸治。

（5）*Managements of accidents during ear acupuncture*.

1）Fainting: It is unnecessary to withdraw the needle if mild fainting takes place. Ask the patient to lie in a horizontal position, rest and to drink some warm boiled water. When severe fainting appears, stop needling immediately and withdraw the needles. Put the patient's head down and stimulate Infratragic Apex, Suboorton, and Oo ciput. After doing so, the condition usually disappears. If treated in combination with moxibustion on Baihui (DU 20) the patient will recover more quickly.

2）Infection of the auricle: Swab 2.5% iodine locally 3 times a day. At the same time, puncture Liver, Shenmen, etc., or mix vinegar with Liushen Wan and apply it to the infected area. Generally, the infection will disappear after 2～3 days of treatment.

3）Auricular perichondritis: Apply an ignited moxa stick to the diseased area with the degree of heat limited to the patient's maximal tolerance. Each treatment lasts 15～30 minutes. Treat thrice per day until the liquid in the focis dissipates. It is necessary to drain the wound if suppuration has taken place in the wound. After draining of all the pus, begin the moxibustion treatment.

第十一节　其他耳穴疗法

Section 11 Other Auricular Therapeutic Methods

1. 耳穴贴压法

耳穴贴压法是指用圆而质硬，表面光滑，适合耳穴面积大小的药籽、药丸或磁珠贴在耳穴上，通过按压刺激耳穴治疗疾病的一种方法。本方法具有安全有效、适应证广和不受条件限制等特点，是近年来最常用的耳穴治疗方法。

（1）操作程序

1）选用圆形，表面光滑，质地坚硬，适合穴位面积大小，对皮肤无毒副作用的物质为贴压物，如王不留行籽、急性子、绿豆、六神丸和磁珠等。

2）将胶布剪成 0.6 厘米×0.6 厘米大小数块备用。

3）用碘酊、乙醇严格消毒耳郭。

4）左手固定耳郭，右手持探棒按压所选穴位，使之留下压痕，然后将粘有贴压物的胶布贴敷在压痕上，并按压数秒钟，至出现发热、酸、胀或放射等针感为止。

5）贴压顺序自上而下，由前往

后；以贴压患侧穴位为主，或双侧同时贴压。

6）耳穴的分布在耳郭的正面和背面一致，因此，大部耳穴均可在两侧同时贴压以增加刺激强度和疗效。此法尤其适宜于头痛、背痛、关节酸痛等痛症。

7）每贴压 1 次，可留置 3～7天，贴压期间，嘱患者每天按压 2～3 次，每次 3～5 分钟，至有酸、胀、热或放射感为止。

8）下次贴压前一天取下贴压物，并用温水清洗耳郭。

1. Auricular Taping

Auricular taping consists of taping small, round, hard, smooth objects such as mustard seeds, small beans, pills, or ballbearings to particular auricular points. The taped objects are then pressed in order to stimulate the points and attain therapeutic results. This method has been widely used in recent years because of its safety, effectiveness, wide range of applications, and lack of contraindications.

(1) *Procedure*

1) Choose small, round, hard, smooth objects of the appropriate size for stimulating the auricular points. The objects chosen should have no toxic properties or side-effects. Seeds of vaccaria segetalis (mustard) or semen impatiens, mung beans, Liushen pills,

or small ball bearings are all suitable for use in auricular taping.

2) Prepare sufficient adhesive tape cut into pieces 0.5 cm square.

3) Sterilize the auricle with tincture of iodine or alcohol.

4) Sterilize the auricle with one hand. With the other hand use a detection probe (any instrument with a blunt point the size of a matchhead) to press the auricular points hard enough to leave depressions. Tape the seeds to the positive points and press for several minutes until a needling sensation of heat or radiating distension is achieved.

5) Tape the points in order of upper to lower and frontal to dorsal mainly taping the affected side. Bilateral auriculae may be taped simultaneously or during alternate treatment sessions.

6) The distribution of points on the frontal and dorsal surfaces of the auricle is identical. Therefore, the main auricular points may be taped on both sides simultaneously in order to increase stimulation and effectiveness. This method is especially suitable for pain such as headache, backache, and sore joints.

7) Leave the tape and seeds on the auricle for three to seven days. Each point should be pressed for three to five minutes, two to three times each day, until a needling sensation of heat,

pain, or radiating distension is achieved.

8）Remove the tape and seeds the evening before the next treatment and clean the auricle with soap and warm water.

（2）适应证

耳穴贴压法安全、有效、易于接受，临床上广泛用于治疗痛症，炎症性病变，内分泌紊乱，功能性失调、运动障碍及过敏性疾病。对于儿童、老年、体弱及药物过敏者尤为适宜。

（2）*Indications*

Because auricular taping is safe, effective, and easily accepted, it is widely used in clinical practice for the treatment of pain, inflammation, endocrine disturbances, functional disorders, motion sickness, and allergic reactions. It is especially suitable for children, aged people and patients with weak constitutions or drug allergies.

（3）耳穴贴压的正常反应

贴压耳穴后，由于年龄、性别、体质等的差异，可出现不同反应。常见的有局部酸、麻、胀、痛、热或放射传导等。有些患者可出现患部肌肉不自主运动、热流感和舒适感。许多患者感到精力充沛，食欲增加，睡眠改善，所有反应说明取穴准确，方法得当，预后良好。

（3）*Normal reaction to auricular taping therapy*

Reactions to auricular taping therapy are varied owing to differences in constitution, age, and sex. The most common reactions include localized sensations of pain, heat, numbness, and distension. Radiating pain may occur in some cases. Some people may experience reflex muscle reactions or a sensation of flowing heat and comfort in the corresponding body areas. Many people feel vigorous, have a good appetite and sleep well after taping. All of these reactions indicate that the therapeutic method and points chosen were correct and that the prognosis is favorable.

（4）耳穴贴压异常现象的处理和预防

1）晕针：由于病员精神紧张、空腹、久病体虚、疲劳过度，或医者取穴不准，手法不当，可出现不同程度的晕针现象。

耳穴贴压疗法中轻度和中度晕针较多见，重度晕针罕见。晕针可能发生在贴压过程中，也可发生在贴压一段时间后，轻度者，让患者平卧，喝热水或糖水，消除紧张情绪，待恢复后可继续贴压。中度者，先取下贴压物，患者平卧呈头低脚高位，解开衣领及裤带（冬天注意保暖），针刺皮质下和肾上腺，必要时应配合其他急救措施。

耳穴贴压导致晕针的因素以过度疲劳，饥饿，久病体弱多见，因紧张而导致者较少。因此，针对上述易发晕针因素进行预防尤为重要。对有易发因素的初诊患者，贴压前后应休息片刻，采用卧位，取穴宜少，手法适度，并告诉患者可能出现的晕针现象和处理方法。

（4）*Prevention and management of abnormal phenomena in auricular taping*.

1）Fainting

Various degrees of fainting may occur due to nervousness, hunger, weak constitution due to long-standing illness, overstrain, or use of inappropriate points of stimulation.

Mild and moderate fainting is common, but severe fainting is quite rare in auricular taping. The fainting may occur either during or after taping. In mild cases the patient should lie down in a horizontal position, drink some hot water or hot sugar water, and relax. The treatment may be continued when the patient recovers. In moderate and severe cases the tape should first be removed. Put the patient in Trendelenburg's position and loosen the collar and belt being careful to keep the patient warm, especially in winter. Puncture Subcortex and Adrenal Gland. Additional emergency treatment should be instituted if necessary.

Fainting caused by overstain, hunger, or weak constitution due to long-standing illness is much more common than that caused by nervousness.

Therefore, care should be taken with those who may have these predisposing conditions. In these cases a period of rest in the clinic before and after taping is necessary. Fewer points are selected, a horizontal position is adopted during taping, and moderate manipulation is given. Additionally, these patients should be informed of the possibility of failting and how to manage it.

2）耳郭感染：因贴压耳穴导致感染的主要原因是患者皮肤对胶布过敏，轻者表现为贴压部位痒、痛、红色丘疹；重者可出现耳郭红肿、局部皮肤溃烂；严重者可致软骨坏死、萎缩，使耳郭畸形。由于耳郭血液循环相对差，一旦感染，尤其波及软骨后则较难治，因此，预防极为重要。对胶布过敏者，可采用脱敏胶布。即使如此，仍有可能出现感染，此时最好改用其他耳穴疗法，如耳穴放血法、耳穴按压法，或耳穴按摩法。

2）Infection of the auricle

The main causes of auricular infection following auricular taping are allergic reactions to the adhesive tape or incomplete sterilization. In mild cases there may be itching and pain in the taped area sometimes accompained by a reddish rash or pimples. In severe cases there may be swelling and redness of the auricle, ulcerative infection of the tape areas, or even necrosis and atrophy of the auricular cartilage resulting in deformity of the auricle. Because of the relatively poor blood circulation in the auriculae, auricular infection is difficult to cure. Therefore, prevention is very important. Hypoallergenic tape should be used when treating people with adhesive allergies. Since infection may still occur in these cases relatively easily, alternative auricular therapies such as auricular blood-letting, pressure, or massage should be considered.

（5）注意事项

1）防止胶布和贴压部位潮湿，以免贴敷张力低而易脱落。

2）对一般胶布过敏者，改用脱敏胶布，并加贴肾上腺和风溪，耳尖放血，或改用其他治疗方法。

3）耳郭有冻疮及炎症者不宜贴压。

4）如果因同时贴双侧耳郭影响睡眠，可两侧轮流贴压。

5）严重心脏病患者禁止贴压。

6）孕妇贴压耳穴时手法宜轻，禁止使用可能诱发子宫收缩的穴位；对有习惯性流产史的孕妇禁止贴压。

7）夏季多汗，贴压时间宜短（3天）；冬季注意耳部保暖。

8）按压耳穴时，禁止搓揉，以防损伤耳郭。

（5）Precaution

1）Avoid exposure of the adhesive tape to moisture. In order to achieve a strong bond with the skin of the ear, apply the tape only after the alcohol used to sterilize the auricle has completely dried.

2）Use hypoallergenic adhesive tape for people with adhesive allergies. At the time of treatment also tape Adrenal Gland, Wind Stream, and puncture Apex of Ear with a three-edged needle to cause bleeding. Alternatively, use other methods such as auricular blood-letting, pressure, or massage.

3）Auricular taping is contraindicated in cases of inflammed or frost bitten auriculae.

4）If sleep is affected because bilateral auriculae have been taped simultaneously, tape each side alternately.

5）Auricular taping is contraindicated for people with severe cardiac disease.

6）Mild manipulation should be adopted for pregnant women. Do not tape points which may cause the uterus to contract. Auricular taping is contraindicated for pregnant women with a history of repeated miscarriage.

7）Because of increased perspiration in summer, tape for a shorter period (three days). In winter, pay attention to keeping the auricule warm.

8）In order to prevent injury to the auricle, do not rub in a sideways or circular motion while pressing the taped auricular points.

2．耳穴放血法

耳穴放血法是采用三棱针、梅花针或蜂针在耳穴区或耳背络脉针刺、切割放血的一种治疗方法。耳穴放血，尤其是耳尖和轮 1～轮 6 部位，能够改善耳郭血液循环，从而促进人体新陈代谢，除用于实热证外，还可用于某些虚证。

2．Auricular Blood-Letting

Auricular blood-letting consists of the use of a three-edged needle, plum blossom needle, or ensiform needle to draw blood from specific auricular points, areas, or collaterals for therapeutic effect. Blood-letting of auricular points, especially Apex of the Ear and Helix 1 to Helix 6, can stimulate blood circulation of the auricula thus improving the metabolism of the entire body. In addition to excessive or heat syndromes, auricular blood-letting is also useful in some deficient syndromes such as insomnia or dizziness.

（1）操作方法

1）按摩耳郭使其充血。

2）严格消毒放血部位及针具。

3）左手固定耳郭放血部位，右手持针具，用三棱针点刺穴位 2 毫米左右，或用梅花针叩刺穴区，或用蜂针切割耳背络脉。

4）挤压放血部位使出血 5～8滴，用消毒干棉球吸附出血。

5）一般病症，两耳郭穴位轮流放血，急症可双侧同时放血。

6）一般病症，每周 2 次，急症可 1 天 1 次。

（1）*Manipulation*

1）Massage the auricle to cause congestion of blood.

2）Strictly sterilize the needles and the area to be punctured.

3）Holding the auricle with one hand, use the other hand to either puncture the chosen points 2 mm deep with a three-edged needle, heavily tap the chosen areas with a plum blossom needle or incise the chosen collaterals on the dorsal surface with an ensiform needle.

4）Pinch the auricle to express five to eight drops of blood. Absorb the blood with sterilized dry cotton.

5）Puncture bilateral sides alternately for general cases or simultaneously for acute cases.

6）Treat twice a week for general cases or once every other day for acute cases.

（2）常用耳郭放血部位及其适应证

1）耳尖：用三棱针在耳尖放血具有显著的祛风清热、通经止痛之功，临床上广泛用于发热，炎性病变，神经官能症，高血压，皮肤病，各种痛症，眼病及耳鸣，耳聋等。由于耳尖部位血管丰富，操作方法容易掌握，因此，是最理想的耳郭放血部位。

2）肝阳：用三棱针在肝阳放血具有平肝熄风之功，常用于肝阳上亢所致的头晕，头痛，目眩，耳鸣等。

3）屏尖：用三棱针在屏尖放血有清热，止痛，镇静之功，用于发热，各种炎性病变，神经官能症。

4）耳背沟：用梅花针叩刺耳背沟出血有降压作用，用于治疗因高血压所致头晕，头痛，目眩，视物昏花及耳鸣等。

5）耳背络脉：用蜂针在耳背络脉放血具有显著的祛风清热作用，常用于治疗皮肤病及炎性病症。

6）轮1～轮6：用三棱针点刺轮1～轮6穴位具有显著的清热之功，常用于治疗各种急性病。

7）其他部位：对实证、热证，所有耳穴均可采用放血方法。例如，用梅花针叩刺面颊区可治疗痤疮，扁平疣，黄褐斑及面部美容；用三棱针点刺肺区及病变对应部位治疗皮肤病。

（2）*Commonly used points and their indications*

1）Apex of Ear: Blood-letting of Apex of Ear with a three-edged needle is useful for relieving heat, eliminating wind, relieving pain, tranquilizing the mind, brightening the eyes, and benefiting the ears. It is widely used in clinical practice for treating fever, inflammatory infections, neuroses, hypertension, skin diseases, allergic reactions, pain, optic problems, tinnitus, and deafness. It is the most ideal point for blood-letting because the blood vessels here are plentiful and the manipulation is easily matered.

2）Liver-Yang: Blood-letting of Liver-Yang with a three-edged needle can calm the liver to arrest endogenous wind, so it is useful in the treatment of headache, vertigo, and tinnitus caused by hyperactivity of the liver-yang.

3）Apex of Tragus: Blood-letting of Apex of Tragus with a three-edged needle relieves heat and pain and has a tranquilizing effect. It is used in the treatment of fever, inflammatory infections, and neuroses.

4）Groove of Dorsal Surface: Tapping Groove of Dorsal Surface with a plum blossom needle to cause bleeding can lower the blood pressure. It is useful in the treatment of dizziness, vertigo, headache, blurred vision, and tinnitus caused by hypertension.

5）Collaterals on the Dorsal Surface: Incising the collaterals with an ensiform needle to draw blood eliminates wind and relieves heat. It is used for treating cases of skin diseases and inflammatory infection.

6）Helix 1 to Helix 6: Blood-letting is contraindicated in cases of immunological insufficiency or hemorrhagic diseases such as hemophilia, primary thrombocylopenic purpura, and aplastic anemia.

7）Other points: Blood-letting can be used on all the auricular points to treat excessive heat syndromes. Needles are chosen according to the position of the points to be treated. For example, Cheek is tapped with a plum blossom needle for acne, flat wart, chloasm, or cosmetic purposes. Lung is punctured with a three-edged needle for skin diseases.

（3）注意事项

1）放血前按摩耳郭，使血管扩张，易于出血。

2）严格消毒放血部位及针具，防止耳郭感染。

3）采用三棱针放血时，不宜刺入太深，以免损伤耳郭软骨。

4）出血量以 5~8 滴为宜，对大实证、大热证者，可适当增加放血量。热证患者因血流加快，容易放血，且出血量较多，有如泉涌者，其效更佳。

5）耳背络脉需多次放血者，应从络脉的远端开始。

6）免疫功能不全及各种出血性疾病，如血友病，原发性血小板减少性紫癜及再生障碍性贫血患者禁止使用此法。

（3）*Precautions*

1）Massage the auricle before puncturing to dilate the blood vessels and make blood-letting easier.

2）Strictly sterilize the needles and the areas to be punctured in order to avoid infection of the auricle.

3）In order to avoid damage to the auricular cartilage be careful not to puncture too deeply with the three-edged needle. 2 mm is sufficient.

4）Sufficient blood should be expressed, usually five to eight drops. For severe excessive or heat syndromes slightly more blood should be let. It is very easy to cause bleeding in patients with heat syndrome because the flow of blood is quite rapid. If the blood spurts like a fountain the prognosis is very good.

5）If it is necessary to draw blood repeatedly on the collaterals of the auricular dorsal surface, puncture the distal end first.

6）Auricular blood-letting is contraindicated in cases of immunological insufficiency, hemorrhagic diseases such as hemophilia, primary thrombocylopenic purpura, and aplastic anemia.

3．耳穴点压法

耳穴点压法是指用压痛棒（任何如火柴头大小的钝头棒）点压耳穴治疗疾病的一种方法。临床实践中发现，当用压痛棒或耳穴探测仪诊查耳穴阳性反应时，有些患者的某些症状即刻得到改善，如疼痛减轻或消失，恶心或呕吐停止。本方法具有疏通经络，调和气血，镇静安神之功，适合于各种痛症，慢性病症，软组织损伤及神经衰弱等。

操作方法：每个穴位点压 2～3 分钟，压力由轻到重，以出现热、酸、胀痛或放射等针感为宜。可教病者自行按压，每天 2～3 次。不宜使用顶端尖锐的按压物，以免损伤耳郭。

3. Auricular Pressure

Auricular pressure uses pressure on selected auricular points with a detection probe (any instrument with a blunt point the size of a matchhead) to achieve therapeutic results. It has been found in clinical practice that there is immediate improvement in symptoms in some cases when tender points on the auricle are located and pressed with the detection probe during the diagnostic process. For instance, pain, nausea, and vomiting may be relieved or stopped as soon as the associated points are pressed. This method can activate meridians and collaterals, regulate the qi and blood, and calm the mind. It is suitable for treating pain, chronic illness, injury of the soft tissues, and neurosism.

Manipulation: Press each point for two to three minutes until a needling sensation of heat, pain, or radiating distension is achieved. The pressure may vary from light to heavy. Patients can practice this method themselves at home, pressing the indicated points two to three times each day. Pressing with sharply pointed instruments should be avoided in order to prevent injury to the auricle.

4. 耳郭按摩法

耳郭按摩法是指用双手按摩耳郭的一种治疗方法。长期按摩耳郭，可疏通经络气血，调整脏腑功能，健脑聪耳明目。因此，既可用于治疗神经衰弱、头痛、头晕、视物昏花、耳鸣等病症，又可用于益智强身。《苏沈良方》云："摩熨耳目，以助真气。"道家亦有按摩耳郭以养生的记载。

按摩方法是首先搓热双手掌心，按摩耳郭前后两面。然后双手空握拳，拇指在后，示指在前，沿耳郭前后自上而下按摩。示指的按摩顺序为：耳轮、耳舟、三角窝、对耳轮、耳甲艇、耳甲腔、耳轮脚周围、对耳屏内侧面。耳垂前面针对病情不同，可在相应部位停留一段时间。反复操作数次，至耳郭发热为度，若配合意念，则效果更佳。

4. Auricular Massage

Auricular massage uses massage of the auricle with the hands to achieve therapeutic effects. Long-term massage of the auriculae can activate the meridians and collaterals, regulate the qi and blood, restore the functions of the Zangfu organs, nourish the brain, brighten the eyes, and benefit the ears. It can be used for treating problems such as neurosism, headache, dizziness, blurred vision, tinnitus, as well as for raising the intelligence and improving general fitness. It was recorded in The Effective Prescription of Sushen, Song dynasty (907~1279 A. D.), that massage of the ears can strengthen antipathogenic qi. There are also records of early Taoists using this method for health preservation and longevity.

Manipulation: Rub the palms together until they are warm. Then massage both the frontal and dorsal auricular surfaces between them. With a loose fist, massage both the frontal and dorsal auricular surface from top to bottom with the thumb on the dorsal surface and the index finger on the frontal surface. The index finger should massage the auricular areas in the following order: helix, scapha, triangular fossa, antihelix, superior concha, inferior concha, peripheral crus of the helix, medial side of the antitragus, medial side of the tragus, lobe. The index finger should remain longer on points and areas specific to the patient's condition. The procedure should be repeated several times until the auriculae are hot. The results will be greatly improved if the patient's mind is focused and attention concentrated during the massage.

第十二节 头 针
Section 12 Scalp Acupuncture

头针是在头部的特定区、线（图 2-17）进行针刺治病的一种方法。具有操作简便的特点，临床常用于治疗脑源性疾病。

Scalp acupuncture is a therapeutic method by needling the specific areas or lines of the scalp (Fig. 2-17). It has the advantages of simplicity and covenience in operation and it is often used to treat cerebral diseases clinically.

1. 刺激部位和主治作用

运动区

部位 上点在前后正中线中点向后移 0.5 厘米处，下点在眉枕线和鬓角发际前缘相交处，两点的连线为运动区。将运动区划分五等份，上 1/5 为下肢、躯干运动区，中 2/5 是上肢运动区，下 2/5 是面部运动区（图 2-18）。

主治 运动区上 1/5 治疗对侧下肢瘫痪；中 2/5 治疗对侧上肢瘫痪；下 2/5 治疗对侧中枢性面瘫、运动性失语、流涎、发音障碍。

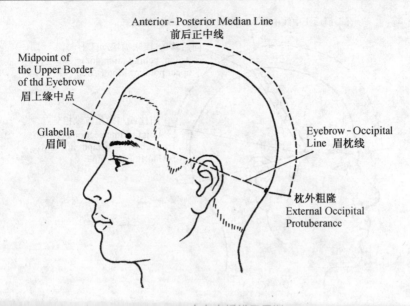

图 2 - 17　头穴定标线示意图

图 2 - 17 头穴定标线示意图

Fig. 2 - 17　The Refence Lines on the Scalp

1. Locations and Indications of the Areas

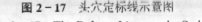

Motor Area

Location: Take the point 0.5 cm posterior to the midpoint of the antero-posterior midline as the upper point and the intersecting point of the eyebrow-occiput line and the anterior border of the natural line of the hair at the temple as the lower point. The connecting line between these two points is the motor area. The area is subdivided into 5 equal parts: the upper 1/5 of this area is the lower limb and trunk motor area, the middle 2/5 is the upper limb motor area, and the lower 2/5 of this area is the face motor area (Fig. 2 - 18).

Indications: The upper 1/5 of the motor area is for contralateral paralysis of the lower limbs the middle 2/5 of this area for contralateral paralysis of the upper limb, and the lower 2/5 of this area for contralateral central facial paralysis, motor aphasia, salivation and dysphonia.

感 觉 区

部位　自运动区后移 1.5 厘米的平行线即为感觉区。上 1/5 是下肢、头、躯干感觉区，中 2/5 是上肢感觉区，下 2/5 是面感觉区（图 2 - 19）。

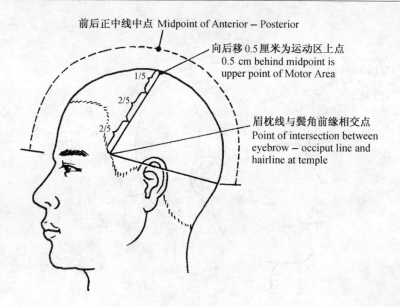

前后正中线中点 Midpoint of Anterior – Posterior

向后移 0.5 厘米为运动区上点
0.5 cm behind midpoint is
upper point of Motor Area

1/5

2/5

2/5

眉枕线与鬓角前缘相交点
Point of intersection between
eyebrow – occiput line and
hairline at temple

图 2 – 18 运动区
Fig. 2 – 18 Motor Area

主治 感觉区上 1/5 治疗对侧腰腿痛，麻木，感觉异常，后头、颈部疼痛和耳鸣；中 2/5 治疗对侧上肢疼痛、麻木、感觉异常；下 2/5 治疗对侧面部麻木、偏头痛、三叉神经痛、牙痛及颞颌关节炎。感觉区配合内脏区（胸腔、胃区、生殖区）可用于有关部位外科手术的头针麻醉。

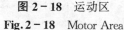

Sensory Area

Location: The parallel line 1.5 cm behind the motor area is the sensory area. The upper 1/5 of this area is the lower limb, head and trunk sensory area. The middle 2/5 of this area is the upper limb sensory area, and the lower 2/5 is the face sensory area (Fig. 2 – 19).

Indications: The upper 1/5 of the sensory area is for contralateral lumbar pain, pain of the leg, numbness, paresthesia, occipital headache, pain in the nape region and tinnitus. The middle 2/5 of this area for contralateral upper limb pain, numbness and paresthesia, and the lower 1/5 of this area for contralateral facial numbness, migraine, trigeminal neuralgia, toothache and temporomandibular arthritis. scalp acupuncture anesthesia employed in surgical operations on relevant parts of the body, the sensory area is used in combination with the visceral areas (the thoracic, gastric and reproduction areas).

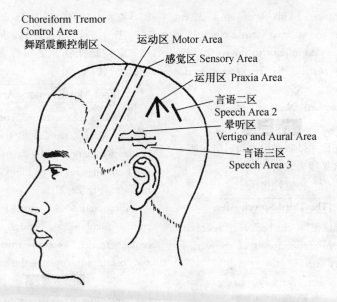

Choreiform Tremor
Control Area
舞蹈震颤控制区

运动区 Motor Area

感觉区 Sensory Area

运用区 Praxia Area

言语二区
Speech Area 2

晕听区
Vertigo and Aural Area

言语三区
Speech Area 3

图 2－19　侧面刺激区

Fig. 2－19　In lateral View

舞蹈震颤控制区

部位　从运动区向前平移 1.5 厘米的平行线。

主治　舞蹈病，震颤麻痹症。一侧病变针对侧，两侧病变针双侧。

Chorea-Trembling Controlled Area

Location：The parallel line 1.5 cm in front of the motor area.

Indications：Chorea, Parkinson's disease. If the symptom is unilateral, needle the contralateral stimulation area. If bilateral, needle bilaterally.

晕　听　区

部位　从耳尖直上 1.5 厘米处，向前、后各引 2 厘米长的水平直线即

该区。

主治　耳鸣，听力减退，头晕，耳源性眩晕等症。

Vertigo-Auditory Area

Location：This area is a 4 cm horizontal straight line located at the site 1.5 cm right above the auricular apex.

Indications：Tinnitus, hypoacusis, vertigo, auditory vertigo, etc.

言语二区

部位　从顶骨结节后下方 2 厘米处引一平行于前后正中线的直线，向下取 3 厘米长的直线。

主治　命名性失语。

The Second Speech Area

Location：This area is a 3 cm straight line starting from a point 2 cm posterior and inferior to the parietal tubercle, paralled to the anteroposterior midline.

Indication：Nominal aphasia.

言语三区

部位　晕听区中点向后引4厘米长的水平线为该区。

主治　感觉性失语。

The Third Speech Area

Location：4 cm backward horizontal line from the midpoint of the vertigo-auditory area.

Indication：Sensory aphasia.

运 用 区

部位　从顶骨结起分别引一垂直线，同时引与该线夹角40°的前后两线，3条线的长度均为3厘米。

主治　失用症。

Usage Area

Location：Take the parietal tubercle as a starting point. Draw a vertical line from the point, at the same time draw the other two lines from the point seperately forwards and backwards, at 40° angle with the vertical line, each of the three lines is 3 cm long.

Indication：Apraxia.

足运感区

部位　在前后正中线的中点旁开左右各1厘米，向后引平行于正中线的3厘米长的直线（图2-20）。

主治　对侧下肢疼痛、麻木、瘫痪，急性腰扭伤，皮质性多尿，夜尿，子宫脱垂等。

Foot Motor Sensory Area

Location：Draw two 3 cm straight lines backwards parallel to the antero-posterior midline. Their starting points are 1 cm bilateral to the midpoint of the midline（Fig.2-20）.

Indications：Contralateral lower limb pain, numbness, paralysis, acute lumbar sprain, cerebro-cortical polyuria, nocturia prolapse of the uterus.

视　区

部位　旁开正中线左右1厘米处，在枕外粗隆水平线向上引平行于前后正中线的4厘米长的直线。

主治　皮质性视力障碍。

Optic Area

Location：Draw a 4 cm straight line upwards paralled to the anteroposterior midline, 1 cm evenly beside the external occipital protuberance.

Indication：Cerebro-cortical visual disturbance.

平　衡　区

部位　旁开正中线左右3.5厘米处，在枕外粗隆水平线向下与正中线平行引4厘米长直线（图2-21）。

主治　小脑疾病引起的平衡障碍。

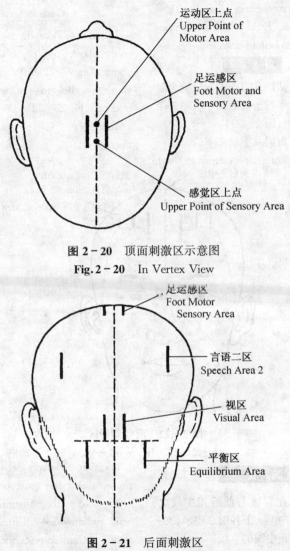

运动区上点
Upper Point of
Motor Area

足运感区
Foot Motor and
Sensory Area

感觉区上点
Upper Point of Sensory Area

图 2 - 20 顶面刺激区示意图

Fig. 2 - 20 In Vertex View

足运感区
Foot Motor
Sensory Area

言语二区
Speech Area 2

视区
Visual Area

平衡区
Equilibrium Area

图 2 - 21 后面刺激区

Fig. 2 - 21 In Posterior View

Balance Area

Location: Draw a 4 cm straight line downwards parallel to the anteroposterior midline, 3.5 cm evenly beside the external occipital protuberance (Fig. 2 – 21).

Indication: Equilibrium disturbance caused by cerebellum disease.

胃   区

部位　从瞳孔直上的发际处为起点，向上引平行于前后正中线的 2 厘米长的直线（图 2 – 22）。

主治　胃痛及上腹部不适。

Gastric Area

Location: Take the hair margin directly above the pupil as a starting point. Draw a 2 cm straight line upwards parallel to the anteroposterior midline (Fig. 2 – 22).

Indications: Gastric pain, epigastric discomfort.

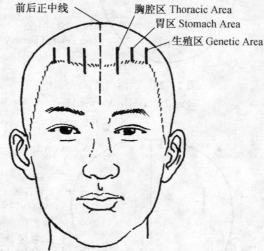

Anterior–Posterior Median Line
前后正中线

胸腔区 Thoracic Area
胃区 Stomach Area
生殖区 Genetic Area

图 2 – 22　前面刺激区
Fig. 2 – 22　In Anterior View

胸　腔　区

部位　在胃区与前后正中线之间，从发际向上、下各引 2 厘米长的平行于前后正中线的直线。

主治　胸痛，胸闷，心悸，冠状动脉供血不足，哮喘，呃逆。

Thoracic Area

Location: Midway between the gastric area and the anteroposterior midline. Take the hair margin as the midpoint and draw a 4 cm straight line parallel to the antero-posterior midline.

Indications: Chest pain, chest stuffiness palpitation, coronary artery insufficiency, asthma, hiccup.

生 殖 区

部位 从额角处向上引平行于前后正中线的 2 厘米长的直线。

主治 功能性子宫出血，盆腔炎，白带多。配足感区治疗子宫脱垂。

Reproduction Area

Location: Draw a 2 cm straight line from the frontal angle upward parallel to the anteroposterior midline.

Indications: Functional uterine bleeding, pelvic inflammation, and leukorrhagia. Prolapse of uterus and others may be treated in association with the foot motor sensory area.

2. 操作方法

(1) 患者取坐位或卧位，取消毒过的 26～28 号 1.5～2.5 寸长的毫针，针尖与头皮呈 30°左右夹角，医者右手拇指、示指捏住针身露出针尖 2 毫米，沿刺激区的方向对准进针点，手指距头皮 5～10 厘米，然后手腕突然用力往掌侧屈曲，使针尖快速冲刺进入头皮下或肌层，再以右手拇指、示指捏住针柄下半部（或将中指扶住针身末端），沿刺激方向推进所需深度；或右手拇指、示指捏住针柄下半部（或中指紧贴针身），左手拇指、示指捏住针身近头皮处，双手协同将针推进至一定深度。推进时，患者有痛感或针下有抵抗感，应将针往后退至皮下，改变角度推进。

(2) 针进入一定的深度后，术者肩、肘、腕关节及拇指固定，示指半屈曲状，用拇指第一节的掌侧面，与示指第一节的桡侧面捏住针柄，然后以示指掌关节不断伸屈，使针身来回快速旋转约 200 次/分钟，每次旋转左右各 2 次。捻转持续 0.5～10 分钟，留针 30 分钟，每隔 5～10 分钟，按上法捻转 1 次即可起针。捻转或留针时，家属协助患者（或患者自己）活动肢体，以加强患肢功能锻炼，有助提高疗效。一般刺激 3～5 分钟后，部分患者在病变部位（或内脏）会出现热、麻、胀、凉、抽动等感应，这种患者的疗效比较好。

(3) 起刺时，如针下无沉紧感，可快速拔出针。即左手持消毒棉球对准针孔附近，右手的中指或无名指沿着针柄快速往下滑，然后拇指和示指捏住针柄快速向外拔出。也可右手边捻转边缓缓出针，起针后必须用消毒干棉球按压针孔片刻，以防出血。

(4) 头针治疗一般每天或隔天针刺 1 次，10～15 次为 1 个疗程。中间休息 1 周左右，再继续下一疗程。

2. Manipulation

(1) Let the patient take a sitting or lying position. Select sterilized filiform needles 1.5～2.5 cun long and at the gauge No. 26～28. Hold the shaft of the needle with the thumb and index finger of the right hand. Exposing the needle tip 2 mm, direct the needle tip at the area to be inserted, and keep the

finger tip 5~10 cm from the scalp and the needle tip 10~20 cm from the point. Then, swiftly insert the needle at a 30° angle to the scalp by sudden and forceful palmar flexion of the wrist into the muscular layer. Then hold the lower half of the needle handle with the thumb and index finger of the right hand (or support the needle shaft with the middle finger). Push the needle along the direction of stimulation to the depth needed. Conversely hold the lower half of the needle handle with the thumb and index finger of the right hand (or support the needle shaft with the middle finger) and grip the portion of the needle near the scalp with the thumb and index finger of the left hand. Push the needle to a certain depth with the two hands acting in coordination. In pushing, if the patient feels pain or there is resistance around the needle, the needle should be withdrawn to the subcutaneous layer for another try in a different direction.

(2) After the needle is inserted to a certain depth, fix the of shoulder, elbow, wrist and thumb, while keeping the index finger at half flexion. Then, hold the needle handle with the palmar side of the thumb and radial side of the index finger. Twirl the needle by continuous and alternate flexion and extension of the metacarpal phalangeal joint

of the index finger at a frequency of about 200 times per minute. Continue the clockwise and anticlockwise turns for 0.5~1 minute. Then, retain the needle for 30 minutes. During retention, twirl the needle in the way mentioned above one time per 5~10 minutes. Finally, withdraw the needle. During twirling or retaining the needle, ask the patient to move his affected limb so as to enhance the therapeutic effect by strengthening functional exercise of the affected limbs. Generally, after stimulation for 3~5 minutes, if the patient has a reaction at the affected area (including heat, numbness, distension, cold or trembling) the patient may get a good therapeutic effect.

(3) In withdrawal, if there is no heavy tight sensation along the needle pull it out swiftly. Hold a sterilized swab with the left hand and direct it at the puncture hole area. Move the middle or ring finger of the right hand downwards along the needle handle smoothly and quickly. Hold the needle handle and pull out the needle quickly with the thumb and index finger (or with the thumb, index and middle fingers. All erndively withdraw the needle slowly while twirling the needle. Then press over the needle hole with a sterilized cotton ball for a moment to prevent bleeding.

(4) In general, scalp needling therapy should be done once a day or every other day. 10～15 treatments make up one course. After one course, discontinue the treatment for a week or so, then begin another course.

3．注意事项

（1）针刺时宜取仰靠坐位或卧位，以防晕针。

（2）消毒要严密，防止感染。

（3）如有高热、急性炎症、心力衰竭等并发症时，不宜立即进行头针治疗，待症状缓解后酌情运用。脑出血患者引起的偏瘫，宜在出血停止、病情稳定后再进行头针治疗。

3．Precaution

（1）The patient should take a lying position or a sitting position to prevent needle fainting.

（2）Strict sterilization should be carried out to prevent infection.

（3）In case the patient has such a complication as high fever, acute inflammation or heart failure, scalp acupuncture is not advisable until the remission of these symptoms. For patients with hemiparalysis caused by cerebral hemorrhage, wait until the bleeding stops and the condition of illness is stable. Then begin treatment with scalp acupuncture.

第十三节　眼　　针

Section 13 Eye Acupuncture

眼针是结合"观眼识病"，根据病变部位，依中医理论，按八卦划分眼区，用毫针刺激眼穴，治疗全身疾病的一种新的针刺疗法。

Eye acupuncture is a newly developed acupuncture method based on the theories "diagnosing diseases by observing the eye" as described in classical chinese medical treatises. This method is useful for treatment of a wide variety of diseases. It utilizes needle stimulation of corresponding eye acupuncture points distributed according to the Bagua.

1．眼针穴位分布及主治

眼针穴位分为8区13穴（图2－23）。眼针穴位分布在距眼眶缘外0.5厘米处，其中每个脏腑相应眼穴点22.5°，而上、中、下焦各占45°。各区所代表的脏腑可以治疗相应的脏腑或经络的病变。如心区能治疗心血管疾病及心经病。

上焦穴区主治膈肌以上疾病，包括头面、五官、上肢、胸背及心脏、肺脏、食管、气管等疾病。

中焦穴区主治膈以下，脐水平以上的疾病，包括腰背部和上腹部及所属区的内脏等疾病。

下焦穴区主治脐水平以下疾病，包括腰骶部、盆腔、臀部、泌尿生殖系统及下肢等疾病。

心包虽在形态上与心有别，但功能上却和心紧密联系，所以眼针穴位无心包。心包经病症可以针心穴。

1. The Locations and Indications of Eye Acupuncture

Eye acupuncture Points are located in eight distinct areas around each eye

with a total of 13 in number (Fig.2-23). The eye acupoints are located 0.5 cm distal to the edge of the eye orbit. Each Zang-organ or Fu-organ point occupies an angle of 22.5 degrees while each area representing the Upper, Middle and Lower Warmers occupies an angle of 45 degrees. Each eye acupoint

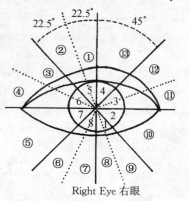
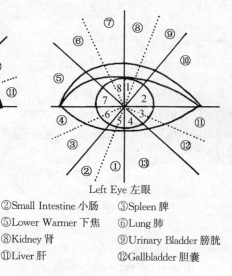

Right Eye 右眼   Left Eye 左眼

①Heart 心   ②Small Intestine 小肠   ③Spleen 脾
④Stomach 胃   ⑤Lower Warmer 下焦   ⑥Lung 肺
⑦Large Intestine 大肠 ⑧Kidney 肾   ⑨Urinary Bladder 膀胱
⑩Upper Warmer 上焦   ⑪Liver 肝   ⑫Gallbladder 胆囊
⑬Middle Warmer 中焦

图 2 - 23 眼针穴位示意图

Fig. 2 - 23 Acupoints of Eye Acupuncture

represents an organ and can be used to treat the Zang and Fu-organs or their related channels and their corresponding diseases. For example, the Heart eye acupoint may be needled to treat diseases of both the cardivascular system and the Heart channel.

The upper warmer eye acupoint is

primarily used to treat diseases above the diaphragm including the head, the five sense organs, upper limbs, back, chest, heart, lungs, esophagus, and trachea.

The middle warmer eye acupoint is mainly used to treat diseases between the levels of the diaphragm and the umbilicus, including the lumbar back region, epigastrium and the internal organs within this area.

The lower warmer eye acupoint is mainly used to treat diseases below the level of the umbilicus including the lumbosacral region, pelvic cavity, buttocks, urogenital system, and the lower limbs.

The pericardium is different from the Heart anatomically but is closely related to it and has similar functions. Hence, there is no specific eye acupoint for the Pericardium, however, diseases of the Pericardium channel can be treated by needling the Heart eye acupoint.

2. 眼针取穴原则

眼针取穴原则是以脏腑经络学说为指导，分为下列五种：

（1）循经取穴：根据中医经络辨证，依疾病症状属何经，即选相应经穴区。如咳嗽气喘，胸闷，上臂前内侧前缘疼痛，属肺经病，即取肺经区。

（2）脏腑辨证取穴：如眩晕属脾虚，痰浊中阻者取脾区；属肝阳上亢者，取肝区；属肾虚者，取肾区。

（3）三焦取穴：根据三焦分布的部位对症取穴。如头面之疾寻上焦，脾胃之患取中焦，腰骶及下肢之疾取下焦。

（4）探穴法：用三棱针柄在眼眶周穴区，用均衡力按压，出现酸、麻、胀、重，或发热、发凉，或不舒

服感，是找到穴位的现象，可在反应点进行针刺。

（5）观眼取穴：是看白睛上血管形状及颜色的改变，不管什么病，只要在眼球区有明显的血管变化，即针该相应穴区。

2. Principles of Selecting Eye Acupoints

Selecting eye acupoints is based on the classical Chinese medical theories regarding Zang-Fu organ systems and the channel systems. There are five methods.

(1) *Corresponding-channel point selection*: This is based on channel differentiation in which the point is selected on the corresponding disease-involved channel. For example, cough, asthma, fullness of the chest, and pain in the anterior medial aspect of the upper limbs are all symptoms of lung channel imbalance. Therefore, the eye acupoint Lung would be selected in treatment.

(2) *Selecting points according to Zang-Fu organ syndrome differentiation*: For example, for vertigo, if caused by phlegm stagnation in the Middle Warmer involving spleen deficiency, choose the eye acupoint Spleen. If it is caused by the hyperactivity of Liver Yang, choose the eye acupoint Liver. If it is caused by kidney defi-

ciency, choose the eye acupoint Kidney.

(3) *Triple Warmer* (*San Jiao*) *point selection*: According to the distribution of the Triple Warmers, choose the corresponding Warmer point. For instance, choose the eye acupoint Upper Warmer for diseases of the head and face, Middle Warmer for diseases of the spleen and stomach and Lower Warmer for diseases of the lumbosacral region and lower limbs.

(4) *Point-detecting method*: Using the end of the handle of a three-edged acupuncture needle press along the eye acupoint area with an "even force". If the patient feels soreness, numbness, tenderness, heaviness or a cold, warm or uncomfortable sensation being caused then you have located an "indicated" point. Needle this sensitive point.

(5) *Eye-inspecting point selection*: When inspecting the changes in shape and coloration of blood vessels in the whites of the eye, if an obvious change is observed, needle the corresponding eye acupoint.

3. 操作方法

(1) 患者取卧位或坐位。根据病情选准眼针穴区，局部常规消毒。

(2) 用 32 号 0.5 寸或 1 寸不锈钢针。以左手拇指或示指压住眼球，并使眼眶皮肤绷紧，右手持针轻轻刺入。

(3) 有针刺反应点者，可以直刺 1~2 分，按经区者可沿皮横刺 2~4 分，但不可超越所刺经区，直刺时达到骨膜即可，以有针感为度，留针 5~30 分钟。

(4) 出针时以左手拇指、示指按住针孔周围，右手迅速将针拔出，用消毒干棉球压住针孔至少 2 分钟以防止出血。

3. Manipulation

(1) Let the patient take a lying or sitting position. Select the correct eye acupoint according to different diseases and sterilize the area routinely.

(2) Use a No. 32, 0.5 or 1.0 inch long stainless steel needle. Press and fix the eyeball with the left thumb or the left index finger and tense the eyelid. Meanwhile, gently insert the needle with the right hand.

(3) When needling an "indicated" point, the needle can be inserted 0.1~0.2 inch in depth perperdicularly. If needling a given region, the needle can be inserted horizontally (transversely) at a depth of 0.2~0.4 cm but not penetrating into another eye acupoint region. When inserting perperdicularly, the tip of the needle may reach the membrane of the bone. Make certain to obtain the needle sensation. Then

retain the needle for 5~30 minutes.

（4）On withdrawl of the needle press the skin around the point with the thumb and index finger of the left hand. Use the right hand to withdraw the needle quickly, then press the punctured point with an alcohol cotton ball for more than 2 minutes to prevent bleeding.

第十四节 腕踝针

Section 14 Wrist-Ankle Acupuncture

腕踝针是在经络学说与神经学说启发下，针刺腕距小腿关节以上的区点治疗疾病的一种方法，操作简单，适应丁常见病的治疗。

Wrist-ankle acupuncture is a therapeutic method, based on the channel theory and neurology, by puncturing the spots proximal to the wrist and ankle to treat diseases. It is simple in operation and suitable to treat common diseases.

1．腕踝针刺激点的定位与主治
（图 2-24，图 2-25）

1. Location and Indications of Wrist-Ankle Acupuncture Points
（Fig. 2-24，Fig.2-25）

定位　前臂掌侧，尺骨内侧缘与尺侧腕屈肌腱间，腕横纹上2指。

主治　前额头痛，眼或鼻病，面肿，牙痛，三叉神经痛，气管炎，胃痛，心脏病，眩晕，失眠，高血压，癔症。

Upper 1

Location: On the palmar aspect of the forearm, between the internal side （ulnar side） of the ulna and the tendon of ulnar flexor muscle of the wrist, two fingers above the transverse crease of the wrist.

Indications: Frontalheadache, eye or nasal disorders, facial swelling, toothache, trigeminal neuralgia, bronchitis, stomachache, heart disease, dizziness, insomnia, hypertension.

上　2

定位　前臂掌侧，掌长肌腱与桡侧腕屈肌腱之间，腕横纹上2指。

主治　前颞头痛，牙痛，颌下肿痛，胸闷，胸痛，哮喘，手心痛，指尖麻木。

Upper 2

Location: On the palmar aspect of the forearm, between the tendon of palmaris longus and the tendon of the radial flexor muscle of the wrist, two fingers above the transverse crease of the wrist.

Indications: Pain of the anterior temple, toothache, submandibular swelling and pain, chest distress and

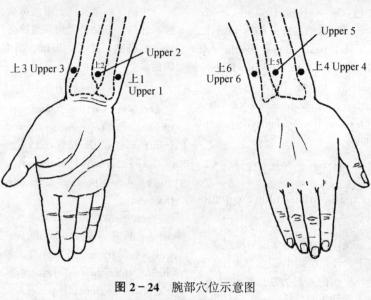

图 2 - 24　腕部穴位示意图

Fig. 2 - 24　Acupoints of Wrist-Puncture

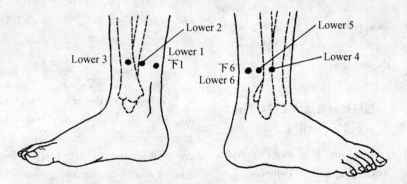

图 2 - 25　踝部穴位示意图

Fig. 2 - 25　Acupoints of Ankle-Acupuncture

pain, asthma, pain in the center of the palm, numbness of the finger tip.

上 3

定位 前臂掌侧，桡动脉桡侧，腕横纹上2指。

主治 高血压，胸痛。

Upper 3

Location: On the palmar aspect of the forearm, radial to radial artery, two fingers above the transverse crease of the wrist.

Indications: Hypertension, chest pain.

上 4

定位 前臂背侧，手掌向内，拇指侧的桡骨缘上，腕横纹上2指。

主治 头顶痛，耳病，下颌关节功能紊乱，肩周炎，胸痛。

Upper 4

Location: On the dorsum of the forearm, with the palm facing inward, at the radial border of the radius, two fingers above the transverse crease of the wrist.

Indications: Parietal headache, ear disorder, functional disorder of mandibular articulation, periathritis of the shoulder joint, pain in the chest.

上 5

定位 腕背面中央，桡、尺骨之间，腕横纹上2指。

主治 后颞部头痛，肩痛，上肢

麻木，瘫痪，震颤，舞蹈病，肘、腕、指关节疼痛。

Upper 5

Location: At the center of the dorsal wrist, between the radius and the ulna, two fingers above the transverse crease of the wrist.

Indications: Pain of the posterior temple, shoulder pain, numbness of the upper limb, paralysis, tremble, chorea, pain of the joints of the elbow, wrist and finger.

上 6

定位 尺骨尺侧缘上，腕横纹上2指。

主治 后头痛，枕顶痛，颈、胸部脊柱及椎旁痛。

Upper 6

Location: At the lateral border of the ulna, two fingers above the transverse crease of the wrist.

Indications: Pain in the back of the head, occipital pain, vertex pain, pain of the neck, chest, spinal column and the area near it.

下 1

定位 跟腱内侧缘，在内、外踝最高点所形成的圈上3横指。

主治 上腹胀痛，脐周痛，痛经，白带，遗尿，阴痒，足跟痛。

Lower 1

Location: At the medial anterior

border of Achilles tendon three fingers above the circle formed by the highest points of the internal and external condyles.

Indications: Pain and distension of the upper abdomen, pain around the umblicus, dysmenorrhea, leukorrhagia, enuresis, pruritus vulvae, and pain in the heel.

下　　2

定位　胫骨内侧后缘，在内、外踝最高点所形成的圈上 3 横指。

主治　肝区痛，侧腹痛，过敏性胸炎。

Lower 2

Location: At the posterior border of the medial side of the shinbone, three fingers above the circle formed by the highest points of the internal and external condyles.

Indications: Hepatalgia, pain in the lateral side of the abdomen, allergic enteritis.

下　　3

定位　胫骨前嵴向内 1 厘米处，在内、外踝最高点所形成的圈上 3 横指。

主治　膝关节内缘痛。

Lower 3

Location: 1 cm medial to the anterior spine of the tibia, three fingers above the circle formed by the highest points of the internal and external

condyles.

Indications: Pain in the medial border of the knee joint.

下　　4

定位　胫骨后嵴与腓骨前缘中点（胫、腓骨之间），在内、外踝最高点所形成的圈上 3 横指。

主治　膝关节痛，股四头肌痛，下肢麻木，过敏，瘫痪，颤动，舞蹈病，膝关节痛。

Lower 4

Location: At the lateral posterior border of the tibia and the anterior border of fibula, three fingers above the circle formed by the highest points of the internal and external condyles.

Indications: Pain in the knee joint, pain of the quadriceps femoris, numbness of the lower limbs, hypersensitivity, paralysis, tremor, chorea, pain of the toe joint.

下　　5

定位　腓骨后缘，在内、外踝最高点所形成的圈上 3 横指。

主治　髋关节痛，踝关节扭伤。

Lower 5

Location: At the lateral posterior border of the fibula, three fingers above the circle formed by the highest points of the internal and external condyles.

Indications: Pain of the hip joint, sprain of the ankle joint.

定位 跟腱外侧缘，在内、外踝最高点所形成的圈上3横指。

主治 急性腰扭伤，腰肌劳损，坐骨神经痛，腓肠肌痛，足前掌痛。

Lower 6

Location: At the lateral border of Achiles tendon, three fingers above the circle formed by the highest points of the internal and external condyles.

Indications: Acute lumbar sprain, lumbar muscle strain, sciatic neuralgia, pain of the gastrocnemius, pain of the anterior plantas.

? 操作方法

操作时，选用已消毒的28～30号1.5～2寸长毫针，进针点常规消毒后，医生左手固定针刺部（腕或踝部）周围皮肤，右手用拇指在下，示指、中指在上夹持针柄，针身与皮肤呈30°角，快速进针。针进入皮肤后，针身贴近皮肤表面，将针身推进在皮下浅表层，针下有松软无痛感为宜。若患者有酸、麻、胀、沉、痛等感觉，说明针身深入筋膜下层，进针过深，宜将针退至皮下浅表部位，或检查针尖是否沿纵行线方向插入，然后作适当偏斜或表浅刺入。进针深度一般为3.5厘米左右，针尖方向一般朝上刺，若病症在手、足部位，针刺方向则可朝下。

进针后不作捻转、提插。留针30分钟，慢性病留针时间可适当延长，一般每天或隔天针刺1次，10次为1个疗程。

2. Manipulation

To the operation, select 1.5～2 cun long No. 28～30 filiform needles for usage. Sterilize the point to be punctured in the routine way. Fix the skin around the area to be punctured (i. e. wrist or ankle) with the left hand and hold the needle handle with the thumb, index and middle fingers of the right hand. Then, swiftly insert the needle at a 30° angle formed by the skin surface and the needle shaft. And then, horizontaly push the needle along the superficial layer of subcutaneous tissue. If there is a soft feeling under the needle causing no pain to the patient this manipulation is better. If the patient complains of soreness, numbness, distension or pain, it indicates the needle has been too deeply inserted or the direction of the needle has been along a vertical straight line. The needle should be withdrawn to the superficial layer of the subcutaneous tissue and pushed shallowly for another try. The direction of insertion should be changed slightly for another try. Generally, the needle is pushed for about 1.2 cun and the direction of the needle tip is upward in puncture. If the disease is located at hand

and foot, the direction of needling may be downwards.

Never twirl, rotate, lift, or thrust the needle after insertion of the needle. Retain the needle for 30 minutes but in chronic diseases the duration of needle retention may be prolonged properly. This acupuncture is done once daily or every other day. One therapeutic course consists of 10 treatments.

第十五节 鬃 针

Section 15 Bristle Acupuncture

鬃针是清宫太医失传已久的治疗眼科疾病的一种有效方法，即以经处理之猪鬃为针，刺入眼部的泪点，治疗某些眼病的一种方法。猪鬃本身含有蛋白质和胶质，蛋白质有营养眼的作用，胶质有收缩血管止血的作用。猪鬃用乙醇浸泡后，形成凝固的蛋白质和胶质，可起杀菌消炎的作用。上泪点紧靠睛明穴，睛明是治疗眼疾要穴。鬃针刺激泪点，可协调眼内的各种功能，又可增加泪液，有益于排除侵入结膜上的异物及眼器产生的瘀血等，并可防止角膜干燥。鬃针治疗眼病方法简便、安全、有效，易于被患者接受。

Bristle acupuncture, which is not handed down from the imperial physicians of Qing dynasty, is an effective method of treating diseases of ophthalmology, in which sterilized bristle is used to stimulate dacryon for treatment of some diseases of the eye. Bristle contains protein and colloid. Protein can supply nutrition to the eye and colloid can contract bloodvessels and stanch bleeding. After bristle is soaked with alcohol, it can form solid protein and colloid to kill bacteria. The upper dacryon is close to Jingming (BL 1) which is an important point for treatment of diseases of the eye. Stimulating dacryon with bristle is able to not only coordinate the function of the eye but also increase tears which are beneficial to eliminate foreign body on the cornea and static blood of the eye thus preventing xerosis corneae. Bristle acupuncture is a simple, safe, effective therapeutic method easily accepted by the patients.

1. 针具

挑选 1 年左右约 15 千克的健康活猪，取颈部之猪鬃用剪刀把猪鬃两端剪掉，留中间 6 厘米长，用洗衣粉洗涤后用热水烫，再用清水清洗，经高压消毒后再用 75% 乙醇浸泡 3 小时即可使用。

1. Needle of Bristle

Choose the bristle of the neck of a one year old healthy pig (about 15 kg). Both ends are cut off with scissors. The middle part of the bristle (about 6 cm) is used as the needle. The needles of the bristle are washed with laundry detergent and hot water. After high pressure sterilization, the bristles are soaked with 75% alcohol for 3 hours. Then the bristles can be used as needles.

2. 操作方法（图 2 - 26）

鬃针主要用于刺泪点，泪点位于目内眦上下脸缘处，为圆形小孔。术者轻轻拨开患者眼睑，暴露泪点，并固定之，然后以另一手之拇指、示指、中指持鬃针之一端刺入泪点，先刺 1.5 毫米，继之斜向鼻侧约 45°，进针 4～15 毫米，局部有酸麻肿胀或流泪即起针。此疗法隔天 1 次，10 次为 1 个疗程，休息 5～7 天后可再进行第 2 个疗程。

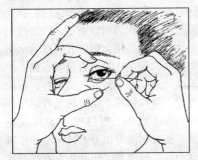

图 2 - 26　鬃针操作示意图
Fig. 2 - 26　Manipulation of Bristle
　　　　　　　Acupuncture

2. Manipulation（Fig. 2 - 26）

Bristle acupuncture is mainly used to stimulate the dacryon which are small round holes located on upper and lower eyelids of the medial sides. The practitioner gently turns over the eyelid in order to expose the dacryon. Fix the eyelid with one hand and hold the bristle with the thumb, index finger and middle finger of the other hand. Insert the bristle into the the dacryon about 1.5 mm. Then continuously insert 4～15 mm at about a 45° angle toward the nose. Take the bristle out if soreness, numbness, heaviness and distension appear at the local area or tears come. One therapeutic course consists of 10 treatments. After taking a rest for 5～7 days, the second therapeutic course can be given.

3. 注意事项

（1）针具消毒要严格，以免感染。

（2）术前应向患者说明治疗过程，取得主动配合，做到"针前安静，针中闭眼，针后望远"。

3. Precautions

（1）Strict sterilization should be given so as to prevent infection.

（2）Before treatment the doctor should give the patient a detailed explanation in order to get active coordination from the patient. The patient should be calm before the treatment. Shut his eyes during the treatment and instruct him to gaze into the distance after the treatment.

4. 适应证

鬃针主要用于治疗眼疾，如近视、乌风内障、暴露赤眼生翳等。

4. Indications

Bristle acupuncture is mainly applied to treat eye diseases such as myopia, glaucoma, lagophthalmic keratitis, etc.

第十六节 指　　针

Section 16 Acupressure

指针是以手指代针在一定的经穴处利用点压的技巧达到治病目的的一种治疗方法。因为这种疗法，主要是运用指尖点刺治病，故又称为指尖点刺法。一般常用于止痛、急救，以及对晕针的患者进行治疗。由于指针安全简便，用途广泛，不需成本，故深受人们的赞誉（图 2－27）。

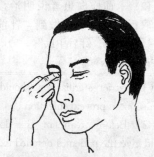

图 2－27　指针示意图
Fig. 2－27 Acupressure

Acupressure is a therapeutic method in which the practitioner uses his finger to press or prick certain acupoints so as to treat diseases. Because this therapeutic method mainly applies the tip of a finger to stimulate acupoints, it is also called finger acupuncture. Acupressure is usually applied to relieve pain, treat emergency cases, and manage needle fainting. It is highly appreciated by people because it is safe and simple, widely applicable, and costs practically nothing (Fig. 2－27).

1. 操作方法

治疗时，患者取坐位或卧位，体位尽可能达到舒适，医者需将两手指甲修整光滑，洗净双手，方可进行指针治疗。手技可分为按压法和点刺法。按压法就是用大拇指深压按在穴位上，并稍用力频频颤动，以加强刺激。点刺法是用大拇指或屈曲的示指尖压在穴位上，稍用力频频点刺。按压法比点刺法刺激强度要大些，一般来说，身体强壮、急性病患者用按压法；身体虚弱、慢性病患者用点刺法。指针刺激可以分为轻刺激和重刺激两种。轻刺激又叫补法，有兴奋作用；重刺激又叫泻法，有抑制作用。选择刺激方法进行治疗的原则是使患者有酸、麻、重、胀的感觉，而又不损伤皮肤为度。

1．Manipulation

In acupressure treatment an appropriate posture, lying or sitting, may be chosen for the patient. Before treatment the practitioner should trim his fingernails and wash his hands. There are two kinds of finger technique, pressing method and pricking method. Pressing method is to press the acupoint with the thumb using appropriate force and frequent trembles to strengthen the stimulation. Pricking method is to prick frequently the acupoint with the thumb or the tip of the curved index finger. Stimulation by pressing method is stronger than that of pricking one. Generally speaking, pressing method is suitable for the patients with strong body or acute disease while pricking method is suitable for patients with weak body or chronic disease. The stimulation of acupressure can be divided into two types, mild and strong. Mild stimulation, which is called supplementation method, has excitative function. Strong stimulation, which is called draining method, has inhibitory function, The principle of treatment with stimulation is that the practitioner makes the patient have the sensation of soreness, numbness, heaviness and distension but not damage the patient's skin.

2．适应证与禁忌证

适用于中暑昏迷、小儿四肢抽搐、中风、感冒、气管炎、神经性头痛、三叉神经痛、关节炎、胃肠炎、神经衰弱、遗尿症、急性结膜炎、鼻炎、扁桃体炎、偏瘫等。肝炎、肾炎、肝脾大、高热及急性传染病、急性风湿症、皮肤病等为禁忌证。

2．Indications and contra in dictions

It is advisable to use acupressure for heat stroke, infantile convulsion, stroke, common cold, tracheitis, headache, trigeminal neuralgia, arthritis, gastroenteritis, nerosism, enuresis, acute conjunctivitis, rhinitis, tonsillitis, hemiplegia, etc. It is inadvisable to apply acupressure to hepatitis, nephritis, hepatomegaly, splenomegaly, high fever, acuteinfectious diseases, dermatosis, etc.

3．注意事项

（1）注意修剪指甲和洗手，以免引起患者皮肤损伤和感染。

（2）治疗时注意室内保温，以防感冒。

（3）操作时精神要集中。

3．Precautions

（1）The practitioner should carefully trim his fingernails and wash his hands so as to avoid damage and infection of the skin.

（2）During the treatment it is important to keep the room warm in order to avoid getting cold.

(3) The practitioner should concentrate his energy and be engrossed in the treatment.

4. 常见病指针处方

（1）感冒：太阳,攒竹,风池,风府,合谷。

（2）偏头痛：头维，太阳，丝竹空，合谷。

（3）鼻塞：迎香，合谷。

（4）咽痛：少商，商阳，关冲，大陵。

（5）咳嗽：大杼，风门，肺俞，列缺。

（6）牙痛：商阳，三间，颊车，合谷。

（7）休克：中冲，劳宫，水沟，内关。

（8）上肢麻木：风池，曲池，合谷，外关。

（9）下肢麻木：风池,风府,阳陵泉,血海。

（10）牙关紧闭：水沟，承浆，颊车，内关。

（11）腹泻：合谷，公孙，足三里，上巨墟。

（12）呕吐：合谷，中冲，劳宫，内关。

（13）中暑：水沟，百会，昆仑，太溪，合谷，曲池。

（14）失眠：三阴交，劳宫，涌泉，申脉，照海，太冲。

（15）嗜睡：申脉，照海，列缺，后溪。

（16）盗汗：劳宫，间使，神门，涌泉。

（17）腹胀：肝俞,胆俞,脾俞,胃俞,公孙。

（18）胁痛：章门，太冲，大敦，肝俞。

（19）腰痛：肾俞，公孙，腰眼，委中。

（20）遗尿：水沟，膀胱俞，曲骨，中极。

（21）遗精：水沟，肾俞，三阴交，会阴。

（22）急性结膜炎：大椎,合谷,丝竹空,足临泣。

（23）手腕痛：外关，阳池，大陵，后溪，腕骨，内关。

（24）膝关节痛：犊鼻，梁丘，阳陵泉，血海，鹤顶，内膝眼。

（25）踝关节痛：解溪，商丘，申脉,丘墟,昆仑。

4. Prescriptions for common diseases

(1) *Common cold*: Taiyang (Ex-HN 5), Cuanzhu (BL 2), Fengchi (GB 20), Fengfu (DU 16), Hegu (L I4).

(2) *Migraine*: Touwei (ST 8), Taiyang (Ex-HN 5), Sizhukong (SJ 23), Hegu (L I4).

(3) *Stuffy nose*: Yingxiang (LI 20), Hegu (L I4).

(4) *Sore throat*: Shaoshang (LU

11), Shangyang (LI 1), Guanchong (SJ 1), Daling (PC 7).

(5) *Cough*: Dashu (BL 11), Fengmen (BL 12), Feishu (BL 13), Lieque (LU 7),

(6) *Toothache*: Shangyang (LI1), Sanjian (LI 3), Jiache (ST 6), Hegu (LI 4).

(7) *Shock*: Zhongchong (PC 9), Laogong (PC 8), Shuigou (DU 26), Neiguan (PC 6).

(8) *Numbness of upper extremity*: Fengchi (GB 20), Quchi (LI 11), Hegu (L I4), Waiguan (SJ 5).

(9) *Numbness of lower extremity*: Fengchi (GB 20), Fengfu (DU 16), Yanglingquan (GB 34), Xuehai (SP 10).

(10) *Lockjaw*: Shuigou (DU 26), Chengjian (RN 24), Jiache (ST 6), Neiguan (PC 6).

(11) *Diarrhea*: Hegu (L I4), Gongsun (SP 4), Zusanli (ST 36), Shangjuxu (ST 37).

(12) *Vomiting*: Hegu (L I4), Zhongchong (PC 9), Laogong (PC 8), Neiguan (PC 6).

(13) *Heat stroke*: Shuigou (DU 26), Baihui (DU 20), Kunlun (BL 60), Taixi (K I3), Hegu (LI 4), Quchi (LI 11).

(14) *Insomnia*: Sanyinjiao (SP 6), Laogong (PC 8), Yongquan (KI 1), Shenmai (BL 62), Zhaohai (KI 6), Taichong (LR 3).

(15) *Lethargy*: Shenmai (BL 62), Zhaohai (KI 6), Lieque (LU 11), Houxi (SI 3).

(16) *Night sweating*: Laogong (PC 8), Jianshi (PC 5), Shenmen (HT 7), Yongquan (KI 1).

(17) *Abdominal distension*: Ganshu (BL 18), Danshu (BL 19), Pishu (BL 20), Weishu (BL 21), Gongsun (SP 4).

(18) *Hypochondriac pain*: Zhangmen (LR 13), Taichong (LR 3), Dadun (LR 1), Ganshu (BL 18).

(19) *Lumbago*: Shenshu (BL 23), Gongsun (SP 4), Yaoyan (Ex-B 7), Weizhong (BL 40).

(20) *Enuresis*: Shuigou (DU 26), Pangguangshu (BL 28), Qugu (RN 2), Zhongji (RN 3).

(21) *Emission*: Shuigou (DU 26), Shenshu (BL 23), Sanyinjiao (SP 6), Huiyin (RN 1).

(22) *Acute conjunctivitis*: Dazhui (DU 14), Hegu (LI 4), Sizhukong (SJ 23), Zulinqi (GB 41).

(23) *Pain in the wrist*: Waiguan (SJ 5), Yangchi (SJ 4), Daling (PC 7), Houxi (SI 3), Wangu (SI 4), Neiguan (PC 6).

(24) *Pain in the knee joint*: Dubi (ST 35), Liangqiu (ST 34), Yanglingquan (GB 34), Heding (EX-LE 2), Neixiyan (EX-LE 4).

（25）*Pain in the ankle joint*：Jiexi
(ST 41), Shangqiu(SP 5), Shenmai(BL
62), Qiuxu(GB 40), Kunlun(BL 60).

第十七节　点穴疗法

Section 17 Digital Point Pressure Therapy

点穴疗法是由中国传统武术中的点穴、打穴、拿穴、踢穴和解穴等动作演化而来的一种推拿疗法，在中国的过去年代比较盛行。武术中的上述点穴法，既是一种击技的进攻手段，又是一种治疗损伤的方法。而点穴疗法则是借鉴了武术击技点穴的技术动作，总结了其医疗点穴的实践经验，并在中医经络、气血学说的指导下用以防治疾病的一种推拿流派。

Digital point pressure therapy, which was popular in the past, evolved from digital acupoint pressing, point-hitting, point-capturing, point-kicking, point-opening and other actions of traditional Chinese martial arts. All the digital point pressing methods mentioned above are taken both as means for attack in striking and as therapy for injury treatment. Taking for reference the technical actions of striking and point-hitting, and based on summarized practical experiences, digital point therapy has become a well-know school of massage in preventing and treating diseases.

1. 基本操作方法

（1）击点法：以中指端，或拇指、示指、中指，或五指捏拢后的指端，在施术部位进行击打点穴的方法，称为击点法或点法。其中根据着力部位不同，又分别称为中指点、三指点与五指点。

轻点时，术者可取坐势；重点时，多取站势。中指击点时的手势与中指按点法相同；三指击点时，拇指、示指、中指指端对齐并拢并捏紧，以三指指端着力；五指击点时，五指指端对齐并拢并捏紧，以五指指端着力。轻度点击时，以腕关节为中心，沉肩，垂肘，先伸腕将手抬起，接着腕关节用力顺势下落，以一种富有弹性的力，对准施术穴点做点状叩击；以中等力度击点时，整个动作要以肘关节为中心环节，沉肩并屈肘90°~100°左右。操作时，先将前臂抬起，并同时伸腕，然后，使前臂与腕用力，快速地顺势下落，以着力指端对准治疗穴点击打；重力型击点时，动作以肩关节为中心，先将整个上肢在肩关节处向上举起，手可高达头以上。此时，屈肘90°左右，腕背伸约30°，接着用力使上肢下落，在这个过程中，前臂在旋前位掌面朝下，腕关节由伸展位顺势向屈曲位过渡，当着力指击打在受术部位时屈腕30°~45°。在进行上述各式击点法时，手指击打到治疗穴后，要随即弹起离开施术部位。

击点法有单点法与节律点法 2 种。单点法是以一次击点动作为一个刺激单元，一般每秒钟点 2～3 次，每次的力度基本一致。节律点法是以一组有固定频率与力度变化的节律性点击为一个刺激单元的手法，常用的有一虚二实、二虚二实、三虚二实或五虚二实等几种形式。虚点时用力轻，速度快；实点时用力重，速度慢。

1. Basic Methods of Manipulation

(1) *Digital-striking method*: Digital-striking method is a manipulation performed by striking the therapeutic region with the operator's middle finger tip, thumb tip, middle fingers, or the tips of his five fingers closed-up. According to the different operating parts, it can be divided into three types: middle-finger striking, three-finger striking, five-finger striking.

In light digital striking manipulation the operator can be in a sitting posture. In heavy digital striking manipulation the operator is frequently in a standing posture. The operation structure of middle-finger striking manipulation is similar to that of middle-finger pressing manipulation; In three-finger striking manipulation, the operator keeps the tips of his thumb, index finger and middle finger at the same level, holds them together, and strikes the operated part with the three tips. In five-finger striking the operator keeps the tips of his thumb and fingers at the same level, holds them together, and strikes the operated part with the tips of his thumb and fingers. In light digital striking manipulation the operator lowers his shoulder and drops his elbow with the motions centering on the wrist joint. He extends his wrist and lifts his hand up, then lowers his wrist joint with the help of gravity and strikes the operated point with elastic force. In moderate digital striking the whole motion is centered on the operator's elbow joint and the operator lowers his shoulder with his elbow flexed about 90 to 100 degrees. In the operation he lifts his forearm up and extends his wrist, then quickly lowers it with his forearm and wrist force aided by gravity and strikes the operated point with the finger tips. In heavy digital striking, its motion is centered on the operator's shoulder joint. First the operator lifts up his upper arm at the shoulder joint and his hand can be above his head. He flexes his elbow about 90 degrees with his dorsal carpal region extended to about 30 degrees, then lowers his upper limb with a great force. In the whole operation, the operator's forearm is in prone position with his palm facing downwards and his wrist joint is also changed from extension to flexion. When the operator strikes the operated region with his fingers, he flexes his wrist about 30 to 45 degrees. In the operation of these striking manipulations, the fingers should be "bounced up" away from the operated part as soon as they touch the operated region.

Digital-striking technique can be divided into two types: single-digital striking and rhythm-digital striking. In single-digital striking one single striking motion is marked as a stimulation unit. Its frequency is 2 to 3 times per second, and the intensity each time should be kept the same. In rhythm-digital striking, a group of rhythmical digital striking are marked as one stimulation unit. Its commonly used patterns are as follows: one weak striking followed by two strong ones, two weak striking followed by two strong ones, three weak striking followed by two strong ones or five weak striking followed by two strong ones, etc. The force in weak striking should be light and quick. The force in strong striking should be heavy and slow.

(2)拍打法:用虚掌拍打体表穴位的手法,称为拍打法。操作时,术者可取坐位或站势。五指并拢,手指伸直,掌指关节略屈,使掌心凹成"虚掌",先将术手抬起,对准治疗部位以一种富有弹性的巧劲向下拍打后,随即弹起,

并顺势将术手抬起到动作开始的位置,以便于进行下一个拍打动作。本法的刺激量也有轻、中、重之分,其动作结构与击点法相似。

(2) *Patting method*: Patting with empty palm on the acupoint of the body surface is called patting method. The practitioner can either be in sitting or in standing position. While operating, the doctor's fingers are closed-up and straightly-stretched. The metacarpophalangeal joints are slightly flexed as to concave the palm to form an empty palm. The practitioner lifts up the operating hand, and pat down the therapeutic region with elastic and skillful strength. Then the hand bounces up right away and restores to its initial position for operation so as to perform the next patting. The stimulus of this therapy can be divided into light, intermediate and heavy types. The structure of this operation is similar to that of digital striking method.

(3)拳击法:沉肩、垂肘,前臂呈旋后位,外侧面对向受术者,术手握成空拳,腕关节伸直,以拳背对准待击部位。操作时,先抬臂、屈肘、屈腕,使手背离开待击部位一定距离,然后,用力朝治疗部位击打。

(3) *Fist-hitting method*: The operator lowers his shoulder and drops the elbow. With his forearm in a backward rotating position and its lateral side fac-

ing the patient, the operating hand is turned into an empty fist. The wrist joint is straightened and the fist back faces the location to be tapped. In operating, the doctor first lifts up his arm, flexes the elbow and wrist and keeps a certain distance between the back of his hand and the region to be tapped. Then, he taps this region with force.

（4）掌击法：包括掌心击法与掌根击法 2 种。掌根击时，四指并拢，拇指外展呈自然屈曲状，腕关节背伸约 45°，使掌根突起对准待击部位；掌心击时，四指并拢，拇指外展，腕、掌指与各指间关节略曲，使整个手掌弯成一浅圆弧形，以与治疗部位——头顶相适应。本法的动作方式与拍法相似。

（4）*Palm-hitting method*: Palm-hitting method includes palm-center-hitting and palm-root-hitting. In the case of palm-root-hitting, the doctor keeps the fingers combined. The thumb is abducted in a natural flexed position, the wrist joint stretched backwards for 45 degrees, and the protruding palmar root directed at the treated region. In case of palm-center-hitting, the doctor keeps the fingers combined. The thumb is abducted and the wrist, metacarpophalangegl, and all manual inter phalangeal joints are slightly flexed so as to turn the palm into a shallow arc

to fit the operated part-the vertex. The operation structure of this manipulation is the same as that of patting method.

（5）小鱼际击法：本法又称侧击法或切打法。操作时，手指、掌及腕关节伸直，拇指自然外展，四指并拢，前臂与手掌取中立位，用小鱼际的尺侧面着力，以单手或双手有节律地交替叩击治疗部位。

（5）*Minor thenar-hitting*: It is also called side-hitting or cut-beating. In operating, the doctor straightly stretches his fingers, palm and wrist joints, with the thumb in a natural abduction. Keeping the fingers combined and the forearm and the palm in a neutral position he pounds the operated region rhythmically and alternatively either with one hand or two hands using the ulnar surface of minor thenar eminance to apply force.

2. 注意事项

（1）防止误伤：治疗前，医生应仔细、全面、正确地诊断病情。对年老体弱的患者，手法要轻柔谨慎，以防导致患者受伤。

（2）防止自伤：操作过程中，医生应该总是采取正确的位置，掌握每一手法的操作要领以防止自伤。

2. Precautions

（1）*Prevention of accidental injuries*: Before treatment, the practitioner should make careful, overall and acurate diagnosis of the illness. For the aged and weak patients, the doctor should operate lightly, softly and carefully so as to prevent injuries.

(2) *Prevention of autolesion*: In the course of the manipulation, practitioners should always take proper postures. A good command of the manipulation principles is necessary to prevent autolesion.

3. 适应证

点穴疗法常用于治疗神经衰弱、失眠、外伤性截瘫、脑性瘫痪、小儿麻痹后遗症、末梢神经炎、感染性多发性神经炎、偏瘫、腰椎间盘突出症、胸闷胸痛，头晕头重等。

3. Indications

Digital point pressure therapy is chiefly used to treat neurosism, insomnia, traumatic paraplegia, cerebral palsy, hysterical paralysis, commenorative sign caused by poliomyelitis, peripheral neuritis, infectious polyradiculitis, hemiparalysis, prolapse of lumbar intervertebral disc, stuffiness and pain in the chest, dizziness, etc.

第十八节　足穴按摩

Section 18 Massage of Foot Acupoint

足穴按摩是对足部特定的穴位进

行按摩以达到促进健康或治疗疾病为目的的一种治疗方法。目前,足穴按摩正在医疗、康复、保健等多方面发挥着重要的作用。随着国内外足穴按摩学术交流的广泛开展,足穴按摩必将以其安全、有效、舒适、无害、无副作用等优点而为世界人民所接受,并为世界人民的健康与长寿作出贡献。

Massage of foot acupoints is a therapeutic method in which the specific acupoints of the foot are massaged for the purpose of improving health or treating diseases. At present, this method is playing a more and more important role in the fields of medical service, rehabil-

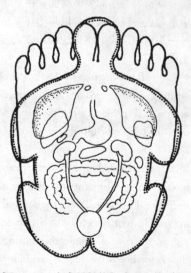

图 2-28　左右足并拢相当于人体缩影

Fig. 2-28　It looks like a sitting person if two feet are put together

itation and health preservation. Along with the nationwide and world-wide academic exchange in massage of foot acupoints, this branch of acupoint therapy will undoubtedly be accepted as a safe, effective, comfortable, harmless and free-of-side-effect therapy by the people of the world and contribute greatly to their health.

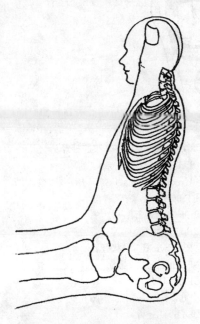

图 2－29 足内侧相当于人的侧身像

Fig. 2－29 The medial side of the foot is similar to the picture of the lateral body

1. 足穴的定位和治疗顺序

人体各脏腑器官在足部都有其相对的穴位，足穴的分布有其一定的规律性。把双脚并拢在一起，可以看成是一个坐着的人（图 2－28）。脚的踇趾，相当于人的头部。脚底的前半部相当于人的胸部，其中包括肺与心脏。脚底中部相当于人的腹部，有胃、肠、胰、肾等器官。右脚有肝、胆；左脚有心、脾等。脚跟部相当于盆腔，有生殖器如子宫、卵巢、前列腺、睾丸、膀胱、尿道、阴道及肛门等。脚的内侧，构成足弓的一条线，相当于人的脊柱，包括颈椎、胸椎、腰椎、骶骨、尾椎。从脚的侧面看相当于一个人的侧位像（图 2－29）。大踇趾相当于头部，踇趾背侧为面部，踇趾跖面为后头部。踇趾根部相当颈，向下依次是胸、腰、骶、臀等部位，踝关节相当于髋关节。足穴的具体定位和治疗顺序如下：

（1）左足底（图 2－30）。
（2）右足底（图 2－31）。
（3）足内侧（图 2－32）。
（4）足外侧（图 2－33）。
（5）足背部（图 2－34）。

1. Location and Sequence of the Treatment of Foot Acupoints

Each organ has its acupoint on the foot. The distribution of the foot acupoints possess a certain regularity. It looks like a sitting person if the two feet

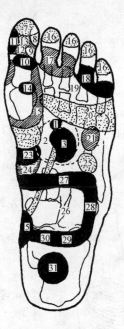

①Adrenal 肾上腺

②Celiac neuroplexus 腹腔神经丛

③Kidney 肾

④Ureter 输尿管

⑤Bladder 膀胱

⑥Urethra, Vagina, Penis 尿道、阴道、阴茎

⑦Frontal sinus 额窦

⑧Trigeminus 三叉神经

⑨Cerebellum, Medulla 小脑、延髓

⑩Cervix 颈部

⑪Nose 鼻

⑫Brain 大脑

⑬Pituitary 垂体

⑭Parathyroid 甲状旁腺

⑮Thyroid 甲状腺

⑯Frontal sinus 额窦

⑰Eye 眼

⑱Ear 耳

⑲Trapezius 斜方肌

⑳Lung and bronchus 肺和支气管

㉑Heart 心

㉒Stomach 胃

㉓Pancreas 胰

㉔Duodenum 十二指肠

㉕Spleen 脾

㉖Small intestine 小肠

㉗Transverse colon 横结肠

㉘Descending colon 降结肠

㉙Rectum 直肠

㉚Anus 肛门

㉛Gonad 性腺

图 2 - 30 左足底穴位示意图

Fig. 2 - 30 Acupoints of Left Sole

(1)Adrenal　肾上腺　　　　　　　　　②Celiac neuroplexus　腹腔神经丛

③Kidney　肾　　　　　　　　　　　　④Ureter　输尿管

⑤Bladder　膀胱　　　　　　　　　　⑥Urethra, Vagina, Penis

　　　　　　　　　　　　　　　　　　　　　尿道、阴道、阴茎

⑦Frontal sinus　额窦　　　　　　　　⑧Trigeminus　三叉神经

⑨Cerebellum, Medulla　小脑，延髓　⑩Cervix　颈部

⑪Nose　鼻　　　　　　　　　　　　　⑫Brain　大脑

⑬Pituitary　垂体　　　　　　　　　　⑭Parathyroid　甲状旁腺

⑮Thyroid　甲状腺　　　　　　　　　⑯Frontal sinus　额窦

⑰Eye　眼　　　　　　　　　　　　　⑱Ear　耳

⑲Trapezius　斜方肌　　　　　　　　⑳Lung and bronchus　肺和支气管

㉑Liver　肝　　　　　　　　　　　　㉒Gallbladder　胆

㉓Stomach　胃　　　　　　　　　　　㉔Pancreas　胰

㉕Duodenum　十二指肠　　　　　　　㉖Small intestine　小肠

㉗Transverse colon　横结肠　　　　　㉘Ascending colon　升结肠

㉙Ileocecal valve　回盲瓣　　　　　　㉚Appendix　阑尾

㉛Gonad　性腺

图 2－31　右足底穴位示意图

Fig. 2－31　Acupoints of Right Sole

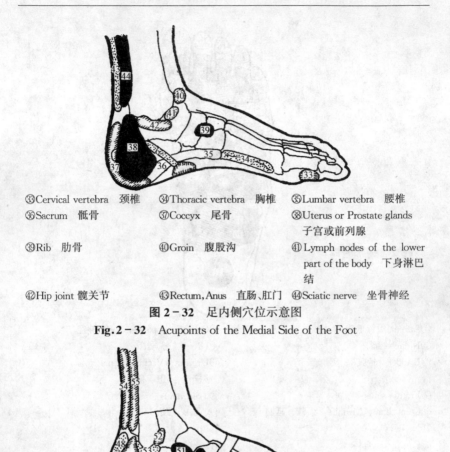

㉝Cervical vertebra 颈椎   ㉞Thoracic vertebra 胸椎   ㉟Lumbar vertebra 腰椎
㊱Sacrum 骶骨   ㊲Coccyx 尾骨   ㊳Uterus or Prostate glands
子宫或前列腺
㊴Rib 肋骨   ㊵Groin 腹股沟   ㊶Lymph nodes of the lower
part of the body 下身淋巴
结
㊷Hip joint 髋关节   ㊸Rectum,Anus 直肠、肛门   ㊹Sciatic nerve 坐骨神经

图 2 - 32   足内侧穴位示意图

Fig. 2 - 32   Acupoints of the Medial Side of the Foot

㊺Shoulder 肩   ㊻Elbow 肘   ㊼Abdomen 腹
㊽Coccyx 尾骨   ㊾Gonad 性腺   ㊿Scapula 肩胛骨
51Rib 肋骨   52Lymph nodes of the upper   53Hip joint 髋关节
part of the body 上身淋巴结
54Lower abdomen 下腹部   55Sciatic nerve 坐骨神经

图 2 - 33   足外侧穴位示意图

Fig. 2 - 33   Acupoints of the Lateral Side of the Foot

⑤Jiexi（ST 41） 解溪

⑤Lymph nodes of the upper part of the body
上身淋巴结

⑤Lymph nodes of the lower part of the body
下身淋巴结

⑤Diaphragm 膈膜

⑥Thymus 胸腺

⑥Trachea 气管

⑥Larynx 喉

⑥Acoustic labyrinth 耳迷路

⑥Chest 胸

⑥Tonsil 扁桃体

⑥Lower palate 下腭

⑥Upper palate 上腭

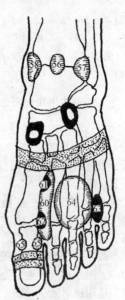

图 2 - 34 足背部穴位示意图

Fig. 2 - 34 Acupoints of the Dorsum of the Foot

are put together（Fig. 2 - 28）. The front part of the sole is like the chest which includes the heart and lung. The middle part of the sole is similar to the abdomen which includes the stomach, intestine, pancreas, kidney, liver and gallbladder on the right foot. The heart and spleen are on the left foot. The heel is similar to the pelvic cavity which includes the uterus, ovary, prostate glands, testis, bladder, urethra, vagina, and anus. The medial side of the foot forms a pitch arc which is similar to the vertebral column including the cervical vertebra, thoracic vertebra, lumbar vertebra, sacrum and coccyx. The medial side of the foot is similar to the picture of the lateral body. The big toe is like the head. The dorsum and medial side of the big toe are like the face. The sole of the big toe is similar to the posterior part of the head. The root of the big toe looks like the cervix and the parts behind the root of the big toe respectively stand for the thorax, waist, sacrum and buttocks. The ankle stands for the hip joint（Fig. 2 - 29）. The location and sequence of treatment of the foot acupoints are as follows:

（1）*Left sole*（Fig. 2 - 30）左足底

（2）*Right sole*（Fig. 2 - 31）右足底

（3）*the medial side of the foot*（Fig. 2 - 32）足内侧

（4）*The lateral side of the foot*（Fig.2－33） 足外侧

（5）*The dorsum of the foot*（Fig.2－34） 足背部

2. 基本手法（图2－35）

（1）单示指扣拳法（图2－36）着力点：示指第一指节背面。施力处：手腕、拳头。适用反射穴：脑、额窦、眼、耳、斜方肌、肺、胃、十二指肠、胰、肝、胆囊、肾上腺、肾、输尿管、膀胱、腹腔神经丛、大肠、心、脾、生殖腺等。

（2）拇指推掌法（图2－37）着力点：拇指指腹。施力处：手腕、手掌。适用反射区：心脏、肩胛骨、肋骨、前列腺（或子宫）、坐骨神经、直肠、肛门等。

（3）扣指法（图2－38）着力点：拇指指尖处。施力处：拇指短展肌、手掌。适用反射区：三叉神经、鼻、小脑、眼、耳、颈、扁桃体、上腭、下腭、甲状旁腺。

（4）捏指法（图2－39）着力点：拇指指腹。施力处：拇指短展肌、手掌。适用反射区：髋关节、腹股沟、肋骨、颈椎、胸椎、腰椎、骶骨、解溪等。

（5）双指钳法（图2－40）着力点：示指远端指骨桡侧。施力处：拇指和示指。适用反射区：甲状旁腺、颈椎。

（6）握足扣指法（图2－41）着力点：示指第一指节背侧。施力处：握拳之手腕，另一手的手指。适用反射区：肾上腺、肾、输尿管等。

（7）单示指钩掌法（图2－42）着力点：示指背面。施力处：拇指固定，示指和手掌用力。适用反射区：甲状腺、耳迷路、胸腺、喉、气管、尾骨、性腺等。

（8）拇指示指扣拳法（图2－43）着力点：为示指第一指关节处。施力处：拇指固定，手腕用力。适用反射区：上身淋巴结、下身淋巴结、横膈膜等。

（9）双掌握推法（图2－44）着力点：大拇指、指腹。施力处：手腕、手掌、前臂。适用反射区：下腹部、尿道、直肠、坐骨神经等。

（10）双指拳法（图2－45）着力点：中指、示指之凸出关节。施力处：手腕。适用反射区：小肠、脑、结肠、直肠。

（11）双拇指扣掌法（图2－46）着力点：为拇指重叠处之指腹。施力处：手腕及拇指。适用反射区：子宫、前列腺、肩、肘等。

（12）推掌加压法（图2－47）着力点：五指指腹。施力处：手掌及手指。适用反射区：胸椎、腰椎、骶骨、尾骨、坐骨神经、尿道等。

2. Basic Methods of Manipulation (Fig.2－35)

（1）*Striking with the index finger* (Fig.2－36)

1）Operating part: The dorsum of the first knuckle of the index finger.

2）Power-applying area: Wrist and fist.

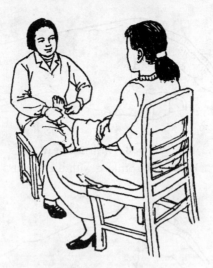

图 2 - 35 操作方法示意图

Fig. 2 - 35 Method of Munipulation

图 2 - 36 单示指扣拳法　　　图 2 - 37 拇指推掌法示意图

Fig. 2 - 36 Striking with the Index Finger　　**Fig. 2 - 37** Pushing with the Thumb

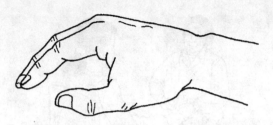

图 2 - 38　扣指法示意图
Fig. 2 - 38　Striking with the Thumb

图 2 - 39　捏指法示意图
Fig. 2 - 39　Pinching with the Thumb

图 2 - 40　双指钳法示意图
Fig. 2 - 40　Clamping with the Index Finger and Thumb

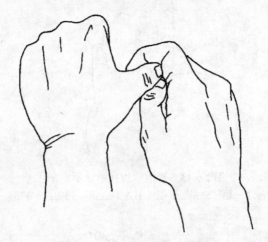

图 2 – 41 握足扣指法示意图

Fig. 2 – 41 Holding the Foot and Striking with the Finger

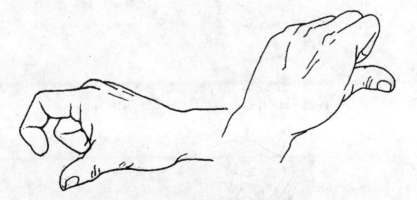

图 2 – 42 单示指钩掌法示意图

Fig. 2 – 42 Hooking with the Index Finger

图 2 - 43   拇指示指扣拳法示意图

Fig.2 - 43 Striking with the Thumb and Index Finger

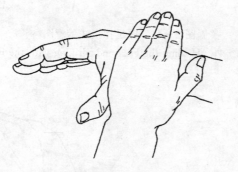

图 2 - 44   双掌握推法示意图

Fig.2 - 44 Holding and Pushing with the Palms

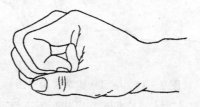

图 2 - 45   双指拳法示意图

Fig.2 - 45 Striking with Two Fingers

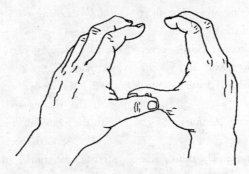

图 2 - 46　双拇指扣掌法示意图
Fig. 2 - 46　Striking with the Thumbs

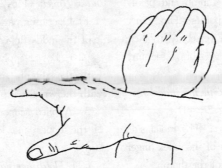

图 2 - 47　推掌加压法示意图
Fig. 2 - 47　Pushing and Pressing with the Palms

3) Applied acupoints: Brain, frontal sinus, eye, ear, trapezius, lung, stomach, duodenum, pancreas, liver, gallbladder, adrenal, kidney, ureter, bladder, celiac neuroplexus, large intestine, heart, spleen, gonad, etc.

(2) *Pushing with the thumb* (Fig. 2 - 37)

1) Operating part: The palmar side of the thumb.

2) Power-applying area: Wrist and palm.

3) Applied acupoints: Heart, scapula, rib, prostate glands (or uterus), sciatic nerve, rectum, anus, etc.

(3) *Striking with the thumb* (Fig. 2 - 38)

1) Operating part: The tip of the thumb.

2) Power-applying area: The short extensor muscle of the the thumb.

3) Applied acupoints: Sciatic nerve, nose, cerebellum, eye, ear, neck, tonsil, upper palate, lower palate, parathyroid, etc.

(4) *Pinching with the thumb* (Fig. 2 – 39)

1) Operating part: The palmar side of the thumb.

2) Power-applying area: The short extensor muscle of thumb and palm.

3) Applied acupoints: Hip joint, groin, rib, cervical vertebra, thoracic vertebra, lumbar vertebra, sacrum, Jiexi (ST 41), etc.

(5) *Clamping with the index finger and thumb* (Fig. 2 – 40)

1) Operating part: The radial side of the distal segment of the index finger and the palmar side of the thumb.

2) Power-applying area: The thumb and the index finger.

3) Applied acupoints: Parathyroid and cervical vertebra.

(6) *Holding the foot and striking with the finger* (Fig. 2 – 41)

1) Operating part: The dorsum of the knuckle of the index finger.

2) Power-applying area: The wrist of the hand of the holding fist and the finger of the other hand.

3) Applied acupoints: Adrenal, kidney and ureter.

(7) *Hooking with the index finger* (Fig. 2 – 42)

1) Operating part: The dorsum of the index finger.

2) Power-applying area: Fixing with the thumb and applying power with the index finger and palm.

3) Applied acupoints: Thyroid, acoustic labyrinth, thymus, larynx, trachea, coccyx, gonad, etc.

(8) *Striking with the thumb and index finger* (Fig. 2 – 43)

1) Operating part: The first knuckle of the index finger.

2) Power-applying area: Fixing with the thumb and applying power with the wrist.

3) Applied acupoints: Lymph nodes of the upper and lower parts of the body.

(9) *Holding and pushing with the palms* (Fig. 2 – 44)

1) Operating part: The thumb and the palmar side of the fingers.

2) Power-applying area: Wrist, palm and forearm.

3) Applied acupoints: Lower abdomen, urethra, rectum, sciatic nerve, etc.

(10) *Striking with two fingers* (Fig. 2 – 45)

1) Operating part: The knuckles of the middle finger and index finger.

2) Power-applying area: Wrist.

3) Applied acupoints: Small intestine, brain, colon, rectum.

(11) *Striking with the thumbs* (Fig.2-46)

1) Operating part: The palmar side of the thumb (one thumb put on the other one).

2) Power-applying: Wrist and thumbs.

3) Applied acupoints: Uterus, prostate glands, shoulder, elbow.

(12) *Pushing and pressing with the palms* (Fig.2-47)

1) Operating part: The palmar side of the fingers.

2) Power-applying area: The palms and fingers.

3) Applied acupoints: Thoracic vertebra, lumbar vertebra, sacrum, coccyx, sciatic nerve, urethra, etc.

3. 注意事项

(1) 足穴定位要准确。
(2) 刺激力度要适当。
(3) 施术时要有节奏感。
(4) 姿势要正确。

3. Precautions

(1) *Location of the foot acupoints should be correct.*

(2) *The force of stimulation should be appropriate.*

(3) *There must be rhythm in the operation.*

(4) *It is important to keep the position correct.*

第十九节　手穴按摩

Section 19 Massage of Hand Acupoints

手穴按摩是对手部特定穴位进行按摩以达到促进健康或治疗疾病为目的的一种治疗方法。每一个手穴都与一定的器官相关，按摩不同的手穴可以治疗与该穴相关器官的疾病。

Massage of hand acupoints is a therapeutic method in which the specific acupoints of the hand are massaged for the purpose of improving health or treating diseases. Each hand acupoint is related with a certain organ. Massage of the different acupoint may treat the disease which is related with the hand acupoints standing for the specific organ.

1. 常用手穴

(1) 手背部（图2-48）。
(2) 手掌部（图2-49）。

1. Commonly Used Hand Acupoints

(1) *The dorsum of the hand* (Fig.2-48).

(2) *The palm of the hand* (Fig.2-49).

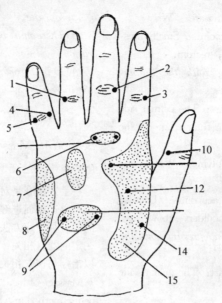

①Lateral part of the head　偏头点

②Vextex of the head　头顶点

③Frontal part of the head　前头点

④Perineum　会阴

⑤Posterior part of the head　后头点

⑥Neck and throat　颈咽区

⑦Chest and abdomen　胸腹区

⑧Vertebra　脊椎反射区

⑨Waist and leg　腰腿点

⑩Eye　眼点

⑪Wulingluo　五零落

⑫Hegu（LI 4）

⑬Vertebra，leg and waist　脊腿腰区

⑭Nose　鼻痛点

⑮Area of the reflex of blood pressure　血压反射区

图 2－48　手背部穴位示意图

Fig. 2－48　Acupoints of the Dorsum of the Hand

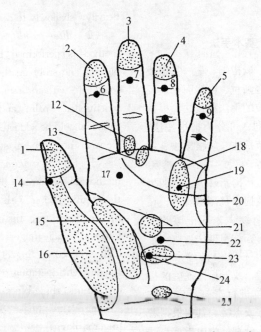

①Lung Meridian 肺经
②Large Intestine Meridian 大肠经
③Pericardium Meridian 心包经
④Sanjiao Meridian 三焦经
⑤Heart Meridian and Small Intestine
　心经、小肠经
⑥Large intestine 大肠
⑦Heart 心
⑧Lung 肺
⑨Kidney 肾
⑩Liver 肝
⑪Life gate 命门
⑫Ear and throat 耳咽区
⑬Palm 手掌

⑭Shaoshang（LU 11） 少商
⑮Stomach, spleen and large intestine
胃脾大肠区
⑯Chest and respiratory organs 胸腔呼
　吸器区
⑰Cough and asthma point 咳喘点
⑱Essence and heart 精心区
⑲Palpitation point 心悸点
⑳Reproductive area 生殖区
㉑Center of the palm 手心
㉒Profuse sweating point 多汗点
㉓Gastrointestinal tract 胃肠点
㉔Jianlisanzhen area 健理三针区
㉕Foot and leg 足腿区

图 2 - 49 手掌部穴位示意图
Fig. 2 - 49 Acupoints of the Palm of the Hand

2．基本手法

（1）按法：以指端、掌、掌根或肘尖着力，先轻渐重、由浅而深地反复按压治疗部位的手法称按法。根据其着力部位不同，可分为拇指按法、中指按法、指节按法、掌根按法、掌按法与肘按法等.

（2）平推法：拇指外展，与四指垂直，以手掌及拇指桡侧缘着力，在施术部位上沿直线做来回推擦的手法，称平推法，亦称掌推法。

（3）击点法：以中指端，或拇指、示指、中指，或五指捏拢后的指端，在施术部位进行击打点穴的方法，称为击点法或点法。其中根据着力部位不同，又分别称为中指点、三指点与五指点。

（4）摩法：用手掌或示指、中指、无名指、小指掌面附着在治疗部位上，以一定的节律做环形抚摩的手法称为摩法。其中，以手掌着力者谓掌摩法；以四指掌面着力操作者称指摩法。

（5）捻法：用拇指与示指夹持住受术者的指、趾等治疗部位，并相对用力做来回搓揉动作，称为捻法。

2. Basic Methods of Manipulation

（1）*Pressing method*: This method is performed by pressing the therapeutic region continuously with the practitioner's finger-tip from lightly to heavily, shallowly to deeply.

（2）*Flat-pushing method*: This method is performed by rectilinearly pushing and srubbing the operated part to and fro with the radial border of the practitioner's palm and thumb. His thumb should be adducted at a right angle with the other fingers.

（3）*Digital-striking method*: This method is performed by striking the therapeutic region with the operator's middle finger tip, tip of the thumb, fore and middle fingers, or the tip of his five closed-up fingers. According to the different operating parts, it can be divided into three types: middle finger striking, three-finger striking, five-finger striking.

（4）*Rubbing method*: This method is performed by rhythmically rubbing the therapeutic part in a circular motion with the palm or the palmar side of the practitioner's finger close to the therapeutic region. Rubbing with the practitioner's palm is called palm rubbing method. Rubbing with the palmar side of the fingers is called finger rubbing method.

（5）*Holding-twisting method*: This method is performed by holding the operated finger with the practitioner's thumb and index finger and rolling-kneading to and fro with relative force.

3．适应证

基本手法可用于治疗心悸、胸闷、胸痛、烦躁、腹痛、恶心、呕吐等。

3. Indications

It is advisable to treat palpitation, thoracic oppression, chest pain, vexation and agitation, headache, abdominal pain, nausea, vomiting, etc.

第二十节 刮痧疗法

Section 20 Guasha Therapy

刮痧即是在人体穴位或皮肤上，用手扯出，或用硬币、汤匙之类物品，刮出一些紫红色、细小似沙粒样的出血点，来治病的方法，民间称刮痧疗法。刮痧疗法所治疗的病通称为痧病。痧病常因夏秋之间感受风寒暑湿之气，壅阻经络，症见恶寒发热、全身胀痛，或上吐下泻，或手足硬直麻木，严重时可出现昏迷。

Guasha, also termed sand scraping, is a therapeutic method in which the practitioner applies his hand to draw a coin or spoon to scrape the patient's acupoints or skin. This causes a purplish red colour or hemorrhagic spots like sand on the patient's skin and is used for treatment of some diseases. Guasha is mainly used to treat sha-syndrome which is a disease caused by the exposure of wind, cold, summer-heat or wetness-evil in summer or autumn leading to the blockage of meridians. It is manifested as chilliness, fever, distension, pain of the body, vomiting, diarrhea, rigidity and numbness of the extremities, and coma in serious cases.

1．操作方法

（1）刮痧法：患者取俯伏位，暴露治疗部位。治疗的常规部位包括背部两侧、颈部、胸壁和腹部。术者右手持硬币或磁汤匙，在冷水里蘸湿后，刮治疗部位。刮痧的方向一般从上至下。刺激的强度可以根据患者的感觉和耐受能力进行适当的调节（图2－50）。

（2）扯痧法：患者取坐位或卧位，术者将手洗净，并备一碗清水。术者用右手拇指、示指或弯曲的示指、中指频频提扯患者皮肤，直至皮肤变成紫红色为止。常规治疗部位包括背部两侧和颈部等。

1. Manipulation

（1）*Scraping method*: The prone sitting posture should be selected for the patient in order to expose the area for treatment. The routine area of treatment with scraping method includes both sides lateral to the posterior median line on the back, neck, nape, chest wall, and abdominal region. The practitioner's right hand holds the coin or spoon to scrap the areas after the tool for scraping has been soaked in cold water. The direction for scraping is gen-

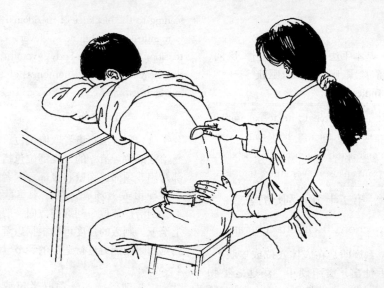

图 2 – 50　刮痧示意图

Fig.2 – 50　Scraping Method

erally from top to bottom. The strength of the manipulation may be regulated according to the patient's sensation and toleration (Fig.2 – 50).

(2) *Drawing method*: The sitting or lying position should be chosen for treatment of the patient. After washing hands and preparing a bowl of water, the practitioner frequently draws the patient's skin. The routine areas include both sides lateral to the posterior median line on the back, neck and nape, etc. with the thumb and index finger or the curved index finger and middle finger of the right hand until the patient's skin becomes a purplish red colour.

2. 注意事项

（1）治疗室要保温，避免患者着凉。

（2）选择体位以患者舒适为原则。

（3）用力不要太重，防止损伤皮肤。

（4）体弱者刮颈部而不刮背部。

2. Precautions

(1) Keep the temperature of the treating room warm in order to avoid getting cold.

(2) The principle of selecting a po-

sition is that the patient should feel comfortable.

(3) Avoid too strong manipulation for the purpose of preventing damage to the skin.

(4) Scraping the nape for emaciated patients instead of scraping the back.

3．适应证

主要用于感冒、中暑、煤气中毒、急性胃肠炎、神经性头痛等。

3．Indications

It is mainly used to treat common cold, heat stroke, gas poisoning, acute gastroenteritis and headache.

第二十一节　穴位棒击疗法

Section 21 Stick-Striking Therapy of Acupoints

穴位棒击疗法是用桑枝制成的治疗棒，击打体表穴位的一种治疗方法。本法具有舒筋通络，活血祛瘀，调和气血等作用。

Stick-striking therapy of acupoints is a therapeutic method by using a stick made of mulberry twigs to strike the acupoints of the body surface. This therapy has the effects of relaxing muscles and tendons and activating the flow of qi and blood in the channels and collaterals, promoting blood circulation to remove blood stasis, and regulating qi and blood, etc.

1．桑枝棒的制法

用细桑枝 12 根（粗约 0.5 厘米），去皮阴干，每根用桑皮纸卷紧，并用线扎紧，然后把桑枝合起来，先用线扎紧，再用桑皮纸层层卷紧并用线绕好，外面用布裹紧缝好即成。要求软硬适中，具有弹性，粗细合用，直径 4.5～5 厘米，长约 40 厘米。

1．The Method of Making Mulberry-Twig Stick

Strip off the bark of 12 thin mulberry twigs (about 0.5 cm thick). Remove the peel and dry them. Roll each twig up tightly with mulberry paper. Tightly tie it with a thread and bundle the twigs up. Again tie them tightly with a thread. Then roll them up tightly with mulberry paper layer upon layer. Then tie it with thread and wrap it with a piece of cloth and sew it. Moderate hardness, elasticity and a combination of thick and thin twigs are required. It is about 4.5 ~ 5 cm in diameter and about 40 cm long.

2．操作方法

本法操作时，用力应果断、快速，击打后将术手立即抬起，叩击的时间要短暂。击打时，手腕既要保持一定的姿势，又要放松，以一种有控制的弹性力进行叩击，使手法既有一定的力度，又使术者感觉缓和舒适。

2. Manipulation

When the stick-striking method is operated, the force used in striking should be in a decisive and swift manner. The practitioner should lift up the operating hand at once after striking. The striking should be very short. In tapping, the doctor should not only keep the wrist in a certain posture, but also relax it. Strike with a controlled elastic force and the patient will feel relaxed and comfortable.

3. 注意事项

（1）切忌用暴力打击，以免给受术者造成不应有的伤痛。

（2）击打时应动作轻柔，以患者能够耐受为度。

（3）治疗过程中，若患者出现头晕、眼花、心慌等感觉时，应立即停止操作，让患者休息片刻。

3. Precautions

（1）Violent striking should be avoided to keep the patient away from unnecessary injury and pain.

（2）Manipulation should be as light and soft as the patient can bear.

（3）During the treatment if the patient feels dizzy, dim-sighted, or palpitation, the practitioner should stop the manipulation at once and let the patient take a rest.

4. 适应证

主要用于治疗风湿痹痛、麻木不仁、肌肉痉挛、肢体瘫痪、肌肉萎缩、头痛、失眠、原发性高血压等。

4. Indications

It is mainly used to treat arthralgia due to wind and dampness, numbness, muscular spasm, paralysis of extremities, myophagism, headache, insomnia, hypertension, etc.

第二十二节　穴位磁疗

Section 22 Magnetization of Acupoints

穴位磁疗是采用一种恒定磁场作用于一定的穴位治疗疾病的一种医疗方法。自从 1969 年以来，许多报道证实穴位磁疗具有消肿、止痒、止泻、平喘等功能。作为一种有效的治疗方法，穴位磁疗现已日益流行。

Magnetization of acupoints is a therapeutic method in which a magnetic field acts on certain acupoints to treat diseases. Since 1969 many reports have proved that magnetization of acupoints has the function of disperse swelling, relieve itching, check diarrhea, and calm panting. Now, as an effective therapeutic method it becomes more and more popular.

1．操作

根据临床的需要，可以选用不同的医用磁体，常用的有圆片形（Φ0.8～2.0厘米）和圆珠形（Φ0.3～0.5厘米）。表面磁场强度2000～3000高斯（Gs）。磁片可直接敷贴在穴位上，再用胶布固定。亦可将磁体置于布袋或皮袋之中，然后固定于穴位上。急性病每2～3天检查1次，慢性病每周检查1次。胶布每3～5天换1次，以防产生皮炎。

1．Manipulation

According to the clinical requirement, different medical magnetic bodies can be chosen, such as a circular magnetic slice (Φ0.8～2.0 cm) or a magnetic sphere (Φ0.3～0.5 cm). The magnetic force of the surace is about 2000～3000 Gs. The circular magnetic slice is put on the acupoint, then covered with adhesive plaster. Another method is to put the magnetic body into cloth or a leather bag. Then fix the bag on the acupoint. Check the patient once per 2～3 days for acute diseases or once per week for chronic diseases. Change the adhesive plaster once per 3～5 days in order to avoid dermatitis.

2．注意事项

（1）为了避免皮肤受损，可在磁体和皮肤之间垫放纱布或薄纸。

（2）患者治疗1周后仍无效，可更换治疗穴位。

2．Precautions

（1）In order to prevent hurting the skin, gauze or paper can be put between the skin and magnetic body.

（2）Change the acupoints if the patient fails to respond to the treatment after a week.

3．适应证

主要用于腰肌劳损、膝关节损伤、头痛、高血压、失眠、支气管哮喘、肠炎、痛经等。

3．Indications

It is mainly used to treat lumbar muscle strain, injury of the knee joint, headache, hypertension, insomnia, bronchial asthma, enteritis, dysmenorrhea, etc.

第二十三节 杵针

Section 23 Pestle Acupuncture

杵针是用一种特殊的针刺激穴位，但不刺入皮肤达到治病目的一种治疗方法。杵刺治疗方法具有调和阴阳、扶正祛邪、行气活血、舒筋通络的功能。

Pestle acupuncture is a therapeutic method by using a specific needle to stimulate acupoints but not to insert the needle into the skin. This method has the functions to harmonize yin and yang, supportright and dispel evil, promote the flow of qi and blood circulation, relax muscle and tendons and remove obstruction from the channels.

1. 杵针针具（图2－51）

（1）结构：杵针是用牛角，优质硬木等材料制作而成，其结构可分为3个部分（图2－52）。

1）针身：手持处称为针身。

2）针柄：杵针两头固定针尖的部位称针柄。

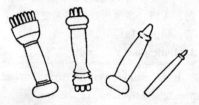

图2－51 杵针针具
Fig.2－51 Needle of Pestle Acupuncture

3）针尖：杵针的尖端部分称为针尖，是杵针直接接触腧穴的部分。

（2）种类：一套杵针工具共有四件：

1）七曜混元件：长10.5厘米，一头呈圆弧形，多作运转手法用。另一头为平行的7个钝爪，多作分理手法用。

2）五星三台杵：长11.5厘米，一头有三脚并排，另一头为梅花形五脚，多作点叩或运转。分理手法用。

3）金刚杵：长10.5厘米，一头为

圆弧形，另一头为钝锥形。多作点叩、升降、开阖手法用。

4）奎星笔：长8厘米，一头为平椭圆形，另一头为钝锥形，多作点叩、升降、开阖手法用。

1. Needle of Pestle Acupuncture (Fig.2－51)

（1）*Structure of the needle*: The needle of pestle acupuncture is made of ox horn or wood. The needle can be divided into three parts (Fig.2－52):

1）Body: The part held by the hand.

2）Handle: The part to fix the tips of the needle.

3）Tip: The sharp part of the needle for touching the acupoints.

（2）*Kinds of needles*: There are four kinds of needle of pestle acupuncture:

1）Seven tip needle: The length of the needle is 10.5 cm. One end is circular shape for the treatment of circular motion. Another end is seven parallel tips for the treatment of flatpushing.

2）Five star and three tip needle: The length of the needle is 11.5cm. There are five heads at one end and three heads at another end. It is mainly used for treatment of circular motion and flat-pushing.

3）Jingang needle: The length of the needle is 10.5 cm. One end is a circular shape and another end is a circular cone. It is mainly used for the treatment of striking, upbearing and downbearing, opening and closing, and circular motion.

4) Pen-shaped needle: The length of the needle is 8.0 cm. One end is a circular shape and another end is a circular cone. It is mainly applied for the treatment of striking, upbearing and downbearing, and opening and closing.

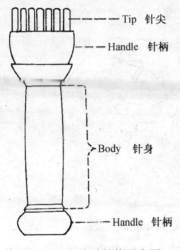

图 2 - 52 杵针结构示意图
Fig. 2 - 52 Structure of Pestle Acupuncture

2. 操作

（1）持杵方法：操作中术者一般都采用双手，右手持针，称为刺手；左手辅助治疗，称为押手。刺手的作用是执持杵针，直接在患者穴位上施杵；押手的作用是固定腧穴，辅助刺手进行治疗。

1）执笔法：拇指、示指持针身，中指靠贴杵柄，如执笔一样（图 2 - 53）。

2）直握法：以右手拇指和其余四指相对握住杵身，如握拳法（图 2 - 53）。

（2）基本手法

1）点叩法：杵尖向施术穴位反复点叩，直至局部皮肤潮红为度。此法宜用于金刚杵或奎星笔杵在面积较小的腧穴上施术。

2）升降手法：行杵时，杵尖接触于腧穴皮肤上，然后一上一下地上推下退，上推为升，下退为降，推则气血向上，退则气血向下。此法一般宜用于金刚杵或奎星笔杵在面积较大的腧穴上施术。

3）开阖手法：杵尖重压在穴位上称为开法，可便气血向四周分散。穴位重压之后，术者逐渐降低穴位压力，但杵尖不离开腧穴皮肤，称为阖法，可使气血还原。一般用于金刚杵或奎星笔杵在面积较小的腧穴上施术。

4）运转手法：杵尖在皮肤上从内向外，然后从外向内运动，或者交替进行顺时针和逆时针运动。主要用于治疗穴位面积较大的部位。

5）分理法：杵尖在腧穴皮肤上，作左右分推，此为分；上下推退，则为理。主要用于治疗穴位面积较大的部位。

2. Manipulation

(1) *Method of holding the needle*

A practitioner generally uses his two hands in the operation. The right hand holding the needle is termed as the "puncturing hand" while the left hand which assists in puncturing by pressing upon the area close to the acupoint is called the "pressing hand".

1) Holding the needle with three fingers: The needle is held with the thumb, index and middle fingers with the thumb opposite to the others like holding a pen (Fig. 2 – 53).

2) Holding the needle with five fingers: The needle is held with the five fingers like holding a fist (Fig. 2 – 53).

(2) *Basic needle performance*

1) Striking method: This method is to use the tip of the needle to strike frequently the acupoints until the local skin becomes red. It is suitable for Jingang and pen-shaped needles to treat the acupoints whose areas are small.

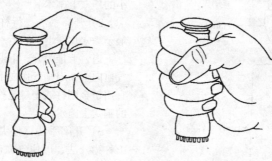

图 2 – 53 持杵方法示意图

Fig. 2 – 53 Method of Holding Pestle Acupuncture

2) Upbearing and downbearing method: In the operation the tip of the needle touches the acupoint with certain force. Then the practitioner pushes the needle upward and downward. When the needle is pushed up ward, the qi and blood also move upward. This is called upbearing method. When the needle is pushed downward, the qi and blood also move downward, This is called downbearing method. It is suitable for Jingang and pen-shaped needles to treat the acupoints whose areas are large.

3) Opening and closing method: Applying the tip of the needle to press the acupoint is called opening method which can disperse qi and blood toward different directions. After the acupoint is pressed, the practitioner slowly de-

creases the pressure of the tip, but the tip of the needle still touches the acupoint. It is called closing method which can restore qi and blood to normal activity. It is suitable for Jingang and pen-shaped needles to treat the acupoints whose areas are small.

4) Moving method: The tip of the needle moves from inside to outside, then from outside to inside, or clockwise and anti-clockwise alternately on the patients skin. It is suitable for the treatment of acupoints whose areas are large.

5) Flat-pushing method: When the tip of the needle is pushed toward right or left on the patient's skin it is called seperate method. When the tip is pushed upward or downward it is called rectifying method. It is suitable for treating the acupoints whose areas are large.

3. 注意事项

（1）患者过度疲劳或饥饿时不宜进行治疗。

（2）孕妇下腹部及腰骶部禁用杵针疗法。

（3）胸、肋、背、腰为重要脏器所在，用力过猛可损伤内脏，故施术者要熟悉穴下的解剖结构，严格把握行杵力度，以免造成损伤。

（4）皮肤有感染、溃破的部位，禁杵。

（5）杵针治疗手法过重，局部皮肤可出现瘀斑，一般不必处理，可以自行消退。

3. Precautions

（1）It is inadvisable to apply pestle acupuncture to patients who are over fatigued or famished.

（2）It is contraindicated to treat acupoints on the lower abdomen and lumbo-sacral region in pregnant women.

（3）Special attention must be paid in treating acupoints on the chest, hypochondrium, back, and loin where the important viscera are located. Too much force may injure the corresponding internal viscera. The practitioner must know the anatomy of acupoints well and control the force in order to prevent accident.

（4）It is not suitable for purulent infected skin or broken and ulcerated skin.

（5）There may be local blood stasis after forceful treatment, which may disappear of its own accord without need of treatment.

4. 适应证

主要用于感冒，哮喘，失眠，头痛，坐骨神经痛，面瘫，神经衰弱，关节炎，痛经等。

4. Indications

It is mainly used to treat common

cold, asthma, insomnia, headache, sciatica, facial paralysis, neurasthenia, arthrits, dysmenorrhea, etc.

第二十四节　蜂针疗法

Section 24 Bee Sting Therapy

蜂针疗法是通过蜂毒和蜂螫对经络腧穴的刺激，达到治病效应的治疗方法。蜂毒具有高度的生物学及药理学活性，蜂针刺激经穴后，经起针刺部位皮下血管的反射性收缩，随即收缩的血管再次扩张，导致皮肤充血，从而提高针刺部位的血液循环，同时通过刺激皮肤末梢神经而促进垂体，使肾上腺素的分泌增加。有利于自主神经调整趋于正常。另外，蜂毒还可刺激人体免疫系统，提高抗病能力。临床上用于治疗心脑血管病、神经病、风湿及类风湿性关节炎有很好的疗效。

So called "Bee Sting Therapy" refers to the use of bee stings and bee poison in stimulating meridians, collaterals and points. Bee poison has a wide range of applications in the realms of both biology and pharmaceuticals. Subsequent to the stimulation of a given area of skin with bee poison, subcutaneous blood vessels in the area contract. As this contraction relaxes, the skin is provided with an increased supply of blood and circulation in the localized area improves. This stimulation of a localized area of skin also stimulates nerve endings in the area, which promotes the pituitary gland and increases production in the adrenal gland. Additionally, bee poison can also stimulate the body's immune system and increase the body's resistence to disease. In the treatment of blood vessel malfunction in the heart and brain, in nerve pain, and in rheumatoid or other forms of arthritis "Bee Sting Therapy" has had remarkable success.

1．针具

一般用家养蜂，根据需要用活蜂蜂针或直接用活蜂螫刺。

1．Needles

Usually bred bees are used and according to circumstances either live bee can be used to sting or else "live bee bee-needle" can be used.

2．操作方法

（1）皮试：将皮肤局部常规消毒后，用蜂针刺入患者内关或间使穴处，1分钟后拔出，30分钟后无全身反应和局部剧烈肿胀、疼痛、皮疹，亦无心悸、乏力、发热、汗出、奇痒等症状，为阴性反应，即可进行蜂针治疗。若出现上述反应，属对蜂毒过敏，不宜施用蜂针疗法。

（2）针刺方法

1）蜂针循经散刺法：局部常规

消毒，将蜂的毒刺从活蜂尾部用游丝镊拔出，夹持蜂针，在患部或与疾病相关的经脉循经散刺4～5穴。做到针不离钳，点刺即出。散刺基本无痛或痛感轻微，对激发调整皮部、经脉经气有特殊功效。此法一般在蜂针治疗第1周采用。

2）蜂针经穴直刺法：取出活蜂的毒刺刺入穴位，留针20分钟再拔出蜂刺。第1次用蜂1只，以后视针刺反应及病情需要逐次增加经穴和活蜂数。运用此法，一般局部均会有肿痛反应，需视反应情况调整蜂针刺激量。

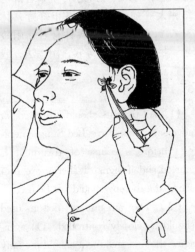

图2-54　活蜂经穴螯刺示意图
ig.2-54　Live Bee Sting Technique

3）活蜂经穴螯刺法：对蜂针疗效较好，且局部反应较轻的患者，可采用活蜂经穴螯刺法。用游丝镊夹住活蜂蜂腰下，直接用蜂针在穴位上螯刺，螯针刺入后能迅速向人体内排出蜂毒，红肿痒痛反应较重，故应严格掌握蜂针剂量及适宜的选择穴位（图2-54）。

（3）疗程：一般隔天或每天1次，7～10天为1个疗程，疗程间休4～10天。

2．Manipulation

（1）*Skin test*：Using either Neiguan（PC 6）or Jianshi（PC 5），first sterilize, then insert the stinger for one minute. If after 30 minutes there has been no anaphylactic response including localized pain, swelling, rash, fatigue, perspiration, fever, anxiety, or itchiness, then treatment can continue. If the above mentioned symptoms are present, this form of treatment is not indicated for the given patient.

（2）*Needling techniques*

1）Meridian line pricking: Sterilize the site to be stung. Using tweezers pull the stinger from the live bee's abdomen. Then insert it into the site of illness or the appropriate meridians at 4～5 points. The needle should not leave tweezers. This form is painless or relatively painless and is especially effective in readjusting qi in the skin, meridians and collaterals. It is usually used in the first week of treatment.

2）Direct pricking of points: Insert

the stinger into the point and leave it in for 20 minutes. The first time only one sting should be used, but afterwards the number of bees and points can be increased according to the patient's reaction to treatment. This form frequently causes swelling and pain so treatment should be adjusted accordingly.

3） Live bee sting technique：Patients who respond well to techniques① and② above or have only mild reactions to bee sting therapy are appropriate candidates for "Live bee sting technique". Using tweezers directly insert stinger into points. Inflammation and swelling may be relatively marked in which case the points used and the amount of poison injected should be monitored closely （Fig. 2－54）.

（3） *Duration of treatment*：Usually a course of treatment lasts 7 to 10 days with treatment each day or every other day and 4 ～ 10 days between courses.

3．注意事项

（1）凡施行蜂针治疗患者，必须先做蜂毒过敏试验，对蜂毒过敏者，不宜施用蜂针疗法。

（2）用蜂针疗法，尤其是活蜂螯刺，应严格掌握剂量，一般首次用一只活蜂，以后每天增加 1～2 只，根据病情反应，患者体质和耐受能力的情况而确定每天用蜂数量，一般最多 1 次不超过 2 5 只。

（3）一般蜂针治疗后可出现一定的毒性反应，如发热，怕冷，乏力，局部瘙痒，皮疹，腋下淋巴结肿大。轻者一般不必处理，可在几天内自行消失；反应较明显者应及时嘱患者多饮温开水、白糖水或蜂糖水，休息片刻可缓解；反应特别明显者除上述补救措施外，发热持续不降宜口服 APC 或肌内注射柴胡注射液；若心悸乏力，可静脉推注 50％ 葡萄糖 40 毫升加维生素 C 500 毫克；若红肿瘙痒难忍，可采用肥皂水冲洗；若淋巴结肿大疼痛者，暂时停止蜂疗，休 3～7 天自然消失，或针合谷、阳陵泉、足三里、太冲等穴，用泻法，或十宣点刺出血。

3．Precautions

（1） All patients should be tested for adverse reactions to "Bee Sting Therapy" before a course of treatment is started and if signs of allergy are present, the therapy should not be used.

（2） The amount of poison used should be closely controlled. On average, the first treatment should use only one bee with each subsequent day increasing 1 ～ 2 bees according to the patient's reaction. As a rule no more than 25 bees should be used in a given session of treatment.

（3） Usually some poisoning reactions

will occur after the use of "Bee Sting Therapy" such as heat, fear of cold, fatigue, localized itching, bruising, skin rash, and swelling of axillary lymph nodes. Mild reactions do not indicate alteration in treatment and will usually disappear naturally within several days. The patient should increase intake of water, sugar water, or honey water and rest. Treatment should be stopped. Patients who react particularly strongly, besides following the above mentioned course of action, should also do the following: For those who suffer long term heat, APC should be taken orally or Bupleurum injection solution should be injected in tramuscularly. Patients suffering anxiety or fatigue should be given intravenous injection of 50% glucose solution 40 mL plus 500 mg of vitamin C. If serious bruising, swelling or itching occurs the localized area should be washed with soapy water. For swelling of lymph nodes the treatment should be stopped for 4 ~ 7 days until swelling recedes and treatment of Hegu (LI 4), Yanglingquan (GB 34), Zusanli (ST 36), Taichong (LR 3), with reducing techniques are indicated or else shixuan (EX-UE) blood letting.

4. 适应证

主要用于中风、面瘫、痹证等。

4. Indications

It is mainly used to treat stroke, facial paralysis, impedimdent pattern, etc.

第三章　常见病的治疗

Chapter Three　Treatment of Common Diseases

第一节　内科疾病

Section 1　Internal Diseases

感冒是以鼻塞，流涕，咳嗽，头痛，发热，恶寒，脉浮为主证的临床常见外感病。一年四季均可发生，但以冬春发病率为高。本病包括现代医学所指的由病毒或细菌感染引起的上呼吸道炎症，流行性感冒等。

1. 风寒感冒

（1）主证　恶寒重，发热轻，头痛，身痛，无汗，鼻塞流清涕，咳嗽痰稀。舌苔薄白，脉浮紧。

（2）治则　祛风散寒，解表宣肺。

（3）治法

1）体针

处方　列缺，风门，风池，合谷。

配穴　头痛加印堂，太阳；鼻塞配迎香。

操作　毫针刺，用泻法。体虚者可用平补平泻手法。留针 15～20 分钟，间歇行针 2～3 次。

2）耳针

处方　肺，内鼻，气管，咽喉，耳尖，三焦，胃，皮质下，肾上腺，脾。

操作　毫针强刺激，留针 10～20 分钟，每次选穴 3～5 个。亦可用耳针埋藏或耳穴压豆方法治疗。

3）拔罐疗法

处方　风门，肺俞。

操作　针刺出针后，可在风门和肺俞拔罐。

4）艾灸

早晚灸大椎，风门，足三里，每次灸 15～20 分钟，此法有益气固表，健运脾胃，增强人体免疫功能，也可用于感冒的预防。

2. 风热感冒

（1）主证　发热重，恶寒轻，头痛，咽喉肿痛，鼻塞清黄涕，咳痰黄稠，口干欲饮。舌苔薄黄，脉浮数。

（2）治则

疏散风热，清利肺气。

（3）治法

1）体针

处方　大椎，曲池，合谷，鱼际，尺泽。

配穴　咽喉肿痛加少商，高热惊厥加十宣。

方法　毫针刺，用泻法。留针

15~20 分钟，间歇行针 2~3 次。

2) 耳针

处方 肺，内鼻，气管，咽喉，耳尖，皮质下，肾上腺，脾。

方法 毫针强刺激，留针 10~20 分钟，每次治疗选 3~5 穴。

3) 三棱针

处方 大椎，少商，十宣。

方法 高热惊厥者可用三棱针点刺放血。

Common Cold

Common cold is a common exogenous disease in the clinic characterized by nasal obstruction and discharge, cough, headache, chills, fever and superficial pulse. It may occur around the year, but more often in winter and spring. This disease includes upper respiratory tract inflammation due to viral or bacterial infection as well as influenza in modern medicine.

1. Wind-cold Type

(1) *Main manifestations*

Severe chills, low fever, headache myalgia, anhidrosis, nasal obstruction and clear nasal discharge, cough with thin sputum, Thin and white tongue coating, supeficial and tense pulse.

(2) *Therapeutic principle*

Eliminate wind, disperse cold from the body surface and promote the function of the lung.

(3) *Treatment*

1) Body acupuncture

Prescription: Lieque (LU 7), Fengmen (BL 12), Fengchi (GB 20), Hegu (LI 4).

Supplementary points: Add Yintang (EX-HN3) and Taiyang (EX-HN5) for headache; and Yingxiang (LI 20) for nasal obstruction.

Method: Use filiform needle to puncture superficially these points with reducing method and retain the needles for 15 ~ 20 minutes, manipulating them 2 ~ 3 times. Even movement method is applied for patients with poor body constitution.

2) Ear acupuncture

Prescription: Lung, Internal nose, Trachea, Throat, Ear apex, Sanjiao, Stomach, Subcortex, Adrenal gland, Spleen.

Method: Use filiform needle with strong stimulation and retain the needles for 10 ~ 20 minutes. Select three to five points for each treatment. Embedding of subcutaneous needle or auricular-seed-pressing therapy may also be used.

3) Cupping therapy

Prescription: Fengmen (BL 12), Feishu (BL 13).

Method: Cupping therapy may be applied to Fengmen (BL 12), Feishu (BL 13) following withdrawal of the needle.

4) Moxibustion

Apply moxibustion to Dazhui (Du 14), Fengmen (BL 12), and Zusanli (ST 36) for 15～20 minutes both in the morning and in the evening. This method can also prevent common cold because it has the effect to strengthen the defensive Qi, promote the function of the spleen and stomach, and strengthen the immune function against the common cold.

2. Wind-heat Type

(1) *Main manifestations*

High fever, slight chills, headache, sore throat, stuffy nose with yellowish discharge, cough with yellow and thick sputum, dry mouth with desire for drinking, thin yellow tougue coating and rapid superficial pulse.

(2) *Therapeutic principle*

Eliminate wind, disperse heat and promote the circulation of lung Qi.

(3) *Treatment*

1) Body acupuncture

Prescription: Dazhui (DU 14), Quchi (LI 11) Hegu (LI 4), Yuji (LU 10), Chize (LU 5).

Supplementary points: Add Shaoshang (LU 11) for sore throat; Shixuan (EX-UE 11) for high fever and convulsion.

Method: Apply filiform needles with reducing method. Retain the needle for 15～20 minutes manipulating them two

to three times.

2) Ear acupuncture

Prescription: Lung, Internal nose, Trachea, Throat, Ear apex, Subcortex, Adrenal gland, Spleen.

Method: Use filiform needle with strong stimulation and retain the needle for 10 ～ 20 minutes. Select three to five points for each treatment.

3) Three-edged needle

Prescription: Dazhui (DU 14), Shaoshang (LU 11), Shixuan (EX-UE11).

Method: Prick the points with a three-edged needle to cause bleeding for high fever and convulsion.

咳　　嗽

凡因感受外邪或脏腑功能失调，而影响肺的正常肃降功能，造成肺气上逆作咳，咳吐痰涎者称为咳嗽。根据发病原因的不同，可分为外感和内伤咳嗽两大类型。外感咳嗽包括风寒咳嗽和风热咳嗽，内伤咳嗽包括痰浊阻肺和肺燥阴虚咳嗽。咳嗽常见于现代医学的上呼吸道感染，急慢性支气管炎，支气管扩张，肺炎，肺结核等。

1. 风寒咳嗽

（1）主证　咳嗽喉痒，痰稀色白，恶寒，发热，无汗，头痛，鼻塞流涕，舌苔薄白，脉浮紧。

（2）治则 疏散风寒,宣肺止咳。

（3）治法

1）体针

处方 列缺,肺俞,合谷,外关。

配穴 头痛加风池,上星;痰多加丰隆;肢体酸楚加昆仑,温溜。

操作 毫针刺,用泻法。留针15～20分钟,间歇行针3～4次。

2）耳针

处方 肺,气管,神门,肾上腺,脾,交感,内鼻。

操作 毫针刺,每次选2～3穴强刺激,留针10～20分钟。亦可采用耳穴贴敷法医治。

3）艾灸

处方 肺俞,外关。

操作 针后加灸,每次15～20分钟。

4）拔罐疗法

处方 肺俞,风门。

操作 坐罐或针上套罐10～20分钟。

2. 风热咳嗽

（1）主证 咳嗽痰黄稠,咽喉肿痛,口渴,发热,恶风,头痛,汗出,舌苔薄黄,脉浮数。

（2）治则 疏风清热,止咳化痰。

（3）治法

1）体针

处方 尺泽,肺俞,大椎,曲池。

配穴 咽痛加少商;汗出加合谷;咳嗽痰多加天突,丰隆。

操作 毫针刺,用泻法。留针15～20分钟,间歇行针2～3次。

2）耳针

处方 肺,气管,神门,枕点,肾上腺,脾,交感,咽喉,内鼻。

操作 每次选2～3穴,用毫针强刺激,留针10～20分钟。

3）三棱针

处方 大椎,少商。

操作 三棱针点刺出血。

3. 痰浊阻肺

（1）主证 咳嗽痰多,痰白而黏,胸闷,纳差,舌苔白腻,脉滑。

（2）治则 调补肺气,健脾化痰。

（3）治法

1）体针

处方 肺俞,脾俞,太白,丰隆。

配穴 咳嗽兼喘加定喘穴;胸脘痞闷加足三里,内关。

操作 毫针刺,用补法或平补平泻法。留针15～20分钟,间歇行针2～3次。

2）耳针

处方 肺,气管,神门,肾上腺,皮质下,交感,脾。

操作 每次选2～3穴,用毫针中等刺激,留针10～20分钟。亦可用耳穴贴敷法。

3）火罐

处方 肺俞，风门，脾俞。

操作 选用坐罐或闪罐法医治，亦可用针上套罐法。

4. 肺燥阴虚

（1）主证 干咳无痰或少痰，痰中带血或咳血，咽干口渴，五心烦热，午后潮热，舌红，苔薄黄少津，脉细数。

（2）治则 益阴润燥，清肺止咳。

（3）治法

1）体针

处方 肺俞，中府，列缺，照海，太冲。

配穴 咳血加孔最，膈俞。

操作 毫针刺，用平补平泻法，太冲用泻法。留针15～20分钟，间歇行针2～3次。

2）耳针

处方 肺，气管，神门，肾上腺，脾，交感，肾。

操作 每次选2～3穴，用毫针中等刺激，留针10～20分钟。

Cough

Cough refers to an abrupt expelling of air with production of sputum due to upward attack of Lung Qi. It is a symptom indicating the impaired function of the lung in its normal descending and dispersing caused by either invasion of exogenous pathogenic factors or dysfunction of the Zangfu organs. According to different causative factors, cough may be divided into two major types, exopathogenic cough and endopathogenic cough. Exopathogenic cough includes wind-cold type and wind-heat type. Endopathogenic cough includes turbid phlegm obstructing the lung type and Yin deficiency with dryness of the lung type. In modern medicine, cough is commoly seen in upper respiratory tract infection, acute and chronic bronchitis, bronchiectasis, pneumonia and tuberculosis.

1. Wind-Cold Type

(1) *Main manifestations*

Cough, itching in the throat, thin and white sputum, aversion to cold, fever, anhidrosis, headache, nasal obstruction and discharge, thin white tongue coating and superficial tense pulse.

(2) *Therapeutic principle*

Eliminate pathogenic wind and cold, promote the lung in dispersing and stop cough.

(3) *Treatment*

1) Body acupuncture

Prescription: Lieque (LU 7), Feishu (BL 13), Hegu (LI 4), Waiguan (SJ 5).

Supplementary points: Add Fengchi (GB 20) and Shangxing (DU 23) for headache, Fenglong (ST 40) for profuse sputum, and Kunlun (BL 60) and Wenliu (LI 7) for general soreness.

Method: Apply filiform needles with reducing method. Retain the needle for 15~20 minutes manipulating them two to three times.

2) Ear acupuncture

Prescription: Lung, Bronchi, Ear-Shenmen, Adrenal gland, Spleen, Sympathetic, Internal nose.

Method: Select two to three points each time and use filiform needles with strong stimulation. Retain the needles for 10 ~ 20 minute. Auricular taping therapy is also applicable.

3) Moxibustion

Prescription: Feishu (BL 13), Waiguan (SJ 5).

Method: After needling, moxibustion is applicable to Feishu (BL 13) and Waiguan (SJ 5) for 15~20 minutes.

4) Cupping therapy

Prescription: Feishu (BL 13), Fengmen (BL 12).

Method: Retaining cupping or cupping with the needle inside the jar is applicable to Feishu (BL 13) and Fengmen (BL 12) for 10~20 minutes.

2. Wind-Heat Type

(1) *Main manifestation*

Cough with yellow thick sputum, sore throat, thirst, fever, aversion to wind, headache, sweating, thin yellow tongue coating, rapid superficial pulse.

(2) *Therapeutic principle*

Eliminate wind-heat, resolve phlegm and cease cough.

(3) *Treatment*

1) Body acupuncture

Prescription: Chize (LU 5), Feishu (BL 13), Dazhui (DU 14), Quchi (LI 11)。

Supplementary points: Add Shaoshang (Lu 11) for sore throat, Hegu (LI 4) for sweating, Tiantu (RN 22) and Fenglong for cough with profuse sputum.

Method: Apply filiform needles with reducing method. Retain the needles for 15~20 minutes manipulating them two to three times.

2) Ear acupuncture

Prescription: Lung, Bronchi, Ear-shenmen, Occiput, Adrenal Gland, Spleen, Sympathetic, Throat, Internal nose.

Method: Select two to three points each time and use filiform needles with strong stimulation. Retain the needles for 10~20 minutes.

3) Three-edged needle

Prescription: Dazhui (DU 14), Shaoshang (LU 11).

Method: Prick the points with a three-edged needle to cause bleeding.

3. Turbid Phlegm Obstructing the Lung Type

(1) *Main manifestation*

Cough with profuse sputum of white colour and sticky quality, fullness sensation in the chest, poor appetite, white greasy tongue coating, and slippery pulse.

(2) *Therapeutic principle*

Reinforce the lung Qi, strengthen the spleen and resolve phlegm.

(3) *Treatment*

1) Body acupuncture

Prescription: Feishu (BL 13), Pishu (BL 20), Taibai (SP 3), Fenglong (ST 40).

Supplementary points: Add Dingchuan (EX-B 1) for cough with asthmatic breathing, Zusanli (ST 36) and Neiguan (PC 6) for fullness sensation in the chest and epigastric region.

Method: Use filiform needles with either the reinforcing or even movement method. Retain the needles for 15~20 minutes manipulating them two to three times.

2) Ear acupuncture

Prescription: Lung, Bronchi, Earshenmen, Adrenal gland, Subcortex, Sympathetic, Spleen.

Method: Select two to three points each time using filiform needles with moderate stimulation. Retain the needles for 10 ~ 20 minutes. Auricular taping therapy is also applicable.

3) Cupping therapy

Prescription: Feishu (BL 13), Fengmen (BL 12), Pishu (BL 20),

Method: Select retaining cupping or succesive flash cupping. Cupping with the needle inside the jar is also applicable.

4. Deficiency of Yin with Dryness of the Lung Type

(1) *Main manifestation*

Dry cough without sputum or with little sputum, spitting blood or coughing blood, dry throat, thirst, feverish palms and soles, tidal fever, red tongue with thin yellow coating that lacks, fluid distribution, thready rapid pulse.

(2) *Therapeutic principle*

Nourish Yin, moisten dryness, clear the lung and stop cough.

(3) *Treatment*

1) Body acupucture

Prescription: Feishu (BL 13), Zhongfu (LU 1), Lieque (LU 7), Zhaohai (KI 6), Taichong (LR 3).

Supplementary points: Add Kongzui (LU 6) and Geshu (BL 17) for hemoptysis.

Method: Apply filiform needle, with even movement to all these points except Taichong (LR 3) which is done with reducing method. Retain the needles for 15 ～ 20 minutes manipulating them two to three times.

2）Ear acupuncture

Prescription Lung, Bronchi, Ear-shenmen, Adrenal gland, Spleen, Sympathetic, Kidney.

Method: Select two to three points each time and use filiform needles with moderate stimulation. Retain the needles for 10～20 minutes.

哮 喘

哮喘是一种发作性的以哮鸣气促，呼气延长，发作时不能平卧为主要临床特征的疾患。哮喘本属两症："哮以声响言"，即以呼吸急促，喉中有哮鸣声为主证，"喘以气息言"，即以呼吸急促，甚至张口抬肩为特征。但两者在临床上每同时举发，难以分开，而且病因病机，治则也大致相似，故作一名为"哮喘"。本病具有反复发作的特点，一年四季都可发作，尤以寒冷季节气候急剧变化时发病较多。哮喘包括现代医学的支气管哮喘，喘息性支气管炎等。

1．风寒型

（1）主证 咳嗽痰稀，呼吸困难，喉中有哮鸣音，伴有恶寒，发热，头痛，无汗，舌苔薄白，脉浮紧。

（2）治则 祛风散寒平喘。

（3）治法

1）体针

处方 肺俞，风门，大椎，列缺，合谷，定喘，人迎。

操作 毫针刺，用泻法。留针15～20分钟，间歇行针2～3次。

2）耳针

处方 平喘，肾上腺，肺，气管，皮质下，交感，神门，内分泌。

操作 每次选3～4穴，毫针强刺激，留针10～15分钟。亦可选用耳穴贴敷法。

3）艾灸

处方 肺俞，膏肓，脾俞，定喘。

操作 用艾炷如枣核大，隔姜灸，每穴3～5壮，不发泡，皮肤微红为度，每天1次。

2．痰热型

（1）主治 呼吸急促，声高气粗，发热面红，痰稠色黄，咳痰不爽，胸闷，渴喜冷饮，小便黄赤，舌苔黄腻，脉滑数。

（2）治则 清热化痰平喘。

（3）治法

1）体针

处方 尺泽，孔最，大椎，丰隆，膻中，合谷，肺俞。

操作 毫针刺，用泻法，留针15～20分钟，间歇行针2～3次。

2）耳针

处方 平喘，肾上腺，肺，气管，咽喉，交感，神门，内分泌。

操作 每次选3～4穴，毫针强刺激，留针10～15分钟。亦可选用耳穴贴敷疗法。

3. 肺气虚

（1）主证　喘促气短，语言无力，咳声低沉，动则汗出，舌质淡，脉濡细。

（2）治则　补益肺气。

（3）治法

1）体针

处方　太渊，肺俞，足三里，太白。

操作　毫针刺，用补法。留针20～30分钟，间歇行针2～3次。

2）耳针

处方　肾上腺、肺、气管，皮质下，交感，神门，内分泌。

操作　每次选穴2～3个，毫针中等强度刺激，留针10～15分钟。亦可选用耳穴贴敷。

3）艾灸

处方　大椎，肺俞，定喘，膻中，足三里定喘，孔最。

操作　每次选2～3穴，用艾条温和灸或回旋灸5～10分钟，每天1次；亦可选用化脓灸。

4. 肾虚型

（1）主证　喘促日久，动则尤甚，喉间痰鸣，气短倦怠，汗出，肢冷，舌质淡，脉沉细。

（2）治则　补肾平喘。

（3）治法

1）体针

处方　大溪，肾俞，肺俞，膻

中，关元。

操作　毫针刺，用补法，留针20～30分钟。

2）耳针

处方　肾上腺，肺，气管，皮质下，交感，内分泌，肾。

操作　每次2～3穴，毫针中等强度刺激，留针10～15分钟；亦可选用耳穴贴敷。

3）艾灸

处方　神门，肺俞，关元。

操作　用艾条温和灸，每次每穴5～10分钟，每天1次；亦可选用化脓灸。

Asthma

Asthma is a common illness mainly characterized by prolonged attacks of dyspnea with wheezing, prolonged expiration and difficulty lying down during an attack. It consists of two disease conditions in the perception of traditional Chinese medicine, i. e. asthma with sound and soundless asthma. The former is marked by asthmatic breathing with a wheezing sound in the throat while the latter by hasty shallow breathing or even with opening the mouth and raising the shoulders in severe cases. Since both may appear at the same time and be actually inseparable, the two are normally called asthma. Their etiology and treatment principle are more or less the same. Asthma may occur in any of the four seasons, especially in cold seasons because of the inclement changes in the weather. It includes bronchial asthma and asthmatic bronchitis in modern medicine.

1. Wind-Cold Type

(1) *Main manifestations*

Cough with thin sputum, difficult respiration, wheezing sound in the throat accompanied by chills, fever, headache, anhidrosis, white tongue coating, superficial tense pulse.

(2) *Therapeutic principle*

Eliminate wind, disperse cold and stop asthma.

(3) *Treatment*

1) Body acupuncture

Prescription: Feishu (BL 13), Fengmen (BL 12), Dazhui (DU 14), Lieque (LU 7), Hegu (LI 4), Dingchuan (EX-B 1), Renying (ST 9).

Method: Use filiform needles with reducing method. Retain the needles for 15~20 minutes manipulating them two to three times.

2) Ear acupuncture

Prescription: Asthma-relief, Adrenal gland, Lung, Trachea, Subcortex, Sympathetic, Ear-shenmen, Endocrine.

Method: Apply filiform needles at three to four points each time with strong stimulation. Retain the needles

for 10~15 minutes. Auricular taping is also applicable.

3) Moxibustion

Prescription: Feishu (BL 13), Gaohuangshu (BL 43) Pishu (BL 20), Dingchun (EX-B 1).

Method: Apply ignited moxa cones similar to the size of date nuts on slices of ginger at the points proposed. Each point is heated with three to five moxa cones to make the local skin turn red without causing any blisters.

2. Phlegm-Heat Type

(1) *Main manifestation*

Shallow breathing in haste with high pitched breathing sound, fever, flushed face, thick yellow sputum that is difficult to be expectorated, stuffy sensation in the chest, thirst with desire for cold drinks, straw coloured urination, yellow greasy tongue coating, rapid slippery pulse.

(2) *Therapeutic principle*

Disperse heat, eliminate phlegm, and stop asthma.

(3) *Treatment*

1) Body acupuncture

Prescription: Chize (LU 5), Kongzui (LU 6), Dazhui (DU 14), Fenglong (ST 40), Tanzhong (RN 17), Hegu (LI 4), Feishu (BL 13).

Method: Apply filiform needles with reducing method. Retain the needles for 15 ~ 20 minutes manipulating them two to three times.

2) Ear acupuncture

Prescription: Asthma-relief, A-drenal gland, Lung, Trachea, Throat, Sympathetic, Ear-shenmen, Endocrine.

Method: Apply filiform needles at three to four points each time with strong stimulation. Retain the needles for 10 ~ 15 minutes. Auricular taping in also applicable.

3. Qi Deficiency of the Lung Type

(1) *Main manifestations*

Reluctant speech, shortness of breath, cough with low pitched sound, sweating on exertion, pale tongue, and soft weak pulse.

(2) *Therapeutic principle*

Strengthen the lung Qi.

(3) *Treatment*

1) Body acupuncture

Prescription: Taiyuan (LU 9), Feishu (BL 13), Zusanli (ST 36), Taibai (SP 3).

Method: Use filiform needles with reinforcing method. Retain the needles for 20 ~ 30 minutes manipulating them two to three times.

2) Ear acupuncture

Prescription: Adrenal gland, Lung, Trachea, Subcortex, Sympathetic, Ear-shenmen, Endocrine.

Method: Apply filiform needles at two to three points each time with moderate stimulation. Retain the needles for 10 ~ 15 minutes. Auricular taping is also advisable.

3) Moxibustion

Prescription: Dazhui (DU 14), Feishu (BL 13), Dingchuan (EX-B 1), Tanzhong (RN 17), Zusanli (ST 36), Kongzui (LU 6).

Method: Select two or three points each time. Give mild-warming or circling moxibustion with the moxa roll to each point for five to ten minutes once a day. Scarring moxibustion is also applicable.

4. Deficiency of the Kidney Type

(1) *Main manifestations*

Dyspnea on exertion after longstanding asthma, severe wheezing, shortness of breath, lassitude and weakness, sweating, cold limbs, pale tongue, deep thready pulse.

(2) *Therapeutic principle*

Strengthen kidney and stop asthma.

(3) *Treatment*

1) Body acupuncture

Prescription: Taixi (KI 3), Shenshu (BL 23), Feishu (BL 13), Tanzhong (RN 17), Guanyuan (RN 4).

Method: Apply filiform needles with reinforcing method and retain the needles for 20～30 minutes.

2）Ear acupuncture

Prescription：Adrenal gland, Lung, Trachea, Subcortex, Sympathetic, Ear-Shenmen, Endocrine, Kidney.

Method：Apply filiform needles at two to three points each time with moderate stimulation and retain the needles for 10～15 minutes. Auricular taping is also applicable.

3）Moxibustion

Prescription：Shenmen（BL 23）, Feishu（BL 13）, Guanyuan（RN 4）.

Method：Apply mild-warming or circling moxibustion with the moxa roll to each point for five to ten minutes once a day. Scarring moxibustion is also applicable.

咳　　血

咳血是肺络受伤所引起的病症，其血由肺而来。以咳嗽痰中带血丝或痰血相兼或纯血鲜红，间夹泡沫为主证。咳血常见于现代医学的支气管扩张，肺脓肿，肺结核，肺癌等。

1.　风热伤肺

（1）主证　喉痒咳嗽，痰中带血，血色鲜红，口渴，咽痛，或有恶寒发热，头痛，舌苔薄黄，脉浮数。

（2）治则　清热润肺，宁络止血。

（3）治法

1）体针

处方　列缺，鱼际，孔最，合谷。

配穴　发热恶寒加大椎、曲池。

操作　毫针刺，用泻法。留针15～20分钟，间歇行针2～3次。

2）耳针

处方　肺，气管，内分泌，皮质下，神门，肾上腺，咽喉。

操作　每次选3～4穴，毫针中等强度刺激，留针10～15分钟。

2.　肝火犯肺

（1）主证　咳嗽，痰中带血或见纯血鲜红，烦躁易怒，胸胁牵痛，口苦而干，大便干燥，小便短赤，舌质红，苔薄黄，脉弦数。

（2）治则　泻肝清肺，相络止血。

（3）治法

1）体针

处方　肺俞，鱼际，孔最，行间，劳宫。

配穴　烦躁易怒加神门，太冲；便秘加支沟。

操作　毫针刺，用泻法。留针15～20分钟，间歇行针2～3次。

2）耳针

处方　肺，气管，心，肾，肝，内分泌，皮质下，神门，肾上腺。

操作　每次选3～4穴，毫针刺，留针10～15分钟；亦可选用耳穴贴敷。

3. 阴虚火旺

（1）主证 干咳痰少，痰中带血或反复咳血，血色鲜红，潮热盗汗，颧部红艳，口干咽燥，形体消瘦，眩晕耳鸣，舌质红，少苔，脉细数。

（2）治则 养阴益肺，清热止血。

（3）治法

1）体针

处方 尺泽，鱼际，然谷，孔最，太溪。

配穴 潮热盗汗加阴郄、大椎。

操作 毫针刺，补泻兼施，尺泽、太溪、然谷用补法，鱼际、孔最用泻法。留针 15～20 分钟，间歇行针 2～3 次。

2）耳针

处方 肺，气管，心，肾，内分泌，皮质下，肾上腺。

操作 每次选 3～4 穴，毫针中等强度刺激，留针 10～15 分钟；亦可选用耳穴贴敷。

Hemoptysis

Hemoptysis is a condition with bleeding originating from the lung caused by impairment of the pulmonary collaterals. It is manifested by cough with blood-stained sputum, bloody sputum or cough with fresh blood involving occasional foam. It is commonly seen in diseases as bronchiectasis, pulmonary abscess, pulmonary tuberculosis, and pulmonary cancer in modern medicine.

1. Wind-Heat Affecting the Lung

（1）*Main manifestation*

Cough with itching sensation in the throat, fresh bloody sputum, thirst and sore throat which may be accompanied by fever with aversion to cold, headache, thin yellowish tongue coating and rapid superficial pulse.

（2）*Therapeutic principle*

Clear up the exogenous pathogenic heat, moisten the lung, ease the collaterals and arrest bleeding.

（3）*Treatment*

1）Body acupuncture

Prescription: Lieque (LU 7), Yuji (LU 10), Kongzui (LU 6), Hegu (LI 4).

Supplementary points: Add Dazhui (DU 14) and Quchi (LI 11) for fever with aversion to cold.

Method: Use filiform needles with reducing method. Retain the needles for 15～20 minutes manipulating them two to three times.

2）Ear acupuncture

Prescription: Lung, Trachea, Endocrine, Subcortex, Ear-Shenmen, Adrenal gland, Throat.

Method: Select three to four points each time for treatment with the use of filiform needles. Apply moderate stimulation and retain needles for 10～15 minutes.

2. Liver Fire Attacking the Lung

(1) *Main manifestations*

Cough, bloody sputum or expectoration of pure fresh blood, restlessness, irritability, pain in the chest and hypochondriac region, dry mouth, bitter taste in the mouth, constipation, scanty urine, red tongue proper with thin yellow coating, and thready rapid pulse.

(2) *Therapeutic principle*

Eliminate fire from the liver and lung, pacify the pulmonary collaterals and stop bleeding.

(3) *Treatment*

1) Body acupuncture

Prescription: Feishu (BL 13), Yuji (LU 10), Kongzui (LU 6), Xingjian (LR 2), Laogong (PC 8).

Supplementary points: Add Shemen (HT 7) and Taichong (LR 3) for restlessness and irritability, and Zhigou (SJ 6) for constipation.

Method: Apply filiform needles with reducing method. Retain needles for 15~20 minutes manipulating them two to three times.

2) Ear acupuncture

Prescription: Lung, Trachea, Heart, Kidney, Liver, Endocrine, Subcortex, Ear-shenmen, Adrenal gland.

Method: Select three to four points

each time. Use filiform needles for treatment and retain the needles for 10~15 minutes. Auricular taping is also applicable.

3. Flaring Fire Due to Yin Deficiency

(1) *Main manifestation*

Dry cough with little sputum, bloody sputum, or constant cough with fresh blood, tidal fever, night sweating, dry mouth and throat, emaciation, dizziness, tinnitus, red tongue proper with less coating, and rapid thready pulse.

(2) *Therapeutic principle*

Nourish pulmonary Yin, eliminate heat and stop bleeding.

(3) *Treatment*

1) Body acupuncture

Prescription Chize (LU 5), Yuji (LU 10), Rangu (KI 2), Kongzui (LU 6), Taixi (KI 3).

Supplementary points: Add Yinxi (HT 6) and Dazhui (DU 14) for tidal fever and night sweating.

Method: Use filiform needles with both reinforcing and reducing methods in the same treatment, i. e. reinforcement for Chize (LU 5), Taixi (KI 3) and Rangu (KI 2), and reduction for Yuji (LU 10) and Kongzui (LU 6). Retain needles for 15~20 minutes manipulating them two to three times.

2）Ear acupuncture

Prescription: Lung, Trachea, Heart, Kidney, Endocrine, Subcortex, Adrenal gland.

Method: Select three to four points each time for treatment with the use of filiform needles. Apply moderate stimulation and retain the needles for 10～15 minutes. Auricular taping is also applicable.

呃　逆

1. 胃中寒冷

（1）主证　呃声沉缓有力，得热则减，遇寒加重，胸膈及胃脘不舒，纳差，小便清长，大便溏薄，舌苔白润，脉迟缓。

（2）治则　祛寒和胃，降逆平呃。

（3）治法

1）体针

处方　膈俞，膻中，内关，足三里，中脘，梁门。

操作　毫针刺，用泻法。留针10～20分钟，间歇行针2～3次。

2）耳针

处方　膈，胃，交感，神门。

操作　毫针强刺激，留针20分钟。

3）拔罐疗法

处方　膈俞，胃俞，中脘。

操作　用坐罐或闪罐法治疗10～15分钟，每天1次。

2. 胃火上逆

（1）主证　呃声洪亮有力，冲逆而出，脘满纳少，呃逆酸臭，小便黄赤，大便秘结，舌苔黄，脉滑数。

（2）治则　清热和胃，降逆平呃。

（3）治法

1）体针

处方　膈俞，膻中，内关，足三里，中脘，加空格陷谷。

操作　毫针刺，用泻法。留针15～20分钟，间歇行针2～3次。

2）耳针

处方　膈，交感，胃，神门。

操作　毫针强刺激，留针15～20分钟。亦可采用耳穴贴敷。

3. 肝气犯胃

（1）主证　呃声连连，脘胁胀满，烦闷不舒，嗳气，胸闷，舌苔薄白，脉弦。

（2）治则　疏肝和胃，降逆平呃。

（3）治法

1）体针

处方　膈俞，膻中，内关，足三里，中脘，太冲，期门。

操作　毫针刺，用泻法。留针15～20分钟，间歇行针2～3次。

2）耳针

处方　膈，交感，胃，肝，神门。

操作　毫针强刺激，留针10～

20 分钟。亦可选用耳穴贴敷。

4. 脾肾阳虚

（1）主证 呃声低长，气不接续，面白少华，食少困倦，气怯神疲，腰膝酸软，手足不温，舌质淡，苔薄白，脉细弱。

（2）治则 温阳和胃，降逆平呃。

（3）治法

1）体针

处方 膈俞，膻中，内关，足三里，中脘，脾俞，肾俞，气海。

操作 毫针刺，用补法。留针 20～30 分钟，间歇行针 2～3 次。

2）耳针

处方 膈，交感，脾，胃，神门。

操作 毫针轻刺激，留针 30 分钟。

3）艾灸

处方 膈俞，足三里，中脘，脾俞，肾俞。

操作 每穴用温和灸或回旋治疗 5～10 分钟，1 日 1 次。

4）拔罐疗法

处方 膈俞，中脘，脾俞，肾俞，气海。

操作 用坐罐或内罐治疗 10～20 分钟，每天 1 次。

Hiccup

Hiccup is a clinical symptom referring to the adverse rise of stomach Qi manifested by an involuntary short, quick sound in the throat. It may occur alone on rare occasions or accompany other body conditions in continuous or paroxysmal attacks. Hiccup is regarded as spasm of the diaphragm in modern medicine. The differentiation and treatment in this section can be referred to for hiccups related to the course of other acute or chronic diseases or that after abdominal operation.

1. Retention of Cold in the Stomach

（1）*Main manifestation*

The hiccup is slow, deep-sounding, forceful, alleviated by warmth and aggravated by cold. It is accompanied by a discomfort in the chest and epigastric region, poor appetite, profuse clear urine, loose stool, white moist tongue coating, and slow pulse.

（2）*Therapeutic principle*

Eliminate cold, pacify the stomach, ease the adverse rise of stomach Qi and relieve hiccup.

（3）*Treatment*

1）Body acupuncture

Prescription: Geshu（BL 17），Tanzhong（RN 17），Neiguan（PC 6），Zusanli（ST 36），Zhongwan（RN 12），Liangmen（ST 21）.

Method: Use filiform needles with reducing method. Retain the needles for 15～20 minutes manipulating them two to three times.

2) Ear acupuncture

Prescription: Diaphram, Stomach, Sympathetic Ear-shenmen.

Method: Apply filiform needles with strong stimulation and retain the needles for 20 minutes.

3) Cupping therapy

Prescription: Geshu (BL 17), Weishu (BL 21), Zhongwan (RN 12).

Method: Use retaining cupping or successive flash cupping for 10 ~ 15 minutes once a day.

2. Ascending of Stomach Fire

(1) *Main manifestation*
The hiccup is loud and forceful in a hasty manner. It is accompanied by a foul and sour smell, fullness sensation in the epigastric region, poor appetite, straw coloured urine, constipation, yellow tongue coating, and rapid slippery pulse.

(2) *Therapeutic principle*
Eliminate heat, pacify the stomach, ease the adverse rise of stomach Qi and relieve hiccup.

(3) *Treatment*

1) Body acupuncture

Prescription: Geshu (BL 17), Tanzhong (RN 17), Neiguan (PC 6), Zusanli (ST 36), Zhongwan (RN 12) Xiangu (ST 43).

Method: Use filiform needles with reducing method. Retain the needles for 15 ~ 20 minutes manipulating them two to three times.

2) Ear acupuncture

Prescription: Diaphragm, Sympathetic, Stomach, Ear-shenmen.

Method: Apply filiform needles with strong stimulation and retain needles for 15 ~ 20 minutes. Auricular taping is also applicable.

3. Perversing of Liver Qi to the Stomach

(1) *Main manifestation*
The continual hiccups are accompanied by eigastric and hypochodriac distension, restlessness, belching, fullness in the chest, thin white tongue coating, and thready pulse.

(2) *Therapeutic principle*
Course the liver, pacify the stomach, ease the adverse rise of stomach Qi and relieve hiccup.

(3) *Treatment*

1) Body acupuncture

Prescription: Geshu (BL 17), Tanzhong (RN 17), Neiguan (PC 6), Zusanli (ST 36), Zhongwan (RN 12), Taichong (LR 3), Qimen (LR 14).

Method: Apply filiform needles with reducing method. Retain the needles for 15 ~ 20 minutes, manipulating them two to three times.

2）Ear acupuncture

Prescription: Diaphragm, Sympathetic, Stomach, Liver, Ear-Shenmen.

Method: Apply filiform needles with strong stimulation and retain the needles 10～20 minutes. Auricular taping is also applicable.

4. Yang Deficiency of the Spleen and Kidney

(1) *Main manifestation*

The low and long hiccup is released with shortness of breath, accompanied by pale complexion, poor appetite, lassitude, soreness and weakness in the lumbar region and knee joints, cold limbs, pale tongue proper with thin white coating, and thin weak pulse.

(2) *Therapeutic principle*

Warm yang, pacify the stomach, ease the adverse rise of stomach Qi and relieve hiccup.

(3) *Treatment*

1）Body acupuncture

Prescription: Geshu（BL 17）, Tanzhong（RN 17）, Neiguan（PC 6）, Zusanli（ST 36）, Zhongwan（RN 12）, Pishu（BL 20）, Shenshu（BL 23）, Qihai（RN 6）.

Method: Use filiform needles with reinforcing method. Retain the needles for 20～30 minutes manipulating them two to three times.

2）Ear acupuncture

Prescription: Diaphragm, Sympathetic, Spleen, Kidney, Ear-shenmen.

Method: Apply filiform needles with mild stimulation and retain the needle for 30 minutes.

3）Moxibustion

Prescription: Geshu（BL 17）, Zusanli（ST 36）, Zhongwan（RN 12）, Pishu（BL 20）, Shenshu（BL 23）

Method: Apply mild-warming moxibustion or rounding moxibustion to each point for 5～10 minutes once a day.

4）Cupping therapy

Prescription: Geshu（BL 17）, Zhongwan（RN 12）, Pishu（BL 20）, Shenshu（BL 23）, Qihai（RN 6）.

Method: Use retain cupping or successive flash cupping for 10～20 minutes once a day.

反胃是以食后脘腹痞满，宿食不化，朝食暮吐，暮食朝吐为主证。本病多见于现代医学的幽门痉挛，幽门梗阻，胃神经官能症等。

1. 脾胃虚寒

（1）主证　食后脘腹胀满，朝食暮吐，暮食朝吐，吐出宿食不化及清稀水液，吐尽始觉舒适，神疲乏力，面色发白，大便稀溏，舌淡苔白，脉细弱。

（2）治则　温中散寒，和胃降逆。

（3）治法

1）体针

处方　脾俞，胃俞，章门，中脘，足三里，内关。

操作　毫针刺，用补法。留针20~30分钟，间歇行针2~3次。

2）耳针

处方　胃，脾，神门，皮质下。

操作　毫针轻刺激，留针20分钟。亦可采用耳穴贴敷。

3）艾灸

处方　脾俞，胃俞，足三里。

操作　每穴用温和灸或回旋灸治疗5~10分钟，每天1次。

4）拔罐疗法

处方　脾俞，胃俞，中脘。

操作　用坐罐或闪罐治疗10~20分钟，每天1次。

2．痰浊阻胃

（1）主证　脘腹胀满，食后尤甚，上腹或有积块，朝食暮吐，暮食朝吐，吐出宿食不化兼有痰涎水饮，或吐白沫，或有眩晕，心下悸，舌苔白滑，脉弦滑。

（2）治则　涤痰化浊，和胃降逆。

（3）治法

1）体针

处方　中脘，丰隆，建里，足三里，内关。

操作　毫针刺，用泻法或平补平

泻法，留针20~30分钟，间歇行针2~3次。

2）耳针

处方　胃，脾，神门，枕，皮质下。

操作　毫针刺，中等强度，留针20分钟。亦可用耳穴贴敷。

3）艾灸

处方　脾俞，胃俞，中脘。

操作　每穴用温和灸治疗5~10分钟，每天1次。

Stomach Reflux

Stomach reflux is characterized by epigastric distension with undigested food and fullness in the abdomen hours after food intake. The patient may vomit the food that he took in the morning in the afternoon, or the food that he took in the previous evening the next morning . Stomach reflux is seen is patients with pylorospasm, prolorochesis and gastroneurosis in terms of modern medicine.

1. Deficient Cold in the Spleen and Stomach

(1) *Main manifestation*

Distension and fullness sensation in the epigastrium and abdomen after meals, vomiting of undigested food and gastric fluid hours after food intake. Relief is attained with thorough vomiting. It is accompanied by lassitude, weakness, pallor complexion, loose stools, pale tongue proper with coating, and thin weak pulse.

(2) *Therapeutic principle*

Warm up the middle Jiao, eliminate cold, pacify the stomach and ease the retroactive stomach Qi.

(3) *Treatment*

1) Body acupunctrue

Prescription: Pishu (BL 20), Weishu (BL 21), Zhangmen (LR 13), Zhongwan (RN 12), Zusanli (ST 36), Neiguan (PC 6).

Method: Apply filiform needles with reinforcing method. Retain the needles for 20~30 minutes manipulating them two to three times.

2) Ear acupuncture

Prescription: Stomach, Spleen, Ear-shenmen, Subcortex.

Method: Apply filiform needles with mild stimulation and retain the needles for 20 minutes. Auricular taping is also applicable.

3) Moxibustion

Prescription: Pishu (BL 20), Weishu (BL 21) Zusanli (ST 36).

Method: Apply mild-warming moxibustion or rounding moxibustion to each point for 5~10 minutes once a day.

4) Cupping therapy

Prescription: Pishu (BL 20), Weishu (BL 21), Zhongwan (RN 12).

Method: Use retain cupping or suc-

cessive flash cupping for 10~20 minutes once a day.

2. Turbid Phlegm Obstructing the Stomanch

(1) *Main manifestation*

Epigastric and abdominal distension worse after meal, possible mass in the upper abdomen, vomiting of food retained in the stomach hours after food intake. The vomiting may involve some watery discharge and foam. It is accompanied by dizziness, palpitation, white slippery tongue, and thready slippery pulse.

(2) *Therapeutic principle*

Resolve the turbid phlegm, pacify the stomach and ease the retroactive stomach Qi.

(3) *Treatment*

1) Body acupuncture

Prescription: Zhongwan (RN 12), Fenglong (ST 40), Jianli (RN 11), Zusanli (ST 36), Neiguan (PC 6).

Method: Apply filiform needles with reducing or even movement method. Retain the needles for 20~30 minutes manipulating the needles two to three times.

2) Ear acupuncture

Prescription: Stomach, Spleen, Ear-shenmen, Occiput, Subcortex.

Method: Apply filiform needles with moderate stimulation and retain the

needles for 20 minutes. Auricular taping is also applicable.

3) Moxibustion

Prescription：Pishu（BL 20），
Weishu（BL 21），Zhongwan（RN
12）.

Method：Apply mild-warming moxibustion to each point for 5～10 minutes
once a day.

噎　膈

噎膈是指饮食吞咽受阻，或食入
即吐的一种病症。噎即噎塞，是吞咽
时梗塞不顺；膈为胸膈梗阻，饮食格
拒不下，或食入即吐。噎证既可单独
出现，又可为膈证的前兆，故以噎膈
并称。噎膈相当于现代医学的幽门梗
阻，食管憩室，食管神经官能症，食
管炎等。亦可见于现代医学的食管
癌，胃癌，贲门癌，贲门痉挛。

1. 痰气交阻

（1）主证　吞咽梗阻，胸膈痞满
隐痛，嗳气呃逆，或呕吐痰涎及食
物，大便艰涩，口干咽燥，体质逐渐
消瘦，舌质红，脉弦细而滑。

（2）治则　开胸膈，调胃气，降
痰浊。

（3）治法

1）体针

处方　天突，膻中，巨阙，内
关，上脘，丰隆。

配穴　胸膈痞满加膈关；大便艰
涩加天枢。

操作　毫针刺，用泻法，留针
20～30分钟，间歇行针2～3次。

2）耳针

处方　神门，胃，食管，膈。

操作　毫针中等强度刺激，留针
30分钟。并可采用耳穴埋针。

2. 痰瘀内结

（1）主证　吞咽困难，胸膈疼
痛，食不能下，甚则滴水难进，进食
即吐，泛吐黏痰，大便坚如羊屎，或
吐下如赤豆汁，或便血，形体消瘦，
肌肤枯燥，舌红少津，脉细涩。

（2）治则　滋阴祛瘀开结，除痰
降逆利膈。

（3）治法

1）体针

处方　膈俞，膈关，膻中，中
脘，照海，关冲。

操作　毫针刺，除照海穴用补法
外，余用泻法。留针15～20分钟，
间歇行针2～3次。

2）耳针

处方　神门，胃，食管，膈，
脾。

操作　毫针中等强度刺激，留针
30分钟。亦可采用耳穴埋针。

3. 气虚阳微

（1）主证　吞咽受阻，饮食难
下，面色㿠白，形寒气短，泛吐涎
沫，面浮足肿，腹胀，舌胖，苔淡
白，脉细弱。

（2）治则　温补脾肾，益气

回阳。

（3）治法

1）体针

处方　脾俞，肾俞，胃俞，气海，膈俞，足三里。

操作　毫针刺，用补法。留针15～30分钟，间歇行针1～2次。

2）耳针

处方　神门，胃，脾，食管，膈，肾。

操作　毫针中等强度刺激，留针30分钟，亦可采用耳穴埋针。

3）艾灸

处方　脾俞，肾俞，膈俞，胃俞。

操作　每穴用温和灸或回旋灸治疗5～10分钟，每天1次。

Dysphagia Syndrome

Dysphagia syndrome refers to a condition characterized by a feeling of obstruction during swallowing and instant vomiting after food intake. The obstructive feeling for swallowing is called Ye while the difficulty in swallowing food and instant vomiting is called Ge in Chinese language. Since the former may not only appear alone in clinic, but also became the pretophase of the latter. These two are collectively known as the dysphagia syndrome in TCM. The syndrome may include such diseases as pylorochesis, esophageal diverticulum, esophageal neurosis, esophagitis, esophageal carcinoma, gastric cancer, cardiac cancer and cardiospasm in modern medicine.

1．Stagnation of Phlegmatic Qi

（1）*Main manifestation*

Feeling of obstruction during swallowing, fullness in the chest and epigastrium, dull pain, belching, hiccup together with vomiting of thin mucous sputum and food substance, severe constipation, dry mouth, progressive loss of weight, red tongue proper, and thready slippery pulse.

（2）*Therapeutic principle*

Relieve fullness in the chest, regulate the stomach Qi and lower the turbid phlegm.

（3）*Treatment*

1）Body acupuncture

Prescription: Tiantu（RN 22），Tanzhong（RN 17），Juque（RN 14），Neiguan（PC 6），Shangwan（RN 13），Fenglong（ST 40）

Supplementary points: Add Geguan（BL 46）for fullness in the chest and epigastrium, and Tianshu（ST 25）for constipation.

Method: Apply filiform needles with reducing method. Retain the needles for 20～30 minutes manipulating them two to three times.

2）Ear acupuncture

Prescription: Ear-shemen, Stomach, Esophagus, Diaphragm.

Method: Use filiform needles with moderate stimulation and retain the needles for 30 minutes. Embedding of subcutaneous needles is also applicable.

2. Retention of Phlegm in the Interior

(1) *Main manifestation*

Dysphagia with pain in the chest and epigastrium, difficulty in swallowing food or water, instant vomiting, vomiting of mucous sputum, and dry stools. It may also accompanied by vomiting of reddish fluid, bloody stools, emaciation, rough dry skin, dry red tongue proper.

(2) *Therapeutic principle*

Nourish Yin, resolve stasis of blood and phlegm, halt reverse of flow of Qi and ease the diaphragm.

(3) *Treatment*

1) Body acupuncture

Prescription: Geshu (BL 17), Geguan (BL 46), Tanzhong (RN 17), Zhongwan (RN 12), Zhaohai (KI 6), Guanchong (SJ 1).

Method: Use filiform needles with reducing method except Zhaohai (KI 6) which is needled with reinforcing method. Retain the needles for 15~20 minutes manipulating them two to three times.

2) Ear acupuncture

Prescription: Ear-shenmen, Stomach, Esophagus, Diaphragm, Spleen.

Method: Use filiform needles with moderate stimulation and retain the needles for 30 minutes. Embedding of subcutaneous needle is also applicable.

3. Exhaustion of Yang Qi

(1) *Main manifestation*

Difficulty in swallowing food, pale complexion, cold limbs, shortness of breath, vomiting of frothy sputum, edema in the face and feet, abdominal distention, flabby tongue, and weak thready pulse.

(2) *Therapeutic principle*

Warm up and tonify the spleen and kidney, strengthen Qi and rescue the patient from collapse of Yang Qi.

(3) *Treatment*

1) Body acupuncture

Prescription: Pishu (BL 20), Shenshu (BL 23) Weishu (BL 21), Qihai (RN 6), Geshu (BL 17), Zusanli (ST 36).

Method: Apply filiform needles with reinforcing method. Retain the needles for 15~30 minutes manipulating them one to two times.

2) Ear acupuncture

Prescription: Ear-shenmen, Stomach, Spleen, Esophagus, Diaphragm, Kidney.

Method: Use filiform needles with moderate stimulation and retain the needles for 30 minutes. Embedding of subcutaneous needles is also applicable.

3）Moxibustion

Prescription: Pishu（BL 20），Shenshu（BL 23），Geshu（BL 17），Weishu（BL 21）.

Method: Apply mild-warming moxibustion or rounding moxibustion to each points for 5～10 minutes once a day.

胃脘痛

胃脘痛又称胃痛。以胃脘部近心窝处经常发生疼痛为主要症状。由于痛近心窝部，故又有心痛、心腹痛之称，但与真心痛有别。现代医学的急、慢性胃炎，胃、十二指肠溃疡，胃神经官能症，胃癌等均属胃脘痛范畴。

1．肝气犯胃

（1）主证 胃脘胀满，攻痛两胁，走窜不定，嗳气频作，呕逆酸苦，苔薄白，脉弦。

（2）治则 疏肝和胃止痛。

（3）治法

1）体针

处方 中脘 内关，期门，足三里，太冲。

操作 毫针刺，用泻法。留针15～20分钟，间歇行针2～3次。

2）耳针

处方 肝，胃，交感，神门，皮质下。

操作 毫针强刺激，留针15～30分钟；亦可采用耳穴贴敷。

2．郁热

（1）主证 胃脘部疼痛，痛势急迫，心烦易怒，泛酸嘈杂，口干口苦，胃脘部有灼热感，舌红苔黄，脉弦数。

（2）治则 清肝泄热，和胃止痛。

（3）治法

1）体针

处方 行间 中脘 内关，足三里，太溪。

操作 毫针刺，用泻法。留针15～20分钟，间歇行针2～3分钟。

2）耳针

处方 胃，交感，神门，肝，皮质下，内分泌。

操作 毫针强刺激，留针15～30分钟。亦可用耳穴贴敷。

3．血瘀

（1）主证 痛有定处而拒按，食后较甚，或见吐血，大便发黑，甚者舌质紫暗，脉涩。

（2）治则 活血通络，和胃止痛。

（3）治法

1）体针

处方 中脘，内关，足三里，公孙，血海，膈俞。

操作 毫针刺，用泻法。留针15～20分钟，间歇行针2～3次。

2）耳针

处方 胃，交感，神门，皮质

下，内分泌。

操作　毫针强刺激，留针 15～30 分钟；亦可采用耳穴贴敷。

4. 饮食停滞

（1）主证　胃脘胀满作痛，嗳腐吞酸，不思饮食，食则痛甚，或呕吐不消化食物，吐后痛减，舌苔厚腻，脉沉实或滑。

（2）治则　消食导滞，和胃止痛。

（3）治法

1）体针

处方　中脘，足三里，梁门，天枢。

操作　毫针刺，用泻法。留针20～30 分钟，间歇行针 2～3 次。

2）耳针

处方　胃，脾，交感，神门，皮质下，内分泌。

操作　毫针刺，强刺激。留针15～30 分钟，亦可用耳穴贴敷。

5. 脾胃虚寒

（1）主证　胃脘隐痛，泛吐清水，喜暖喜按，神疲乏力，四肢欠温，纳食减少，大便溏薄，舌质淡，脉虚弱。

（2）治则　温中健脾，散寒止痛。

（3）治法

1）体针

处方　脾俞，胃俞，章门，中脘，足三里，内关。

操作　毫针刺，用补法。留针20～30 分钟，间歇行针 2～3 次。

2）耳针

处方　脾，胃，交感，神门，十二指肠，皮质下，内分泌。

操作　毫针温和刺激，留针15～30 分钟。亦可采用耳穴贴敷。

3）艾灸

处方　脾俞，胃俞，中脘，足三里。

操用　每穴用温和灸或回旋灸治疗 5～10 分钟，每天 1 次。

4）拔罐疗法

处方　脾俞，胃俞，中脘。

操作　用坐罐或闪罐治疗 10～20 分钟，每天 1 次。

Epigastric Pain

Epigastric pain, also known as gastric pain, refers to a syndrome manifested by frequent pain over the epigastric region. In the ancient times, it was mistakenly called cardiac pain because the painful area was close to the center of the chest. It may commonly be seen in acute and chronic gastritis, gastric or duodenal ulcer, gastroneurosis and gastric cancer in modern medicine.

1. Liver Qi Attacking the Stomach

(1) *Main manifestation*

Epigastric fullness, distention and wandering pain which radiates to the hypochondriac region, frequent belching, acid regurgitation, vomiting, bitter taste in the mouth, thin white tongue coating, and thready pulse.

(2) *Therapeutic principle*

Remove the stagnation of liver Qi, pacify the stomach and relieve pain.

(3) *Treatment*

1) Body acupuncture

Prescription: Zhongwan (RN 12), Neiguan (PC 6), Qimen (LR 14), Zusanli (ST 36), Taichong (LR 3).

Method: Apply filiform needles with reducing method. Retain the needles for 15~20 minutes manipulating them two to three times.

2) Ear acupuncture

Prescription: Liver, Stomach, Sympathetic, Ear-shenmen, Subcortex

Method: Use filiform needles with strong stimulation and retain the needles for 15~30 minutes. Auricular taping is also applicable.

2. Stagnant Heat

(1) *Main manifestation*

Sudden onset of epigastric pain, restlessness, irritability, acid regurgitation, discomfort sensation in the stomach, dry mouth, bitter taste in the mouth, red tongue proper with yellow coating, and rapid thready pulse.

(2) *Therapeutic principle*

Sedate heat from the liver, pacify the stomach and stop pain.

(3) *Treatment*

1) Body acupuncture

Prescription: Xingjian (LR 2), Zhongwan (RN 12), Neiguan (PC 6), Zusanli (ST 36), Taixi (KI 3)

Method: Apply filiform needles with reducing method. Retain the needles for 15 ~ 20 minutes, manipulating them two to three times.

2) Ear acupuncture

Prescription: Stomach, Sympathetic, Ear-shenmen, Liver, Subcortex, Endocrine.

Method: Use filiform needles with strong stimulation and retain the needles for 15 ~ 30 minutes. Auricular taping is also applicable.

3. Stasis of Blood

(1) *Main manifestation*

Fixed pain aggravated by pressing or food intake, bloody vomiting, melena, dark purplish tongue proper, and uneven pulse.

(2) *Therapeutic principle*

Activate blood circulation in the channels and collaterals, pacify the stomach and stop pain.

(3) *Treatment*

1) Body acupuncture

Prescription: Zhongwan (RN 12), Neiguan (PC 6), Zusanli (ST 36), Gongsun (SP 4), Xuehai (SP 10), Geshu (BL 17).

Method: Apply filiform needle with reducing method. Retain the needles for 15 ~ 20 minutes manipulating them two to three times.

2) Ear acupuncture

Prescription: Stomach, Sympathetic, Ear-shenmen, Subcortex, Endocrine.

Method: Use filiform needles with strong stimulation and retain the needles for 15 ~ 30 minutes. Auricular taping is also applicable.

4. Food Retention

(1) *Main manifestation*

Epigastric pain with fullness and distention, belching, acid regurgitation, poor appetite, vomiting of undigested food, pain aggravated after food intake but relieved upon vomiting, thick greasy tongue coating, and deep strong or slippery pulse.

(2) *Therapeutic principle*

Relieve food retention, pacify the stomach and stop pain.

(3) *Treatment*

1) Body acupuncture

Prescription: Zhongwan (RN 12), Zusanli (ST 36), Liangmen (ST 21), Tianshu (ST 25).

Method: Apply filiform needles with reducing method. Retain the needles for 20 ~ 30 minutes, manipulating them two to three times.

2) Ear acupuncture

Prescription: Stomach, Spleen, Sympathetic, Ear-shenmen, Subcortex, Endocrine.

Method: Use filiform needles with strong stimulation and retain the needles for 15 ~ 30 minutes. Auricular taping is also applicable.

5. Deficient Cold in the Spleen and Stomach

(1) *Main manifestion*

Dull pain in the epigastrium that is relieved by warmth and pressure, watery regurgitation, listlessness and weakness, cold limbs, loss of appetite, loose stools, pale tongue proper, and weak pulse.

(2) *Therapeutic principle*

Warm up the middle-Jiao, strengthen the spleen, eliminate cold and stop pain.

(3) *Treatment*

1) Body acupuncture

Prescription: Pishu (BL 20), Weishu (BL 21), Zhangmen (LR 13), Zhongwan (RN 12), Zusanli (ST 36), Neiguan (PC 6).

Method: Apply filiform needles with reinforcing method. Retain the needles for 20 ~ 30 minutes manipulating them two to three times.

2) Ear acupuncture

Prescription: Spleen, Stomach,

Sympathetic, Ear-Shenmen, Duodenum, Subcortex, Endocrine.

Method: Use filiform needles with mild stimulation and retain the needles for 15～30 minutes. Auricular taping is also applicable.

3) Moxibustion

Prescription: Pishu (BL 20), Weishu (BL 21) Zhongwan (RN 12), Zusanli (ST 36)

Method: Apply mild-warming or rounding moxibustion to each point for 5～10 minutes once a day.

4) Cupping Therapy

Prescription: Pishu (BL 20), Weishu (BL 21), Zhongwan (RN 12).

Method: Use retaining cupping or successive flash cupping for 10～20 minutes once a day.

呕 吐

呕吐又名吐逆，是指食物或痰涎等由胃中上逆而出的病症。古人认为：有声有物谓之呕，有物无声谓之吐，有声无物谓之哕（干呕），只吐涎沫谓之吐涎。由于临床呕与吐常兼见，难以截然分开，故合称呕吐。

1. 外邪犯胃

（1）主证 突然呕吐，起病较急，胸闷不舒，兼见恶寒发热，头痛身痛等证，苔白，脉浮。

（2）治则 解表调中止呕。

（3）治法

1) 体针

处方 大椎，合谷，内庭，中脘，内关。

操作 毫针刺，用泻法。留针15～20分钟，间歇行针3～4次。

2) 耳针

处方 胃，交感，神门，枕。

操作 毫针强刺激，留针15～30分钟。

2. 饮食停滞

（1）主证 呕吐酸腐，脘腹胀满，嗳气厌食，腹痛，吐后则舒，大便或溏或结，舌苔腻，脉滑实。

（2）治则 行气消食导滞。

（3）治法

1) 体针

处方 下脘，璇玑，足三里，内关，腹结。

配穴 便秘加支沟；便溏加天枢，上巨墟；腹胀加气海。

操作 毫针刺，用泻法。留针15～20分钟，间歇行针2～3次。

2) 耳针

处方 胃，交感，神门，皮质下。

操作 毫针强刺激，留针15～30分钟。

3. 肝气犯胃

（1）主证 呕吐吞酸，嗳气频作，胸胁满痛，烦闷不舒，常因精神刺激而使病情加重，舌苔薄腻，脉弦。

（2）治则　疏肝和胃止呕。

（3）治法

1）体针

处方　上脘，阳陵泉，太冲，梁门，内关，足三里。

操作　毫针刺，用泻法。留针15～20分钟，间歇行针3～4次。

2）耳针

处方　胃，肝，脾，交感，神门，皮质下。

操作　毫针刺，每次3～4穴，强刺激，留针15～30分钟。

4. 脾胃虚弱

（1）主证　面色㿠白，饮食稍多即吐，时作时止，倦怠乏力，纳少，大便溏薄，舌质淡，脉濡弱。

（2）治则　健脾温中和胃。

（3）治法

1）体针

处方　脾俞，胃俞，中脘，章门，足三里，公孙，内关。

操作　毫针刺，用补法。留针20～30分钟，间歇行针2～3次。

2）耳针

处方　胃，脾，交感，神门，皮质下。

操作　每次选3～4穴用毫针刺，留针15～30分钟。

3）艾灸

处方　脾俞，胃俞，中脘，足三里。

操作　每穴用温和灸或回旋灸治

疗5～10分钟，每天1次。

4）拔罐疗法

处方　脾俞，胃俞，中脘。

操作　坐罐或闪罐治疗10～20分钟，每天1次。

5. 胃阴不足

（1）主证　呕吐反复发作，或时作干呕，口燥咽干，似饥而不欲食，舌红少津，脉细数。

（2）治则　滋养胃阴，降逆止呕。

（3）治法

1）体针

处方　胃俞，阴陵泉，足三里，内关，公孙，内庭。

配穴　呕吐不止加金津、玉液；口燥咽干加照海、阴郄。

操作　毫针刺，内庭穴用泻法，余用补法。留针15～20分钟，间歇行针2～3次。

2）耳针

处方　胃，交感，肝，神门，皮质下。

操作　毫针轻刺激，留针15～30分钟；亦可采用耳穴贴敷。

3）三棱针

处方　金津，玉液。

操作　三棱针点刺出血。

Vomiting

Vomiting is a condition referring to the casting up of food substance or gastric fluid from the stomach through the mouth. The concept of vomiting in traditional Chinese medicine has a much broader context. According to records in classics, the simple term of vomiting is futher divided into noisy vomiting with food substance, non-sounding vomiting with food substance, noisy nausea without food substance or gastric fluid, and simple vomiting of gastric fluid. In general, the Chinese concept of vomiting includes both vomiting and nausea. Since both may often accompany one and the other clinically, only the word vomiting is adopted.

1. Exogenous Pathogenic Invasion Into the Stomach

(1) *Main manifestation*

Vomiting characterized by sudden casting up of food, discomfort in the chest accompanied by aversion to cold, fever, headache and general pain, white tongue coating and superficial pulse.

(2) *Therapeutic principle*

Relieve superficial symptoms and signs, regulate Qi of the middle-Jiao and stop vomiting.

(3) *Treatment*

1) Body acupuncture

Prescription: Dazhui (DU 14), Hegu (LI 4), Neiting (ST 44), Zhongwan (RN 12), Neiguan (PC 6).

Method: Use filiform needles with reducing method. Retain the needles for 15～20 minutes manipulating them three to four times.

2) Ear acupuncture

Prescription: Stomach, Sympathetic, Ear-shenmen, Occiput.

Method: Apply filiform needles with strong stimulation and retain needles for 15～30 minutes.

2. Food Retention in the Stomach

(1) *Man manifestation*

Vomiting characterized by casting up of sour fluid or food substance, epigastric distension and fullness, frequent belching, abdominal pain lessened by vomiting, dry or loose stools, greasy tongue coating, and slippery full pulse.

(2) *Therapeutic principle*

Activate Qi circulation, promote digestion and remove food retention.

(3) *Treatment*

1) Body acupuncture

Prescription: Xiawan (RN 10), Xuanji (RN 21), Zusanli (ST 36), Neiguan (PC 6), Fujie (SP 14).

Supplementary points: Add Zhigou (SJ 6) for constipation, Tianshu (ST 25) and Shangjuxu (ST 37) for loose stools, Qihai (RN 6) for abdominal distension.

Method: Apply filiform needles with reducing method. Retain the needles for 15～20 minutes manipulating them two to three times.

2) Ear acupuncture

Prescription: Stomach, Sympathetic, Ear-shenmen, Subcortex.

Method: Apply filiform needles with strong stimulation and retain the needles for 15~30 minutes.

3. Liver Qi Attacking the Stomach

(1) *Main manifestation*

Vomiting characterized by casting up of sour fluid or food substance, frequent belching, pain and distention in the hypochondriac region, suffocating sensation often aggravated by emotional disturbances, thin greasy tongue coating and wiry pulse.

(2) *Therapeutic principle*

Soothe the liver, pacify the stomach and check vomiting.

(3) *Treatment*

1) Body acupuncture

Prescription: Shangwan (RN 13), Yanglingquan (GB 34), Taichong (LR 3), Liangmen (ST 21), Neiguan (PC 6), Zusanli (ST 36).

Method: Apply filiform needles with reducing method. Retain the needles for 15~20 minute, manipulating them three to four times.

2) Ear acupuncture

Prescription: Stomach, Liver, Spleen, Sympathetic, Ear-shenmen, Subcortex.

Method: Apply filiform needles at three to four points each time with strong stimulation and retain the needles for 15~30 minutes.

4. Deficiency of the Spleen and Stomach

(1) *Main manifestation*

Pallor complexion, instant vomiting with repeated attack, lassitude, weakness, poor appetite, loose stools, pale tongue proper, and weak soft pulse.

(2) *Therapeutic*

Principle warm up the middle-Jiao, strengthen the spleen and pacify the stomach.

(3) *Treatment*

1) Body acupuncture

Prescription: Pishu (BL 20), Weishu (BL 21), Zhongwan (RN 12). Zhangmen (LR 13), Zusanli (ST 36), Gongsun (SP 4), Neiguan (PC 6).

Method: Apply filiform needles with reinforcing method. Retain the needles for 20~30 minutes manipulating them two to three times.

2) Ear acupuncture

Prescription: Stomach, Spleen, Sympathetic, Ear-Shenmen, Subcortex.

Method: Apply filiform needles at three to four points each time and retain the needles for 15~30 minutes.

3) Moxibustion

Prescription: Pishu (BL 20), Weishu (BL 20), Zhongwan (RN 12), Zusanli (ST 36).

Method: Use mild-warming moxibustion or rounding moxibustion to each point for 5~10 minutes, once a day.

4) Cupping Therapy

Prescription: Pishu (BL 20), Weishu (BL 20), Zhongwan (RN 12).

Method: Apply retaining cupping or succesive flash cupping for 10~20 minutes once a day.

5. Yin Difficiency of the stomach

(1) *Main manifestation*

The vomiting appears in repeated attacks. It is accompanied by dryness in the mouth and throat, anorexia despite hunger, red tongue proper, lacking fluid distribution, and rapid thready pulse.

(2) *Therapeutic Principle*

Nourish stomach Yin and sedate the abnormal ascending of stomach Qi and check vomiting.

(3) *Treatment*

1) Body acupuncture

Prescription: Weishu (BL 21), Yinlingquan (SP 9), Zusanli (ST 36), Neiguan (PC 6), Gongsun (SP 4), Neiting (ST 44).

Supplementary points: Add Jinjin (EX-HN 12) and Yuye (EX-HN 13) for continuous vomiting, Zhaohai (KI 6) and Yinxi (HT 6) for dryness in the mouth and throat.

Method: Apply filiform needles with reinforcing method except Neiting (ST 44) which is needled by reducing method. Retain the needles for 15~20 minutes manipulating them two to three times.

2) Ear acupuncture

Prescription: Stomach, Sympathetic, Liver, Ear-shenmen, Subcortex.

Method: Apply filiform needles with mild stimulation and retain the needles for 15~30 minutes. Auricular taping is also applicable.

3) Three-edged needle

Prescription: Jinjin (EX-HN 12), Yuye (EX-HN 13).

Method: Prick the points with a three-edged needle to cause bleeding.

腹　　痛

腹痛是指胃脘以下，耻骨毛际以上部位发生疼痛的症状而言。在临床上极为常见，可伴发于多种脏腑疾病。本节所述腹痛常见于现代医学的急、慢性肠炎，胃肠痉挛，肠神经官能症，消化不良性腹痛等。外科和妇科疾病所致腹痛，可参阅有关篇章。

1．热邪内积

（1）主证　腹痛、腹胀拒按，便

秘或大便不爽，伴有发热口渴，尿黄，舌苔黄腻，脉滑数或沉实。

（2）治则　清热通腑，理气止痛。

（3）治法

1）体针

处方　天枢，气海，合谷，足三里，内庭。

操作　毫针刺，用泻法。留针15～20分钟，间歇行针3～4次。

2）耳针

处方　大肠，小肠，腹，神门，皮质下。

操作　毫针强刺激，留针15～30分钟。

2. 寒邪内积

（1）主证　痛势急剧，喜温恶冷，大便溏薄，腹中雷鸣，小便清长，饮食减少，口不渴，四肢不温，舌苔薄白，脉沉紧或沉迟。

（2）治则　温中散寒止痛。

（3）治法

1）体针

处方　中脘，神阙，足三里，合谷。

配穴　脐腹痛剧加气海，三阴交；大便溏薄加天枢，大肠俞。

操作　毫针刺，用泻法。留针20～30分钟，间歇行针2～3次。

2）耳针

处方　大肠，小肠，腹，神门，皮质下。

操作　毫针强刺激，留针15～

30分钟。

3）艾灸

处方　神阙。

操作　采用隔姜灸，每次灸5～10壮。

3. 饮食停滞

（1）主证　腹痛，腹胀拒按，厌食，吞酸嗳气，便秘或腹泻，矢气腐臭，泻后痛减，舌苔灰腻，脉滑。

（2）治则　消食导滞，和中止痛。

（3）治法

1）体针

处方　下脘，梁门，公孙，足三里，里内庭。

操作　毫针刺，用泻法。留针15～30分钟，间歇行针2～3次。

2）耳针

处方　大肠，小肠，脾，腹，神门。

操作　毫针强刺激，留针10～20分钟。

4. 脾阳不振

（1）主证　腹痛绵绵，时作时止，痛时喜按，喜热恶冷，大便溏泄，神疲肢倦，舌质淡，边有齿龈，苔薄白，脉沉细。

（2）治则　温中散寒，益气健脾。

（3）治法

1）体针

处方　脾俞，胃俞，中脘，章

门，足三里，气海，关元。

操作 毫针刺，用补法。留针15～30分钟，间歇行针2～3次。

2）耳针

处方 脾，大肠，小肠，神门，皮质下。

操作 毫针温和刺激，留针20～30分钟。亦可用耳穴贴敷。

3）艾灸

处方 脾俞，胃俞，气海，足三里。

操作 采用温和灸或回旋灸治疗5～10分钟，每天1次。

4）拔罐疗法

处方 脾俞，胃俞，气海，关元。

操作 用坐罐或闪罐治疗10～20分钟；每天1次。

Abdominal Pain

Abdominal pain refers to the pain involving the area below the epigastrium and above the suprapubic hair margin. Clinically, it is a very common symptom encountered in various Zangfu disorders. It can be seen in both acute and chronic enteritis, gastrointestinal spasm, intestinal neurosis and indigestion in terms of modern medicine. For the treatment of acute abdominal pain due to surgical and gynecological diseases refer to the contents in the related sections.

1. Accumulation of Heat in the Interior

(1) *Main manifestation*

Fullness and pain of the abdomen which cannot be pressed, constipation or dyschezia acompanied by fever, thirst, dark urine, yellowish greasy coating of the tongue, smooth and rapid pulse or deep and forceful pulse.

(2) *Therapeutic principle*

Clear away heat to relax the bowels and relieve the pain.

(3) *Treatment*

1) Body acupuncture

Prescription: Tianshu (ST 25), Qihai (RN 6), Hegu (LI 4), Zusanli (ST 36), Neiting (ST 44)

Method: Apply filiform needles with reducing method. Retain the needles for 15～20 minutes manipulating them three to four times.

2) Ear acupuncture

Prescription: Large intestine, Small intestine, Abdomen, Ear-shenmen, Subcortex.

Method: Apply filiform needles with strong stimulation and retain the needles for 15～30 minutes.

2. Accumulation of Cold in the Interior

(1) *Main manifestation*

Sudden onset of severe abdominal pain relieved by warmth and aggravated by cold, loose stools, borborygmus, profuse clear urine, poor appetite, absence of thirst, cold limbs, thin white tongue coating and deep tense or deep slow pulse

(2) *Therapeutic principle*

Warm up the middleJiao, eliminate cold and stop pain.

(3) *Treatment*

1) Body acupuncture

Prescription: Zhongwan (RN 12), Shenque (RN 8), Zusanli (ST 36), Hegu (LI 4).

Supplementary points: Add Qihai (RN 6) and Sanyinjiao (SP 6) for pain in the umbilicus, Tianshu (ST 25) and Dachangshu (BL 25) for loose stools.

Method: Apply filiform needles with reducing method. Retain the needles for 20～30 minutes manipulating them two to three times.

2) Ear acupuncture

Prescription: Large Intestine, Small Intestine, Abdomen, Ear-shenmen, Subcortex.

Method: Use filiform needles with strong stimulation and retain the needles for 15～30 minutes.

3) Moxibustion

Prescription: Shenque (RN 8).

Method: Use moxibustion with ginger, 5～10 moxa cones each time.

3. Retention of Food

(1) *Main manifestation*

Pain and fullness of the abdomen which cannot be pressed, anorexia, regurgitation of acid, belching, constipation or diarrhea, wind from the bowels with stinky smell, relieved pain after diarrhea, greyish greasy coating of the tongue, smooth pulse.

(2) *Therapeutic principle*

Promote digestion and regulate the functions of the stomach and intestine to relieve the pain.

(3) *Treatment*

1) Body acupuncture

Prescription: Xiawan (RN 10), Liangmen (ST 21), Gongsun (SP 4), Zusanli (ST 36), Lineiting (Extra).

Method: Apply filiform needles with reducing method. Retain the needles for 15～30 minutes manipulating them two to three times.

2) Ear acupuncture

Prescription: Large Intestine, Small Intestine, Spleen, Abdomen, Ear-shenmen.

Method: Apply filiform needles with strong stimulation and retain 10～20 minutes.

4. Deficiency of Spleen Yang

(1) *Main manifestation*

The lingering abdominal pain appears intermittently. It responds to pressure and warmth but is aggravated by cold, acompanied by loose stools, listlessness, weakness of the four limbs, pale tongue with teethmarks on the edge, and a deep thready pulse.

(2) *Therapeutic principle*

Warm up the middleJiao, eliminate cold, and strengthen spleen Qi.

(3) *Treatment*

1) Body acupuncture

Prescription: Pishu (BL 20), Weishu (BL 21), Zhongwan (RN 12), Zhangmen (LR 13), Zusanli (ST 36), Qihai (RN 6), Guanyuan (RN 4).

Method: Apply filiform needles with reinforcing method. Retain the needles for 15～30 minutes manipulating them two to three times.

2) Ear acupuncture

Prescription Spleen, Large Intestine, Small Intestine, Ear-shenmen, Subcortex.

Method: Use filiform needles with mild stimulation and retain the needles for 20～30 minutes. Auricular taping is also applicable.

3) Moxibustion

Prescription: Pishu (BL 20), Weishu (BL 21) Qihai (RN 6), Zusanli (ST 36).

Method: Use mild-warming moxibustion or rounding moxibustion for 5～10 minutes once a day.

4) Cupping Therapy

Prescription: Pishu (BL 20), Weishu (BL 21), Qihai (RN 6), Guanyuan (RN 4).

Method: Apply retaining cupping or succesive flash cupping for 10～20 minutes once a day.

腹　胀

腹胀是指以腹部胀满不舒为主证的疾患，甚则兼见腹痛，嗳气，呕吐。本病多因胃肠功能失调所致。现代医学的胃下垂，肠麻痹，肠梗阻，胃肠神经官能症，急性胃扩张等病出现以腹胀为主症时均可参考本篇辨证治疗。

1. 实证

(1) 主证　腹部胀满不减，腹满拒按，甚至腹痛，嗳气，口臭，小便黄赤，大便秘结，或有发热，呕吐，舌苔黄厚，脉滑数有力。

(2) 治则　通调腑气。

(3) 治法

1) 体针

处方　中脘，天枢，足三里，上巨墟。

操作　毫针刺，用泻法。留针15～20分钟，间歇行针2～3次。

2) 耳针

处方　脾，胃，大肠，小肠，交感，皮质下。

操作　毫针中度刺激，留针15～20分钟。亦可采用耳穴贴敷。

2．虚证

（1）主证　腹胀喜按，肠鸣，便溏，纳减，神疲乏力，尿清，舌淡苔白，脉弱。

（2）治则　健脾和胃，理气消胀。

（3）治法

1）体针

处方　建里，天枢，足三里，太白，关元，中脘。

操作　毫针刺，用补法。留针15～30分钟，间歇行针2～3次。

2）耳针

处方　脾，胃，交感，大肠，小肠。

操作　毫针温和刺激，留针15～30分钟，亦可采用耳穴贴敷。

3）艾灸

处方　胃俞，脾俞，大肠俞，小肠俞，关元，足三里。

操作　用温和灸或回旋灸每穴治疗5～10分钟，每天1次。

Abdominal Distention

Abdominal distention is characterized by a discomfort sensation and fullness in the abdomen. In severe cases, it also causes local pain, belching and vomiting. It is mostly the consequence of gastrointestinal dysfunction. For abdominal distention appearing as a major symptom in such diseases as gastroptosis, enteroparalysis, intestinal obstruction, gastroneurosis and acute gastrectasis, the treatment presented in this part can be taken as reference.

1. Repletion Pattern

（1）*Main manifestation*

Persistent distention and fullness in the abdomen which may also cause abdominal pain, aggravated by pressure. It is accompanied by belching, foul breath, dark yellow urine, constipation or occasional fever and vomiting, yellow thick tongue coating, and slippery rapid and forceful pulse.

（2）*Therapeutic principle*

Promote the Qi circulation of the stomach and intestines.

（3）*Treatment*

1）Body Acupuncture

Prescription：Zhongwan（RN 12）Tianshu（ST 25）Zusanli（ST 36），Shangjuxu（ST 37）.

Method：Apply filiform needles with reducing method. Retain the needles for 15～20 minutes manipulating them two to three times.

2）Ear acupuncture

Prescription：Spleen，Stomach，Large Intestine，Small Intestine，Sympathetic，Subcortex.

Method：Apply filiform needles with moderate stimulation and retain the needles for 15～20 minutes. Auricular taping is also applicable.

2. Vacuity Pattern

(1) *Main manifestation*
Abdominal distention relieved by pressure, borborygmus, loose stools, poor appetite, lassitude, listlessness, clear urine, pale tongue with white coating and forceless pulse.

(2) *Therapeutic principle*
Strengthen the spleen, pacify the stomach, regulate Qi circulation and relieve distention.

(3) *Treatment*
1) Body acupuncture
Prescription: Jianli (RN 11), Tianshu (ST 25), Zusanli (ST 36), Taibai (SP 3), Guanyuan (RN 4) Zhongwan (RN 12).
Method: Apply filiform needles with reinforcing method. Retain needles for 15~30 minutes manipulating them two to three times.

2) Ear acupuncture
Prescription: Spleen, Stomach, Sympathetic, Large Intestine, Small Intestine.
Method: Apply filiform needles with mild stimulation and retain the needles for 15~30 minutes. Auricular taping is also applicable.

3) Moxibustion
Prescription: Weishu (BL 21), Pishu (BL 20), Dachangshu (BL 25), Xiaochangshu (B 27), Guanyaun (RN 4), Zusanli (ST 36).
Method: Use mild-warming moxibustion or rounding moxibustion to each point for 5~10 minutes once a day.

泄　泻

泄泻是指大便次数增多，粪质溏薄，完谷不化，甚至泻如水样的一种病症。根据临床表现可分为急性和慢性腹泻。本病一年四季均可发生，但以夏秋两季较多见。泄泻与现代医学的腹泻含义相似，可见于急、慢性肠炎，肠结核，肠功能紊乱，结肠过敏等。

1. 寒湿型

(1) 主证 泄泻清稀，甚则如水样，肠鸣腹痛，脘闷食少，身寒喜温，口不渴，舌淡苔白，脉沉迟或濡缓。

(2) 治则 温中利湿。

(3) 治法
1) 体针
处方 天枢，建里，气海，上巨墟，阴陵泉。
操作 毫针刺，用泻法。留针15~20分钟。间歇行针2~3次。

2) 耳针
处方 大肠，小肠，神门，交感，腹。
操作 毫针强刺激，留针15~20分钟；亦可采用耳穴贴敷。

3) 艾灸
处方 建里，气海，天枢。
操作 采用隔姜灸每穴5~10壮，每天1次。

2．湿热型

（1）**主证**　泄泻腹痛，泻下急迫或泻而不爽，粪色黄褐，气味臭秽，肛门灼热，烦热口渴，小便短赤，舌苔黄腻，脉滑数或脉濡数。

（2）**治则**　清热利湿。

（3）**治法**

1）体针

处方　中脘，天枢　阴陵泉，内庭，曲池。

操作　毫针刺，用泻法。留针15～20分钟，间歇行针2～3次。

2）耳针

处方　大肠，小肠，胃，神门，交感，腹。

操作　毫针强刺激，留针15～20分钟；亦可采用耳穴贴敷。

3．伤食

（1）**主证**　腹痛肠鸣，泻下粪臭如败卵，泻后痛减，脘腹胀满，嗳腐酸臭，不思饮食，矢气频作，舌苔垢浊或腻，脉滑。

（2）**治则**　消食导滞止泻。

（3）**治法**

1）体针

处方　天枢，中脘，璇玑，里内庭，足三里。

配穴　嗳腐酸臭加内关、内庭。

操作　毫针刺，用泻法。留针15～20分钟，间歇行针2～3次。

2）耳针

处方　大肠，小肠，神门，胃，

脾，交感。

操作　毫针强刺激，留针15～20分钟。

4．脾虚

（1）**主证**　大便时溏时泻，迁延反复，完谷不化，食欲减退，食后脘闷不舒，稍进油腻食物，则大便次数明显增加，面色萎黄，神疲倦怠，舌苔白腻，脉濡缓。

（2）**治则**　健脾止泻。

（3）**治法**

1）体针

处方　脾俞，章门，太白，中脘，足三里，天枢。

操作　毫针刺，用补法，留针15～20分钟，间歇行针1～2次。

2）耳针

处方　大肠，小肠，脾，胃，神门。

操作　毫针弱刺激，留针15～20分钟；亦可采用耳穴贴敷。

3）艾灸

处方　脾俞，天枢，足三里，中脘。

操作　采用温和灸或回旋灸每穴治疗5～10分钟，每天1次。

4）拔罐疗法

处方　脾俞，大肠俞，小肠俞，关元。

操作　采用坐罐或闪罐治疗10～20分钟，每天1次。

5．肝脾不调

（1）主证 腹痛即泻，泻后而痛不减，每当精神刺激，情绪紧张之时，即发生腹痛泄泻，泻时常有脘胁痞闷，嗳气，苔薄，脉弦。

（2）治则 疏肝理气，健脾和胃止泻。

（3）治法

1）体针

处方 肝俞，太冲，脾俞，章门，天枢，足三里，内关。

操作 毫针刺，平补平泻。留针15～20分钟；间歇行针2～3次。

2）耳针

处方 脾，肝，交感，神门，胃，大肠，小肠。

操作 毫针中等强度刺激，留针15～20分钟；亦可采用耳穴贴敷。

6．肾虚

（1）主证 黎明前脐腹作痛，肠鸣即泻，泻后则安，形寒肢冷，腰膝酸软，舌苔白，脉沉细。

（2）治则 温补脾肾止泻。

（3）治法

1）体针

处方 肾俞，命门，关元，脾俞，天枢，上巨墟。

操作 毫针刺，用补法。留针15～30分钟，间歇行针1～2次。

2）耳针

处方 肾，脾，小肠，大肠，交感，神门。

操作 毫针弱刺激，留针15～20分钟；亦可采用耳穴贴敷。

3）艾灸

处方 肾俞，命门，关元，脾俞。

操作 采用温和灸或回旋灸每穴治疗5～10分钟，每天1次。

4）拔罐疗法

处方 肾俞，脾俞，关元。

操作 采用坐罐治疗10～20分钟。每天1次。

Diarrhea

Diarrhea refers to increased number of loose stools with undigested food or even watery stools. According to the clinical manifestations and duration, it is divided into acute and chronic types. The condition may occur in any of the four seasons but is more common in the summer and autumn. Similar to that described in modern medicine, it may be seen in such diseases as acute and chronic enteritis, intestinal tuberculosis, intestinal dysfunction and irritable bowel.

1. Cold-damp Type

（1）*Main manifestation*

Loose stools or even watery stools, abdominal pain, borborygmus, general cold sensation with desire for warmth, absence of thirst, pale tongue proper with white coating, and deep slow or soft pulse.

(2) *Therapeutic principle*

Warm up the middle-Jiao and resolve dampness.

(3) *Treatment*

1) Body acupuncture

Prescription: Tianshu(ST 25), Jianli (RN 11),Qihai(RN 6),Shangjuxu(ST 37),Yinlingquan(SP 9).

Method: Apply filiform needles with reducing method. Retain the needles for 15 ~ 20minutes manipulating them two to three times.

2) Ear acupuncture

Prescription: Large Intestine, Small Intestine, Ear-shenmen, Sympathetic, Abdomen.

Method: Apply filiform needles with strong stimulation and retain the needles for 15 ~ 20 minutes. Auricular taping is also applicable.

3) Moxibustion

Prescription: Jianli (RN 11), Qihai (RN 6), Tianshu (ST 25)

Method: Apply moxibustion with ginger, 5 ~ 10 moxa cones at each point once a day.

2. Damp-heat Type

(1) *Main manifestation*

Loose stools with abdominal pain, urgent bowel movement or that with difficulty, yellow stools with odour, feverish sensation in the anus, restlessness, thirst, short scanty urine, yellow greasy tongue coating, and rapid slippery or rapid soft pulse.

(2) *Therapeutic principle*

Eliminate heat and resolve dampness.

(3) *Treatment*

1) Body acupuncture

Prescription: Zhongwan (RN 12), Tianshu(ST 25), Yinlingquan(SP 9), Neiting(ST 44),Quchi(LI 11).

Method: Apply filiform needles with reducing method. Retain the needles for 15 ~ 20 minutes manipulating them two to three times.

2) Ear acupuncture

Prescription: Large Intestine, Small Intestine, Stomach, Ear-shenmen, Sympathetic, Abdomen.

Method: Use filiform needles with strong stimulation and retain the needles for 15 ~ 20 minutes. Auricular taping is also applicable.

3. Food Retention Type

(1) *Main manifestation*

Abdominal pain, borborygmus, fetid stools, lessened pain after releasing stools, fullness and distention in the epigastric region, belching with mouth odour, poor appetite, frequent passing of wind, sticky greasy tongue coating, and slippery pulse.

(2) *Therapeutic principle*

Promote digestion, remove food retention and stop diarrhea.

(3) *Treatment*

1) Body acupuncture

Prescription: Tianshu (ST 25), Zhongwan (RN 12), Xuanji (RN 21), Lineiting (Extra), Zusanli (ST 36).

Supplementary point: Add Neiguan (PC 6) and Neiting (ST 44) for belching with sour smell.

Method: Apply filiform needles with reducing method. Retain the needles for 15~20 minutes manipulating them two to three times.

2) Ear acupuncture

Prescription: Large Intestine, Small Intestine, Ear-shenmen, Stomach, Spleen, Sympathetic.

Method: Apply filiform needles with strong stimulation and retain the needles for 15~20 minutes.

4. Spleen Deficiency Type

(1) *Main manifestation*

Prolonged and reccurent loose stools with undigested food, decrease of appetite, fullness sensation in the epigastric region after food intake, apparent increase of bowel movement soon after intake of greasy or oily food, sallow complexion, white sticky tongue coating, and soft slow pulse.

(2) *Therapeutic principle*

Strengthen the spleen and stop diarrhea.

(3) *Treatment*

1) Body acupuncture

Prescription: Pishu (BL 20), Zhangmen (LR 13), Taibai (SP 3), Zhongwan (RN 12), Zusanli (ST 36), Tianshu (ST 25).

Method: Apply filiform needles with reinforcing method. Retain the needles for 15~20 minutes manipulating them one to two times.

2) Ear acupuncture

Prescription: Large Intestine, Small Intestine, Spleen, Stomach, Ear-shenmen.

Method: Apply filiform needles with mild stimulation and retain the needles for 15~20 minutes. Auricular taping is also applicable.

3) Moxibustion

Prscription: Pishu (BL 20), Tianshu (ST 25) Zusanli (ST 36), Zhongwan (RN 12).

Method: Use mild-warming moxibustion or rounding moxibustion to each point for 5~10 minutes once a day.

4) Cupping Therapy

Prescription: Pishu (BL 20), Dachangshu (BL 25), Xiaochangshu (BL 27), Guanyuan (RN 4).

Method: Use retaining cupping or succesive flash cupping for 10~20 minutes once a day.

5. Liver and Spleen Derangement Type

(1) *Main manifestation*

Bowel movement stimulated by abdominal pain that still remains the same after bowel movement, recurrent diarrhea due to emotional disturbance or stress. The accompanying symptoms and signs include discomfort sensation in the hypochondriac region during diarrhea, belching, thin tongue coating, and wiry pulse.

(2) *Therapeutic principle*

Soothe the liver Qi, strengthen the spleen, pacify the stomach and stop diarrhea.

(3) *Treatment*

1) Body acupuncture

Prescription: Ganshu (BL 18), Taichong (LR 13), Pishu (BL 20), Zhangmen (LR 13), Tianshu (ST 25), Zusanli (ST 36), Neiguan (PC 6).

Method: Apply filiform needles with even movement method. Retain the needles for 15~20 minutes manipulating them two to three times.

2) Ear acupuncture

Prescription: Spleen, Liver, Sympathetic, Ear-shenmen, Stomach, Large Intestine, Small Intestine.

Method: Apply filiform needles with moderate stimulation and retain the needles for 15~20 minutes. Auricular taping is also applicable.

6. Kidney Deficiency Type

(1) *Main manifestation*

Borborygmus and diarrhea with abdominal pain just before dawn, comfortable sensation after bowel movement, cold limbs, soreness and weakness in the knee joint and lumbar region, white tongue coating and deep thready pulse.

(2) *Therapeutic principle*

Warm up and tonify the spleen and kidney and stop diarrhea.

(3) *Treatment*

1) Body acupuncture

Prescription: Shenshu (BL 23), Mingmen (DU 4), Guanyuan (RN 4), Pishu (BL 20), Tianshu (ST 25), Shangjuxu (ST 37).

Method: Apply filiform needles with reinforcing method. Retain the needles for 15~30 minutes manipulating them one to two times.

2) Ear acupuncture

Prescription: Kidney, Spleen, Small Intestine, Large Intestine, Sympathetic, Ear-shenmen.

Method: Apply filiform needles with mild stimulation and retain the needles for 15~20 minutes. Auricular taping is also applicable.

3) Moxibustion

Prescription: Shenshu (BL 23), Mingmen (DU 4), Guanyuan (RN 4), Pishu (BL 20).

Method: Use mild-warming moxibustion or rounding moxibustion to each point for 5～10 minutes once a day.

4）Cupping Therapy

Prescription：Sheshu（BL 23），Pishu（BL 20），Guanyuan（RN 4）.

Method：Use retaining cupping for 10～20 minutes once a day.

痢 疾

痢疾是夏秋季节常见的肠道传染病。以大便次数增多，腹痛里急后重，痢下赤白脓血为特征。临床分为湿热痢，寒湿痢，噤口痢，休息痢等。现代医学的细菌性痢疾，中毒性痢疾，阿米巴痢疾，慢性非特异性溃疡性结肠炎等，均可参照本节辨证治疗。

1．湿热痢

（1）主证 腹痛，里急后重，下痢赤白相杂，赤多白少，日数次或十余次，肛门灼热，小便短赤，甚者身发高热，心烦口渴，舌苔黄腻，脉滑数。

（2）治则 清热导滞，调气行血。

（3）治法

1）体针

处方 天枢，上巨墟，曲池，内庭，合谷。

配穴 发热加大椎；里急后重甚者加气海。

操作 毫针刺，用泻法。留针15～20分钟，间歇行针2～3次。

2）耳针

处方 大肠，小肠，胃，神门，直肠下段。

操作 毫针强刺激，留针10～15分钟。

2．寒湿痢

（1）主证 腹痛拘急，痢下赤白黏冻，白多赤少或为纯白冻，里急后重，喜暖畏寒，兼有胸脘痞闷，口淡不渴，舌苔白腻，脉沉迟。

（2）治则 温化寒湿，行气和血。

（3）治法

1）体针

处方 中脘，天枢，气海，上巨墟，阴陵泉。

操作 毫针刺，平补平泻。留针15～20分钟，间歇行针2～3次。

2）耳针

处方 大肠，小肠，胃，腹，神门。

操作 毫针中等强度刺激，留针10～15分钟。

3）艾灸

处方 气海，天枢，中脘。

操作 采用温和灸或温针灸治疗10～15分钟。

3．噤口痢

（1）主证 痢下赤白，饮食不进，恶心呕吐，腹痛或胸腹胀满，舌苔黄腻，脉濡数。

（2）治则 和胃开噤。

（3）治法

1）体针

处方 中脘，合谷，内关，内庭，天枢。

操作 毫针刺，用泻法。留针15～20分钟，间歇行针2～3次。

2）耳针

处方 大肠，小肠，胃，耳神门。

操作 毫针中等强度刺激，留针10～15分钟。

4．休息痢

（1）主证 下痢时作时止，或轻或重，缠绵难愈，常因饮食不慎，过于劳累，或感受外邪而使其痢下加重，兼有倦怠乏力，怯冷嗜卧，腹胀纳差，舌淡苔腻，脉濡软或虚大。

（2）治则 清热导滞，调气行血。

（3）治法

1）体针

处方 脾俞，胃俞，大肠俞，关元，天枢，足三里。

操作 毫针刺，用补法。留针15～30分钟，间歇行针1～2次。

2）耳针

处方 大肠，小肠，脾，肾，神门，胃。

操作 毫针中等强度刺激，留针10～15分钟；亦可采用耳穴贴敷。

3）艾灸

处方 脾俞，胃俞，关元。

操作 温和灸或温针灸治疗10～15分钟，每天1次。

Dysentery

Dysentery is an intestinal epidemic disease that occurs more in the summer and fall time. It is characterized by abdominal pain, tenesmus and frequent bowel movements containing blood and mucous. Clinically, it is divided into damp-heat desentery, dampcold dysentery, fasting dysentery and chronic recurrent dysentery. The differentiation and treatment in this section can be used as reference for bacillary, toxic and amebic dysenteries, and chronic nonspecific ulerative colitis in modern medicine.

1. Damp-heat Type

（1）*Main manifestation*

Abdominal pain, tenesmus, stools with pus and mucous that run up to several or even more than ten times a day, burning sensation in the anus, scanty and dark urine, high fever in severe cases, restlessness, thirst, yellow greasy tongue coating, and rapid slippery pulse.

（2）*Therapeutic principle*

Eliminate damp-heat, regulate Qi circulation and activate blood.

（3）*Treatment*

1）Body acupuncture

Prescription: Tianshu（ST 25）, Shangjuxu（ST 37）, Neiting（ST 44）, Hegu（LI 4）.

Supplementary points: Add Dazhui (DU 14) for fever, and Qihai (RN 6) for tenesmus sensation.

Method: Apply filiform needles with reducing method. Retain the needles for 15～20 minutes manipulating them two to three times.

2) Ear acupuncture

Prescription: Large Intestine, Small Intestine, Stomach, Ear-shenmen, Lower portion of rectum.

Method: Apply filiform needles with strong stimulation and retain the needles for 10～15 minutes.

2. Cold-damp Type

(1) *Main manifestation*

Spasmodic pain in the abdomen, white mucous or mixed with small amount of blood in the stools, tenesmus, aversion to cold preferring warmth, fullness in the chest and epigastrium, tastelessness, absence of thirst, white greasy tongue coating and deep slow pulse.

(2) *Therapeutic principle*

Eliminate cold by warming and resolve dampness, promote Qi and blood circulation.

(3) *Treatment*

1) Body acupuncture

Prescirption: Zhongwan (RN 12), Tianshu (ST 25), Qihai (RN 6), ShangJuxu (ST 37), Yinlingquan (SP 9)。

Method: Apply filiform needles with even movement method. Retain the needles for 15～20 minutes manipulating them two to three times.

2) Ear acupuncture

Prescription: Large Intestine, Small Intestine, Stomach, Abdomen. Ear-shenmen.

Method: Apply filiform needles with moderate stimulation and retain the needles for 10～15 minutes.

3) Moxibustion

Prescription: Qihai (RN 6), Tianshu (ST 25), Zhongwan (RN 12).

Method: Use mild-warming moxibustion or moxibustion with warming needles for 10～15 minutes.

3. Fasting Dysentery

(1) *Main manifestation*

Frequent stools containing blood and pus, total loss of appetite, nausea and vomiting, abdominal pain, distention and fullness in the chest and abdomen, yellow greasy tongue coating, and soft rapid pulse.

(2) *Therapeutic principle*

Pacify the stomach and restore the appetite.

(3) *Treatment*

1) Body acupuncture

Prescription: Zhongwan (RN 12), Hegu (LI 4), Neiguan (PC 6), Neiting (ST 44), Tianshu (ST 25).

Method: Apply filiform needles with reducing method. Retain the needles for 15~20 minutes manipulating them two to three times.

2) Ear acupuncture

Prescription: Large Intestine, Small Intestine, Stomach, Ear-shenmen.

Method: Use filiform needles with moderate stimulation and retain the needles for 10~15 minutes.

4. Chronic Recurrent Dysentery

(1) *Main manifestation*
This kind of dysentery is intermittent from time to time in a lingering course. It worsens with improper diet, overstrain or invasion of exogenous pathogenic factors, general lassitude and cold limbs. It is accompanied by somnolence, poor appetite, pale tongue proper with greasy coating, and soft or full deficient pulse.

(2) *Therapeutic principle*
Strengthen the spleen, replenish Qi and remove stagnation.

(3) *Treatment*
1) Body acupuncture

Prescription: Pishu (BL 20), Weishu (BL 21), Dachangshu (BL 25), Guanyuan (RN 4), Tianshu (ST 25), Zusanli (ST 36).

Method: Apply filiform needles with reinforcing method. Retain the needles for 15~30 minutes manipulating them

one to two times.

2) Ear acupuncture

Prescription: Large Intestine, Small Intestine, Spleen, Kidney, Ear-shenmen, Stomach.

Method: Apply filiform needles with moderate stimulation and retain the needles for 10~15 minutes. Auricular taping is also applicable.

3) Moxibustion

Prescription: Pishu (BL 20), Weishu (BL 21), Guanyuan (RN 4).

Method: Apply mild-warming moxibustion or moxibustion with warming needle for 10~15 minutes once a day.

便　秘

便秘是指大便秘结不通，排便间隔时间延长，或欲大便而艰涩不畅的一种病症。本病多见于现代医学的习惯性便秘或暂时性肠蠕动功能失调之便秘，以及肛门直肠疾患所引起的便秘等。

1. 热秘

（1）主证　大便干结，排便困难，3~5天排便1次，或时间更长，发热，口渴，口臭，小便短赤，厌食，舌苔干黄，脉滑实有力。

（2）治则　清热润肠通便。

（3）治法

1）体针

处方　合谷，曲池，内庭，天枢，腹结，上巨墟。

配穴　烦热口渴加少府，廉泉；口臭加承浆。

操作　毫针刺，用泻法。留针15～20分钟，间歇行针2～3次。

2）耳针

处方　大肠，腹，直肠，三焦。

操作　毫针强刺激，留针15～20分钟；亦可采用三棱针胃和耳尖放血。

2．气秘

（1）主证　大便秘结，脘腹胀满疼痛，嗳气频作，不思饮食，苔薄腻，脉弦。

（2）治则　顺气导滞。

（3）治法

1）体针

处方　中脘，天枢，行间，阳陵泉，支沟。

配穴　胁痛甚者加期门，日月；腹胀甚者加大横。

操作　毫针刺，用泻法。留针15～20分钟，间歇行针2～3次。

2）耳针

处方　大肠，直肠，腹，皮质下，三焦，肝。

操作　毫针中等强度刺激，留针15～20分钟；亦可采用耳穴贴敷。

3．虚秘

（1）主证　便秘，排便时汗出气短，面色苍白无华，头晕目眩，唇甲色淡，心悸乏力，舌淡苔薄，脉细弱。

（2）治则　益气养血，润肠通便。

（3）治法

1）体针

处方　脾俞，胃俞，关元，气海，足三里。

配穴　多汗加阴郄；心悸加内关。

操作　毫针刺，用补法。留针20～30分钟，间歇行针1～2次。

2）耳针

处方　大肠，小肠，脾，皮质下，直肠，肺。

操作　毫针弱刺激，留针15～30分钟。亦可采用耳穴贴敷。

3）艾灸

处方　神阙，气海，脾俞。

操作　用温和灸或回旋灸每穴治疗10～15分钟，每天1次。

4．冷秘

（1）主证　大便艰涩，不易排出，甚则脱肛，腹中或有冷痛，面色青白，手足不温，喜热怕冷，小便清长，舌淡苔白，脉沉迟。

（2）治则　补肾助阳，温腑通便。

（3）治法

1）体针

处方　神阙，气海，照海，肾俞，天枢。

操作　毫针刺，用补法。留针20～30分钟，间歇行针1～2次。

2）耳针

处方　大肠，小肠，直肠，肾，皮质下。

操作　采用温和灸或回旋灸每穴

治疗 10~15 分钟。

3）拔罐疗法

处方　肾俞，气海，关元。

操作　采用坐罐或闪罐治疗 10~20 分钟，每天 1 次。

Constipation

Constipation is a condition manifested by prolonged intervals of dry of compacted feces from the intestines or urgent desire for immediate bowel movement but with difficulty in defecating. It commonly includes habitual constipation, constipation due to peristalsis dysfunction and constipation due to rectum or anus disorders in modern medicine.

1. Heat Constipation

(1) *Main manifestation*

Constipation, difficult defecation, one defecation every 3 to 5 days or even longer, fever, thirst, foul breath, scanty dark urine, anorexia, yellow and dry tongue coating, slippery replete and forceful pulse.

(2) *Therapeutic principle*

Clear away the heat and moisten the intestine to relieve constipation.

(3) *Treatment*

1) Body acupuncture

Prescription: Hegu (LI 4), Quchi (LI 11), Neiting (ST 44), Tianshu (ST 25), Fujie (SP 14), Shangjuxu (ST 37).

Supplementary points: Add Shaofu (HT 8) and Lianquan (RN 23) for excessive heat with thirst and Chengjian (RN 24) for foul breath.

Method: Apply filiform needles with reducing method. Retain the needles for 15~20 minutes manipulating them two to three times.

2) Ear acupuncture

Prescription: Large Intestine, Abdomen, Rectum, San Jiao

Method: Apply filiform needles with strong stimulation and retain the needles for 15 ~ 20 minutes. Stomach and Apex of the Ear punctured with a three-deged needle to cause bleeding is also applicable.

2. Qi Constipation

(1) *Main manifestation*

Constipation, fullness and distending pain in the abdomen and hypochonriac regions, frequent belching, loss of appetite, thin and greasy tongue coating, wiry pulse.

(2) *Therapeutic principle*

Smooth Qi flow and remove stagnation.

(3) *Treatment*

1) Body acupuncture

Prescription: Zhongwan (RN 12), Tianshu (ST 25), Xingjian (LR 2), Yanglingquan (GB 34), Zhigou (SJ 6).

Supplementary points: Add Qimen (LR 14) and Riyue (GB 24) for severe pain in the hypochondriac region and Daheng (SP 15) for severe abdominal distention.

Method: Apply filiform needles with reducing method. Retain the needles for 15～20 minutes manipulating them two to three times.

2) Ear acupuncture

Prescription: Large Intestine, Rectum, Abdomen, Subcortex, San Jiao, Liver.

Method: Apply filiform needles with moderate stimulation and retain the needles for 15～20 minutes. Auricular taping is also applicable.

3. Deficient Constipation

(1) *Main manifestation*

Constipation, sweat and shortness of breath during defecation, pale and lustreless complexion, dizziness, blurred vision, pale lips and nails, palpitation, lassitude, pale tongue with thin coating, thready and weak pulse.

(2) *Therapeutic principle*

Tonify Qi and nourish blood, moisten the intestine and relieve constipation.

(3) *Treatment*

1) Body acupuncture

Prescription: Pishu (BL 20), Weishu (BL 21), Guanyuan (RN 4), Qihai (RN 6), Zusanli (ST 36).

Supplementary points: Add Yinxi

(HT 6) for profuse sweating and Neiguan (PC 6) for palpitation.

Method: Apply filiform needles with reinforcing method. Retain the needles for 20～30 minutes manipulating them one to two times.

2) Ear acupuncture

Prescription: Large Intestine, Small Intestine, Spleen, Subcortex, Rectum, Lung.

Method: Apply filiform needles with mild stimulation and retain the needles for 15～30 minutes. Auricular taping is also applicable.

3) Moxibustion

Prescription: Shenque (RN 8), Qihai (RN 6), Pishu (BL 20).

Method: Apply mild-warming moxibustion or rounding moxibustion to each point for 10～15 minutes once a day.

4. Cold Constipation

(1) *Main manifestation*

Dry stool difficult to discharge, prolapse of rectum in severe cases, occasional pain in the abdomen, pallid complexion, cold limbs with a desire for warmth, copious clear urine, pale tongue with white coating, and deep slow pulse.

(2) *Therapeutic principle*

Reinforce kidney Yang, warm up the intestine and promote bowel movements.

(3) *Treatment*

1) Body acupuncture

Prescription: Shenque (RN 8), Qihai (RN 6), Zhaohai (KI 6), Shenshu (BL 23), Tianshu (ST 25).

Method: Apply filiform needles with reinforcing method. Retain the needles for 20~30 minutes manipulating them one to two times.

2) Ear acupuncture

Prescription: Large Intestine, Small Intestine, Rectum, Kidney, Subcortex.

Method: Use filiform needles with mild stimulation and retain the needles for 20 ~ 30 minutes. Auricular taping is also applicable.

3) Moxibustion

Prescription: Shenque (RN 8), Qihai (RN 6), Shenshu (BL 23).

Method: Apply mild moxibustion or rounding moxibustion to each point for 10~15 minutes.

4) Cupping Therapy

Prescription: Shenshu (BL 23), Qihai (RN 6), Guanyuan (RN 4).

Method: Use retaining cupping or successive flash cupping for 10 ~ 20 minutes once a day.

脱　　肛

脱肛是指直肠下端脱出肛门之外而言。多见于老人、小儿或久病体弱的患者。本病与现代医学的直肠脱垂相似。

1．脾虚下陷

(1) 主证　长期泄泻，直肠黏膜脱出，伴面色萎黄，心悸气短，神疲乏力，舌质淡，苔薄白，脉细弱。

(2) 治则　补益气血。

(3) 治法

1) 体针

处方　百会，长强，大肠俞，气海，足三里。

操作　毫针刺，用补法。留针15~30分钟，间歇行针2~3次。

2) 耳针

处方　直肠下段，大肠，脑，脾，肾上腺。

操作　毫针弱刺激，留针15~30分钟。亦可采用耳穴贴敷或埋针。

3) 艾灸

处方　气海，百会，足三里。

操作　采用温和灸或回旋灸每穴灸治10~15分钟。亦可采用温针灸治疗。

2．阴虚火旺

(1) 主证　直肠黏膜脱出，肛门疼痛，伴口干咽燥，便秘尿赤，舌红苔薄，脉数。

(2) 治则　养阴清火。

(3) 治法

1) 体针

处方　百会，气海，白环俞，承山，孔最，郄门。

操作　毫针刺，用补法。留针15~20分钟，间歇行针2~3次。

2）耳针

处方 直肠下段，大肠，脑，肾，肾上腺。

操作 毫针中等强度刺激，留针15～20分钟；亦可采用耳穴贴敷或埋针治疗。

3．湿热下注

（1）主证 直肠脱出，肛门灼热、肿痛，兼有面赤身热，口干口臭，胸脘痞闷，腹胀便结，小便短赤，舌红苔黄腻，脉濡数。

（2）治则 清泄湿热。

（3）治法

1）体针

处方 百会，长强，承山，委中，丰隆，阴陵泉。

配穴 腹胀便结加天枢；因痔疾而致脱肛加二白穴。

操作 毫针刺，用泻法。留针15～20分钟；间歇行针2～3次。

2）耳针

处方 直肠下段，皮质下，脾，神门。

操作 毫针中等强度刺激，留针15～20分钟；亦可采用耳穴贴敷。

3）三棱针

操作 在第3腰椎至第2腰椎之间，脊柱中线旁开1～1.5寸外纵线上，任选一点进行挑治。

Prolapse of Rectum

Prolapse of rectum refers to the condition in which the lower portion of the rectum is prolapsed out of the anus, mainly seen in aged patients, children or those with poor body constitution due to certain lingering diseases. The condition described here is similar to rectum prolapse in modern medicine.

1. Prolapse Due to Deficiency of the Spleen

(1) *Main manifestation*

Long history of diarrhea, prolapse of rectum mucosa, accompanied by sallow complexion, palpitation and shortness of breath, mental weakness and fatigue, pale tongue with thin white coating, thready and feeble pulse.

(2) *Therapeutic principle*

Invigorate the blood and QI.

(3) *Treatment*

1) Body acupuncture

Prescription: Baihui (DU 20), Changqiang (DU 1), Dachangshu (BL 25), Qihai (RN 6), Zusanli (ST 36).

Method: Apply filiform needles with reinforcing method. Retain the needles for 15～30 minutes manipulating them two to three times.

2) Ear acupuncture

Prescription: Lower rectum, Large Intestine, Brain, Spleen, Adrenal gland.

Method: Apply filiform needles with mild stimulation and retain the needles for 15～30 minutes. Auricular taping or subcutaneous needle is also applicable.

3) Moxibustion

Prescription: Qihai (RN 6), Baihui (DU 20) Zusanli (ST 36).

Method: Apply mild-warming moxibustion or rounding moxibustion to each point for 10~15 minutes. Moxibustion with warming needle is also applicable.

2. Intense Fire Due to Yin Deficiency

(1) *Main manifestation*

Prolapse of rectal mucosa, pain in the anus, accompanied by dry mouth and thirst, constipation, dark urine, red tongue with thin coating, rapid pulse.

(2) *Therapeutic principle*

Nourish yin and remove fire.

(3) *Treatment*

1) Body acupuncture

Prescription: Baihui (DU 20), Qihai (RN 6), Baihuanshu (BL 30), Chengshan (BL 57), Kongzui (LU 6), Ximen (PC 4).

Method: Apply filiform needles with reinforcing method. Retain the needles for 15~20 minutes manipulating them two to three times.

2) Ear acupuncture

Prescription: Lower rectum, Large Intestine, Brain, Kidney, Adrenal gland.

Method: Apply filiform needles with moderate stimulation and retain the needles for 15~20 minutes. Auricular taping or subcutaneous needle is also applicable.

3. Damp-heat Attacking the Lower-Jiao

(1) *Main manifestation*

Prolapse of the rectum involved with swelling and burning pain in the anus. It is accompanied by flushed face, fever, dry mouth with foul breath, chest and epigstric fullness, abdominal distention, scanty yellow urine, red tongue proper with yellow greasy coating, and soft rapid pulse.

(2) *Therapeutic principle*

Eliminate damp-Heat.

(3) *Treatment*

1) Body acupuncture

Prescription: Baihui (DU 20), Changqiang (DU 1), Chengsha (BL 57), Weizhong (BL 40), Fenglong (ST 40), Yinlingquan (SP 9).

Supplementary points: Add Tianshu (ST 25) for abdominal distention and Erbai (EX-UE 2) for prolapse of rectum due to hemorrhoids.

Method: Apply filiform needles with reducing method. Retain the needles for 15~20 minutes manipulating them two to three times.

2) Ear acupuncture

Prescription: Lower rectum, Subcortex, Spleen, Ear-shenmen.

Method: Use filiform needles with moderate stimulation and retain the needle for 15～20 minutes. Auricular taping is also applicable.

3) Three-edged needle

Method: Prick any point on the longtitudinal line between the 3rd and 2nd lumbar vertebrae 1～1.5 Cun lateral to the spinal column.

黄　疸

黄疸是以目黄、肤黄、尿黄为主证的疾患，其中尤以目黄为主要特征。临床甚为常见，多发于儿童及青壮年。本病与现代医学所述的黄疸含义相同，包括肝细胞性黄疸，阻塞性黄疸，溶血性黄疸等。

1. 阳黄

（1）主证　发病急，病程短。目肤色黄，鲜明如橘，发热，口渴，小便黄赤短少，大便秘结，身重腹满，胸闷呕恶，舌苔黄腻，脉弦数。若热毒内陷可见神昏、发斑、出血等重证。若湿重于热则黄疸欠鲜明，发热较轻，脘痞便溏，口渴不甚，苔腻微黄，脉濡数。

（2）治则　疏泄肝胆，清热化湿。

（3）治法

1）体针

处方　至阳，腕骨，肝俞，胆俞，阳陵泉，太冲，阴陵泉，内庭。

配穴　热重加大椎；腹胀便秘加天枢、大胸俞；神昏加人中、中冲、少冲；脘闷便溏加足三里。

操作　毫针刺，用泻法。留针20～30分钟，间歇行针2～3次。

2）耳针

处方　肝，胆，脾，胃，膈，耳迷根，腹。

操作　毫针中等强度刺激，留针10～20分钟；亦可采用耳穴贴敷或埋针治疗。

3）电针

处方　同体针。

操作　每次选2～4穴，选用疏波或疏密波，输出电量为中等度刺激，频率40～60次/分钟。每天1次，每次15～30分钟，10次为1疗程。

4）穴位注射

处方　肝俞，脾俞，中都。

操作　每穴注射板蓝根注射液0.5～1毫升，隔天1次，10次为1疗程。

2. 阴黄

（1）主证　起病缓，病程长，目肤俱黄，其色晦暗或如烟熏，神疲身倦，畏寒纳少，恶心欲吐，口淡不渴，脘痞，大便不实，舌淡苔腻，脉沉迟。

（2）治则　健脾利胆，温化寒湿。

（3）治法

1）体针

处方　脾俞，胆俞，至阳，中脘，足三里，三阴交。

配穴　神疲畏寒加气海、命门；大便溏泄加天枢、关元。

操作　毫针刺，平补平泻。留针

20～30分钟，间歇行针2～3次。

2) 耳针

处方 脾，胃，肝，胆，膈，耳迷根，皮质下。

操作 毫针中等强度刺激，留针15～20分钟；亦可采用耳穴贴敷或埋针治疗。

3) 艾灸

处方 脾俞，中脘，三阴交，胆俞。

操作 每穴用温和灸或回旋灸治疗10～15分钟；亦可采用温针灸。

4) 穴位注射

处方 肝俞，脾俞，中都。

操作 每穴注射板蓝根、丹参或维生素 B_1、维生素 B_{12} 注射液0.5～1毫升，隔天1次，10次为1疗程。

Jaundice

Jaundice is a condition characterized by yellow pigmentation of the sclera and skin as well as dark yellow coloured urine. The yellow sclera is considered as the main sign in the clinic. Jaundice is mostly seen in the infantile, the young and the middle aged. The condition described here is the same as that related in modern medicine, including hepatocelular jaundice, obstructive jaundice, hemolytic jaundice, etc.

1. Yang Jaundice

(1) *Main manifestation*

The onset of jaundice is abrupt with very short duration. The symptoms and signs include yellow sclera and skin that is as apparent as orange skin, fever, thirst, short scanty urine, constipation, general heavy sensation, abdominal distention, fullness in the chest, nausea, yellow greasy tongue coating, and wiry pulse. Loss of consciousness, skin eruptions and hemorrhage will appear if the heat attacks the interior of the body. There will be less jaundice, milder fever, fullness in the epigastrium, moderate thirst, slightly yellow greasy tongue coating, and soft rapid pulse if dampness is more severe than heat as the causative factor of the jaundice.

(2) *Therapeutic principle*

Soothe the Qi of the liver and gallbladder, eliminate heat and resolve dampness.

(3) *Treatment*

1) Body acupuncture

Prescription: Zhiyang (DU 9), Wangu (SI 4), Ganshu (BL 18), Danshu (BL 19), Yanglingquan (GB 34), Taichong (LR 3), Yinliquan (SP 9), Neiting (ST 44).

Supplementary points: Add Dazhui (DU 14) for severe heat, Tianshu (ST 25) and Dachangshu (BL 25) for abdominal distention and constipation, Renzhong (DU 26), Zhongchong (PC 9) and Shaochong (HT 9) for loss of consciousness, Zusanli (ST 36) for epigastric fullness and loose stools.

Method: Apply filiform needles with reducing method. Retain needles for 20~30 minutes manipulating them two to four times.

2) Ear acupuncture

Prescription: Liver, Gallbladder, Spleen, Stomach, Diaphragm, Vegus nerve, Abdomen.

Method: Apply filiform needles with moderate stimulation and retain the needles for 15~20 minutes. Auricular taping or subcutaneous needle is also applicable.

3) Electroacupuncture

Prescription: Same as that of body acupuncture.

Method: Two to four points are selected each treatment session. An electric stimulation with a low or irregular wave, a frequency at 40~60 turns/min, and a medium strength intensity is given for 15~30 minutes daily. Ten treatment sessions constitute a therapeutic course.

4) Point injection

Prescription: Ganshu (BL 18), Pishu (BL 20), Zhongdu (LR 6).

Method: Inject 0.5to 1ml Isatis Injection into each point. The treatment is given once every other day. 10 treatments make a course.

2. Yin Jaundice

(1) *Main manifestation*

The onset of the jaundice is slow over a long duration. The main symptoms and signs include yellow sclera and skin which may appear grey dark as if being smoked, general lassitude, aversion to cold, anorexia, nausea, vomiting, tastelessness in the mouth, no thirst, epigastric distention, unformed stools, pale tongue proper, greasy tongue coating, and deep slow pulse.

(2) *Therapeutic principle*

Strengthen the spleen, promote bile excretion, eliminate cold and resolve dampness.

(3) *Treatment*

1) Body acupuncture

Prescription: Pishu (BL 20), Danshu (BL 19), Zhiyang (DU 9), Zhongwan (RN 12), Zusanli (ST 36), Sanyinjiao (SP 6).

Supplementary points: Add Qihai (RN 6) and Mingmen (DU 4) for general lassitude and aversion to cold, and Tianshu (ST 25) and Guanyuan (RN 4) for loose stools.

Method: Apply filiform needles with even movement method. Retain the needles for 20~30 minutes manipulating them two to three times.

2) Ear acupuncture

Prescription: Spleen, Stomach, Liver, Gallbladder, Diaphragm, Vegus nerve, Subcortex.

Method: Apply filiform needles with

moderate stimulation and retain the needles for 15～20 minutes. Auricular taping or subcutaneous needles is also applicable.

3）Moxibustion

Prescription：Pishu（BL 20）, Zhongwan（RN 12）, Sanyinjiao（SP 6）, Danshu（BL 19）.

Method：Apply mild-warming or rounding moxibustion to each point for 10 ～ 15 minutes. Moxibustion with warming needle is also applicable.

4）Point injection

Prescription：Ganshu（BL 18）, Pishu（BL 20）, Zhongdu（LR 6）.

Method：Inject 0.5～1mL Isatis Injection, Salvia Injection or Vit. B$_1$, Vit. B$_{12}$ Injection into each point. The treatment is given once every other day. 10 treatments make a course.

胁　痛

胁痛是指一侧或两侧胁肋疼痛而言，可见于现代医学的肝、胆疾患及肋间神经痛等。

1．肝气郁结

（1）主证　胁肋胀痛，走窜不定，常因情志波动而发作和加甚。伴有胸闷不舒，饮食减少，嗳气频作，易怒，少寐，舌苔薄白，脉弦。

（2）治则　疏肝解郁，理气止痛。

（3）治法

1）体针

处方　期门，肝俞，太冲，支沟，阳陵泉。

配穴　胸闷嗳气加中脘、胃俞；少寐加大陵、神门。

操作　毫针刺，用泻法。留针15～20分钟，间歇行针2～3次。

2）耳针

处方　肝，胆，神门，胸。

操作　毫针中等强度刺激，留针15～20分钟；亦可采用耳穴贴敷。

2．肝胆湿热

（1）主证　胁痛偏于右侧，如刺如灼，急性发作时伴有恶寒发热，口苦，心烦，恶心呕吐，目赤或目黄身黄，小便黄赤，舌红，苔黄，脉弦数。

（2）治则　清热化湿，疏肝利胆。

（3）治法

1）体针

处方　期门，日月，支沟，阳陵泉，丘墟，行间。

配穴　热重加关冲，恶心呕吐加中脘、内关；心烦加郄门。

操作　毫针刺，用泻法。留针15～20分钟，间歇行针2～3次。

2）耳针

处方　肝，胆，神门，胸，皮质下。

操作　毫针中等强度刺激，留针15～20分钟；亦可采用耳穴贴敷。

3）皮肤针

处方　胁肋部痛点，及与痛点成水平的背俞穴上中下3个腧穴。

操作　轻刺激，叩至皮肤潮红为度，并加拔火罐。

3．瘀血停积

（1）主证　胁痛如刺，痛处不移，入夜更甚，疼痛拒按，胁肋下或见痞块，舌质紫暗，脉沉涩。

（2）治则　活血通络，行气止痛。

（3）治法

1）母体针

处方　膈俞，肝俞，太冲，三阴交，期门，支沟。

配穴　跌仆损伤可结合痛部取其阿是穴。

操作　毫针刺，用泻法，留针15～20分钟，间歇行针2～4次；亦可采用皮肤针。

2）耳针

处方　肝，胆，神门，胸，皮质下。

操作　毫针中等强度刺激，留针15～20分钟。亦可采用耳穴贴敷或皮肤针。

4．肝阴不足

（1）主证　两胁隐隐作痛，其痛绵绵不休，口干心烦，头晕目眩，潮热，自汗，舌红少苔，脉细数。

（2）治则　滋阴养血，和络止痛。

（3）治法

1）体针

处方　肝俞，肾俞，期门，太冲，足三里，三阴交。

配穴　潮热加膏肓，头晕目眩加百会，风池。

操作　毫针刺，用补法。留针20～30分钟，间歇行针1～2次。

2）耳针

处方　肝，胆，神门，胸。

操作　毫针弱刺激，留针20～30分钟。亦可采用耳穴贴敷或埋针治疗。

Hypochondriac Pain

Hypochondriac pain refers to a painful sensation either on one side or both sides of the hypochondrium. It is included in hepatopathy, biliary disorders, intercostal neuralgia, etc. in modern medicine.

1. Stagnation of Liver Qi

(1) *Main manifestation*
Distention and wandering pain in the hypochondriac region aggravated by emotional upset, accompanied by fullness sensation in the chest, poor appetite, frequent belching, irritability, poor sleep, thin white coating, and wiry pulse.

(2) *Therapeutic principle*
Soothe the liver, regulate Qi circulation and stop pain.

(3) *Treatment*

1) Body acupuncture

Prescription: Qimen (LR 14), Ganshu (BL 18), Taichong (LR 3), Zhigou (SJ 6), Yanglingquan (GB 34).

Supplementary Points: Add Zhongwan (RN 12) and Weishu (BL 21) for fullness sensation in the chest and belching, Daling (PC 7) and Shen-men (HT 7) for poor sleep.

Method: Apply filiform needles with reducing method. Retain the needles for 15～20 minutes manipulating them two to three times.

2) Ear acupuncture

Prescription: Liver, Gallbladder, Ear-shenmen, Chest.

Method: Apply filiform needles with moderate stimulation and retain the needles for 15～20 minutes. Auricular taping is also applicable.

2. Damp-heat Retention in the Liver and Gallbladder

(1) *Main manifestation*

Stabbing pain with burning sensation particularly on the right hypochondriac region is accompanied by chills and fever during the acute pain, bitter taste in the mouth, irritability, nausea and vomiting, congested eyes, short scanty urine, red tongue proper with yellow coating, and wiry rapid pulse.

(2) *Therapeutic principle*

Clear heat, resolve dampness, soothe the liver and promote the function of the gallbladder.

(3) *Treatment*

1) Body acupuncture

Prescription: Qimen (LR 14), Riyue (GB 24), Zhigou (SJ 6), Yanglingquan (GB 34), Qiuxu (GB 40), Xingjian (LR 2).

Supplementary points: Add Guan-chong (SJ 1) for severe fever, Zhong-wan (RN 12) and Neiguan (PC 6) for nausea and vomiting, and Ximen (PC 4) for restlessness.

Method: Apply filiform needles with reducing method. Retain the needles for 15～20 minutes manipulating them two to three times.

2) Ear acupuncture

Prescription: Liver, Gallbladder, Ear-shemen, Chest, Subcortex.

Method: Apply filiform needles with moderate stimulation and retain the needles for 15～20 minutes. Auricular taping is also applicable.

3) Plum-blossom needling

Prescription: Tenderness in the hypochondriac region and three Back-Shu points at the same level, respectively superior, inferior and horizontal to the tender point.

Method: Tap gently till local redness with moisture appears which is then followed by cupping.

3. Blood Stasis

(1) *Main manifestation*

Localized pain with pricking sensation aggravated at night, severe pain worse by pressing, also possible hypochondriac mass, dark purplish tongue proper and deep choppy pulse.

(2) *Therapeutic principle*

Activate the circulation of Qi and blood, resolve blood stasis and stop pain.

(3) *Treatment*

1) Body acupuncture

Prescription: Geshu (BL 17), Ganshu (BL 18), Taichong (LR 3), Sanyinjiao (SP 6), Qimen (LR 14), Zhigou (SJ 6).

Supplementary points: Add local Ashi points provided that the pain in the hypochondrium is ascribed to traumatic factors.

Method: Apply filiform needles with reducing method. Retain the needles for 15~20 minutes manipulating them two to four times. Plumblossom needling is also applicable.

2) Ear acupuncture

Prescription: Liver, Gallbadder, Ear-shenmen, Chest, Subcortex.

Method: Apply filiform needles with moderate stimulation and retain the needles for 15~20 minutes. Auricular taping or subcutaneous needles is also applicable.

4. Deficiency of Liver Yin

(1) *Main manifestation*

Dull pain of a lingering nature in both hypochondriac regions, dry mouth, restlessness, blurred vision, dizziness, afternoon fever, spontaneous sweating, red tongue with less coating, and thin rapid pulse.

(2) *Therapeutic principle*

Nourish Yin and blood, regulate Qi circulation and relieve pain.

(3) *Treatment*

1) Body acupuncture

Prescription: Ganshu (BL 18), Shenshu (BL 23), Qimen (LR 14), Taichong (LR 3), Zusanli (ST 36), Sanyinjiao (SP 6).

Supplementary points: Add Gaohuangshu (BL 43) for tidel fever, Baihui (DU 20) and Fengchi (GB 20) for dizziness and vertigo.

Method: Apply filiform needles with reinforcing method. Retain the needles for 20~30 minutes manipulating them once or twice.

2) Ear acupuncture

Prescription: Liver, Gallbladder, Ear-shenmen, Chest.

Method: Use filiform needles with mild stimulation and retain the needles for 20~30 minutes. Auricular taping or subcutaneous needle is also applicable.

眩　　晕

眩晕是目眩与头晕的总称。目眩即眼花或眼前发黑，视物模糊；头晕即感觉自身或外界景物旋转，站立不稳。两者常同时并见，故统称为眩晕。轻者闭目即可停止；重者如坐车船，旋转不定,不能站立或伴有恶心、呕吐、汗出、甚则晕倒。

1. 痰湿中阻

（1）主证 眩晕倦怠或头重如蒙，恶心欲吐，胸脘痞闷，口黏不渴，少食多梦，肢体麻木，舌苔白腻，脉濡滑。

（2）治则 健脾和胃，化痰除湿。

（3）治法

1）体针

处方 中脘，脾俞，足三里，丰隆，百会，内关。

操作 毫针刺，平补平泻或泻法。留针 15～20 分钟，间歇行针 2～3 次。

2）耳针

处方 脾，神门，内耳，皮质下。

操作 毫针中等强度刺激，留针 15～30 分钟；亦可采用耳穴贴敷。

2. 肝阳上亢

（1）主证 眩晕耳鸣，头痛且胀，每因烦劳或恼怒而加重，面红目赤，急躁易怒，失眠多梦，口苦，舌红，苔薄黄，脉弦数。

（2）治则 滋阴潜阳，平肝熄风。

（3）治法

1）体针

处方 风池，太冲，侠溪，肝俞，肾俞，太溪。

操作 毫针刺，肾俞，太溪，肝俞用补法，风池，太冲，侠溪用泻法。留针 20～30 分钟，间歇行针 3～4次。

2）耳针

处方 肝，神门，皮质下，内耳。

操作 毫针中等强度刺激，留针 15～30 分钟；亦可采用耳穴贴敷。

3. 气血亏虚

（1）主证 头晕眼花，动则加剧，劳累即发，面色㿠白，精神不振，心悸失眠，唇甲不华，气短懒言，四肢无力，纳呆，舌质淡，脉细弱。

（2）治则 补气益血，健脾益胃。

（3）治法

1）体针

处方 足三里，三阴交，脾俞，肾俞，关元，百会。

操作 毫针刺，用补法。留针 15～30 分钟，间歇行针 2～3 次。

2）耳针

处方 脾，肝，神门，皮质下，内耳，肾。

操作 毫针轻刺激，留针 15～30 分钟；亦可采用耳穴贴敷。

3）艾灸

处方 脾俞，足三里，关元，肾俞。

操作 用温和灸或回旋灸治疗 10～15 分钟；亦可采用温针灸治疗。

4）拔罐疗法

处方 脾俞，关元。

操作 选用坐罐治疗 10～20 分钟。

4. 肾精亏虚

（1）主证 眩晕健忘，腰膝酸软，遗精耳鸣，失眠多梦。偏于阳虚者则四肢不温，舌质淡，脉沉细；偏于阴虚者则五心烦热，盗汗，舌质红，脉弦细。

（2）治则　补肾培元。

（3）治法

1）体针

处方　肾俞，关元，太溪，足三里。

操作　毫针刺，用泻法。留针15～30分钟，间歇行针1～3次。

2）耳针

处方　肾，神门，皮质下，内耳。

操作　毫针刺，轻刺激，留针15～30分钟。

Dizziness

Dizziness is the general term for blurred vision and vertigo. The former refers to visionary sparkling or the blurring of vision with darkness appearing in front of the eyes. The latter refers to a subjective feeling that the body or surrounding objects are turning around with difficulty to keep balance. They are always mentioned together since both may appear at the same time. Mild dizziness may be stopped by instant closing of the eyes. In severe cases, the patient feels as if he is on a fast-moving train or sailing boat that makes him unable to stand firmly. It may be accompanied by nausea, vomiting, sweating or fainting in more severe conditions. Dizziness may be seen in many cases in modern medicine such as auditory vertigo, cerebral arteriosclerosis, hypertension, hypotension, vertebrobasilar ischemia, anemia, neurasthenia and those cerebral conditions with dizziness as the main symptom. For the above mentioned conditions, the differentiation and treatment in this section can be referred to.

1. Phlegm-damp Obstruction in the Middle-Jiao

(1) *Main manifestation*

Dizziness, lassitude, heaviness of head, nausea, vomiting, fullness in the chest and epigastrium, sticky mouth with no thirst, poor appetite, dream-disturbed sleep, numbness of the limbs, white greasy tongue coating, and soft slippery pulse.

(2) *Therapeutic principle*

Strengthen spleen, pacify the stomach, eliminate phlegm and resolve the dampness.

(3) *Treatment*

1) Body acupuncture

Prescription: Zhongwan (RN 12), Pishu (BL 20), Zusanli (ST 36), Fenglong (ST 40), Baihui (DU 20), Neiguan (PC 6).

Method: Apply filiform needles with even movement method or with reducing method and retain the needles for 15～20 minutes. Manipulate them two to three times.

2) Ear acupuncture

Prescription: Spleen, Ear-shenmen,

Inner ear, Subcortex.

Method: Apply filiform needles with moderate stimulation and retain the needles for 15～30 minutes. Auricular taping is also applicable.

2. Hyperactivity of Liver Yang

(1) *Main manifestation*

1) Body acupuncture

Prescription: Fengchi (GB 20), Taichong (LR 3), Xiaxi (GB 43), Ganshu (BL 18), Shenshu (BL 23), Taixi (KI 3).

Method: Apply filiform needles with reinforcing method at Shenshu (BL 23), Taixi (KI 3), and Ganshu (BL 18) and reducing method at Fengchi (GB 20), Taichong (LR 3) and Xiaxi (GB 43). Retain the needles for 20 ～ 30 minutes manipulating them three to four times.

2) Ear acupuncture

Prescription: Liver, Ear-shenmen, Subcortex, Inner ear.

Method: Apply filiform needles with moderate stimulation and retain the needles for 15～30 minutes. Auricular taping is also applicable.

3. Deficiency of Qi and Blood

(1) *Main manifestation*

Dizziness, blurred vision aggravated by exertion or overstrain, pale complexion, poor spirit, palpitation and insomnia, pale lips and nails, shortness of breath, reluctant speech, weak limbs, poor appetite, pale tongue proper, and thin weak pulse.

(2) *Therapeutic principle*

Invigorate Qi, nourish blood, strengthen the spleen and stomach.

(3) *Treatment*

1) Body acupuncture

Prescription: Zusanli (ST 36), Sanyinjiao (SP 6), Pishu (BL 20), Shenshu (BL 23), Guanyuan (RN 4), Baihui (DU 20).

Method: Apply filiform needles with reinforcing method. Retain the needles for 15～30 minutes manipulating them two to three times.

2) Ear acupuncture

Prescription: Spleen, Liver, Ear-shenmen, Subcortex, Inner ear, Kidney.

Method: Apply filiform needles with mild stimulation and retain the needles for 15 ～ 30 minutes. Auricular taping is also applicable.

3) Moxibustion

Prescription: Pishu (BL 20), Zusanli (ST 36), Guanyuan (RN 4), Shenshu (BL 23).

Method: Use mild-warming moxibustion or rounding moxibustion for 10～15 minutes. Moxibustion with warming needle is also applicable.

4) Cupping Therapy

Prescription: Pishu (BL 20),

Guanyuan（RN 4）.

Method：Use retaining cupping for 10～20 minutes.

4．Deficiency of Kidney Essence

(1) *Main manifestation*

Dizziness, poor memory, weakness of the lumbus and knees, seminal emission, tinnitus, and poor sleep. Patients with kidney Yang deficiency may also have cold limbs, pale tongue proper with thin deep pulse. Patients with kidney Yin deficiency may also have feverish palms, soles and chest, night sweating, red tongue proper with thin wiry pulse.

(2) *Therapeutic principle*

Reinforce Kidney and tonify the Yuan-Source Qi.

(3) *Treatment*

1) Body acupuncture

Prescription：Shenshu（BL 23）, Guanyuan（RN 4）, Taixi（KI 3）, Zusanli（ST 36）.

Method：Apply filiform needles with reinforcing method. Retain the needles for 15～30 minutes manipulating them one to three times.

2) Ear acupuncture

Prescription：Kidney, Ear-shenmen, Subcortex, Inner ear.

Method：Apply filiform needles with mild stimulation and retain the needles for 15～30 minutes.

中 风

中风是以突然昏仆，不省人事，或半身不遂，语言不利，口角㖞斜为主症的一种疾病。因其起病急骤，变化多端，犹如风之善行而数变的特征相似，故类比称为中风，又称"猝中"。现代医学的脑出血，脑血栓形成，脑栓塞，蛛网膜下腔出血，脑血管痉挛等病及其后遗症，均可参照本节辨证治疗。

1．风中经络

(1) 主证　半身不遂，肌肤不仁，口眼㖞斜，舌强语塞，舌苔白腻，脉弦滑。

(2) 治则　疏风通络，调和气血。

(3) 治法

1) 体针

处方　百会，足三里，合谷，风府，人迎。

配穴　上肢瘫痪加肩髃，曲池，外关；下肢瘫痪加环跳，阳陵泉，风市；口眼㖞斜加颊车，地仓，下关，合谷，太冲；语言不利加哑门，廉泉。

操作　毫针刺，平补平泻。留针20～30分钟，间歇行针1～3次。

2) 头皮针

处方　运动区，言语区。

操作　毫针刺，每10分钟捻针3～5分钟。留针30～40分钟。

2．风中脏腑

闭证

（1）主证　突然昏仆，神识昏昧，两手紧握，牙关紧闭，面赤气粗，喉中痰鸣，二便不通，脉弦滑有力。

（2）治则　开窍熄风，清火豁痰。

（3）治法

1）体针

处方　百会，水沟，丰隆，太冲，涌泉，十二井穴。

配穴　牙关紧闭者加下关，颊车，合谷；舌强语塞加哑门，廉泉，通里。

操作　毫针刺，用泻法。留针20～40分钟，间歇行针3～5次。十二井穴可用三棱针点刺出血。

2）头针

处方　运动区，感觉区，语言区，足运感区。

操作　毫针沿皮下刺入0.5～1寸，频频捻针，捻转角度在180度以内，频率为200次/分钟以上。

脱证

（1）主证　突然昏仆，神识昏昧，目合口张，鼻鼾息微，四肢软瘫，小便失禁，舌痿软，脉细弱。重者四肢逆冷，面红如妆，脉来浮大。

（2）治则　补益元气，回阳固脱。

（3）治法

1）艾灸

处方　神阙，气海，关元。

操作　艾炷灸之，不拘壮数，以汗收、肢温、脉起为度。

2）体针

处方　水沟，内关，太渊，足三里，百会。

操作　毫针刺，用补法。留针20～30分钟，间歇行针1～2次。

Windstroke

Windstroke refers to a disease characterized by sudden fainting with loss of consciousness, hemiplegia, slurred speech, and deviation of the eyes and mouth. Because of its abrupt onset and drastic changes bearing the wandering and changing nature of wind, it acquires the term windstroke by convention. For many diseases such as cerebral hemorrhage, cerebral thrombosis, cerebral embolism, subarachnoid hemorrhage, cerebral angiospasm as well as their sequelae, the differetiation and treatment in this section can be referred to.

1. Windstroke Attacking the Channels and Collaterals

（1）*Main manifestation*
Hemiplegia, numbness, deviation of the mouth and eyes, stiff tongue, dysarthria, greasy coating of the tongue, stringy and smooth pulse.

（2）*Therapeutic principle*
Dispel the wind to promote the flow of Qi and blood in the channel.

（3）*Treatment*

1）Body acupuncture
Prescription: Baihui（DU 20），Zusanli（ST 36），Hegu（LI 4），Fengfu

(DU 16), Renying (ST 9).

Supplementary points: Add Jianyu (LI 15), Quchi (LI 11), Waiguan (SJ 5) for hemiplegia involving the upper limb, Huantiao (GB 30), Yanglingquan (GB 34), Fengshi (GB 31) for hemiplegia involving the lower limb, Jiache (ST 6), Dicang (ST 4), Xiaguan (ST 7), Hegu (LI 4) and Taichong (LR 3) for deviation of the eye and mouth, Yamen (DU 15) and Lianquan (RN 23) for poor speech conducting.

Method: Apply filiform needles with even movement method. Retain the needles for 20～30 minutes manipulating them one to three times.

2) Scalp acupuncture

Prescription: Motor area, Speech area.

Method: Apply filiform needles with continuous rotating for three to five minutes out of every ten minutes and retain the needles for 30～40 minutes.

2. Windstroke Attacking the Zangfu Tense Syndrome

(1) *Main manifestations*

Falling down with loss of consciousness, tightly closed hands and clenched jaws, flushed face, coarse breahing, rattling in the throat, retention of urine, constipation, red tongue with thick yellow or dark grey coating, string-taut rolling and forceful pulse.

(2) *Therapeutic principle*

Bring back resuscitation, quench the wind, eliminate fire and clear up phlegm.

(3) *Treatment*

1) Body acupuncture

Prescription: Baihui (DU 20), Shuigou (DU 26), Fenglong (ST 40), Taichong (LR 3), Yongquan (KI 1), Twelve Jing-well points on both hands (LU 11, HT 9, PC 9, LI 1, SJ 1, SI 1).

Supplementary points: Add Xiaguan (ST 7), Jiache (ST 6), Hegu (LI 4) for clenched jaws, Yamen (DU 15), Lianquan (RN 23), and Tongli (HT 5) for aphasis and stiffness of tongue.

Method: Apply filiform needles with reducing method. Retain the needles for 20～40minutes manipulating them three to five times. The Jing well points are pricked with a three-edged needle to cause bleeding.

2) Scalp acupuncture

Prescription: Motor area, Sensory area, Speech area, Foot-kinesthetic Sensory area.

Method: Insert filiform needles into the areas selected. Push beneath the scalp for 0.5～1cun and twist at a frequency of above 200 times per minute. within an amplitude of a half round.

Flaccid Syndrome

(1) *Main manifestation*

Falling down in a fit, sudden loss of consciousness with mouth agape and eyes closed, soring but feeble breathing, flaccid paralysis of limbs, incontinence of urine, flaccid tongue, thready, weak pulse. In severe cases there are cold limbs, flushing of face, fading or big floating pulse.

(2) *Therapeutic principle*

Reinforce Yuan-source Qi and restore Yang Qi from collapse.

(3) *Treatment*

1) Moxibustion

Prescription: Shenque (RN 8), Qihai (RN 6), Guanyuan (RN 4).

Method: Apply ignited moxa cones at these points till the sweating stop, increase of body temperature and repulsation disregarding the number of moxa cones that will be used in the treatment.

2) Body acupuncture

Prescription: Shuigou (DU 26), Neiguan (PC 6), Taiyuan (LU 9), Zusanli (ST 36), Baihui (DU 20).

Method: Apply filiform needles with reinforcing method. Retain the needles for 20 ~ 30 minutes manipulating them one to two times.

口眼㖞斜

口眼㖞斜又称面瘫。以单纯性的一侧面颊筋肉弛缓、口眼㖞斜为主证。任何年龄均可发病，但以青壮年为多见。本病相当于现代医学的周围性面神经麻痹，亦称 Bell 氏麻痹。

1. 主证

起病突然，多发于一侧。发病后病侧面部板滞不适，眼睑闭合不全，流泪，口角下垂，漱口漏水，不能蹙额、皱眉、鼓腮、闭眼、示齿和吹口哨等。部分患者有耳后、耳下疼痛或偏侧头痛，严重时可出现舌前 2/3 味觉减退或消失，听觉过敏等症，舌苔薄白，脉浮紧或浮缓。

2. 治则

疏风通络，调和气血。

3. 治法

(1) 体针

处方　风池，翳风，阳白，四白，太阳，地仓，颊车，迎香，合谷，内庭。

配穴　眼睑闭合不全加攒竹、瞳子髎；人中沟㖞斜加水沟；颏唇沟㖞斜加承浆或夹承浆；示齿不能加巨髎；耳后疼痛加完骨，外关。

操作　毫针刺，平补平泻。留针15~20 分钟，间歇行针 1~3 次或初期用泻法，后期用补法；亦可用透刺法，阳白透鱼腰，地仓透颊车，太阳透下关。

(2) 皮肤针

处方　阳白，太阳，四白，地仓，颊车。

操作　轻刺激，叩至皮肤潮红为度，隔天 1 次。此法适用于恢复期及其后遗症。

（3）拔罐疗法

处方　颊车，下关，太阳。

操作　毫针刺后用小型火罐拔，隔 2～3 天 1 次，亦可用皮肤针叩刺后，用小型火罐吸拔，每次拔 5～10 分钟。

（4）发泡灸

处方　翳风，太阳，颊车。

操作　将中药制成的药膏贴敷于穴位上，患部有一种热感，甚至烧灼痛，贴敷 2～3 小时后将药膏撕掉，此时局部皮肤轻者紫红，甚者可见有大小不等的水泡，出现水泡者，用三棱针点破使水流尽，一般无需特殊处理。

（5）挑治

处方　取患侧腮内膜咬合线。

操作　令患者先用盐水漱口，以清洁口腔，并尽量将口张大。医者左手拇指、示指用纱布拿住患侧口角，该手余指按压腮部，使其内侧面向口方向翻转，右手持消毒三棱针由内向外点刺咬合线，使其微出血。间隔 0.5 寸左右挑 1 针，挑至口角内侧即完毕。挑治后避受风寒，可热敷患部，5～7 天挑 1 次。

Deviation of the Eye and Mouth

Deviation of eye and mouth, also called facial paralysis, is manifested by deviated eye and mouth and unilateral looseness of facial muscles. It may happen in patients at any age but more common in the young and the middle aged. The disease is the same as peripheral facial paralysis (Bell's paralysis) in modern medicine.

1. Main Manifestation

The onset of the disease is abrupt, mostly affecting only one side of the face. Subsequently the patient feels a stiff and numb sensation on the affected side of the face. This is accompanied by incomplete closure of the eye, lacrimation, drop of the mouth corner, salivation and inability to frown, to raise the eyebrow, to blow out the cheek, to close the eye, to show the teeth or to whistle. Some patients may also complain of pain in the posteriolnferior auricular region and migraine. In severe cases, there may appear hypogeusthesia or ageusia on the anterior 2/3 of the tongue.

2. Therapeutic Principle

Eliminate wind, remove obstruction from the channels and collaterals and regulate Qi and blood circulation.

3. Treatment

(1) *Body acupuncture*

Prescription：Fengchi (GB 20), Yifeng (SJ 17), Yang bai (GB 14), Sibai (ST 2), Taiyang (EX-HN 5), Dicang (ST 4), Jiache (ST 6), Yingxiang (LI 20), Hegu (LI 4), Neiting (ST 44).

Supplementary points: Add Zanzhu (BL 2) and Tongziliao (GB 1) for incomplete closure of the eye, Chengjiang (RN 24) or Jiachengjiang (Extra) for deviation of the mentolabial sulcus, Juliao (ST 3) for difficulty showing the teeth, Wangu (GB 12) and Waiguan (SJ 5) for pain in the posterioinferior auricular region.

Method: Apply filiform needles with even movement method. Retain the needles for 15~20 minutes manipulating the needles one to three times. Or, apply reducing method in the early period of the treatment and reinforcing method for later period of treatment. Penetrating method may also be applied from Yang bai (GB 14) to Yuyao (Extra) from Dicang (ST 4) to Jiache (ST 6), and from Taiyang (EX-HN 5) to Xiaguan (ST 7).

(2) *Plum-blossom needling therapy*

Prescription: Yangbai (GB 14), Taiyang (EX-HN 5) Sibai (ST 2), Dicang (ST 4), Jiache (ST 6).

Method: Tap these points with gentle stimulation till local redness appears once every other day. This kind of treatment is suitable for rehabilitation or sequela of facial paralysis.

(3) *Cupping*

Prescription: Jiache (ST 6), Xiaguan (ST 7), Taiyang (EX-HN 5)

Method: Apply cupping with small sizes of cups after acupuncture treatment every two to three days. Each point is cupped for five to ten minutes. Cupping can also be applied after tapping with the plum-blossom needles.

(4) *Scar-causing plastering*

Prescription: Yifeng (ST 17), Taiyang (EX-HN 5), Jiache (ST 6)

Method: Stick the herbal plasters on the above mentioned areas. The patient will soon feel a feverish sensation or even burning sensation in the local area. Remove the plasters in two to three hours. At this time there will be a purplish colour in the local area. Some patients may have blisters of different sizes. Prick the blisters with a three-edged needle to let out the fluid in the blisters. No special handling is necessary.

(5) *Pricking therapy*

Prescription: The line of occulation at the buccal mucosa at the affected side.

Method: Ask the patient to clean his mouth with water and to open it as largely as possible. Take some cloth to hold the angle of mouth at the affected side with the thumb and the index finger of the left hand. Press the cheek of the affected side with the other fingers of the hand and prick the line with a three-edged needle held by another hand from posterior outwards to cause slight bleeding. Every 0.5 cun portion of the line is pricked from the inside towards the outside until the internal side of the angle of the mouth is reached. The patient is advised to apply hot compress to the affected area and to avoid being attacked by wind-cold evils. The treatment is given once every five to seven days for three sessions as a course.

胸　痹

胸痹是指胸中憋闷疼痛而言，轻者仅感胸闷如塞，重者胸痛如绞，并有短气、喘息等症。肺部为心肺两脏所居，故本病的发生多与心肺功能失常有关。本病主要见于现代医学的冠心病。如慢性支气管炎、肺气肿等以胸痛为主证时，亦可参照本篇辨证治疗。

1. 虚寒

（1）主证　胸痛彻背，心悸，胸闷短气，恶寒肢冷，受寒则甚，舌苔白滑或腻，脉沉细。

（2）治则　助阳散寒，行气活血。

（3）治法

1）体针

处方　心俞，巨厥，厥阴俞，膻中，内关，通里。

操作　毫针刺，用补法或平补平泻法。留针 20～30 分钟，间歇行针 2～3 次。

2）耳针

处方　心，神门，交感，肺，胸，肾。

操作　毫针中等强度刺激，留针20 分钟，亦可采用耳穴贴敷或埋针治疗。

3）艾灸

处方　肺俞，风门，心俞，厥阴俞。

操作　采用温和灸或回旋灸治疗10～15 分钟。亦可采用温针灸。

4）拔罐疗法

处方　心俞，肺俞，厥阴俞。

操作　采用坐罐治疗 10～20 分钟，每天 1 次。

2. 痰浊

（1）主证　胸闷如窒，痛引肩背，气短喘促，咳嗽，痰多黏腻色白，脘腹痞满，纳呆，肢体疲倦，舌苔白腻，脉濡缓。

（2）治则　通阳祛痰化浊。

（3）治法

1）体针

处方　巨厥，膻中，郄门，建里，丰隆，三阴交。

配穴　背痛加脾俞、心俞；气短加灸气海俞、内关。

2）耳针

处方　心，小肠，神门，交感，胸，皮质下，脾。

操作　毫针中等强度刺激，留针20 分钟；亦可采用耳穴贴敷。

3. 血瘀

（1）主证　胸痛如刺，或绞痛阵发，痛彻肩背，胸闷短气，心悸，唇紫，舌质暗，脉细涩或结代。

（2）治则　活血化瘀止痛。

（3）治法

1）体针

处方　至阳，阴郄，心俞，巨
厥，膈俞，膻中。

操作　毫针刺，用泻法。留针
15～30 分钟，间歇行针 2～3 次。

2）耳针

处方　心，神门，交感，皮质
下，胸，肺。

操作　毫针中等强度刺激，留针 20
分钟；亦可采用耳穴贴敷或埋针治疗。

3）三棱针

处方　少冲，中冲。

操作　三棱针点刺出血。

Chest Bi-Syndrome

Chest Bi-syndrome refers to suffocating sensation, fullness and pain in the chest. There is only fullness as if the chest is being oppressed in mild cases, but angina pectoris, shortness of breath and asthmatic breathing in severe cases. Since chest cavity is the anatomical residence of the heart and lungs, chest Bi-syndrome is closely related to the dysfunction of these two organs. Chest Bi-syndrome is commonly seen in coronary heart disease in modern medicine. If the chest pain occurs as a major symptom in case of chronic bronchitis, pulmonary emphysema, etc. the differentiation and treatment in this section can be referred to.

1. Deficient Cold

（1）*Main manifestation*

Chest pain aggravated by cold and radiating towards the back, palpitation, fullness sensation in the chest, shortness of breath, aversion to cold, white greasy tongue coating, and deep thin pulse.

（2）*Therapeutic principle*

Activate Yang, eliminate cold and promote the circulation of Qi and blood.

（3）*Treatment*

1）Body acupuncture

Prescription：Xinshu （BL 15）, Juque （RN 14）, Jueyinshu （BL 14）, Tanzhong （RN 17）, Neiguan （PC 6）, Tongli （HT 5）.

Method：Apply filiform needles.

Add needles with reinforcing or even movement method. Retain the needles for 20～30 minutes manipulating them two to three times.

2）Ear acupuncture

Prescription：Heart, Ear-shenmen, Sympathetic, Lung, Chest, Kidney.

Method：Apply filiform needles with moderate stimulation and retain the needles for 20 minutes. Auricular taping or subcutaneous needle is also applicable.

3）Moxibustion

Prescription：Feishu （BL 18）, Fengmen （BL 12）, Xinshu （BL 15）, Jueyinshu （BL 14）.

Method：Use mild-warming moxibustion or rounding moxibustion for 10~15 minutes. Moxibustion with warming needle is also applicable.

4) Cupping therapy

Prescription: Xinshu (BL 15), Feishu (BL 18), Jueyinshu (BL 14).

Method: Use retaining cupping for 10~20 minutes once a day.

2. Turbid Phlegm Retention

(1) *Main manifestation*

Stuffy sensation in the chest, chest pain radiating towards the back and shoulder, palpitation, shortness of breath, dyspnea, cough, profuse white sticky sputum, fullness in the epigastrium and abdomen, poor appetite, listlessness, white greasy tongue coating, and soft slow pulse.

(2) *Therapeutic principle*

Promote Yang Qi and resolve the pathogenic turbid dampness.

(3) *Treatment*

1) Body acupuncture

Prescription: Juque (RN 14), Tanzhong (RN 17), Ximen (PC 4), Jianli (RN 11), Fenglong (ST 40), Sanyinjiao (SP 6).

Supplementary points: Add Pishu (BL 20), Xinshu (BL 15) for spinal pain, and moxibustion at Qihai (RN 6) and Neiguan (PC 6) for shortness of breath.

Method: Apply filiform needles with reducing method. Retain the needles for 15~30 minutes manipulating them two to three times.

2) Ear acupuncture

Prescription: Heart, Small Intestine, Ear-shenmen, Sympathetic, Chest, Subcortex, Spleen.

Method: Apply filiform needles with moderate stimulation and retain the needles for 20 minutes. Auricular taping is also applicable.

3. Blood Stasis

(1) *Main manifestation*

Paroxysmal pricking pain or colic pain in the chest radiating towards the shoulder and back, fullness of the chest, shortness of breath, palpitation, purplish lips, dark tongue proper, and thin uneven or intermittent pulse.

(2) *Therapeutic principle*

Activate Yang, eliminate cold and promote the circulation of Qi and blood.

(3) *Treatment*

1) Body acupuncture

Prescription: Zhiyang (DU 9), Yinxi (HT 6), Xinshu (BL 15), Juque (RN 14), Geshu (BL 17), Tanzhong (RN 17).

Method: Apply filiform needles with reducing method. Retain the needles for 15~30 minutes manipulating them two to three times.

2) Ear acupuncture

Prescription: Heart, Ear-Shenmen, Sympathetic, Subcortex, Chest, Lung.

Method: Apply filiform needles with moderate stimulation and retain the needles for 20 minutes. Auricular taping or subcutaneous needle is also applicable.

3) Three-edged needle

Prescription: Shaochong (HT 9), Zhongchong (PC 9).

Method: Prick these points with a three-edged needle to cause bleeding.

惊　悸

惊悸又名心悸、怔忡。以患者自感心中急剧跳动，惊慌不安，不能自主为主证。一般多呈阵发性，每因情志波动或劳累而发作加重。常见于现代医学中的各种原因引起的心律失常，心脏神经官能症，甲状腺功能亢进和贫血等。

1. 心神不宁

（1）主证　心悸，善惊易恐，烦躁不宁，多梦易醒，纳食减少，舌苔薄白，脉细数。

（2）治则　宁心安神镇惊。

（3）治法

1）体针

处方　神门，心俞，内关，间使，巨厥，大陵。

操作　毫针刺，用补法。留针15～30分钟，间歇行针1～2次。

2）耳针

处方　心，交感，神门，皮质下，胸。

操作　毫针轻刺激，留针15～20分钟；亦可采用耳穴贴敷。

2. 痰火内动

（1）主证　心悸时发时止，烦躁不宁，胸闷，头晕，失眠多梦，易惊神恍，口苦，咳嗽，咳痰黏稠，小便黄，大便不爽，舌苔黄腻，脉滑数。

（2）治则　清火化痰，宁心安神。

（3）治法

1）体针

处方　灵道，郄门，肺俞，尺泽，丰隆，阳陵泉。

配穴　失眠多梦，心神恍惚加厉兑；烦躁不宁加间使；便秘加大肠俞。

操作　毫针刺，用泻法。留针15～20分钟，间歇行针2～3次。

2）耳针

处方　心，交感，神门，皮质下。

操作　毫针中等强度刺激，留针15～20分钟；亦可采用耳穴贴敷。

3. 血瘀

（1）主证　心悸持续多年，日渐加重，动则气喘，心痛时作，面色黄瘦，甚至出现形寒肢冷，咳喘不能平卧，冷汗，浮肿，唇舌紫暗，脉细涩结代。

（2）治则　活血化瘀，强心定悸。

（3）治法

1）体针

处方 内关，曲泽，少海，膈俞，气海。

操作 毫针刺，平补平泻。留针15～30分钟，间歇行针1～2次。

2）耳针

处方 心，交感，神门，皮质下，小肠。

操作 毫针中等强度刺激，留针15～20分钟；亦可采用耳穴贴敷。

3）电针

处方 内关，郄门，心俞，足三里，三阴交。

操作 每次2穴，选用疏密波，中等刺激以患者能耐受为度。每天1次，每次15～30分钟。

4. 气血不足

（1）主证 心悸不安，难以自主，气短乏力，面色不华，头晕目眩，舌质淡，脉细弱或结代。

（2）治则 补养气血定悸。

（3）治法

1）体针

处方 心俞，巨厥，膈俞，脾俞，足三里，气海，神门，内关。

配穴 头晕目眩者加百会，风池。

操作 毫针刺，用补法。留针15～30分钟，间歇行针2～3次。

2）耳针

处方 心，交感，神门，皮质下，脾。

操作 毫针轻刺激，留针15～20分钟；亦可采用耳穴贴敷。

3）艾灸

处方 心俞，脾俞，膈俞，足三里，气海。

操作 采用温和灸或回旋灸治疗10～15分钟，每天1次。亦可采用温针灸。

5. 阴虚

（1）主证 心悸怔忡，失眠多梦，手足心发热，颧红，潮热盗汗，口干咽燥，或口舌生疮，舌绛少津，脉细数。

（2）治则 补心阴，宁心神。

（3）治法

1）体针

处方 心俞，肝俞，神门，内关，三阴交，太溪。

操作 毫针刺，用补法。留针15～20分钟，间歇行针2～3次。

2）耳针

处方 心，交感，皮质下，神门。

操作 毫针轻刺激，留针15～20分钟；亦可采用耳穴贴敷。

Palpitation

Palpitation is a cardiac condition characterized by unduely rapid heart beat with nervousness and anxiety. It generally occurs in paroxysmal attacks. It is often found in arrhythmia due to any disease, cardioneurosis, hyperthyroidism, anemia, etc, in modern medicine. Such attacks or their aggravated conditions are often the consequence of emotional disturbance or overstrain.

1. Heart-mind Disturbance

(1) *Main manifestation*

Palpitation, eassily frightened or fear, restlessness, dream-disturbed sleep that often wakens the patient, poor appetite, thin white tongue coating, and rapid thready pulse.

(2) *Therapeutic principle*

Calm the heart and mind and sedate frightenings.

(3) *Treatment*

1) Body acupuncture

Prescription: Shenmen (HT 7), Xinshu (BL 15), Neiguan (PC 6), Jianshi (PC 5), Juque (RN 14), Daling (PC 7).

Method: Apply filiform needles with reinforcing method. Retain the needles for 15～30 minutes manipulating them one to two times.

2) Ear acupuncture

Prescription: Heart, Sympathetic, Ear-shenmen, Subcortex, Chest.

Method: Apply filiform needles with mild stimulation and retain the needles for 15～20 minutes. Auricular taping is also applicable.

2. Plegm-fire Disturbance

(1) *Main manifestation*

Intermittent palpitation, restlessness, fullness sensation in the chest, dizziness, insomnia with dream-disturbed sleep, easily frightened, bitter taste in the mouth, cough with sticky sputum, yellow urine, slightly dry stools, yellow greasy tongue coating, and rapid slippery pulse.

(2) *Therapeutic principle*

Eliminate fire, resolve phlegm and calm the heart and mind.

(3) *Treatment*

1) Body acupuncture

Prescription: Lingdao (HT 4), Ximen (PC 4), Feishu (BL 13), Chize (LU 5), Fenglong (ST 40), Yanglingquan (GB 34).

Supplementary points: Add Lidui (ST 45) for in somnia, dreamdisturbed sleep and forgetfulness, Jianshi (PC 5) for restlessness, and Dachangshu (BL 25) for constipation.

Method: Apply filiform needles with reducing method. Retain the needles for 15～20 minutes manipulating them two to three times.

2) Ear acupuncture

Prescription: Heart, Sympathetic, Ear-Shenmen, Subcortex.

Method: Apply filiform needles with moderate stimulation and retain the needle for 15～20 minutes. Auricular taping is also applicable.

3. Blood Stasis

(1) *Main manifestation*

Worsening palpitation over the years, asthmatic breathing upon exertion, occasional cardiac pain, sallow emaciated complexion, and thready choppy pulse. In severe cases, there may appear cold limbs, asthmatic breathing that makes it difficult for the patient to lie down, cold sweating, and puffiness.

(2) *Therapeutic principle*
Activate blood, resolve blood stasis, strengthen the heart and ease palpitation.

(3) *Treatment*

1) Body acupuncture

Prescription: Neiguan (PC 6), Quze (PC 3), Shaohai (HT 3), Geshu (BL 17), Qihai (RN 6).

Method: Apply filiform needles with even movement method. Retain the needles for 15～30 minutes manipulating them one to two times.

2) Ear acupuncture

Prescription: Heart, Sympathetic, Ear-shenmen, Subcortex, Small intestine.

Method: Apply filiform needles with moderate stimulation and retain the needle for 15～20 minutes. Auricular taping is also applicable.

3) Electroacupuncture

Prescription: Neiguan (PC 6), Ximen (PC 4), Xinshu (BL 15), Zusanli (ST 36), Sanyinjiao (SP 6).

Method: Employ two points each session and apply electric stimulation at medium strength with sparse-dense wave for fifteen to thirty minutes once daily.

4. Qi Blood Deficiency

(1) *Main manifestation*
Palpitation, restlessness, shortness of breath, lassitude, pale complexion, dizziness, vertigo, pale tongue proper, and weak thready or choppy pulse.

(2) *Therapeutic principle*
Strengthen Qi, nourish blood and sedate palpitation.

(3) *Treatment*

1) Body acupuncture

Prescription: Xinshu (BL 15), Juque (RN 14), Geshu (BL 17), Pishu (BL 20), Zusanli (ST 36), Qihai (RN 6), Shenmen (HT 7), Neiguan (PC 6).

Supplementary points: Add Baihui (DU 20) and Fengchi (GB 20) for dizziness and vertigo.

Method: Apply filiform needles with reinforcing method. Retain the needles for 15～30 minutes manipulating them two to three times.

2) Ear acupuncture

Prescription: Heart, Sympathetic, Ear-shenmen, Subcortex, Spleen.

Method: Apply filiform needles with mild stimulation and retain the needles for 15～20 minutes. Auricular taping is also applicable.

3) Moxibustion

Prescription: Xinshu (BL 15), Pishu (BL 20), Geshu (BL 17), Zusanli (ST 36), Qihai (RN 6).

Method: Apply mild-warming moxibustion or rounding moxibustion for 10～15 minutes once a day. Moxibustion with warming needle is also applicable.

5. Yin Deficiency

(1) *Main manifestation*
Palpitation, insomia and dreaminess, feverish sensation in the palms and soles, flushing of the zygomatic region, hectic fever, night perspiration, dry mouth and throat, boils of the lips and the tongue, dry and deep red tongue, thready and rapid pulse.

(2) *Therapeutic principle*
Promote blood circulation to relieve the pain and mental stress.

(3) *Treatment*
1) Body acupuncture
Prescription: Xinshu (BL 15), Ganshu (BL 18), Shenmen (HT 7), Neiguan (PC 6), Sanyinjiao (SP 6), Taixi (KI 3).

Method: Apply filiform needles with reinforcing method. Retain the needles for 15～20 minutes manipulating them two to three times.

2) Ear acupuncture
Prescription: Heart, Sympathetic, Subcortex, Ear-shenmen.

Method: Apply filiform needles with mild stimulation and retain the needles for 15～20 minutes. Auricular taping is also applicable.

不寐即失眠，是以经常不能获得正常的睡眠为特征的一种病症。并常兼见头晕，头痛，心悸，健忘等证。不寐的临床表现不一，轻者入寐困难；或寐而多梦易惊，时寐时醒，或醒后不能再寐；严重者整夜不能入寐。

1. 心脾两虚

（1）主证　夜来不易入寐，寐则多梦易醒，心悸健忘，体倦神疲，面色不华，饮食无味，脘痞便溏，舌质淡，苔薄白，脉细弱。

（2）治则　补益心脾，养血安神。

（3）治法
1）体针　脾俞，心俞，隐白，神门，三阴交。

配穴　健忘者加志室，百会。

操作　毫针刺，用补法。留针15～30分钟，间歇行针2～3次。

2）耳针
处方　皮质下，交感，神门，心，脾，内分泌。

操作　毫针轻刺激，留针30分钟；亦可采用耳穴贴敷或埋针治疗。

3）艾灸
处方　脾俞，心俞，三阴交。

操作　采用温和灸治疗10～15分钟，每天1次。

4）皮肤针

处方 四神聪，安眠穴，夹脊穴。

操作 轻刺激，叩至皮肤微红为度，从上向下，每次叩打2～3遍，隔天1次。

5）拔罐疗法

处方 脾俞，心俞。

操作 采用坐罐治疗10～20分钟，每天1次。

2．心肾不交

（1）主证 心烦不寐，头晕耳鸣，口干津少，五心烦热，健忘，心悸，梦遗腰酸，舌质红，苔少，脉细数。

（2）治则 交通心肾。

（3）治法

1）体针

处方 心俞，肾俞，太溪，大陵，神门，照海。

配穴 头晕加风池；耳鸣加听宫，遗精加志室。

操作 毫针刺，补泻兼施。留针15～30分钟，间歇行针2～3次。

2）耳针

处方 皮质下，交感，神门，心，肾。

操作 毫针中等强度刺，留针30分钟；亦可采用耳穴贴敷。

3）皮肤针

处方 四神聪，安眠穴，夹脊穴。

操作 轻刺激，叩至皮肤微红为度，夹脊穴从上向下每次叩打2～3遍，隔天1次。

3．胃气不和

（1）主证 夜寐不安多梦，心中懊憹，脘腹胀满或胀痛，时有恶心或呕吐，嗳腐吞酸，大便不爽，舌苔黄腻、脉滑或弦。

（2）治则 健脾和胃，利湿化痰。

（3）治法

1）体针

处方 中脘，丰隆，足三里，历兑，隐白，神门。

配穴 懊憹，呕恶者加内关。

操作 毫针刺，用泻法。留针15～30分钟，间歇行针2～3次。

2）耳针

处方 皮质下，交感，神门，胃，腹，内分泌。

操作 毫针中等强度刺激，留针30分钟；亦可采用耳穴贴敷。

4．肝火上扰

（1）主证 入睡困难，头晕头胀，多烦易怒。或伴有目赤，口苦，胁痛等，舌苔薄黄，脉弦数。

（2）治则 清肝泻火，滋阴潜阳。

（3）治法

1）体针

处方 肝俞，胆俞，行间，足窍阴，神门。

配穴 目赤者加太阳。

操作 毫针刺，用泻法。留针15～20分钟，间歇行针2～3次。太阳穴可用三棱针点刺出血。

2）耳针

处方　肝，皮质下，交感，神门，内分泌。

操作　毫针轻刺激，留针30分钟，亦可采用耳穴贴敷。

3）皮肤针

处方　四神聪，安眠穴，夹脊穴。

操作　轻刺激，叩至皮肤微红为度，夹脊穴从上向下每次叩打2～3遍，隔日1次。

Insomnia

Insomnia is a condition that makes the patient unable to acquire normal hours of sleep. It is usually accompanied by dizziness, headache, palpitation and poor memory. However, insomnia does present different clinical manifestations. In mild cases, there may be difficulty in falling a sleep, dreamdisturbed sleep that often wakes up the patient with fright or makes him unable to fall a sleep again. In severe cases, there is often no sleep for the whole night.

1. Deficiency of Heart and Spleen

(1) *Main manifestation*

Difficulty in falling asleep, dream-disturbed sleep, palpitation, poor memory, lassitude, listlessness, sallow complexion, poor appetite, epigastric distension, loose stools, pale tongue with thin white coating, thready weak pulse.

(2) *Therapeutic principle*

Reinforce the heart and spleen, nourish blood and calm the mind.

(3) *Treatment*

1) Body acupuncture

Prescription: Pishu (BL 20), Xinshu (BL 15), Yinbai (SP 1), Shenmen (HT 7), Sanyinjiao (SP 6).

Supplementary points: Add Zhishi (BL 52) and Baihui (BL 20) for poor memory.

Method: Apply filiform needles with reinforcing method. Retain the needles for 15～30 minutes manipulating them two to three times.

2) Ear acupuncture

Prescription: Subcortex, Sympathetic, Ear-Shenmen, Heart, Spleen, Endocrine.

Method: Apply filiform needles with mild stimulation and retain the needles for 30 minutes. Auricular taping or subcutaneous needle is also applicable.

3) Moxibustion

Prescription: Pishu (BL 20), Xinshu (BL 15), Sanyinjiao (SP 6).

Method: Apply mild-warming moxibustion for 10～15 minutes once a day.

4) Plum-blossom needling therapy

Prescription: Sishencong (EX-HN 1), Anmian, Huatuojiaji.

Method: Tap with mild stimulation until local redness appears. Tap the Huatuojiaji points from top down to the bottom repeatedly for two to three times. Treatment is given once every other day.

5) Cupping Therapy

Prescription: Pishu (BL 20), Xinshu (BL 15).

Method: Apply retaining cupping for 10~20 minutes once a day.

2. Dysharmony Between the Heart and Kidneys

(1) *Main manifestation*

Poor sleep, restlessness, dizziness, tinnitus, dry mouth with lack of fluid, feverish sensation in the palms and soles, poor memory, palpitation, seminal emission, lumbar soreness, red tongue proper with less coating, and thin rapid pulse.

(2) *Therapeutic principle*

Regain the harmony between heart and kidney.

(3) *Treatment*

1) Body acupuncture

Prescription: Xinshu (BL 15), Shenshu (BL 23), Taixi (KI 3), Daling (PC 7), Shenmen (HT 7), Zhaohai (KI 6).

Supplementary points: Add Fengchi (GB 20) for dizziness, Tinggong (SI 19) for tinnitus, and Zhishi (BL 52) for seminal emission.

Method: Apply filiform needles with both reinforcing and reducing method. Retain the needles for 15~30 minutes

manipulating them two to three times.

2) Ear acupuncture

Prescription: Subcortex, Sympathetic, Ear-shenmen, Heart, Kidney.

Method: Apply filiform needles with moderate stimulation and retain the needles for 30 minutes. Auricular taping is also applicable.

3) Plum-blossom needling therapy

Prescription: Sishencong (EX-HN 1), Anmian, Huatuojiaji.

Method: Tap with mild stimulation until local redness appears. Tap Huatuojiaji from top down to the bottom repeatedly two to three times. Treatment is given once every other day.

3. Derangement of Stomach

(1) *Main manifestation*

Poor sleep disturbed by dreams, feverish sensation in the chest, distention or distending pain in the epigastrium and abdomen, occasional nausea, vomiting, belching, acid regurgitation, difficult defecation, yellow greasy tongue coating, and slippery or wiry pulse.

(2) *Therapeutic principle*

Strengthen the spleen and stomach, eliminate dampness and resolve phlegm.

(3) *Treatment*

1) Body acupuncture

Prescription: Zhongwan (RN 12), Fenglong (ST 40), Zusanli (ST 36), Lidui (ST 45), Yinbai (SP 1),

Shenmen (HT 7).

Supplementary points: Add Neiguan (PC 6) for feverish sensation in the chest and nausea.

Method: Apply filiform needles with reducing method. Retain the needles for 15~30 minutes manipulating them two to three times.

2) Ear acupuncture

Prescription: Subcortex, Sympathetic, Ear-shenmen, Stomach, Abdomen, Endocrine.

Method: Apply filiform needles with moderate stimulation and retain the needles for 30 minutes. Auricular taping is also applicable.

4. Flaring up of Liver Fire

(1) *Main manifestation*

Difficulty in falling a sleep, dizziness, head distention, restlessness, shortness of temper, probable congested eyes, bitter taste in the mouth and hypochondriac pain, thin yellow tongue coating, and wiry rapid pulse.

(2) *Therapeutic Principle*

Eliminate liver fire, moisten yin and sedate hyperactive Yang.

(3) *Treatment*

1) Body acupuncture

Prescription: Ganshu (BL 18), Danshu (BL 19), Xingjian (LR 2), Zuqiaoyin (GB 44), Shenmen (HT 7).

Supplementary points: Add Taiyang (EX-HN 5) for congested eyes.

Method: Apply filiform needles with reducing method. Retain the needles for 15~20 minutes manipulating them two to three times. Taiyang (EX-HN 5) can be pricked with a three-edged needle to cause bleeding.

2) Ear acupuncture

Prescription: Liver, Subcortex, Sympathetic, Ear-shenmen, Endocrine.

Method Apply filiform needles with mild stimulation and retain the needles for 30 minutes. Auricular taping is also applicable.

3) Plum-blossom needling therapy

Prescription: Sishencong (EX-HN 1) Anmian, Huatuojiaji.

Method: Tap with mild stimulation until local redness appears. Tap Huatuojiaji points from top down to the bottom repeatedly two to three times. Treatment is given once every other day.

多　寐

多寐亦称"嗜睡"、"嗜卧"。以不分昼夜，时时欲睡，呼之能醒，醒后复睡为特征。现代医学的发作性睡病，神经官能症，精神病的某些患者，其临床症状与多寐类似者可参考本篇辨证治疗。

1．湿盛困脾

（1）主证 昏昏欲睡，头蒙如裹，肢体沉重，倦怠乏力，胸痞脘闷，纳少泛恶，或见浮肿，舌苔白腻，脉濡缓。

（2）治则 健脾祛湿醒神。

（3）治法

1）体针

处方 中脘，丰隆，阴陵泉，百会，太阳。

配穴 纳少泛恶加足三里、内关。

操作 毫针刺，用补法或平补平泻。留针 15～20 分钟，间歇行针 2～3 次。

2）耳针

处方 脾，交感，皮质下。

操作 毫针中等强度刺激，留针 20 分钟。

2．脾气不足

（1）主证 食后困倦嗜睡，肢体倦怠，必须少睡片刻，醒后似略常人，面色萎黄，纳少便溏，苔薄白，脉虚弱。

（2）治则 健脾益气醒脑。

（3）治法

1）体针

处方 脾俞，中脘，隐白，足三里，解溪，百会。

操作 毫针刺，用补法。留针 20～30 分钟，间歇行针 1～2 次。

2）艾灸

处方 脾俞，章门，足三里。

操作 采用温和灸或回旋灸治疗 10～15 分钟，每天 1 次。

3．阳气虚衰

（1）主证 整日嗜睡懒言，精神疲惫，畏寒肢冷，健忘，舌淡苔薄，脉沉细无力。

（2）治则 益气温阳。

（3）治法

1）体针

处方 膏肓俞，肾俞，气海，三阴交，大钟，申脉。

配穴 健忘加神门。

操作 毫针刺，用补法。留针 15～30 分钟，间歇行针 1～2 次。

2）耳针

处方 脾，肾，内分泌，皮质下，心。

操作 毫针轻刺激，留针 20～30 分钟。亦可采用耳穴贴敷。

3）艾灸

处方 肾俞，气海，三阴交，膏肓俞。

操作 采用温和灸或回旋灸治疗 10～15 分钟。亦可采用温针灸治疗。

4）拔罐疗法

处方 肾俞，膏肓俞，气海。

操作 针刺后采用坐罐治疗 5～10 分钟，隔日 1 次。

4．瘀血阻滞

（1）主证 时时欲睡，头晕头痛，肢体困倦，记忆力减退，或有头部外伤史，舌质紫暗或有瘀斑，脉沉涩。

（2）治则 活血通络，醒脑提神。

（3）治法

1）体针

处方 膈俞，肝俞，合谷，太冲，太阳，百会。

操作 毫针刺，用泻法。留针15~20分钟，间隔行针2~3次。

2）耳针

处方 交感，神门，皮质下，心。

操作 毫针中等强度刺激，留针20分钟。

Somnolence

Somnolence, known as sleepiness or drowsiness, is characterized by low spirit with drowsiness that bothers the patient all day long, being easily waken during the state of drowsiness and falling asleep soon after the awakened state. In modern medicine, such conditions as paroxysmal sleeping, neurosis and psychosis with similar symptoms to somnolence, the differentiation and treatment in this section can be referred to.

1. Excessive Dampness Accumulating in the Spleen

（1）*Main manifestation*

Drowsiness as if the head is wrapped up, general heavy sensation, lassitude, fullness sensation in the chest, anorexia, nausea or puffiness, white greasy tongue coating and soft slow pulse.

（2）*Therapeutic principle*

Strengthen the spleen, resolve dampness and invigorate the spirit.

（3）*Treatment*

1）Body acupuncture

Prescription: Zhongwan（RN 12），Fenglong（ST 40），Yinlingquan（SP 9），Baihui（DU 20），Taiyang（EX-HN 5）.

Supplementary points: Add Zusanli（ST 36）and Neiguan（PC 6）for poor appetite and nausea.

Method: Apply filiform needles with reinforcing or even movement method. Retain needles for 15~20 minutes manipulating them two to three times.

2）Ear acupuncture

Prescription: Spleen, Sympathetic, Subcortex.

Method: Apply filiform needles with moderate stimulation and retain the needles for 20 minutes.

2. Deficiency of Spleen Q

（1）*Main manifestation*

Sleepiness after meals, general lassitude that is relieved after quarters of sleeping, sallow complexion, poor appetite, loose stools, thin white tongue coating, and deficient weak pulse.

（2）*Therapeutic principle*

Strengthen spleen Qi and clear the mind

（3）*Treatment*

1）Body acupuncture

Prescription: Pishu（BL 20）, Zhangmen（LR 13）, Yinbai（SP 1）, Zusanli（ST 36）, Jiexi（ST 41）, Baihui（DU 20）.

Method: Apply filiform needles with reinforcing method. Retain the needles for 20～30 minutes manipulating them one to two times.

2）Moxibustion

Prescription: Pishu（BL 20）, Zhangmen（LR 13）, Zusanli（ST 36）.

Method: Apply mild warming moxibustion or rounding moxibustion for 10～15 minutes once a day.

3. Deficiency and Decline of Yang Qi

(1) *Main manifestation*

Full drowsiness in the day, reluctant speech, poor spirit, cold limbs, poor memory, pale tongue proper, yellow coating, and feeble thready pulse.

(2) *Therapeutic principle*

Reinforce and warm up the Yang Qi

(3) *Treatment*

1）Body acupuncture

Prescription: Gaohuangshu（BL 43）, Shenshu（BL 23）, Qihai（RN 6）, Sanyinjiao（SP 6）, Dazhong（KI 4）, Shenmai（BL 62）.

Supplementary points: Add Shenmen（HT 7）for poor memory.

Method: Apply filiform needles with reinforcing method. Retain the needles for 15～30 minutes manipulating them once or twice.

2）Ear acupuncture

Prescription: Spleen, Kidney, Endocrine, Subcortex, Heart.

Method: Apply filiform needles with mild stimulation and retain the needles for 20～30 minutes. Auricular taping is also applicable.

3）Moxibustion

Prescription: Shenshu（BL 23）, Qihai（RN 6）, Sanyinjiao（SP 6）, Gaohuangshu（BL 43）.

Method: Apply mild-warming moxibustion or rounding moxibustion for 10～15 minutes. Moxibustion with warming needle is also applicable.

4）Cupping Therapy

Prescription: Shenshu（BL 23）, Gaohuang shu（BL 43）, Qihai（RN 6）.

Method: Apply retaining cupping after acupuncture treatment once every other day. Each point is cupped for five to ten minutes.

4. Blood Stasis Obstruction

(1) *Main manifestation*

Drowsiness from time to time, dizziness, headache, general lassitude, poor memory, dark purplish tongue proper with purplish spots, and deep unsmooth pulse. Some patients may have tramatic history of the head.

(2) *Therapeutic principle*

Activate blood circulation, remove obstruction from the channels and collaterals, clear the mind and invigorate the spirit.

(3) *Treatment*

1) Body acupuncture

Prescription: Geshu (BL 17), Ganshu (BL 18), Hegu (LI 14), Taichong (LR 3), Taiyang (EX-HN 5), Baihui (DU 20)

Method: Apply filiform needles with reducing method. Retain the needles for 15~20 minutes manipulating them two to three times.

2) Ear acupuncture

Prescription: Sympathetic, Earshenmen, Subcortex, Heart.

Method: Apply filiform needles with moderate stimulation and retain the needles for 20 minutes.

健　忘

健忘是指记忆力减弱，遇事易忘的一种病症。常见于现代医学的神经衰弱，脑动脉硬化等疾病。

1. 心脾两虚

（1）主证　遇事善忘，精神倦怠，四肢无力，心悸少寐，纳呆气短，声低语怯，面色少华，舌苔薄白或白腻，舌质淡，有齿痕，脉细弱无力。

（2）治则　养心健脾。

（3）治法

1) 体针

处方　心俞，脾俞，膈俞，气海。

操作　毫针刺，用补法。留针20~30分钟，间歇行针1~2次。

2) 耳针

处方　心，神门，脑点，交感，脾。

操作　毫针轻刺激，留针20分钟。

3) 艾灸

处方　心俞，脾俞，膈俞。

操作　采用温和灸或回旋灸治疗10~15分钟，每天1次。

2. 心肾不交

（1）主证　遇事善忘，腰痠腿软，或有遗精，头晕耳鸣，或手足心热，心烦失眠，舌质红，苔薄白，脉细数。

（2）治则　交通心肾。

（3）治法

1) 体针

处方　心俞，太溪，肾俞，劳宫，神门。

操作　劳宫、神门用泻法，心俞、肾俞、太溪用补法。毫针刺，留针20分钟，间歇行针1~2次。

2) 耳针

处方　心，肾，神门，交感，脑点。

操作　毫针轻刺激，留针20分钟，亦可采用耳穴贴敷。

3. 年老神衰

（1）主证　遇事善忘，形体衰惫，神志恍惚，气短乏力，腰痠腿软，纳少尿频，心悸少寐，舌苔薄白，脉细弱无力。

（2）治则 补肾养心，健脾益智。

（3）治法

1）体针

处方 肾俞，太溪，心俞，脾俞，四神聪。

操作 毫针刺，用补法。留针20～30分钟，间歇行针1～2次。

2）耳针

处方 心，脑点，神门，交感。

操作 毫针轻刺激，留针20分钟。

3）艾灸

处方 肾俞，心俞，脾俞，太溪。

操作 采用温和灸或回旋灸治疗10～15分钟，每天1次。

4．痰瘀痹阻

（1）主证 遇事善忘，兼见语言迟缓，神思欠敏，表情呆钝，舌上有瘀点，舌苔白腻，脉滑或细涩。

（2）治则 补心气，化痰瘀。

（3）治法

1）体针

处方 丰隆，足三里，神门，大陵，三阴交，行间。

操作 毫针刺，用泻法。留针15～20分钟，间歇行针2～3次。

2）耳针

处方 脾，心，神门，交感，脑点。

操作 毫针轻刺激，留针15～20分钟。亦可采用耳穴贴敷。

Poor Memory

Poor memory refers to a condition characterized by hypomnesia and forgetfulnss. In modern medicine it can be seen in patients suffering from neurasthenia and cerebral arteriosclerosis.

1. Deficiency of Heart and Spleen

(1) *Main manifestation*
Forgetfulness, listlessness, weakness of the four limbs, palpitation, poor sleep and appetite, shortness of breath, low voice, pallor complexion, pale tongue proper with teeth marks on the edge, thin white or white greasy tongue coating, and weak thready pulse.

(2) *Therapeutic principle*
Nourish heart and strengthen spleen.

(3) *Treatment*

1) Body acupuncture

Prescription: Xinshu (BL 15), Pishu (BL 20), Geshu (BL 17), Qihai (RN 6).

Method: Apply filiform needles with reinforcing method. Retain the needles for 20～30 minutes manipulating them one to two times.

2) Ear acupuncture

Prescription: Heart, Ear-shenmen, Brainstem, Sympathetic, Spleen.

Method: Apply filiform needles with mild stimulation and retain the needles for 20 minutes.

3) Moxibustion

Prescription: Xinshu (BL 15), Pishu (BL 20), Geshu (BL 17).

Method: Apply mild-warming or rounding moxibustion for 10～15 minutes once a day.

2. Dysharmony Between Heart and Kidney

(1) *Main manifestation*

Forgetfulness, lumbar soreness, knee joint weakness or seminal emission, dizziness, tinnitus, or feverish sensation in the palms and soles, restlessness, poor sleep, red tongue proper, and thin rapid pulse.

(2) *Therapeutic principle*

Regain the harmony between the heart and kidney.

(3) *Treatment*

1) Body acupuncture

Prescription: Xinshu (BL 15), Taixi (KI 3), Shenshu (BL 23), Laogong (PC 8), Shenmen (HT 7).

Method: Apply reducing method at Laogong (PC 8) and Shenmen (HT 7) and reinforcing method at Xinshu (BL 15), Shenshu (BL 23) and Taixi (KI 3). Use filiform needles and retain the needles for 20 minutes manipulating them one to two times.

2) Ear acupuncture

Prescription: Heart, Kidney, Ear-shenmen, Sympathetic, Brainstem.

Method: Apply filiform needles with mild stimulation and retain the needles for 20 minutes. Auricular taping is also applicable.

3. Aging-related Poor spirit

(1) *Main manifestation*

Forgetfulness, poor appetite, lassitude, trance, shortness of breath, lumbar soreness, knee joint weakness, frequent urination, palpitation, poor sleep, thin white tongue coating, and weak thready pulse.

(2) *Therapeutic principle*

Reinforce kidney, nourish heart, strengthen spleen and promote intelligence.

(3) *Treatment*

1) Body acupuncture

Prescription: Shenshu (BL 23), Taixi (KI 3), Xinshu (BL 15), Pishu (BL 20), Sishencong (EX-HN 1).

Method: Apply filiform needles with reinforcing method. Retain the needles for 20～30 minutes manipulating them one to two times.

2) Ear acupuncture

Prescription: Heart, Brainstem, Ear-shenmen, Sympathetic.

Method: Apply filiform needles with mild stimulation and retain the needles for 20 minutes.

3) Moxibustion

Prescription：Shenshu（BL 23），Xinshu（BL 15），Pishu（BL 20），Taixi（KI 3）.

Method：Apply mild-warming moxibustion or rounding moxibustion for 10～15 minutes once a day.

4．Phlegm-fluid and Stasis Obstruction

（1）*Main manifestation*

Forgetfulness, low speech, dull response, ecchymosis over the tongue, white greasy tongue coating, and slippery or thin rapid pulse.

（2）*Therapeutic principle*

Strengthen heart Qi and resolve phlegm.

（3）*Treatment*

1）Body acupuncture

Prescription：Fenglong（ST 40），Zusanli（ST 36），Shenmen（HT 7），Daling（PC 7），Sanyinjiao（SP 6），Xingjian（LR 2）.

Method：Apply filiform needles with reducing method. Retain the needles for 15～20 minutes manipulating them two to three times.

2）Ear acupuncture

Prescription：Spleen, Heart, Earshenmen, Sympathetic, Brainstem.

Method：Apply filiform needles with mild stimulation and retain the needles for 15～20 minutes. Auricular taping is also applicable.

癫　狂

癫与狂都是精神失常的疾病。癫证是以精神抑郁，表情淡漠，沉默痴呆，语无伦次，静而少动为特征；狂证以精神亢奋，狂躁打骂，喧扰不宁，动而多怒为特征。癫属阴，狂属阳，两者在病理上有一定联系，病情亦可互相转化，故常并称为癫狂。本病包括现代医学的精神分裂症，反应性精神病，脑器质性疾病引起的精神障碍等。

1．癫证

（1）主证　发病缓慢，初起先有精神苦闷，神志呆滞，继则言语错乱，喜怒无常或终日不语，喜静多睡，不知秽洁，不思饮食，甚者妄见妄闻，舌苔薄腻，脉弦细或弦滑。

（2）治则　疏肝解郁，化痰开窍。

（3）治法

1）体针

处方　神门，大陵，心俞，肝俞，脾俞，太冲，丰隆，膻中。

配穴　不思饮食加中脘，足三里；喜怒无常加间使；妄见加睛明；妄闻加听宫。

操作　毫针刺，平补平泻。留针15～30分钟，间歇行针2～3次。

2）耳针

处方　心，皮质下，枕，脑点，额，神门，交感。

操作　毫针轻刺激，留针15～20分钟，亦可采用耳穴贴敷或埋针治疗。

2. 狂证

（1）主证　发病急速，病前亦见烦躁易怒，少睡少食，继而狂躁好动，气力倍增，高声叫骂，弃衣奔走，终日不眠，甚至毁物打人，不避亲疏，舌苔黄腻，脉弦滑而数。

（2）治则　清心，豁痰，醒脑。

（3）治法

1）体针

处方　大椎，风府，水沟，丰隆，间使，劳宫。

操作　毫针刺，用泻法。留针15～30分钟，间歇行针2～4次。大椎可用三棱针点刺出血。

2）耳针

处方　心，皮质下，肾，枕，额，神门，交感。

操作　毫针强刺激，不留针；亦可采用耳穴贴敷或埋针治疗。

3）电针

处方　定神（人中沟下1/3与2/3交界处），百会，头颞（太阳穴后上1寸，与耳尖平行，咬牙时颞肌突出处）。

操作　每天针刺2～4次，用脉冲电，电压6伏，用较高频率间断通电，患者局部肌肉抽搐，麻胀感强，施术时严密观察患者情况，调节电流量及通电时间。一般2～3天可控制症状，然后减少电针次数。

Maniac Depression and Insanity

Both maniac depression and mental insanity are considered abnormal conditions of the mental state. The former is characterized by a quiet physical state such as emotional dejection, apathy, dull or incoherent speech. The later is characterized by a hyperactive physical and mental state such as restlessness, abnormally hyperactive mentality, excessive motor activity or violent behavior. Maniac depression is Yin in nature while mental insanity is Yang in nature. Pathologically, there is certain relationship between them. Conditions of both may intertransform. Therefore, both are always mentioned together. In modern medicine, it may include schizophrenia, reactive psychosis and mental disorders caused by cerebral organic conditions.

1. Maniac Depression

（1）*Main manifestation*

A gradual onset. At the beginning, the patient may experience some emotional dejection and mental dullness. The subsequent manifestations include incoherent speech, abnormal mood changing such as excessive joy or anger, somnolence, no sense to mind Sanitation, no desire for food, illusions, thin greasy tongue coating, and thready thin, or thready slippery pulse.

（2）*Therapeutic principle*

Soothe the stagnant liver Qi, resolve

the phlegm and regain the function of the heart to house the mind.

(3) *Treatment*

1) Body acupuncture

Prescription: Shenmen (HT 7), Daling (PC 7), Xinshu (BL 15), Ganshu (BL 18), Pishu (BL 20), Taichong (LR 3), Fenglong (ST 40), Tanzhong (RN 17).

Supplementary points: Add Zhongwan (RN 12) and Zusanli (ST 36) for no desire for food, Jianshi (PC 5) for abnormal joy or anger, Jingming (BL 1) for photism, and Tinggong for auditory hallucination.

Method: Apply filiform needles with even movement method. Retain the needles for 15 ~ 30 minutes manipulating them two to three times.

2) Ear acupuncture

Prescription: Heart, Subcortex, Occipital, Brainstem, Forehead, Earshenmen, Sympathetic.

Method: Apply filiform needles with mild stimulation and retain needles for 15 ~ 20 minutes. Auricular taping or subcutaneous needle is also applicable.

2. Mental Insanity

(1) *Main manifestation*

The sudden onset of mental insanity is often characterized by irritability, less sleep and no desire for food. The subsequent manifestations include excessive mental activity, increased physical energy with violent behavior and rage shouting, running around in the nude, destroying surrounding objects and harming familiar or unfamiliar persons for no reason at all. Yellow greasy tongue coating and rapid thready slippery pulse.

(2) *Therapeutic principle*

Clear the heart, dispel the phlegm and resuscitate the mind.

(3) *Treatment*

1) Body acupuncture

Prescription: Dazhui (DU 14), Fengfu (DU 16), Shuigou (DU 26), Fenglong (ST 40), Jianshi (PC 5), Laogong (PC 8).

Method: Apply filiform needles with reducing method. Retain the needles for 15 ~ 30 minutes manipulating them two to four times. Dazhui (DU 14) may be pricked with a three-edged needle to cause bleeding.

2) Ear acupuncture

Prescription: Heart, Subcortex, Kidney, Occipital, Forehead, Earshenmen, Sympathetic.

Method: Apply filiform needles with strong stimulation and without needling retention. Auricular taping or subcutaneous needle is also applicable.

3) Electroacupuncture

Prescription: Dingshen (extra point, at philtrum, at the junction of lower 1/3 and upper 2/3 of the philtrum), Baihui (DU 20), Tounie (extra point, 1 cun superior to Taiyang, EX-HN 5).

Method: Following needling, electrical stimulation by intermittent electric pulse at a comparatively high frequency and at a voltage of 6 is applied to the needles inserted in the points. This causes local muscular spasm and induces numbness and distension to the patient. During the electroacupuncture, the patient's response should be observed closely and the intensity of the stimulation adjusted according to the patient's needling sensation and tolerance. The puncture is given two to four times daily. Generally speaking, after accepting the electroacupuncture for two or three days, the patient's symptoms and signs will be relieved obviously and the frequency of giving the electroacupuncture can be decreased.

痫　证

痫证是一种发作性神志失常的疾病，俗称"羊痫风"。以突然仆倒，昏不知人，口吐涎沫，两目上视，肢体抽搐，或口中如猪羊叫声，醒后如常人为主要临床特征。

1. 发作期

(1) 主证　发作时，常先觉头晕头痛，胸闷欠伸，旋即昏倒仆地，神志不清，面色苍白，牙关紧急，两目上视，手足抽搐，口吐涎沫，并发出类似猪羊叫声，甚至二便失常，不久渐渐苏醒，症状消失，除感疲乏无力外，饮食起居如常，舌苔白腻，脉多弦滑。

(2) 治则　化痰开窍，平肝熄风。

(3) 治法

1) 体针

处方　水沟，鸠尾，大椎，间使，太冲，丰隆。

配穴　发作昏迷不醒者加涌泉，气海。

操作　毫针刺，用泻法。留针15～20分钟，间歇行针2～3次。一般先刺水沟，再针太冲和涌泉，提插捻转至神志清醒为止。

2) 电针

处方　内关，合谷。

操作　每穴用密波刺激15～20分钟。

2. 休止期

(1) 主证　发作后，精神委靡，面色不华，头晕，心悸，食少，痰多，腰痠肢软，舌质淡，苔白，脉细滑。

(2) 治则　养心安神，健脾益肾。

(3) 治法

1) 体针

处方　心俞，印堂，神门，三阴交，太溪，腰奇。

配穴　白昼多发作者加申脉；夜间多发作者加照海；痰多加丰隆。

操作　毫针刺，用补法或平补平

泻法。留针 20～30 分钟，间歇行针
1～2 次。

2）挑治

处方 长强穴。

操作 常规消毒后，以左手将穴
位局部组织捏起，右手持三棱针重刺
长强穴及前后左右各 1 针，四点距长
强穴各 15 毫米，然后挤压使局部出
血，如此每周针刺 1 次，10 次为 1
疗程，前后疗程间休 1 个月，最多者
为 3 个疗程。

Epilepsy

Epilepsy, a mental disorder of
paroxysmal attacks, is characterized by
sudden falling down in a fit, mouthful
of foam, eyes staring upward, convulsions and utterances like domesticated
pigs and sheep. However, the patients
appear normal when they regain consciousness.

1. During the seizure

(1) *Main manifestation*

Patient first experiences dizziness,
headache and suffocating sensation in
the chest. This is then followed by a
sudden falling down with loss of consciousness, pallor complexion,
clenched jaws, upward staring of the
eyes, limb convulsions, mouthful of
foam, utterances like pigs or sheep,
and even incontinence of urine and feces. Not long after that, the patient
regains consciousness and becomes
asymptomatic. Apart from the fatigue
and weakness the patient appears normal. The tongue coating is white
greasy and the pulse is thready and slippery.

(2) *Therapeutic principle*

Dissolve the phlegm to resuscitate the
patient, soothe the liver and quench
the wind.

(3) *Treatment*

1) Body acupuncture

Prescription: Shuigou (DU 26),
Jiuwei (RN 15), Dazhui (DU 14),
Jianshi (PC 5), Taichong (LR 3),
Fenglong (ST 40).

Supplementary points: Add Yongquan
(KI 1) and Qihai (RN 6) for loss of
consciousness during the seizure.

Method: Apply filiform needles with
reducing method. Retain the needles
for 15～20 minutes manipulating them
two to three times. Generally,
Shuigou (DU 26) is punctured first.
This is followed by puncturing Taichong
(LR 3) and Yongquan (KI 1) with
lifting, thrusting and rotating until the
patient resuscitates.

2) Electroacupuncture

Prescription: Neiguan (PC 6),
Hegu (LI 4).

Method: Apply dense wave to the
points for fifteen to twenty minutes.

2. After the Seizure

(1) *Main manifestation*

Listlessness, lustreless complexion, dizziness, palpitation, loss of appetite, profuse sputum, lumbar soreness and knee weakness, pale tongue proper with white greasy coating, and thin slippery pulse.

(2) *Therapeutic Principle*

Nourish the heart, calm the mind, strengthen the spleen and reinforce the kidney.

(3) *Treatment*

1) Body acupuncture

Prescription: Xinshu (BL 15), Yintang (EX-HN 3), Shenmen (HT 7), Sanyinjiao (SP 6), Taixi (KI 3), Yaoqi (EX-B 9).

Supplementary points: Add Shenmai (BL 62) if attacks mostly take place in the daytime, Zhaohai (KI 6) if attacks mostly take place at night, and Fenglong (ST 40) for profuse sputum.

Method: Apply filiform needles with reinforcing or even movement method. Retain the needles for 20～30 minutes manipulating them one to two times.

2) Breaking with three-edged needle

Prescription: Changqiang (DU 1).

Method: After a local routine sterilization, hold the local tissure with the left hand. Heavily prick Changqiang (DU 1) and 4 points 15 mm respectively anterior, posterior, left and right to Changqiang (DU 1) with the three-edged needle held by the right hand. Press the local area to cause bleeding. The treatment is given once every week for ten times as a course. Three courses is the maximum. The intermittent period between two courses is one month.

郁　证

郁证是由于情志忧郁，气滞不畅所引起的病症的总称。以心情抑郁，情绪不宁，胸部满闷，胁肋胀痛或易怒欲哭；或咽中如有异物梗阻等为主要症状。现代医学的癔病，神经官能症，更年期综合征等均可参见本节辨证治疗。

1. 肝气郁结

(1) 主证　精神抑郁，情绪不宁，胸闷胁痛，腹胀嗳气，不思饮食或腹痛呕吐，大便正常，舌苔薄腻，脉弦。

(2) 治则　疏肝解郁，理气调中。

(3) 治法

1) 体针

处方　膻中，肝俞，太冲，中脘，足三里，公孙。

操作　毫针刺，平补平泻。留针15～20分钟，间歇行针2～3次。

2) 耳针

处方　肝，皮质下，脑点，内分泌，神门，心。

操作　毫针轻刺激，留针10～20分钟；亦可采用耳穴贴敷或埋针治疗。

2．气郁化火

（1）主证　性情急躁易怒，胸胁胀满，口苦而干，或头痛，目赤，耳鸣，或吞酸嘈杂，大便秘结，舌质红，脉弦数。

（2）治则　清肝泄火解郁，理气和中健胃。

（3）治法

1）体针

处方　行间，侠溪，支沟，阳陵泉，上脘，足三里。

操作　毫针刺，用泻法。留针15～20分钟，间歇行针2～3次。

2）耳针

处方　心，肝，皮质下，枕，脑点，内分泌，神门。

操作　毫针刺，轻刺激，留针15～20分钟；亦可采用耳穴贴敷或埋针治疗。

3．痰气郁结

（1）主证　精神抑郁，胸部闷塞，咽中不适，如有物阻，咳之不出，咽之不下，但饮食吞咽不困难，舌苔薄腻，脉弦滑。

（2）治则　疏肝行气，开郁化痰。

（3）治法

1）体针

处方　天突，膻中，内关，丰隆，太冲。

操作　毫针刺，平补平泻。留针15～20分钟，间歇行针2～3次。

2）耳针

处方　肝，心，脑点，内分泌，神门，枕。

操作　毫针刺，轻刺激，留针15～20分钟；亦可采用耳穴贴敷。

4．阴血不足

（1）主证　无故悲伤，喜怒无常，多疑善惊，心悸烦躁，睡眠不安等，或有突发胸闷，呃逆，暴喑，抽搐等症，严重者可昏迷，僵仆，苔薄白，脉弦细。

（2）治则　调肝养血，宁心安神。

（3）治法

1）体针

处方　太冲，神门，心俞，内关，三阴交，巨厥。

配穴　暴喑加通里，廉泉；呃逆加天突；抽搐加合谷，阳陵泉；昏厥僵仆加水沟，涌泉。

操作　毫针刺，平补平泻，留针15～20分钟，间歇行针1～2次。

2）耳针

处方　心，皮质下，枕，肝，脑点，内分泌，神门。

操作　毫针轻刺激，留针15～20分钟；亦可采用耳穴贴敷或埋针。

Melancholy

Melancholy is a general term for diseases caused by emotional depression and Qi stagnation. Its main symptoms are depression, restlessness, fullness sensation in the chest, distending pain in the hypochondrium, irritability or feeling of a lump in the throat. Diseases such as hysteria, neurosis and menopause syndrome in modern medicine can be treated according to the differentiation and treatment in this section.

1. Liver Qi Stagnation

(1) *Main manifestation*

Emotional depression, restlessness, fullness in the chest and distending pain in the hypochondrium, abdominal distention and eructation, anorexia or abdominal pain, nausea and vomiting, thin greasy tongue coating, and wiry pulse.

(2) *Therapeutic principle*

Soothe the liver Qi and regulate the Qi circulation of the middle-Jiao.

(3) *Treatment*

1) Body acupuncture

Prescription: Tanzhong (RN 17), Ganshu (BL 18), Taichong (LR 3), Zhongwan (RN 12), Zusanli (ST 36), Gongsun (SP 4).

Method: Apply filiform needles with even movement method. Retain the needles for 15 ~ 20 minutes manipulating them two to three times.

2) Ear acupuncture

Prescription: Liver, Subcortex, Brainstem, Endocrine, Ear-shenmen, Heart.

Method: Apply filiform needles with mild stimulation and retain the needles

for 15 ~ 20 minutes. Auricular taping or subcutaneous needle is also applicable.

2. Qi Stagnation Turning into Fire

(1) *Main manifestation*

Irritable temper, fullness in the chest and hypochondriac region, dryness and bitter taste in the mouth, headache, congested eyes, tinnitus, aid regurgitation, constipation, red tongue proper and rapid wiry pulse.

(2) *Therapeutic principle*

Eliminate liver fire, soothe the liver Qi, regulate Qi circulation and pacify the middle-Jiao.

(3) *Treatment*

1) Body acupuncture

Prescription: Xingjian (LR 2), Xiaxi (GB 43), Zhigou (SJ 6), Yanglingquan (GB 34), Shangwan (RN 13), Zusanli (ST 36).

Method: Apply filiform needles with reducing method. Retain the needles for 15 ~ 20 minutes manipulating them two to three times.

2) Ear acupuncture

Prescription: Heart, Liver, Subcortex, Occipital, Brainstem, Endocrine, Ear-shenmen.

Method: Apply filiform needles with mild stimulation and retain the needles for 15 ~ 20 minutes. Auricular taping or subcutaneous needle is also applica-

ble.

3. Phlegmatic Qi Stagnation

(1) *Main manifestation*

Depression, chest fullness, discomfort sensation of the throat with a lump feeling but no difficulty in swallowing, thin greasy tongue coating, and wiry slippery pulse.

(2) *Therapeutic principle*

Soothe the liver, promote Qi circulation and resolve phlegm.

(3) *Treatment*

1) Body acupuncture

Prescription: Tiantu (RN 22), Tanzhong (RN 17), Neiguan (PC 6), Fenglong (ST 40), Taichong (LR 3).

Method: Apply filiform needles with even movement method. Retain the needles for 15~20 minutes manipulating them two to three times.

2) Ear acupuncture

Prescription: Liver, Heart, Brainstem, Endocrine, Ear-shenmen, Occipital.

Method: Apply filiform needles with mild stimulation and retain the needles for 15~20 minutes. Auricular taping is also applicable.

4. Blood Deficiency

(1) *Main manifestation*

Frequent sorrow without any obvious causes, abnormal joy or rage, unreasonable suspicion or fear, palpitation and irritability, unsound sleep, thin white tongue coating, and wiry pulse. Sometimes, there may be sudden fullness sensation in the chest, hiccups, sudden loss of voice, and convulsions. In severe cases, there may be sudden syncope.

(2) *Therapeutic principle*

Regulate the liver, nourish blood and calm the heart and mind.

(3) *Treatment*

1) Body acupuncture

Prescription: Taichong (LR 3), Shenmen (HT 7), Xinshu (BL 15), Neiguan (PC 6), Sanyinjiao (SP 6), Juque (RN 14).

Supplementary points: Add Tongli (HT 5) and Lianquan (RN 23) for horseness of voice, Tiantu (RN 22) for hiccup, Hegu (LI 4), Yang Lingquan (GB 34), Shuigou (DU 26) and Yongquan (KI 1) for syncope.

Method: Apply filiform needles with even movement method. Retain the needles for 15~20 minutes manipulating them one to two times.

2) Ear acupuncture

Prescription: Heart, Subcortex, Occipital, Liver, Brainstem, Endocrine, Ear-shenmen.

Method: Apply filiform needles with mild stimulation and retain the needles for 15～20minutes. Auricular taping or subcutaneous needle is also applicable.

头　痛

头痛系患者的一种自觉症状，可见于多种急慢性疾病中。本篇所述头痛，是指外感或内伤杂病以头痛为主证者。如属某一疾病过程中所出现的兼证，不属本节讨论范围。头痛可见于现代医学中感染性发热性疾病，高血压，颅内疾病，神经官能症，偏头痛等多种疾病。

1. 风邪外袭

（1）主证　恶风头痛，痛可及项背部。如头痛剧烈，刺痛，痛处不移，兼有脉弦，苔薄白者又称"头风"。

（2）治则　疏风通络，活血止痛。

（3）治法

1）体针

处方　风池，头维，百会，合谷。

配穴　前头痛配上星、阳白、印堂；后头痛配天柱、昆仑、后溪；侧头痛配太阳、率谷、外关；头顶痛配通天、脑空、太冲。

操作　毫针刺，用泻法。留针15～20分钟，间歇行针2～3次。疼痛剧烈发作时，持续行针至疼痛减轻或消失。

2）耳针

处方　皮质下，额，枕，太阳，神门。

操作　毫针中等强度刺激，留针15～20分钟。亦可用耳背静脉放血。

3）皮肤针

处方　太阳，印堂，阿是穴。

操作　重刺激，叩至局部皮肤出血。

2. 肝阳上亢

（1）主证　头痛眩晕，多烦易怒，睡眠不宁，面红目赤，口苦，舌红，苔薄黄，脉弦有力。

（2）治则　平肝降逆，熄风潜阳。

（3）治法

1）体针

处方　风池，悬颅，太阳，行间，侠溪，太溪。

配穴　目赤加关冲点刺放血；心烦易怒加肝俞、间使。

操作　毫针刺，用泻法。太溪穴用补法。留针10～20分钟，间歇行针2～3次。太阳穴可用三棱针点刺出血。

2）耳针

处方　肝，皮质下，神门，额，枕。

操作　毫针中等强度刺激，留针15～20分钟。亦可在耳背静脉放血。

3）皮肤针

处方　太阳，印堂，阿是穴。

操作　皮肤针重刺激，叩至局部皮肤发红。

3. 痰浊

（1）主证　头额昏痛如裹，胸脘痞闷，恶心，甚则呕吐痰涎，便溏，舌苔白腻，脉弦滑。

（2）治则　化痰降浊，通络止痛。

（3）治法

1）体针

处方 中脘，丰隆，百会，印堂，悬钟。

配穴 呕吐痰涎加内关；便溏加天枢。

操作 毫针刺，用泻法。留针15～20分钟，间歇行针2～3次。

2）耳针

处方 皮质下，额，枕，太阳，神门，脾。

操作 毫针中等强度刺激，留针15～20分钟；亦可采用耳穴贴敷或埋针治疗。

4. 气血亏虚

（1）主证 头痛头晕，痛热绵绵，遇劳则甚，休息痛减，神疲气短，心悸健忘，食欲不振，面色少华，舌淡，苔薄白。

（2）治则 益气养血，和络止痛。

（3）治法

1）体针

处方 肝俞，脾俞，肾俞，膈俞，气海，百会，足三里，三阴交。

操作 毫针刺，用补法。留针20～30分钟，间歇行针1～2次。

2）耳针

处方 肝，额，枕，神门，脾。

操作 毫针轻刺激，留针15～20分钟；亦可采用耳穴贴敷或埋针治疗。

5. 血瘀

（1）主证 头痛如刺，经久不愈，痛处固定不移，视物花黑，记忆力减退，舌有紫斑，脉细涩。

（2）治则 活血化瘀，行气定痛。

（3）治法

1）体针

处方 合谷，三阴交，膈俞，阿是穴。

配穴 眉棱痛加攒竹；侧头痛加太阳；后头痛加玉枕；头顶痛加四神聪。

操作 毫针刺，平补平泻或补泻兼施。合谷用补法，余穴用泻法或平补平泻法。留针15～20分钟，间歇行针2～3次。阿是穴可用三棱针点刺出血。

2）耳针

处方 皮质下，额，枕，太阳，神门。

操作 毫针强刺激，留针15～20分钟。严重头痛者可在耳背静脉放血。

3）皮肤针

处方 太阳，印堂，阿是穴。

操作 皮肤针叩至局部皮肤发红。

Headache

Headache is a subjective symptom that may appear in many acute and chronic diseases. The headache stated here refers to that as a main symptom in many exogenous or miscellaneous internal diseases. It does not include the headache as an accompanying symptom in the progression of certain diseases.

Headache can be seen in many infectious diseases with fever in modern medicine such as hypertension, intracranial diseases, psychoneurosis and migraine.

1. Invasion of Collateral by Wind-Pathogen

(1) *Main manifestation*

Headache occuring on exposure to wind, the pain may extend to the nape of the neck and back regions. If it is a violent, boring and fixed pain, accompanied by string-taut pulse and thin white tongue coating, such a syndrome is also termed "head wind".

(2) *Therapeutic principle*

Dispel wind, remove obstruction in the meridians and collaterals, regulate Qi and blood and relieve the pain.

(3) *Treatment*

1) Body acupuncture

Prescription: Fengchi (GB 20), Touwei (ST 8), Baihui (DU 20), Hegu (LI 4).

Supplementary points: Add Shangxing (DU 23), Yangbai (GB 14) and Yintang (Extra) for frontal headache, Tianzhu (BL 10), Kunlun (BL 60) and Houxi (ST 3) for occipital headache, Taiyang (EX-HN 3), Shuaigu (GB 8) and Waiguan (SJ 5) for temporal headache, Tongtian (BL 7), Naokong (GB 19) and Taichong (LR 3) for pain in the vertex.

Method: Apply filiform needles with reducing method. Retain the needles for 15 ~ 20 minutes manipulating them two to three times. If the pain is severe during the attack continue to manipulate the needles until the pain lessens.

2) Ear acupuncture

Prescription: Subcortex, Vertex, Occipital, Taiyang, Ear-shenmen.

Method: Apply filiform needles with moderate stimulation and retain the needles for 15 ~ 20 minutes. Pricking the veins on the ear dorsum is also applicable for severe headaches.

3) Plum-blossom needle therapy

Prescription: Taiyang (EX-HN 5), Yintang (EX-HN 3), Ashi points.

Method: Use the plum-blossom needle to tap in the local area until the skin turns red.

2. Hyperactivity of Hepatic Yang

(1) *Main manifestation*

Headache, dizziness, irritability, shortness of temper, poor sleep, redness of the face, congested eyes, bitter taste in the mouth, red tongue proper, thin yellow tongue coating, and wiry forceful pulse.

(2) *Therapeutic Principle*

Soothe liver, sedate Yang and quench the wind.

(3) *Treatment*

1) Body acupuncture

Prescription: Fengchi (GB 20), Xuanlu (GB 5), Taiyang (EX-HN 5), Xingjian (LR 2), Xiaxi (GB 43), Taixi (KI 3).

Supplementay points: Add Guanchong (SJ 1) for pricking for congestion in the eyes, Ganshu (BL 18) and Jianshi (PC 5) for restlessness and shortness of temper.

Method: Apply filiform needles with reducing method except Taixi (KI 3) that is punctured with reinforcing method. Retain the needles for 10~20 minutes manipulating them two to three times. Taiyang (EX-HN 5) may also be applied with three-edged needle to cause bleeding.

2) Ear acupuncture

Prescription: Liver, Subcortex, Ear-shenmen, Vertex, Occipital.

Method: Apply filiform needles with moderate stimulation and retain the needles for 15~20 minutes. Pricking the veins on the ear dorsum is also applicable for severe headache.

3) Plum-blossom needle therapy

Prescription: Taiyang (EX-HN 5), Yintang (EX-HN 3).

Method: Use plum-blossom needles to tap in the local area until the skin turns red.

3. Turbid Phlegm

(1) *Main manifestation*

Pain in the forehead as if the head is wrapped up, fullness sensation in the chest, nausea, vomiting of saliva in severe cases, loose stools, white greasy tongue coating, and wiry slippery pulse.

(2) *Therapeutic principle*

Resolve phlegm and sedate the turbidity, remove obstruction.

(3) *Treatment*

1) Body acupuncture

Prescription: Zhongwan (RN 12), Fenglong (ST 40), Baihui (DU 20), Yintang (EX-HN 3), Xuanzhong (GB 39).

Supplementary points: Add Neiguan (PC 6) for vomiting of saliva, Tianshu (ST 25) for loose stools.

Method: Apply filiform needles with reducing method. Retain the needles for 15~20 minutes manipulating them two to three times.

2) Ear acupuncture

Prescription: Subcortex, Vertex, Occipital, Taiyang, Ear-shenmen, Spleen.

Method: Apply filiform needles with moderate stimulation and retain the needles for 15~20 minutes. Auricular taping or subcutaneous needle is also applicable.

4. Qi and Blood Deficiency

(1) *Main manifestation*

Headache, dizziness, lingering pain worsened by overstrain and alleviated by rest, lassitude, shortness of breath, palpitation, poor memory, poor appetite, pallor complexion, pale tongue proper, thin white coating, and thready feeble pulse.

(2) *Therapeutic principle*

Reinforce Qi, nourish blood, promote channel circulation and stop pain.

(3) *Treatment*

1) Body acupuncture

Prescription: Ganshu (BL 18), Pishu (BL 20), Shenshu (BL 23), Geshu (BL 17), Qihai (RN 6), Baihui (DU 20), Zusanli (ST 36), Sanyinjiao (SP 6).

Method: Apply filiform needles with reinforcing method. Retain the needles for 20～30 minutes manipulating them one to two times.

2) Ear acupuncture

Prescription: Liver, Vertex, Occipital, Ear-shenmen, Spleen.

Method: Apply filiform needles with mild stimulation and retain the needles for 15～20 minutes. Auricular taping or subcutaneous needle is also applicable.

5. Blood Stasis

(1) *Main manifestation*

A fixed stabbing headache that lasts for a long time, blurring of vision, poor

memory, purplish spots on the tongue, and thready pulse.

(2) *Therapeutic principle*

Activate blood, resolve blood stasis, promote Qi circulation and stop pain.

(3) *Treatment*

1) Body acupuncture

Prescription: Hegu (LI 4), Sanyinjiao (SP 6), Geshu (BL 17), Ashi points.

Supplementary points: Add Zanzhu (BL 2) for pain in the superciliary ridge, Taiyang (EX-HN 5) for migraine, Yuzhen (BL 9) for occipital headache and Sishencong (EX-HN 1) for pain in the vertex.

Method: Apply filiform needles with even movement method or both reinforcing and reducing methods. Hegu (LI 4) is applied with reducing method and the rest of the points with even movement method. Retain the needles for 15～20 minutes manipulating them two to three times. Ashi points are applied with a three-edged needle to cause bleeding.

2) Ear acupuncture

Prescription: Subcortex, Vertex, Occipital, Taiyang, Ear-shenmen.

Method: Apply filiform needles with strong stimulation and retain the needles for 15～20 minutes. Pricking the veins on the ear dorsum is also applicable for the severe headache.

3）Plum-blossom needle therapy

Prescription：Taiyang（EX-HN 5），Yintang（EX-HN 3），Ashi points.

Method：Use the plum-blossom needles to tap in the local area until the skin turns red.

面　　痛

面痛指面部一定部位出现阵发性、短暂性、烧灼样剧烈疼痛而言。本病多发于一侧面部的额部、上颌部或下颌部，两侧俱痛者极少见。初起每次疼痛时间较短，间隔时间较长，久则发作次数越来越频，疼痛程度越来越重。发病年龄多在中年以后，女性患者较多。面痛相当于现代医学的三叉神经痛。

1. 风寒

（1）主证　面颊疼痛，面部时抽掣、眴动，遇寒发作或痛甚，得热痛减，兼有头痛，恶寒，鼻流清涕，舌苔薄白，脉弦紧。

（2）治则　祛风散寒止痛。

（3）治法

1）体针

处方　风池，风府，列缺，攒竹，太阳，颊车，下关。

操作　毫针刺，用泻法。留针15～30分钟，间歇行针2～3次。

2）耳针

处方　面颊，上颌，前额，神门，交感，皮质下。

操作　毫针刺，强刺激，留针20～30分钟；亦可采用耳穴贴敷。

2. 风热

（1）主证　面颊火灼样疼痛，面部发热，目赤流泪，烦躁，口干咽燥，苔薄黄，脉弦数。

（2）治则　祛风清热止痛。

（3）治法

1）体针

处方　大椎，曲池，攒竹，阳白，四白，合谷，承浆，颊车。

操作　毫针刺，用泻法。留针15～30分钟，间歇行针2～4次。

2）耳针

处方　面颊，上颌，额，下颌，前额，神门，皮质下。

操作　毫针强刺激，留针20～30分钟；亦可采用耳穴贴敷。

3. 肝胃实热

（1）主证　面颊火灼样疼痛，烦躁易怒，口苦，目赤，眩晕，胸膈满闷，胁下胀，便秘，舌红质干，苔黄厚，脉弦数或洪数。

（2）治则　清热平肝，调胃止痛。

（3）治法

1）体针

处方　行间，内庭，头维，中渚，四白，合谷，承浆，翳风，陷谷。

操作　毫针刺，用泻法。留针15～30分钟，间隔行针2～4次。

2）耳针

处方　面颊，上颌，下颌，前

额，神门，交感，皮质下。

操作　毫针强刺激，留针 20～30 分钟；亦可采用耳穴贴敷。

4. 阴虚火旺

（1）主证　面颊疼痛，反复发作，颧红，皮肤粗糙，头晕目眩，五心烦热，形体消瘦，舌红，苔少，脉细数。

（2）治则　滋阴平肝，清热止痛。

（3）治法

1）处方　风池，太溪，四白，颧髎，承浆，颊车，下关。

操作　毫针刺，太溪用补法外，余用泻法。留针 15～30 分钟，间歇行针 2～4 次。

2）耳针

处方　面颊，上颌，下颌，额，神门，交感，皮质下。

操作　毫针强刺激，留针 20～30 分钟；亦可用耳穴贴敷。

Facial Pain

Facial pain refers to severe aching that may be paroxysmal, temporal or burning in the facial region. It mostly affects one side of the face in the lateral aspect of the forehead, superior maxillary bone or inferior maxillary bone, but rarely affects both sides. At the beginning, the attack of aching only lasts for a short time with very long intervals. The longer the history, the more frequent attacks there will be. Facial pain is often complained by patients in their middle ages but more common in middle aged women. It is similar to trigeminal neuralgia in modern medicine.

1. Wind-cold

（1）*Main manifestation*

Painful cheek, facial muscular spasm and twitching, aggravation of pain or new attack due to exposure to cold and alleviated by warmth. The accompanying symptoms and signs include headache, aversion to cold, nasal discharge, thin white tongue coating, and wiry tense pulse.

（2）*Therapeutic principle*

Dispel wind, disinhibit cold and relieve pain.

（3）*Treatment*

1）Body acupuncture

Prescription：Fengchi（GB 20），Fengfu（DU 16），Lieque（LU 7），Zanzhu（BL 2），Taiyang（EX-HN 5），Jiache（ST 6），Xiangu（ST 43）.

Method：Apply filiform needles with reducing method. Retain the needles for 15～30 minutes manipulating them two to three times.

2）Ear acupuncture

Prescription：Cheek, Superior Maxillary, Forehead, Ear-Shenmen, Sympathetic, Subcortex.

Method: Apply filiform needles with strong stimulation and retain the needles for 20 ~ 30 minutes. Auricular taping is also applicable.

2. Wind-heat

(1) *Main manifestation*

Burning pain in the cheek, feverish sensation on one side of the face, congestion of the eyes, running tears, restlessness, dry mouth and throat, thin yellow tongue coating, and wiry rapid pulse.

(2) *Therapeutic Principle*

Dispel wind, dissipate heat and relieve pain.

(3) *Treatment*

1) Body acupuncture

Prescription: Dazhui (DU 14), Quchi (LI 11), Zanzhu (BL 2), Yangbai (GB 14), Sibai (ST 2), Hegu (LI 4), Chengjiang (RN 24), Jiache (ST 6)

Method: Apply filiform needles with reducing method. Retain the needles for 15 ~ 30 minutes manipulating them two to four times.

2) Ear acupuncture

Prescription: Cheek, Superier Maxillary, Vertex, Inferior Maxillary, Forehead, Ear-Shenmen, Subcortex.

Method: Apply filiform needles with strong stimulation and retain the needles for 20 ~ 30 minutes. Auricular taping is also applicable.

3. Excess Heat from the Liver and Stomach

(1) *Main manifestation*

Burning pain in the cheek, restlessness with shortness of temper, bitter taste in the mouth, congestion of the eye, dizziness and vertigo, fullness sensation in the chest, distention in the hypochondriac region, constipation, dry red tongue proper, thick yellow coating, and wiry rapid or full rapid pulse.

(2) *Therapeutic principle*

Disperse heat, calm the liver, regulate stomach and stop pain.

(3) *Treatment*

1) Body acupuncture

Prescription: Xingjian (LR 2), Neiting (ST 44), Touwei (ST 8), Zhongzhu (SJ 3), Sibai (ST 2), Hegu (LI 4), Chengjian (RN 24), Yifeng (SJ 17), Xiangu (ST 43).

Method: Apply filiform needles with reducing method. Retain the needles for 15 ~ 30 minutes manipulating them two to four times.

2) Ear acupuncture

Prescription: Cheek, Superior Maxillary, Inferior Maxillary, Forehead, Ear-Shenmen, Sympathetic, Subcortex.

Method: Apply filiform needles with

stong stimulation and retain the needles for 20 ~ 30 minutes. Auricular taping is also applicable.

4. Hyperactivity of Fire due to Yin Deficiency

(1) *Main manifestation*

Pain in the cheek in repeated attacks, redness in the cheek, rough facial skin, dizziness, blurring of vision, feverish sensation in the palms and soles, emaciation, red tongue proper with less coating, and thin rapid pulse.

(2) *Therapeutic principle*

Nourish yin, emolliate the liver, clear heat and stop pain.

(3) *Treatment*

1) Body acupuncture

Prescription: Fengchi (GB 20), Taixi (KI 3), Sibai (ST 2), Quanliao (SI 18), Chengjiang (RN 24), Jiache (ST 6), Xiaguan (ST 7).

Method: Apply filiform needles with reducing method except Taixi (KI 3) which is used with reinforcing method. Retain the needles for 15 ~ 30 minutes manipulating them two to four times.

2) Ear acupuncture

Prescription: Cheek, Superior Maxillary, Inferior Maxillary, Forehead, Ear-Shenmen, Sympathetic, Subcortex.

Method: Apply filiform needles with strong stimulation and retain the needles for 20 ~ 30 minutes. Auricular taping is also applicable.

痹 证

痹有闭阻不通之意。凡处邪侵袭经络，气血闭阻运行不畅，引起以肢体、关节、肌肉等处疼痛、痠楚、麻木、关节肿大和屈伸不利为主要症状的病症，统称为痹证。本病在临床上较为常见，具有渐进性或反复发作的特点。现代医学的风湿热，风湿性关节炎，痛风，风湿性肌纤维炎等病，均属本证范畴。

1. 辨证

(1) 行痹

肢体关节肌肉疼痛痠楚，游走不定，上下左右走窜疼痛，以腕、肘、膝、踝处为甚，关节运动不利，或见恶寒发热，舌苔薄腻，脉浮弦。

(2) 痛痹

肢体关节肌肉疼痛剧烈，甚者如刀割锥刺，痛有定处，得热痛减，遇寒加剧，日轻夜重，关节屈伸不利，局部不红不热，常有冷感，舌苔薄白，脉弦紧。

(3) 着痹

肢体关节肌肉痠痛沉重，痛处较为固定，肌肤麻木不仁，易受阴雨气候影响而加重，舌苔白腻，脉濡缓。

(4) 热痹

肢体关节疼痛，局部灼热红肿，痛不可近，活动受限，可涉及一个或多个关节，兼有发热，口渴，心烦，喜冷，恶热等症状，舌苔黄，脉滑数。

（5）顽痹

痹症历时较长，反复发作，骨节僵硬变形，关节附近呈黯黑色，疼痛剧烈，停著不移，不可屈伸，或疼痛麻木，或关节红肿，兼见发热，口渴，尿短赤，或关节冰凉，寒冷季节而痛剧，得热而安，舌质紫暗有瘀斑，脉细涩。

2. 治则

扶正祛邪，疏通经络，祛风散寒化湿。

3. 治法

（1）体针

处方

肩部　肩髃，肩髎，臑俞，合谷。

肘部　曲池，天井，尺泽，外关。

腕部　阳溪，阳池，外关，腕骨。

髀部　环跳，居髎，悬钟。

股部　秩边，承扶，殷门，昆仑。

膝部　梁丘，血海，膝眼，阳陵泉，阴陵泉。

踝部　解溪，商丘，昆仑，太溪，丘墟。

腰脊背部　身柱，腰阳关，夹脊穴，大椎。

配穴　行痹加风池，血海，膈俞；痛痹加关元，肾俞；着痹加脾俞，足三里，阴陵泉；热痹加大椎，曲池，委中；顽痹加脾俞，肝俞，肾俞，膈俞，大杼。

操作　毫针刺，用泻法或平补平泻法。留针 20～30 分钟，间歇行针 2～3 次。

（2）耳针

处方　神门，内分泌，肾上腺，肝，脾，肾，耳尖。

（3）皮肤针

处方　脾俞，肝俞，肾俞，膈俞，夹脊穴。

操作　中等强度刺激，叩至局部微红为度，隔天 1 次。

（4）艾灸

处方　神厥。

操作　切 2 分厚的姜片，在中心用针穿数孔，置于神厥穴，以艾炷施灸，每次 5～7 壮。本法适应于痛痹，着痹，顽痹。

（5）拔罐疗法

处方　肾俞，脾俞，肝俞。

操作　采用坐罐或闪罐治疗 10～20分钟，每天 1 次。热痹不宜采用。

Bi Syndrome

Bi is a Chinese concept. Bi syndrome means obstruction. Conditions characterized by the following chief manifestations such as aching, numbness and heavy sensation involving the limbs, joints and muscles as well as swollen joints and limited movement due to poor circulation. As well, obstruction of Qi and blood caused by exogenous pathogenic invasion into the channels and collaterals are in general called Bi syndromes. Bi syndromes, commonly seen in the clinic, also bear the characteristics of progressive pain or pain in repeated attacks. The concept of Bi syndrome in traditional Chinese medicine covers rheumatic fever, rheumatic arthritis, rheumtoid gout and rheumatic myofibrositis in modern medicine.

1. Differentiation

(1) *Wandering Bi Syndrome*

The main manifestations include wandering pain and soreness in the body limbs, joints and muscles, particuarly in the wrist joints, elbow, knee and ankle areas. As well limited movements of the joints, or fever with aversion to cold, thin greasy tongue coating, and superficial wiry pulse.

(2) *Painful Bi Syndrome*

The chief manifestation includes severe pain in the limbs and joints as if being stabbed or pricked in worse cases, fixed pain that is alleviated by warmth but aggravated by cold, better in the daytime but worse at night, limited movements of the joints, no local redness or feverish sensation, cold sensation in the affected parts, thin white tongue coating, and wiry tense pulse.

(3) *Fixed Bi Syndrome*

The chief manifestation include pain and heavy sensation in relatively fixed areas of body limbs or joints, numbness of the muscles, aggravation of the condition in rainy days, white greasy tongue coating, and soft slow pulse.

(4) *Febrile Bi Syndrome*

The chief manifestations include painful limb or joints, local burning sensation with redness, pain worsened by touching, limited movement involving one or several joints, fever, thirst, restlessness, desire for cold drinks, aversion to heat, yellow tongue coating, and slippery rapid pulse.

(5) *Stubborn Bi Syndrome*

The main manifestations include a long history of repeated attacks that have already deformed the affected joints. Some of the joint areas may have black spots. It also has severe pain in the local areas, limited movement, soreness and numbness, redness and swelling of the joints, fever, thirst, short scanty urine, or cold sensation in the joints, worsened condition in the cold seasons, alleviation of pain by warmth, purplish dark tongue with purplish spots, and thready hesitant pulse.

2. Therapeutic principle

Strengthen the antipathogemic Qi, remove wind and cold from the channels and collaterals and resolve dampness.

3. Treatment

(1) *Body acupuncture*

Prescription Based on location of pain

Shoulder: Jianyu (LI 15), Jianliao (SJ 14), Naoshu (SI 10), Hegu (LI 4).

Elbow: Quchi (LI 11), Tianjing (SJ 10), Chize (LU 5), Waiguan (SJ 5).

Wrist: Yangxi (LI 5), Yangchi (SJ 4), Waiguan (SJ 5), Wangu (SJ 4).

Hip: Huantiao (GB 30), Juliao (GB 29), Xuanzhong (GB 29).

Femur: Zhibian (BL 54), Chengfu (BL 36), Yinmen (BL 37), Kunlun (BL 60)

Knee: Liangqiu (ST 34), Xuehai (SP 10), Xiyan (EX-LE 5), Yangingquan (GB 34), Yinlingquan (SP 9).

Ankle: Jiexi (ST 41), Shangqiu (SP 5), Kunlun (BL 60), Taixi (KI 3), Qiuxu (GB 40).

Back and Lumbar region: Shenzhu (DU 12), Yaoyangguan (DU 3), Dazhui (DU 14), Huatuojiaji (Extra).

Supplementary points: Add Fengchi (GB 20), Xuehai (SP 10) and Geshu (BL 17) for wandering Bi syndrome, Guanyuan (RN 4) and Shenshu (BL 23) for painful Bi syndrome, Pishu (BL 20), Zusanli (ST 36) and Yanglingquan (GB 34) for fixed Bi syndrome, Dazhui (DU 14), Quchi (LI 11) and Weizhong (BL 40) for febrile Bi syndrome, Pishu (UB 20), Ganshu (BL 18), Shenshu (BL 23), Geshu (BL 17) and Dashu (BL 11) for stubborn Bi syndrome.

Method: Apply filiform needles with reducing or even movement method. Retain the needles for $20 \sim 30$ minutes manipulating them two to three times.

(2) *Ear acupuncture*

Prescription: Ear-shenmen, Endocrine, Adrenal Gland, Liver, Spleen, Kidney, Apex of Ear.

Method: Apply filiform needles with stong stimulation and retain the needles for 15 - 20 minutes. Apex of Ear may be pricked with a three-edged needle to cause bleeding.

(3) *Plum-blossom needle therapy*

Prescription: Pishu (BL 20), Ganshu (BL 18), Shenshu (BL 23), Geshu (BL 17), Huatuojiaji ( ).

Method: Tap the above mentioned areas with moderate stimulation until local redness appears, once every other day.

(4) *Moxibustion*

Prescription: Shenque (RN 8).

Method: Cut ginger slices in 2 mm thickness and prick many holes with a needle on the ginger slice to be put over Shenque (RN 8). Ignite five to seven pieces of moxa cones at the point in order. This method is applicable for painful, fixed and stubborn Bi syndromes.

(5) *Cupping Therapy*

Prescription: Shenshu (BL 23), Pishu (BL 23), Guanyan (RN 4).

Method: Apply retaining cupping or successive flash cupping for 10 ~ 20 minutes once a day. Febrile Bi syndrome is not applicable.

痿　证

痿证是以肌肉萎缩或痿软及运动障碍为特征的疾病，常见于现代医学的多发性神经炎，急慢性脊髓炎，进行性肌萎缩，重症肌无力，周期性麻痹，肌营养不良症，癔症性瘫痪及外伤性瘫痪等。

1. 辨证

（1）肺热

主证　下肢肌肉痿软，运动受限，伴见发热，咳嗽，易怒，口渴，尿黄短，舌红苔黄，脉细数或滑数。

（2）湿热

主证　小腿痿软微肿，触之微热，全身重着，胸闷脘痞，尿黄短，尿时疼痛，舌苔黄腻，脉濡数。

（3）外伤

主证　外伤之后，肢体痿瘫，或伴见二便失禁，脉涩，淡红或暗紫舌，苔薄或薄白。

（4）肝肾阴虚

主证　下肢痿软，运动受限，腰部酸软无力，遗精，滑精，带下，头晕眼花，舌质红，脉细数。

2. 治则

疏通气血，滋润筋骨。如果热邪或湿热之邪在肺是主要病因，应以泻法清热；肝肾阴虚，施以补法；外伤者平补平泻。

3. 治法

（1）体针

处方

上肢　肩髃，曲池，合谷，外关。

下肢　髀关，环跳，血海，梁丘，足三里，阳陵泉，解溪，悬钟。

配穴　肺热加尺泽，肺俞；湿热加脾俞，阴陵泉；肝肾阴虚加膈俞，肾俞；外伤加相应于受损脊柱处的夹脊穴；大便失禁加大肠俞，次髎。

操作　毫针刺，肺热和湿热者用泻法，肝肾阴虚者用补法，外伤者用平补平泻法。留针15~30分钟，间歇行针2~3次。

（2）头针

处方　运动区，运用区，足运感区。

操作　毫针与头皮呈30°左右夹角，快速刺入皮下，然后沿刺激区快速推进到相应的深度。进针后，使针体来回快速旋转200次/分钟左右，捻转持续0.5~1分钟，然后静留针5~10分钟重复捻转，用同样的方法再捻转2次，即可起针。

（3）皮肤针

处方　肺俞，肝俞，脾俞，胃

俞，肾俞或沿手足阳明经线叩刺。

操作　轻刺激，叩至皮肤呈现红晕为度，隔天 1 次。

Wei Syndrome

The Wei syndrome is characterized by flaccidity or atrophy of the limbs with motor impairment. It is often complained about by patients suffering from polyneuritis, acute and chronic myelitis, progressive myatrophy, myasthenia gravis, periodic paralysis, muscular trophoneurosis, hysterical paralysis and paralysis due to traumatic injuries in terms of modern medicine.

1. Differentiation

(1) *Heat in the lung*

Main manifestation

Muscular flaccidity of the lower limbs with motor impairment, accompanied by fever, cough, irritability, thirst, scanty and brownish urine, reddened tongue with yellow coating, thready and rapid or rolling and rapid pulse.

(2) *Damp Heat*

Main manifestation

Flaccid or slightly swollen legs, a little hot sensation on touch, general heaviness, sensation of fullness in the chest and epigastric region, painful urination, hot and brownish urine, yellow sticky tongue coating, soft and rapid pulse.

(3) *Trauma*

Main manifestation

History of trauma, flaccid paralytic limbs, may be accompanied with incontinence of urine and feces, relaxed or hesitant pulse, pink or dark purplish tongue, thin or thin white coating.

(4) *Deficiency of Yin of the Liver and Kidneys*

Main manifestation

Muscular flaccidity of the lower limbs with motor impairment, combined with soreness and weakness of the lumbar region, seminal emission, prospermia, dizziness, blurring of vision, reddened tongue, thready and rapid pulse.

2. Therapeutic Principle

Promote circulation of Qi in the meridians and nourish the tendons and bones. If heat or damp heat in the lung is the main etiological factor, reducing method should be used to dissipate heat. In case of deficiency of Yin in the liver and kidney, reinforcing method should be employed. For trauma, puncture the points on the affected side with even movement.

3. Treatment

(1) *Body acupuncture*

Prescription

Upper limb: Jianyu (LI 15), Quchi (LI 11), Hegu (LI 4), Waiguan (SJ 5).

Lower limb: Biguan (ST 31), Huantiao (GB 30), Xuehai (SP 10), liangqiu (ST 34), Zusanli (ST 36), Yanglingquan (GB 34), Jiexi (ST 41), Xuanzhong (GB 39).

Supplementary points: Add Chize (LI 5) for heat in the lung, Pishu (BL 20), Yinlingquan (SP 9) for damp heat, Ganshu (BL 18) and Shenshu (BL 23) for deficiency of Yin in the liver and kidneys, Huantojiaji at the corresponding level of spinal injury for trauma, Dachangshu (BL 25), Ciliao (BL 32) for incontinence of feces.

Method: Apply filiform needle with reducing method for heat in the lung and damp heat, reinforcing method for deficiency Yin of the liver and kidney, even movement method for trauma. Retain the needles for 15~30 minutes manipulating them two to three times.

(2) *Scalp acupuncture*

Prescription: Motor area, Voluntary movement area, Leg motor and Sensory area.

Method: Filiform needle is inserted in an angle of 30° to the scalp swiftly. Then inserted further along the area stimulated to (not rotating) a requisite portion. Once the needle is in place, it should be twirled 200 times per minute. Twirling may be continued for 0.5 to 1 minute after which the needle is left in

place for 5 to 10 minutes, then twirled again. After repeating this procedure twice the needle may be withdrawn.

(3) *Plum-blossom needle therapy*

Prescription: Feishu (BL 13), Ganshu (BL 18), Pishu (BL 20), Weishu (BL 21), Shenshu (BL 23) or along the Yangming channels of the foot and hand.

Method: Use the plum-blossom needle to tap gently until local redness appears. Treatment is given once every other day.

腰　　痛

腰痛又称腰脊痛。疼痛的部位或在脊中，或在一侧，或在腰脊旁，是临床常见的证候之一。本病多见于现代医学的腰部软组织损伤，肌肉风湿，以及脊柱病变等。

1. 寒湿外侵

(1) 主证　腰痛常发生于感受寒湿之后，雨天加剧，腰背肌肉重着，仰俯不利，疼痛向臀部和下肢放射，患处寒冷，舌苔白腻，脉沉弱或沉迟。

(2) 治则　散寒祛湿，温经通络。

(3) 治法

1) 体针

处方　肾俞，关元俞，腰阳关，委中，次髎，大肠俞。

操作　毫针刺，平补平泻。留针15~20分钟，间歇行针2~3次。

2) 耳针

处方 腰椎,骶椎,神门,皮质下。

操作 毫针强刺激,留针 20 分钟;亦可采用耳穴贴敷。

3)艾灸

处方 肾俞,关元俞,腰阳关。

操作 采用温和灸或回旋灸治疗 10～20 分钟,每天 1 次;亦可采用温针灸治疗。

4)拔罐疗法

处方 肾俞,腰阳关,次髎,关元俞。

操作 采用坐罐或闪罐治疗 10～20分钟,每天 1 次。

2. 肾虚

(1)主证 腰痛迁延,起病缓慢,伴见腰膝酸软,劳累加剧,休息缓解。肾阳虚者可有下腹抽掣感,面色㿠白,肢冷,舌苔白,脉沉细或沉迟;肾阴虚者可有烦躁失眠,口咽干燥,面红,五心烦热,舌红少苔,脉细弱或细数。

(2)治则 益肾气,强腰脊。

(3)治法

1)体针

处方 肾俞,命门,志室,太溪,委中。

操作 毫针刺,用补法。留针 20～30 分钟,间歇行针 1～2 次。

2)耳针

处方 肾,神门,皮质下,腰椎,骶椎。

操作 毫针强刺激,留针 20 分钟;亦可采用耳穴贴敷。

3)艾灸

处方 肾俞,命门,志室。

操作 采用温和灸或回旋灸治疗 10～20 分钟;亦可采用温针灸。本法仅适合于肾阳虚者。

4)拔罐疗法

处方 肾俞,命门,次髎。

操用 用坐罐或闪罐治疗 10～20 分钟,每天 1 次。

3. 外伤

(1)主证 腰部外伤史,通常固定于腰部某一部位拘急疼痛,压之或运动时疼痛加剧,舌淡红或暗紫,脉弦涩。

(2)治则 通经活血,祛瘀止痛。

(3)治法

1)体针

处方 阿是穴,膈俞,次髎,委中,后溪,水沟。

操作 毫针刺,用泻法。留针 15～30 分钟,间歇行针 3～4 次。

2)耳针

处方 腰椎,骶椎,神门,皮质下。

操作 毫针强刺激,留针 20 分钟;亦可采用耳穴贴敷。

3)三棱针

处方 阿是穴。

操作 三棱针点刺阿是穴出血,然后拔火罐,使瘀尽出。

Lumbar Pain

Lumbar pain, also broadly known as lumbospinal pain, may involve either the spine, or one or both sides of the lumbar region. It is a commonly encountered condition in the clinic. Lumbar pain ofter refers to soft tissure injury, muscular rheumatism and lumbar disc degeneration in modern medicine.

1. Lumbar Pain due to Cold-damp Invasion

(1) *Main manifestation*

Low back pain usually occuring after exposure to cold and damp and aggravated on rainy days, heavy sensation and stiffness of the muscles in the dorsolumbar region, limitation of extension and flexion of the back, pain radiating downwards to the buttocks and lower limbs, cold feeling of the affected area, white and stickly tongue coating, deep and weak, or deep and slow pulse.

(2) *Therapeutic principle*

Warm up the channels and collaterals, eliminate cold and resolve dampness.

(3) *Treatment*

1) Body acupuncture

Prescription: Shenshu (BL 23), Guanyuanshu (BL 26), Yaoyangguan (DU 3), Weizhong (BL 40), Ciliao (BL 32), Dachangshu (BL 25).

Method: Apply filiform needles with even movement method. Retain the needles for 15~20 minutes manipulating them two to three times.

2) Ear acupuncture

Prescription: Lumbar Vertebra, Sacral Vertebra, Ear-shenmen, Subcortex.

Method: Apply filiform needles with strong stimulation for 20 minutes. Auricular taping is also applicable.

3) Moxibustion

Prescription: Shenshu (BL 23), Guanyuanshu (BL 26), Yaoyangguan (DU 3).

Method: Apply mild warming moxibustion or rounding moxibustion for 10~20 minute once a day. Moxibustion with warming needle is also applicable.

4) Cupping therapy

Prescription: Shenshu (BL 23), Yaoyangguan (DU 3), Ciliao (BL 32), Guanyuanshu (BL 26).

Method: Apply retaining cupping or successive flash cupping for 10 ~ 20 minutes once a day.

2. Deficiency of the Kidney

(1) *Main manifestation*

Insidious onset of protracted pain and soreness accompanied by lassitude and weakness of the loins and knees, aggravated by fatigue and alleviated by bed rest. In case of deficiency of kidney Yang, cramp-like sensation in the lower abdomen, pallor, normal taste in the mouth, cold limbs, pale tongue, deep thready or deep slow pulse. In case of kidney Yin insufficiency, irritability, insommia, dry mouth and throat, flushed face, feverish sensation in the chest, palms and soles, reddened tongue proper with scanty coating, thready weak or thready rapid pulse.

(2) *Therapeutic rinciple*

Tonify kidney Qi and strengthen the lumbar region.

(3) *Treatment*

1) Body acupuncture

Prescription: Shenshu (BL 23), Mingmen (DU 4), Zhishi (BL 52), Taixi (KI 3), Weizhong (BL 40).

Method: Apply filiform needles with reinforcing method. Retain the needles for 20～30 minutes manipulating them one to two times.

2) Ear acupuncture

Prescription: Kidney, Ear-Shenmen, Subcortex, Lumbar Vertebra, Sacral Vertebra.

Method: Apply filiform needles with strong stimulation and retain the needles for 20 minutes. Auricular taping is also applicable.

3) Moxibustion

Prescription: Shenshu (BL 23), Mingmen (DU 4), Zhishi (BL 52).

Method: Apply mild-warming moxibustion or rounding moxibustion for 10～20 minutes. Moxibustion with warming needle is also applicable. This method is only suitable for deficiency of kidney Yang.

4) Cupping Therapy

Prescription: Shenshu (BL 23), Mingmen (DU 4), Ciliao (BL 32).

Method: Apply retain cupping or successive flash cupping for 10～20 minutes once a day.

3. Trauma

(1) *Main manifestation*

History of sprain of the lumbar region, rigidity and pain of the lower back which is generally fixed in a certain area, aggravated by pressure and by turning the body, pink or dark purplish tongue proper, string-taut hesitant pulse.

(2) *Therapeutic principle*

Activate blood circulation, remove obstruction from the channels and collaterals, resolve blood stasis and stop pain.

(3) *Treatment*

1) Body acupuncture

Prescription: Ashi points, Geshu (BL 17), Ciliao (BL 32), Weizhong (BL 40), Houxi (SI 3), Shuigou (DU 26).

Method: Apply filiform needles with reducing method. Retain the needles for 15～30 minutes manipulating them three to four times.

2) Ear acupuncture

Prescription: Lumbar Vertebra,

Sacral Vertebra, Ear-shenmen, Sub-cortex.

Method: Apply filiform needles with strong stimulation and retain the needles for 20 minutes. Auricular taping is also applicable.

3) Three-edged needle

Prescription: Ashi Points.

Method: Prick Ashi points with a three-edged needle followed by cupping in order to suck out as much stagnant blood as possible.

消　渴

消渴是以多饮，多食，多尿，形体消瘦或尿有甜味为特征的病症。现代医学称之为糖尿病。

1. 上消

（1）主证　烦渴多饮，口干舌燥，兼见尿多，食多，舌尖红，苔薄黄，脉洪数。

（2）治则　清热润肺，生津止渴。

（3）治法

1) 体针

处方　少府，心俞，太渊，肺俞，脘下俞，廉泉，承浆。

操作　毫针刺，平补平泻。留针15～20分钟，间歇行针2～3次。

2) 耳针

处方　胰，内分泌，胃，肺，神门。

操作　毫针刺，轻刺激，留针15～20分钟；亦可采用耳穴贴敷。

3) 皮肤针

处方　肺俞，心俞，夹脊穴，胃

脘下俞。

操作　皮肤针轻刺激，叩至皮肤微红为度，隔天1次。

2. 中消

（1）主证　食量倍增，消谷善饥，嘈杂，烦热，多汗，形体消瘦，或大便干结，兼见多饮，多尿，舌苔黄燥，脉象滑数。

（2）治则　清胃泻火，养阴保津。

（3）治法

1) 体针

处方　内庭，三阴交，脾俞，胃俞，胃脘下俞。

配穴　嘈杂反酸加中脘、内关。

操作　毫针刺，平补平泻，留针15～20分钟，间歇行针2～3次。

2) 耳针

处方　胰，内分泌，脾，胃，神门，三焦。

操作　毫针轻刺激，留针20分钟；亦可采用耳穴贴敷。

3) 皮肤针

处方　脾俞，胃俞，夹脊穴。

操作　皮肤针轻刺激，叩至皮肤微红为度，隔天1次。

3. 下消

（1）主证　小便频数，量多而略稠，口干舌燥，渴而多饮，头晕，目糊，颧红，虚烦，善饥而食不甚多，腰膝酸软，舌质红，脉细数。久病阴虚及阳，可兼见面色黧黑，畏寒肢冷，尿量特多，男子阳痿，女子经闭，舌质淡，苔白，脉沉细无力。

（2）治则 养津固肾。

（3）治法

1）体针

处方 太溪，太冲，肝俞，肾俞，胃脘下俞。

配穴 阳虚者加命门。

操作 毫针刺，肾俞，胃脘下俞用补法；太溪，太冲，肝俞用泻法。留针20分钟，间隔行针1～2次。

2）耳针

处方 肾，胰，内分泌，三焦，神门。

操作 毫针轻刺激，留针15～20分钟；亦可采用耳穴贴敷。

3）皮肤针

处方 肾俞，肝俞，胃脘下俞，夹脊。

操作 轻刺激，叩至皮肤微红为度，隔天1次。

Diabetic Syndrome

Diabetic syndrome is a condition characterized by polydipsia, polyphagia, polyuria and sweet urine. It is called diabetes in modern medicine.

1. Upper-Jiao Diabetes

(1) *Main manifestation*

Thirst with desire to drink, dry mouth and tongue, accompanied by profuse urine, polydipsia, redness in the tip of the tongue, thin yellow tongue coating, and full rapid pulse.

(2) *Therapeutic principle*

Eliminate heat and moisten Lung, engender liquid, and allay thirst.

(3) *Treatment*

1) Body acupuncture

Prescription: Shaofu (HT 8), Xinshu (BL 15), Taiyuan (LU 9), Feishu (BL 13), Weiguanxiashu (Extra), Lianquan (RN 23), Changjiang (RN 24).

Method: Apply filiform needles with even movement method. Retain the needles for 15～20 minutes manipulating them two to three times.

2) Ear acupuncture

Prescription: Pancreas, Endocrine, Stomach, Lung, Ear-shenmen.

Method: Apply filiform needles with mild stimulation and retain the needles for 15～20 minutes. Auricular taping is also applicable.

3) Plum-blossom needle therapy

Prescription: Feishu (BL 13), Xinshu (BL 15), Huatuojiaji, Weiguanxiashu (Extra).

Method: Use a plum-blossom needle to tap on the areas with gentle stimulation until local redness appears once every other day.

2. Middle-Jiao Diabetes

(1) *Main manifestation*

Great increase of appetite, insatiable hunger, discomfort sensation in the stomach, restlessness with feverish

sensation, profuse sweating, emaciation, dry stools accompanied by profuse
drinking of water, polyuria, dry yellow tongue coating, and rapid slippery
pulse.

(2) *Therapeutic Principle*

Clear the stomach and drain fire, nourish Yin and safegurd liquids.

(3) *Treatment*

1) Body acupuncture

Prescription: Neiting (ST 44),
Sanyinjiao (SP 6), Pishu (BL 20),
Weishu (BL 21), Weiguanxiashu
(Extra).

Supplementary points: Add Zhongwan (RN 12) and Neiguan (PC 6) for
gastric discomfort sensation with acid
regurgitation and polyorexia.

Method: Apply filiform needles with
even movement method. Retain the
needles for 15～20 minutes manipulating them two to three times.

2) Ear acupuncture

Prescription: Pancreas, Endocrine,
Spleen, Stomach, Ear-shenmen, Sanjiao.

Method: Apply filiform needles with
mild stimulation and retain the needles
for 20 minutes. Auricular taping is also
applicable.

3) Plum-blossom needle therapy

Prescription: Pishu (BL 20),
Weishu (BL 21), Huatuojiaji.

Method: Use a plum-blossom needle

to tap on the areas with gentle stimulation until local redness appears once every other day.

3. Lower-Jiao Diabetes

(1) *Main manifestation*

Frequent urination in heavy quantity
and turbid quality, dry mouth and
tongue, desire for profuse drinking,
dizziness, blurring of vision, red
cheeks, restlessness due to Yin deficiency, insatiable hunger but poor appetite, soreness and weakness of the
lumbus and knees, red tongue proper,
and rapid thready pulse. There will be
dark complexion, aversion to cold,
profuse urinary discharge, pale tongue
proper with white coating, and deep
thready weak pulse if the chronic Yin
deficiency has affected Yang of the
body. There will be impotence and a-
menorrhea respectively as well.

(2) *Therapeutic principle*

Nourish liquid and secure the kidneys.

(3) *Treatment*

1) Body acupuncture

Prescription: Taixi (KI 3), Tai-
chong (LR 3), Ganshu (BL 18),
Shenshu (BL 23), Weiguanxiashu
(Extra).

Supplementary point: Add Mingmen
(DU 4) for Yang deficiency.

Method: Apply filiform needles with
reinforcing method to Shenshu (BL

23) and Weiguanxiashu (Extra), with reducing method to Taixi (KI 3), Taichong (LR 3) and Ganshu (BL 18). Retain the needles for 20 minutes manipulating them one to two times.

2) Ear acupuncture

Prescription: Kidney, Pancreas, Endocrine, Sanjiao, Ear-shenmen.

Method: Apply filiform needles with mild stimulation and retain the needles for 15~20 minutes. Auricular taping is also applicable.

3) Plum-blossom needle therapy

Prescription: Shenshu (BL 23), Ganshu (BL 18), Weiguanxiashu (Extra), Huatuojiaji.

Method: Use a plum-blossom needle to tap on the areas with gentle stimulation until local redness appears once every other day.

脚　气

脚气是以两脚软弱无力，脚胫肿满强直，或虽不肿满而缓弱麻木，步履艰难为特征的一种疾病。因病从脚起，故名脚气。本病包括现代医学所称的维生素 B_1 缺乏所致的脚气病。此外如营养不良，多发性神经炎等，凡具有类似证候的疾患，均可参照本篇辨证治疗。

1. 湿脚气

（1）主证　足胫浮肿，脚趾疼痛麻木，其势逐渐向上蔓延，腿膝沉重酸软，步行乏力，行动不便。偏于寒

湿者，则足胫怯寒喜温；偏于湿热者，则足胫灼热喜凉，或有恶寒，发热，小便短少，舌苔白腻或浮黄，脉濡数。

（2）治则　疏通经络，清化湿热。

（3）治法

1）体针

处方　足三里，三阴交，阳陵泉，八风。

配穴　恶寒发热加合谷，大椎，外关；小便短少加阴陵泉，昆仑。

操作　毫针刺，用泻法。留针20~30分钟，间歇行针 2~3 次。偏寒者可针灸并用，每穴灸 10~15 分钟。偏湿热者八风穴可点刺出血。

2）耳针

处方　趾，踝，膝，脾，神门。

操作　毫针中等强度刺激，留针20分钟，亦可采用耳穴贴敷。

2. 干脚气

（1）主证　两足无力，腿膝麻木疼痛，时感筋肉挛急，活动欠利，足胫肌肉逐渐萎缩，甚至顽麻萎废，便秘溲黄，舌质淡红，苔薄白或少苔，脉细数。

（2）治则　益阴养血。

（3）治法

1）体针

处方　解溪，阴市，复溜，照海，血海，悬钟。

配穴　筋肉挛急加承山；腰痛加委中；膝肿加膝眼，风市。

操作　毫针刺，用补法。留针

20 分钟，间歇行针 1~2 次。

2）耳针

处方   趾，踝，膝，胃，脾，肺，神门。

操作   毫针中等强度刺激，留针 20 分钟。亦可用耳穴贴敷。

3．脚气冲心

（1）主证   足胫肿痛或萎细麻木，步行乏力，突然气急，心悸，恶心呕吐，胸中懊恼，重证则神昏烦躁，语言错乱，唇舌发绀，脉细数无力。

（2）治则   降气泻肺，泄毒宁心。

（3）治法

1）体针

处方   尺泽，膻中，劳宫，神门，足三里，涌泉。

配穴   神昏加人中；虚脱加气海，关元。

操作   毫针刺，平补平泻，留针 15~20 分钟，间歇行针 1~2 次。

2）耳针

处方   心,肾,趾,踝,膝,神门。

操作   毫针轻刺激，留针 20 分钟；亦可采用耳穴贴敷。

Beriberi

Beriberi refers to flaccid feet and lower portion of the legs. It may also refer to weakness and numbness of the feet even though there may not be any swelling involved. Since the condition starts from the feet, this condition has been named feet flaccidity or beriberi.

It includes feet conditions due to Vit. B_1 deficiency in modern medicine. The differentiation and treatment here can be referred to for other feet conditions that bear similar manifestations such as feet malnutrition and polyneuritis.

1. Damp Beriberi

(1) *Main manifestation*

Swelling of the dorsum of the feet, pain and numbness of toes which gradually affects the legs, soreness and heaviness of the feet and knee joints, weakness of the feet with difficulty in walking. There will be a cold sensation in the feet that responds to warmth if cold-damp is more prevlent. There will be feverish sensation in the dorsum of the feet that responds to cooling if the damp-heat is more prevalent. Other manifestations may include fever with aversion to cold, short scanty urine, white greasy or slightly yellow tongue coating, rapid soft pulse.

(2) *Therapeutic principle*

Promote Qi and blood circulation in the channels and collaterals, clear up heat and resolve dampness.

(3) *Treatment*

1) Body acupuncture

Prescription: Zusanli (ST 36), Sanyinjiao (SP 6), Yanglingquan (GB 34), Bafeng (EX-LE 10).

Supplementary points: Add Hegu

(LI 4), Dazhui (DU 14) and Waiguan (SJ 5) for fever with aversion to cold, Yinlingquan (SP 9) and Kunlun (BL 60) for short scanty urine.

Method: Apphy filiform needles with reducing method. Retain the needles for 20 ~ 30 minutes manipulating them two to three times. Moxibustion can be applied for 10 ~ 15 minutes if cold-damp is prevalent. Pricking with a three-edged needle at Bafeng (Extra) can be applied for beriberi due to severe damp-heat.

2) Ear acupuncture

Prescription: Toe, Ankle, Knee, Spleen, Ear-Shenmen.

Method: Apply filiform needles with moderate stimulation and retain the needles for 20 minutes. Auricular taping is also applicable.

2. Dry Beriberi

(1) *Main manifestation*

Weakness of both feet, numbness and pain of the legs and knees with occasional tendon spasm, limited movement, gradual atrophy of foot muscles or even severe atrophy of foot muscles, constipation, yellow urinary discharge, slightly red tongue proper, thin white tongue coating or slightly coated tongue, and rapid thready pulse.

(2) *Therapeutic principle*

Nourish Yin and blood.

(3) *Treatment*

1) Body acupuncture

Prescription: Jiexi (ST 41), Yinshi (ST 33), Fuliu (KI 7), Zhaohai (KI 6), Xuehai (SP 10), Xuanzhong (GB 39).

Supplementary points: Add Chengshan (BL 57) for muscular spasm, Weizhong (BL 40) for lumbar pain, Xiyan (EX-LE 5) and Fengshi (GB 31) for swollen knee.

Method: Apply filiform needles with reinforcing method. Retain the needles for 20 minutes manipulating them one to two times.

2) Ear acupuncture

Prescription: Toe, Ankle, Knee, Stomach, Spleen, Lung, Ear-shenmen.

Method: Apply filiform needles with moderate stimulation and retain the needles for 20 minutes. Auricular Aaping is also applicable.

3. Beriberi Affecting the Heart

(1) *Main manifestation*

Swelling, pain or numbness with atrophy and weakness during walking, sudden onset of shortness of breath, palpitation, nausea, vomiting, suffocating sensation in the chest, restlessness and even loss of consciousness in severe cases, disorderly speech, purplish lips, rapid thready pulse of a feeble nature

(2) *Theurapeutic principle*

Promote the function of lung in descending and dispersing and clear away damp-heat from the heart.

(3) *Treatment*

1) Body acupuncture

Prescription: Chize (LU 5), Tanzhong (RN 17), Laogong (PC 8), Shenmen (HT 7), Zusanli (ST 36), Yongquan (KI 1).

Supplementary points: Add Renzhong (DU 26) for loss of conciousness, Qihai (RN 6) and Guanyuan (RN 4) for collapse of yang Qi.

Method: Apply filiform needles with even movement. Retain the needles for 15~20 minutes manipulating them one to two times.

2) Ear acupuncture

Prescription: Heart, Kidney, Toe, Ankle, Knee, Ear-shenmen.

Method: Apply filiform needles with mild stimulation and retain the needles for 20 minutes. Auricular taping is olso applicable.

鼓　　胀

鼓胀是因腹部胀大如鼓而得名。以腹部胀大，皮色苍黄，甚则腹皮青筋暴露，四肢不肿或微肿为特征。临床上根据证候表现不同，一般分为气鼓、水鼓、血鼓三类。本证可见于现代医学多种疾病的晚期，如肝硬化、结核性腹膜炎、腹腔内肿瘤等疾病发生腹水，而出现类似鼓胀的证候时，均可参照本篇辨证治疗。

1. 气鼓

（1）主证　腹部膨隆，肿胀，肤色不变，按之陷而即起，恼怒后胀势更剧，嗳噫或转矢气则舒，腹部叩之如鼓，脘胁痞满，小便短黄，大便不爽或秘结，苔薄白，脉弦细。

（2）治则　疏肝理气，和中消胀。

（3）治法

1）体针

处方　膻中，中脘，气海，足三里，天枢，太冲。

配穴　便秘加腹结；胁痛加阳陵泉，支沟；尿黄加阴陵泉。

操作　毫针刺，用泻法。留针20~30分钟，间歇行针2~3次。

2）耳针

处方　肝，胃，大肠，小肠，皮质下。

操作　毫针中等强度刺激，留针15~20分钟；亦可用耳穴贴敷。

2. 水鼓

（1）主证　腹部胀大如蛙腹，皮肤光亮，按之凹陷，移时不起，或有下肢水肿，脘腹肿胀，面色滞黄，怯寒，神倦，小便不利，大便溏薄，苔白腻，脉沉缓。

（2）治则　健脾益肾，调气行水。

（3）治法

1）体针

处方 脾俞，肾俞，水分，复溜，公孙。

配穴 大便溏薄加天枢，上巨墟；怯寒灸命门，气海。

操作 毫针刺，补泻兼施，脾俞、肾虚多用补法，余穴用泻法。留针20～30分钟，间歇行针2～3次。

2) 耳针

处方 脾，肾，三焦，大肠，小肠，皮质下。

操作 毫针中等强度刺激，留针15～20分钟；亦可采用耳穴贴敷。

3) 艾灸

处方 水分，脾俞。

操作 采用温和灸或温针灸治疗10～20分钟。

3. 血鼓

(1) 主证 脘腹胀大坚硬，脐周青筋暴露，胁下肿块，痛如针刺，皮肤甲错，面色黄滞晦暗，或见赤丝缕缕，头颈胸臂可出现血痣、潮热，口干不欲引饮，大便或见黑色，舌质紫暗，或有瘀斑，脉细弦或涩。

(2) 治则 活血化瘀，行气利水。

(3) 治法

1) 体针

处方 期门，章门，石门，三阴交。

配穴 肿胀加梁门；黄疸加阳纲；潮热加太溪，膏肓。

操作 毫针刺，用泻法。留针20～30分钟，间歇行针3～4次。

2) 耳针

处方 肝，肾，胰，大肠，小肠，三焦，艇中。

操作 毫针刺，每次选4～5穴。中等强度刺激，留针15～20分钟；亦可采用耳穴贴敷。

Drum Belly

Drum belly is a term applied in traditional Chinese medicine referring to abnormal abdominal distention like a drum hence the name. It is characterized by distended abdomen and yellowish skin. There are visible green vessels on the abdomen with normal limbs or slightly swollen limbs. According to the different clinical manifestations, drum belly is generally divided into Qi distention, water distention and blood distention. The condition described here can be seen in the advanced stage of various chronic disease in terms of modern medicine such as hepatocirrhosis, tubercular peritonitis, and abdominal tumor. The differentiation and treatment in this section can be referred to for similar symptoms and signs appearing in the above conditions.

1. Qi distention

(1) *Main manifestation*

Abdominal and epigastric fullness and distention, unchanged abdominal skin colour, depression upon pressure but soon rebounding when the hand is removed, aggravation of distention during emotional upset, alleviation by belching, sighing or passing gas, percussing sound on the abdomen, fullness sensation in the epigastric and hypochondriac regions, short yellow urine, dry stools or constipation, thin white tongue coating, and wiry thready pulse.

(2) *Therapeutic principle*

Soothe the liver Qi, pacify the stomach and relieve distention.

(3) *Treatment*

1) Body acupuncture

Prescription: Tanzhong (RN 17), Zhongwan (RN 12), Qihai (RN 6), Zusanli (ST 36), Tianshu (ST 25), Taichong (LR 3).

Supplementary points: Add Fujie (SP 14) for constipation, Zhigou (SJ 6) and Yanlingquan (SP 34) for hypochondriac pain, and Yinlingquan (SP 9) for yellow urine.

Method: Apply filiform needles with reducing method. Retain the needles for 20~30 minutes manipulating them two to three times.

2) Ear acupuncture

Prescription: Liver, Stomach, Large Intestine, Small Intestine, Subcortex.

Method: Apply filiform needles with moderate stimulation and retain the needles for 15~20 minutes. Auricular taping is also applicable.

2. Water Distention

(1) *Main manifestation*

Abdominal distention like the belly of a frog, lustrous abdominal colour, depression that is slow to rebound, occasional edema in the lower limbs, distention in epigastric and abdominal areas, pallor complexion, aversion to cold, lassitude, difficult urination, loose stools, white greasy tongue coating, and deep slow pulse.

(2) *Therapeutic principle*

Strengthen the spleen and tonify the kidney, promote Qi circulation and enhance water discharge.

(3) *Treatment*

1) Body acupuncture

Prescription: Pishu (BL 20), Shenshu (BL 23), Shuifen (RN 9), Fuliu (KI 7), Gongsun (SP 4).

Supplementary points: Add Tianshu (ST 25) and Shangjuxu (ST 37) for loose stools, and Mingmen (DU 4) and Qihai (RN 6) for aversion to cold.

Method: Apply filiform needles with both reinforcing and reducing method. Pishu (BL 20) and Shenshu (BL 23) are applied with reinforcing method. The rest of the points are applied with reducing method. Retain the needles for 20~30 minutes manipulating them two to three times.

2) Ear acupuncture

Prescription: Spleen, Kidney, Sanjiao, Large Intestine, Small Intestine, Subcortex.

Method: Apply filiform needles with moderate stimulation and retain the needles for 15～20 minutes. Auricular taping is also applicable.

3) Moxibustion

Prescription: Shuifen (RN 9), Pishu (BL 20).

Method: Apply mild-warming moxibustion or moxibustion with warming needle to the points for 10～20 minutes.

3. Blood Distention

(1) *Main manifestation*

Distention in the abdomen and epigastrium with hard abdominal wall, visible vessels surrounding the umbilicus, mass in the hypochondriac region with pricky pain, scaled skin, dim complexion or dark pallor complexion with red threads, bloody moles appearing on the neck, chest and arms, tidal fever, dry mouth with no desire for drinks, occasional black stools, purplish dark tongue proper with possible stagnant spots, hesitant or wiry thready pulse.

(2) *Therapeutic principle*

Activate blood, resolve stasis, promote Qi circulation and water discharge.

(3) *Treatment*

1) Body acupuncture

Prescription: Qimen (LR 14),

Zhangmen (LR 13), Shimen (RN 5), Sanyinjiao (SP 6).

Supplementary points: Add Liangmen (ST 21) for distention, Yanggang (BL 48) for jaundice, and Taixi (KI 3) and Gaohuangshu (BL 43) for tidal fever.

Method: Apply filiform needles with reducing method. Retain the needles for 20～30 minutes manipulating them three to four times.

2) Ear acupuncture

Prescription: Liver, Kidney, Pancreas, Large Intestine, Small Intestine, Sanjiao, Auricular Concha.

Method: Apply filiform needles with moderate stimulation at 4～5 points each time and retain the needles for 15～20 minutes. Auricular taping is also applicable.

水　肿

水肿是指人体水液潴留，泛溢肌肤，引起头面、眼睑、四肢、腹部，甚至全身水肿而言。根据病因及临床证候可分为阳水与阴水两类。本病包括现代医学的急慢性肾炎，充血性心力衰竭，内分泌失调以及营养障碍等疾病所出现的水肿。

1. 阳水

（1）主证　多为急性发作，初起面目浮肿，继则四肢及全身皆肿，按之凹陷恢复较快，皮肤光泽，阴囊肿亮，小便不利，或伴有胸中烦闷，咳嗽气粗，肢体酸楚，舌苔白滑而润，脉浮滑或浮数。

（2）治则　疏风清热，宣肺利水。

（3）治法

1）体针

处方　肺俞，三焦俞，偏历，阴陵泉，外关，合谷。

操作　毫针刺，用泻法。留针15～20分钟，间歇行针2～3次。

2）耳针

处方　肺，膀胱，皮质下，肝。

操作　毫针中等强度刺激，留针20分钟。亦可采用耳穴贴敷。

2．阴水

（1）主证　发病多渐起，初起足跗微肿，继则面、腹各部均渐浮肿，腰以下为甚，按之凹陷恢复较慢，皮肤晦暗，小便短少。兼有脘痞便溏，神疲怯寒，四肢倦怠，舌质淡，苔白，脉沉细或迟。

（2）治则　健脾温肾，助阳利水。

（3）治法

1）体针

处方　脾俞，肾俞，水分，气海，太溪，足三里。

配穴　脘痞加中脘；便溏加天枢。

操作　毫针刺，用泻法或平补平泻法。留针15～30分钟，间歇行针2～3次。

2）耳针

处方　肝，脾，肾，肺，膀胱，皮质下。

操作　毫针中等强度刺激；留针

20分钟；亦可用耳穴贴敷。

3）艾灸

处方　气海，脾俞，肾俞，足三里。

操作　采用温和灸或回旋灸治疗15～20分钟，每天1次。

Edema

Edema refers to retention of fluid in the body resulting in puffiness of the head, face, eyelids, limbs, abdomen and even the general body. It can be divided into Yang edema and Yin edema in terms of etiology and pathogenesis. The condition elaborated here includes edema caused by acute and chronic nephritis, congestive heart failure, endocrine disorder and dystrophy in modern medicine.

1. Yang Edema

(1) *Main manifestation*

It is acute in nature, characterized by incipient puffiness of the face, eyelids, and limbs affecting the general body, skin lustre, swelling of the scrotum, and dysuria. Depressions appearing upon hand pressure may rebound quickly. The accompanying symptoms and signs include fullness sensation in the chest, cough, uneven breathing, soreness and aching of the limbs, white slippery tongue coating with moisture, superficial slippery or superficial rapid pulse.

(2) *Therapeutic principle*

Eliminate wind, clear up heat, disperse lung and promote water metabolism.

(3) *Treatment*

1) Body acupuncture

Prescription: Feishu (BL 13), Sanjiaoshu (BL 22), Pianli (LI 6), Yinlingquan (SP 9), Waiguan (SJ 5), Hegu (LI 4).

Method: Apply filiform needles with reducing method. Retain the needles for 15~20 minutes manipulating them two to three times.

2) Ear acupuncture

Prescription: Lung, Urinary bladder, Subcortex, Liver.

Method: Apply filiform needles with moderate stimulation and retain the needles for 20 minutes. Auricular taping is also applicable.

2. Yin Edema

(1) *Main manifestation*

It is characterized by a slow onset, light swelling of the face in the incipient stage which then spreads to the abdomen and the whole body, especially the areas below the waist. Depressions appearing upon hand pressure rebound slowly. The acompanying symptoms and signs include scant urine, epigastric distention, loose stools, lassitude, aversion to cold, weak limbs, pale tongue proper with white coating, deep thready or deep slow pulse.

(2) *Therapeutic principle*

Tonify the spleen and warm up the kidney to strengthen the yang Qi in steaming water.

(3) *Treatment*

1) Body acupuncture

Prescription: Pishu (BL 20), Shenshu (BL 23), Shuifen (RN 9), Qihai (RN 6), Taixi (KI 3), Zusanli (ST 36).

Supplementary points: Add Zhongwan (RN 12) for epigastric distention, and Tianshu (ST 25) for loose stools.

Method: Apply filiform needles with reinforcing or even movement method. Retain the needles for 15~30 minutes manipulating them two to three times.

2) Ear acupuncture

Prescription: Liver, Spleen, Kidney, Lung, Urinary Bladder, Subcortex.

Method: Apply filiform needles with moderate stimulation and retain the needles for 20 minutes. Auricular taping is also applicable.

3) Moxibustion

Prescription: Qihai (RN 6), Pishu (BL 20), Shenshu (BL 23), Zusanli (ST 36).

Method: Apply mild-warming moxibustion or rounding moxibustion for 15~20 minutes once a day.

淋 证

淋证是以小便频急，淋漓不尽，

尿道涩痛，小腹拘急，痛引脐中为特征的病症。根据病机和症状的不同，临床一般分为热淋、石淋、血淋、气淋、膏淋等类型。本病常见于现代医学中的泌尿系统疾病，如肾盂肾炎，膀胱炎，肾结核，泌尿系统结石，急慢性前列腺炎，膀胱癌以及乳糜尿等病症。

1. 辨证

（1）热淋

主证　起病多急，小腹频数，点滴而下，尿色黄赤，灼热刺痛，急迫不爽，痛引脐中，或伴腰痛拒按，或有恶寒发热，口苦，便秘，舌质红，苔黄腻，脉濡数。

（2）石淋

主证　尿中时夹沙石，小便滞涩不畅，或尿不能卒出，窘迫难忍，痛引少腹，或尿时中断，或腰痛如绞，牵引少腹，连及外阴，尿中带血，苔薄白或黄，脉弦或数。

（3）血淋

主证　尿色红赤，或夹紫暗血块，溲频短急，灼热痛剧，滞涩不利，甚则尿道满急疼痛，牵引脐腹，舌尖红，苔薄黄，脉数有力。

（4）气淋

主证　少腹及会阴部胀痛不适，排尿乏力，小便断续，甚则点滴而下，尿频溲清，少气懒言，腰酸神疲，舌淡，苔薄白，脉细弱。

（5）膏淋

主证　小便混浊不清，呈乳糜色，置之沉淀如絮状，上有浮油如脂，或夹凝块，或混血液，尿时不畅，灼热疼痛，或腰酸膝软，头昏无力，舌质红，苔白微腻，脉濡数或细数。

2. 治则

调理膀胱气机，清热利尿通淋。

3. 治法

（1）体针

处方　膀胱俞，中极，阴陵泉，行间，太溪。

配穴　热淋加合谷，外关；石淋加委阳，然谷；血淋加血海，三阴交；气淋加气海，水道；膏淋加气海俞，肾俞，百会。

操作　毫针刺，用泻法或平补平泻法，留针15～30分钟，间歇行针2～3次。

（2）耳针

处方　膀胱，肾，交感，枕，肾上腺，内分泌。

操作　毫针刺，每次选3～4穴，强刺激，留针20～30分钟；亦可用耳穴贴敷。

Lin Syndrome

Lin syndrome refers to a condition characterized by frequent, incontinent urinary discharge with pain, spasm of the lower abdomen, and umbilical pain. According to the different etiology and pathogenesis in the clinic, it is divided into five types altogether. They include heat Lin, stone Lin, blood Lin, Qi Lin and turbid Lin syndromes. Lin syndrome is mainly seen in some urinary system diseases with abnormal stimulation or infections of the urethra, such as pyelonephritis, cystitis, renal tuberculosis, stones in the urinary bladder, and chylous urine.

1. Differentiation

(1) *Heat Lin*

Main manifestation

Rapid onset of urinary dripping, frequent urination, dark yellow urine with feverish and painful sensation, hasty urinary discharge, pain involving the umbilicus, or fever with aversion to cold, bitter taste in the mouth, red tongue proper with yellow greasy tongue coating and rapid soft pulse.

(2) *Stone Lin*

Main manifestation

Difficult urination with occasional sandy substance in the urine, dysuria with pain involving the lower abdomen difficult to tolerate, or on and off urinary discharge with stabbing lumbar pain that involves both the lower abdomen and external genitalia, occasional bloody urine, thin white or yellow tongue coating, wiry or rapid pulse.

(3) *Blood Lin*

Main manifestation

Short reddish urine or with dark purplish clots, severe burning pain, difficulty in discharging the urine, distending pain in the urethra in severe cases which involves the umbilicus, red tongue tip, thin yellow tongue coating, rapid forceful pulse.

(4) *Qi Lin*

Main manifestation

Distending pain in the lower abdomen and pubic region, weakness in discharge of urine, frequent dripping of clear urine, reluctant speech, poor spirit, lumbar soreness, pale tongue with thin white coating, and weak thready pulse.

(5) *Turbid Lin*

Main manifestation

Turbid milky urine that soon sediments with catkin substance at the bottom, fatty oily substance at the surface of the urine container with coagulation, bloody difficult urinary discharge with feverish pain, soreness in the lumbar region and knees, dizziness, lassitude, red tongue proper, slightly white greasy coating, soft rapid or rapid thready pulse.

2. Therapeutic principle

Regulate the Qi mechanism of the urinary bladder, eliminate heat and promote urinary discharge

3. Treatment

(1) *Body acupuncture*

Prescription: Pangguangshu (BL 28), Zhongji (RN 3), Yinlingquan (SP 9), Xingjian (LR 2), Taixi (KI 3).

Supplementary points: Add Hegu (LI 4) and Waiguan (SJ 5) for heat Lin, Weiyang (BL 39) and Rangu (KI 2) for stone Lin, Xuehai (SP 10) and Sanyinjiao (SP 6) for blood Lin, Qihai (RN 6) and Shuidao (ST 28) for Qi Lin, Qihai (RN 6), Shenshu (BL 23) and Baihui (DU 20) for turbid Lin.

Method: Apply filiform needles with reducing or even movement. Retain the needles for 15～30 minutes manipulating them two to three times.

(2) *Ear acupuncture*

Prescription: Urinary Bladder, Kidney, Sympathetic, Occipital Bone, Adrenal Gland, Endocrine.

Method: Apply filiform needles at three to four points with strong stimulation and retain the needles for 20～30 minutes. Auricular taping is also applicable.

遗　精

遗精是指不因性交而精液常自行泄出的病症。有梦而遗者名为梦遗，无梦而遗精，甚至清醒时精液流出者名为滑精。一般成年未婚男子或婚后久旷者偶有遗精，属生理现象，不能作为病态。现代医学的前列腺炎，神经衰弱，精囊炎以及某些病症引起的

遗精，一般可参考本节内容辨证治疗。

1. 阴虚火旺

（1）主证　梦泄时作，恶热烦躁，手足心热，面赤，舌边尖红，脉细数。

（2）治则　清心降火，益肾涩精。

（3）治法

1) 体针

处方　心俞，神门，肾俞，太溪，关元，志室。

配穴　体倦乏力，精神不振加足三里；头晕加百会；小便赤痛，淋漓遗精者加阴陵泉，三阴交。

操作　毫针刺，补泻兼施，心俞，神门用泻法，余穴用补法。留针20～30分钟，间歇行针2～3次。

2) 耳针

处方　精宫，内分泌，神门，心，肾。

操作　毫针轻刺激，留针20分钟；亦可用耳穴贴敷。

2. 肾虚不固

（1）主证　遗精频作，无梦居多，甚至滑精，伴有腰酸腿软，头晕耳鸣，舌质淡，苔白，脉沉弱。

（2）治则　补益肾气，固涩精关。

（3）治法

1) 体针

处方　肾俞，三阴交，关元，气海，太溪，足三里。

操作　毫针刺，用补法，留针

20～30 分钟，间歇行针 2～3 次；亦可针灸并用。

2）耳针

处方　精宫，内分泌，神门，脾，心，肾，肝。

操作　毫针轻刺激，留针 20 分钟；亦可采用耳穴贴敷。

Seminal Emission

Seminal emission refers to ejaculation in the male without sexual intercourse. Specially, nocturnal emission which happens during dreams in sleep. Spermatorrhea happens when the patient has no dreams during sleep. However, occasional seminal emission in adult males, married or unmarried, is not considered as a disease condition. For seminal emission caused by prostatitis, neurasthenia, seminal vesiculitis and other diseases in modern medicine, the differentiation and treatment in this section can be referred to.

1. **Hyperactivity of Fire due to Yin Deficiency**

(1) *Main manifestation*

Frequent emission, aversion to heat, restlessness, feverish sensation in palms and soles, flushed face, red margin and tip of the tongue, thready and rapid pulse.

(2) *Therapeutic principle*

Sedate heart fire, nourish Yin and consolidate sperm.

(3) *Treatment*

1) Body acupuncture

Prescription: Xinshu (BL 15), Shenmen (HT 7), Shenshu (BL 23), Taixi (KI 3), Guanyuan (RN 4), Zhishi (BL 52).

Supplementary points: Add Zusanli (ST 36) for lassitude and poor spirit, Baihui (DU 20) for dizziness, Yinlingquan (SP 9) and Sanyinjiao (SP 6) for short scanty or dripping of urine.

Method: Apply filiform needle with both reinforcing and reducing methods. Xinshu and Shenmen (HT 7) are used with reducing method and the rest of the points with reinforcing method. Retain the needles for 20～30 minutes manipulating them two to three times.

2) Ear acupuncture

Prescription: Sperm palace, Endocrine, Ear-shenmen, Heart, Kidney.

Method: Apply filiform needles with mild stimulation and retain the needles for 20 minutes. Auricular taping is also applicable.

2. **Unconsolidation due to Kidney Deficiency**

(1) *Main manifestation*

Frequent seminal emission which takes place in most cases when the patient is dreamless, spermatorrhea, accompanied with lassitude in the loins and legs, dizziness, tinnitus, pale tongue with white fur, deep and weak pulse.

(2) *Therapeutic* principle

Tonify the kidney Qi and regain consolidation over the sperm gate.

(3) *Treatment*

1) Body acupuncture

Prescription: Shenshu (BL 23), Sanyinjiao (SP 6), Guanyuan (RN 4), Qihai (RN 6), Taixi (KI 3), Zusanli (ST 36).

Method: Apply filiform needles with reinforcing method. Retain the needles for 20～30 minutes manipulating them two to three times. Moxibustion can be combined with acupuncture treatment.

2) Ear acupuncture

Prescription: Sperm Palace, Endocrine, Ear-shenmen, Spleen, Heart, Kidney, Liver.

Method: Apply filiform needles with mild stimulation and retain the needles for 20 minutes. Auricular taping is also applicable.

阳　痿

阳痿是指男子阴茎痿弱不起，临房时举而不坚或坚而不久的一种病症。现代医学的性神经衰弱和某些慢性疾病表现以阳痿为主证者，可参考本篇内容辨证治疗。

1. 湿热下注

(1) 主证　阴茎痿软不能勃起，阴囊潮湿臊臭，兼见口苦或渴，小便热赤，下肢酸困，舌苔腻，脉濡数。

(2) 治则　清利湿热。

(3) 治法

1) 体针

处方　中极，三阴交，阴陵泉，行间，足三里。

操作　毫针刺，用泻法。留针15～20分钟，间歇行针2～3次。

2) 耳针

处方　精宫，外生殖器，睾丸，内分泌，肝。

操作　毫针中等强度刺激，留针20分钟；亦可采用耳穴贴敷。

3) 电针

处方　第1组：次髎，然谷。

第2组：关元，三阴交。

操作　2组可交替使用，用低频脉冲电流，每次通电3～5分钟，每日1～2次，6～10次为1疗程。

2. 心脾亏虚

(1) 主证　阴茎痿软，或勃起不坚，伴见心悸气短，神疲乏力，面色萎黄，胃纳不佳，舌质淡，脉细弱。

(2) 治则　补益心脾。

(3) 治法

1) 体针

处方　关元，三阴交，蠡沟，神门。

操作　毫针刺，用补法。留针20～30分钟，间歇行针1～2次。

2) 耳针

处方　精宫，外生殖器，睾丸，内分泌，心，脾。

操作　毫针轻刺激，留针 20～30 分钟。亦可采用耳穴贴敷。

3. 命门火衰

（1）主证　阴茎痿弱不举，或举而不坚，面色㿠白，形寒肢冷，头晕目眩，精神不振，腰腿酸软，小便频数，舌淡苔白，脉沉细。如兼心脾损伤者，则有心悸胆怯，失眠等。

（2）治则　补肾壮阳。

（3）治法

1）体针

处方　肾俞，命门，关元，三阴交，太溪。

配穴　心脾亏损加心俞，大陵；头晕目眩加百会，足三里。

操作　毫针刺，用补法。针天元时针尖向阴部方向斜刺，使针感放射至前阴部。留针 20～30 分钟，间歇行针 2～3 次。

2）耳针

处方　精宫，外生殖器，肾，睾丸，内分泌，皮质下。

操作　毫针中等强度刺激，留针20 分钟。亦可采用耳穴贴敷。

3）艾灸

处方　关元，肾俞，命门。

操作　采用温和灸或回旋灸治疗15～20 分钟；亦可采用温针灸。

Impotence

Impotence refers to weakness of the penis erecting during sexual intercourse. It is characterized by poor erecting or erection that lasts only for seconds. For impotence as a main symptom due to sexual neurasthenia or some other chormic diseases, the differentiation and treatment in this section can be referred to.

1. Downward Flowing Damp-heat

（1）*Main manifestation*
Inability of the penis to erect and wet scrotum with foul smell. It may be accompanied by bitter taste in the mouth, thirst, short scanty urine, soreness in the lower limbs, greasy tongue coating, and rapid soft pulse.

（2）*Therapeutic principle*
Eliminate damp-heat.

（3）*Treatment*

1）Body acupuncture

Prescription: Zhongji（RN 3），Sanyinjiao（SP 6），Yinlingquan（SP 9），Xingjian（LR 2），Zusanli（ST 36）.

Method: Apply filiform needles with reducing method. Retain the needles for 15～20 minutes manipulating them two to three times.

2）Ear acupuncture

Prescription: Sperm palace, External genitalia, Testis, Endocrine, Liver.

Method: Apply filiform needles with moderate stimulation and retain the needles for 20 minutes. Auricular taping is also applicable.

3) Electroacupuncture

Prescription:

Group I : Ciliao (BL 32), Rangu (KI 2).

Group II: Guanyuan (RN 4), Sanyinjiao (SP 6).

Method: The two groups may be used alternatively. Low-frequency pulse current is adopted. Electrify the points for 3 ~ 5 minutes each treatment, 1~2 treatments a day. 6~10 treatments make up a course.

2. Deficiency of Heart and Spleen

(1) *Main manifestation*

Failure of the penis in erection, weak erection, accompanied with palpitation, shortness of breath, listlessness, sallow complexion, loss of appetite, pale tongue, thin and weak pulse.

(2) *Therapeutic principle*

Supplement the heart and spleen.

(3) *Treatment*

1) Body acupuncture

Prescription: Guanyuan (RN 4), Sanyinjiao (SP 6), Ligou (LI 5), Shenmen (HT 7).

Method: Apply filiform needles with reinforcing method. Retain the needles for 20 ~ 30 minutes manipulating them one to two times.

2) Ear acupuncture

Prescription: Seminal Palace, External Genitalia, Testis, Endocrine, Heart, Spleen.

Method: Apply filiform needles with mild stimulation and retain the needles for 20 ~ 30 minutes. Auricular taping is also applicable.

3) Moxibustion

Prescription: Guanyuan (RN 4), Shenshu (BL 23).

Method: Apply mild-warming moxibustion or rounding moxibustion for 10~20 minutes once a day.

3. Life Gate Fire Decline

(1) *Main manifestation*

Poor erecting of penis or erection that lasts only for seconds, pallor complexion, cold limbs, dizziness, blurring of vision, poor spirit, soreness in the lumbar region and knee joints, frequent urination, pale tongue proper with white coating, and deep thready pulse. There will also be palpitation and insomma if the impairment of heart and spleen is involved.

(2) *Therapeutic principle*

Reinforce kidney Yang and warm up the Lower Jiao.

(3) *Treatment*

1) Body acupuncture

Prescription: Shenshu (BL 23), Mingmen (DU 4), Guanyuan (RN 4), Sanyinjiao (SP 6), Taixi (KI 3).

Supplementary points: Add Xinshu

(BL 15), Daling (PC 7) for deficiency of both heart and spleen, Baihui (DU 20) and Zusanli (ST 36) for dizziness and blurring of vision.

Method: Apply filiform needles with reinforcing method. Retain the needles for 20～30 minutes manipulating them two to three times. Direct the needle towards the pubic region in order to let the needling sensation radiate to the penis when Guanyuan (RN 4) is needled.

2) Ear acupuncture

Prescription: Sperm Palace, External Genitalia, Kidney, Testis, Endocrine, Subcortex.

Method: Apply filiform needles with moderate stimulation and retain the needles for 20 minutes. Auricular taping is also applicable.

3) Moxibustion

Prescription: Guanyuan (RN 4), Shenshu (BL 23), Mingmen (DU 4).

Method: Apply mild-warming moxibustion or rounding moxibustion for 15～20 minutes. Moxibustion with warming needle is also applicable.

遗　尿

遗尿是指 3 周岁以上的儿童反复出现不随意的排尿,多在睡眠中发生,醒后方觉,故又称尿床。由于 3 岁以下儿童脑髓未充,正常的排尿习惯尚未形成,亦可发生遗尿,不属病态。中医认为,本证多因肾阳不足,或病后脾肺两虚,气虚失摄所致。常见于现代医学所指的儿童或成人神经功能紊乱和泌尿系统病变所致的小便失禁。

1. 肾阳不足

(1) 主证　睡中遗尿,形体消瘦,神疲畏冷,面色㿠白,腰痛膝软,舌质淡,脉沉迟无力。

(2) 治则　温补肾阳。

(3) 治法

1) 体针

处方　肾俞,膀胱俞,关元,气海,太溪,中极,三阴交。

操作　毫针刺,用补法。留针20～30分钟,间隔行针1～2次。

2) 耳针

处方　肾,膀胱,尿道,皮质下,交感。

操作　毫针轻刺激,留针20分钟,亦可采用耳穴贴敷。

3) 艾灸

处方　肾俞,膀胱俞,关元,三阴交。

操作　采用温和灸或温针灸治疗10～15分钟,每天1次。

2. 脾肺气虚

(1) 主证　遗尿,面色㿠白,呼吸气短,精神倦怠,四肢乏力,食欲不振,大便稀溏,舌质淡,脉缓或沉细。

(2) 治则　补益脾肺。

(3) 治法

1）体针

处方　脾俞，肺俞，太渊，足三里，气海，三阴交。

操作　毫针刺，用补法。留针20～30分钟，间歇行针1～2次。

2）耳针

处方　脾，肺，肾，膀胱，尿道，皮质下，交感。

操作　毫针轻刺激，留针20分钟；亦可用耳穴贴敷。

3）艾灸

处方　脾俞,肺俞,足三里,气海。

操作　采用温和灸或温针灸治疗10～15分钟，每天1次。

Enuresis

Enuresis refers to that involuntary passage of urine in children over 3 occurs especially during sleeping at night. The victim is not aware of it until he or she is awake. So it is also called bedwetting. It may occur in children under 3 resulting from insufficiency of the cerebrospinal cord and unforming of regular passage of urine. This is not considered as an illness. Traditional Chinese medicine holds that the major causes of the disease are deficiency of kidney Yang, insufficiency of both the spleen and lung after illness, and loss of retaining power due to deficiency of Qi. It is often seen in children and adults with neural dysfunction and pathological changes of the urinary system in terms of modern medicine.

1. Deficiency of Kidney Yang

（1）*Main manifestation*

Enuresis during sleep, emaciation, lassitude, cold limbs, pallor complexion, soreness and weakness of the lumbar region and knees, pale tongue proper, and deep slow weak pulse.

（2）*Therapeutic principle*

Warm up the kidney Yang.

（3）*Treatment*

1) Body acupuncture

Prescription：Shenshu（BL 23）, Pangguanshu（BL 28）, Guanyuan（RN 4）, Qihai（RN 6）, Taixi（KI 3）, Zhongji（RN 3）, Sanyinjiao（SP 6）.

Method：Apply filiform needles with reinforcing method. Retain the needles for 20～30 minutes manipulating them one to two times.

2) Ear acupuncture

Prescription Kidney, Urinary bladder, Urethra, Subcortex, Sympathetic.

Method：Apply filiform needles with mild stimulation and retain the needles for 20 minutes. Auricular taping is also applicable.

3) Moxibustion

Prescription：Shenshu（BL 23）, Pangguangshu（BL 28）, Guanyuan（RN 4）, Sanyinjiao（SP 6）.

Method：Use mild-warming moxibustion or moxibustion with warming needle for 10~15 minutes once a day.

2. Qi Defeciency of the Lung and Kidney

(1) *Main manifestation*

Enuresis, pallor complexion, shortness of breath, lassitude, weakness of the four limbs, poor appetite, loose stools, pale tongue proper, and slow or deep thready pulse.

(2) *Therapeutic principle*

Reinforce spleen and lung.

(3) *Treatment*

1) Body acupuncture

Prescription: Pishu (BL 20), Feishu (BL 13), Taiyuan (LU 9), Zusanli (ST 36), Qihai (RN 6), Sanyinjiao (SP 6).

Method: Apply filiform needles with reinforcing method. Retain the needles for 20 ~ 30 minutes manipulating then one to two times.

2) Ear acupuncture

Prescription: Spleen, Lung, Kidney, Urinary bladder, Urethra, Subcortex, Sympathetic.

Method: Apply filiform needles with mild stimulation and retain the needles for 20 minutes. Auricular taping is also applicable.

3) Moxibustion

Prescription: Pishu (BL 20), Feishu (BL 13), Zusanli (ST 36),

Qihai (RN 6).

Method: Apply mild-warming moxibustion or moxibustion with warming needle for 10~15 minutes once a day.

小便失禁

小便失禁是指在清醒状态下不能控制排尿，而尿液自行排出的病症。多见于老人、妇女及病后。常见于现代医学的神经功能紊乱，泌尿系统慢性疾患和脑血管意外、脊髓损伤等引起的小便失控。

1. 肾阳虚衰

（1）主证 小便失禁，尿意频频，尿后余沥，形体消瘦，神疲肢冷，面色㿠白，腰痛肢软，舌质淡，脉沉迟无力。

（2）治则 温补肾阳。

（3）治法

1) 体针

处方 肾俞，膀胱俞，关元，气海，中极，太溪，三阴交。

操作 毫针刺，用补法。留针20~30分钟，间隔行针1~2次。

2) 耳针

处方 膀胱，尿道，皮质下，交感，肾。

操作 毫针轻刺激，留针20分钟。

3) 艾灸

处方 肾虚，膀胱俞，关元，三阴交。

操作 采用温和灸或回旋灸治疗15~20分钟，每天1次。

2. 肺脾气虚

（1）主证　小便失禁，面色㿠白，呼吸气短，神疲乏力，食欲不振，大便稀溏，舌质淡，脉缓或沉细。

（2）治则　补益脾肺。

（3）治法

1）体针

处方　脾俞，肺俞，太渊，足三里，气海，三阴交。

操作　毫针刺，用补法。留针20～30分钟，间歇行针1～2次。

2）耳针

处方　肺，脾，肾，膀胱，尿道，皮质下，交感。

操作　毫针轻刺激，留针15分钟。

3）艾灸

处方　肺俞,脾俞,足三里,气海。

操作　采用温和灸或回旋灸治疗15～20分钟，每天1次。

3. 湿热下注

（1）主证　小便失禁，小便频数灼热，小便短少而臭，或滴涩淋漓，腰酸低热，苔薄腻，脉细数。

（2）治则　清利湿热。

（3）治法

1）体针

处方　膀胱俞，中极，阴陵泉，足通谷，委阳，三阴交。

操作　毫针刺，用泻法。留针15～20分钟，间歇行针2～3次。

2）耳针

处方　膀胱，尿道，皮质下，交感，肾，脾。

操作　毫针中等强度刺激，留针15～20分钟；亦可采用耳穴贴敷。

4. 下焦蓄血

（1）主证　小便淋漓失禁，腹满胀痛，可触及包块，舌质紫暗，苔薄，脉涩或细数。

（2）治则　活血化瘀。

（3）治法

1）体针

处方　中极，次髎，三阴交，气海，膈俞。

操作　毫针刺，用泻法。留针20～30分钟，间歇行针3～4次。

2）耳针

处方　膀胱，尿道，皮质下，交感，肾。

操作　毫针轻刺激，留针15分钟；亦可采用耳穴贴敷。

Urinary Incontinence

Urinary incontinence refers to involuntary urinary discharge when the patient is conscious of it. It is mostly seen in aged patients, women patients or patients who survived some morbid condition. In modern medicine, it is often seen in urinary incontinence caused by disorder of nervous function, chronic diseases of the urinary system as well as cerebrovascular accident, cerebritis and spinal cord injury.

1. Deficiency of Kidney Yang

(1) *Main manifestation*

Urinary incontinence or frequent urination with dripping of urine, emaciation, lassitude, cold limbs, pallor complexion, soreness and weakness of the lumbar region and kness, pale tongue proper, and deep slow weak pulse.

(2) *Therapeutic* principle

Warm up the kidney Yang.

(3) *Treatment*

1) Body acupuncture

Prescription: Shenshu (BL 23), Pangguangshu (BL 28), Guanyuan (RN 4), Qihai (RN 6), Zhongji (RN 3), Taixi (KI 3), Sanyinjiao (SP 6).

Method: Apply filiform needles with reinforcing method. Retain the needles for 20～30 minutes manipulating them one to two times.

2) Ear acupuncture

Prescription: Urinary bladder, Urethra, Subcortex, Sympathetic, Kidney.

Method: Apply filiform needles with mild stimulation and retain the needles for 20 minutes.

3) Moxibustion

Prescription: Shenshu (BL 23), Pangguanshu (BL 28), Guanyuan (RN 4), Sanyinjiao (SP 6).

Method: Apply mild-warming moxibustion or rounding moxibustion for 15～20 minutes once a day.

2. Qi Deficiency of the Lung and Spleen

(1) *Main manifestation*

Urinary incontinence, pallor complexion, shortness of breath, lassitude, weakness of the four limbs, poor appetite, loose stools, pale tongue proper, and slow or deep thready pulse.

(2) *Therapetic* principle

Reinforce the Lung and Spleen.

(3) *Treatment*

1) Body acupuncture

Prescription: Pishu (BL 20), Feishu (BL 13), Taiyuan (LU 9), Zusanli (ST 36), Qihai (RN 6), Sanyinjiao (SP 6).

Method: Apply filiform needles with reinforcing method. Retain the needles for 20～30 minutes manipulating them one to two times.

2) Ear acupuncture

Prescription: Lung, Spleen, Kidney, Urinary bladder, Urethra, Subcortex, Sympathetic.

Method: Apply filiform needles with mild stimulation and retain the needles for 15 minutes.

3) Moxibustion

Prescription: Feishu (BL 13), Pishu (BL 20), Zusanli (ST 36),

Qihai (RN 6).

Method: Apply mild-warming or rounding moxibustion for 15~20 minutes once a day.

3. Downward Flowing of Damp-heat

(1) *Main manifestation*

Urinary incontinence, frequent urination with burning sensation in the urethra, short scanty urine with odour, dripping urine, lumbar soreness, low grade fever, thin greasy tongue coating, and rapid thready pulse.

(2) *Therapeutic* principle

Eliminate damp-heat from the lower-jiao.

(3) *Treatment*

1) Body acupuncture

Prescription: Pangguangshu (BL 28), Zhongji (RN 3), Yinlingquan (SP 9), Zutonggu (BL 66), Weiyang (BL 39), Sanyinjiao (SP 6).

Method: Apply filiform needles with reducing method. Retain the needles for 15~20 minutes manipulating them two to three times.

2) Ear acupuncture

Prescription: Urinary bladder, Urethra, Subcortex, Sympathetic, Kidney, Spleen.

Method: Apply filiform needles with moderate stimulation and retain the needles for 15~20 minutes. Auricular taping is also applicable.

4. Blood Stasis in the Lower-Jiao

(1) *Main manifestation*

Dripping of urine and urinary incontinence, abdominal distention with dull pain, masses felt by palpating, dark purplish tongue proper, and hesitant or rapid thready pulse.

(2) *Therapeutic* principle

Activate blood circulation and resolve stasis of blood.

(3) *Treatment*

1) Body acupuncture

Prescription: Zhongji (RN 3), Ciliao (BL 32), Sanyinjiao (SP 6), Qihai (RN 6), Geshu (BL 17).

Method: Apply filiform needles with reducing method. Retain the needles for 20~30 minutes manipulating the needles three to four times.

2) Ear acupuncture

Prescription: Urinary bladder, Urethra, Subcortex, Sympathetic, Kidney.

Method: Apply filiform needles with mild stimulation and retain the needles for 15 minutes. Auricular taping is also applicable.

癃　　闭

癃闭是指以排尿困难，少腹胀痛，甚则小便不通为主证的一种疾病。癃，指小便不畅，点滴而出，病势较缓者；闭，指小便闭塞，点滴不通，病势较急者。本病可见于现代医学中各种原因所引起的尿潴留。

1. 肾气虚弱

（1）主证　小便淋沥，排出无力，面色㿠白，神气怯弱，腰部酸痛，四肢乏力，舌质淡，脉沉细而迟弱。

（2）治则　补肾利尿。

（3）治法

1）体针

处方　肾俞，三阴交，阴谷，三焦俞，气海，委阳。

配穴　腰部酸楚加腰阳关，命门。

操作　毫针刺，用补法。留针20～30分钟，间歇行针2～3次。

2）耳针

处方　膀胱，肾，尿道，三焦，交感，皮质下。

操作　毫针中等强度刺激，留针20～30分钟；亦可采用耳穴贴敷。

3）艾灸

处方　肾俞，三焦俞，气海。

操作　采用温和灸或回旋灸治疗15～20分钟，亦可用温针灸。

2. 膀胱湿热

（1）主证　小便阻塞不通或短少，小腹胀满，口渴不欲饮，舌质红，苔黄，脉数。

（2）治则　清热利湿。

（3）治法

1）体针

处方　膀胱俞，中极，三阴交，阴陵泉。

操作　毫针刺，用泻法。留针15～20分钟，间歇行针2～3次。

2）耳针

处方　膀胱，尿道，三焦，枕。

操作　毫针中等强度刺激，留针15～20分钟；亦可采用耳穴贴敷。

3. 瘀血阻塞

（1）主证　小便阻塞不通，小腹胀满疼痛，舌有瘀点，脉涩。

（2）治则　行瘀散结，通利小便。

（3）治法

1）体针

处方　膀胱俞，中极，三阴交，水泉，水道，气海。

操作　毫针刺，平补平泻或泻法。留针15～20分钟，间歇行针2～3次。

2）耳针

处方　膀胱，尿道，三焦，交感，皮质下。

操作　毫针中等强度刺激，留针20～30分钟。亦可采用耳穴贴敷。

3）电针

处方　维道。

操作　毫针刺，针沿皮向曲骨方向透刺2～3寸，疏密波，通电20～30分钟。

4）指压

处方　关元。

操作　右手掌心对准脐部，以中指点按关元穴，左手拇指压于右手中指第1节，两手由轻渐重半稳施加压

力，着力点在关元穴，同时嘱患者排
尿，如有小便流溢，应继续加压，待
其排空后，再缓缓将手松开。

Retention of Urine

Retention of urine refers to difficult
urination, distending pain in the lower
abdomen and even blockage of urine. It
clinically includes the mild condition of
difficult urinary discharge with dripping
and obstructed urinary discharge with
distending and urgent feeling in severe
cases. It can be seen in uroschesis due
to various causes in modern medicine.

1. Deficiency of Kidney Qi

(1) *Main manifestation*

Forceless dribbling of urine, pallor
complexion, listlessness, lumbar soreness, weakness of the four limbs, pale
tongue proper, and deep thready pulse
which is particular weak in the kidney
region.

(2) *Therapeutic* principle

Reinforce kidney and promote urinary
discharge.

(3) *Treatment*

1) Body acupuncture

Prescription: Shenshu (BL 23),
Sanyinjiao (SP 6), Yingu (KI 10),
Sanjiaoshu (BL 22), Qihai (RN 6),
Weiyang (BL 39).

Supplementary points: Add Yaoyangguan (DU 3) and Mingmen (DU 4) for
soreness in the lumbar region.

Method: Apply filiform needles with
reinforcing method. Retain the needles
for 20 ~ 30 minutes manipulating them
two to three times.

2) Ear acupuncture

Prescription: Urinary bladder, Kidney, Urethra, Sanjiao, Sympathetic,
Subcortex.

Method: Apply filiform needles with
moderate stimulation and retain the
needles for 20 ~ 30 minutes. Auricular
taping is also applicable.

3) Moxibustion

Prescription: Shenshu (BL 23),
Sanjiaoshu (BL 22), Qihai (RN 6).

Method: Apply mild-warming or
rounding moxibustion for 15 ~ 20
minutes. Moxibustion with warming
needle is also applicable.

2. Damp-heat Retention in Urinary Bladder

(1) *Main manifestation*

Obstructed discharge of urine or short
scanty urine, distention in the lower
abdomen, thirst with no desire for
drinking, red tongue proper, yellow
coating and rapid pulse.

(2) *Therapeutic* principle

Elimination of damp-heat.

(3) *Treatment*

1) Body acupuncture

Prescription: Pangguangshu (BL
28), Zhongji (RN 3), Sanyinjiao

(SP 6), Yinlingquan (SP 9).

Method: Apply filiform needles with reducing method. Retain the needles for 15～20 minutes manipulating them two to three times.

2) Ear acupuncture

Prescription: Urinary bladder, Urethra, Sanjiao, Occipital.

Method: Apply filiform needles with moderate stimulation and retain the needles for 15～20 minutes. Auricular taping is also applicable.

3. Obstruction of Blood Stasis

(1) *Main manifestation*

Obstruction of urine, pain and distention in the lower abdomen, purplish spots on the tongue and hesitant pulse.

(2) *Therapeutic* principle

Resolve stasis and promote urinary discharge.

(3) *Treatment*

1) Body acupuncture

Prescription: Pangguangshu (BL 28), Zhongji (RN 3), Sanyinjiao (SP 6), Shuiquan (KI 5), Shuidao (ST 28), Qihai (RN 6).

Method: Apply filiform needles with even movement or reducing method. Retain the needles for 15～20 minutes manipulating them two to three times.

2) Ear acupuncture

Prescription: Urinary bladder, Urethra, Sanjiao, Sympathetic, Subcor-tex.

Method: Apply filiform needles with moderate stimulation and retain the needles for 20～30 minutes. Auricular taping is also applicable.

3) Electroacupuncture

Prescription: Weidao (GB 28).

Method: Apply filiform needles at Weidao (GB 28) horizontally towards Qugu (RN 2) for about two to three cun distance, then followed by electric stimulation with dense-sparse wave for 20～30 minutes.

4) Pressing with finger

Prescription: Guanyuan (RN 4).

Method: Direct the patient's umbilicus with the center of the right palm. Press on Guanyuan (RN 4) with the middle finger of the hand. Press the first portion of the middle finger of the right hand with the thumb of the left hand. The pressure given by the doctor is gradually increased with stress on Guanyuan (RN 4) while the patient is asked to urinate at the same time. If urine is found out of the urethra the pressure is continuously increased until little urine is in the bladder. Then the doctor releases the fingers from the patient slowly.

汗　　证

汗证是指由于人体阴阳失调，营卫不和，腠理不固而引起汗液外泄的病症。本节主要讨论自汗、盗汗两种。自汗以时时汗出，动则尤甚为主证；盗汗以睡中汗出，醒来即止为特征。汗证可见于现代医学的多种疾病。如甲状腺功能亢进，自主神经功能紊乱，低血糖，结核病，风湿热及某些传染病的发作期和恢复期等出现自汗、盗汗者，均可参见本节辨证治疗。

1. 自汗

（1）主证　时时汗出，动则尤甚，身冷畏寒，甚则冷汗，或兼有心悸，气短，神疲乏力，脘腹胀闷，苔白或微黄，脉虚弱无力。

（2）治则　补阳固表止汗。

（3）治法

1）体针　复溜，合谷，膏肓俞，肺俞，脾俞，足三里，气海。

配穴　心悸气短者加内关，脘腹胀闷加中脘。

操作　毫针刺，复溜用泻法，余穴用补法。留针 15～20 分钟，间歇行针 1～2 次。

2）耳针

处方　肺，交感，内分泌，肾上腺。

操作　毫针中等强度刺激，留针 15～20 分钟。亦可采用耳穴贴敷。

2. 盗汗

（1）主证　睡则汗出，醒则汗止，面赤颧红，五心烦热，舌红少苔，脉细数。

（2）治则　滋阴降火止汗。

（3）治法

1）体针

处方　太溪，阴郄，三阴交，复溜。

操作　毫针刺，平补平泻。留针 15～20 分钟，间歇行针 1～2 次。

2）耳针

处方　心，肺，交感，内分泌，肾上腺。

操作　毫针中等强度刺激，留针 15～20 分钟，亦可用耳穴贴敷。

Sweat Syndrome

Sweat syndrome is a condition of poor opening and closing of skin pores with heavy perspiration due to the imbalance of Yin and Yang of the body and dysharmony between the nutritive and defensive systems. This section mainly covers spontaneous sweating and night sweating. The former is characterized by perspiration that worsens by exertion while the latter is characterized by perspiration during sleep at night that stops by itself when the patient is a wakened. Sweat syndrome can be seen in many diseases in modern medicine. The differentiation and treatment elaborated here can be referred to for both spontaneous sweating and night sweating as a symptom in such diseases as hyperthyroidism, vegetative nerve dysfunction, hypoglycemia, tuberculosis, rheumatic fever as well as spontaneous and night sweating seen in acute and rehabilitative stage of some infectious diseases.

1. Spontaneous sweating

(1) *Main manifestation*

Continuous sweating without any exertion or worse on exertion, and cold limbs with cold sweat in severe cases. It may be accompanied by palpitation, shortness of breath, lassitude, distension in abdominal and epigastric regions, white, or slightly yellow tongue coating, and deficient feeble pulse.

(2) *Therapeutic* principle

Reinforce Yang, strengthen the superficial portion of the body to stop sweating.

(3) *Treatment*

1) Body acupuncture

Prescription: Fuliu (KI 7), Hegu (LI 4), Gaohuangshu (BL 43), Feishu (BL 13), Pishu (BL 20), Zusanli (ST 36), Qihai (RN 6).

Supplementary points: Add Neiguan (PC 6) for palpitation and shortness of breath, Zhongwan (RN 12) for fullness and distention in the abdominal and epigastric regions.

Method: Apply filiform needles with reducing method at Fuliu (KI 7) and reinforcing method at the rest of the points. Retain the needles for 15 ~ 20 minutes manipulating them one to two times.

2) Ear acupuncture

Prescription: Lung, Sympathetic, Endocrine, Adrenal gland.

Method: Apply filiform needles with moderate stimulation and retain the needles for 15 ~ 20 minutes. Auricular taping is also applicable.

2. Night Sweating

(1) *Main manifestation*

Continuous sweating during sleep that stops when the patient is awake, red cheeks, feverish sensation in the palms and soles, red tongue proper with less coating than normal, and rapid thready pulse.

(2) *Therapeutic* principle

Nourish Yin, sedate fire and stop sweating.

(3) *Treatment*

1) Body acupuncture

Prescription: Taixi (KI 3), Yinxi (HT 6), Sanyinjiao (SP 6), Fuliu (KI 7).

Method: Apply filiform needles with even movement method. Retain the needles for 15 ~ 20 minutes manipulating them one to two times.

2) Ear acupuncture

Prescription: Heart, Lung, Sympathetic, Endocrine, Adrenal gland.

Method: Apply filiform needles with moderate stimulation and retain the needles for 15 ~ 20 minutes. Auricular taping is also applicable.

无 脉 证

无脉证是指寸口脉搏动减弱或消失的一种证候，亦可见于下肢的趺阳脉。本病常见于现代医学的多发性大动脉炎、闭塞性动脉粥样硬化症、血栓闭塞性脉管炎、动脉栓塞等多种疾病。

1. 主证

寸口脉搏减弱或消失，兼有头晕，视力模糊，臂膊倦怠乏力，麻木酸痛，感觉发凉，指端发紫。严重者可见抽搐、昏迷等。若病发下肢其症状与上肢大致相同，但见趺阳脉搏减弱或消失。

2. 治则

调气活血，祛瘀复脉。

3. 治法

（1）体针

处方　太渊，人迎，大陵，内关，尺泽。

配穴　头晕加风池，百会；视力模糊加睛明；手臂麻木酸痛加曲池，合谷；病发下肢加足三里，隐白，委中，冲阳。

操作　毫针刺，平补平泻。留针15～20分钟，间歇行针2～3次。

（2）耳针

处方　神门，心，肾，脾，皮质下，内分泌，上肢，肾上腺。

操作　毫针轻刺，留针10～15分钟。亦可用耳穴贴敷。

Pulseless Syndrome

Pulseless syndrome refers to a weakness or disappearance of pulse at Cunkou that is one cun distal to the end of the radial artery. Such a condition may also take place at the ulnar artery at the ankle. It can be seen in many diseases in modern medicine such as multiple aorto-arteritis, atherosclerosis obliterans, thromboangitis obliterans, arterial embolism, etc.

1. Main manifestation

Weakened or faint pulse at Cunkou, dizziness, blurring of vision, lassitude, weakness of the arms, numbness, soreness and cold sensation in the arms, and purplish colour of the finger tips. Convulsions and loss of conciousness may also take place if the condition is severe. The symptoms and signs for pulseless syndrome involving the lower limbs are similar to those of the upper limbs.

2. Therapeutic principle

Regulate Qi and activate blood and resolve stasis to restore normal pulsation.

3. Treatment

（1）*Body acupuncture*

Prescription   Taiyuan （LU 9）, Renying （ST 9）, Daling （PC 7）, Neiguan （PC 6）, Chize （LU 5）.

Supplementary points: Add Fengchi （GB 20） and Baihui （DU 20） for dizziness, Jingming (BL 1) for blurring of vision, Quchi (LI 11) and Hegu (LI 4) for numbness and soreness of the arm, Zusanli (ST 36), Yinbai (SP 1), Weizhong (BL 40) and Chongyang (ST 42) for pulseless syndrome of the lower limbs.

Method: Apply filiform needles with even movement method. Retain the needles for 15～20 minutes manipulating them two to three times.

(2) *Ear acupuncture*

Prescription: Ear-shenmen, Heart, Kidney, Spleen, Subcortex, Endocrine, Upper limb, Adrenal Gland.

Method: Apply filiform needles with mild stimulation and retain the needles for 10～15 minutes. Auricular taping is also applicable.

疟　疾

疟疾是以寒战、壮热、休作有时为特征的一种传染性疾病。根据其发作间歇的时间长短不同又分为日疟、间日疟、三日疟。如久疟不愈，胁下痞块，触之可得者称为疟母。本病多发于夏秋季节，其他季节也有散在发病。

1. 主证

寒战壮热，发作有时，先呵欠乏力，继而寒战，寒去则内外皆热，甚则高热，神昏谵语，头痛如裂，面赤颧红，胸胁痞满，口苦而干，烦渴引饮，终则遍身出汗，热退身凉，舌苔

薄腻而黄，脉弦数。久疟不愈，时发时止无定时，面色㿠白，倦怠乏力，头目眩晕，肢体羸瘦，胁下形成痞块。

2. 治则

通调督脉，和解少阳，祛邪截疟。

3. 治法

(1) 体针

处方　大椎，陶道，后溪，液门，后溪，间使。

配穴　高热神昏谵语加十二井穴点刺；久疟加脾俞，膏肓俞；痞块加章门，痞根。

操作　毫针刺，用泻法。留针15～20分钟，间隔行针3～4次。针刺应在疟疾发作前2～3小时进行。

(2) 耳针

处方　肾上腺，皮质下，内分泌，神门，肝，脾，胆，耳尖。

操作　毫针刺，每次选3～5穴，强刺激，留针15～20分钟。耳尖采用三棱针点刺出血，均在发作前2～3小时施治，亦可用耳穴贴敷或埋针治疗。

(3) 艾灸

处方　脾俞，膏肓俞，痞根。

操作　采用温和灸或温针灸治疗久疟胁下有痞块者，每穴15～20分钟，可灸5～7壮。

(4) 拔罐疗法

处方　大椎，陶道，至阳。

操作　先用三棱针点刺出血，随即拔火罐，隔日一次。本法可单独使

用，若配合针灸应用效果更佳。

（5）三棱针

处方　委中（BL 40）。

操作　于发作前 1～2 小时，将患者腘窝部常规消毒后，用三棱针点刺放血 1 毫升左右，然后用干棉球压迫止血。每次取一侧，左右交替。

Malaria

Malaria is an infectious disease characterized by shivering chills and strong fever at regular intervals. This condition can be divided into quotidian malaria, tertian malaria and quartan malaria according to the interval between every two attacks. There may be some palpable mass in the hypochondriac region in chronic cases. This is medically called malaria with splenomegaly. Malaria, more common in summer and autumn, may also sporadically occur in other seasons.

1. Main manifestation

Shivering chills and fever appear at regular intervals. They often start with yawning and forcelessness and then with shivering chills. When the chills retreat general fever takes place. In severe cases there can be high fever, coma, delirium, headache, red cheeks, fullness in the hypochondriac region, bitter taste, dryness in the mouth, thirst with desire for drinking, and sweating by the end of the attack. The

body feels cool again when the fever stops. The tongue coating is thin, yellow and greasy, and the pulse is wiry and rapid. There may also appear pallor complexion, lassitude, blurring of vision, dizziness, emaciation, and mass in the hypochondriac region if the malaria lasts for a long period of time with irregular intervals.

2. Therapeutic

Regulate Qi of the Du channel, eliminate the pathogenic factors from Shaoyang and stop malaria.

3. Treatment

(1) *Body acupuncture*

Prescription: Dazhui (DU 14), Taodao (DU 13), Yemen (SJ 2), Houxi (SJ 3), Jianshi (PC5).

Supplementary points: Add 12 Jingwell points with pricking for high fever, coma and delirium, Pishu (BL 20) and Gaohuangshu (BL 22) for lingering malaria, and Zhangmen (LR 13) and Pigen (Extra) for hypochondriac mass.

Method: Apply filiform needles with reducing method. Retain the needles for 15～20 minutes manipulating them three to four times. Treatment is given two to three hours in advance to the next attack of malaria when acupuncture is used to treat such a condition.

(2) *Ear acupuncture*

Prescription: Adrenal gland, Subcortex, Endocrine, Ear-Shenmen, Liver, Spleen, Gallbladder, Ear apex.

Method: Apply filiform needles with strong stimulation at three to five points and retain the needles for 15 ～ 20 minutes, Ear apex is pricked with a three-edged needle to cause bleeding. Treatment is given two to three hours in advance of the next attack. Auricular taping or subcutaneous needle is also applicable.

(3) *Moxibustion*

Prescription: Pishu (BL 20), Gaohuangshu (BL 22), Pigen (EX-B4).

Method: Apply mild-warming moxibustion or moxibustion with warming needle for 15 ～ 20 minutes if the lingering malaria has already caused hypochondriac mass. Five to seven moxa cones can also be applied at the above points.

(4) *Cupping Therapy*

Prescription: Dazhui (DU 14), Taodao (DU 13), Zhiyang (DU 9).

Method: Prick these points with a three-edged needle to cause bleeding. This is then followed by cupping. Treatment is given once every other day. This method can be applied independently or combined with other treatments which will help to produce a better therapeutic effect.

(5) *Three-edged needle*

Prescription: Weizhong (BL 40).

Method: The treatment is given two hours prior to the onset of the paroxysm. A routine and local sterilization is given to the politeal fossa. Then the point is pricked with a three-edged needle to cause letting out of about 1 mL of blood. After that, the needle hole is pressed to stop bleeding with a dry sterilized cotton ball. Only one side is pricked at each session and the two sides are pricked alternately.

流行性感冒

流行性感冒是由流感病毒引起的一种急性呼吸道传染病，多流行于冬季。主要表现为恶寒，高热，头痛，周身酸痛，乏力，食欲不振及恶心，呕吐，并伴有鼻塞，流涕，干咳及咽痛等症状。

中医认为本病为外感风寒或风热之邪，经皮肤及鼻侵袭肺脏，从而导致肺失宣降所致。风寒型临床表现特点为恶寒重，发热轻，周身疼痛，鼻塞流清涕；风热型临床表现特点为发热重，恶寒轻，头痛，口渴，咽痛，鼻塞，流稠涕而黄。

1. 体针

处方 大椎，合谷，太阳，足三里。

配穴 风寒者加风池；风热者加曲池，少商。

操作 毫针刺，用泻法，留针15～20分钟，间歇行针2～4次。

2. 耳针

处方 肺，内鼻，咽喉，耳尖，屏尖，额。

操作 毫针中等强度刺激，留针15～20分钟。高热者可用三棱针耳尖和屏尖点刺出血，亦可采用耳穴贴敷。

3. 三棱针

处方 少商。

操作 三棱针点针出血。此法适用于感冒属于风热的患者。

4. 拔罐疗法

处方 风门，大椎，肺俞。

操作 穴位拔罐，也可针上套罐，留罐10～15分钟，本法宜于流感属于风热者。

Influenza

Influenza is an acute communicable disease of the respiratory tract caused by the influenza virus, usually occurring epidemically in the winter. It is marked by sudden onset of high fever, chills, headache, soreness of the entire body, lassitude, poor appetite, nausea, and vomiting, usually accompanied by nasal obstruction, nasal discharge, dry cough, and sore throat.

According to traditional Chinese medicine, influenza is caused by epidemic exogenous pathogens such as wind-cold or wind-heat invading the lungs through the skin and nose. Therefore the lungs cannot perform their function of dispersal and descending normally. Influenza caused by wind-cold is characterized by severe chills, mild fever, soreness of the entire body, and nasal obstruction with dilute discharge. Influenza caused by wind-heat is characterized by high fever, mild chills, headache, thirst, sore throat, and nasal obstruction with scanty yellowish discharge.

1. Body acupuncture

Prescription: Dazhui (DU 14), Hegu (LI 4), Taiyang (Extra 1), Zusanli (S 36).

Supplementary points: Add Fengchi for wind-cold type, Quchi (LI 11) and Shaoshang (LU 11) for wind-heat type.

Method: Apply filiform needles with reducing method. Retain the needles for 15～20 minutes manipulating them two to four times.

2. Ear acupuncture

Prescription: Lung, Internal nose, Throat, Apex of ear, Apex of tragus, Forehead.

Method: Apply filiform needles, with moderate stimulation and retain the needles for 15～20 minutes. For high fever, Apex of Ear and Apex of tragus are pricked with a three-edged needle to cause bleeding. Auricular taping is also applicable.

3. Three-edged needle

Prescription: Shaoshang (LU 11).

Method: Prick the point with a three-edged needle to cause bleeding. It is suitable for wind-heat type of influenza.

4. Cupping

Prescription: Fengmen (BL 12), Dazhui (DU 14), Feishu (BL 13).

Method: Apply cupping on the acupoints which are being punctured with the needles or not for 10~15 minutes. This treatment is suitable for wind-cold type of influenza.

流行性腮腺炎

流行性腮腺炎是由流行性腮腺炎病毒导致的腮腺非化脓性急性炎症性传染病。多发于儿童,常流行于冬春季节。主要临床表现为发热,恶寒,头痛,一侧或双侧腮腺肿大疼痛,其肿大以耳垂为中心,边缘不清,触之有弹性感及轻度压痛。一般预后良好,但治疗欠妥或不及时,亦可引起脑膜炎、睾丸炎、卵巢炎等。

中医认为本病主要由于风温毒邪侵袭三焦和胆经,引起气血阻滞于腮部所称。中医称之为"痄腮"。

1. 体针

处方 外关,颊车,曲池,下关,合谷,翳风,痄腮穴。

配穴 睾丸肿痛加太冲,曲泉,三阴交;高热加少商。

操作 毫针刺,用泻法。留针20~30分钟,间歇行针3~4次。针翳风时,针尖斜向患处;针颊车时向大迎方向透刺。

2. 耳针

处方 对屏尖,颌,颊,内分泌,三焦,胆,耳尖。

操作 毫针强刺激,留针15~20分钟。耳尖可用三棱针点刺出血,亦可用耳穴贴敷。

3. 灯草灸法

处方 角孙。

操作 用灯心草两根蘸植物油,点燃后,对准角孙穴,快速烧灼皮肤,一点即起,当听到一响声即可。一般1次治疗即可消肿。如灸后肿未全消时,次日可重复1次。

4. 电针

处方 合谷,少商,患侧腮腺炎刺激点(肿大腮腺上缘处)。

操作 针呈45°角,由肿大腮腺上缘刺入,深1~1.5寸,通电10~15分钟,起针后再刺双侧少商出血,双侧合谷毫针刺。

5. 三棱针

处方 少商。

操作 三棱针点刺出血。本法尤其适宜于高热患者。

Mumps

Mumps, nonpurulent inflammation

of the parotid gland, is an acute communicable disease caused by the mumps virus. It occurs most commonly in children and is usually epidemic in the winter and spring. Symptoms include fever, aversion to cold, headache, swelling and pain in unilateral or bilateral parotid regions with the center in the ear lobe and with unclear border. The swollen mass has elasticity and slight tenderness if touched. The prognosis is generally good, but if appropriate and timely treatment is not given there may be complications including meningitis, testitis or ovaritis with possible subsequent sterility.

According to traditional Chinese medicine, mumps is caused by exogenous wind-heat and pathogens which invade the San Jiao and gallbladder meridians thus obsrueting Qi and blood in the parorid glands. This disease is termed "zha sai" in traditional Chinese medicine.

1. Body acupuncture

Prescription: Waiguan (SJ 5), Jiache (ST 6), Quchi (LI 11), Xiaguan (ST 7), Hegu (LI 4), Yifeng (SJ 17), Zhasai (Extra point)

Supplementary points: Add Taichong (LR 3), Ququan (LR 8) and Sanyinjiao (SP 6) for swelling and pain in the testicles, Shaoshang (LU 11) for high fever.

Method: Apply filiform needles with reducing method. Retain the needles for 20～30 minutes manipulating them three to four times. When puncturing at Yifeng (SJ 11) the needle tip is directed to the affected site while puncturing at Jiache (ST 6) the needling direction is towards Daying (ST 5).

2. Ear acupuncture

Prescription: Antitragic, Apex, Jaw, Cheek, Endocrine, San Jiao, Gallbladder, Apex of ear.

Method: Apply filiform needles with strong stimulation and retain the needles for 15～20 minutes. Apex of ear may be pricked with a three-edged needle to cause bleeding. Auricular taping is also applicable.

3. Moxibustion with rush pith (Medulla Junci)

Prescription: Jiaosun (SJ 20)

Method: Two pieces of rush pith soaked with vegetable oil are ignited and aimed at the point Jiaosun (SJ 20). Remove them quickly as soon as there is a sound of skin burning. Usually the swelling will subside after one treatment. The treatment can be repeated the next day if the swelling is not completely gone.

4. Electroacupuncture

Prescription: Hegu (LI 4),

Shaoshang (LU 11), the stimulation point of mumps (at the upper border of the swollen parotid region).

Method: Insert a needle obliquely 1～1.5 cun deep at an angle of 45° into the upper border of the swollen parotid region. Connect the needle with an electric current from an electric therapeutic unit for 10～15 minutes. After withdrawal of the needle, prick Shaoshang (LU 11) bilaterally to cause bleeding and puncture Hegu (LI 4) bilaterally.

5. Three-edged Needle

Prescription: Shaoshang (LU 11).

Method: Apply a three-edged needle to cause bleeding. This method is especially suitable for high fever.

细菌性痢疾

细菌性痢疾是由志贺菌属所引起的肠道传染病，多见于夏秋季。传染源是患者和带菌者。病菌通过污染的食物、水、餐具等而传染。其主要病变为结肠黏膜化脓性炎症。临床上以全身中毒症状，腹痛，腹泻，里急后重和黏液脓血便为主要表现。本病属中医"痢疾"范畴。

1. 体针

处方 足三里，合谷，天枢，上巨墟。

配穴 发热加曲池，大椎；恶心加内关，中脘；里急后重加大肠俞，白环俞，长强。

操作 毫针刺，用泻法，留针15～20分钟。慢性病例用补法。

2. 耳针

处方 大肠，小肠，胃，脾，交感，神门。

操作 毫针强或中等度刺激，留针20～30分钟，每天1～2次；亦可用耳穴贴敷。

3. 艾灸

处方 神厥，天枢，关元，足三里，上巨墟，小肠俞。

操作 用艾卷回旋灸或温和灸，亦可用艾炷隔姜或隔蒜灸，以及神阙隔盐灸。每穴每次用艾卷点10～15分钟，或艾炷灸3～5壮，每天1～2次。本法对急性菌痢无高热者效果较好，对慢性菌痢坚持长期灸治优于其他方法。

4. 三棱针

处方 大椎，脾俞，大肠俞。

操作 三棱针点刺出血，然后再加拔火罐。

Bacillary Dysentery

Bacillary dysentery is an infectious disease of the intestinal tract caused by Shigella. It commonly occurs in summer and autumn. The sources of infection are patients and bacteria carriers. The disease is transmitted by means of contact with contaminated food, water and tableware. The major pathological change is purulent inflammation of the colonic mucosa. Clinically fever, abdominal pain, diarrhea, tenesmus and bloody purulent stools are major manifestations. This disease belongs to the category or "Li Ji" (dysentery) in traditional Chinese medicine.

1. Body Acupuncture

Prescription: Zusanli (ST 36), Hegu (LI 4), Tianshu (ST 25), Shangjuxu (ST 37).

Supplementary points: Add Quchi (LI 11) and Dazhui (DU 14) for fever, Neiguan (PC 6) and Zhongwan (RN 12) for nausea, Dachangshu (BL 25), Baihuanshu (BL 30) and Changqiang (DU 1) for tenesmus.

Method: Apply filiform needles with reducing method. Retain the needles for 15~20 minutes. For chronic cases the points are punctured with reinforcing method.

2. Ear Acupuncture

Prescription: Large Intestine, Small Intestine, Stomach, Spleen, Sympthetic, Shenmen.

Method: Apply filiform needles with strong or moderate stimulation and retain the needles for 20 ~ 30 minutes with 1~2 treatments a day. Auricular taping is also applicable.

3. Moxibustion

Prescription: Shenque (RN 8), Tianshu (ST 25), Guanyuan (RN 4), Zusanli (ST 36), Shangjuxu (ST 37), Xiaochangshu (BL 27).

Method: Apply the circling moxibustion or mild-warming moxibustion with the moxa roll, or ginger moxibustion or garlic moxibustion, or moxibustion with some salt on Shenque (RN 8) one to two times daily. Give moxibustion to each point with the moxa roll for 10~15 minutes or with the moxa cone until 3~5 cones have been burnt out. Moxibustion is effective in treatment of acute bacillary desentery without high fever and provides a better effect in treating chronic bacillary dysentery compared with other treatment methods.

4. Three-edged needle

Prescription: Dazhui (DU 14), Pishu (BL 20), Dachangshu (BL 25).

Method: Prick the points with a three-edged needle to cause bleeding and apply cupping on the pricked points.

病毒性肝炎

病毒性肝炎主要有甲型、乙型和丙型肝炎三种，均由肝炎病毒引起。人群对本病普遍易感。临床上以食欲减退、肝区疼痛乏力等为主要表现，亦可有发热、黄疸以及不同程度的肝功能损害。本病属于中医"黄疸"、"肝郁"、"胁痛"、"症积"等范畴。

1. 体针

处方 至阳,肝俞,胆俞,阳陵泉,足三里。

配穴 黄色鲜明者加内庭,太冲;黄色晦暗如烟熏者加脾俞,中脘,三阴交;胁痛者加期门,支沟,内关;腹部胀满者加中脘。

操作 毫针刺,用泻法。留针20~30分钟,间歇行针2~4次。

2. 耳针

处方 肝,胆,脾,胃,神门,交感,三焦,耳迷根。

操作 每次选3~4穴,毫针强刺激,捻转毫针至耳朵发热,然后留针20~30分钟;亦可用耳穴贴敷。

3. 电针

处方 至阳,肝俞,胆俞,足三里。

操作 每次治疗选用2~4穴,采用疏波或疏密波,输出电量为中等度刺激,频率40~60次/分钟。每天1次,每次15~30分钟,10次为1个疗程。

Viral Hepatitis

Viral hepatitis, caused by hepatitis viruses, can be mainly divided into three types: Type A, Type B and Type C hepatitis. Clinically, the major symptoms are poor appetite, hepatalgia and fatigue. Fever and jaundice may occur. Liver function tests show various degrees of hepatic damage. In traditional Chinese medicine this disease belongs to the categories of "Jaundice", "stagnation of liver-Qi" "hypochondriac pain" and "mass in the abdomen".

1. Body Acupuncture

Prescription: Zhiyang (DU 9), Ganshu (BL 18), Danshu (BL 19), Yinlinquan (GB 34), Zusanli (ST 36).

Supplementary points: Add Neiting (ST 44) and Taichong (LR 3) for lustrous yellow skin, Pishu (BL 20), Zhongwan (RN 12) and Sanyinjiao (SP 6) for dusky yellow skin, Qimen (LR 14), Zhigou (SJ 6) and Neiguan (PC 6) for hypochondriac pain, Zhongwan (RN 12) for abdominal distension.

Method: Apply filiform needles with reducing method. Retain the needles for 20~30 minutes manipulating them 2~4 times.

2. Ear Acupuncture

Prescription: Liver, Gallbladder, Spleen, Stomach, Shenmen, Sympathetic, Sanjiao, Ermigen.

Method: Select 3~4 points for each treatment and apply filiform needles with strong stimulation. Twist the needles until the ear feels warm, then retain the needles for 20~30 minutes. Auricular taping is also applicable.

3. Electroacupuncture

Prescription: Zhiyang (DU 9), Ganshu (BL 18), Dashu (BL 19), Zusanli (ST 36).

Method: 2 ~ 4 points are selected each treatment session. Use an electric stimulation with a low or irregular wave with a frequency at 40~60 turns/min. A medium strength is given for 15~30 minutes daily. 10 treatment sessions make up a therapeutic course.

艾 滋 病

艾滋病是近年来发现的一种在世界范围内传播的疾病，病死率颇高。其病因已知为病毒感染所致，但至今病毒分离培养仍未获得成功。目前西医尚无有效治疗方法。本病多见于同性恋者和吸毒者。婴儿和儿童亦可被感染。主要通过性接触、输血、注射及母婴等方式传播。艾滋病似可属于中医"温热病"、"虚劳"等范畴。

1. 体针

处方 足三里，膏肓俞，大椎，神门，筑宾，膈俞。

配穴 食欲不振，体重减轻加脾俞，胃俞，中脘；慢性腹泻加天枢，大肠俞，上巨墟，神阙；发热加曲池；盗汗加复溜，阴郄；咳嗽加中府，肺俞；瘙痒性皮肤炎加膈俞，血海，曲池；倦怠乏力加气海，三阴交，肺俞，肾俞。

操作 毫针刺，用补法或平补平泻法，强刺激，留针 20 ~ 30 分钟，间歇行针 2~3 次。

2. 耳针

处方 脾，肾，内分泌，皮质下，神门，胃，肺，枕，大肠，小肠。

操作 每次选 3~5 穴，毫针重刺激，留针 30 分钟；亦可用耳穴贴敷。

3. 艾灸

处方 膏肓俞，足三里，膈俞，脾俞。

操作 用温和灸或回旋灸治疗 10~15 分钟，每天 1 次。

Acquired Immunodeficiency Syndrome (AIDS)

AIDS is a worldwide infectious disease discovered in recent years. Its case-fatality is very high. AIDS is known to be a viral infection but the isolation and culture of the virus have not been successful. Western medicine has had no effective treatment for the disease yet. AIDS is frequently found in homosexuals and drug addicts. It also occurs in infants and children. AIDS is mainly transmitted by means of sexual contact, infusion, injection and mother-to-infant. This disease, in traditional Chinese medicine probably pertains to the categories of "epidemic febrile diseases", "consumptive diseases," etc.

1. Body Acupuncture

Prescription: Zusanli (ST 36), Gaohuangshu (BL 43), Dazhui (DU 14), Shenmen (HT 7), Zhubin (KI 9), Geshu (BL 17).

Supplementary points: Add Pishu (BL 20), Weishu (BL 21) and Zhongwan (RN 12) for anorexia and loss of body weight, Tianshu (ST 25), Dachangshu (BL 25), Shangjuxu (ST 37) and Shenque (RN 8) for chronic diarrhea, Quchi (LI 11) for fever, Fuliu (KI 7) and Yinxi (HT 6) for night sweat, Zhongfu (LU 1) and Feishu (BL 13) for cough, Geshu (BL 17), Xuehai (SP 10) and Quchi (LI 11) for pruritic dermatitis, Qihai (RN 6), Sanyinjiao (SP 6), Feishu (BL 13) and Shenshu (BL 23) for lassitude and listlessness.

Method: Apply filiform needles with reinforcing or even movement method. Retain the needles for 20~30 minutes manipulating them 2~3 times.

2. Ear Acupuncture

Prescription: Spleen, Kidney, Endocrine, Subcortex, Shenmen, Stomach, Lung, Occiput, Large Intestine, Small Intestine.

Method: Select 3~5 points for each treatment, Apply filiform needles with strong stimulation and retain the needles for 30 minutes. Auricular taping is also applicable.

3. Moxibustion

Prescription: Gaohuangshu (BL 43), Zusanli (ST 36), Geshu (BL 17), Pishu (BL 20).

Method: Apply mild-warming moxibustion or rounding moxibustion for 10~15 minutes once a day.

支气管哮喘

支气管哮喘系一发作性肺部过敏性疾病。其发病多因吸入或接触过敏源所致。常见过敏原为植物花粉、灰尘、昆虫（如螨）和病原菌等。发作时多由于支气管平滑肌痉挛、黏膜水肿和分泌液增多而导致气道阻塞，以致出现严重呼吸困难。如哮喘持续长时间不能缓解，称为"哮喘持续状态"。支气管哮喘好发于青少年。本病属中医"哮"、"喘"范畴。

1. 体针

处方 膻中，孔最，鱼际，肺俞，定喘。

配穴 患者呼吸急促，喉间哮鸣，甚至张口抬肩不能平卧者加丰隆，太白；患者喘促日久，咳声低弱，语言无力动则喘甚者加膏肓俞，气海，肾俞，太溪，足三里；食欲不振，大便稀溏者加脾俞，三阴交。

操作 毫针刺，平补平泻。留针20~30分钟，间歇行针2~4次。

2. 耳针

处方 对屏尖，肺，气管，支气

管，肾，下屏尖，神门，交感。

操作　每次选2～3穴，留针30分钟，亦可采用耳穴贴敷。

3．艾灸

处方　大椎，肺俞，定喘，天突，膻中，足三里，孔最。

操作　用艾条温和灸或回旋灸，每次2～4穴，每穴灸5～10分钟，每天1次；亦可艾炷隔姜灸，每次2～4穴，每穴灸5～7壮，每天1次。若用化脓灸，疗效亦佳，即在穴位处涂上大蒜汁，将黄豆般或碗豆般大小艾炷置于其上，为减少患者疼痛，医者可用手轻轻拍打施灸处周围，以分散注意力，或穴位常规消毒后，注射1%普鲁卡因0.5～1毫升后，再涂上大蒜汁置黄豆般大小艾炷灸之。每次施灸5～9壮，灸毕后贴上消毒敷料，待局部化脓。一般于夏季伏天（7～9月）灸治，隔天1次，每次1～3穴，3次1个疗程，每年灸1疗程。

4．电针

处方　孔最，鱼际，定喘，肺俞，合谷，天突，膻中，内关。

操作　每次取2～4穴，上穴交替使用，多采用密波（也可用连续波），5分钟后改用疏密波刺激量可由中等度逐渐增加到强刺激。根据病情需要每天1～2次，也可隔天1次，每次15～60分钟，10次为1个疗程。

5．挑治

处方　崇翼穴（第6颈椎棘突下的崇骨穴旁开5分），喘息穴（大椎穴旁开1寸）。

操作　患者俯坐，上穴常规消毒，用三棱针挑破0.1～0.5厘米，每穴连挑3针，患者自觉如弹弦感，皮肤略有出血。挑后用碘酊消毒，外盖消毒纱布，每隔3～5天挑治1次，连续10次为1个疗程。

Bronchial Asthma

Bronchial asthma is an episodic allergic pulmonary disease. The attack is mostly induced by the inhalation of or contact with allergens such as pollens, dust, insects（such as mite），etc. During the attack, patients have severe dyspnea which is due to spasm of bronchial smooth muscles, swelling of the bronchial mucosa, and hypersecretion of the mucus leading to bronchial obstruction. When the attack can not be relieved for a long time it is called "status asthmaticus". The disease is often seen in children and teenagers. In traditional Chinese medicine, it is attributable to the categories of "bronchial wheezing" and "dyspnea".

1．Body Acupuncture

Prescription：Tanzhong（RN 17），Kongzui（LU 6），Yuji（LU 10），Feishu（B 13），Ding chuan（EX-

B 1).

Supplementary points: Add Feng-long (ST 40) and Taibai (SP 3) for patients with rapid breathing, wheezing in the throat, and unable to lie flat with the mouth open and the shoulders lifted, Gaohuangshu (BL 34), Qihai (RN 6), Shenshu (BL 23), Taixi (KI 3) and Zusanli (ST 36) for patients with short and rapid breathing for a long time, weak and low sounding cough, feeble voice, more severe wheezing on exertion, Pishu (BL 20) and Sanyinjiao (SP 6) for poor appetite and loose stools.

Method: Apply filiform needles with even movement method. Retain the needles for 20~30 minutes manipulating them 2~4 times.

2. Ear Acupuncture

Prescription: Antitragic Apex, Lung, Trachea, Bronchi, Kidney, Infratragic Apex, Shenmen, Symthetic.

Method: 2~3 points are selected for each treatment. Retain the needles for 30 minutes. Auricular taping is also applicable.

3. Moxibustion

Prescription: Dazhui (DU 14), Feishu (BL 13), Dingchuan (EX-B 1), Tiantu (RN 22), Tanzhong (RN 17), Zusanli (ST 36), Kongzui (LU 6).

Method: 2~3 acupoints are selected each treatment session. Mild-warming or circling moxibustion with the moxa roll is given to each point for 5 ~ 10 minutes once daily, or ginger moxibustion is given to each point with 5 ~ 7 cones once daily. Additional, scarring moxibustion is also effective. Smear some garlic juice over the point. Place a moxa cone like a yellow bean in size on the acupoint and ignite it. In order to relieve the possible pain caused by burning the patient, gently tap the area around the acupoint during moxibustion or inject 0.5 ~ 1 mL of procanie into the acupoint area before moxibustion. Five to nine cones are used for each acupoint each session. After moxibustion, the acupoint is covered by a sterilized dressing. Generally, scarring moxibustion is given during the period from July to September once every other day. Moxibustion is given to 1 ~ 3 acupoints in each session, and 3 sessions constitute 1 therapeutic course. The next course is given the next year.

4. Electroacupuncture

Prescription: Kongzui (LU 6), Yuji (LU 10), Dingchuan (EX-B 1), Feishu (BL 13), Hegu (LI 4), Tiantu (RN 22), Tanzhong (RN 17), Neiguan (PC 6).

Method: Electroacupuncture is given to $2 \sim 4$ points each treatment. Dense wave is administered in the first 5 minutes and irregular wave the rest of the time. The stimulation gradually increased from medium to is large intensity. The electroacupuncture is applied for $15 \sim 60$ minutes, $1 \sim 2$ times daily or once every other day. 10 treatment sessions constitute a therapeutic course.

5. Breaking Therapy

Prescription: Chongyi (Extra, 0.5 cun lateral to Chonggu which is located below the spinous process of the sixth cervical vertebra), Chuanxi (Extra, 1 cun lateral to Dazhui DU 14).

Method: The patient is in a prone-sitting position. After local and routine sterilization, break the skin of the acupoint $0.1 \sim 0.5$ cm with the three-edged needle. Consecutively break the fibrous tissues of each point for three times. During pricking the patient may feel like a string is being flicked and the skin may bleed slightly. After breaking, sterilize the pricked area with iodine and cover it with a sterilized dressing. The pricking therapy is given once per $3 \sim 5$ days and 10 times constitutes a therapeutic course.

急性支气管炎

急性支气管炎是由细菌、病毒感染或物理化学刺激引起的气管或支气管的急性炎症。初起常有上呼吸道感染的症状，如发热、恶寒、身痛等。咳嗽为其主要症状，开始为干咳，$1 \sim 2$ 天后咳出少量黏痰或稀薄痰液，并逐渐转为脓痰或白黏痰。病程很少超过 1 个月。本病属中医"外感咳嗽"的范畴。

1. 体针

处方　肺俞，列缺，合谷。

配穴　咽喉肿痛加少商；发热加大椎，曲池。

操作　毫针刺，用泻法。留针 $15 \sim 20$ 分钟，间歇行针 $2 \sim 3$ 次。

2. 耳针

处方　气管，肺，神门，枕，交感，下屏尖。

操作　每次选 $2 \sim 3$ 个穴，毫针中等或强刺激，留针 30 分钟；亦可用耳穴贴敷。

3. 线香灸疗

处方　天突，风门，大椎，肺俞。

操作　线香点燃后，快速按在上述穴位上进行粹烫，点灸时听到皮肤表面发出一声微响声即可，每穴 1 次。对急性支气管炎喉痒咳嗽有良效。

4. 水针

处方　定喘，曲池，尺泽，丰隆，足三里，风门，肺俞。

操作 选用维生素 B_1 100 毫克，或鱼腥草注射液 2 毫升，或黄连素注射液 4 毫升，亦可用胎盘组织液，每次取 2～3 穴，每穴注射 0.5 毫升，每天 1 次。

Acute Bronchitis

Acute bronchitis is an acute inflammation of the trachea or bronchi. It is caused by a bacterium, virus, physical or chemical irritation. At the onset, it usually presents with symptoms of infection of the upper respiratory tract such as fever, aversion to cold, general aching, etc. Cough is the main symptom. At the beginning it is a nonproductive cough which becomes a productive cough. The cough produces a little sticky sputum or thin sputum after 1～2 days, gradually becoming a purulent sputum or white and sticky sputum. The course of the disease seldom goes beyond one month. It belongs to the category of "cough due to exopathy" in traditional Chinese medicine.

1. Body Acupuncture

Prescription: Feishu (BL 13), Lieque (LU 7), Hegu (LI 4).

Supplementary points: Add Shaoshang (LU 1) for sore throat, Dazhui (DU 14) and Quchi (LI 11) for fever.

Method: Apply filiform needles with reducing method. Retain the needles for 15 - 20 minutes manipulating them

two to three times.

2. Ear Acupuncture

Prescription: Bronchi, Lung, Shenmen, Occiput, Sympathetic, Infratragic Apex.

Method: Select 2～3 points for each treatment. Apply filiform needles with moderate or strong stimulation and retain the needles for 30 minutes. Auricular taping is also applicable.

3. Moxibustion with Thread Incense

Prescription: Tiantu (RN 12), Fengmen (BL 12), Dazhui (DU 14), Feishu (BL 13).

Method: Thread incense is ignited and directly pressed over the points mentioned above, and removed quickly as soon as there is a sound of skin burning. Moxibustion treatment is given to each point once only leading to an effective result for acute bronchitis, itching of the throat, and cough.

4. Point-injection

Prescription: Dingchuan (EX-B 1), Quchi (LI 11), Chize (LU 5), Fenglong (ST 40), Zusanli (ST 36), Fengmen (BL 12), Feishu (BL 13).

Method: Select Vitamin B_1, 100mg, Houttuynia Injection Solution, 2mL, Berberian Injection Solution, 4mL, Injection Solution Made of Placental Tissue.

Two or three points are injected with

0.5mL of drug solution from any one of the drugs mentioned above once a day for 10 times as a course.

慢性支气管炎

慢性支气管炎是由支气管感染、物理化学因素刺激或过敏所致的慢性支气管炎症。患者以中年以上居多。临床上病情迁延、反复发作为其特点。每年发病持续时间至少 3 个月，并连续 2 年以上。久病者常引起慢性阻塞性肺气肿和慢性肺心病。本病属中医"咳嗽"、"痰饮"、"哮"、"喘"等范畴。

1. 体针

处方　丰隆，肺俞，脾俞，太渊，足三里，肾俞。

操作　毫针刺，平补平泻。留针 15～20 分钟，间隔行针 2～3 次。

2. 耳针

处方　肝，神门，肺，气管，皮质下，下屏尖。

操作　毫针中等强度刺激，留针 15～20 分钟；亦可采用耳穴贴敷。

3. 艾灸

处方　天突，风门，肺俞，大椎，膏肓。

操作　采用艾炷灸，3～5 天治疗 1 次，5 次为 1 疗程，或艾条灸，每天 1 次，每次 5～10 分钟，以皮肤潮红为度。

4. 水针

处方　定喘，曲池，尺泽，丰隆，足三里，风门，肺俞，脾俞，神门。

操作　选用维生素 B_1 100 毫克，或鱼腥草注射液 2 毫升，或黄连素注射液 4 毫升，亦可用胎盘组织液，每次取 2～3 穴，每穴注射 0.5 毫升，每天 1 次。

5. 三棱针

处方　大椎。

操作　先局部常规消毒，然后用三棱针点刺大椎穴，并在其四周约 6 厘米处各刺 2 针（上下左右共 8 针），以微出血为佳，然后用中型玻璃火罐，燃乙醇棉球或纸片投入罐内，罩于应拔部位上 10～20 分钟。

Chronic Bronchitis

The disease is a chronic inflammation of the bronchi due to infection, physical and chemical irritants or allergic agents. The majority of the patients are of middle age or greater. It is characterized by a chronic course and recurrent episodes. The episode of attack lasts at least 3 month each year for more than 2 years. In some chronic cases, the disease may progress to chronic obstructive emphysema and chronic pulmonary heart disease. In traditional Chinese medicine, this disease is related to the categories of "cough", "phlegm retention", "asthma" and so on.

1. Body Acupuncture

Prescription: Fenglong (ST 40), Feishu (BL 13), Pishu (BL 20), Taiyuan (LU 9), Zusanli (ST 36), Shenshu (BL 23).

Method: Apply filiform needles with even movement. Retain the needles for 15~20 minutes manipulating them two to three times.

2. Ear Acupuncture

Prescription: Liver, Shenmen, Lung, Trachea, Subcortex, Infratragic Apex.

Method: Apply filiform needles with moderate stimulation and retain the needles for 15~20 minutes. Auricular taping is also applicable.

3. Moxibustion

Prescription: Tiantu (RN 12), Fengmen (BL 12), Feishu (BL 13), Dazhui (DU 14), Gaohuang (BL 43).

Method: Moxibustion with moxa cones is given once per three to five days and five times constitutes one therapeutic course. Or moxibustion with the moxa roll is given until the local skin becomes reddish (for about 5 ~ 10 minutes) once a day.

4. Point-injection

Prescription: Dingchuan (EX-B 1), Quchi (LI 11), Chize (LU 5), Fen-glong (ST 40), Zusanli (ST 36), Fengmen (BL 12), Feishu (BL 13), Pishu (BL 20), Shenmen (BL 23).

Method: Select Vitamin B_1 100mg, Houttuynia Injection Solution, 2mL, Berberian Injection Solution, 4mL, Injection Solution Made of Placental Tissues.

Two or three points are injected with 0.5mL of a drug solution from any one of the drugs mentioned above once daily, and for 10 times as a course.

5. Three-edged Needle

Prescription: Dazhui (DU 14).

Method: Give routine sterilization, then prick the point and eight other points respectively 6cm above, below, left and right to it with the three-edged needle to cause slight bleeding. After pricking, select a medium size glass jar and apply cupping with it on the pricked site for 10~20 minutes.

急性胃肠炎

急性胃肠炎是一种因暴饮、暴食或食入不洁食物引起的肠道急性炎症，多发于夏秋季节。临床以突然腹痛、腹泻及呕吐为主要症状。病者每天腹泻可达 10 次或更多，大便稀薄或水样。呕吐严重者，可引起水和电解质紊乱，继之可出现血压下降或肌肉抽搐等症状。本病属于中医"泄泻"、"呕吐"、"霍乱"等范畴。

1．体针

处方　中脘，天枢，内关，足三里。

配穴　严重者腹泻呕吐者加曲泽，委中。

操作　中脘穴垂直进针 1~1.5 寸，得气后留针 3~5 分钟，然后退至皮下，用横刺角度向上脘透刺 1~1.5 寸；复将针退至皮下，直刺建里穴，留针 2~3 分钟，再退至皮下横刺左右阴都、梁门，针刺 1.5~2 寸。中脘一针四周透六穴，诸穴均用泻法。

2．耳针

处方　胃，大肠，小肠，脾，交感，神门，耳尖。

操作　选用 3~4 穴，毫针强刺激，留针 15~20 分钟。耳尖可点刺出血以减轻炎症和疼痛，亦可采用耳穴贴敷。

3．艾灸

处方　中脘，天突，内关，足三里。

操作　用艾炷隔姜灸，每日 1 次，每次 2~3 穴，每穴 3~5 壮，或艾条温和灸及回旋灸，每次 15~20 分钟，每天 1 次。本法适宜于患者突然腹痛腹泻，大便稀薄或呈水样，恶心呕吐，苔白腻，脉濡者。

4．三棱针

操作　适宜于感冒或暴食冷饮诱发者。初起头痛，全身发胀，胃脘痛如刀绞，可见心窝、腰背两旁有疹，顶稍带黄白透明点，出现于皮毛，或稍陷于皮内。耳三棱针行挑刺，皮肤常规消毒，针对疹子以 30°~40°角刺入 2 分许，旋将针尖向上挑起，拨出白色蚕丝样的纤维，反复 4~5 次，以拨出更多纤维为度，挑完一个疹子，再挑第二个，直到胀痛消失或大减为止。

Acute Gastroenteritis

Acute gastroenteritis is an acute inflammation of the intestines caused by overindulgence in food, alcohol or consumption of contaminated food, occurring mainly in summer and autumn. It is characterized by sudden onset of abdominal pain, diarrhea, and vomiting. Dilute or watery stool is passed ten or more times each day. In cases with severe vomiting, disturbance of the water and electrolyte balance with subsequent lowered blood pressure or muscle spasm may occur. It pertains to the categories of "diarrhea", "vomiting" and "cholera morbus" in traditional Chinese medicine.

1. Body Acupuncture

Prescription: Zhongwan (RN 12), Tianshu (ST 25), Neiguan (PC 6), Zusanli (ST 36).

Supplementary points: Add Quze (PC 3) and Weizhong (BL 40) for severe vomiting and diarrhea.

Method: Puncture Zhongwan (RN 12) perpendicularly about 1~1.5 cun. Retain the needle for 3~5 minutes after the arrival of Qi. Then lift the needle tip to the subcutaneous area and pierce Shangwan (RN 13) 1~1.5 cun horizontally. Again lift the needle tip to the subcutaneous area, then puncture Jianli (RN 11) perpendicularly and retain the needle for 2~3 minutes. Lift the needle tip again to the subcutaneous area and pierce horizontal about 1.5 ~ 2 cun Yindu (KI 19) and Liangmen (ST 21) of both left and right sides. The reducing method is adopted during the process, that is, puncturing Zhongwan (RN 12) and then piercing the six points around it. Apply reducing method to all points.

2. Ear Acupuncture

Prescription: Stomach, Large Intestine, Small Intestine, Spleen, Sympathetic, Shenmen, Apex of Ear.

Method: Select 3~4 points. Apply filiform needles with strong stimulation and retain the needles for 15 ~ 20 minutes. Apex of Ear may be pricked to cause bleeding for relieving inflammation and pain. Auricular taping is also applicable.

3. Moxibustion

Prescription: Zhongwan (RN 12), Tianshu (ST 25), Neiguan (PC 6), Zusanli (ST 36).

Method: Apply ginger moxibustion until 3 ~ 5 moxa cones have burnt on each point. Alternatively apply mild-warming or circling moxibustion with the moxa roll to each point for 15~20 minutes once a day. This method is suitable for patients with acute abdominal pain and diarrhea, thin or watery stools, nausea, vomiting, white and greasy tongue coating, soft pulse.

4. Three-edged Needle

Method: This treatment is suitable for the patients induced by common cold or by over-drinking of cold fluid. It is manifested by colic epigastric pain with headache and general distension at the beginning, followed by papules with yellow, white and transparent spots on the heads of the papules which are distributed over the skin of the areas of the xiphoid process, the upper and lower back. Following a routine and local sterilization, insert a three-edged needle into the papule about 0.2 cun deep at an angle of 30°~40° formed by the needle and the local skin surface. Make the needle shaft tilted and moving upward to break the white and silk fibers until many broken. After one papule is pricked, the next one is pricked in the same way.

慢性胃炎

本病是以胃黏膜非特异性慢性炎症为主要病理变化的慢性胃部疾病。其病因不十分清楚，可能与服用刺激性药物和食物、胆汁反流、口腔炎症有关；亦有人认为和自身免疫有关。慢性胃炎可分为原发性和继发性两大类。前者又分为浅表性、萎缩性和肥厚性三种类型；后者多和溃疡病、胃癌等并存。慢性胃炎好发于中年以上人群。本病属于中医"痞"、"胃脘痛"等范畴。

1. 体针

处方　内关，中脘，足三里。

配穴　患者胃脘隐痛，喜按喜暖者加脾俞，胃俞，公孙；脘腹胀痛者加阳陵泉，太冲，期门；上腹部刺痛者加肝俞，膈俞，三阴交。

操作　毫针刺，平补平泻。留针15～20分钟，间歇行针2～4次。

2. 耳针

处方　胃，肝，皮质下，内分泌，三焦，腹。

操作　每次选用2～3穴，毫针中等强度刺激，留针15～30分钟。亦可采用耳穴贴敷。

3. 水针

处方　足三里，内关，脾俞，胃俞。

操作　选用生理盐水5毫升，或维生素 B_6、维生素 B_{12} 2毫升。采用1种注射液每次注射1～2穴，每天1次。

4. 三棱针

处方　胃俞，中脘，脾俞。

操作　常规消毒后，三棱针挑破皮肤。外盖消毒纱布。

5. 拔罐疗法

处方　中脘，脾俞，胃俞，气海。

操作　采用坐罐或闪罐治疗10～15分钟，每天1次。

Chronic Gastritis

Chronic gastritis is a chronic gastric lesion, pathologically characterized by nonspecific chronic inflammation of the gastric mucosa. Its etiology is not well understood but is possibly related to administration of irritating drugs, food, bile regurgitation, buccal inflammation or autoimmunity. Chronic gastritis can be divided into two categories, primary and secondary. The former is further categorized into superficial, atrophic and hypertrophic types. The latter often complicates gastroduodenal ulcer and gastric cancer. Chronic gastritis occurs most frequently in middle-aged people. This disease in traditional Chinese medicine pertains to the categories of "feeling of fullness in the upper abdomen" and "stomachache".

1. Body Acupuncture

Prescription: Neiguan (PC 6), Zhongwan (RN 12), Zusanli (ST 36).

Supplementary points: Add Pishu (BL 20), Weishu (BL 21) and Gongsun (SP 4) for patients with dull pain in the epigastrium relieved by pressure and warming, Yanglingquan (GB 34), Taichong (LR 3) and Qimen (LR 14) for patients with distending pain in the epigastrium, Ganshu (BL 18), Geshu (BL 17), Sanyinjiao (SP 6) for patients with stabbing pain in the epigastrium.

Method: Apply filiform needles with even movement. Retain the needles for 15~20 minutes manipulating them two to four times.

2. Ear Acupuncture

Prescription: Stomach, Liver, Subcortex, Endocrine, San jiao, Abdomen.

Method: Select 2 ~ 3 points. For each treatment apply filiform needles with moderate stimulation and retain the needles for 15 ~ 30 minute. Auricular taping is also applicable.

3. Point-injection

Prescription: Zusanli (ST 36), Neiguan (PC 6), Pishu (BL 20), Weishu (BL 21).

Method: Select Normal Saline, 5mL, or Vitamin B_6 2mL, or Vitamin B_{12}, 2mL. 1 ~ 2 points are injected with one kind of solution mentioned above once a day.

4. Three-edged Needle

Prescription: Weishu (BL 21), Zhongwan (RN 12), Pishu (BL 20).

Method: Break the skin of the points with a three-edged needle after routine sterilization. Cover the area with a sterilized dressing.

5. Cupping Therapy

Prescription: Zhongwan (RN 12), Pishu (BL 20), Weishu (BL 21), Qihai (RN 6).

Method: Apply retaining cupping or successive flash cupping for 10 ~ 15 minutes once a day.

胃 下 垂

胃小弯角切迹低于髂嵴连线以下，十二指肠壶腹部向左偏移时称为"胃下垂"。多因胃膈韧带、肝胃韧带及腹肌松弛所致。临床主要表现为腹胀，饭后加重，平卧减轻，腹痛，恶心，嗳气，食欲减退，大便或稀或干等，上腹部可扪及腹主动脉搏动。胃肠钡餐造影可帮助诊断。本病属于中医"胃脘痛"、"嗳气"，"嘈杂"等范畴。

1. 体针

处方 中脘，足三里，气海，关

元，天枢，脾俞，胃俞，大横，下脘。

操作　毫针刺，平补平泻或补法。留针 20～30 分钟，间歇行针 2～3 次。

2．耳针

处方　胃，脾，肝，神门。

操作　毫针中等强度刺激，留针 30 分钟；亦可采用耳穴贴敷。

3．电针

处方　中脘，气海，关元，足三里，提胃，胃上。

操作　每次取 2～4 穴，断续波或疏密波，腹部穴位先通电，下肢穴位后通电，电流输出量为中等度，每天 1 次，每次 15～30 分钟。

4．艾灸

处方　百会，足三里，关元，气海，中脘，胃俞，脾俞，天枢，三阴交。

操作　艾条温和灸或回旋灸，亦可针上加灸。每次 2～4 穴，治疗 15～20 分钟，每天 1 次。

5．水针

处方　中脘，足三里，下脘。

操作　每次 2 穴注射三磷腺苷 0.8 毫升，1 周 2 次，20 次为 1 个疗程。

Gastroptosis

Gastroptosis refers to the condition in which the notch of the angle of the lesser curvature of the stomach is under the level of the inter-iliac-crest line and the duodenal bulb moves to the left. It is caused mainly by a flaccid gastrophrenic ligament, hepatogastric ligament and abdominal muscles. The main clinical manifestations are abdominal distension which is aggravated after meals and relieved while lying flat, abdominal pain, nausea, belching, anorexia, either loose or dry stools. Abdominal aortic pulsation can be felt on the epigastrium by palpation. Barium meal examination of the gastrointestinal tract may support diagnosis of the disease. The disease belongs to the categories of "epigastric pain", "belching" and "gastric discomfort with acid regurgitation" in traditional Chinese medicine.

1. Body Acupuncture

Prescription: Zhongwan (RN 12), Zusanli (ST 36), Qihai (RN 6), Guanyuan (RN 4), Tianshu (ST 25), Pishu (BL 20), Weishu (BL 21), Daheng (SP 15), Xiawan (RN 10).

Method: Apply filiform needles with even movement or reinforcing method. Retain the needles for 20～30 minutes manipulating them 2～3 times.

2. Ear Acupuncture

Prescription: Stomach, Spleen,

Liver, Shenmen.

Method: Apply filiform needles with moderate stimulation and retain the needles for 30 minutes. Auricular taping is also applicable.

3. Electroacupuncture

Prescription: Zhongwan (RN 12), Qihai (RN 6), Guanyuan (RN 4), Zusanli (ST 36), Tiwei [Extra, 4 cun lateral to Zhongwan (RN 12)], Weishang [Extra, 4 cun lateral to Xiawan (RN 10)].

Method: Electroacupuncture is given to two to four points once a day with intermittent or irregular stimulation and medium strength output current applied for $15\sim30$ minutes on each point. The current is connected with the points first on the abdomen and second on the lower extremities.

4. Moxibustion

Prescription: Baihui (DU 20), Zusanli (ST 36), Guanyuan (RN 4), Qihai (RN 6), Zhongwan (RN 12), Weishu (BL 21), Pishu (BL 20), Tianshu (ST 25), Sanyinjiao (SP 6).

Method: Apply mild-warming or circling moxibustion or moxibustion with warming needle to $2\sim4$ points for $15\sim20$ minutes once a day.

5. Point-injection

Prescription: Zhongwan (RN12), Zusanli (ST36), Xiawan (RN10).

Method: Two points are injected with A.T.P, 0.8mL, twice a week. 20 treatment sessions constitute a therapeutic course.

消化性溃疡

消化性溃疡通常指胃或十二指肠壁的圆形或椭圆形缺损，主要发生在胃幽门部和十二指肠壶腹部。主要表现为上腹部规律性疼痛，伴有嗳气、反酸、恶心、呕吐及食欲不振。疼痛发作与进食有关，胃溃疡疼痛在进食后30~90分钟出现，至下一餐前已消失；十二指肠溃疡疼痛在进餐后3~4小时出现，持续至下次进餐，进餐后疼痛减轻或消失。中医称之为"胃痛"。

1. 体针

处方 中脘，足三里，内关，胃俞，肝俞，公孙，下脘。

操作 毫针刺，平补平泻。留针15~20分钟，间歇行针2~4次。

2. 耳针

处主 胃，十二指肠，腹，脾，肝，交感，皮质下，神门。

操作 毫针中等强度刺激，留针15~30分钟。亦可采用耳穴贴敷。

3. 艾灸

处方 内关，中脘，足三里，肝俞，胃俞。

操作 适宜于胃痛隐隐，喜温喜按，纳少神疲，大便溏薄等虚寒性胃脘痛。可单用，亦可在针刺后再灸。

用隔姜灸、隔附子饼灸，或艾条悬灸，温针灸。每次灸1~2小时，每天1次。一般灸后都能迅速止痛，若坚持长时间的施灸，可获良好效果。

4. 皮肤针

处方 足太阳膀胱经第一侧线（眷正中线旁开1.5寸）和第二侧线（眷正中线旁开3寸），中脘，足三里，内关。

操作 皮肤针中等强度刺激上述部位，每天1次。

5. 皮内针

处方 胃俞，脾俞，中脘。

操作 首先将皮内针、镊子及欲埋针的部位皮肤进行消毒。操作时医生左手拇指、示指将所刺部位皮肤撑开，右手持镊子夹住针柄，对准穴位垂直刺进真皮后，与经脉循行呈交叉方向，沿皮横刺入皮内，针身埋入皮内0.5~1厘米，然后用胶布将露在皮外的针柄粘贴固定。埋针的时间视季节而定，夏天一般留置1~2天，秋冬季节可留置3~5天。撤针埋针期间可每天用手按压数次，每次1~2分钟，以增强刺激提高疗效。

Peptic Ulcer

Peptic ulcer refers to circular or oval lesions on the wall of the stomach or duodenum occuring primarily on the gastric pylorus or the duodenal bulb. Peptic ulcer is marked by regularly occuring pain in the epigastric region accompanied by belching, acid regurgitation, nausea, vomiting, and poor appetite. Onset of pain is generally related to intake of food. In cases of gastric ulcer, pain is usually occurring 30 minutes to two hours after eating and disappearing sometimes before the next meal. In cases of duodenal ulcer, the pain usually starts three to four hours after eating and is relieved after eating the next meal. It belongs to the category of "epigastric pain" in traditional Chinese medicine.

1. Body Acupuncture

Prescription: Zhongwan (RN 12), Zusanli (ST 36), Neiguan (PC 6), Weishu (BL 21), Ganshu (BL 18), Gongsun (SP 4), Xiawan (RN 10).

Method: Apply filiform needles with even movement. Retain the needles for 15~20 minutes manipulating them two to four times.

2. Ear Acupuncture

Prescription: Stomach, Duodenum, Abdomen, Spleen, Liver, Sympathetic, Subcortex, Shenmen.

Method: Apply filiform needles with moderate stimulation and retain the needles for 15~30 minutes. Auricular taping is also applicable.

3. Moxibustion

Prescription: Neiguan (PC 6), Zhongwan (RN 12), Zusanli (ST

36), Ganshu (BL 18), Weishu (BL 21).

Method: Moxibustion treatment is suitable for epigastric pain of deficiency-cold type manifested by dull pain in the epigastrium which may be relieved by pressure and warmth, poor appetite, general lassitude and loose stools. 3～5 points are employed each treatment session and moxibustion may be applied singly or after puncturing. The ginger or monkshood-cake moxibustion, suspended moxibustion, or mild-warming moxibustion is given 1～2 hours once daily. Generally, the pain is relieved immediately after the moxibustion, and a better effect will be achived if a long period of treatment is given.

4. Plum-blossom Needle

Prescription: The four lines respectively 1.5 cun and 3 cun lateral to the posterior median line on the back, Zhongwan (RN 12), Zusanli (ST 36), Neiguan (PC 6).

Method: Apply a plum-blossom needle to tap the areas mentioned above with moderate stimulation once a day.

5. Acupuncture With the Intradermal Needle

Prescription: Weishu (BL 21), Pishu (BL 20), Zhongwan (RN 12).

Method: Sterilize the intradermal needle, forceps and skin area to be punctured. Push the skin at the acupoint area in two opposite directions with the thumb and index finger of the left hand. Hold the needle perpendicularly directly into the acupoint to the dermis. Then, horizontal puncture in a direction crossing the meridian course along the skin and embed the needle shaft 0.5～0.1cm inside the skin. Finally, fix the handle of the needle left outside on the skin with a piece of adhesive plaster. The duration of embedment varies with the season. Generally, 1～2 days in summer and 3～5 days in autumn or winter. During the embedding period, the patient should press the thumb-tack needle several times daily each time lasting 1～2 minutes.

胃肠神经官能症

胃肠神经官能症是由高级神经功能紊乱所致的胃肠功能障碍。临床主要以胃肠症状为主，同时伴有失眠，多梦，健忘，神经过敏等症状。该病属中医"胃脘痛"、"呕吐"、"嗳气"、"泄泻"等范畴。

1. 体针

处方 内关，中脘，天枢，足三里，太冲，脾俞，肝俞。

操作 毫针刺，平补平泻，留针15～20分钟，间隔行针2～3次。

2．耳针

处方　胃，小肠，大肠，腹，脾，肝，皮质下。

操作　毫针中等强度刺激，留针30 分钟。亦可用耳穴贴敷。

3．艾灸

处方　中脘，天枢，足三里，脾俞。

操作　温和灸或回旋灸治疗 10～15 分钟，每日 1 次。

4．水针

处方　内关，足三里，脾俞。

操作　维生素 B_1 2 毫升穴位注射，2 天 1 次。

Gastrointestinal Neurosis

Gastrointestinal neurosis is gastrointestinal disorder due to higher nervous activity dysfunction. It is characterized mainly by gastrointestinal symptoms accompanied with insomnia, dream-disturbed sleep, amnesia, nervousness, etc. It pertains to the categories of "epigastric pain", "vomiting", "belching" and "diarrhea" in traditional Chinese medicine.

1. Body Acupuncture

Prescription: Neiguan (PC 6), Zhongwan (RN 12), Tianshu (ST 25), Zusanli (ST 36), Taichong (LR 3), Pishu (BL 20), Ganshu (BL 18).

Method: Apply filiform needles with even movement and retain the needles for 15～20 minutes manipulating them 2～3 times.

2. Ear Acupuncture

Prescription: Stomach, Small Intestine, Large Intestine, Abdomen, Spleen, Liver, Subcortex.

Method: Apply filiform needles with moderate stimulation and retain the needles for 30 minutes. Auricular taping is also applicable.

3. Moxibustion

Prescription: Zhongwan (RN 12), Tianshu (ST 25), Zusanli (ST 36), Pishu (BL 20).

Method: Apply mild-warming or rounding moxibustion for 10 ～ 15 minutes once a day.

4. Point-injection

Prescription: Neiguan (PC 6), Zusanli (ST 36), Pishu (BL 20).

Method: Vitamin B_1 2mL is injected into the points once every other day.

慢性非特异性溃疡性结肠炎

本病亦称溃疡性结肠炎。其病因不明，近来认为与自身免疫有关。病变侵犯直肠、乙状结肠和降结肠，是一种非特异性炎症，主要累及黏膜层，情绪紧张、精神创伤和对某些食物过敏可诱发本病。患者女多于男。

本病中医属"泄泻"、"赤白痢"等范畴。

1. 体针

处方　大肠俞，中脘，足三里，天枢，脾俞。

操作　毫针刺，平补平泻，留针15～30分钟，间歇行针2～4次。

2. 耳针

处方　大肠，小肠，直肠，腹，内分泌，神门，脾。

操作　毫针中等强度刺激，留针20～30分钟；亦可用耳穴贴敷。

3. 艾灸

处方　中脘，足三里，脾俞，天枢。

操作　温和灸或回旋灸治疗10～30分钟，每天1次。本法适宜于脾胃虚弱和脾肾阳虚者。

Chronic Nonspecific Ulcerative Colitis

This disease is also termed ulcerative colitis. Its etiology is still unknown but in recent years has been associated with autoimmunity. The pathological change attacks the rectum, sigmoid colon and descending colon. It is a kind of nonspecific inflammation which primarily involves the mucosal layer. Precipitating factors include emotional tonus, psychic trauma and allergy to certain foods. It occurs more frequently in males than in females. In traditional Chinese medicine the disease is categorized as "diarrhea", "dysentery", etc.

1. Body Acupuncture

Prescription: Dachangshu (BL 25), Zhongwan (RN 12), Zusanli (ST 36), Tianshu (ST 25), Pishu (BL 20).

Method: Apply filiform needles with even movement. Retain the needles for 15～30 minutes manipulating them two to four times.

2. Ear Acupuncture

Prescription: Large Intestine, Small Intestine, Rectum, Abdomen, Endocrine, Shenmen, Spleen.

Method: Apply filiform needles with moderate stimulation and retain the needles for 20～30 minutes. Auricular taping is also applicable.

3. Moxibustion

Prescription: Zhongwan (RN 12), Zusanli (ST 36), Pishu (BL 20), Tianshu (ST 25).

Method: Apply mild-warming or rounding moxibustion for 10 ～ 30 minutes once a day. It is suitable for insuffiency of the spleen and stomach and insufficiency of the spleen-Yang and kidney-Yang.

高 血 压

高血压是临床常见病症，以动脉血压升高为特点。根据病因病机可分为原发性和继发性两类。原发性高血压是指病因尚未明确，以动脉血压升高为主要临床表现的一种独立疾病，症状有头痛，头晕，耳鸣，面色潮红，失眠，易怒，重者可出现视物昏花，心悸，气短，健忘，手指麻木，甚则中风。病者常有高血压家族史，高级神经中枢失调在本病中占主导地位。继发性高血压是指继发于某些器质性病变的高血压病，如肾病，心脏病及内分泌系统的疾病，高血压仅是这些疾病的一个症状，所以又称为症状性高血压。本病属于中医"头痛"、"眩晕"范畴。

1．体针

处方　曲池，太冲，足三里，三阴交，内关。

配穴　头痛加太阳，风池；失眠心悸加通里，神门；头重肢困加丰隆。

操作　毫针刺，平补平泻，留针20～30分钟，间歇行针2～4次。

2．耳针

处方　皮质下，交感，神门，耳尖，降压沟。

操作　毫针中等强度刺激，留针30分钟；亦可用耳穴贴敷。

3．皮肤针

处方　取颈后至尾骶脊柱两侧常现刺激区，气管两侧。

操作　从上而下轻度或中度叩刺。

4．三棱针

处方　大椎，曲泽，委中，太阳。

操作　大椎穴附近常规消毒后，用三棱针刺入皮下，挑拨1～3次出针，随后将火罐扣于穴上，拔罐15分钟左右。或取曲泽，委中，太阳刺血，每次1穴（双侧），3～5天治疗1次，每次出血量5～10毫升。

5．头针

处方　足运感区（双），胸腔区，血管舒缩区。

操作　每天1次，5～10次为1疗程。

Hypertension

Hypertension is a commonly seen complaint in clinical practice. It is characterized by high blood pressure of the arterial system and is classified into primary and secondary types according to etiology and pathogenesis. Primary hypertension refers to hypertension with no clear cause. It is an independent disease marked by high blood pressure of the arterial system. Other manifestations include headache, dizziness, tinnitus, flushed face, insomnia, and irritability. In severe cases, blurred vision, palpitation, shortness of breath, poor memory, numbness of the fingers, or even stroke may occur. There is often a family history of hypertension. The primary pathogenesis of primary hypertension is disorder of the central nervous system.

Secondary hypertension refers to hypertension occurring secondary to organic problems such as nephric, cardiac, or endocrinal disorder. In these cases, hypertension is a symptom of the disease, therefore, secondary hypertension is also called symptomatic hypertension. Traditional Chinese medicine classifies hypertension as "headache" or "vertigo".

1. Body Acupuncture

Prescription: Quchi (LI 11), Taichong (LR 3), Zusanli (ST 36), Sanyinjiao (SP 6), Neiguan (PC 6).

Supplementary points: Add Taiyang (EX-HN 5) and Fenchi (GB 20) for headache, Tongli (HT 5) and Shenmen (HT 7) for insomnia and palpitation, Fenglong (ST 40) for heaviness in the head and weakness of the limbs.

Method: Apply filiform needles with even movement. Retain the needles for 20~30 minutes manipulating them 2~4 times.

2. Ear Acupuncture

Prescription: Subcortex, Sympathetic, Shenmen, Apex of ear, Groove for lowering blood pressure, Liver.

Method: Apply filiform needles with moderate stimulation and retain the needle for 30 minutes. Auricular taping is also applicable.

3. Plum-blossom Needle

Prescription: The regular stimulation area beside the spinal column, the area beside the trachea.

Method: Tap with a plum-blossom needle on the areas gently or moderately from top to bottom once a day.

4. Three-edged Needle

Prescription: Dazhui (DU 14), Quze (PC 3), Weizhong (BL 40), Taiyang (EX-HN 5).

Method: After routine and local sterilization prick the areas around Dazhui (DU14) with the three-edged needle and shake the needle one to three times at each point. Following withdrawal of the needle, apply cupping to Dazhui (DU 14) area for about 15 minutes. Alternatively select Quze (PC 3), Weizhong (BL 40) and Taiyang (EX-HN 5) alternately, pricking one pair of points to cause bleeding 5~10 mL each treatment session. Give the treatment once per 3~5 days.

5. Scalp Acupuncture

Prescription: Foot motor sensory area (bilateral), Thoracic area, Vasomotor area.

Method: Give the treatment once a day. 5 ~ 10 treatment, make up a course.

冠 心 病

冠心病是冠状动脉粥样硬化性心脏病的简称，世界各国特别是发达国家患病率甚高，我国近年来亦有上升趋势。本病的易患因素为高血压、高血脂、糖尿病和吸烟等。按世界卫生组织的诊断标准，冠心病的分类诊断为：①原发心脏骤停；②心绞痛；③心肌梗死；④冠心病心力衰竭；⑤心律失常。本章重点阐述心绞痛和心肌梗死，属于中医"胸痹"、"胸痛"、"真心痛"、"厥心痛"等范畴。

1．体针

处方　心俞，厥阴俞，内关，膻中，郄门，足三里，神堂，通里。

操作　毫针刺，补泻兼施。留针20～30分钟，间歇行针2～4次。

2．耳针

处方　心，胸，皮质下，交感，小肠，肝，脑。

操作　毫针中等强度刺激，留针20～30分钟。亦可采用耳穴贴敷。

3．艾灸

处方　膻中，膈俞，心俞，足三里。

操作　艾灸每穴施治10～15分钟，每天1次。

4．水针

处方　双侧内关。

操作　哌替啶（度冷丁）10毫克，加入注射用水，稀释至5毫升，用6.5号针头垂直刺入内关穴，得气后强刺激，每穴注药2.5毫升。如疼痛不缓解，30分钟后可以此法将药注入双侧间使穴。

Coronary Heart Disease

Coronary heart disease is the abbreviation of coronary atherosclerotic heart disease. The incidense is high in all countries, especially in developed countries. Recently, the incidence in China has been increasing. The risk factors for coronary heart disease are hypertension, hyperlipemia, diabetes mellitus and cigarette smoking. According to the diagnostic criteria made by the WHO, coronary heart disease can be divided into: ①primary sudden cardiac arrest ②angina pectoris ③myocardiac infarction ④heart failure due to coronary heart disease ⑤and arrhythma. In this section only angina pectoris and myocardiac infarction are described. This disease, in traditional Chinese medicine, pertains to the categories of "obstruction of Qi in the chest", "Chest pain", "myocardiac infarction" and "precordial pain with cold limbs".

1. Body Acupuncture

Prescription: Xinshu（BL 15），Jueyinshu（BL 14），Neiguan（PC 6），Tanzhong（RN 17），Ximen（PC 4），Zusanli（ST 36），Shentang（BL

44）, Tongli（HT 5）.

Method: Apply filiform needles with both reinforcing and reducing methods, Retain the needles for 20～30 minutes manipulating them 2～4 times.

2. Ear Acupuncture

Prescription: Heart, Chest, Subcortex, Sym-psathetic, Small Intestine, Liver, Brain.

Method: Apply filiform needles with moderate stimulation and retain the needles for 20～30 minutes. Auricular taping is also applicable.

3. Moxibustion

Prescription: Tanzhong（RN 17）, Geshu（BL 17）, Xinshu（BL 15）, Zusanli（ST 36）.

Method: Moxibustion with the moxa roll is given to each point for 10～20 minutes once a day.

4. Point Injection

Prescription: Neiguan（PC 6）（bilateral）.

Method: Pethidine（Dolantin）10 mg of dolantin with water to make a 5 mL solution for injection. Puncture Neiguan（PC 6）perpendicularly with No. 6.5 needle. A strong stimulation is given after arrival of Qi. 2.5mL of this solution is injected into each of the two points. If the patient still feels pain, this kind of solution may be injected into Jianshi（PC 5）（bilateral）

in the same way 30 minutes later.

高脂蛋白血症

血中脂质包括胆固醇、三酰甘油（甘油三脂）、磷脂和非脂化脂肪酸四种。血中脂质增高主要指胆固醇和三酰甘油增高，并与动脉粥样硬化关系密切。由于血中脂质是以脂蛋白形式转运，所以高脂血症亦常反映高脂蛋白血症。本症属中医"眩晕"、"痰浊"等范畴。

1. 体针

处方　曲池，内关，三阴交，足三里，丰隆，太白，阳陵泉。

配穴　伴高血压头胀痛，眩晕，耳鸣，面红目赤加刺太冲；口渴多饮，消谷善饥加刺内庭；畏寒肢冷，尿少身肿加刺太溪，阴陵泉，肾俞等穴。

操作　毫针刺，补泻并用。留针20～30分钟，间歇行针2～3次。

2. 耳针

处方　肝，交感，内分泌，脾。
操作　毫针中等强度刺激，留针20～30分钟；亦可采用耳穴贴敷。

3. 艾灸

处方　足三里，悬钟。
操作　用直接米粒灸法，灸双侧足三里，悬钟（交替使用），每周1次，每次3壮，致使三度烧伤起泡化脓，若破皮者，隔日换药1次，直至结痂形成瘢痕，以10次为1个疗程，均只作 1 个疗程。

Hyperlipoproteinemia

Blood lipids are composed of cholesterol, triglycerides, phospholipids and free fatty acids. Hyperlipemia mainly implies the elevation of cholesterol and triglycerides in the plasma and is closely related to atherosclerosis. As blood lipids are transported in the form of lipoproteins, hyperlipemia also manifests as hyperlipoproteinemia. It is included in the categories of "vertigo", "Phlegm syndrome" and others in traditional Chinese medicine.

1. Body Acupuncture

Prescription: Quchi (LI 11), Neiguan (PC 6), Sanyinjiao (SP 6), Zusanli (ST 36), Fenglong (ST 40), Taibai (SP 3), Yanglingquan (GB 34).

Supplementary points: Add Taichong (LR 3) for hypertension with distending pain in the head, dizziness, tinnitus, flushed face and congested eye, Neiting (ST 44) for thirst, polydipsia, ravenous appetite, excessive hunger, and Taixi (KI 3), Yinlingquan (SP 9) and Shenshu (BL 23) for aversion to cold, cold extremities, oliguria and edema.

Method: Apply filiform needles with both reinforcing and reducing methods. Retain the needles for 20~30 minutes

manipulating them 2~3 times.

2. Ear Acupuncture

Prescription: Liver, Sympathetic, Endocrine, Spleen.

Method: Apply filiform needles with moderate stimulation and retain the needles for 20~30 minutes. Auricular taping is also applicable.

3. Moxibustion

Prescription: Zusanli (ST 36), Xuanzhong (GB 39).

Method: Left and right points are employed alternately. Direct moxibustion with rice-sized cones are given until three cones are burnt in each point causing local third degree burns, blisters and purulence. If the local area is broken, it is covered with a dressing and the dressing is replaced with a new one every other day until a scar is formed. The moxibustion is given once per week and ten sessions constitute a course.

心律失常

心律失常是指由心律起源部位、心搏频率与节律及冲动传导等方面异常所致的病症。常见的有心动过速、心动过缓和心律不齐。本病属中医"心悸"、"怔忡"等范畴。

1. 体针

处方　内关，神门，心俞，厥阴俞，肾俞，至阳，足三里。

操作 毫针刺，平补补泻。留针20～30分钟，间歇行针2～3次。

2．耳针

处方 心，脑，神门，皮质下，肾，小肠。

操作 毫针轻刺激，留针20～30分钟，亦可采用耳穴贴敷。

3．电针

处方 内关，郄门，心俞，足三里，三阴交。

操作 每次2穴，选用疏密波，中等强度刺激，以患者能耐受为度。每天1次，每次15～30分钟。

Arrhythmia

Any abnormality in the starting portion of heart-stroke, heart rate, rhythm, or cardiac conduction is called arrhythmia in which tachycardia, bradycardia and irregular heart rate are more common. It belongs to the categories of "palpitation", "Severe palpitation" and others in traditional Chinese medicine.

1. Body Acupuncture

Prescription: Neiguan (PC 6), Shenmen (HT 7), Xinshu (BL 15), Jueyinshu (BL 14), Shenshu (DU 12), Zhiyang (DU 9), Zusanli (ST 36).

Method: Apply filiform needles with even movement. Retain the needles for 20～30 minutes manipulating them 2～3 times.

2. Ear Acupuncture

Prescription: Heart, Brain, Shenmen, Subcortex, Kidney, Small Intestine.

Method: Apply filiform needles with mild stimulation and retain the needles for 20～30 minutes. Auricular taping is also applicable.

3. Electroacupuncture

Prescription: Neiguan (PC 6), Ximen (PC 4), Xinshu (BL 15), Zusanli (ST 36), Sanyinjiao (SP 6).

Method: Employ two points each session and apply electric stimulation at medium strength with sparse-dense wave tolerable to the patient. Treatment is given for 15～30 minutes once a day.

病态窦房结综合征

病态窦房结综合征是由各种原因引起的窦房结及其周围组织缺血、变性、纤维化等病变，从而导致以显著窦性心动过缓为主要表现的一种心律紊乱。病变严重或侵犯房室交界传导系统，称为双节病变或全传导系统病变。本病属中医"脉迟"、"心悸"、"眩晕"、"胸痹"、"厥证"等范畴。

1．体针

处方 内关，心俞，足三里，神门，郄门。

操作 毫针刺,用补法。留针 20~30 分钟,间歇行针 2~3 次。

2. 耳针

处方 心,肾,交感,皮质下,小肠。

操作 毫针轻刺激,留针 20~30 分钟;亦可用耳穴贴敷。

3. 艾灸

处方 心俞,肾俞,足三里,三阴交。

操作 温和灸或回旋灸治疗 10~15 分钟,每天 1 次。

4. 电针

处方 内关,郄门,心俞,足三里。

操作 每次选 2 个穴位,选用疏密波,中等刺激,每天 1 次,每次 15~30 分钟。

Sick Sinus Syndrome

Sick sinus syndrome is the ischemia, degeneration and fibrosis of the sinoatrial node and its adjacent tissue induced by various causes resulting in marked sinus bradycardia as a major manifestation. In severe cases or in patients whose atrioventricular conductive junction system is also affected, it is called double nodal dysfunction or dysfunction of the whole cardiac conduction system. The syndrome is included in the categories of "slow pulse", "palpitation", "vertigo", "obstruction of Qi in the chest," "Cold limbs", etc.

1. Body Acupuncture

Prescription: Neiguan (PC 6), Xinshu (Bl 15), Zusanli (ST 36), Shenmen (HT 7), Ximen (PC 4).

Method: Apply filiform needles with reinforcing method. Retain the needles for 20~30 minutes manipulating them 2~3 times.

2. Ear Acupuncture

Prescription: Heart, Kidney, Sympathetic, Subcortex, Small Intestine.

Method: Apply filiform needles with mild stimulation and retain the needles for 20~30 minutes. Auricular taping is also applicable.

3. Moxibustion

Prescription: Xinshu (BL 15), Shenshu (BL 23), Zusanli (ST 36), Sanyinjiao (SP 6).

Method: Apply mild-warming or rounding moxibustion for 10~15 minutes once a day.

4. Electroacupuncture

Prescription: Neiguan (PC 6), Ximen (PC 4), Xinshu (BL 15), Zusanli (ST 36).

Method: Select 2 points each session and apply electric stimulation at medium strength with sparse-dense wave for 15~30 minutes once a day.

慢性风湿性心脏病

慢性风湿性心脏病是由于风湿病反复发作引起的心脏瓣膜损害，临床主要表现为心悸，呼吸困难，咳血，甚至水肿。本病属于中医"心痹"、"心悸"、"怔忡"、"水肿"等范畴。

1. 体针

处方　心俞，厥阴俞，内关，神门，足三里。

配穴　心痛，两颧紫红，唇甲青灰，舌质青紫，或有瘀斑，脉细涩或结代加血海，膈俞，少海；神疲乏力，气短自汗加脾俞，气海，膈俞；水肿，咳嗽气短，手足不温加肾俞，命门水分，膻中。

操作　毫针刺，用补法或平补平泻法。留针20~30分钟，间歇行针2~3次。

2. 耳针

处方　心，肺，神门，脾，肾，交感。

操作　毫针轻刺激，留针20~30分钟。

3. 艾灸

处方　心俞，厥阴俞，足三里。

操作　温和灸或回旋灸治疗10~15分钟，每天1次。

Chronic Rheumatic Heart Disease

The disease is a valvulopathy due to repeated attacks of rheumatism. The main clinical manifestations are palpitation, dyspnea, hemoptysis, even edema, etc. It belongs to categories of "obstruction of the heart-Qi", "palpitation", "severe palpitation", "edema" and others in traditional Chinese medicine.

1. Body Acupuncture

Prescription: Xinshu (BL 15), Jueyinshu (BL 14), Neiguan (PC 6), Shenmen (HT 7), Zusanli (ST 36).

Supplementary points: Add Xuehai (SP 10), Geshu (BL 17) and Shaohai (HT 3) for precordial pain, violent redness of zygomatic regions, bluish grey lips and nails, blue-purple tongue, tongue with ecchymoses, uneven or knotted and intermittent pulse, Pishu (BL 20), Qihai (RN 6) and Geshu (BL 17) for lassitude, shortness of breath, spontaneous perspiration, Shenshu (BL 23), Mingmen (DU 4), Shuifen (RN 9) and Tangzhong (RN 17) for edema, cough shortness of breath, and cold limbs.

Method: Apply filiform needles with reinforcing or even movement method. Retain the needles for 20~30 minutes manipulating them 2~3 times.

2. Ear Acupuncture

Prescription: Heart, Lung, Shenmen, Spleen, Kidney, Sympathetic.

Method: Apply filiform needles with mild stimulation and retain the needles for 20~30 minutes.

3. Moxibustion

Prescription: Xinshu (BL 15), Jueyinshu (BL 14), Zusanli (ST 36).

Method: Apply mild-warming or rounding moxibustion for 10~15 minutes once a day.

心脏神经官能症

心脏神经官能症又称神经血循环衰弱症或奋力综合征，为高级神经功能失调引起的心脏血管功能性疾病，多发生于青壮年，女性多于男性。其特点为心前区钝痛，持续数小时或数天，或心尖处针刺状疼痛，持续 1~5 分钟，多在劳累或精神紧张后诱发或加重，其他症状包括易于疲劳，心悸，气短，焦虑，烦躁，汗出，手震颤及麻木等。本病多属于中医"心痛"、"心悸"等范畴。

1. 体针

处方　心俞，内关，膻中，郄门，足三里，通里。

操作　毫针刺，平补平泻法。留针 20~30 分钟，间歇行针 2~3 次。

2. 耳针

处方　心，内分泌，交感，脑，神门，肝。

操作　毫针中等强度刺激，留针 30 分钟；亦可采用耳穴贴敷。

3. 艾灸

处方　百会。

操作　艾卷悬灸百会穴 10~15 分钟。每天 1 次。

Cardiac Neurosis

Cardiac neurosis, also called neurocirculatory asthenia or effort syndrome, is a functional disorder of the cardiovascular system caused by disturbance of the central nervous system. It occurs mainly in adults and more often in females than in males. It is characterized by precordial dull pain lasting several hours or days, or stabbing pain in the apical region of the heart lasting one to five minutes. It is induced or aggravated primarily by exertion or nervousness. Other symptoms may include lassitude, palpitations, shortness of breath, anxiety, restlessness, mild fever, perspiration, or trembling and numbness of the hands. It belongs to the categories of "Chest pain", and "Palpitation" in traditional Chinese medicine.

1. Body Acupuncture

Prescription: Xinshu (BL 15), Neiguan (PC 6), Tanzhong (RN 17), Ximen (PC 4), Zusanli (ST 36), Tongli (HT 5).

Method: Apply filiform needles with

even movement. Retain the needles for 20~30 minutes manipulating them 2~3 times.

2. Ear Acupuncture

Prescription: Heart, Endocrine, Sympathetic, Brain, Shenmen, Liver.

Method: Apply filiform needles with moderate stimulation and retain the needles for 30 minutes. Auricular taping is also applicable.

3. Moxibustion

Prescription: Baihui (DU 20).

Method: Moxibustion with a moxa stick is given to Baihui (DU 20) for 10~15 minutes once a day.

4. Plum blossom Needle

Prescription: The Du meredian and the branches of the Urinary Bladder meridian on the back.

Method: Tap the channels from above downwards 5~7 times to cause erytherma and a little oozing of blood.

急性肾炎

急性肾炎是一种免疫反应性疾病，多由乙型溶血性链球菌感染后体内产生免疫复合物沉积于肾小球所致，亦可为其他病原体感染引起，或为其他疾病表现的一部分。本病多见于儿童，男多于女。大多数患者病后可以恢复，少数迁延不愈转为慢性肾炎。急性肾小球肾炎多属于中医"风水"范畴。

1. 体针

处方　列缺，曲池，合谷，三阴交，风池。

操作　毫针刺，用泻法。留针20~30分钟，间歇行针2~4次。

2. 耳针

处方　肾，内分泌，膀胱，肺。

操作　毫针中等强度刺激，留针20~30分钟。

3. 皮肤针

处方　足太阳膀胱经第一侧线和第二侧线。

操作　从上至下中等强度叩击5~7遍，隔天1次。

Acute Nephritis

Acute nephritis is an immunoreactive disease caused by the deposition of an immune complex in the glomeruli mainly after hemolytic streptococcal infection. The disease can also be caused by other organisms, or is involved as part of the manifestations of other diseases. It occurs mostly in children with males predominating. Most patients can recover completely. A few cases may progress to chronic nephritis. This disease pertains to the category of "wind edema" in traditional Chinese medicine.

1. Body Acupuncture

Prescription: Lieque (LU 7),

Quchi (LI 11), Hegu (LI 4), Sany-injiao (SP 6), Fengchi (GB 20).

Method: Apply filiform needles with reducing method. Retain the needles for 20～30 minutes manipulating them 2～4 times.

2. Ear Acupuncture

Prescription: Kidney, Endocrine, Urinary Bladder, Lung.

Method: Apply filiform needles with moderate stimulation and retain the needles for 20～30 minutes.

3. Plum-blossom Needles

Prescription: The four lines respectively 1.5 cun and 3 cun lateral to the posterior median line on the back.

Method: Tap the areas from top to bottom with moderate stimulation 5～7 times once every other day.

慢性肾炎

慢性肾炎是由多种病因所引起的一种变态反应性疾病。患者可由急性肾炎演变而来，但多无急性肾炎病史。好发于中青年，病程长，预后较差。本病属中医"水肿"、"虚劳"、"腰痛"等范畴。

1. 体针

处方　脾俞，肾俞，三阴交，太溪。

操作　毫针刺，用补法。留针20～30分钟，间歇行针2～3次。

2. 耳针

处方　肾，膀胱，脾，内分泌。

操作　毫针中等强度刺激，留针30分钟；亦可用耳穴贴敷。

3. 水针

处方　肾俞，脾俞，足三里。

操作　每次2穴注射胎盘组织液2毫升。

4. 艾灸

处方　肾俞，脾俞，命门，足三里。

操作　温和灸治疗10～15分钟，每天1次。适宜于水肿，腰膝酸软，四肢不温者。

Chronic Nephritis

Chronic nephritis is an allergic disease caused by a wide variety of etiological factors. Only a small percentage of cases are obviously due to the progression of acute nephritis. The majority of patients with chronic nephritis have no history of acute nephritis. The disease is common in young adults and middle aged people. Its course is long and the prognosis is poor. In traditional Chinese medicine this disease is categorized as "edema", "consumptive disease", "lumbago", etc.

1. Body Acupuncture

Prescription: Pishu (BL 21),

Shenshu（BL 23）, Sanyinjiao（SP 6）, Taixi（KI 3）.

Method: Apply filiform needles with reinforcing method. Retain the needles for 20～30 minutes manipulating them 2～3 times.

2. Ear Acupuncture

Prescription: Kidney, Urinary Bladder, Spleen, Endocrine.

Method: Apply filiform needles with moderate stimulation and retain the needles for 30 minutes. Auricular taping is also applicable.

3. Point Injection

Prescription: Shenshu（BL 23）, Pishu（BL 21）, Zusanli（ST 36）.

Method: Two points are injected with Injection Solution Made of Placental Tissues 2 mL.

4. Moxibustion

Prescription: Shenshu（BL 23）, Pishu（BL 21）, Mingmen（DU 4）, Zusanli（ST 36）.

Method: Apply mild-warming moxibustion for 10～15 minutes, once a day, It is suitable for edema, soreness and weakness of the loins, knees, and cold extremities.

风湿性关节炎

　　风湿性关节炎是一种与链球菌感染有关的反复发作的关节结缔组织性疾病。多发于冬春季节，女性较男性多见。临床特点为多发性，游走性及对称性大关节炎。主要累及膝、肩、肘、腕和髋等关节。病变部位可见红、肿、热、痛。炎症消退后，关节功能可恢复正常，不留任何畸形。中医称之为痹证，病因风寒湿三种病气相合侵犯人体，引起气血阻滞，筋脉失养所致。

1. 体针

　　处方　足三里，商丘，肾俞，曲池。

　　配穴　肩部疼痛加肩髃，肩贞，臑俞；肘部疼痛配曲池，合谷，天井，外关，尺泽；腕部疼痛加阳池，阳谷，阳溪，外关；髋部疼痛加环跳，居髎，悬钟；股部疼痛加秩边，承扶，阳陵泉，膝阳关；踝部疼痛加商丘，丘墟，昆仑，太溪。

　　操作　毫针刺，用泻法。留针20～30分钟，间歇行针2～3次。

2. 耳针

　　处方　关节相应部位，神门，肝，脑，肾，心。

　　操作　每次选3～5穴，毫针强刺激，留针30分钟；亦可用耳穴贴敷。

3. 艾灸

　　处方　足三里，肾俞，脾俞。

　　操作　用温和灸或回旋灸治疗10～15分钟，每天1次。

Rheumatic Arthritis

Rheumatic arthritis refers to a frequently recurring collagen disorder of the joints caused primarily by Streptococcus rheumatosis bacteria. It occurs mainly in spring and autumn and more often in females than in males. It is marked by multiple, shifting, and symmetrical inflammation of the major joints including the knees, ankles, shoulders, elbows, wrists, and hips. The affected area is usually red, swollen, hot, and painful. The joints may recover normal function with no residual deformity when the inflammation is relieved. Traditional Chinese medicine considers rhematic arthritis to be a "Bi syndrome" caused primarily by exogenous wind, cold, and dampness. These three pathogens combine to attack the body leading to obstruction of Qi and blood and insufficient nourishment of the joints and tendons.

1. Body Acupuncture

Prescription: Zusanli (ST 36), Shangqiu (SP 5), Shenshu (BL 23), Quchi (LI 11).

Supplementary points: Add Jianyu (LI 15), Jianzhen (SI 9) and Naoshu (SI 10) for pain in the shoulder joints, Quchi (LI 11), Hegu (LI 4), Tianjing (SJ 10), Waiguan (SJ 5) and Chize (LU 5) for pain in the elbow; Yangchi (SJ 4), Yanggu (SI 5), Yangxi (LI 5) and Waiguan (SJ 5) for pain in the wrist, Renzhong (DU 26), Shenshu (BL 23) and Yaoyangguan (DU 3) for pain in the lumber region, Huantiao (GB 30), Juliao (GB 29) and Xuanzhong (GB 39) for pain in the hip joint, Zhibian (BL 54), Chengfu (BL 36) and Yanglingquan (GB 34) for pain in the thigh region, Dubi (ST 35), Liangqiu (ST 34), Yanglingquan (GB 34) and Xiyangguan (GB 33) for pain in the knee joint, Shangqiu (SP 5), Qiuxu (GB 40), Kunlun (BL 60) and Taixi (KI 3) for pain in the ankle.

Method: Apply filiform needles with reducing method. Retain the needles for 20～30 minutes manipulating them 2～3 times.

2. Ear Acupuncture

Prescription: The area corresponding to the joints, Shenmen, Liver, Brain, Kidney, Heart.

Method: 3～5 point are used for each treatment. Apply filiform needles with strong stimulation and retain the needles for 30 minutes. Auricular taping is also applicable.

3. Moxibustion

Prescription: Zusanli (ST 36), Shenshu (BL 23), Pishu (BL 20).

Method: Apply mild-warming or rounding moxibustion for 10～15 minutes once a day.

类风湿性关节炎

类风湿性关节炎是一种因自身免疫导致的多关节非化脓性炎症。多发于青壮年，女性较男性多见。临床特点为多发性、对称性的小关节的慢性炎症，两手近端指间关节和掌指关节受累最常见，其次为足趾、踝和腕关节受累。一些不典型病变可发肘、肩、膝和髋等大关节部。病变初期，受累关节疼痛，僵硬，肿胀，压痛，晨起时明显，轻度活动后症状减轻；中期则上述关节部症状加重，关节肿胀，呈梭形；晚期则关节强硬，畸形，关节周围的肌肉萎缩。全身症状可见乏力，消瘦，低热，食欲不振及轻度贫血。本病属于中医"痹证"的范畴。

1. 体针

处方 以局部选穴为主，配合循经取穴。

脊椎关节 取人中，殷门，大椎，委中穴，脊椎两侧相应节段部位。

肩关节 取肩髃，肩髎，曲池，天宗，臂臑，阿是穴。

肘关节 取曲池，少海，外关，合谷，阿是穴。

腕关节 取阳池，阳溪，腕骨，合谷，养老，阿是穴。

腰骶关节 取腰阳关，委中，昆仑，大肠俞，阿是穴。

髋关节 取环跳，秩边，阳陵泉，阿是穴。

膝关节 取内、外膝眼，委中，鹤顶，阴陵泉，阳陵泉。

踝关节 取解溪，丘墟，商丘，太冲，太溪，昆仑，阿是穴。

操作 每次取穴 3～5 个，毫针刺，补法和泻法并用，留针 20～30 分钟，间隔行针 2～4 次。

2. 耳针

处方 神门，脑，肾，内分泌，相应区压痛点。

操作 毫针中等强度刺激，留针 30 分钟。

3. 艾灸

处方 大椎。

操作 艾条直接熏大椎，每次 2 小时以上。灸感达到命门穴以下，加熏灸命门穴。

4. 皮肤针

处方 肿胀区，脊椎两侧。

操作 叩刺肿胀区，脊椎两侧自上而下叩刺。

Rheumatoid Arthritis

Rheumatoid arthritis is a non-suppurative inflammation of the small joints caused primarily by autoimmunity. It occurs mainly in young people and adults, more often in females than in males. Rheumatoid arthritis is characterized by chronic, multiple, and symmetrical inflammation of the small joints. The paracentral interphalangeal joints of the hands are most commonly affected followed by the joints of the toes, ankles, and wrists. In some atypical cases, major joints such as the elbows, shoulders, knees, and hips may be affected. In the initial stage, there is pain, rigidity, swelling, and tenderness of the affected joints most severe in the morning and gradually lessening with mild movement. In the intermediate stage, symptoms worsen with the joints becoming swollen and fusiform. In the advanced stage, stiffness and deformity of the affected joints may be accompanied by atrophy of the surrounding muscles. General symptoms may include lassitude, emaciation, mild fever, poor appetite, and mild anemia. Traditional Chinese medicine classifies rheumatoid arthritis as "Bi syndrome".

1. Body Acupuncture

Prescription: The local points are taken as the main points and distal points along the meridian as the adjuvant. The points are selected according to the disease portion as follows:

Vertebra joints: Renzhong (DU 26), Dazhui (DU 14), Weizhong (BL 40), Yinmen (BL 51). Bilateral sides of corresponding vertebral joint areas.

Shoulder joints: Jianyu (LI 15), Jianliao (SJ 14), Quchi (LI 11), Tianzong (SI 11), Binao (LI 14), tender spots at the local area.

Elbow joints: Quchi (LI 11), Shaohai (HT 3), Waiguan (SJ 5), Hegu (LI 4), tender spots at the local area.

Wrist joints: Yangchi (SJ4), Yangxi (LI 5), Wangu (SI 4), Hegu (LI 4), Yanglao (SI 6), tender spots at the local area.

Lumbosacral joints: Yaoyangguan (DU 3), Weizhong (BL 40), Kunlun (BL 6), Dachangshu (BL 25), tender spot at the local area.

Hip joints: Huantiao (GB 30), Zhibian (BL 54), Yanglingquan (GB 34), tender spots at the local area.

Knee joints: Internal and external Xiyan (EX-LE 4, 5), Weizhong (BL 40), Heding (EX-LE 2), Yinlingquan (SP 9), Yanglingquan (GB 34).

Ankle joints: Jiexi (ST 41), Qiuxu (GB 40), Shangqiu (SP 5), Taichong (LR 3), Taixi (KI 3), Kunlun (BL 60), tender spots at the local area.

Method: 3~5 points or tender spots are employed each treatment session. Apply filiform needles with both reinforcing and reducing methods. Retain the needles for 20~30 minutes manipulating them 2~4 times.

2. Ear Acupuncture

Prescription: Shenmen, Brain, Kidney, Endocrine, corresponding tender spots on the auricle.

Method: Apply filiform needles with moderate stimulation and retain the needles for 30 minutes.

3. Moxibustion

Prescription: Dazhui (DU 14).

Method: Moxibustion with a moxa stick is applied to Dazhui (DU 14) for more than two hours until the moxibustion sensation induced to the patient is propagated to the area below Mingmen (DU 4). Moxibustion is given to Mingmen (DU 4) additionally.

4. Plum-blossom Needle

Prescription: Swelling and distension area, bilateral sides of the spinal vertebra.

Method: Tap on the local swelling and distension areas or at the bilateral sides of the spinal vertebra from the top towards the bottom.

三叉神经痛

三叉神经痛是指发生在三叉神经分布区的短暂性阵发性剧痛。多见于青壮年，女性多于男性，多累及三叉神经的第二支和第三支，第一支很少受累。其特点为受累部位疼痛突然发作，如电击、针刺、刀割或烧灼样，

疼痛常因说话、咀嚼、洗脸、刷牙、受凉或触及面部板击点而触发。其他症状有面肌抽搐、流涎和流泪。疼痛持续数秒或数分钟后消失，间歇期无任何不适。本病属中医"牙痛"、"头痛"范畴。

1. 体针

处方　下关，颊车，地仓，夹承浆（地仓穴直下，承浆旁开1寸），太阳，阳白，四白，攒竹，合谷，中渚，内庭，足临泣，太冲。

操作　每次选穴3~5个，毫针刺，用泻法，留针20~30分钟，间歇行针2~4次。

2. 耳针

处方　面颊，颌，牙，三焦，皮质下，神门，耳尖。

操作　毫针强刺激，留针30分钟，亦可用耳穴贴敷。

3. 电针

处方　下关，颊车，攒竹，合谷，中渚。

操作　用密波或疏密波，电流量缓慢增加，至患者能耐受为度，每次20~30分钟。每天1次。

4. 水针

处方　四白，攒竹，下关。

操作　维生素 B_1 1毫升（100毫克）穴位注射，隔2~3天1次。

Trigeminal Neuralgia

Trigeminal neuralgia refers to transient paroxysmal megalgia of the trigeminal nerve pathway. It occurs mainly in adults and more often in females than in males. Usually affected branches are the second and third branches of the trigeminal nerve. The first branch is rarely involved. Trigeminal neuralgia is marked by sudden onset of stabbing or burning pain along the pathway of the affected nerve usually evoked by speaking, chewing, washing the face, brushing the teeth, catching cold, or touching "trigger points" on the face. Other manifestations include facial spasm, salivation, and lacrimation. The pain usually spontaneously disappears after several seconds or minutes with no discomfort between episodes. Traditional Chinese medicine classifies trigeminal neuralgia as "toothache" and "headache".

1. Body Acupuncture

Prescription: Xiaguan (ST 7), Jiache (ST 6), Dicang (ST 4), Jianchengjian〔Extra, below Dicang (ST 4), 1 cun lateral to Chengjian (RN 24)〕, Taiyang (EX-HN 5), Yangbai (GB 14), Sibai (ST 2), Cuanzhu (BL 2), Hegu (LI 4), Zhongzhu (SJ 3), Neiting (ST 44), Zulinqi (GB 41), Taichong (LR 3).

Method: 3~5 points are employed each treatment session. Apply filiform needles with reducing method. Retain the needles for 20~30 minutes manipulating them 2~4 times.

2. Ear Acupuncture

Prescription: Cheek, Jaw, Teeth, Sanjiao, Subcortex, Shenmen, Apex of Ear.

Method: Apply filiform needles with strong stimulation and retain the needles for 30 minutes. Auricular taping is also applicable.

3. Electroacupuncture

Prescription: Xiaguan (ST 7), Jiache (ST 6), Cuanzhu (BL 2), Hegu (LI 4), Zhongzhu (SJ 3).

Method: The intensity of electric stimulation with dense wave or dense-sparse wave is adjusted from weak gradually to maximum so that the patient can tolerate it without pain. The electric stimulation lasts for 20~30 minutes per session and the treatment is given once a day.

4. Point Injection

Prescription: Sibai (ST 2), Cuanzhu (BL 2), Xiaguan (ST 7).

Method: The points are injected with Vitamin B_1 1 mL (100mg), once every 2~3 days。

周围性面神经麻痹

周围性面神经麻痹是因茎乳突孔

内急性非化脓性面神经炎所致的疾病。临床表现为突然口眼㖞斜，一侧眼睑不能闭合，不能皱眉，流泪，流涎，不能鼓腮吹气，面肌有麻木感，耳下或乳突常有疼痛，有的病例尚伴患侧舌 2/3 味觉障碍，但无肢体瘫痪等。中医称之为"口眼㖞斜"。

1. 体针

处方　地仓，颊车，阳白，合谷，上巨墟，四白，颧髎。

配穴　乳突部疼痛加翳风；鼻唇沟平坦加迎香；人中沟㖞斜加水沟；颏唇沟㖞斜加承浆。

操作　毫针刺，用泻法。留针30 分钟，间歇行针 2～4 次。

2. 耳针

处方　面颊，眼，口，皮质下。

操作　毫针中等强度刺激，留针30 分钟；亦可用耳穴贴敷。

3. 艾灸

处方　地仓，颊车，阳白，四白，承浆。

操作　用艾卷温和灸，或针上加灸，或隔姜灸，每次每穴 5～7 壮，或每穴灸 10～15 分钟，每天 1～2次。本法适宜于面瘫伴有肢体不温，食欲不振，口不渴，面色苍白，小便量多色清，舌淡苔白，脉沉细，或迟而无力者。

4. 电针

处方　地仓透颊车，丝竹空透攒竹，四白透迎香，阳白透鱼腰。

操作　先针第一穴，获针感后，退至皮下，以 30 度角透刺后，通电5～10 分钟，以瘫痪肌肉出现收缩现象为佳。每天或隔天 1 次。

5. 拔罐疗法

处方　下关，牵正，太阳，阳白，承浆，颊车。

操作　每次取 2～3 穴，用小号火罐以闪火法拔罐 10 分钟，隔天1 次。

6. 三棱针

处方　患侧腮内膜咬合线。

操作　令患者先用盐水漱口，以清洁口腔，并尽量将口张大。医者左手拇指、示指用纱布拿住患侧口角，该手余指按压腮部，使其内侧面向口方向翻转，右手持消毒三棱针由内向外点刺咬合线，使其微出血。间隔0.5 寸左右挑 1 针，挑至口角内侧即完毕。挑治后避风寒，可热敷患部，5～7 天挑 1 次。

Peripheral Facial Paralysis

Peripheral facial paralysis is caused by an acute nonsuppurative inflammation of the facial nerve in the stylomastoid foramen. It is manifested clinically by sudden onset of deviation of eye and mouth, incomplete closure of eye in the affected side, inability to frown, salivation, inability to blow out the cheek, facial numbness, and pain in the mastoid region. In some cases, dysgeusia in the tongue in the affected side may be seen but no paralysis of extremities is found. It is termed " deviation of mouth and eye" in traditional Chinese medicine.

1. Body Acupuncture

Prescription: Dicang (ST 4), Jiache (ST 6), Yangbai (GB 14), Hegu (LI 4), Shangjuxu (ST 37), Sibai (ST 2), Quanliao (SI 18).

Supplementary points: Add Yifeng (SJ 17) for mastoidalgia, Yingxiang (LI 20) for shallow nasolabial groove, Shuigou (DU 26) for deviation of the philtrum, Chengjiang (RN 24) for deviation of the mentolabial sulcus.

Method: Apply filiform needles with reducing method. Retain the needles for 30 minutes manipulating them 2~4 times.

2. Ear Acupuncture

Prescription: Cheek, Eye, Mouth, Subcortex.

Method: Apply filiform needles with moderate stimulation and retain the needles for 30 minutes. Auricular taping is also applicable.

3. Moxibustion

Prescription: Dicang (ST 4), Ji-

ache (ST 6), Yangbai (GB 14), Sibai (ST 2), Chengjiang (RN 24).

Method: Apply mild-warming moxibustion with a moxa stick, moxibustion with warming needle, or ginger moxibustion is applied to each point for 10~15 minutes or 5~7 cones once or twice a day. This method is suitable for facial paralysis accompanied by cold body and limbs, poor appetite with no thirst, pale complexion, abundant pale urine, pale tongue with whitish coating, deep and small or slow and forceless pulse, and for those acupuncture is not effective. 3 ~ 5 points are employed each treatment session.

4. Electroacupuncture

Prescription: Dicang (ST 4) piercing towards Jiache (ST 6), Sizhukong (SJ 23) piercing towards Zanzhu (BL 2), Sibai (ST 2) piercing towards Yingxiang (LI 20), Yangbai (GB 14) piercing towards Yuyao (Extra).

Method: Puncture the first point, lift the needle tip to the subcutaneous area after arrival of Qi. Then pierce the second point at the angle of 30°. Send electrical current to them for 5 ~ 10 minutes. It is recommended to see the contraction of the paralytic muscles. Give the treatment once every day or every other day.

5. Cupping

Prescription: Xiaguan (ST 7), Qianzheng (EX-HN 16), Taiyang (EX-HN 5), Yangbai (GB 14), Chengjiang (RN 24), Jiache (ST 6).

Method: 2~3 points are employed each treatment session. Small jars are selected and flashing method is applied to each point for 10 minutes once every other day.

6. Three-edged Needle

Prescription: The line of occlusion at the buccal mucosa at the effected side.

Method: Ask the patient to clean his mouth with water and open it as largely as possible. Take some cloth to hold the angle of mouth at the affected side with the thumb and the index finger of the left hand. Press the cheek of the affected side with the other fingers of the hand and prick the line with a three-edged needle from posterior outwards to cause slight bleeding. Every 0.5 cun portion of the line is pricked from the inside towards the outside until the internal side of the angle of the mouth is reached. The patient is advised to apply hot compresses to the affected area and to avoid being attacked by wind-cold evils. The treatment is given once every 5~7 days for 3 sessions as a course.

面肌抽搐

面肌抽搐系指单侧面部肌肉阵发性不自主地抽搐。多数病例发病原因不明，少数为面瘫后遗症。抽搐多从眼轮匝肌开始，逐渐扩散至同侧面部，尤以口角处抽搐明显。多数病例入睡后抽搐即停止，少数仍存在。中医认为本病多因外风或内风所导致。

1. 体针

处方 风池，合谷，足三里，百会。

操作 毫针刺，平补平泻，留针30分钟，间歇行针2~4次。

2. 耳针

处方 面颊，眼，口，皮质下，神门，三焦。

操作 毫针中等强度刺激，留针30分钟。

3. 水针

处方 翳风，地仓，颊车。

操作 穴位注射维生素 B_1 100毫克，隔天1次。

Facial Spasm

Facial spasm is an involuntary, paroxysmal spasm of the unilateral facial muscles. Although some cases are sequelae of facial paralysis, most do not have a clear and definite cause. The spasm usually originates in the orbicular muscle of the eye and gradually spreads to its homolateral facial muscles. Spasm of the angle of the mouth is most apparent. The spasm may spontaneously stop after sleep but in some cases it persists. According to traditional Chinese medicine, facial spasm is caused by either exogenous wind or endogenous wind.

1. Body Acupuncture

Prescription: Fengchi (GB 20), Hegu (LI 4), Zusanli (ST 36), Baihui (DU 20).

Method: Apply filiform needle with even movement method. Retain the needles for 30 minutes manipulating them 2~4 times.

2. Ear Acupuncture

Prescription: Cheek, Eye, Mouth, Subcortex, Shenmen, Sanjiao.

Method: Apply filiform needles with moderate stimulation and retain the needles for 30 minutes.

3. Point Injection

Prescription: Yifeng (SJ 17), Dicang (ST 4), Jiache (ST 6).

Method: The points are injected with Vitamin B_1 100mg once every other day.

肋间神经痛

肋间神经痛是指因肋间神经炎性病变导致一个或几个肋间部位疼痛。发病多由胸膜炎、肺炎、肋软骨炎、带状疱疹及外伤等引起肋间神经炎。表现特点为病损肋间神经分布呈针刺样或闪电样持续性疼痛，可放射至腰背部，疼痛因咳嗽、深呼吸而加重。局部感觉过敏和压痛。中医称之为"肋痛"。

1. 体针

处方　丘墟，支沟，阳陵泉，行间，内关，胸 5~10 夹脊穴。

操作　选 3~5 个穴，毫针刺，用泻法，留针 20~30 分钟，间歇行针 2~4 次。

2. 耳针

处方　胸，胸椎，肝，神门，耳尖。

操作　毫针中等强度刺激，留针30 分钟。亦可用耳穴贴敷。

3. 皮肤针

处方　患处肋间隙，脊柱两侧，锁骨上窝。

操作　皮肤针叩击上述部位，每次 5~10 分钟，每天 1 次。

Intercostal Neuralgia

Intercostal neuralgia refers to pain in one or more intercostal spaces caused by inflammation of the intercostal nerves. It is caused mainly by pleuritis, pneumonia, costal chondritis, herpes zoster, or chest trauma resulting in inflammation of the intercostal nerves. It is marked by persistent stabbing pain along the pathway of the affected intercostal nerves, radiating to the lumbar region of the affected side and aggravated by coughing or deep breathing. Localized hyperesthesia and tenderness are also present. It pertains to the category of "pain in hypochondriac region" in traditional Chinese medicine.

1. Body Acupuncture

Prescription: Qiuxu (GB 40), Zhigou (SJ 6), Yanglingquan (GB 34), Xingjian (LR 2), Neiguan (PC 6), Jiaji (EX-B2, T5~10).

Method: Select 3~5 points. Apply filiform needles with reducing method. Retain the needles for 20~30 minutes manipulating them 2~4 times.

2. Ear Acupuncture

Prescription: Chest, Thoracic Vertebrae, Liver, Shenmen, Apex of Ear.

Method: Apply filiform needles with moderate stimulation and retain the needles for 30 minutes. Auricular taping is also applicable.

3. Plum-blossom Needle

Prescription: Intercostal space of the affected region, the skin lateral to the spinal column of both sides, the skin over the supraclavicular fossa.

Method: Tap on the areas with strong stimulation for 5~10 minutes once a day.

坐骨神经痛

坐骨神经痛为临床常见的腰腿痛。主要表现为沿坐骨神经走行的放射性疼痛，疼痛如刀割样或烧灼样，每于行走、弯腰、咳嗽时加重，病变常累及一侧。根据病因可分为原发性和继发性，原发性坐骨神经痛是坐骨神经本身因感染而发生病变；继发性坐骨神经痛是因受坐骨神经邻近组织病变影响所致，如腰椎间盘突出症、骶髂关节炎、髋关节炎及盆腔病变。本病属于中医"痹证"。

1. 体针

处方　大肠俞，肾俞，次髎，委中，环跳，阳陵泉，悬钟，殷门，阿是穴。

配穴　腰部压痛明显者加腰阳关，痛久不愈加人中。

操作　每次选3~5穴，毫针刺，用泻法。留针20~30分钟，间歇行针2~4次。

2. 耳针

处方　坐骨神经，腰骶椎，臀，神门，膀胱。

操作　毫针强刺激，留针20~30分钟，亦可用耳穴贴敷。

3. 电针

处方　阳陵泉，委中，环跳，足三里。

操作　针刺得气后通电20分钟，采用密波或疏密波，每天1次。

4. 水针

处方　环跳，殷门，委中，阳陵泉，悬钟，颊车，腰 2~4 夹脊穴。

操作　每次选用 2~3 穴，每穴注射当归或红花注射液 1 毫升，隔天1 次。

5. 皮肤针

处方　腰骶两侧，臀，下肢足太阳及足少阳循行线。

操作　三棱针叩刺，每天 1 次。

Sciatica

Sciatica is a commonly occuring lumbocrural pain frequently seen in clinical practice. It is marked by stabbing or burning pain radiating along the pathway of the sciatic nerve aggravated by walking, bending, or coughing. Usually only one side is affected. Sciatica is classified into primary and secondary types. Primary sciatica is caused by infection affecting the sciatic nerve itself. Secondary sciatica is caused by disease or disorder of the tissues adjacent to the sciatic nerve such as prolapse of the lumbar intervertebral disc, sacroiliitis, coxitis, or pelvic infection. Traditional Chinese medicine classifies sciatica as "bi syndrome".

1. Body Acupuncture

Prescription: Dachangshu (BL 25), Shenshu (BL 23), Ciliao (BL 32), Weizhong (BL 40), Huantiao (GB 30), Yanglingquan (GB 34), Xuanzhong (GB 39), Yinmen (BL 37), Ashi points。

Supplementary points: Add Yaoyangguan (DU 3) for obviously tender manifestation at the lower part of the back, Renzhong (DU 26) for prolonged pain.

Method: Select 3~5 points. Apply filiform needles with reducing method. Retain the needles for 20~30 minutes manipulating them 2~4 times.

2. Ear Acupuncture

Prescription: Sciatic Nerve, Lumbosacral Vertebra, Buttock, Shenmen, Urinary Bladder.

Method: Apply filiform needles with strong stimulation and retain the needles for 20~30 minutes. Auricular taping is also applicable.

3. Electroacupuncture

Prescription: Yanglingquan (GB 34), Weizhong (BL 40), Huantiao (GB 30), Zusanli (BL 36).

Method: Insert the needles into the points. After arrival of Qi, electrify them for 20 minutes with a dense wave or a sparse-dense wave. Give the treatment once a day.

4. Point Injection

Prescription: Huantiao (GB 30), Yinmen (BL 37), Weizhong (BL 40), Yanglingquan (GB 34), Xuanzhong （GB 39）, Jiaji （EX-BZ, L 2～4）。

Method：2～3 points are employed each session. Radix Angelicae Sinesis Injection or Safflower Injection, 1 mL, is injected into each point. The treatment is given once every other day.

5．Plum-blossom Needle

Prescription: Bilateral sides of the lumbosacral spine, buttock, courses of the Foot-Taiyang meridian and Foot-Shaoyang meridian.

Method：Tap the areas with a plum-blossom needles, once a day.

红斑性肢痛病

红斑性肢痛病系因迷走神经兴奋过度引起的末梢血管病症。多发于冬季，女性多于男性。临床特点为病变部位阵发性皮肤色红，怕热及灼痛或刺痛，夜间、行走或遇热加重。多数累及两足，少数累及双手。缓解期内病变部位仍可有轻度麻木、疼痛。本病属于中医"痹证"。

1．体针

处方　行间，内庭，侠溪，陷谷。

操作　毫针刺，用泻法。留针30分钟，间歇行针2～4次。

2．耳针

处方　神门，枕，耳尖，心，肺。

操作　毫针强刺激，留针30分钟；亦可用耳穴贴敷。

3．皮肤针

处方　肿痛区。

操作　皮肤针叩刺肿痛区，1天1次。

Erythromelalgia

Erythromelalgia is a problem of the capillary tips caused by vagotonia. It occurs mainly in winter and more often in females than in males. It is marked by paroxysmal burning or stabbing pain, redness of the extremities, aversion to heat, and is aggravated at night by walking, or by exposure to heat. There may be mild numbness and pain during the remission stage. The feet are affected much more often than hands. Traditional Chinese medicine classifies erythromelalgia as "bi syndrome".

1．Body Acupuncture

Prescription: Xingjian （LR 2）, Neiting （ST 44）, Xiaxi （GB 43）, Xiangu （ST 43）.

Method：Apply filiform needles with reducing method. Retain the needles for 30 minutes manipulating them 2～4 times.

2．Ear Acupuncture

Prescription: Shenmen, Occiput, Apex of Ear, Heart, Liver.

Method: Apply filiform needles with

strong stimulation and retain the needles for 30 minutes. Auricular taping is also applicable.

3. Plum-blossom Needle

Prescription: The areas of swelling and pain.

Method: Tap the areas of swelling and pain with a plum-blossom needle once a day.

雷 诺 病

雷诺病系因末梢小动脉痉挛引起末梢血液循环障碍而致的一种病症。多见于青年妇女，常因寒冷、情绪刺激或内分泌障碍等因素而诱发。部分患者有家族史。临床特点为四肢末端对称性、间歇性改变，多累及上肢。发作时，病变部位肤色苍白，继之紫暗，伴有局部寒冷、麻木及刺痛，数小时或数日后，皮肤颜色转为潮红，变暖，最后肤色恢复正常。本病属于中医"痹证"。

1. 体针

处方　内庭，侠溪，尺泽，足三里，合谷，曲池，外关，少海，阳池，阳溪。

操作　毫针刺，用泻法，留针30分钟，间歇行针 2～4 次。

2. 耳针

处方　交感，皮质下，耳尖，心，肺。

操作　毫针强刺激，留针 30 分钟；亦可用耳穴贴敷。

3. 皮肤针

处方　患处。

操作　皮肤针叩刺患处，每次 5～10 分钟，每天 1 次。

Raynaud's Disease

Raynaud's disease is a disorder of the peripheral circulation caused by spasm of the peripheral arterioles. It occurs mainly in young women and is usually induced by cold, mental injury, or endocrine dysfunction. There may be a family history of Raynaud's disease as well. Raynaud's disease is marked by symmetrical, intermittent change in the color of the extremities, most often the hands. During onset, the skin of the affected areas first becomes pale and then deep purple in color with accompanying localized coldness, numbness, and stabbing pain. After several hours or days the skin becomes warm and its color returns to normal. Traditional Chinese medicine classifies Raynaud's disease as "bi syndrome".

1. Body Acupuncture

Prescription: Neiting (ST 44), Xiaxi (GB 44), Chize (LU 5), Zusanli (ST 36), Hegu (LI 4), Quchi (LI 11), Waiguan (SJ 5), Shaohai (HT 3), Yanchi (SJ 4), Yangxi (LI 5).

Method: Apply filiform needles with

reducing method. Retain the needles for 30 minutes manipulating them 2~4 times.

2. Ear Acupuncture

Prescription：Sympathetic, Subcortex, Apex of Ear, Heart, Liver.

Method：Apply filiform needles with strong stimulation and retain the needles for 30 minutes. Auricular taping is also applicable.

3. Plum-blossom Needle

Prescription：Affected area.

Method：Tap the affected area with a plum-blossom needle for 5~10 minutes once a day.

神经衰弱

神经衰弱是临床上最常见的一种神经官能症，多见于青壮年，女性多于男性。本病主要由于长期精神紧张，如抑郁、焦虑、恼怒或用脑过度，引起大脑皮质兴奋和抑制功能失调所致。症状包括失眠，多梦，心悸，烦躁，头晕，头痛，汗出，食欲不振，精神委靡，倦怠及健忘等。本病属中医"失眠"范畴。

1．体针

处方　神门，劳宫，太溪，三阴交，足三里。

操作　毫针刺，用泻法，留针20~30分钟，间歇行针2~4次。

2．耳针

处方　心，神门，皮质下，脑。

操作　毫针强刺激，留针30分钟；亦可用耳穴贴敷。

3．艾灸

处方　百会。

操作　每晚睡前用艾卷悬灸百会穴10~15分钟。

Neurosism

Neurosism is one of the most commonly seen neuroses in clinical practice, occurring mainly in adults and more often in females than in males. It is caused primarily by protracted mental injury, resulting in an imbalance between excitement and inhibition of the cortex. Manifestations include insomnia, nightmares, palpitation, restlessness, irritability, dizziness, headache, perspiration, poor appetite, listlessness, lassitude, and poor memory. Traditional Chinese medicine refers to neurosism as insomnia.

1. Body Acupuncture

Prescription：Shenmen（HT 7），Laogong（PC 8），Taixi（KI 3），Sanyinjiao（SP 6），Zusanli（ST 36）.

Method：Apply filiform needles with reducing method. Retain the needles for 20~30 minutes manipulating them 2~4 times.

2. Ear Acupuncture

Prescription: Heart, Shenmen, Subcortex, Brain.

Method: Apply filiform needles with strong stimulation and retain the needles for 30 minutes. Auricular taping is also applicable.

3. Moxibustion

Prescription: Baihui (DU 20).

Method: Moxibustion with a moxa stick is given to Baihui (DU 20) for 10~15 minutes before the patient goes to bed.

癔 症

癔症是由精神刺激不良暗示引起的功能性疾病，多见于青年，女性多于男性。首次癔症发作常与精神创伤有关。临床表现多样，例如：精神障碍包括情志暴发如哭笑无常，癔症性晕厥或缄默，躯体障碍包括癔症性瘫痪，癔症性失音，癔症性痉挛，癔症性失明，癔症性耳聋及癔球症；内脏器官功能障碍包括神经性呕吐，神经性厌食，神经性呃逆及神经性尿频等。本病属于中医"郁病"范畴。

1. 体针

处方 人中，内关，合谷，太冲，神门，后溪。

操作 毫针刺，用泻法。留针20~30分钟，间歇行针3~5次。

2. 耳针

处方 心，神门，脑，内分泌。

操作 毫针强刺激，留针20~30分钟。

3. 电针

处方 第一组：人中，百会；第二组：大椎，风池。

操作 每次选用一组，针后通以脉冲电流5~20分钟，每天1次。

Hysteria

Hysteria is a functional disorder caused by mental injury occuring primarily in young people and more often in females than in males. The first hysterical attack is usually related to psychic trauma. Manifestations are various. For example, mental disorders including emotional outburst such as irrational laughing or crying, hysterical syncope, or mutism; physical problems including hysterical paralysis, aphonia, spasm, blindness, deafness, and globus hystericus; and internal disorders including nervous vomiting, anorexia, hiccups, and frequent urination. Traditional Chinese medicine classifies hysteria as "Yu syndrome".

1. Body Acupuncture

Prescription: Renzhong (DU 26), Neiguan (PC 6), Hegu (LI 4), Taichong (LR 3), Shenmen (HT 7),

Houxi（SI 3）。

Method：Apply filiform needles with reducing method. Retain the needles for 20～30 minute manipulating them 3～5 times.

2. Ear Acupuncture

Prescription： Heart， Shenmen， Brain， Endocrine.

Method：Apply filiform needles with strong stimulation and retain the needles for 20～30 minutes.

3. Electroacupuncture

Prescription：Group Ⅰ：Renzhong （DU 26），Baihui（DU 20）；Group Ⅱ：Dazhui（DU14），Fenchi（GB 20）.

Method：Select one group for each treatment. Send the pulsating electric current to the points for 5～20 minutes after needling. Give the treatment once a day.

精神分裂症

精神分裂症是最常见的一种精神病。其病因迄今尚未明了，一般认为与遗传因素、环境因素等有关。多发于青年人，男女发病率无明显差异。本病属中医"郁证"、"癫"、"狂"等范畴。

1. 体针

处方　内关，神门，百会，丰隆，天窗，三阴交。

配穴　幻听加听宫，翳风；幻视加攒竹，肝俞，丝竹空，睛明；狂躁不安加行间，劳宫，人中，涌泉。

操作　毫针刺，用泻法，不留针，每天1次。

2. 耳针

处方　心，脑，神门，内分泌，枕，肝，胃。

操作　毫针强刺激，不留针。

3. 电针

处方　第一组：人中，百会；第二组：大椎，风池。

操作　每次选一组穴，针后通电5～20分钟，每天1次。

Schizophrenia

Schizophrenia is the most common from of psychosis. Its etiology has not been well understood despite many years of studies. Generally, genetic and environmental factors are considered to be involved in causing the disease. Schizophrenia frequently occurs in young adults. The ratio of incidence between males and females is roughly equal. In traditional Chinese medicine this disease is included in the categories of "melancholia", "depressive psychosis", "mania", etc.

1. Body Acupuncture

Prescription： Neiguan（PC 6）, Shenmen（HT 7）, Baihui（DU 20）, Fenglong（ST 40）, Tianchuang（SI

16), Sanyinjiao (SP 6).

Supplementary points: Add Tinggong (SI 19) and Yifeng (SJ 17) for auditory hallucination, Cuanzhu (BL 12), Ganshu (BL 18), Sizhukong (SJ 23) and Jingming (BL 1) for visual hallucination, Xingjian (LR 2), Laogong (PC 8), Renzhong (DU 26) and Yongquan (KI 1) for excessive motor activity.

Method: Select 2 ~ 4 points each treatment session. Apply filiform needles with reducing method. The needles are not retained. The treatment is given once a day.

2. Ear Acupuncture

Prescription: Heart, Brain, Shenmen, Endocrine, Occiput, Liver, Stomach.

Method: Apply filiform needles with strong stimulation. The needles are not retained.

3. Electroacupuncture

Prescription: Group I: Renzhong (DU 26), Baihui (DU 20); Group II: Dazhui (DU 14), Fengchi (GB 20).

Method: Apply one group for each treatment. Use the pulsating electric current to the points for 5~20 minutes after needling. Give the treatment once a day.

脑血管意外后遗症

脑血管意外后遗症是指由急性脑血管疾患所致的肢体瘫痪，语言不利，口眼㖞斜等症。本病属中医"中风"范畴。

1. 体针

处方　百会，三阴交，风府，天窗。

配穴　上肢瘫加肩髃，曲池，外关，合谷；下肢瘫加环跳，阳陵泉，足三里，绝骨；口角㖞斜加地仓，颊车。

操作　毫针刺，平补平泻，留针30分钟，间歇行针2~4次。

2. 耳针

处方　心，脑，神门，皮质下。

操作　毫针轻刺激，留针30分钟；亦可采用耳穴贴敷。

3. 头针

处方　对侧运动区，感觉区，足运感区，语言区。

操作　毫针沿皮刺，间歇捻针，留针30分钟，或通电50分钟，以患肢出现热、麻、胀、抽动感应为好。

4. 电针

处方　肩髃，合谷，曲池，环跳，风池，颊车，阳白。

操作　选2~3对穴位，进针捻转得气或出现针感向远端扩散后再通电，用疏波或断续波，电流强度以患者能耐受为度，每次通电20分钟，每天1次。

Cerebrovascular Accident Sequelae

Cerebrovascular accident sequelae

refers to hemiplegia, slurred speech, deviation of the mouth and eye, and other symptoms caused by acute cerebrovascular diseases. It pertains to the category of "wind stroke" in traditional Chinese medicine.

1. Body Acupuncture

Prescription: Baihui (DU 20), Sanyinjiao (SP 6), Fengfu (DU 16), Tianchuang (SI 16).

Supplementary points: Add Jianyu (LI 15), Quchi (LI 11), Waiguan (SJ 5) and Hegu (LI 4) for paralysis of the upper limbs, Huantiao (GB 30), Yanglingquan (GB 34), Zusanli (ST 36) and Juegu (GB 39) for paralysis of the lower limbs, Dicang (ST 4) and Jiache (ST 6) for deviation of the mouth and eyes.

Method: Apply filiform needles with even movement method. Retain the needles for 30 minutes manipulating them 2~4 times.

2. Ear Acupuncture

Prescription: Heart, Brain, Shenmen, Subcortex.

Method: Apply filiform needles with mild stimulation and retain the needles for 30 minutes. Auricular taping is also applicable.

3. Scalp Acupuncture

Prescription: Contralateral motor area, sensory area, foot motor sensory area, speech area.

Method: Use filiform needles to puncture the areas along the skin. Twirl the needles at intervals. Retain them for 30 minutes or electrify them for 50 minutes. It is better for the patient to feel warm, numb, distending and subsultory on the affected limb.

4. Electroacupuncture

Prescription: Jianyu (LI 15), Hegu (LI 4), Quchi (LI 11), Huantiao (GB 30), Fengchi (GB 20), Jiache (ST 6), Yangbai (GB 14).

Method: 2~3 pairs of points are punctured first. Following the needling sensation which is propagated to the distal end of the extremities, a tolerable electric current with sparse wave or intermittent wave is given to the needles in the points for 20 minutes once a day.

甲状腺功能亢进

甲状腺功能亢进（简称甲亢）为自身免疫和精神创伤引起甲状腺腺体增生和甲状腺素分泌过多所致，20～40岁女性多见。临床表现以交感神经兴奋性和代谢率增高为特点，症状包括易于激动，手和舌震颤，倦怠，食欲亢进，消瘦，大便频，怕热及多汗，体征有轻度或中度弥漫性甲状腺肿大，伴有震颤与血管性杂音，心脏可出现期前收缩，阵发性心动过速，心房颤动及突眼。一些病例症状不典型，甚至出现与甲亢典型症状相反的表现，如精神委靡，皮肤干冷，食欲不振及心动过缓等。

1．体针

处方 足三里，三阴交，太冲，神门，内关。

操作 毫针刺，平补平泻，留针30 分钟，间歇行针 2～4 次。

2．耳针

处方 颈，肝，脾，肾，内分泌，皮质下，交感。

操作 毫针中等强度刺激，留针30 分钟，亦可采用耳穴贴敷。

Hyperthyroidism

Hyperthyroidism is caused by autoimmunity or psychic trauma resulting in thyroid gland enlargement and hypersecretion of thyroxin. It is marked by hyperexcitation of the sympathetic nervous system and hypermetabolism. It occurs primarily in adult females. Manifestations include irritability, trembling of the fingers and tongue, lassitude, polyphagia, emaciation, frequent defecation, aversion to heat, and profuse perspiration. Signs include mild or moderate diffuse thyroid gland enlargement, tremor, vascular murmur, premature heartbeat, paroxysmal tachycardia, atrial fibrillation, and exophthalmus. In some atypical cases there may be symptoms other than the usual manifestations of hyperthyroidism, such as listlessness, dry or cold skin, poor appetite, or bradycardia. In traditional Chinese medicine it is categorized as "goiter" or "palpitation".

1. Body Acupuncture

Prescription: Zusanli (ST 36), Sanyinjiao (SP 6), Taichong (LR 3), Shenmen (HT 7), Neiguan (PC 6).

Method: Apply filiform needles with even movement. Retain the needles for 30 minutes manipulating them 2～4 times.

2. Ear Acupuncture

Prescription: Neck, Liver, Spleen, Kidney, Endocrine, Subcortex, Sympathetic.

Method: Apply filiform needles with moderate stimulation and retain the needles for 30 minutes. Auricular taping is also applicable.

糖 尿 病

糖尿病是一种常见的代谢内分泌疾病，其主要病理改变为胰岛素绝对或相对不足，引起糖、脂肪、蛋白质等代谢紊乱，并可继发水、电解质和酸碱平衡方面失调。本病按发病年龄和临床表现以及对胰岛素的需求，可分为许多类型。中医称之为"消渴"。

1．体针

处方 胰俞，脾俞，胃俞，肾俞，三阴交，内关，中脘。

配穴 口干加廉泉，承浆；视物模糊加光明。

操作 毫针刺，平补平泻，留针

30 分钟，间歇行针 2~4 次。

2. 耳针

处方 内分泌，肾，脾，口，缘中，皮质下。

操作 毫针中等强度刺激，留针30 分钟。亦可用耳穴贴敷。

3. 电针

处方 胰俞，肾俞，脾俞，胃俞，三阴交。

操作 每次选用 2 穴，密波或疏密波治疗 20 分钟，隔天 1 次。

4. 皮肤针

处方 脊椎两侧区域。

操作 三棱针叩刺 10~15 分钟，每天 1 次。

5. 水针

处方 胰俞，肾俞。

操作 每穴注射维生素 B_1 0.5 毫升，每天 1 次。

Diabetes Mellitus

Diabetes mellitus is a common metabolic endocrinopathy resulting from absolute or relative deficiency of insulin and leading to disturbances of carbohydrate, fat and protein metabolism. The disease is frequently followed by water-electrolyte imbalance and acid-base disturbance. According to the age of the patients clinical manifestations and requirements for insulin, diabetes mellitus can be divided into many types. In traditional Chinese medicine the disease is categorized as "Xiao Ke" which means diabetes.

1. Body Acupuncture

Prescription: Yishu (Extra), Pishu (BL 20), Weishu (BL 21), Shenshu (BL 23), Sanyinjiao (Sp 6), Neiguan (PC 6), Zhongwan (RN 12).

Supplementary points: Add Lianquan (RN 23) and Chengjiang (RN 24) for dry mouth, Guangming (GB 37) for blurred vision.

Method: Apply filiform needles with even movement method. Retain the needles for 30 minutes manipulating them 2~4 times.

2. Ear Acupuncture

Prescription: Endocrine, Kidney, Spleen, Mouth, Midpoint of Rim, Subcortex.

Method: Apply filiform needles with moderate stimulation and retain the needles for 30 minutes. Auricular taping is also applicable.

3. Electroacupuncture

Prescription: Yishu (Extra), Shenshu (BL 23), Pishu (BL 20), Weishu (BL 21), Sanyinjiao (SP 6).

Method: Two points are employed each treatment session. Apply dense wave or dense-sparse wave for 20 minutes once every other day.

4. Plum-blossom Needle

Prescription: Bilateral sides of the spine.

Method: Tap the areas with a three-edged needle for $10\sim15$ minutes once a day.

5. Point Injection

Prescription: Yishu (Extra), Shenshu (BL 23).

Method: Each point is injected with Vitamin B$_1$ 0.5mL, once a day.

尿　崩　症

尿崩症是由于抗利尿激素缺乏引起肾小管重吸收水的功能障碍而致的一种病症。临床以多尿，烦渴，多饮及低密度尿为主要表现。可分为两种类型，特发性者病因不明确，少数有家族史；继发性者可因下丘脑及神经垂体占位病变及颅脑损伤或感染等因素导致。本病属中医"消渴"范畴。

1. 体针

处方　少府，太渊，三阴交，内庭，肾俞。

操作　毫针刺，平补平泻，留针30分钟，间歇行针2～3次。

2. 耳针

处方　肾，膀胱，脾，口，皮质下，内分泌。

操作　毫针轻或中等强度刺激，留针30分钟。

Diabetes Insipidus

Diabetes insipidus is a dysfunction of the system of water resorption by the renal tubules caused by insufficient diuretic hormone. It is marked by polyuria, thirst, polydipsia, and hyposthenuria. It is classified into idiopathic and secondary types. The idiopathic type has no clear and definite cause although there may be a family history of diabetes insipidus. The secondary type is caused by diseases of the hypothalamus, neurohypophysis, head injury, or infection. The disease belongs to the category of "Xiao Ke" in traditiona Chinese medicine.

1. Body Acupuncture

Prescription: Shaofu (HT 8), Taiyuan (LU 9), Sanyinjiao (SP 6), Neiting (ST 44), Shenshu (BL 23).

Method: Apply filiform needles with even movement method. Retain the needles for 30 minutes manipulating them $2\sim3$ times.

2. Ear Acupuncture

Prescription: Kidney, Urinary Bladder, Spleen, Mouth, Subcortex, Endocrine.

Method: Apply filiform needles with mild or moderate stimulation and retain the needles for 30 minutes.

肥　胖　症

肥胖症是由多种因素引起的一种共同的临床表现，包括神经功能障碍，内分泌失调，代谢功能紊乱，饮食失调，药物或遗传等。其特点为体内脂肪过多沉积，超过标准体重20%以上。中医认为本病主要由于脾虚，引起痰湿积聚于内所致。

1. 体针

处方 梁丘，公孙，足三里，天枢，三阴交，脾俞，丰隆。

操作 毫针刺，用泻法。留针30分钟，间歇行针2～3次。

2. 耳针

处方 内分泌，脾，肾，饥点，口，神门，三焦。

操作 毫针中等强度刺激，留针30分钟；亦可用耳穴贴敷。

Obesity

Obesity is a commonly occuring condition caused by various factors including nervous dysfunction, endocrine disorder, metabolic disturbance, improper diet, drugs, or heredity. It is marked by excessive fat deposits resulting in weight twenty percent or more than the standard. According to traditional Chinese medicine obesity is caused by deficiency of the spleen resulting in accumulation of dampness and phlegm in the interior.

1. Body Acupuncture

Prescription: Liangqiu (ST 34), Gongsun (SP 4), Zusanli (ST 36), Tianshu (ST 25), Sanyinjiao (SP 6), Pishu (BL20), Fenglong (ST 40).

Method: Apply filiform needles with reducing method. Retain the needles for 30 minutes manipulating them 2～3 times.

2. Ear Acupuncture

Prescription: Endocrine, Spleen, Kidney, Hunger, Mouth, Shenmen, San Jiao.

Method: Apply filiform needles with moderate stimulation and retain the needles for 30 minutes. Auricular taping is also applicable.

再生障碍性贫血

再生障碍性贫血是由于不同病因（部分原因不明）引起的一组骨髓造血障碍综合征。临床上以全血细胞减少为特征，表现为贫血、出血和感染。好发于青壮年，男较女多见。本病属中医"虚劳"、"血证"等范畴。

1. 体针

处方 悬钟，足三里，合谷，命门，心俞。

操作 毫针刺，用补法。留针30分钟，间歇行针2～3次。

2. 耳针

处方 心，肝，肾，脾，皮质下，内分泌。

操作 毫针轻刺激，留针30

分钟。

3．艾灸

处方　大椎，心俞，足三里，关元，膏肓。

操作　温和灸治疗 10～15 分钟，每天 1 次。

4．皮肤针

处方　心俞，肝俞，脾俞，肾俞，夹脊穴。

操作　三棱针叩刺 10～15 分钟，每天 1 次。

Aplastic Anemia

Aplastic anemia is a clinical syndrome caused by a variety of etiological factors (some of them are unknown) which lead to hematopoietic disorder of the bone marrow. Clinically, it is characterized by panhematopenia resulting in anemia, hemorrhage and infections. The disease often occurs in young adults. It is more common in males than in females. In traditional Chinese medicine it is categorized as "consumptive disease", "blood trouble", etc.

1．Body Acupuncture

Prescription: Xuanzhong (GB 39), Zusanli (ST 36), Hegu (LI 4), Mingmen (DU 4), Xinshu (BL 15).

Method: Apply filiform needles with reinforcing method. Retain the needles for 30 minutes manipulating them 2～3 times.

2．Ear Acupuncture

Prescription: Heart, Liver, Kidney, Spleen, Subcortex, Endocrine.

Method: Apply filiform needles with mild stimulation and retain the needles for 30 minutes.

3．Moxibustion

Prescription: Dazhui (DU 14), Xinshu (BL 15), Zusanli (ST 36), Guanyuan (RN 4), Gaohuang (BL 43).

Method: Apply mild-warming moxibustion for 10～15 minutes once a day.

4．Plum-blossom Needle

Prescription: Xinshu (BL 15), Ganshu (BL 18), Pishu (BL 20), Shenshu (BL 23), Jiaji (EX-13).

Method: Tap the areas with a plum-blossom needle for 10～15 minutes once a day.

血小板减少性紫癜

血小板减少性紫癜是一种自身免疫性疾病，发病中脾脏因素亦起到一定作用。本病多见于青少年，女性多于男性，属中医"肌衄"，"发斑"等范畴。

1．体针

处方　膈俞，脾俞，足三里，血海，三阴交。

操作 毫针刺，用补法。留针30分钟，间歇行针2~3次。

2．耳针

处方 心，脾，内分泌，肾。

操作 毫针轻刺激，留针30分钟，亦可用耳穴贴敷。

Thrombocytopenic Purpura

Thrombocytopenic purpura is an autoimmune disease. It also involves the spleen and often occurs in children and young adults. The incidence in females is higher than in males. In traditional Chinese medicine the disease is categorized as "subcutaneous hemorrhage", "Purpura", etc.

1. Body Acupuncture

Prescription: Geshu (BL 17), Pishu (BL 20), Zusanli (ST 36), Xuehai (SP 10), Sanyinjiao (SP 6).

Method: Apply filiform needles with reinforcing method. Retain the needles for 30 minutes manipulating them 2~3 times.

2. Ear Acupuncture

Prescription: Heart, Spleen, Endocrine, Kidney.

Method: Apply filiform needles with mild stimulation and retain the needles for 30 minutes. Auricular taping is also applicable.

白细胞减少症

周围血液中白细胞数持续低于4×10⁹/升，中性粒细胞百分比正常或稍减少，称为白细胞减少症。多数情况下，白细胞减少症是由中性粒细胞减少所致，若粒细胞绝对值低于（1.8~2）×10⁹/升称为粒细胞减少症。本病属中医"眩晕"、"虚劳"等范畴。

1．体针

处方 足三里，三阴交，血海，膈俞。

操作 毫针刺，用补法，留针30分钟，间歇行针2~3次。

2．耳针

处方 交感，内分泌，肾，肝，脾。

操作 毫针轻刺激，留针30分钟。

3．艾灸

处方 大椎，肾俞，足三里。

操作 温和灸治疗10~15分钟，每天1次。

Leukopenia

Leukopenia exists when the number of the white blood cells in the peripheral circulation is continuously lower than $4 \times 10^9/L$ and the percentage of neutrophilic granulocytes is normal or slightly decreased. In most cases the disease is related to the decrease of neutrophilic granulocytes. Granulocytopenia is defined as when the absolute number of granulocytes

is below（1.8～2）×10⁹/L. In traditional Chinese medicine this disease is
grouped into the categories of "vertigo",
"consumptive disease", etc.

1. Body Acupuncture

Prescription：Zusanli（ST 36），
Sanyinjiao（SP 6），Xuehai（SP 10），
Geshu（BL 17）.

Method：Apply filiform needles with
reinforcing method. Retain the needles
for 30 minutes manipulating them 2～3
times.

2. Ear Acupuncture

Prescription：Sympathetic, Endocrine, Kidney, Liver, Spleen.

Method：Apply filiform needles with
mild stimulation and retain the needles
for 30 minutes.

3. Moxibustion

Prescription：Dazhui（DU 14），
Shenshu（BL 23），Zusanli（ST 36）.

Method：Apply mild-warming moxibustion for 10～15 minutes once a day.

第二节　外科和皮肤科疾病

Section 2　Surgical and Derma-
tological Diseases

急性淋巴管炎

急性淋巴管炎多由溶血性链球菌
自破损的皮肤或其他感染灶蔓延到邻
近的淋巴管而引起的急性炎症。中医
称之为"红丝疔"。

1. 体针

处方　身柱，灵台，足三里，合
谷，委中。

配穴　高热加曲池，大椎；神昏
谵语加人中和十宣；烦躁加关冲。

操作　毫针刺，用泻法，留针
20～30分钟，间歇行针3～4次。

2. 耳针

处方　神门，皮质下，肾上腺，
肺。

操作　毫针强刺激，留针20～
30分钟。

3. 皮肤针

处方　局部红线。

操作　皮肤叩刺10～15分钟，
每天1次。

4. 三棱针

处方　委中，中冲。

操作　三棱针点刺出血。

5. 拔罐疗法

操作　灵台穴常规消毒后，用三
棱针点刺出血，吸拔火罐。如见有红
线，沿红丝起止点常规消毒后，用三
棱针从终点开始至起点，每隔2～3
厘米点刺出血，然后拔罐。

Acute Lymphangitis

Acute lymphangitis is a kind of acute
inflammatory   disease   caused   by
hemolytic streptococcus entering the

broken skin or other infected focus and spreading to the adjacent lymphatic vessels. Traditional Chinese medicine call this disease "red-streaked infection".

1. Body Acupuncture

Prescription: Shenzhu (DU 12), Lingtai (DU 10), Zusanli (ST 36), Hegu (LI 4), Weizhong (BL 40).

Supplementary points: Add Quchi (LI 11), Dazhui (DU 14) for high fever, Renzhong (DU 26) and Shixuan (EX-UE 11) for loss of consciousness and delirium, Guanchong (SJ 1) for restlessness.

Method: Apply filiform needles with reducing method. Retain the needles for 20 ~ 30 minutes manipulating them 3~4 times.

2. Ear Acupuncture

Prescription: Shenmen, Subcortex, Adrenal gland, Lung.

Method: Apply filiform needles with strong stimulation and retain the needles for 20~30 minutes.

3. Plum-blossom Needle

Prescription: Local red thread.

Method: Tap the local red thread with a plum blossom needle for 10~15 minutes once a day.

4. Three-edged Needle

Prescription: Weizhong (BL 40), Zhongchong (PC 9).

Method: Prick the points with a three-edged needle to cause bleeding.

5. Cupping

Prescription: Lingtai (DU 10).

Method: After routine disinfection at Lingtai (DU 10), prick the point with a three-edged needle to cause bleeding. Then cupping is given. If a red thread appears, disinfect the line routinely. Prick the line from the beginning to the end every 2 ~ 3 centimetres away. Then do cupping.

颈部淋巴结结核

颈部淋巴结结核是由结核杆菌侵入颈部淋巴结引起的慢性特异性炎症。因其结核累累如贯珠之状，故中医称之为"瘰疬"。

1. 体针

处方 期门，内关，行间，肩井，足临泣，天井，百劳。

配穴 项部瘰疬加翳风；颈部瘰疬加臂臑，手三里；腋下瘰疬加肘尖，阳辅。

操作 毫针刺，用泻法，留针10~15分钟，间歇行针2~3次。针刺适宜于颈淋巴结核的初、中期，对溃破者不适宜。

2. 艾灸

处方 百劳，天井。

操作 小艾炷各灸5~7壮，1天1次。适宜于颈淋巴结核的早期阶段。

Tuberculosis of Cervical Lymph Nodes

Tuberculosis of cervical lymph nodes is a kind of chronic specific inflammation caused by the infection of microbacterio tuberculosis that attacks the cervical lymph nodes. Since the tubercles are like chains of pearls hanging around, traditional Chinese medicine calls it "scrofula".

1. Body Acupuncture

Prescription: Qimen (LR 14), Neiguan (PC 6), Xingjian (LR 2), Jianjing (GB 21), Zulinqi (GB 41), Tianjing (SJ 10), Jingbailao (EX-HN 15).

Supplementary points: Add Yifeng (SJ 17) for scrofula in the nape, Binao (LI 14), Shousanli (LI 10) for scrofula in the neck, and Zhoujian (EX-UE 1) and Yangfu (GB 38) for scrofula in the auxillary fossa.

Method: Apply filiform needles with reducing method. Retain the needles for 10~15 minutes manipulating them 2~3 times. Acupuncture is generally suggested for treating scrofula in the first two stages, not for the advanced stage when ulceration has already taken place.

2. Moxibustion

Prescription: Jingbailao (EX-HN 15) and Tianjing (SJ 10).

Method: The points are applied with 5~7 small cones once a day. It is suitable for scrofula in the first stage.

带状疱疹

带状疱疹是由带状疱疹病毒感染引起的一种急性疱疹性皮肤病。临床特点为发病急剧，密集的水疱群，沿着一侧神经分布区呈带状排列，伴有神经痛，常发于胸、腰、腹部。中医称为"缠腰丹"、"火带疮"、"蛇串疮"、"蜘蛛疮"等。

1. 体针

处方　内庭，公孙，外关，侠溪，委中，足三里。

配穴　纳呆加中脘；疱疹在腰以上者加膈俞；疱疹在腰以下者加血海，阳陵泉。

操作　毫针刺，用泻法。留针20~30分钟，间歇行针4~6次。

2. 耳针

处方　肾上腺，神门，皮质下，相应区。

操作　毫针强刺激，留针15~20分钟，间歇行针3~4次。亦可用耳穴压丸。

3. 艾灸

处方　足三里。

操作　艾条灸足三里穴20分钟，每天1次。

Herpes Zoster

Herpes zoster is a kind of acute herpetic skin infection caused by herpes zoster virus. Its clinical characteristic is the acute onset of the disease with groups of crowded blisters arranged in a zonary fashion along one side of the nerve distribution. It is accompanied with nerve pain on the chest, waist and abdomen. This disease is called "chan yao dan", "huo dai chuang", "she chuan chuang", and "zhizhu chuang" in traditional Chinese medicine.

1. Body Acupuncture

Prescription: Neiting (ST 44), Gongsun (SP 4), Waiguan (SJ 5), Xiaxi (GB 43), Weizhong (BL 40), Zusanli (ST 36)

Supplementary points: Add Zhongwan (RN 12) for poor appetite, Geshu (BL 17) for herpes zoster appearing in areas above the waist, and Xuehai (SP 10) and Yanglingquan (GB 34) for herps zoster appearing in areas below the waist.

Method: Apply filiform needles with reducing method. Retain the needles for 20~30 minutes manipulating them 4~6 times.

2. Ear Acupuncture

Prescription: Adrenal Gland, Shenmen, Subcortex, corresponding areas.

Method: Apply filiform needles with strong stimulation for 15~20 minutes manipulating them 3~4 times. Auricular taping is also applicable.

3. Moxibustion

Prescription: Zusanli (ST 36).

Method: Apply moxibustion at the point for 20 minutes once a day.

荨 麻 疹

荨麻疹是一种以皮肤出现风团为主要表现的过敏性皮肤病，临床特点为皮肤出现风团，多骤然发作，迅速消退，愈后不留痕迹，有剧烈瘙痒感和灼热感；可反复发作，迁延日久。中医称之为"隐疹"，"风疹块"，"游风"等。

1. 体针

处方　曲池，血海，三阴交，风市，足三里，风池，大椎，合谷，阴陵泉。

操作　毫针刺，用泻法。留针30分钟，间歇行针3~4次。

2. 耳针

处方　神门，肺，肾上腺，内分泌，交感，大肠。

操作　毫针强刺激，留针30分钟。

3. 艾灸

处方　血海，三阴交，足三里，大椎，合谷，阴陵泉，脾俞，肺俞。

操作　每次选3~5穴，用艾条温和灸或回旋灸每穴灸15分钟，亦

可用艾炷灸，每穴灸 5～8 壮。每天
1 次。

4．皮肤针

处方   夹脊，风池，血海，风
门，委中，肺俞，三阴交，足三里。
操作   中等强度叩刺，1 日 1 次。

5．拔罐

处方   神门。
操作   用一枚大头针扎入塑料
盖，将乙醇棉球插到大头针上并点
燃，立即将玻璃瓶罩在上面，待吸力
不紧后取下，连续拔 3 次，每天 1
次，3 天为 1 个疗程。

6．三棱针

处方   大椎，血海。
配穴   疹发于上肢加曲池；疹发
于下肢加风市，委中；疹发于背部加
膈俞，风门。
操作   先在局部按揉，使其达到
红润充血，常规消毒，然后用三棱针
点刺，当血溢出，速用闪火法将玻璃
火罐吸附在穴位上，并左右旋转，使
出血量增加，留罐 15 分钟，隔天 1
次，7 次为 1 个疗程。

Urticaria

Urticaria is a kind of allergic skin disease with skin wheals as the main manifestation. The clinical manifestations are the appearance of wheals over the skin with sudden onset and rapid disappearance, leaving no trace after recovery. There is a sensation of severe itching and burning heat on the affected part. Urticaria can attack repeatedly and last for a long time. In traditional Chinese medicine this disease is called "hidden eruption", "wind eruption", "wandering wind evils", etc.

1. Body Acupuncture

Prescription: Quchi (LI 11), Xuehai (SP 10), Sanyinjiao (SP 6), Fengshi (GB 31), Zusanli (ST 36), Fenchi (GB 20), Dazhui (DU 14), Hegu (LI 4), Yinlingquan (SP 9).

Method: Apply filiform needles with reducing method. Retain the needles for 30 minutes manipulating them 3～4 times.

2. Ear Acupuncture

Prescription: Shenmen, Lung, Adrenal Gland, Endocrine, Sympathetic, Large Intestine.

Method: Apply filiform needles with strong stimulation and retain the needles for 30 minutes

3. Moxibustion

Prescription: Xuehai (SP 10), Sanyinjiao (SP 6), Zusanli (ST 36), Dazhui (DU 14), Hegu (LI 4), Yinlingquan (SP 9), Pishu (BL 20), Feishu (BL 13).

Method: Select 3～5 points each treatment session. Apply mild-warming or circling moxibustion with a moxa stick to each point for 15 minutes. Or moxibustion with moxa cones is performed to each point using 5~8 cones. The treatment is given once a day for seven days as a course.

4. Plum-blossom Needle

Prescription: Jiaji (EX-B 2), Fengchi (GB 20), Xuehai (SP 10), Fengmen (BL 12), Weizhong (BL 40), Feishu (BL 13), Sanyinjiao (SP 6), Zusanli (ST 36).

Method: Tap the areas with medium strength stimulation once a day.

5. Cupping

Prescription: Shenmen (RN 8).

Method: A glass bottle and a plastic lid in which a pin is inserted are selected. The lid is placed on the point and an alcohol cotton ball is attached around the pin and ignited. Immediately, the glass bottle is covered over the lid for cupping. The procedure is repeated three times. The treatment is given once a day for three days as a course.

6. Three-edged Needle

Prescription: Dazhui (DU 14), Xuehai (SP 10).

Supplementary points: Add Quchi (LI 11) for disease at the upper limbs, Fengshi (GB 31) and Weizhong (BL 40) for that at the lower limbs, Geshu (BL 17) and Fengmen (BL 12) for that at the upper back.

Method: First massage is performed over the local affected area to cause congestion and routine local sterilization is given. Then, the points selected are pricked with a three-edged needle. When bleeding is caused by pricking, cupping with glass bottles to the points is applied and the bottles are turned left and right to cause more bleeding. The bottles are retained at each point for 15 minutes. The treatment is given once every other day for seven sessions as a course。

湿疹是由多种内外因素作用于特异性机体而引起的一种过敏性皮肤病。其特点为多型性皮肤损害，并伴有剧烈瘙痒。分为两种类型。急性者主要累及头面，四肢屈侧，皮损表现为水肿性红斑；丘疹，水泡，糜烂渗液，结痂或感染。病程一般2~3周，但有复发倾向。慢性者主要累及手，耳后，阴囊及小腿，皮损表现为皮肤粗糙，肥厚，皮纹深，色素沉着并有鳞屑抓痕。中医称婴儿湿疹为"奶癣"，"胎敛疮"；称外耳湿疹为"旋耳疮"；称局限性湿疹为"湿毒疮"；称阴囊湿疹为"肾囊风"，"绣球风"；肘腘部湿疹为"四弯风"。

1. 体针

处方 曲池，血海，三阴交，大椎，足三里，合谷，委中，外关。

操作 每次选用3~5穴，毫针

刺，急性病例用泻法，慢性病例用补法。留针 20 ~ 30 分钟，间歇行针 2~4 次。

2. 耳针

处方　肺，三焦，大肠，内分泌，肾上腺，风溪，心。

配穴　急性湿疹加耳尖；慢性湿疹加肝，肾。

操作　毫针中等或强刺激，留针 30 分钟。亦可用耳穴贴敷。

3. 艾灸

处方　曲池，血海，三阴交，委中，大椎，足三里，外关，阳陵泉。

操作　每次选 3~5 穴，采用温和灸或回旋灸治疗 20 分钟。或用艾炷灸，每穴灸 3 ~ 5 壮。每天治疗 1 次。

4. 水针

处方　足三里，曲池。

操作　每穴注射 0.1 毫克维生素 B_{12}，每天 1 次。

Eczema

Eczema is an allergic skin condition with various internal and external causes marked by pleomerphic skin lesions accompanied by severe itching. It is classified into acute and chronic types. Acute eczema affects primarily the craniofacial region and flexion aspects of the extremities. Skin lesions may exhibit edematous erythema, pimples, vesicles, oozing erosion, scabs, or infection. The condition usually lasts 2 ~ 3 weeks but may recur after recovery. Chronic eczema mainly affects the hands retroauricular regions, scrotum, vulva, and legs. Skin lesions may exhibit pachylosis, pachydermia, deep dermatoglyph, pigmentation with scales, and scratch marks. Chronic eczema may occur primarily or develop from subacute eczema. In traditional Chinese medicine eczema in infants is called "infantile eczema", eczema on the external ear is called "eczema of the external ear", eczema on the local area is called "noxious eczema", eczema on the scrotum is called "scrotal eczema", eczema in the elbow and popliteal fossa is called "atopic eczema", etc.

1. Body Acupuncture

Prescription：Quchi (LI 11), Xuehai (SP 10), Sanyinjiao (SP 6), Dazhui (DU14), Zusanli (ST 36), Hegu (LI 4), Weizhong (BL 40), Waiguan (SJ 5).

Method：Select 3 ~ 5 points each treatment session. Apply filiform needles with reducing method for acute cases and reinforcing method for chronic cases. Retain the needles for 20 ~ 30 minutes manipulating them 2~4 times.

2. Ear Acupuncture

Prescription: Lung, San jiao, Large Intestine, Endocrine, Adrenal Gland, Wind Stream, Heat, Shenmen, Occiput, Center of Ear.

Supplementary points: Add Apex of Ear for acute eczema, Liver and Kidney for chronic eczema.

Method: Apply filiform needles with moderate or strong stimulation and retain the needles for 30 minutes. Auricular taping is also applicable.

3. Moxibustion

Prescription: Quchi (LI 11), Xuehai (SP 10), Sanyinjiao (SP 6), Weizhong (BL 4), Dazhui (DU 4), Zusanli (ST 36), Waiguan (SJ 5), Yanglingquan (GB 34).

Method: Select 3 ~ 5 points each treatment session. Apply mild-warming or circling moxibustion for 20 minutes. Alternatively, moxibustion with moxa cones is applied to each point using 3 ~ 5 cones. The treatment is given once a day.

4. Point Injection

Prescription: Zusanli (ST 36), Quchi (LI 11).

Method: Inject 0.1mg of vitamin B_{12} into each point once a day.

皮肤瘙痒症

皮肤瘙痒症为多种疾病的一种共同皮肤病症，如内分泌障碍，寄生虫病，肝病，肾病，肿瘤。老年性者称

之为老年性皮肤瘙痒症。随着病情的发展，因搔抓而出现抓痕，痂皮，色素沉着，甚至苔藓化。分为局限性和全身性。前者多发于阴囊，肛门，女阴处。中医称之为"痒风"。

1. 体针

处方　曲池，血海，合谷，三阴交，足三里，大椎，风池。

操作　毫针刺，用泻法，或平补平泻法。留针 30 分钟，间歇行针 2~4 次。

2. 耳针

处方　肺，肝，神门，枕，皮质下，耳中，耳尖。

操作　毫针强刺激，留针 30 分钟；亦可用耳穴贴敷。

3. 艾灸

处方　风池，足三里，血海，曲池，肺俞。

操作　艾条温和灸或回旋灸每穴治疗 10~15 分钟，每天 1 次。

4. 水针

处方　曲池，足三里，三阴交。

操作　每穴注射 0.1 毫克维生素 B_{12}，隔天 1 次。

Cutaneous Pruritus

Cutaneous Pruritus is a common skin problem that may occur secondary to various diseases such as endocrine dysfunction, parasitosis, diabetes mellitus, hepatic illness, nephric disorders, or tumors. In the elderly it is referred to as pruritus senilis. Cutaneous pruritus is marked in the initial stage by paroxysmal itching without skin lesions. As the condition develops, scratch marks, scabs, pigmentation or lichenification due to extensive scratching may appear. The condition may be either localized, appearing mainly on the scrotum, vulva, and anus, or general. It is called "yang feng" (Pruritus) in traditonal Chinese medicine.

1. Body Acupuncture

Prescription: Quchi (LI 11), Xuehai (SP 10), Hegu (LI 4), Zusanli (ST 36), Sanyinjiao (SP 6), Dazhui (Du 14), Fengchi (GB 20).

Method: Apply filiform needles with reducing or even movement method. Retain the needles for 30 minutes manipulating them 2~4 times.

2. Ear Acupuncture

Prescription: Lung, Liver, Shenmen, Occiput, Subcortex, Center of Ear, Apex of Ear.

Method: Apply filiform needles with strong stimulation and retain the needles for 30 minutes. Auricular taping is also applicable.

3. Moxibustion

Prescription: Fenchi (GB 20), Zusanli, (ST 36), Xuehai (SP 10), Quchi (LI 11), Feishu (BL 13).

Method: Apply mild-warming or rounding moxibustion with a moxa stick to each point for 10~15 minutes once a day.

4. Point Injection

Prescription: Quchi (LI 11), Zusanli (ST 36), Sanyinjiao (SP 6).

Method: Inject 0.1mg of vitamin B_{12} into each point once every other day.

神经性皮炎

　　神经性皮炎是一种常因情绪变化、局部摩擦而诱发的痒性皮肤神经官能症。皮肤损害呈苔藓样变，并伴有阵发性瘙痒。病变初期，局部先痒，继则因搔抓日久而出现圆形或多角形丘疹，密集成簇。随着病情发展，可出现皮纹加深，皮嵴突起，皮肤肥厚，呈棕色变。可分为局限型和播散型。前者较多见，好发于颈侧与颈后、肘、前臂伸侧、骶、股内侧、小腿腓侧等处。后者可见于头面、肩、四肢及躯干部。中医称之为"牛皮癣"、"摄领疮"等。

1. 体针

　　处方　委中，风门，曲池，血海，三阴交，合谷，肺俞，阳陵泉。

　　操作　每次选3~4穴，毫针刺，用泻法或补法。留针30分钟，间歇行针2~4次。

2．耳针

处方 肺，肝，内分泌，肾上腺，风溪，心，神门，枕，皮质下，耳尖。

操作 毫针中等强度或强刺激，留针 30 分钟；亦可采用耳穴贴敷。

3．艾灸

处方 曲池，血海，三阴交，肺俞，阿是穴。

操作 艾条温和灸每穴治疗 20～30 分钟，每天 1 次。

4．皮肤针

处方 患处选用几条经纬线，每条线相距约 0.5 厘米。

操作 皮损处进行经纬线叩刺，每条线叩刺 3 次，或在皮损局部由外向内围刺，以出血为度。每天治疗 1 次。

Neurodermatitis

Neurodematitis is a type of itching dermatoneurosis usually induced by mental injury or localized physical irritation. It is marked by lichenoid skin lesions accompanied by paroxysmal itching. In the initial stage there is localized itching with dense groups of falciform pimples occuring as the result of extensive scratching. As the condition develops deep dermatoglyph, dermal ridging, and brown pachydermatomy appear. Neurodermatitis is classified into localized and disseminated types. The former is much more common and occurs primarily on the bilateral sides and back of the neck, the elbows, the extension aspect of the forearms, the sacral region, the medial sides of the thighs, and the fibular aspect of the legs. The latter occurs mainly in the craniofacial region the shoulders, the extremities, or the trunk. This disease is called "miu pi xian" or "she ling chuang" (neurodermatitis) in traditional Chinese medicine.

1. Body Acupuncture

Prescription: Weizhong (BL 40), Fengmen (BL 12), Quchi (LI 11), Xuehai (SP 10), Sanyinjiao (SP 6), Hegu (LI 4), Feishu (BL 13), Yanglingquan (GB 34).

Method: Select 3 ~ 4 points each treatment session. Apply filiform needles with reducing or reinforcing method. Retain the needles for 30 minutes manipulating them 2 ~ 4 times.

2. Ear Acupuncture

Prescription: Lung, Liver, Endocrine, Adrenal Gland, Wind Stream, Heart, Shenmen, Occiput, Subcortex, Apex of Ear.

Method: Apply filiform needles with moderate or strong stimulation and retain the needles for 30 minutes. Auricular taping is also applicable.

3. Moxibustion

Prescription: Quchi (LI 11), Xue-hai (SP 10), Sanyinjiao (SP 6), Feishu (BL 13), Ashi points.

Method: Apply mild-warning moxibustion with a moxa stick to the points for 20~30 minutes each treatment session. The treatment is given once a day.

4. Plum-blossom Needle

Prescription: Select several lines at the affected region, some of them being perpendicular and some horizontal, the distance between two parallel and near lines being 0.5 cm。

Method: Tap each line 3 times at each treatment session. Alternatively give surrounding tapping on the affected region towards its center to cause bleeding. The treatment is given once a day or once every other day.

寻常痤疮

寻常痤疮是青春期的常见病。它由皮脂分泌亢进，毛囊口上皮增生及角化过度，引起皮脂积聚并继发细菌感染所致。多发于青少年，常累及面、胸等处。皮肤损害有毛囊性丘疹，脓疱，硬结或囊肿等。皮损常此起彼伏，缠绵难愈，有的可拖延数年，甚至十余年。

1. 体针

处方   肺俞，血海，大椎，胃俞，曲池，合谷，太阳，足三里，三阴交。

操作   每次选用3~5穴，毫针刺，用泻法。留针20~30分钟，间歇行针2~4次。

2. 耳针

处方   肺，胃，大肠，内分泌，缘中，肾上腺，耳尖。

配穴   瘙痒者加心，神门，耳中。

操作   毫针强刺激，留针30分钟。耳尖穴可用三棱针点刺出血；亦可用耳穴贴敷。

3. 三棱针

处方   大椎，肺俞，胃俞。

操作   医生以手在应刺部位揉搓数分钟，使其局部充血，皮肤常规消毒后，用三棱针速刺出血，隔天1次。

4. 皮肤针

处方   大椎，肺俞，曲池，血海。
操作   叩刺出血，每周2次。

Acne Vulgaris

Acne vulgaris is a common problem of adolescence. It is caused by hypersteatosis combined with proliferation and hyperkeratosis of the epithelia of the follicular orifices. This leads to accumlation of sebum cutaneum and subsequent bacterial infection. Usually affected areas are the face and chest.

Skin lesions include pimples, pustules, folliculorum, scleroma, and cysts. It rises one after another and may not be cured for several years or even more than ten years.

1. Body Acupuncture

Prescription: Feishu (BL 13), Xuehai (SP 10), Dazhui (DU 14), Weishu (BL 21), Quchi (LI 11), Hegu (LI 4), Taiyang (EX-HN 5), Zusanli (ST 36), Sanyinjiao (SP 6).

Method: Select 3 ~ 5 points each treatment session, apply filiform needles with reducing method. Retain the needles for 20 ~ 30 minutes manipulating them 2 ~ 4 times.

2. Ear Acupuncture

Prescription: Lung, Stomach, Large Intestine, Endocrine, Midpoint of Rim, Adrenal Gland, Apex of Ear.

Supplementary points: Add Heart, Shenmen, Center of Ear for itching.

Method: Apply filiform needles with strong stimulation and retain the needle for 30 minutes. Apex of Ear may be pricked with a three-edged needle to cause bleeding. Auricular taping is also applicable.

3. Three-edged Needle

Prescription: Dazhui (DU 14), Feishu (BL 13), Weishu (BL 21).

Method: Following twisting the region to be pricked for several minutes to cause local congestion give local and routine sterilization. Prick the point gently to cause bleeding. The treatment is given once every other day.

4. Plum-blossom Needle

Prescription: Dazhui (DU 14), Feishu (BL 13), Quchi (LI 11), Xuehai (SP 10).

Method: Tap the points to cause bleeding, twice every week.

脂溢性皮炎

脂溢性皮炎是在皮脂溢出基础上发生的一种慢性皮肤炎性病症。与皮脂分泌过多、感染、代谢障碍等有关。临床分干性和湿性两种类型，干性表现特点为淡黄红色斑片，表面附有糠状油脂性鳞屑。湿性由干性演变而来，皮损呈湿疹样，可见糜烂、渗出、结痂。好发于青壮年，常累及头、面、颈、腋、胸等处。中医称之为"白屑风"，"面游风"。

1. 体针

处方 肺俞，曲池，血海，三阴交，风门，大椎，合谷，足三里。

操作 每次选3~5穴，毫针刺，用泻法。留针30分钟，间歇行针2~4次。

2. 耳针

处方 病变相对应部位，肺，大肠，三焦，肝，脾，内分泌，皮质下，交感。

操作　毫针强刺，留针30分钟；亦可用耳穴贴敷。

3．皮肤针

处方　风池，血海，肺俞，三阴交。

操作　皮肤针叩刺10～15分钟，每天1次。

Seborrheic Dermatitis

Seborrheic dermatitis is a chronic inflammatory condition of the sebaceous glands of the skin occurring in conjunction with hypersteatosis, infection, or metabolic dysfunction. It is classified into dry and moist types. The dry type is marked by yellowish-red patches covered with pityroid oleoginous scales. The moist type develops from the dry type with eczematoid skin lesions displaying erosion, oozing, and scabbing. This problem occurs mainly in young people and adults. Usually affected areas are the head, face, neck, axilla, and chest. In traditional Chinese medicine it is called "bai xie feng", "mian you feng" (seborrheic dermatitis or seborrheic eczema).

1. Body Acupuncture

Prescription：Feishu (BL 13), Quchi (LI 11), Xuehai (SP 10), Sanyinjiao (SP 6), Fengmen (BL 12), Dazhui (DU 14), Hegu (LI 4), Zusanli (ST 36).

Method：Select 3 ～ 5 points each treatment session. Apply filiform needles with reducing method. Retain the needles for 30 minutes manipulating them 2～4 times.

2. Ear Acupuncture

Prescription：Areas corresponding to the affected regions, Lung, Large Intestine, San jiao, Liver, Spleen, Endocrine, Subcortex, Sympathetic.

Method：Apply filiform needles with strong stimulation and retain the needles for 30 minutes. Auricular taping is also applicable.

3. Plum-blossom Needle

Prescription：Fengchi (GB 20), Xuehai (SP 10), Feishu (BL 13), Sanyinjiao (SP 6).

Method：Tap the points with a plum-blossom needle for 10 ～ 15 minutes once a day.

多形性红斑

多形性红斑是皮肤的一种急性病症。好发于青壮年，多见于春秋季节。其发生可能与病灶感染、药物、食物、寒冷等因素引起的过敏反应有关。皮损呈多形性，包括丘疹、水肿性红斑、中央性水疱或虹彩形红斑。好发于手脚背及四肢远端处。轻者仅局部瘙痒，重者可出现黏膜糜烂及高热，头痛，关节痛等全身症状。中医称之为"猫眼疮"、"雁疮"。

1. 体针

处方　曲池，合谷，委中，血海，三阴交，肺俞。

操作　毫针刺，用泻法。留针20~30分钟，间歇行针2~4次。

2. 耳针

处方　肺，内分泌，肾上腺，风溪，交感，病变对应部位，耳尖。

操作　毫针强刺激，留针30分钟，间歇行针2~4次。三棱针耳尖穴点刺出血。亦可用耳穴贴敷。

3. 皮肤针

处方　夹脊，血海，肺俞，大椎，三阴交。

操作　皮肤针中等强度刺激15~20分钟，每天1次。

Erythema Multiforme

Erythema multiforme is an acute inflammatory condition of the skin occuring mainly in young people and adults and usually in the spring and autumn. It may occur in conjunction with allergic reaction due to localized infection, drug sensitivity, food, or cold. Skin lesions are pleomorphic and may exhibit pimples, edematous erythema, central vesicles, or erythema iris. Usually, affected areas are the dorsum of the hands, feet and the distal ends of the extremities. In mild cases there is only localized itching. In severe cases mucosal erosion and general symptoms such as high fever, headache, and arthralgias may occur. This disease is called "mao yan chuang" and "yan chuang" (erythema multiforme) in traditional Chinese medicine.

1. Body Acupuncture

Prescription: Quchi (LI 11), Hegu (LI 4), Weizhong (BL 40), Xuehai (SP 10), Sanyinjiao (SP 6), Feishu (BL 13).

Method: Apply filiform needles with reducing method. Retain the needles for 20~30 minutes manipulating them 2~4 times.

2. Ear Acupuncture

Prescription: Lung, Endocrine, Adrenal Gland, Wind Stream, Sympathetic, areas corresponding to the affected regions, Apex of Ear.

Method: Apply filiform needles with strong stimulation and retain the needles for 30 minutes manipulating them 2~4 times. Apex of Ear may be pricked with a three-edged needle to cause bleeding. Auricular taping is also applicable.

3. Plum-blossom Needle

Prescription: Jiaji (EX-B 2), Xuehai (SP 10), Feishu (BL 13), Dazhui (DU 14), Sanyinjiao (SP 6).

Method: Apply a plum-blossom needle to tap the points with medium strength stimulation for 15～20 minutes once a day.

玫瑰糠疹

玫瑰糠疹是一种急性自限性红斑鳞屑性皮肤病。其临床特点为：发于躯干部，呈指甲大红色屑斑，春秋季多见，多发于青壮年，可自然消退。中医称之为"风癣"、"血疳"。

1. 体针

处方　足三里，曲池，天枢，肺俞，血海，风池，风门。

操作　毫针刺，用泻法。留针20～30分钟，间歇行针 2～4 次。

2. 耳针

处方　肺，内分泌，肾上腺，脑，交感，胃。

操作　毫针强刺激，留针 30 分钟；亦可用耳穴压丸。

3. 皮肤针

处方　夹脊，血海，风门，肺俞，三阴交，足三里。

操作　皮肤针叩刺 15～20 分钟，每天 1 次。

Pityriasis Rosea

Pityriasis rosea is an acute self-limited skin disease characterized by many red maculae and scales. Its clinical symptom is that it often occurs on the trunk in spring and autumn. The size of the red macula is as large as a finger nail. This disease is most common in young and middle-aged people. It can disappear spontaneously. In traditional Chinese medicine it is known as "feng xian" or "xue gan" (pityriasis rosea).

1. Body Acupuncture

Prescription: Zusanli (ST 36), Quchi (LI 11), Tianshu (ST 25), Feishu (BL 13), Xuehai (SP 10), Fengchi (GB 20), Fengmen (BL 12).

Method: Apply filiform needles with reducing method. Retain the needles for 20～30 minutes manipulating them 2～4 times.

2. Ear Acupuncture

Prescription: Lung, Endocrine, Adrenal Gland, Brain, Sympathetic, Stomach.

Method: Apply filiform needles with strong stimulation and retain the needles for 30 minutes. Auricular taping is also applicable.

3. Plum-blossom needle

Prescription: Jiaji (EX-B 2), Xuehai (SP 10), Fengmen (BL 12), Feishu (BL 13), Sanyinjiao (SP 6), Zusanli (ST 36).

Method: Tap the points with a plum-blossom needle for 15 ～ 20 minutes once a day.

硬　皮　病

硬皮病是由皮肤硬化而致的皮肤

结缔组织病。分局限性和系统性两种类型。一般经过红肿、硬化、萎缩三个阶段。晚期受累皮肤常与深部组织粘连，可造成相应器官的功能障碍。中医称之为"皮痹"、"皮痹疽"。

1. 体针

处方 血海，风门，委中，肺俞，三阴交，足三里，大椎。

操作 毫针刺，用泻法。留针30分钟，间歇行针2~4次。

2. 耳针

处方 肺，肾上腺，内分泌，交感，耳尖。

操作 毫针强刺激，留针30分钟。耳尖可点刺出血；亦可用耳穴贴敷。

3. 水针

处方 肺俞，三阴交，足三里。

操作 每穴注射0.5毫升丹参注射液，每天1次。

Scleroderma

Scleroderma is a kind of skin disease of connective tissue caused by sclerosis of the skin. It is divided into two types, localized and systemic types. Generally it undergoes three stages, red swelling, sclerosis and atrophy. At the advanced stage the affected skin will be adhered to the deep tissue and produce afunctional disturbance of corresponding organs. This disease is called "pi bi" and "pi bi ju" (scleroderma).

1. Body Acupuncture

Prescription: Xuehai (SP 10), Fengmen (BL 12), Weizhong (BL 40). Feishu (BL 13), Sanyinjiao (SP 6), Zusanli (ST 36), Dazhui (DU 14).

Method: Apply filiform needles with reducing method. Retain the needles for 30 minutes manipulating them 2~4 times.

2. Ear Acupuncture

Prescription: Lung, Adrenal Gland, Endocrine, Sympathetic, Apex of Ear.

Method: Apply filiform needles with strong stimulation and retain the needles for 30 minutes. Apex of Ear may be pricked to cause bleeding. Auricular taping is also applicable.

3. Point Injection

Prescription: Feishu (BL 13), Sanyinjiao (SP 6), Zusanli (ST 36).

Method: 0.5 mL of salvia miltiorrhiza injection solution is injected into each point once a day.

疖 病

疖为金黄色葡萄球菌侵入毛囊及周围皮脂腺引起的急性化脓性炎症。多发及反复发作者称为疖病。糖尿病，慢性肾炎，营养不良，湿疹，痱子及虱病患者易患本病。初期表现为鲜红色圆锥形丘疹，逐渐变大成为硬节，伴有明显疼痛。最后硬节化脓，有时病灶中央有一腐肉栓，栓脱脓出，疼痛缓解，愈后结疤。急性期可见恶寒，发热，头痛，食欲不振，甚则出现败血症。多发于面，颈后，背及臀部。

1. 体针

处方　大椎，曲池，合谷，外关，足三里，风池，身柱，灵台，委中。

操作　毫针刺，用泻法。留针15～30分钟，间歇行针3～4次，每天1次。委中穴点刺放血。

2. 耳针

处方　肺，心，内分泌，神门，耳尖。

配穴　面部生疖加大肠和胃；颈后部生疖加膀胱和胰胆。

操作　毫针强刺激，留针30分钟，耳尖点刺出血。

Furunculosis

A furuncle is an acute purulent inflammation of the hair follicle and its peripheral sebaceous glands caused by the staphylococcus aureus bacteria. Cases of multiple or frequently recurring furuncles are referred to as furunculosis. People with diabetes mellitus, chronic nephritis, malnutrition, eczema, prickly heat, or pediculosis are at particularly high risk for this disorder. Furunculosis is marked in the initial stage by bright red conic papular eruptions which gradually enlarge and turn into scleroma accompanied by severe pain. The scleroma eventually suppurates, sometimes with a slough embolus in the center of the lesion. When the embolus drops off pus is discharged. The pain is alleviated and a scar often remains after healing. General symptoms in the acute stage include chills, fever, headache, poor appetite, or even hematosepsis. The furuncles usually occur on the face, back of the neck, and buttocks.

1. Body Acupuncture

Prescription: Dazhui (DU 14), Quchi (LI 11), Hegu (LI 4), Waiguan (SJ 5), Zusanli (ST 36), Fengchi (GB 20), Shenzhu (DU 12), Lingtai (DU 10), Weizhong (BL 40).

Method: Apply filiform needles with reducing method. Retain the needles for 15～30 minutes manipulating them 3～4 times once every day. Weizhong (BL 40) is pricked to cause bleeding.

2. Ear Acupuncture

Prescription: Lung, Heart, Endocrine, Shenmen, Apex of Ear.

Supplementary points: Add Large Intestine and Stomach for furuncle on the face, Urinary Bladder, Pancreas and Gallbladder for furuncle on the back of the neck.

Method：Apply filiform needles with strong stimulation and retain the needles for 30 minutes. Apex of Ear may be pricked to cause bleeding.

酒 渣 鼻

酒渣鼻系指发生在鼻、鼻侧、眉间或颊部的慢性炎症性皮肤病。其发生可能与胃肠功能紊乱，内分泌失调，饮食刺激，慢性病灶感染等有关。在不同阶段，分别表现为红斑、丘疹、脓疱或鼻赘。好发于成年人。

1. 体针

处方 肺俞，胃俞，大椎，曲池，血海，地仓，大迎，膈俞。

操作 毫针刺，用泻法。留针30分钟，间歇行针 2～4 次。

2. 耳针

处方 肺，胃，内分泌，肾上腺，风溪，神门，耳尖，大肠。

操作 毫针强刺激，留针 30 分钟，间歇行针 2～4 次；亦可采用耳穴贴敷。

3. 皮肤针

处方 患处。

操作 局部消毒后，皮肤针叩刺患处 15～20 分钟。每周 2 次。

4. 穴位注射

处方 迎香，曲池。

操作 每穴注射 0.5～1 毫升 丹参注射液，每周 2 次。

Brandy Nose

Brandy nose refers to chronic inflammation of the skin of the nasal, paranasal, glabellar or buccal regions. It is caused by gastrointestinal disturbances, endocrine disorder, food sensitivities, or chronic local infection. It is marked in different stages by erythema, pimples, pustules, and rhinophyma successively. It usually occurs in adults.

1. Body Acupuncture

Prescription：Feishu（BL 13），Weishu（BL 21），Dazhui（DU 14），Quchi（LI 11），Xuehai（SP 10），Dicang（ST 4），Daying（ST 5），Geshu（BL 17）.

Method：Apply filiform needles with reducing method and retain the needles for 30 minutes manipulating them 2～4 times.

2. Ear Acupuncture

Prescription：Lung, Stomach, Endocrine, Adrenal Gland, Wind Stream, Shenmen, Apex of Ear, Large Intestine.

Method：Apply filiform needles with strong stimulation. Retain the needles for 30 minutes manipulating them 2～4 times. Auricular taping is also applicable.

3. Plum-blossom Needle

Prescription：The affected area.

Method：After local sterilization tap the affected area with a plum-blossom needle for 15 ~ 20 minutes twice a week.

4. Point Injection

Prescription: Yingxiang (LI 20), Quchi (LI 11).

Method: Inject 0.5~1 mL of salvia miltiorrhiza injection solution into each point twice a week.

黄　褐　斑

黄褐斑是一种后天局限性皮肤黑色素沉着病。可能与慢性病症，内分泌紊乱，月经不调，日晒等诱发皮肤黑色素细胞功能亢进有关。性成熟期后的女性易患此病。皮损特点为淡褐色或深褐色斑片，分布于前额、颧部、颊部、鼻部、口周围部，左右对称，略呈蝴蝶形。中医称之为"面尘"、"鼾黑斑"等。

1. 体针

处方　合谷，曲池，三阴交，足三里，风门。

操作　毫针刺，用泻法。留针20~30分钟，间歇行针2~3次。

2. 耳针

处方　肝　脾，胃，肾，内分泌，肾上腺，缘中。

操作　毫针中等强度刺激，留针20~30分钟；亦可用耳穴贴敷。

Chloasma

Chloasma refers to acquired, localized, cutaneous melanosis. It may be caused by chronic illness, endocrine disorder, irregular menstruation, or overexposure to the sun leading to hyperfunction of the cutaneous melanocytes. Adult women are especially susceptible to this problem. Affected skin is marked by dark or light brown patches with a clearly delineated border, symmetrically distributed in the shape of a butterfly and covering the forehead, zygomatic, buccal, nasal, and perioral regions. It is called "mianchen" (dusty complexion), "Liheiban" and "Liheiyanzhen" (chlosma) in traditional Chinese medicine.

1. Body Acupuncture

Prescription: Hegu (LI 4), Quchi (LI 11), Sanyinjiao (SP 6), Zusanli (ST 36), Fengmen (BL 12).

Method: Apply filiform needles with reducing method. Retain the needles for 20~30 minutes manipulating them 2~3 times.

2. Ear Acupuncture

Prescription: Liver, Spleen, Stomach, Kidney, Endocrine, Adrenal Gland, Midpoint of Rim.

Method: Apply filiform needles with moderate stimulation and retain the needles for 20~30 minutes. Auricular taping is also applicable.

白　癜　风

白癜风是一种后天性局限性皮肤

色素脱失病，以皮肤出现无自觉症状的不规则白斑为特征。中医亦称之为"白癜风"，"白癜"或"白驳风"。

1. 体针

处方 合谷，曲池，风池，膈俞，肝俞，太冲，三阴交，隐白，人迎。

操作 毫针刺，平补平泻，留针15～20分钟，间歇行针2～3次。

2. 皮肤针

处方 患处。

操作 常规消毒后，用皮肤针轻叩，至皮肤红晕，立刻吸拔火罐。

3. 耳针

处方 肺，脾，心，神门，皮质下，肾上腺。

操作 毫针刺，强刺激，留针10～15分钟；亦可用耳穴贴敷。

Vitiligo

Vitiligo is an acquired skin disease of localized pigment loss. It is characterized by irregular white patches on the skin without subjective symptoms. This disease is called "baidianfeng" or "baidian" or "baibofeng" (vitiligo) in traditional Chinese medicine.

1. Body Acupuncture

Prescription: Hegu (LI 4), Quchi (LI 11), Fengchi (GB 20), Geshu (BL 17), Ganshu (BL 18), Taichong (LR 3), Sanyinjiao (SP 6), Yinbai (SP 1), Renying (ST 9).

Method: Apply filiform needles with even movement method. Retain the needles for 15～20 minutes manipulating them 2～3 times.

2. Plum-blossom Needle

Prescription: Local points in the affected areas of the body.

Method: After doing routine disinfection, tap with a plum-blossom needle until local redness of the skin appears. This is then followed by cupping.

3. Ear Acupuncture

Prescription: Lung, Spleen, Heart, Shenmen, Subcortex, Adrenal Gland.

Method: Apply filiform needles with strong stimulation and retain the needles for 10～15 minutes. Auricular taping is also applicable.

疣

疣是发生于皮肤浅表的小赘生物，好发于手背及面部，一般无自觉症状。

1. 体针

处方 曲池，合谷，支正，大骨空，大椎，血海，肝俞。

操作 毫针刺，用泻法，留针20～30分钟，间歇行针2～3次。

2. 耳针

处方 肺，屏间，胆，神门，下屏尖，患部相应部位。

操作 毫针强刺激，留针20～

30 分钟。

3．艾灸

处方　疣表面。

操作　用干燥艾绒搓成圆锥形，置于疣表面，灸 3～5 壮。圆锥底面直径应比疣之表面大 2～3 毫米。如过大则损伤正常组织过多，过小则疣之根部未受烧灼，可能复发。治疗时应选择原发之母疣。母疣治愈后，其继发的小疣常可自行脱落。

4．火针

处方　选疣 3～5 枚。

操作　常规消毒后，用火针从疣之中心点灸至根底部。

Wart

Wart, a kind of small neoplasm at the superficial portion of skin, mostly affects the dorsum of the hand and face without subjective symptoms and signs in general.

1．Body Acupuncture

Prescription：Quchi (LI 11), Hegu (LI 4), Zhizheng (SI 7), Dagukong (EX-UE 5), Dazhui (DU 14), Xuehai (SP 10), Ganshu (BL 18).

Method：Apply filiform needles with reducing method. Retain the needles for 20～30 minutes manipulating them 2～3 times.

2．Ear Acupuncture

Prescription：Lung, Intertragus, Gallbladder, Shenmen, Infratragic Apex, the corresponding parts of the diseased area.

Method：Apply filiform needles with strong stimulation and retain the needles for 20～30 minutes.

3．Moxibustion

Prescription：The surface of the wart.

Method：Dried moxa wool is made into a moxa cone and is put on the surface of the wart. 3～5 cones are applicable. The diameter of the cone bottom should be 2～3 mm larger than the wart surface. If it is too big, it is possible to damage the normal tissue too. If it is too small, the wart base will not be burnt. Therefore, it is possible to have a recurrence. It is advisable to choose the primary mother wart. After the mother wart is healed, the secondary small wart will drop automatically.

4．Cauterized Needle

Prescription：3～5 warts.

Method：After routine disinfection, puncture the warts with a cauterized needle to the base of the warts.

鸡　　眼

鸡眼多发于足底部，其根深陷肉里，状似鸡眼，故而得名。

1．体针

处方　鸡眼局部。

操作　以鸡眼为中心，毫针围刺，针刺深度以达鸡眼的基底部为准，亦可针后加灸。

2. 火针

处方　鸡眼中心。

操作　常规消毒后，取火针直刺鸡眼中心，深度以直达其基底部为止；或用火针于鸡眼之左右上下，各刺 1 针，深度同上。每隔 2～3 天 1次，直至鸡眼自然脱落。

Clavus

Clavus refers to deep-rooted skin infections on the plantar region. Clavus looks like cook eyes hence the name.

1. Body Acupuncture

Prescription: Local points.

Method: Apply filiform needles surrounding the clavus at the depth to the base of the clavus. Moxibustion is also applicable after needling.

2. Cauterized Needle

Prescription: Local clavus point.

Method: After routine disinfection insert the cauterized needle to the center of clavus until reaching the base. Cauterized needles may also be used to puncture from the surrounding sides towards the center at the similar depth. Treatment is given once every 2 ～ 3 days until natural casting off of the clavus.

腱鞘囊肿

腱鞘囊肿多发生在关节或肌腱附近，尤以腕关节背面、掌面、足背、膝的侧面及腋窝多见。囊肿局部隆起、光滑，触之有饱满感或波动感，局部不痛或稍有酸痛，无力。

1. 局部扬刺

处方　患处。

操作　用 28 号或 26 号毫针，在囊肿的正中及周围、上下、左右各刺1 针，深达肿块底部，中等度捻转，留针 10 分钟左右，期间加强捻转 1次。出针后可挤压或揉按肿块处，或配合局部艾炷灸 3 壮，使其充血为度；或加压包扎 2～3 天；若囊肿再度出现，可按原法再刺，一般 1～2次或 3～5 次即能消退自行吸收。

2. 火针

处方　囊肿之高点。

操作　常规消毒后，用 26 号粗毫针在酒精灯上烧红，当顶焠刺，出针后立即挤出囊内液体，刺后加灸20～30 分钟，隔天 1 次。

Ganglion

Ganglion occurs usually near joints or tendons, especially at the dorsal and palmar aspect of the wrist joints, dorsum of the foot, lateral side of the knee, and popliteal fossa. It is manifested by smooth protuberance with no pain or with soreness and forcelessness at the affected region. A full or undulatory sensation is felt by touching it.

1. Centro-Square Needling (Scattering Pricking)

Prescription: The affected region.

Method: No. 28 or No. 26 needles are selected. One needle is inserted into the spot at the center of the affected region, and another four needles are respectively inserted into four points which are at the border of the cyst respectively above, below, left and right to the center of the cyst. The needles are pushed towards the center of the basis of the ganglion and twisted at medium strength. Then, the needles are retained for approximately ten minutes and twisted once during the retention for strengthening the needling sensation. After withdrawal of the needles the cyst or protuberance is pressed, squeezed using massaged, or moxibustion is applied to it using three cones causing local congestion. Alternatively, a compression bandage is placed on it for two or three days. If the protuberance occurs again, the same puncture method is applied. Ganglion is usually cured by treatment of 1~5 sessions.

2. Cauterized Needle

Prescription: Top of the ganglion.

Method: After routine disinfection use a 26 gauge needle to quickly insert into the ganglion after heating it on an alcohol lamp. After withdrawal of the needle press the inserted ganglion to let the fluid come out. This is then followed by moxibustion for 20 ~ 30 minutes. Treatment is given once every other day.

皮脂腺囊肿

皮脂腺囊肿中医称为“脂瘤”。其囊内充满豆腐渣样物质。

1. 局部拘针

处方　囊肿四周。

操作　局部消毒后，用 26 号粗毫针从囊肿的最高点刺入，然后再从上、下、左、右四个方向，向中心行围针刺，出针后即加挤压，挤出胶状黏液，加灸 30 分钟。

2. 火针

处方　囊肿之高点。

操作　常现消毒后，用 26 号粗毫针在酒精灯上烧红，当顶焠刺，出针后立即挤压出囊内液体，刺后加灸 20~30 分钟。

Wen

Wen is called atheroma in traditional Chinese medicine. Inside the wen there exists some matter that looks like bean curd residue.

1. Centro-Square Needling

Prescription: Local points surrounding the wen.

Method: After routine disinfection in the local area use a 26 gauge needle to insert first from the top to the bottom, then from the surrounding directions to the center of the wen. Squeeze the points after withdrawing the needles until fluid flows out. This is followed by thirty minutes of moxibustion.

2. Cauterized Needle

Prescription: Top of the wen.

Method: After routine disinfection use a 26 gauge needle to quickly insert into the wen after heating it on an alcohol lamp. After withdrawal of the needle, press the inserted wen to let the fluid come out. This is then followed by moxibustion for 20 ~ 30 minutes. Treatment is given once every other day.

急性乳腺炎

急性乳腺炎是因金黄色葡萄球菌引起的乳腺急性化脓性炎症。多发于初产哺乳期，常在产后 3~4 周发生。病者发病前常有乳头皲裂，乳头内陷，乳房受挤压或乳汁瘀积等诱因。病变初期，乳房红肿疼痛，局部变硬且有压痛，数天后炎性肿块软化形成脓肿。全身症状可见高热、寒战、头痛、恶心、食欲不振，甚则败血症。中医称之为"乳痈"。

1. 体针

处方　肩井，乳根，膻中，足三里，内关。

操作　毫针刺，用泻法。留针

20~30 分钟，间歇行针 3~4 次。

2. 耳针

处方　胸，胸椎，胃，肝，内分泌，皮质下，神门，耳尖。

操作　毫针强刺激，留针 20 分钟。耳尖用三棱针点刺出血。亦可用耳穴贴敷。

3. 艾灸

处方　肩井，乳根，曲池，手三里，足三里。

操作　每穴温和灸治疗 5~10 分钟，每天 1 次或 2 次。多与针刺、拔火罐配合。

4. 三棱针

处方　在患者背部第 7 颈椎以下至第 12 胸椎以上的部位，寻找直径为 0.5 厘米的红疹。

操作　对所有红疹及周围皮肤进行常规消毒后，用三棱针刺破红疹，以手挤压，使之出血少许。

Acute Mastitis

Acute mastitis is an acute suppurative inflammation of the breast caused by Staphylococcus aureus. It occurs primarily in primiparae women while breast-feeding with onset usually occuring three to four weeks after delivery. There is often a history of cracked nipple, inverted nipple, or glactostasis before onset. In the initial stage, the breast is red and swollen with localized hard and tender regions. After several days, the hard inflammed mass softens and an abscess is formed. General symptoms may include high fever, chills, headache, nausea, poor appetite, and even septicemia. It is called "ruyong" in traditional Chinese medicine.

1. Body Acupuncture

Prescription: Jianjing (GB 21), Rugen (ST 18), Tanzhong (RN 17), Zusanli (ST 36), Neiguan (PC 6).

Method: Apply filiform needles with reducing method. Retain the needles for 20～30 minutes manipulating them 3～4 times.

2. Ear Acupuncture

Prescription: Chest, Thoracic Vertebrae, Stomach, Liver, Endocrine, Subcortex, Shenmen, Apex of Ear.

Method: Apply filiform needles with strong stimulation and retain the needles for 20 minutes. Apex of Ear may be pricked with a three-edged needle to cause bleeding. Auricular taping is also applicable.

3. Moxibustion

Prescription: Jianjing (GB 21), Rugen (ST 18), Quchi (LI 11), Shousanli (LI 10), Zusanli (ST 36).

Method: Mild warming moxibustion with a moxa stick is applied to each point for 5～10 minutes. Treatment is given once or twice daily. Usually, puncturing or cupping is additionally applied in coordination.

4. Three-edged Needle

Prescription Look for red rashes which are 0.5 cm in diameter, discoloured by pressing with the finger, on the back below the level of the 7th cervical vertebra and above the level of the 12th thoracic vertebra.

Method: After giving local and routine sterilization to the rashes, prick the rashes with a three-edged needle and press and squeeze them to cause slight bleeding.

乳腺囊性增生病

乳腺囊性增生病是指因乳管和腺泡上皮增生形成囊肿所致的一种病症。40 岁以上妇女易患本病，并常有月经不调，不孕或流产史。临床特点为乳房胀痛，有周期性。因情绪刺激或经前加重，经后减轻或消失。乳房肿块常为多发性，多在无意中发现，肿块呈圆形、椭圆形或分叶状，质韧，边界不清，与周围组织无粘连。情绪或经期变化可影响肿块。本病属中医"乳癖"、"乳中结核"范畴。

1. 体针

处方　太冲，屋翳，膻中，合谷，肩井，肿块局部。

操作 毫针刺，用泻法，肿块局部中心刺1针，周围边缘上下左右各刺1针，留针20分钟。

2. 耳针

处方 胸，胸椎，肝，胃，内分泌，缘中，皮质下，内生殖器，神门。

操作 毫针强刺激，留针20分钟；亦可用耳穴贴敷。

Cystic Hyperplasia of the Breast

Cystic hyperplasia of the breast refers to cytogenesis of the mammary tubes caused by hyperplasia and acinar epithelia. It occurs primarily in women above forty years old who have a history of irregular menstruation, infertility, or miscarriage. It is marked by periodic descending pain in the breast, aggravated by mental injury or before menstruation and alleviated after menstruation. Masses in the breast occur multiply and may be circular, oval, or lobulated with an indistinct border and adhesion to peripheral tissues. The masses may vary with the menstrual cycle and state of mind. This disease belongs to the categories of "rupi" and "ruzhong jiehe" in traditional Chinese medicine.

1. Body Acupuncture

Prescription: Taichong (LR 3), Wuyi (ST 15), Tanzhong (RN 12), Hegu (LI 4), Jiajing (GB 2), points around the nodules on the breast.

Method: Apply filiform needles with reducing method and puncture a filiform needle into the centre of the nodule and four filiform needles around the nodule. Retain the needles for 20 minutes.

2. Ear Acupuncture

Prescription: Chest, Thoracic Vertebrae, Liver, Stomach, Endocrine, Midpoint of Rim, Subcortex, Internal Genitals, Shenmen.

Method: Apply filiform needles with strong stimulation and retain the needles for 20 minutes. Auricular taping is also applicable.

胆 囊 炎

胆囊炎是指胆囊的急、慢性炎症。急性胆囊炎临床特点为突发右上腹持续性疼痛，阵发性加剧，并向右肩背部放射，常伴有恶心、呕吐及发热。多见于中年女性，常在饱餐或进食油腻食物后发作。慢性胆囊炎患者多有急性胆囊炎病史，急性发作时，其症状与急性胆囊炎相似，缓解期主要表现为进食后上腹部胀满不适，嗳气及厌食油腻，常伴有右肩背部隐痛，在站立、运动或冷水浴后加重。本病属中医"胁痛"范畴。

1. 体针

处方 日月，期门，肝俞，胆俞，内关，阳陵泉，太冲。

配穴 持续高热加合谷，曲池，大椎；恶心呕吐加足三里，中脘，丘墟。

2. 耳针

处方 胰胆，肝，腹，脾，胃，三焦，耳迷根，内分泌，耳尖。

操作 毫针强刺激，留针30分钟。耳尖可用三棱针点刺出血；亦可采用耳穴贴敷。

Cholecystitis

Cholecystitis is an acute or chronic inflammation of the gallbladder. The acute type is marked by sudden persistent pain in the right upper abdomen with paroxysmal exacerbation and radiation to the right shoulder and back. It is usually accompanied by nausea, vomiting, and fever. It occurs primarily in middle-aged women and is usually induced by overindulgence in greasy food. There is usually a history of acute cholecystitis in cases of chronic cholecystitis. The manifestations of an acute attack of chronic cholecystitis are similar to those of acute cholecystitis. The remission stage of chronic cholecystitis is marked by distension and discomfort in the upper abdomen after eating, belching, and aversion to greasy food , usually accompanied by dull pain in the right shoulder and back which is aggravated by standing, motion, or cold showers. Traditional Chinese medicine classifies cholecystitis as hypochondriac pain.

1. Body Acupuncture

Prescription: Riyue (GB 24), Qimen (LR 14), Ganshu (BL 18), Danshu (BL 19), Neiguan (PC 6), Yanglingquan (GB 34), Taichong (LR 3).

Supplementary points: Add Hegu (LI 4), Quchi (LI 11) and Dazhui (DU 14) for persistent high fever, Zusanli (ST 36), Zhongwan (RN 12) and Qiuxu (GB 40) for nausea and vomiting.

Method: Apply filiform needles with reducing method. Retain the needles for 30 minutes manipulating them 3～4 times.

2. Ear Acupuncture

Prescription: Pancreas, Gallbladder, Liver, Abdomen, Spleen, Stomach, San jiao, Root of Ear, Vagus, Endocrine, Apex of Ear.

Method: Apply filiform needles with strong stimulation and retain the needles for 30 minutes. Apex of Ear may be pricked with a three-edged needle to cause bleeding. Auricular taping is also applicable.

胆道蛔虫症

本病是因肠道蛔虫钻入胆道所导致的急腹症。临床主要表现为发作性上腹部或剑突下剧烈绞痛，并有向上钻顶样感觉，突起突止，常伴有恶心，呕吐。剑突下偏右方可有深压痛，但无腹肌紧张。胆道蛔虫症属中医"蛔厥"范畴。

1. 体针

处方Ⅰ 迎香透四白；中脘透梁门，天枢。

配穴 呕吐加内关、足三里；吐蛔虫加关元、太冲。

操作 毫针刺，用泻法。留针30分钟，间歇行针4～5次。疼痛缓解后，口服陈醋40毫升。

处方Ⅱ 第7胸椎夹脊穴或至阳。

操作 快速进针，针尖向上斜刺1～1.4寸，均匀地提插捻转，持续运针10分钟，留针30分钟，使针感向上下传导。其中夹脊穴左右取双侧，垂直刺入皮下，以65度角斜向胸椎刺入1寸左右，使针尖抵达脊柱骨膜，行小幅度捻转泻法，以患者胸腹部有宽松感止，留针20～30分钟。

2. 耳针

处方 胆，肝，神门，交感，十二指肠。

操作 毫针强刺激，留针30分钟；亦可用耳穴贴敷。

Biliary Ascariasis

The disease is an acute abdominal disease caused by the ascarids which enter the biliary tract from the intestinal tract. The main clinical manifestations are severe paroxysmal colic pains of the upper abdomen or right below the xiphoid process which seems to run upward, appearing and disappearing suddenly, accompanied often with nausea and vomiting. There is a deep tenderness right to and below the xiphoid process but no rigidity of abdominal muscles. The disease pertains to the category of "huijue" (colic caused by ascarids) in traditional Chinese medicine.

1. Body Acupuncture

Prescription Ⅰ: Yingxiang (LI 20) penetrating through Sibai (ST 2), Zhongwan (RN 12) penetrating through Liangmen (ST 21), and Tianshu (ST 25).

Supplementary points: Add Neiguan (PC 6) and Zusanli (ST 36) for vomiting, Guanyuan (RN 4) and Taichong (LR 3) for vomiting ascarides.

Method: Apply filiform needles with reducing method. Retain the needles for 30 minutes manipulating them 4～5 times. After relieving pain the patient should take 40 mL of mature vinegar.

Prescription Ⅱ: Huatuojiaji (Extra 15) at the seventh thoracic vertebra or Zhiyang (DU 9)

Method: Insert the needles rapidly. Puncture obliquely upward, 1～1.4 cun. Lift, thrust and twist the needle gently for 10 minutes. Retain the needles for 30 minutes making the needling sensation conduct upwards and downwards. Select one Huatuojiaji (Extra 15) respectively on both left and right sides. Insert the needles perpendicularly into the skin, Then puncture obliquely at an angle of 65° about 1 cun towards the thoracic vertebra making the tip reach the vertebral periosteum. Reducing by twisting gently with small amplitude is given until the patient feels a relaxing sensation in the chest and abdomen. Retain the needles for 20~30 minutes.

2. Ear Acupuncture

Prescription: Gallbladder, Liver, Shenmen, Sympathetic, Duodenum.

Method: Apply filiform needles with strong stimulation and retain the needles for 30 minutes. Auricular taping is also applicable.

胰 腺 炎

胰腺炎是指胰腺的急、慢性炎性病变。急性胰腺炎是由于胰液溢出胰管外后，作用于胰腺本身及其周围组织所引起的炎症。临床特点为突然发生上腹刀割样持续疼痛，阵发性加剧，并向腰部及左肩部放射，伴有恶心、呕吐、发热、多汗，甚则手足搐搦或中毒性休克。多见于青壮年，常因胆道蛔虫或结石，暴饮暴食或情绪刺激而诱发。慢性胰腺炎临床特点为上腹部反复发作性剧痛，向腰背及左肩部放射，一般持续 4~5 天。间歇期可无症状，或仅感上腹部隐痛或不适。部分患者表现为长期上腹部持续性疼痛，并逐渐加重，有的患者可无腹痛症状。多见于中年人，男性多于

女性，有胆囊炎、胆管炎、胆石症和急性胰腺炎病史及嗜酒者易患此症。本病属中医"腹痛"范畴。

1. 体针

处方　上脘，中脘，足三里，下巨墟，地机。

配穴　呕吐加内关；发热加合谷；黄疸加阳陵泉；腹痛加梁门，章门，内庭，日月，期门。

操作　毫针刺，用泻法。留针60~90 分钟，每 5~10 分钟间歇行针 1 次。

2. 耳针

处方　胰胆，脾，胃，三焦，腹，内分泌，肾上腺，神门。

操作　毫针强刺激，留针 40 分钟；亦可用耳穴贴敷。

Pancreatitis

Pancreatitis refers to acute or chronic inflammation of the pancreas. Acute pancreatitis is caused by pancreatic secretions which overflow from the pancreatic duct resulting in inflammation of the pancreas and its peripheral tissue. Acute pancreatitis is marked by suddenly occuring, persistent stabbing pain in the left upper abdomen with paroxysmal exacerbation and radiation to the lumbar region, back, and left shoulder usually accompanied by nausea, vomiting, fever, profuse perspiration, and even tetany or toxic shock. It occurs primarily in young people and adults and is usually induced by biliary ascariasis, roundworm, overindulgence in food or alcohol, or mental injury. Chronic pancreatitis is marked by frequently re-curring severe pain in the upper ab-domen radiating to the lumbar region, back, left shoulder, and usually lasting for 4 ~ 5 hours. During the remission stage there may be no symptoms or mi-nor dull pain in the upper abdomen. Some cases are marked by protracted, persistent, gradually-worsening pain in the upper abdomen while others may have no pain at all. Chronic pancreati-tis occurs mainly in middle aged people and more often in males than in fe-males. Alcoholics and those with a his-tory of cholecystitis, cholangitis, cholelithiasis, or acute pancreatitis are at high risk for chronic pancreatitis. Traditional Chinese medicine classifies pancreatitis as abdominal pain.

1. Body Acupuncture

Prescription: Shangwan (RN 13), Zhongwan (RN 12), Zusanli (ST 36), Xiajuxu (ST 39), Diji (SP 8).

Supplementary points: Add Neiguan (PC 6) for vomiting, Hegu (LI 4) for fever, Yanglingquan (GB 34) for Jaundice, Liangmen (ST 21), Zhangmen (LR 13), Neiting (ST 44), Riyue (GB 24), and Qimen (LR 14) for abdominal pain.

Method: Apply filiform needles with reducing method. Retain the needles for 60 ~ 90 minutes manipulating them once every 5 ~ 10 minutes.

2. Ear Acupuncture

Prescription: Pancreas, Gallblad-der, Spleen, Stomach, Sanjiao Ab-domen, Endocrine, Adrenal Gland, Shenmen.

Method: Apply filiform needles with strong stimulation and retain the needles for 40 minutes. Auricular taping is also applicable.

胆 石 症

胆石症为常见急腹症之 。结石在胆囊与胆管内形成，主要与胆汁瘀积、胆道感染或胆固醇代谢障碍有关。多发于中年人，女性多于男性。病者常有反复发作及持续性上腹部隐痛史。在静止期，可无任何症状，或仅感右上腹轻微钝痛；在活动期，临床表现常因结石位置不同而异，但共同症状为左上腹阵发性绞痛，向左肩放射。其他常见症状有厌油腻，恶心，呕吐，口苦，纳呆及发热。本病属中医"胁痛"范畴。

1. 体针

处方 日月，期门，中脘，胆俞，足三里，阳陵泉，丘墟。

配穴 绞痛加合谷；呕吐加内关；高热加曲池；黄疸加至阴。

操作 毫针刺，用泻法。留针
30 分钟，间歇行针 3～5 次。

2. 耳针

处方 神门，交感，肝，胆囊，
十二指肠。

操作 毫针强刺激，留针 30 分
钟；亦可用耳穴贴敷。

Cholelithiasis

Cholelithiasis, or gall stones, is a commonly seen acute abdominal condition. The formation of stones in the gallbladder or biliary ducts is due primarily to cholestasis, infection of the biliary tract, or metabolic disturbance of cholesterol. It occurs mainly in middle-aged people and more often in females than in males. There is usually a history of frequently recurring and persistent dull pain in the upper abdomen. During remission, there may be no symptoms or mild dull pain in the right upper abdomen. During the active stage, manifestations differ according to the location of the stones. The most common symptom is paroxysmal colic pain in the right upper abdomen radiating to the right shoulder. Other commonly seen symptoms include aversion to greasy food, nausea, vomiting, bitter taste in the mouth, poor appetite, and fever. Traditional Chinese medicine classifies cholelithiasis as hypochondriac pain.

1. Body Acupuncture

Prescription: Riyue (GB 24), Qimen (LR 14), Zhongwan (RN 12), Danshu (BL 19), Zusanli (ST 36), Yanglingquan (GB 34), Qiuxu (GB 40).

Supplementary points: Add Hegu (LI 4) for colic pain, Neiguan (PC 6) for vomiting, Quchi (LI 11) for high fever, Zhiyin (BL 67) for jaundice.

Method: Apply filiform needles with reducing method. Retain the needles for 30 minutes manipulating them 3～5 times.

2. Ear Acupuncture

Prescription: Shenmen, Sympathetic, Liver, Gallbladder, Duodenum.

Method: Apply filiform needles with strong stimulation and retain the needles for 30 minutes. Auricular taping is also applicable.

溃疡病穿孔

溃疡病急性穿孔是溃疡病较常见
的严重并发症之一，以青壮年男性为
多见。主要表现为突然发生上腹部剧
痛，持续加重，并逐渐波及全腹，变
动体位时腹痛加剧；烦躁不安、血压
下降、汗出、肢冷、脉搏急促等休克
症状；腹式呼吸变浅（或消失）、腹
肌强直、压痛、反跳痛明显加剧。肝
浊音界缩小或消失，肠鸣音减弱或消
失，叩诊可出现腹腔内移动性浊音。

1. 体针

处方　足三里，中脘，梁门，内关。

操作　毫针刺，用泻法。留针 1 小时，每 15 分钟间歇行针 1 次。

2. 耳针

处方　腹，胃，交感，神门，内分泌。

操作　毫针强刺激，留针 30 分钟。

Acute Perforation of Peptic Ulcer

Acute perforation of peptic ulcer is one of the common severe complications seen in peptic ulcer cases. Most of them are found in young and middle-aged male patients. The main manifestations are sudden attacks of severe pain in the upper abdomen. The pain is persistent and progressive and gradually involves the whole abdomen. The pain becomes worse in changing the body position. The patients may have manifestations of shock such as restlessness, hypotension, cold limbs, profuse sweating, and rapid pulse. Physical examination may reveal abdominal muscular tension, prominent tenderness, rebounding tenderness, shifting dullness, decrease or disappearance of hepatic dullness. In traditional Chinese medicine this disease is classfied as percordial pain with cold limbs or stomachache.

1. Body Acupuncture

Prescription: Zusanli (ST 36), Zhongwan (RN 12), Liangmen (ST 21), Neiguan (PC 6).

Method: Apply filiform needles with reducing method. Retain the needles for 1 hour manipulating them once every 15 minutes. 3~4 treatments daily.

2. Ear Acupuncture

Prescription: Abdomen, Stomach, Sympathetic, Shenmen, Endocrine.

Method: Apply filiform needles with strong stimulation and retain the needles for 30 minutes.

肠 梗 阻

肠腔内容物不能顺利通过肠道称之为肠梗阻。本病是常见的急腹症，具有病因复杂，病情多变，发展迅速等特点。主要表现为突然发作的阵发性腹痛，呕吐剧烈，常吐出胆汁、粪水；腹胀，可见肠型，无排便，无排气，肠鸣音阵发性亢进，有气过水声者为单纯机械性梗阻；腹痛呕吐持续加剧，则出现腹肌紧张，触痛明显，肠鸣音反而减弱，血压下降，汗出肢冷，气促脉疾者为绞窄性梗阻；若腹胀明显，而腹痛、呕吐不明显及肠鸣音减弱，无排气者，可能为麻痹性梗阻。中医称之为"关格"、"肠结"等。

1. 体针

处方　足三里，内庭，大横，合谷，中脘。

配穴　发热加曲池；腹痛加内关，章门；腹胀或小腹痛加关元，气海。

操作　毫针刺，用泻法。留针20～30分钟，间歇行针3～5次。每4～6小时治疗1次。

2. 耳针

处方　腹，小肠，大肠，交感，神门，皮质下。

操作　毫针强刺激，留针30分钟。

3. 水针

处方　足三里。

操作　双侧足三里注射新斯的明0.25毫克。本法适宜于麻痹性肠梗阻。

4. 肠套叠指压复位法

操作　患者取仰卧位，屈膝。术者站于患者左侧，右手触及套叠包块后，将示指、中指、无名指和小指自然伸直，使小指外侧面按压在套入肠管解剖部位之远端头部（包块上部），由轻到重地做按揉动作。重按后，小指抬起的同时无名指重按压，无名指抬起时中指按压，中指抬起时示指按压，示指抬起时再小指按压。轮流交替按压，缓缓按揉包块不停，直到套入肠管完全退出，包块消失。再用右手大鱼际在右下腹壁作轻柔和缓的回旋按摩，促使回盲部水肿消失。

5. 颠簸疗法

操作　患者取膝肘位，尽量加大膝肘的距离，充分暴露腹部。术者立于病床右侧或将担架放于地上，虚骑患者之上，让患者放松腹肌，先作腹部按摩，使患者适应后，两手合抱患者腹部，托起后再骤然放松，反复操作并逐渐增大幅度，以患者能忍受为度。重点颠簸区在脐部或脐下区。颠簸数次后，可将腹部左右摇晃，如此反复进行，每次5～10分钟，间歇15～30分钟，至少要连续进行3次。本法适宜于早期肠扭转。

Intestinal Obstruction

The phenomenon where the contents in the intestines can not pass through the intestinal canal smoothly is called intestinal obstruction. It is commonly seen as a case of acute abdomen with features of complicated etiology, variable states and rapid development. The main manifestations are sudden attacks of paroxysmal abdominal pain, severe vomiting with biliary juice or feces. In cases of simple intestinal obstruction the patient may have abdominal fullness, constipation and no gas passing. Physical examination reveals visible peristalsis, paroxysmal hyperactivity of bowel sounds and sounds of air passing water.

In cases of strangulated intestinal obstruction the patient may have persistent and severe vomiting and abdominal pain. Physical examination reveals tenderness and abdominal muscular tension, diminution of bowel sounds, hypotension, cold limbs, profuse sweating, rapid breathing and rapid pulse. Patients with paralytic intestinal obstruction may have prominent fullness of the abdomen, diminution of bowel sounds, no gas passing, and have only mild abdominal pain and vomiting. This disease is called "guange" (obstruction and rejection), "changjie" (knotted intestine) in traditional Chinese medicine.

1. Body Acupuncture

Prescription: Zusanli (ST 36), Neiting (ST 44), Daheng (SP 15), Hegu (LI 4), Zhongwan (RN 12).

Supplementary points: Add Quchi (LI 11) for fever, Neiguan (PC 6) and Zhangmen for abdominal pain, Guanyuan (RN 4) and Qihai (RN 6) for abdominal fullness and lower abdominal pain.

Method: Apply filiform needles with reducing method. Retain the needles for 20~30 minutes manipulating them 3~5 times. One treatment every 4~6 hours.

2. Ear Acupuncture

Prescription: Abdomen, Small Intestine, Large Intestine, Sympathetic, Shenmen, Subcortex.

Method: Apply filiform needles with strong stimulation and retain the needles for 30 minutes.

3. Point Injection

Prescription: Zusanli (ST 36).

Method: Inject 0.25mg of neostigmine into both points of Zusanli (ST 36). It is suitable for paralytic ileus.

4. Reduction of Intussusception with Fingerpressure Therapy

Method: The patient should lie on his back and bend the knee joints. The doctor should stand on the left side of the patient and use his right hand to press the intussusceptive mass. stretching his forefinger, middle finger, ring finger, and little finger naturally, let the lateral aspect of the little finger press the distal head which runs into the anatomic site of the intestinal canal (ie. the upper part of the mass). The pressing and rubbing should be from mild to heavy. After heavy pressing, lift the little finger and press heavily with the ring finger. Then lift the ring finger and press with the middle finger. Lift the middle finger and press with the forefinger, Lift the forefinger and press with the little finger. Repeat with fingers till the mass disappears completely. Then use the thenar of the right hand to press the right lower abdomen gently and massage rotatingly in order to let the edema of ileocecum disappear.

5. Jolty Therapy

Method: The patient should take the knee-elbow position to expand the distance between the knee and the elbow and to expose the abdomen fully. The doctor should stand on the right side of the patient's bed or astride the patient who lies on a stretcher on the floor. Let the patient relax his or her abdominal muscles and after that, start to massage the patient's abdomen till the patient has got used to this practice. Hold the patient's abdomen and lift it up and then suddenly get loose. Repeat this process continuously and increase the amplitude gradually. How long this process should last depends on the patient's endurance. The key jolty area is the umbilical region or the abdominal region below the umbilicus. After jolting several times shake the abdomen from right to left or vice versa and continue the jolting. After $5\sim10$ minutes of each process take a $15\sim30$ minutes-rest. The whole course should at least consist of three successive processes. It is suitable for early volvulus.

阑　尾　炎

阑尾炎是指阑尾的急、慢性炎性病变。急性阑尾炎表现特点为早期移动性腹痛，即初起上腹或脐周疼痛，数小时后移动至右下腹部，疼痛呈持续性，阵发性加剧。亦有少数患者腹痛一开始就在右下腹部。其他症状有恶心、呕吐、食欲不振、便秘、腹泻及发热。慢性阑尾炎表现特点为反复发作性或持续性右下腹隐痛，常因剧烈运动，行走过久或饮食不节而诱发或加重。可伴有上腹部胀痛不适，便秘或大便次数多。慢性阑尾炎患者多有典型急性阑尾炎病史。本病属于中医"腹痛"和"肠痈"的范畴。

1. 体针

处方　足三里，阑尾穴，下巨墟，天枢，上巨墟，阿是穴。

配穴　恶心，呕吐加内关，上脘，中脘；发热加合谷，曲池。

操作　毫针刺，用泻法，留针$20\sim30$分钟，间歇行针$3\sim5$次。

2. 耳针

处方　神门，交感，阑尾，腹，小肠，大肠，肺。

操作　毫针强刺激，留针30分钟。

3. 艾灸

处方　气海，阑尾穴。

操作　温和灸治疗$10\sim15$分钟，每天1次或2次。

4. 水针

处方　足三里，阑尾穴。

操作　患者取仰卧屈膝或屈膝端坐位，穴位常规消毒后，用5毫升注射器吸入注射用蒸馏水2~4毫升，以较快速度将针刺入3~4厘米，探索穴位刺激点，待有酸重麻胀感时，即将蒸馏水缓慢注入，患者立即感到沉重的麻酸胀感，沿经前外侧传至足背以至足趾。视病情每天注射1~2次，直至痊愈为止。

Appendicitis

Appendicitis is an acute or chronic inflammation of the appendix. Acute appendicitis is marked in the initial stage by shifting abdominal pain. It starts in the upper abdomen or umbilical region and moves after several hours to the right lower abdomen and becomes persistent with paroxysmal exacerbation. A small number of cases may experience pain in the right lower abdomen at onset. Other manifestations include nausea, vomiting, poor appetite, constipation, diarrhea, and fever. Chronic appendicitis is marked by frequently recurring or persistent dull pain in the right lower abdomen. It is usually induced or aggravated by exertion or improper diet and accompanied by distending pain or discomfort in the upper abdomen, constipation, or frequent defecation. There is often a history of acute appendicitis. Traditional Chinese medicine classifies appendicitis as abdominal pain and intestinal abscess.

1. Body Acupuncture

Prescription: Zusanli (ST 36), Lanweixue (EX-LE 7), Xiajuxu (ST 39), Tianshu (ST 25), Shangjuxu (ST 37), Ashi point.

Supplementary points: Add Neiguan (PC 6), Shangwan (RN 13) and Zhongwan (RN 12) for nausea and vomiting, Hegu (LI 4) and Quchi (LI 11) for fever.

Method: Apply filiform needles with reducing method. Retain the needles for 20 ~ 30 minutes manipulating them 3 ~ 5 times.

2. Ear Acupuncture

Prescription: Shenmen, Sympathetic, Appendix, Abdomen, Small Intestine, Large Intestine, Lung.

Method: Apply filiform needles with strong stimulation and retain the needles for 30 minutes.

3. Moxibustion

Prescription: Qihai (RN 6), Lanweixue (EX-LE 7).

Method: Apply mild-warming moxibustion for 10 ~ 15 minutes once or twice a day.

4. Point Injection

Prescription: Zusanli (ST 36),

Lanweixue (EX-LE 7).

Method: The patient is in the supine position with genuflex or in sitting position with genuflex. Local and routine sterilization is given. A needle in a 5 mL syringe with 2~4 mL of water for injection is inserted quickly into the acupoint to a depth of 3~4 cm. When needling sensations such as soreness, heaviness, numbness and distension are induced, the water is injected slowly into the point and the patient's needling sensation will be increased and propagated to the dorsum of the foot or even to the toes. The injection is given one or two times daily according to the patient's condition until the disease is cured.

痔　疮

痔疮是因痔静脉回流障碍，引起直肠末端黏膜下和肛管皮下的静脉丛发生扩张、曲张形成的静脉团。根据静脉团的位置不同可分为三种类型。内痔表现特点为排便出血，痔核脱出，若痔核合并感染时，则疼痛剧烈。外痔表现特点为肛门异物感，若痔静脉破裂或有血栓形成则有剧烈疼痛。混合痔兼有内、外痔的特点，但病情较严重。

1. 体针

处方　长强，承山，大肠俞，白环俞。

操作　毫针刺，平补平泻。留针30 分钟，间歇行针 3~4 次。

2. 耳针

处方　直肠下端，大肠，痔点，皮质下，脾，肾上腺。

操作　毫针强刺激，留针 20 分钟；亦可用耳穴贴敷。

3. 三棱针

处方　大肠俞，肾俞，次髎，或腰骶部脊柱两侧，突出皮面，状如大头针帽大小的红褐色小点，或上唇系带周围瘀血点。

操作　常规消毒后，三棱针点刺引起出血少许，每 3 天 1 次。

4. 激光疗法

处方　痔核局部。

操作　用氦-氖激光对准痔核部位，直接照射 15~20 分钟，每天 1~2 次。

Hemorrhoids

Hemorrhoids refers to venous masses caused by backflow obstruction of the hemorrhoidal veins. This results in dilation and varicosity of the submucosal venous plexus of the blind end of the rectum and the submucosal venous plexus of the anal canal. It is classified into three types according to the location of the venous masses. Internal hemorrhoids are marked by bleeding during defecation, prolapse of the hemorrhoids, or severe pain when complicated by infection. External hemorrhoids are marked by the sensation of a foreign body in the anus, and severe pain aggravated by defecation, walking, or sitting, any of which may cause thrombosis or splitting of the hemorrhoidal veins to occur. Mixed hemorrhoids has characteristics of both internal and external hemorrhoids but the condition is more severe than either alone.

1. Body Acupuncture

Prescription: Changqiang (DU 1), Chengshan (BL 57), Dachangshu (BL 25), Baihuanshu (BL 30).

Method: Apply filiform needles with even movement method and retain the needles for 30 minutes manipulating them 3~4 times.

2. Ear Acupuncture

Prescription: Lower Rectum, Large Intestine, Pile Spot, Subcortex, Spleen, Adrenal Gland.

Method: Apply filiform needles with strong stimulation and retain the needles for 20 minutes. Auricular taping is also applicable.

3. Three-edged Needle

Prescription: Dachangshu (BL 25), Shenshu (BL 23), Ciliao (BL 32), the red brown spots about 0.2 cm in diameter beside the lumbosacral vertebrae, or the stagnant spots on the upper labial frenulum.

Method: After routine disinfection use a three-edged needle to prick the points to cause a tiny amount of bleeding. Treatment is given once every three days.

4. Laser Therapy

Prescription: Hemorrhoids spot.

Method: Radiate the hemorrhoids spot with He-Ne laser beams for 15~20 minutes once or twice daily.

膀　胱　炎

膀胱炎是因细菌感染引起膀胱壁的急性或慢性炎症改变。急性膀胱炎临床特点为起病急骤，出现尿频、尿急、尿痛及下腹部疼痛，伴肉眼血尿及脓尿。尿频以白天为重。慢性膀胱炎的症状与急性的相似，反复发作，但程度较轻。本病属中医"淋病"范畴。

1. 体针

处方　膀胱俞，中极，阴陵泉，三阴交。

操作　毫针刺，用泻法。留针30分钟，间歇行针2~4次。

2. 耳针

处方　膀胱，尿道，腹，盆腔，肾，内分泌，神门，耳尖。

操作　毫针强刺激，留针30分钟；亦可采用耳穴贴敷。

Cystitis

Cystitis is an acute bacteria caused inflammation of the internal wall of the urinary bladder. Acute cystitis is marked by sudden onset of lower abdominal pain and frequent, dripping, and painful urination, accompanied by macroscopic blood in the urine and pyuria. Frequency of urination is higher during the day than at night. The manifestation of chronic cystitis are similar to or milder than those of acute cystitis and recur frequently. Traditional Chinese medicine classifies cystitis as "lin syndrome".

1. Body Acupuncture

Prescription: Pangguangshu (BL 28), Zhongji (RN 3). Yinlingquan (SP 9), Sanyinjiao (SP 6).

Method: Apply filiform needles with reducing method. Retain the needles for 30 minutes manipulating them 2～4 times.

2. Ear Acupuncture

Prescription: Urinary Bladder, Urethra, Abdomen, Pelvis, Kidney, Endocrine, Shenmen, Apex of Ear.

Method: Apply filiform needles with strong stimulation and retain the needles for 30 minutes. Auricular taping is also applicable.

附 睾 炎

附睾炎多为泌尿生殖系统感染经输精管蔓延至附睾急、慢性炎性病变。急性附睾炎多发于青壮年，常累及单侧。临床特点为发病急，患侧阴囊肿胀、坠痛，并向下腹及腹股沟部放射。伴有发热、恶寒等全身症状。慢性附睾炎表现特点为附睾持续性隐痛，坠痛，并向下腹及腹股沟部放射。伴有发热，恶寒等全身症状。慢性附睾炎表现特点为附睾持续性隐痛，下坠感，时有急性发用。病者常有慢性前列腺炎，长期留置导尿管或急性附睾炎病史。

1. 体针

处方　气海，关元，归来，三阴交，曲骨，气冲。

操作　毫针刺，用泻法。留针30分钟，间歇行针3～4次。

2. 耳针

处方　内生殖器，外生殖器，盆腔，腹，肝，肾，内分泌，肾上腺，屏尖，耳尖。

操作　毫针刺，强刺激，留针30分钟；亦可用耳穴贴敷。

Epididymitis

Epididymitis is an acute or chronic inflammation of the epididymides caused primarily by urogenital infection spreading to the epididymides through the spermatic ducts. Acute epididymitis occurs mainly in young people and adults usually unilaterally. It is marked by sudden swelling and sinking pain in the affected testicle, the pain radiating to the lower abdomen and groin. Accompanying general symptoms include chills and fever. Chronic epididymitis is marked by persistent dull pain and sinking sensation in the affected testicle with periodic acute attacks. There is usually a history of chronic prostatitis, acute epididymitis or long-term indwelling catheter.

1. Body Acupuncture

Prescription：Qihai（RN 6）, Guanyuan（RN 4）, Guilai（ST 29）, Sanyinjiao（SP 9）, Qugu（RN 2）, Qichong（ST 30）.

Method：Apply filiform needles with reducing method. Retain the needles for 30 minutes manipulating them 3～4 times.

2. Ear Acupuncture

Prescription：Internal Genitals, External Genitals, Pelvis, Abdomen, Liver, Kidney, Endocrine, Adrenal Gland, Apex of Antitragus, Apex of Ear.

Method：Apply filiform needles with strong stimulation and retain the needles for 30 minutes. Auricular taping is also applicable.

前列腺炎

前列腺炎是指前列腺的急、慢性病症。急性前列腺炎多见于青壮年，其临床特点为起病急、高热、寒战、尿频、尿急、尿痛、腰骶及会阴部胀痛或剧痛。常因饮酒过度，性生活不当，会阴损伤，感冒或急性尿道炎而诱发。慢性前列腺炎临床特点为轻度尿频，排尿烧灼感，终末尿混浊及腰骶、会阴和阴部坠痛。可伴有阳痿、早泄等性功能障碍及神经衰弱症状。病者常有急性前列腺炎病史。本病属中医"淋证"范畴。

1. 体针

处方　关元，中极，三阴交，三焦俞，足三里，阴陵泉。

操作　毫针刺，用泻法。留针30分钟，间歇行针 3～4 次。

2. 耳针

处方　艇角，尿道，肾，三焦，肝，内分泌，神门。

操作　毫针强刺激，留针 30 分钟；亦可用耳穴贴敷。

Prostatitis

Prostatitis is an acute or chronic inflammation of the prostate gland. Acute prostatitis occurs mainly in young people and adults and is marked by frequent, painful, or dripping urination, sudden high fever, chills, and distending or severe pain in the lumbosacral region and perineum. It is usually caused by overindulgence in alcohol, excessive sexual activity, suppression of ejaculation, injury of the perineum, acute urethritis, or the common cold. Chronic prostatitis is marked by increased frequency of urination, burning sensation during urination, turbid terminal urine, and sinking pain in the lumbosacral region, perineum, and scrotum. It may be accompanied by sexual dysfunction including pain during ejaculation or impotence, and neurosism. There is usually a history of acute prostatitis. Traditional Chinese medicine classifies prostatitis as "Lin syndrome".

1. Body Acupuncture

Prescription: Guanyuan (RN 4), Zhongji (RN 3), Sanyinjiao (SP 6), Sanjiaoshu (BL 22), Zusanli (ST 36), Yinlingquan (SP 9).

Method: Apply filiform needles with reducing method. Retain the needles for 30 minutes manipulating them 3~4 times.

2. Ear Acupuncture

Prescription: Angle of Superior Concha, Urethra, Kidney, Sanjiao, Liver, Endocrine, Shenmen.

Method: Apply filiform needles with strong stimulation and retain the needles for 30 minutes. Auricular taping is also applicable.

前列腺增生症

前列腺增生症是老年人常见病症，也是引起尿潴留，泌尿系统感染和尿毒症的常见原因。病变初期，表现为尿频，以夜间为著，并逐渐加重。继则出现排尿困难，尿流细，尿淋漓或尿流中断。病变后期可出现急性尿潴留或充盈性尿失禁。本病属中医"淋证"范畴。

1. 体针

处方　膀胱俞，中极，阴陵泉，三阴交，大敦。

操作　毫针刺，用泻法。留针30分钟，间歇行针3~4次。

2. 耳针

处方　艇角，尿道，肾，三焦，肝，内分泌，皮质下。

操作　毫针强刺激，留针30分钟；亦可采用耳穴贴敷。

Hyperplasia of the Prostate

Hyperplasia of the prostate is a common problem in older men. It is also a common cause of such disorders as retention of urine, urinary tract infection, and uremia. It is marked in the initial stage by frequent urination, more severe at night and worsening over time. As the condition develops, difficulty in urination, weak urinary stream, urinary stuttering, or interrupted urination may occur. In the advanced stage, there may be acute urinary retention or incontinence. Traditional Chinese medicine classifies hyperplasia of the prostate as "Lin syndrome."

1. Body Acupuncture

Prescription: Pangguangshu (BL 28), Zhongji (RN 3), Yinlingquan (SP 9), Sanyinjiao (SP 6), Dadun (LR 1).

Method: Apply filiform needles with reducing method. Retain the needles for 30 minutes manipulating them 3~4 times.

2. Ear Acupuncture

Prescription: Angle of Superior Concha, Urethra, Kidney, Sanjiao, Liver, Endocrine, Subcortex.

Method: Apply filiform needles with strong stimulation and retain the needles for 30 minutes. Auricular taping is also applicable.

泌尿系结石

泌尿系结石是指发生在肾、输尿管、膀胱和尿道等泌尿系统部位的结石症。肾结石的临床特点为腰部持续性钝痛，有时呈阵发性绞痛，疼痛向背及下腹部放射。输尿管结石的临床特点为阵发性剧烈绞痛，沿输尿管向下放射至会阴及大腿内侧，常伴有烦躁不安，恶心、呕吐及大汗出。肾和输尿管结石多发生于 20～40 岁男性，单侧多见。膀胱和尿道结石临床特点为小便淋漓不畅，或尿流突然中断，伴有尿痛及血尿，疼痛可放射到会阴及阴茎头处。如果结石阻塞尿道，则会发生急性尿潴留。膀胱和尿道结石多发于 10 岁以下男孩及患前列腺肥大的老年人。中医称本病为"石淋"。

1. 体针

处方　肾俞，膀胱俞，足三里，关元，中极，三阴交，阴陵泉，水道。

操作　毫针刺，用泻法。留针20～30分钟，间歇行针4～5次。

2. 耳针

处方　肾，输尿管，膀胱，尿道，腹，三焦，交感，神门。

操作　毫针强刺激，留针30分钟。

3. 电针

处方　肾俞，膀胱俞，关元，水道。

操作　肾俞或膀胱俞连接阴极，关元或水道连接阳极。取患侧上下两个穴位，强度由弱变强，至患者能耐受为度，持续 20～30 分钟，每天1～2 次。

Urinary Stones

Urinary stones occur in the urinary tract, including the kidney, urinary bladder, ureters, and urethra. Nephrolithiasis, or kidneys stones are marked by persistent dull pain or paroxysmal colicky pain in the lumbar region radiating to the back and lower abdomen. Ureterolithiasis, or ureter stones are marked by paroxysmal severe colicky pain radiating downward along the ureters to the perineum and medial side of the thighs, usually accompanied by restlessness, nausea, vomiting, and profuse perspiration. Both kidney and ureter stones occur primarily in men twenty to forty years old. Usually only one side is affected. The presence of stones in the urethra or bladder is marked by dripping or interrupted urination, accompanied by pain and blood in the urine. The pain may radiate to the perineum and glans of the penis or clitoris. Acute retention of urine may occur if there are stones blocking the urethra. Bladder and urethral stones occur primarily in boys younger than ten years old and older men with prostate hyperplagia. Urinary stones are referred to as "stonelin" in traditional Chinese medicine.

1. Body Acupuncture

Prescription: Shenshu (BL 23), Pangguangshu (BL 28), Zusanli (ST 36), Guanyuan (RN 4), Zhongji (RN 3), Sanyinjiao (SP 6), Yinlingquan (SP 9), Shuidao (ST 28).

Method: Apply filiform needles with reducing method. Retain the needles for 20～30 minutes manipulating them 4～5 times.

2. Ear Acupuncture

Prescription: Kidney, Ureter, Urinary Bladder, Urethra, Abdomen, Sanjiao, Sympathetic, Shenmen.

Method: Apply filiform needles with strong stimulation and retain the needles for 30 minutes.

3. Electroacupuncture

Prescription: Shenshu (BL 23), Pangguangshu (BL 28), Guanyuan (RN 4), Shuidao (ST 28).

Method: The therapeutic electrode (－) is connected with Shenshu (BL 23) or Pangguanshu (BL 28), while the (＋) with Guanyuan (RN 4) or Shuidao (ST 28). Select the upper and lower points of the affected side for needling. The intensity of the needling should be from weak to strong and it must be as strong as the patient can bear. Then sustain the needling for 20～30 minutes 1 or 2 times a day.

颈 椎 病

颈椎病是由于颈椎间盘退行性变骨质增生，压迫颈神经根或脊髓所致。多发于 40 岁以上，病者常有颈部外伤、劳损或落枕病史。临床表现特点为颈肩部持续性针刺样疼痛，疼痛常向一侧或双侧上肢放射，夜间颈部后弯或咳嗽时加重，卧床或提肩可使疼痛减轻。其他症状可见头晕，恶心，呕吐，手臂及手指麻木或胸前区疼痛。

1. 体针

处方　风池，秉风，肩髃，曲池，外关，合谷，后溪，颈部夹脊。

操作　毫针刺，平补平泻。留针

30 分钟，间歇行针 2～4 次。

2. 耳针

处方　颈椎，肝，肾，神门。

操作　毫针轻刺激，留针 30 分钟，亦可采用耳穴贴敷。

3. 皮肤针

处方　颈部夹脊穴。

操作　轻刺激，叩击皮肤潮红为度，隔天 1 次。

Cervical Spondylopathy

Cervical spondylopathy is caused by degeneration and hyperosteogeny of cervical intervertebral discs resulting in compression of the cervical root nerves or spinal cord. It occurs primarily in people over forty years old. There is often a history of cervical trauma, strain, or stiff neck. Clinically, cervical spondylopathy is marked by persistent stabbing pain in the cervical region and shoulder often radiating to one or both arms and worsening at night. It is aggravated by backward bending of the neck and coughing, and alleviated by lying down or lifting the shoulders. Additional manifestations include dizziness, nausea, vomiting, numbness of the forearms and fingers, and pain in the anterior pectoral region.

1. Body Acupuncture

Prescription: Fengchi (GB 20), Bingfeng (SI 12), Jianyu (LI 15), Quchi (LI 11), Waiguan (SJ 5), Hegu (LI 4), Houxi (SI 3), Cevical Huatuojiaji points.

Method: Apply filiform needles with even movement. Retain the needles for 30 minutes manipulating them 2 ~ 4 times.

2. Ear Acupuncture

Prescription: Cervical Vertebrae, Liver, Kidney, Shenmen.

Supplementary points: Add Occiput for dizziness, Cardia for nausea and vomiting, positive points on the scaphoid fossa for numbness and pain of the arms and fingers.

Method: Apply filiform needles with mild stimulation and retain the needles for 30 minutes. Auricular taping is also applicable.

3. Plum-blossom Needles

Prescription: Cervical Huatojiaji points

Method: Tap with mild stimulation once every other day until local redness appears.

肋软骨炎

肋软骨炎是指肋软骨的慢性非特异性炎症。多见于青壮年，常有胸部外伤，突然过力牵拉，慢性震动及呼吸道感染等诱因。好发于第 2、第 3 肋软骨。临床表现为患处肋软骨肿胀高起，持续性钝痛，疼痛随咳嗽、深呼吸或胸肩活动加重。疼痛持续 1 个月左右可自行消失，但易复发。

1. 体针

处方　行间，足三里，足窍阴，太冲，丘墟，阳陵泉，内关。

操作　毫针刺，用泻法。留针 30 分钟；间歇行针 3～4 次。

2. 耳针

处方　胸，胸椎，肝，胰胆，肾，神门。

操作　毫针强刺，留针 30 分钟；亦可采用耳穴贴敷，强刺激。

3. 皮肤针

处方　患处。

操作　皮肤针叩至局部潮红，隔天 1 次。

Costal Chondritis

Costal chondritis is a chronic nonspecific inflammation of the costal cartilage. It occurs primarily in young people and adults and is usually induced by chest trauma or infection of the respiratory tract. Usually affected areas are the costal cartilage of the second and third ribs. Manifestations include swelling and eminence of the affected costal cartilage and persistent dull pain aggravated by coughing, deep breathing, or movement of the chest or shoulders. The pain may spontaneously disappear after approximately one month but recurs easily. Traditional Chinese medicine classifies costal chondritis as "hypochondriac pain".

1. Body Acupuncture

Prescription: Xingjian (LR 2), Zusanli (ST 36), Zuqiaoyin (GB 44), Taichong (LR 3), Qiuxu (GB 40), Yanglingquan (GB 34), Neiguan (PC 6).

Method: Apply filiform needles with reducing method. Retain the needles for 30 minutes manipulating them 3～4 times.

2. Ear Acupuncture

Prescription: Chest, Thoracic Vertebrae, Liver, Pancreas, Gallbladder, Kidney, Shenmen.

Method: Apply filiform needles with strong stimulation and retain the needles for 30 minutes. Auricular taping with strong stimulation is also applicable.

3. Plum-blossom Needle

Prescription: Affected areas.

Method: Tap the affected areas with a plum-blossom needle until local redness appears once every other day.

肩关节周围炎

肩关节周围炎为肩周肌肉、肌腱及关节囊等软组织的慢性炎症和退行性变。多发于 50 岁以上，女性多见。临床表现以疼痛及肩关节活动受限，如外展、外旋、后伸及上举等时出现疼痛和受限为特点。疼痛可向颈和上臂放射，日轻夜重。严重者肩关节活动可完全消失及肌肉萎缩。

1. 体外

处方 肩髃，肩髎，曲池，天宗，臂臑。

操作 毫针刺，用泻法。留针30分钟，间歇行针3～4次。

2. 耳针

处方 肩，锁骨，小肠，大肠，三焦，肝，脾，肾，神门。

操作 毫针强刺激，留针30分钟，亦可采用耳穴贴敷。

3. 艾灸

处方 患处，大椎，命门。

操作 用点燃的艾条在痛处及大椎、命门穴处巡回熏灸15～20分钟，每天1次。

4. 皮肤针

处方 局部肿胀处。

操作 皮肤针叩刺患处10～15分钟，每天1次。

Scapulohumeral Periarthritis

Scapulohumeral periarthritis is a chronic retrograde inflammation of the soft tissues, including muscles, tendons, and joint capsules peripheral to the shoulder joint. It occurs primarily in people above fifty years old and more often in females than in males. It is marked by pain and limited abduction, outward rotation, backward extension, and raising of the shoulder joint. The pain may radiate to the neck and upper arm. The pain also lessens during the day and worsens at night. In severe cases the shoulder joint may become completely frozen with resulting atrophy of the shoulder muscles.

1. Body Acupuncture

Prescription: Jianyu (LI 15), Jianliao (SJ 14), Quchi (LI 11), Tianzong (SI 11), Binao (LI 14).

Method: Apply filiform needles with reducing method. Retain the needles for 30 minutes manipulating them 3～4 times.

2. Ear Acupuncture

Prescription: Shoulder, Clavicle, Small Intestine, Large Intestine, San-Jiao, Liver, Spleen, Kidney, Shenmen.

Method: Apply filiform needles with strong stimulation and retain the needles for 30 minutes. Auricular taping is also applicable.

3. Moxibustion

Prescription: Affected region, Dazhui (DU 14), Mingmen (DU 4).

Method: Apply rounding moxibustion with a moxa stick for 15～20 minutes once a day.

4. Plum-blossom Needle

Prescription: Local swelling and distension area.

Method: Tap on the affected are a with a plum-blossom needle for 10~15 minutes once a day.

肱骨外上髁炎

肱骨外上髁炎,俗称"网球肘",系因腕伸肌腱起点扭伤或劳损所致。多见于青壮年,从事木工或网球运动等职业的人易患此种病症。临床特点为肘关节外侧疼痛,常向前臂外侧或肩部放射,握拳或拧毛巾时疼痛加剧。肱骨外上髁处压痛明显,但无肿胀及关节活动障碍。中医称之为"肘劳"。

1. 体针

处方 曲池,少海,外关,合谷。

操作 毫针刺,用泻法。留针30分钟,间歇行针3~4次。

2. 耳针

处方 肘,三焦,肝,神门。

操作 毫针强刺激,留针30分钟;亦可采用耳穴贴敷。

3. 艾灸

处方 患处。

操作 用温和灸治疗患处15~20分钟,每天1次。

External Humeral Epicondylitis

External humeral epicondylitis, commonly called tennis elbow, is caused by sprain or strain of the base of the carpal extensor muscle. It occurs mainly in young people and adults. Carpenters and tennis players are at especially high risk for this condition. External humeral epicondylitis is marked by pain on the lateral side of the elbow joint, usually radiating to the lateral side of the forearm or shoulder and aggravated when making a fist or wringing a towel. There is severe tenderness on the external humeral epicondyle but no swelling or impairment of joint movement. It is termed "Zhoulao" in traditional Chinese medicine.

1. Body Acupuncture

Prescription: Quchi (LI 11), Shaohai (HT 3), Waiguan (SJ 5), Hegu (LI 4).

Method: Apply filiform needles with reducing method. Retain the needles for 30 minutes manipulating them 3~4 times.

2. Ear Acupuncture

Prescription: Elbow, Sanjiao, Liver, Shenmen.

Method: Apply filiform needles with strong stimulation and retain the needles for 30 minutes. Auricular taping is also applicable.

3. Moxibustion

Prescription: Affected area.

Method：Apply mild-warming moxibustion to the affected area for 15～20 minutes once a day.

急性软组织损伤

急性软组织损伤是指四肢关节或躯体部的软组织如肌肉、肌腱、韧带及血管等因扭、挫导致的损伤。损伤部位常发生于肩、肘、腕、指、髋、膝和踝。临床表现为受伤部位肿胀、疼痛及关节活动障碍。

1. 体针

处方　以受伤的局部或邻近穴位为主，配合相应的远端循经取穴。

操作　毫针刺，用泻法。留针30分钟，间歇行针3～4次。

2. 耳针

处方　相应耳穴区，神门，脑，肝，脾，心。

操作　毫针强刺激，留针30分钟。

3. 艾灸

处方　受损区。

操作　用艾卷温和灸治疗受伤局部15分钟，或每穴施艾炷4～6壮；亦可用温针灸。

4. 拔罐疗法

处方　受损局部。

操作　用坐罐治疗10～20分钟，每天1次。

Acute Soft Tissue Injury

Acute soft tissue injury refers to sprain or contusion of the soft tissue, including the muscles, tendons, ligaments, or joint capsules. It usually occurs on the shoulder, elbow, wrist, fingers, lumbus, hip, knee, or ankle. Manifestations include swelling, pain, and impaired joint movement.

1. Body Acupuncture

Prescription：The points at the injured area and adjacent area are taken as the main points and the distal points of the involved meridian as the adjuvant.

Method：Apply filiform needles with reducing method. Retain the needles for 30 minutes manipulating them 3～4 times.

2. Ear Acupuncture

Prescription：Corresponding auricular region, Shenmen, Brain, Liver, Spleen, Heart.

Method：Apply filiform needles with strong stimulation and retain the needles for 30 minutes.

3. Moxibustion

Prescription：The injured region.

Method：Apply mild-warming moxibustion with a moxa stick or moxibustion with moxa cones to the injured region for 15 minutes or using 4～6 cones. Moxibustion with warming needle is also applicable.

4. Cupping

Prescription: The injured region.

Method: Apply retaining cupping to the injured region for $10 \sim 20$ minutes once a day.

腰肌劳损

腰肌劳损是腰部的一种慢性病症。临床特点为腰部间歇性或持续性酸、痛、沉重，适当活动或休息后减轻，久立、久坐或阴雨寒冷天气加重。病者常有急性腰部扭伤史、长期弯腰工作或感受风寒湿等。本病属于中医"腰痛"的范畴。

1. 体针

处方　肾俞，腰阳关，委中，阳陵泉。

操作　毫针刺，平补平泻，留针30分钟，间歇行针 3～4 次。

2. 耳针

处方　肾，膀胱，肝，脾，神门。

操作　毫针轻刺激，留针30分钟；亦可用耳穴贴敷。

3. 艾灸

处方　肾俞，阳陵泉，委中。

操作　用温和灸治疗 15～20 分钟，每天 1 次。

4. 拔罐

处方　患处，肾俞，腰阳关。

操作　采用坐罐或闪罐治疗 10～20分钟，每天 1 次。

Lumbar Muscle Strain

Lumbar muscle strain refers to chronic lower back pain. It is marked by intermittent or persistent soreness, pain, and heaviness in the lumbar region alleviated after appropriate movement and aggravated by extended sitting or standing or cold and rainy weather. There is usually a history of acute lumbar sprain, work involving extensive standing or bending or invasion by wind-cold or cold-damp. It belongs to the category of "lumbar pain" in traditional Chinese medicine.

1. Body Acupuncture

Prescription: Shenshu (BL 23), Yaoyangguan (DU 3), Weizhong (BL 40), Yanglingquan (GB 34).

Method: Apply filiform needles with even movement. Retain the needles for 30 minutes manipulating them $3 \sim 4$ times.

2. Ear Acupuncture

Prescription: Kidney, Urinary Bladder, Liver, Spleen, Shenmen.

Method: Apply filiform needles with mild stimulation and retain the needles for 30 minutes. Auricular taping is also applicable.

3. Moxibustion

Prescription: Shenshu (BL 23),

Yaoyangguan （DU 3）, Weizhong (BL 40).

Method: Apply mild-warming moxibustion for 15～20 minutes once a day.

4. Cupping

Prescription: Affected area, Shenshu（BL 23）, Yaoyangguan（DU 3）.

Method: Apply retaining cupping or successive flash cupping for 10～20 minutes once a day.

第三节　妇科疾病

Section 3 Gynecological Diseases

功能性子宫出血

功能性子宫出血系指因性腺功能障碍引起子宫异常出血，但无全身和生殖器官器质性病变。分为排卵型和无排卵型。无排卵型多见于青春期及更年期，表现特点为月经周期不规则，经期长短不定，经血量多或淋漓不尽；排卵型多见于育龄期妇女，表现特点为月经周期缩短或正常，经期正常或延长，经血量多少不定。本病属于中医"崩漏"的范畴。

1. 体针

处方　隐白，通里，关元，三阴交，中极。

配穴　经来量多，色紫红，味臭秽，夹有瘀块，腹痛拒按，大便秘结，口渴，舌质红，苔黄，脉弦数有力者加血海，水泉；经来量多，或淋漓不断，色淡质稀，少腹冷痛，面色㿠白，神疲乏力，倦怠嗜卧，胃纳减少，舌质淡，苔白滑，脉细弱者加脾俞，足三里；经色鲜红，质稠量少，头晕耳鸣，五心烦热，舌红无苔，脉细数者加内关，太溪。

操作　毫针刺，平补平泻，留针20～30分钟，间歇行针3～4次。

2. 耳针

处方　内生殖器，盆腔，腹，肝，脾，内分泌，缘中，皮质下。

配穴　腹痛加神门；烦躁易怒加胸。

操作　毫针轻刺激，留针30分钟；亦可用耳穴贴敷。

3. 艾灸

处方　气海，关元，肾俞，脾俞，隐白。

操作　每穴用温和灸治疗10～20分钟，每天1次。

4. 皮肤针

处方　膈俞，肝俞，脾俞，胃俞，肾俞，足三里，三阴交，关元，隐白。

操作　三棱针中等强度刺激，隔天1次。

5. 水针

处方　关元，三阴交，中极，血海。

操作　每穴注射维生素 B_{12} 0.5毫升，每天1次。

6. 三棱针

处方　隐白，大敦。

操作　三棱针点刺出血，隔天 1
次。

7. 头针

处方　生殖区。

操作　毫针与头皮成 30 度角快
速进针，留针 1～2 小时，间歇行针
3 次。

Dysfunctional Uterine Bleeding

Dysfunctional uterine bleeding refers
to abnormal uterine bleeding caused by
gonadal dysfunction but with no accompanying organic or genital problems. It
is classified into ovulatory and anovulatory types. The anovulatory type occurs primarily during adolescence or climacteric and is marked by irregular
menstrual cycles and periods with unusually profuse or scanty menstrual
blood. The ovulatory type occurs primarily during the reproductive period of
life and is marked by short menstrual
cycles with long periods or normal
length cycles and periods with unusually
scanty or profuse menstrual blood. The
disease belongs to the category of "Ben-
glou" in traditional Chinese medicine.

1. Body Acupuncture

Prescription: Yinbai (SP 1),
Tongli (HT 5), Guanyuan (RN 4),
Sanyinjiao (SP 6), Zhongji (RN 3).

Supplementary points: Add Xuehai
(SP 10) and Shuiquan (KI 5) for
profuse, purple-red menses with clots
in it, smell, abdominal pain aggravated by pressure, constipation, thirst,
red tongue with yellow coating, taut,
rapid and forceful pulse, Pishu (BL
20) and Zusanli (ST 36) for profuse
bleeding or continuous scanty bleeding
marked by light red and thin blood,
cold and pain in the lower abdomen,
pallor, lassitude, listlessness, loss of
appetite, pale tongue with white and
slippery coating, thin and weak pulse,
Neiguan (PC 6) and Taixi (KI 3) for
bright red menses, scanty and thick
blood, dizziness, tinnitus, dysphoria
with feverish sensation in the chest,
palms and soles, red tongue without
coating, thin and rapid pulse.

Method: Apply filiform needles with
even movement method. Retain the
needles for 20～30 minutes manipulating them 3～4 times.

2. Ear Acupuncture

Prescription: Internal Genitals,
Pelvis, Abdomen, Liver, Spleen,
Endocrine, Midpoint of Rim, Subcor-
tex.

Supplementary points: Add Shenmen for abdominal pain, Chest for restlessness and irritability.

Method：Apply filiform needles with mild stimulation and retain the needles for 30 minutes. Auricular taping is also applicable.

3. Moxibustion

Prescription：Qihai（RN 6）, Guanyuan（RN 4）, Shenshu（BL 23）, Pishu（BL 20）, Yinbai（SP 1）.

Method：Apply mild-warming moxibustion to each point for 10 ~ 20 minutes once a day.

4. Plum-blossom Needle

Prescription：Geshu（BL 17）, Ganshu（BL 18）, Pishu（BL 20）, Weishu（BL 21）, Shenshu（BL 23）, Zusanli（ST 36）, Sanyinjiao（SP 6）, Guanyuan（RN 4）, Yinbai（SP 1）.

Method：Tap on the points with a plum-blossom needle and apply medium strength stimulation once every other day.

5. Point Injection

Prescription：Guanyuan（RN 4）, Sanyinjiao（SP 6）, Zhongji（RN 3）, Xuehai（SP 10）.

Method：Inject 0.5 mL of vitamin B_{12} into each point once a day.

6. Three-edged Needle

Prescription：Yinbai（SP 1）, Dadun（LR 1）.

Method：Prick the points with a three-edged needle to cause bleeding once every other day.

7. Scalp Acupuncture

Prescription：Reproduction Area.

Method：Apply filiform needle to insert at an angle of 30° to the scalp swiftly and retain the needles for 1 ~ 2 hours manipulating them 3 times.

痛　经

痛经是一种以月经期间或其前后小腹疼痛为特点的常见妇科病症。分为原发性和继发性。原发性痛经是指从月经初潮起就有小腹部疼痛，但无生殖器官器质性病变者，与子宫发育不全、精神紧张及内分泌失调有关；继发性痛经是指月经初潮时并无痛经，以后起病者，与内生殖器官的器质性病变有关。临床症状为小腹阵发性绞痛，多见于月经初期，疼痛常向外阴、肛门及腰背部放射，常常伴有恶心、呕吐、头痛、头晕，甚则面色苍白、汗出、手足厥冷。

1. 体针

处方　三阴交，中极，气海，关元，归来，足三里。

配穴　小腹冷痛，经量少伴血块者加血海；小腹胀痛者加太冲，内关，阳陵泉；腹痛绵绵，头晕耳鸣，经色淡者加照海，肾俞，曲泉。

操作　毫针刺，平补平泻，留针30分钟，间歇行针3~4次。

2. 耳针

处方   内生殖器，盆腔，腹，肝，内分泌，缘中，皮质下，神门。

操作   毫针强刺激，留针 30 分钟；亦可采用耳穴贴敷。

3. 艾灸

处方   关元，曲骨，三阴交。

操作   月经来潮前 1～2 天或月经来潮时，采用隔姜灸或艾条灸，每次每穴 3～5 壮或 10～15 分钟，每天 1～2 次。

4. 腕踝针

处方   双侧下 1。

操作   采用 1.5 寸长 30 号毫针，医者左手拇指、示指舒张皮肤，右手持针对准应刺部位，使针体与皮肤呈 30 度角，刺透皮后，将针放平贴近皮肤表面，循纵线向上沿皮下平刺入 1.4 寸左右，留针 30 分钟。

5. 电针

处方   关元，中极，三阴交，气海，肾俞。

操作   每次选 2 个穴位，采用疏密波或密波治疗 10～20 分钟，中等强度刺激，每天 1 次。

6. 水针

处方   肾俞，气海，关元，三阴交，血海。

操作   每穴注射当归注射液 0.5 毫升，每天 1 次。

7. 激光疗法

处方   关元   中极，足三里，太溪，交信。

操作   每穴用氦-氖激光直接照射 5 分钟，每天 1 次。

Dysmenorrhea

Dysmenorrhea is a commonly seen gynecological disorder marked by pain in the lower abdominal region before, during or after menstruation. It is classified into primary and secondary types. In primary dysmenorrhea lower abdominal pain commences with onset of the menarche with no abnormal genital conditions present. It is caused primarily by hypoplasia of the uterus, mental injury, or endocrine disorder. In secondary dysmenorrhea lower abdominal pain commences some time after the menarche. It is caused primarily by organic problems of the internal genitals. Manifestations of both primary and secondary dysmenorrhea include cramps in the lower abdominal region during menstruation, sometimes radiating to the vulva, anus, and back, and often accompanied by nausea, vomiting, headache, dizziness, pale complexion, and sweating and coldness of the hands and feet.

1. Body Acupuncture

Prescription: Sanyinjiao (SP 6), Zhongji (RN 3), Qihai (RN 6), Guanyuan (RN 4), Guilai (ST 29), Zusanli (ST 36).

Supplementary points: Add Xuehai (SP 10) for coldness and pain at the lower abdomen and scanty menses with clots, Taichong (LR 3), Neiguan (PC 6), and Yanglingquan (GB 34) for distension and pain at the lower abdomen, Zhaohai (KI 6), Shenshu (BL 23), and Ququan (LR 8) for dull pain in the abdomen, dizziness, tinnitus, and thin menses.

Method: Apply filiform needles with even movement method. Retain the needles for 30 minutes manipulating them 3~4 times.

2. Ear Acupuncture

Prescription: Internal Genitals, Pelvis, Abdomen, Liver, Endocrine, Midpoint of Rim, Subcortex, Shenmen.

Method: Apply filiform needles with strong stimulation and retain the needles for 30 minutes. Auricular taping is also applicable.

3. Moxibustion

Prescription: Guanyuan (RN 4), Qugu (RN 2), Sanyinjiao (SP 6).

Method: Apply ginger moxibustion to each point using 3~5 cones or moxibustion with a moxa stick to each point for 10~15 minutes at the period one or two days before the menstruation or on menstruation once or twice a day.

4. Wrist-Ankle Puncture

Prescription: Bilateral lower 1.

Method: Stretch the local skin with the thumb and index finger of the left hand. Insert a No. 30 needle 1.5 cun long held with the right hand into the skin at an angle of 30° to the skin. After piercing through the skin, place the needle horizontally and push it beneath the skin upwards for 1.4 cun. Then, it is retained for 30 minutes.

5. Electroacupuncture

Prescription: Guanyuan (RN 4), Zhongji (RN 3), Sanyinjiao (SP 6), Qihai (RN 6), Shenshu (BL 23).

Method: Select 2 points each treatment session. Apply dense-sparse wave or dense wave to each point for 10~20 minutes with medium strength stimulation once a day.

6. Point Injection

Prescription: Shenshu (BL 23), Qihai (RN 6), Guanyuan (RN 4), Sanyinjiao (SP 6), Xuehai (SP 10).

Method: Inject 0.5 mL of Radix Angelicae Sinensis injection into each point once a day.

7. Laser Therapy

Prescription: Guanyuan (RN 4),

Zhongji（RN 3）, Zusanli（ST 36）, Taixi（KI 3）, Jiaoxin（KI 8）.

Method: Radiate each point with He-Ne laser beams for 5 minutes once a day.

闭　　经

女子年逾 18 岁尚未行经，或月经周期建立后又连续停经达 3 个月以上者称为闭经。前者称原发性闭经，后者称继发性闭经。

1. 体针

处方　合谷，阴交，照海，气冲，血海。

操作　毫针刺，平补平泻，留针20～30 分钟，间歇行针 3～4 次。

2. 耳针

处方　内生殖器，内分泌，缘中，神门，皮质下，肝，肾，盆腔。

操作　毫针中等强度刺激，留针30 分钟。亦可采用耳穴贴敷。

3. 电针

处方　归来，三阴交，中极，地机。

操作　每穴采用疏波或疏密波治疗 10～20 分钟，每天 1 次。

4. 皮肤针

处方　肝俞，脾俞，肾俞，足三里，三阴交，关元，血海，照海。

操作　皮肤针中等强度叩刺10～20分钟，隔天 1 次。

5. 艾灸

处方　腰俞，照海。

操作　每穴用温和灸治疗 10～15 分钟，每天 1 次。

Amenorrhea

By amenorrhea it is meant primary a-menorrhea and secondary amenorrhea. The former applies to those who are not yet 18 years old and have never men-struated, while the latter refers to those whose menses have ceased for over three months after the formation of menstrual cycle.

1. Body Acupuncture

Prescription: Hegu（LI 4）, Yinjiao（RN 7）, Zhaohai（KI 6）, Qichong（ST 30）, Xuehai（SP 10）.

Method: Apply filiform needles with even movement method. Retain the needles for 20～30 minutes manipulating them 3～4 times.

2. Ear Acupuncture

Prescription: Internal Genitals, En-docrine, Midpoint of Rim, Shenmen, Subcortex, Liver, Kidney, Pelvis.

Method: Apply filiform needles with medium strength stimulation and retain the needles for 30 minutes. Auricular taping is also applicable.

3. Electroacupuncture

Prescription: Guilai（ST 29）, Sanyinjiao（SP 6）, Zhongji（RN 3）,

Diji（SP 8）.

Method：Apply sparse wave or dense-sparse wave to the points for 10～20 minutes once a day.

4. Plum-blossom Needle

Prescription：Ganshu（BL 18），Pishu（BL 20），Shenshu（BL 23），Zusanli（ST 36），Sanyinjiao（SP 6），Guanyuan（RN 4），Xuehai（SP 10），Zhaohai（KI 6）.

Method：Tap the points with a three-edged needle. Apply medium strength stimulation for 10～20 minutes once every other day.

5. Moxibustion

Prescription：Yaoshu（DU 2），Zhaohai（KI 6）.

Method：Apply mild-warming moxibustion to each point for 10～15 minutes, once a day.

经前期综合征

经前期综合征是指月经前出现的一系列症候群，主要由于精神紧张引起大脑皮质下中枢和自主神经系统功能失调，以及性激素紊乱所致。临床表现为精神紧张，神经过敏，注意力不集中，抑郁，焦虑，易怒，失眠，头痛，手足及颜面浮肿，恶心，呕吐，腹痛，腹泻，小腹坠痛，乳房胀疼，甚则发红，发热。

1. 体针

处方 太冲，三阴交，中极，肝俞。

操作 毫针刺，用泻法，留针20分钟，间歇行针3～4次。

2. 耳针

处方 内生殖器，内分泌，缘中，神门，皮质下，肝。

配穴 有精神症状者加心；有胃肠症状者加胃和贲门；小腹痛者加腹，盆腔；乳房胀痛者加胸。

操作 毫针强刺激，留针30分钟，亦可采用耳穴贴敷或耳穴自我按摩。

3. 皮肤针

处方 肝俞，三阴交，心俞，胆俞，太冲。

操作 三棱针叩刺20分钟，每天1次。

4. 电针

处方 内关，神门，足三里，通里。

操作 每穴采用疏密波中等强度刺激5～10分钟，每天1次。

Premenstrual Syndrome

Premenstrual syndrome refers to a series of symptoms occuring in some women for several days before each menstrual period. It is caused by dysfunction of the cerebral subcortex, the autonomic nervous system and disturbance of the sex hormones. Manifestations include nervousness, depression, anxiety, irritability, insomnia, headache, swelling of the hands, face, or feet, nausea, vomiting, diarrhea, cramps or sinking pain in the lower abdomen, lower back pain, and painful swelling, redness or fever of the breasts.

1. Body Acupuncture

Prescription: Taichong (LR 3), Sanyinjiao (SP 6), Zhongji (RN 3), Ganshu (BL 18).

Method: Apply filiform needles with reducing method. Retain the needles for 20 minutes manipulating them 3～4 times.

2. Ear Acupuncture

Prescription: Internal Genitals, Endocrine, Midpoint of Rim, Shenmen, Subcortex, Liver.

Supplementary points: Add Heart for mental symptoms, Stomach and Cardia for gastrointestinal problems, Abdomen and Pelvis for lower abdominal pain, Chest for painful swelling of the breasts.

Method: Apply filiform needles with strong stimulation and retain the needles for 30 minutes. Auricular taping or auricular self-massage may also be practiced.

3. Plum-blossom Needle

Prescription: Ganshu (BL 18), Sanyinjiao (SP 6), Xinshu (BL 15),

Danshu (BL 19), Taichong (LR 3).

Method: Tap the points with a plum-blossom needle for 20 minutes once a day.

4. Electroacupuncture

Prescription: Neiguan (PC 6), Shenmen (HT 7), Zusanli (ST 36), Tongli (HT 5).

Method: Apply sparse-dense wave and medium strength stimulation to each point for 5～10 minutes once a day.

更年期综合征

更年期综合征是指部分妇女在更年期因卵巢功能逐渐衰退，引起内分泌及自主神经功能紊乱所致的一系列症状。因创伤、手术、盆腔放射治疗而丧失卵巢功能者亦可罹患本病。临床表现多样。心血管系统症状可见间歇性颜面、颈、胸潮红，发热，心悸，心前区不适或疼痛，肢端蚁行感、麻木、疼痛。精神症状有烦躁、易怒、焦虑、失眠多梦，肥胖，水肿等代谢失常症状亦可出现。本病属于中医"绝经前后诸证"。

1. 体针

处方 内关，通里，后溪，足三里，三阴交，太冲。

配穴 潮热，汗出，烦怒者加行间，足临泣，太溪，复溜；心悸，心慌，失眠，健忘者加神门，肝俞，心俞。

操作　毫针刺，用泻法或平补平泻法，留针 20～30 分钟，间歇行针 3～4 次。

2. 耳针

处方　内生殖器，肾，肝，内分泌，皮质下，神门。

配穴　失眠者加目 1 目 2，枕；心悸者加心，胸；水肿者加脾，艇中。

操作　毫针中等强度刺激，留针 30 分钟。亦可用耳穴贴敷。

3. 皮肤针

处方　心俞，肝俞，照海，三阴交，足三里。

操作　皮肤针每穴叩刺 5～10 分钟，隔天 1 次。

4. 电针

处方　内关，太冲，神门，足三里。

操作　疏密波中等强度刺激，每天 10～15 分钟，每天 1 次。

Menopausal Syndrome

Menopausal syndrome refers to a series of symptoms occuring in some women during the climacteric. It is caused by a gradual decline of ovarian function leading to disturbance of the endocrine and autonomic nervous systems. Women with anovarism due to trauma, surgery, or pelvic radiotherapy may also experience this condition.

Manifestations are various. Cardiovascular symptoms include intermittent flushing and sensations of heat on the face, neck and chest, accompanied by profuse perspiration (popularly know as hot flashes), palpitation, discomfort or pain in the precardial region, formication, and numbness or pain of the extremities. Mental symptoms include restlessness, irritability, anxiety, insomnia, and poor memory. Symptoms of metabolic dysfunction such as obesity and edema may also occur. It belongs to the category of syndrome before or after menopause.

1. Body Acupuncture

Prescription: Neiguan (PC 6), Tongli (HT 5), Houxi (SI 3), Zusanli (ST 36), Sanyinjiao (SP 6), Taichong (LR 3).

Supplementary points: Add Xiangjian (LR 2), Zulinqi (GB 41), Taixi (KI 3), Fuliu (K I7) for tidal fever with sweating and irritability, Shenmen (HT 7), Ganshu (BL 18), Xinshu (BL 15) for palpitation, insomnia and poor memory.

Method: Apply filiform needles with reducing or even movement method. Retain the needles for 20～30 minutes manipulating them 3～4 times.

2. Ear Acupuncture

Prescription: Internal Genitals,

Kidney, Liver, Endocrine, Subcortex, Shenmen.

Supplementary points: Add Eye 1 Eye 2 and Occiput for insomnia, Heart and Chest for palpitation, Spleen and Central Superior Concha for edema.

Method: Apply filiform needles with medium strength stimulation and retain the needles for 30 minutes. Auricular taping is also applicable.

3. Plum-blossom Needle

Prescription: Xinshu (BL 15), Ganshu (BL 18), Zhaohai (KI 6), Sanyinjiao (SP 6), Zusanli (ST 36).

Method: Apply a plum-blossom needle to tap each point for 5～10 minutes once every other day.

4. Electroacupuncture

Prescription: Neiguan (PC 6), Taichong (LR 3), Shenmen (HT 7), Zusanli (ST 36).

Method: Apply spare-dense wave and medium strength stimulation to each point for 10～15 minutes once a day.

白带异常

白带异常是指白带的量和质的异常，可见于多种内、外生殖器病症。单纯白带量多见于排卵前期，行经前后，妊娠期及应用雌激素后；脓性白带，黄色黏稠，有臭味，多因外生殖器官的炎性病变所致；血性白带常见于老年性阴道炎，宫颈息肉及肿瘤。

1. 体针

处方　带脉，白环俞，次髎，关元，归来，三阴交。

配穴　白带量多质稠无臭，纳少，便溏，倦怠，体胖，舌淡苔白腻，脉弱者加脾俞，公孙；带下色白，量多质稀，淋漓不断，腰部酸痛，小腹发凉，兼头目眩晕，小便清长，舌淡苔薄，脉沉细者加肾俞，太溪；带下黏稠色黄，或夹有血液，量多而气腥秽，阴部作痒，口干舌苦，小便短赤，舌红苔黄，脉弦滑数者加阴陵泉，丰隆。

操作　毫针刺，实证用泻法，虚证用补法。留针 30 分钟，间歇行针 3～4 次。

2. 耳针

处方　内生殖器，外生殖器，盆腔，三焦，内分泌，缘中，皮质下，肾上腺。

操作　毫针中等强度刺激，留针 30 分钟；亦可采用耳穴贴敷。

3. 艾灸

处方　带脉，关元，三阴交，脾俞，肾俞。

操作　温和灸或隔蒜灸治疗 10～15分钟。本法适宜于脾虚或肾虚者。

4. 腕踝针

处方　双侧下 2。

操作　患者仰卧。采用 30 号 1.5 寸毫针，医者用拇指、示指、中指共持针柄，针体与皮肤表面呈 30 度角，用拇指端轻旋针柄，使针尖进入皮肤。过皮后即将针放平，贴近皮肤表面，针尖向上顺直线沿皮下表线进针。进针速度稍缓慢，如有阻力或出现酸、麻、胀、疼等感觉，则表示针刺太深而已入肌层，应将针退至皮下，重新刺入。进针入皮下的长度一般为 1.4 寸，留针 20～30 分钟，每天治疗 1 次。

Leukorrhagia

Leukorrhagia refers to abnormal change of the vaginal secretions. It is a common symptom of various diseases and disorders of both the internal and external female genitals. Simple leukorrhagia with profuse, thin, clear vaginal discharge, occurs mainly during the preovulatory phase before or after the menstrual period during pregnancy or after administration of estrogen. Yellowish, sticky, strong-smelling vaginal discharge occurs primarily in the presence of inflammation of either the internal or external genitals. Bloody vaginal discharge occurs primarily in the presence of senile vaginitis, cervical polyps, or tumors.

1. Body Acupuncture

Prescription: Daimai (GB 26), Baihuanshu (BL 30), Ciliao (BL 32), Guanyuan (RN 4), Guilai (ST 29), Sanyinjiao (SP 6).

Supplementary points: Add Pishu (BL 20) and Gongsun (SP 4) for profuse thick and white vaginal discharge without smell, poor appetite, loose stools, thicle and pale tongue with white and sticky coating, and weak pulse, Shenshu (BL 23) and Taixi (KI 3) for profuse and continuous thin and white vaginal discharge, soreness and pain of the lower back, cold sensation at the lower abdomen, dizziness, excessive urine, pale tongue with thin coating, and deep and thready pulse, Yinlingquan (SP 9) and Fenglong (ST 40) for profuse yellow and thick mucous vaginal discharge with smell or with blood, itching in the vulva, thirst and bitter taste in the mouth, scanty and yellow urine, red tongue with yellow coating, and string-taut smooth and rapid pulse.

Method: Apply filiform needles with reducing method for repletion pattern or reinforcing method for vacuity pattern. Retain the needles for 30 minutes manipulating them 3～4 times.

2. Ear Acupuncture

Prescription: Internal Genitals, External Genitals, Pelvis, Abdomen, Sanjiao, Endocrine, Midpoint of Rim, Subcortex, Adrenal Gland.

Method: Apply filiform needles with medium strength stimulation and retain the needles for 30 minutes. Auricular taping is also applicable.

3. Moxibustion

Prescription: Daimai (GB 26), Guanyuan (RN 4), Sanyinjiao (SP 6), Pishu (BL 20), Shenshu (BL 23).

Method: Apply mild-warming moxibustion or garlic moxibustion to the points for 10～15 minutes. It is suitable for spleen deficiency or kidney deficiency.

4. Wrist-Ankle Puncture

Prescription: Bilateral Lower 2.

Method: Ask the patient to lie supine. Hold a 1.5 cun long needle with the thumb, index and middle fingers and insert it through the skin at an angle of 30° to the skin. Then, slowly push it horizontally upwards along the skin. If feeling the resistance around the needle tip or inducing soreness, numbness, distension and pain to the patient, lift the needle to the area beneath the skin and make another try because these phenomena indicate that the needle is inserted too deep to the muscular layer. Generally, insert the needle 1.4 cun deep and retain it for 20～30 minutes. The treatment is given once a day.

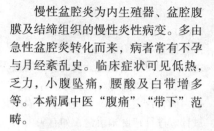

慢性盆腔炎为内生殖器、盆腔腹膜及结缔组织的慢性炎性病变。多由急性盆腔炎转化而来，病者常有不孕与月经紊乱史。临床症状可见低热，乏力，小腹坠痛，腰酸及白带增多等。本病属中医"腹痛"、"带下"范畴。

1. 体针

处方　三阴交，中极，归来，足三里，关元。

操作　毫针刺，用泻法。留针30分钟，间歇行针3～4次。

2. 耳针

处方　盆腔，内生殖器，腹，三焦，脾，肝，内分泌，肾上腺，神门，耳尖。

操作　毫针强刺激，留针30分钟；亦可用耳穴贴敷。

3. 水针

处方　中极，归来，关元，三阴交。

操作　每穴注射当归注射液1毫升，每天1次。

4. 激光疗法

处方　中极，气海，关元，肾俞。

操作　每穴用氦-氖激光直接照射5分钟，每天1次。

Chronic Pelvic Inflammation

Chronic pelvic inflammation refers to

chronic inflammation of the internal genitals, pelvis, peritoneum, and pelvic connective tissues. It usually develops from acute pelvic inflammation and there is often a history of sterility or menstrual disorder. Manifestations include mild fever, fatigue, sinking pain in the lower abdomen, lower back pain, and profuse vaginal discharge. Traditional Chinese medicine classifies chronic pelvic inflammation as abdominal pain or leukorrhagia.

1. Body Acupuncture

Prescription: Sanyinjiao (SP 6), Zhongji (RN 3), Guilai (ST 29), Zusanli (ST 36), Guanyuan (RN 4).

Method: Apply filiform needles with reducing method. Retain the needles for 30 minutes manipulating them 3~4 times.

2. Ear Acupuncture

Prescription: Pelvis, Internal Genitals, Abdomen, Sanjiao, Spleen, Liver, Endocrine, Adrenal Gland, Shenmen, Apex of Ear.

Method: Apply filiform needles with strong stimulation and retain the needles for 30 minutes. Auricular taping is also applicable.

3. Point Injection

Prescription: Zhongji (RN 3), Guilai (ST 29), Guanyuan (RN 4), Sanyinjiao (SP 6).

Method: Inject 1 mL of Radix Angelicae Sinensis injection into each point once a day.

4. Laser Therapy

Prescription: Zhongji (RN 3), Qihai (RN 6), Guanyuan (RN 4), Shenshu (BL 23).

Method: Radiate each point with He-Ne laser beams for 5 minutes once a day.

子宫脱垂

子宫脱垂系指子宫从正常位置下降，使子宫颈达到坐骨棘突水平以下，甚至子宫全部脱出阴道口外。常伴有阴道前后壁膨出。病变初期，脱出的子宫在卧床后可自行还纳。随着病情的发展，脱垂的子宫不能还纳而暴露在阴道口外，并常伴有大便困难、尿潴留或尿失禁、尿路感染等。

1. 体针

处方 百会，气海，足三里，关元，肾俞，三阴交，归来。

操作 毫针刺，用补法。留针30分钟，间歇行针2~3次。

2. 耳针

处方 内生殖器，盆腔，腹，肾，脾，肝。

配穴 大便困难者加肺，大肠；尿潴留或失禁者加膀胱；尿路感染者加内分泌，肾上腺。

操作 毫针轻刺激，留针30分

钟，间歇行针 2～3 次；亦可用耳穴贴敷。

3. 艾灸

处方　百会，气海，肾俞，脾俞。

操作　每穴用温和灸治疗 10 分钟，每天 1 次。

Prolapse of the Uterus

Prolapse of the uterus refers to descent of the uterus from the normal position with the cervix dropping to below the level of the ischial spine. In extreme cases the entire uterus may extrude out of the vaginal opening. Prolapse of the uterus is usually accompanied by prolapse of both the anterior and posterior vaginal walls in the initial stage the prolapsed uterus may spontaneously return to normal when a horizontal position is assumed. But with development of the condition, the prolapsed uterus remains exposed outside of the vaginal opening with accompaning difficulty in defecation, urinary retention, incontinence, or urinary tract infection.

1. Body Acupuncture

Prescription: Baihui (DU 20), Qihai (RN 6), Zusanli (ST 36), Guanyuan (RN 4), Shenshu (BL 23), Sanyinjiao (SP 6), Guilai (ST 29).

Method: Apply filiform needles with reinforcing method. Retain the needles for 30 minutes manipulating them 2～3 times.

2. Ear Acupuncture

Prescription: Internal Genitals, Pelvis, Abdomen, Kidney, Spleen, Liver.

Supplementary points: Add Lung and Large Intestine for difficulty in defecation, Urinary Bladder for urinary retention or incontinence, Endocrine and Adrenal Gland for urinary tract infection.

Method: Apply filiform needles with mild stimulation. Retain the needles for 30 minutes manipulating them 2～3 times. Auricular taping is also applicable.

3. Moxibustion

Prescription: Baihui (DU 20), Qihai (RN 6), Shenshu (BL 23), Pishu (BL 20).

Method: Apply mild-warming moxibustion to each point for 10 minutes once a day.

不　孕　症

女子结婚后，夫妇同居 2 年以上，配偶生殖功能正常，未避孕而不受孕者，称原发性不孕。如曾生育或流产后，未避孕而又 2 年以上不再受孕者，称继发性不孕。

1. 体针

处方 次髎，涌泉，商丘，三阴交，曲骨。

操作 毫针刺，虚证用补法，实证用泻法。留针20～30分钟，间歇行针2～4次。

2. 耳针

处方 内分泌，肾，皮质下，内生殖器。

操作 毫针轻刺激，留针30分钟。

3. 艾灸

处方 内关，三阴交。

操作 每穴采用温和灸治疗15～20分钟，每天1次。

4. 电针

处方 气海，关元，水道，三阴交。

操作 每穴用疏密波治疗20分钟，隔天1次。

Sterility

Primary sterility means that married women who live together with their spouse with normal genital functions for over two years fail to be pregnant without contraception. Secondary sterility refers to the fact that women fail to be pregnant over two years after previous delivery or miscarriage without contraception.

1. Body Acupuncture

Prescription: Ciliao (BL 32), Yongquan (KI 1), Shangqiu (SP 5), Sanyinjiao (SP 6), Qugu (RN 2).

Method: Apply filiform needles with reinforcing method for vacuity pattern or reducing method for repletion pattern. Retain the needles for 20～30 minutes manipulating them 2～4 times.

2. Ear Acupuncture

Prescription: Endocrine, Kidney, Subcortex, Internal Genitals.

Method: Apply filiform needles with mild stimulation and retain the needles for 30 minutes.

3. Moxibustion

Prescription: Neiguan (PC 6), Sanyinjiao (SP 6).

Method: Apply mild-warming moxibustion to each point for 15～20 minutes once every other day.

4. Electroacupuncture

Prescription: Qihai (RN 6), Guanyuan (RN 4), Shuidao (ST 28), Sanyinjiao (SP 6).

Method: Apply sparse-dense wave to each point for 20 minutes once every other day.

妊娠恶阻

妊娠恶阻又称妊娠呕吐。临床以恶心，呕吐，头晕，厌食或食入即吐为主要特征，是最常见的早期妊娠反应。多在怀孕 3 个月以后逐渐消失。

1．体针

处方　内关，足三里，中脘，胃俞。

操作　毫针刺，虚证用补法，实证用泻法。留针 20～30 分钟，间歇行针 2～4 次。

2．耳针

处方　胃，脾，肝，神门。

操作　毫针轻刺，留针 30 分钟；亦可用耳穴贴敷。

3．艾灸

处方　中脘，足三里，巨阙。

操作　每穴用温和灸治疗 10～15 分钟，每天 1 次。

Morning Sickness

Morning sickness, also know as pregnant vomiting, is symptomized by nausea, vomiting, dizziness, anorexia or vomiting right after food intake. It is virtually the early reaction of pregnancy which gradually subsides during the first three months of pregnancy.

1. Body Acupuncture

Prescription：Neiguan (PC 6)，Zusanli (ST 36)，Zhongwan (RN 12)，Weishu (BL 21).

Method：Apply filiform needles with reinforcing method for vacuity pattern or reducing method for repletion pattern. Retain the needles for 20～30 minutes manipulating them 2～4 times.

2. Ear Acupuncture

Prescription：Stomach, Spleen, Liver, Shenmen.

Method：Apply filiform needles with mild stimulation and retain the needles for 30 minutes. Auricular taping is also applicable.

3. Moxibustion

Prescription：Zhongwan (RN 12)，Zusanli (ST 36)，Juque (RN 14).

Method：Apply mild-warming moxibustion to each point for 10～15 minutes once a day.

胎位不正

胎位不正是指妊娠 28 周后，胎儿在子宫内的位置异常。常见于经产妇或腹壁松弛的孕妇，本身多无自觉症状。临床后容易出现并发症。因骨腔狭窄，子宫畸形等原因引起的胎位不正，不属本病的治疗范畴。

1．艾灸

处方　至阴。

操作　嘱孕妇解松腰带，排空小便仰卧床上，用艾条两根点燃后，同时分别在至阴穴距 2～3 厘米处悬灸，以局部充血为度，每天 1 次，每次 15～20 分钟。

2．耳针

处方　子宫，下脚端，交感，

脑，肝，脾，腹。

操作　毫针轻刺，留针 30 分钟；亦可用耳穴贴敷。

Malposition of Fetus

Malposition of fetus refers to the abnormal fetal position in the uterus after 28 weeks of gestation. It is an asymptomatic condition commonly seen in multipara women or those with lax abdominal wall. Complications will appear when the parturient is not adjusted. Malposition of fetus related to structure of constricted pelvis or uterine deformity is beyond the therapeutic scope of acupuncture discussed here.

1. Moxibustion

Prescription: Zhiyin (BL 67).

Method: Let the patient loosen her clothing and evacute the urine from her bladder. She should lie supine in bed. Then, hold two moxa sticks respectively 2～3 cm bilaterally to Zhiyin (BL 67). Ignite them for moxibustion for 15～20 minutes causing local congestion. The treatment is given once a day.

2. Ear Acupuncture

Prescription: Uterus, Triangular Fossa, Sympathetic, Brain, Liver, Spleen, Abdomen.

Method: Apply filiform needles with mild stimulation and retain the needles for 30 minutes. Auricular taping is also applicable.

滞　产

产妇临产总产程超过 24 小时者，称为滞产。多因产力异常，或胎位异常等因素造成，如因子宫畸形，头盆不称引起的滞产，不属针灸治疗范围。

1. 体针

处方　合谷，三阴交，秩边。

操作　毫针刺，气血虚弱者用补法，气滞血瘀者用泻法，留针 20～30 分钟，间歇行针 2～4 次。

2. 耳针

处方　子宫，内分泌，肾，皮质下。

操作　毫针中等强度刺激，留针 30 分钟。

Protracted Labour

Protracted labour refers to a delivery with parturition of more than 24 hours. It is often due to abnormal contraction of the womb or malposition of the fetus. However, protracted labour caused by other factors such as uterine deformity and cephalopelvic disproportion is not suggested for treatment by means of acupuncture.

1. Body Acupuncture

Prescription: Hegu (LI 4), Sanyinjiao (SP 6), Zhibian (BL 54), Zhiyin (BL 27).

Method: Apply filiform needles with reinforcing method for patients with dificiency of Qi and blood or reducing method for patients with stagnation of Qi and stasis of blood. Retain the needles for 20～30 minutes manipulating them 2～4 times.

2. Ear Acupuncture

Prescription: Uterus, Endocrine, Kidney, Subcortex.

Method: Apply filiform needles with medium strength stimulation and retain the needles for 30 minutes.

胎盘滞留

胎盘滞留是指胎儿娩出之后，胎盘在 30 分钟之内尚未娩出者。

1. 体针

处方　关元，独阴，三阴交，合谷。

操作　毫针刺，气虚者用补法，血瘀者用泻法。留针 30 分钟，间歇行针 3～5 次。

2. 艾灸

处方　三阴交，关元，独阴。

操作　每穴温和灸治疗 10～15 分钟。

3. 电针

处方　合谷，三阴交。

操作　采用疏密波治疗 30 分钟。

Retention of Placenta

Retention of placenta refers to the delayed relief of placenta 30 minutes after the delivery.

1. Body Acupuncture

Prescription: Guanyuan (RN 4), Duyin (EX-LE 11), Sanyinjiao (SP 6), Hegu (LI 4).

Method: Apply filiform needles with reinforcing method for patients with Qi deficiency or reducing method for patients with blood stasis. Retain the needles for 30 minutes manipulating them 3～5 times.

2. Moxibustion

Prescription: Sanyinjiao (SP 6), Guanyuan (RN 4), Duyin (EX-LE 11).

Method: Apply mild-warming moxibustion to each point for 10～15 minutes.

3. Electroacupuncture

Prescription: Hegu (LI 4), Sanyinjiao (SP 6).

Method: Apply sparse-dense wave for 30 minutes.

恶露不绝

产后胞宫内的余血浊液经阴道排出，谓之恶露。3 周左右干净，若产后超过 3 周恶露仍淋漓不断者，称为恶露不绝或恶露不止。

1. 体针

处方　三阴交，关元，足三里。

操作 毫针平补平泻，留针20～30分钟，间歇行针3～4次。

2. 耳针

处方 子宫，神门，内分泌，脾，交感，皮质下，肝。

操作 毫针中等强度刺激，留针30分钟；亦可采用耳穴贴敷。

Lochia

Lochia refers to vaginal discharge of cellular debris, mucus and blood following childbirth. The complete discharge needs three weeks time. Persistent vaginal discharge over three weeks after delivery is called lochiorrhea.

1. Body Acupuncture

Prescription: Sanyinjiao (SP 6), Guanyuan (RN 4), Zusanli (ST 36).

Method: Apply filiform needles with even movement. Retain the needles for 20～30 minutes manipulating them 3～4 times.

2. Ear Acupuncture

Prescription: Uterus, Shenmen, Endocrine, Spleen, Sympathetic, Subcortex, Liver.

Method: Apply filiform needles with moderate stimulation and retain the needles for 30 minutes. Auricular taping is also applicable.

子 痫

妊娠后期或正值临产时，或新产后发生突然眩晕仆倒，昏不知人，四肢抽搐，全身强直，牙关紧闭，双目上视，少时自醒，醒后复发，状如癫痫发作，故称"子痫"，或称"妊娠痫证"。

1. 体针

处方 水沟，内关，风池，太冲，三阴交，照海，涌泉。

操作 毫针刺，水沟，内关，风池，太冲用泻法，三阴交，照海，涌泉用补法，留针15～20分钟。

2. 耳针

处方 神门，肝，肾，脑点，皮质下。

操作 毫针中等强度刺激，留针15～20分钟。

Eclampsia Gravidarm

Eclampsia gravidarm may occur in the third trimester of pregnancy, eutopic parturient or even after childbirth. It is a condition characterized by sudden fainting, loss of consciousness, convulsions, general lassitude, trismus, general rigidity and upward staring of the eyes. This condition ends up with self-recovery in a few minutes which is then followed by another similar attack resembling epileptic attacks.

1. Body Acupuncture

Prescription: Shuigou (DU 26), Neiguan (PC 6), Fengchi (GB 20), Taichong (LR 3), Sanyinjiao (SP

6）, Zhaohai（KI 6）, Yongquan（KI 1）.

Method：Apply filiform needles with reducing method for Shuigou（DU 26）, Neiguan（PC 6）, Fengchi（GB 20）and Taichong（LR 3）, but reinforcing method for Sanyinjiao（SP 6）, Zhaohai（KI 6）and Yongquan（KI 1）. Retain the needles for 15～20 minutes.

2.Ear Acupuncture

Prescription：Shenmen, Liver, Kidney, Brain stem, Subcortex.

Method：Apply filiform needles with moderate stimulation and retain the needles for 15～20 minutes.

产后腹痛

产后以小腹疼痛为主证者，称为"产后腹痛"，亦称"儿枕痛"。以经产妇较为多见，常在产后 1～2 天出现。

1. 体针

处方　中极，三阴交，足三里，关元。

操作　毫针刺，平补平泻。留针 20～30 分钟，间歇行针 3～4 次。

2. 耳针

处方　子宫，肾，神门，内分泌。

操作　毫针中等强度刺激，留针 30 分钟。

3. 艾灸

处方　关元，三阴交，归来，气海。

操作　每穴用温和灸治疗 10～20 分钟，每天 1 次。

4. 水针

处方　三阴交。

操作　穴位注射 0.25％普鲁卡因注射液 2～3 毫升。

Puerperal Pain

Puerpera pain refers to the pain in the lower abdomen in puerperium. It is mostly complained by multipara women within 1～2 days after the delivery. This condition is also called baby pillow pain in traditional Chinese medicine.

1.Body Acupuncture

Prescription：Zhongji（RN 3）, Sanyinjiao（SP 6）, Zusanli（SP 36）, Guanyuan（RN 4）.

Method:Apply filiform needles with even movement. Retain the needles for 20～30 minutes manipulating them 3～4 times.

2.Ear Acupuncture

Prescription：Uterus, Kidney, Shenmen, Endocrine.

Method：Apply filiform needles with moderate stimulation and retain the needles for 30 minutes.

3.Moxibustion

Prescription：Guanyuan（RN 4）,

Sanyinjiao（SP 6），Guilai（ST 29），Qihai（RN 6）.

Method：Apply mild-warming moxibustion to each point for $10\sim20$ minutes once a day.

4. Point Injection

Prescription：Sanyinjiao（SP 6）.

Method：Inject $2\sim3$ mL of 0.25% procaine hydrochloride into the point.

乳　少

产后乳汁甚少或全无，称为"乳少"，亦称"缺乳"或"乳汁不行"。

1. 体针

处方　膻中，少泽，乳根，三阴交，足三里。

操作　毫针刺，平补平泻，留针 $15\sim20$ 分钟，间歇行针 $2\sim3$ 次。

2. 耳针

处方　胸，内分泌，交感，脾，胃。

操作　毫针中等强度刺激，留针 $10\sim15$ 分钟；亦可用耳穴贴敷。

3. 皮肤针

处方　脾俞，胃俞，乳根，三阴交。

操作　每穴皮肤针叩刺 $5\sim10$ 分钟，每天 1 次。

Lactation Deficiency

Lactation deficiency refers to low production of milk after childbirth.

The nomenclature for lactation deficiency in traditional Chinese medicine is lack of milk of halted milkflow.

1. Body Acupuncture

Prescription：Tanzhong（RN 17），Shaoze（SI 1），Rugen（ST 18），Sanyinjiao（SP 6），Zusanli（ST 36）.

Method：Apply filiform needles with even movement method. Retain the needles for $15\sim20$ minutes manipulating them $2\sim3$ times.

2. Ear Acupuncture

Prescription：Chest, Endocrine, Sympathetic, Spleen, Stomach.

Method：Apply filiform needles with moderate stimulation and retain the needles for $10\sim15$ minutes. Auricular taping is also applicable.

3. Plum-blossom Needle

Prescription：Pishu（BL 20），Weishu（BL 21），Rugen（ST 18），Sanyinjiao（SP 6）.

Method：Tap each point with a plum-blossom needle for $5\sim10$ minutes once a day.

第四节　儿科疾病

Section 4 Pediatric Diseases

厌 食 症

少儿厌食症是指小儿较长时间的食欲减退或消失，多与全身性疾病、消化系统疾病、精神因素及不良饮食习惯等因素有关。中医称之为"厌食"。

1. 体针

处方　脾俞，足三里，三阴交，气海，胃俞。

操作　毫针刺，用补法。留针30分钟，间歇行针2~3次。

2. 耳针

处方　胃，脾，小肠，肝，腹，内分泌，皮质下。

操作　毫针中等强度刺激，留针30分钟。

3. 三棱针

处方　四缝。

操作　三棱针点刺出血，2周1次。

4. 艾灸

处方　脾俞，胃俞，中脘。

操作　每穴温和灸治疗10~15分钟，每天1次。

5. 皮肤针

处方　背部脊正线旁开1.5寸和3寸共4条直线。

操作　皮肤针叩刺背部四线10~20分钟，每天1次。

Anorexia

Anorexia in children is characterized by loss of or regressive appetite associated with general or digestive diseases, psychic factors and bad feeding habits. This disease is call "yanshi" in traditional Chinese medicine.

1. Body Acupuncture

Prescription: Pishu (BL 20), Zusanli (ST 36), Sanyinjiao (SP 6), Qihai (RN 6), Weishu (BL 21).

Method: Apply filiform needles with reinforcing method. Retain the needles for 30 minutes manipulating them 2~3 times.

2. Ear Acupuncture

Prescription: Stomach, Spleen, Small Intestinal, Liver, Abdomen, Endocrine, Subcortex.

Method: Apply filiform needles with moderate stimulation and retain the needles for 30 minutes.

3. Three-edged Needle

Prescription: Sifeng (EX-UE 10).

Method: Prick the point with a three-edged needle to cause bleeding once every two weeks.

4. Moxibustion

Prescription: Pishu (BL 20), Weishu (BL 21), Zhongwan (RN 12).

Method: Apply mild-warming moxibustion to each point for 10 ~ 15 minutes once a day.

5. Plum-blossom Needle

Prescription: The four lines respectively 1.5 cun and 3 cun lateral to the posterior median line on the back.

Method: Tap the four lines with a plum-blossom needle for 10 ～ 20 minutes once a day.

婴儿腹泻

婴儿腹泻是指婴儿大便次数的增加。引起急性腹泻的原因可能与饮食因素、细菌感染或其毒素作用或病毒感染有关。婴儿迁延性腹泻病程可在1个月以上，常与肠道感染未获控制或滥用各种抗生素引起菌群失调有关。本病属中医"泄泻"范畴。

1. 体针

处方　四缝，足三里，气海，三阴交，中脘。

操作　毫针平补平泻，不留针。

2. 耳针

处方　胃，脾，三焦，大肠，小肠。

操作　毫针中等强度刺激，亦可用耳穴贴敷。

3. 艾灸

处方　天枢，中脘，神厥。

操作　每穴温和灸治疗5～7壮，每天1次。

4. 激光疗法

处方　天枢，中脘，气海。

操作　每穴用氦-氖激光照射3分钟，每天1次。

5. 水针

处方　足三里。

操作　穴位注射维生素 B_1 50～100 毫克，隔天1次。

Infantile Diarrhea

This diarrhea refers to increased frequency and volume of defecation. Acute diarrhea may be associated with improper intake, bacterial infection, or viral infection. The course of diarrhea of persisting type is usually over 4 weeks and it is often caused by uncontrolled intestinal infections or induced by flora imbalance resulting from abused antibiotics. In traditional Chinese medicine, this disease is categorized as "Xiexie" (diarrhea).

1. Body Acupuncture

Prescription: Sifeng (EX-UE 10), Zusanli (ST 36), Qihai (RN 6), Sanyinjiao (SP 6), Zhongwan (RN 12).

Method: Apply filiform needles with even movement but without needling retention.

2. Ear Acupuncture

Prescription: Stomache, Spleen, Sanjiao, Large Intestine, Small Intestine.

Method: Apply filiform needles with moderate stimulation. Auricular taping is also applicable.

3. Moxibustion

Prescription: Tianshu (ST 25), Zhongwan (RN 12), Shengue (RN 8).

Method: Apply mild-warming moxibustion to each point using 5~7 cones once a day.

4. Laser Therapy

Prescription: Tianshu (ST 25), Zhongwan (RN 12), Qihai (RN 6).

Method: Radiate the points with He-Ne laser beams for 3 minutes once a day.

5. Point Injection

Prescription: Zusanli (ST 36).

Method: Inject 50~100mg of vitamin B$_1$ into the point once every other day.

小儿疳疾

疳疾是由喂养不当，或因多种疾病的影响，使脾胃受损，气液耗伤，临床以全身虚弱羸瘦为其主要特征。其发病年龄以5岁以下的小儿较多见。小儿疳疾包括现代医学的营养不良和维生素缺乏症等。

1. 体针

处方　中脘，脾俞，胃俞，足三里，四缝，天枢。

操作　毫针刺，用补法，不留针。

2. 皮肤针

处方　脾俞，胃俞，足三里，三阴交，四缝，华佗夹脊穴。

操作　三棱针中等强度刺激，叩打至皮肤充血红润为度。

3. 三棱针

处方　四缝。

操作　三棱针点刺出血。

Infantile Malnutrition

Infantile malnutrition is related to either improper nursing or the affect of various illnesses which have weaken the function of the spleen and stomach and over consumed Qi and blood. It is mainly characterized by general deficiency and emaciation bothering children mostly under the age of five. It includes dystopia and vitamin deficiency in modern medicine.

1. Body Acupuncture

Prescription: Zhongwan (RN 12), Pishu (BL 20), Weishu (BL 21), Zusanli (ST 36), Sifeng (EX-UE 10), Tianshu (ST 25).

Method: Apply filiform needles with reinforcing method without needling retention.

2. Plum-blossom Needle

Prescription: Pishu (BL 20), Weishu (BL 21), Zusanli (ST 36), Sanyinjiao (BL 22), Sifeng (EX-UE

10), Huatuojiaji (V 7~V 17).

Method: Apply plum-blossom needle tapping with moderate stimulation until local redness with moisture appears.

3. Three-edged Needle

Prescription: Sifeng (EX-UE 10).

Method: Apply a three-edged needle to prick the point to cause bleeding.

小儿瘘证

小儿瘘证又称小儿麻痹证、婴儿瘫。是由于感受时邪疫毒而引起的一种急性传染病。其主要临床表现为早期症状类似感冒,有发热,头痛,咽红,咳嗽,或伴有恶心呕吐,腹泻及全身肌肉疼痛。继而出现肌肉弛缓,肢体瘘软瘫痪,肌肉萎缩,运动障碍等。瘫痪肢体以单侧下肢为多见,发病年龄尤以 5 岁以下的婴幼儿为最多,多流行于夏秋两季,相当于现代医学脊髓灰质炎后遗症。

1. 体针

处方

上肢取穴 肩髃,曲池,手三里,合谷。

下肢取穴 ·环跳,髀关,伏兔,足三里,阳陵泉,三阴交。

配穴 腕下垂加外关,中泉;足下垂加解溪;足内翻加悬钟;足外翻加照海。

操作 毫针刺,用补法,留针15~20 分钟,每天 1 次。

2. 艾灸

处方 脾俞,胃俞,三阴交,足三里,手三里。

操作 每穴用温和灸治疗 10~15 分钟,每天 1 次。

Infantile Wei Syndrome

Infantile Wei syndrome, also known as infantile paralysis, is a kind of acute infectious disease caused by the invasion of seasonal epidemics. Its incipient manifestations are similar to those of common cold such as fever, headache, and congestion in the throat. These may be accompanied by cough, nausea, vomiting, diarrhea and general muscle pain. The incipient symptoms and signs are then followed by muscular flaccidity, acroparalysis, myophagism and dyscinesia. It mostly affects unilateral lower limbs in children predominantly under the age of five. The incidence of infantile paralysis is high in summer and autumn similar to the sequelae of policmyelitis in modern medicine.

1. Body Acupuncture

Prescription

(1) Upper Limb Paralysis: Jianyu (LI 15), Quchi (LI 11), Shousanli (LI 10), Hegu (LI 4).

(2) Lower Limb Paralysis: Huantiao (GB 30), Biguan (ST 31), Futu

（ST 32），Zusanli（ST 36），Yanglingquan（GB 34），Sanyinjiao（SP 6）.

Supplementary points: Add Waiguan（SJ 5），Zhong quan（Extra）for wrist-drop, Jiexi（ST 41）for foot drop, Xuan zhong（GB 39）for adduction, and Zhaohai（KI 6）for abduction.

Method: Apply filiform needles with reinforcing method. Retain the needles for 15~20 minutes, once a day.

2. Moxibustion

Prescription: Pishu（BL 20），Weishu（BL 21），Sanyinjiao（SP 6），Zusanli（ST 36），Shousanli（LI 10）.

Method: Apply mild-warming moxibustion to each point for 10 ~ 15 minutes once a day.

儿童多动综合征

儿童多动综合征，或称为脑功能轻微障碍综合征，是儿童期常见的一种神经精神系统病症。表现特点为活动过多，注意力不集中，情绪不稳，认知障碍等，但患儿智能接近或完全正常。可有中枢神经系统微细的功能异常。多数患儿在青春期后症状明显减轻或消失。常见病因为遗传因素，分娩异常（如难产、窒息）及出生后疾病等。

1. 体针

处方　百会，太冲，足三里，神门，三阴交。

操作　毫针刺，平补平泻。留针30分钟，间歇行针2~3次。

2. 耳针

处方　肾，肝，心，脾，胃，皮质下，额，神门，枕。

操作　毫针轻刺激，留针30分钟；亦可用耳穴贴敷。

Childhood Hyperkinetic Syndrome

Childhood hyperkinetic syndrome, also called minimal brain dysfunction, is a common developmental problem of childhood. It is characterized by hyperactivity, distractability, excessive mood swings, and cognitive difficulty. However, intelligence is close to or completely normal and sometimes superior. Minimal dysfunction of the central nervous system may be present. In most cases, all symptoms diminish or disappear spontaneously with maturation. Common causes include heredity, abnormal or difficult labor resulting in oxygen deprivation, or disease in infancy.

1. Body Acupuncture

Prescription: Baihui（DU 20），Taichong（LR 3），Zusanli（ST 36），Shenmen（HT 7），Sanyinjiao（SP 6）.

Method: Apply filiform needles with even movement. Retain the needles for

30 minutes manipulating them $2 \sim 3$ times.

2. Ear Acupuncture

Prescription： Kidney, Liver, Heart, Spleen, Stomach, Subcortex, Forehead, Shenmen, Occiput.

Method: Apply filiform needles with mild stimulation and retain the needles for 30 minutes. Auricular taping is also applicable.

智力迟钝

智力迟钝是儿科常见的神经精神系统病症。在儿童生长发育期内，患儿智力明显落后于同龄者的平均水平，且智能发育始终不能成熟，是导致人类伤残的一个主要因素。发病原因可能为严伤、遗传等，但有40%～75%的病例发病原因不明。

1. 体针

处方　百会，心俞，三阴交，四神聪，风池，内关，大椎，足三里。

操作　毫针刺，用补法。留针20～30分钟，间歇行针2～3次。

2. 耳针

处方　肾，肝，脾，皮质下，肾上腺，内分泌，额，颞，枕。

操作　毫针轻刺激，留针30分钟；亦可用耳穴贴敷。

Mental Retardation

Mental retardation is a developmental disability that becomes apparent during childhood. Intelligence lags behind children of the same age gourp and never completely matures. Causes of mental retardation include birth trauma and heredity, but $40\% \sim 75\%$ of cases have no clear and definite cause.

1. Body Acupuncture

Prescription： Baihui （DU 20）, Xinshu （BL 15）, Sanyinjiao （SP 6）, Sishencong （EX-HN 1）, Fengchi （GB 20）, Neiguan （PC 6）, Dazhui （DU 14）, Zusanli （ST 36）.

Method： Apply filiform needles with reinforcing method. Retain the needles for $20 \sim 30$ minutes manipulating them $2\sim3$ times.

2. Ear Acupuncture

Prescription： Kidney, Liver, Spleen, Subcortex, Adrenal Gland, Endocrine, Forehead, Temple, Occiput.

Method： Apply filiform needles with mild stimulation and retain the needles for 30 minutes. Auricular taping is also applicable.

小儿遗尿

遗尿又称遗溺、尿床，是指3周岁以上的小儿在睡眠中小便不能自行控制而自遗，醒后方觉的一种病症。若因疲劳过度，或精神紧张，或因睡前多饮而偶然发生遗尿者，则不属病态。

1．体针

处方　中极，关元，三阴交，肾俞，膀胱俞，三阴交，足三里，百会。

操作　毫针强刺激，留针 20～30 分钟，间歇行针 2～3 次。

2．耳针

处方　肾，膀胱，脾，脑点，肺，皮质下。

操作　每次 2～3 穴毫针轻刺激，留针 20 分钟；亦可用耳穴贴敷。

3．艾灸

处方　肾俞，膀胱俞，百会，足三里，三阴交。

操作　每穴温和灸治疗 10～15 分钟，每天 1 次。

4．头针

处方　两侧足运感区。

操作　间歇捻针，留针 15 分钟，每天 1 次。

Enuresis

Enuresis, also know as bed-wetting, refers to the involuntary discharge of urine during sleep in children over three years old. Such children are not aware of the bed-wetting unless they are waken up. It is usually related to fatigue or mental stress. However, bed-wetting due to excessive drinking of water on occasions is not considered as a disease condition.

1．Body Acupuncture

Prescription： Zhongji （RN 3）, Guanyuan （RN 4）, Sanyinjiao （SP 6）, Shenshu （BL 23）, Pangguangshu （BL 28）, Zusanli （ST 36）, Baihui （DU 20）.

Method： Apply filiform needles with reinforcing method. Retain the needles for 20～30 minutes manipulating them 2～3 times.

2．Ear Acupuncture

Prescription： Kidney, Urinary bladder, Spleen, Brain, Stem, Lung, Subcortex.

Method： Apply filiform needles at 2～3 points each time with moderate stimulation. Retain the needles for 20 minutes. Auricular taping is also applicable.

3．Moxibustion

Prescription： Shenshu （BL 23）, Pangguangshu （BL 28）, Baihui （DU 20）, Zusanli （ST 36）, Sanyinjiao （SP 6）.

Method： Apply mild-warming moxibustion to each point for 10 ～ 15 minutes once a day.

4．Scalp Acupuncture

Prescription： Bilateral sensorimotor area of the foot.

Method： Apply filiform needles with

intermittent stimulation for 15 minutes once a day.

夜   啼

夜啼系指患儿夜晚啼哭过于频繁，多见于智力发育障碍的 3 岁以内婴儿。

1. 体针

处方 印堂，百会，足三里，三阴交，神门。

操作 毫针刺，平补平泻，不留针。

2. 耳针

处方 神门，肝，脾，三焦。

操作 毫针中等强度刺激，不留针；亦可用耳穴贴敷。

3. 艾灸

处方 百会，印堂，足三里，大椎，内关。

操作 每穴温和灸治疗 10 分钟，每天 1 次。

4. 推拿

处方 百会，安眠，内关，足三里。

操作 每穴每晚揉 20 次。

Night Crying

Night crying is a disorder in infants who cry frequently during the night. It often occurs in children under the age of three usually due to mental underdevelopment.

1. Body Acupuncture

Prescription: Yintang (EX-HN 3), Baihui (DU 20), Zusanli (ST 36), Sanyinjiao (SP 6), Shenmen (HT 7).

Method: Apply filiform needles with even movement without needle retention.

2. Ear Acupuncture

Prescription: Shenmen, Liver, Spleen, San Jiao.

Method: Apply filiform needles with moderate stimulation without needle retention. Auricular taping is also applicable.

3. Moxibustion

Prescription: Baihui (DU 20), Yintang (EX-HN 3), Zusanli (ST 36), Dazhui (DU 14), Neiguan (PC 6).

Method: Apply mild-warming moxibustion to each point for 10 minutes once a day.

4. Massage

Prescription: Baihui (DU 20), Anmian (Ex-HN 17), Neiguan (PC 6), Zusanli (ST 36).

Method: Knead each point 20 times every night.

猩 红 热

猩红热中医称为"丹痧"。临床

以发热，咽喉肿痛，全身伴有弥漫性
猩红色皮疹，疹后脱皮为主要特征。
多见于冬春季节，以 2～8 岁的儿童
发病率最高。

1. 体针

　　处方　风池，曲池，合谷，列
缺，大椎，关冲。

　　操作　毫针刺，用泻法，不留
针。

2. 耳针

　　处方　神门，肺，胃，耳尖，
脾。

　　操作　毫针强刺激，不留针；亦
可用耳穴贴敷。

3. 三棱针

　　处方　大椎，关冲。
　　操作　三棱针点刺出血。

Scarlet Fever

Scarlet fever is called the red rash in traditional Chinese medicine. It is characterized by fever, swelling, sore throat, diffusing scarlet erythema of the general body and subsequent casting off of scaled skin. It usually occurs in winter and spring with a high incidence in children aged from two to eight years old.

1. Body Acupuncture

Prescription: Fengchi (GB 20), Quchi (LI 11), Hegu (LI 4), Lieque (LU 7), Dazhui (DU 14), Guanchong (SJ 1).

Method: Apply filiform needles with reducing method without needle retention.

2. Ear Acupuncture

Prescription: Shenmen, Lung, Stomach, Apex of Ear, Spleen.

Method: Apply filiform with strong stimulation but without needling retention. Auricular taping is also applicable.

3. Three edged Needle

Prescription: Dazhui (DU 14), Guanchong (SJ 1).

Method: Prick the points with a three-edged needle to cause bleeding.

小儿惊风

　　惊风又称惊厥，俗称抽风，是小
儿时期常见的一种病症。系多种原因
及多种疾病引起，临床以四肢抽搐，
颈项强直，甚则角弓反张或意识不清
等为特征。多发生于 5 岁以下的小
儿，年龄越小，发病率越高。

1. 体针

　　处方　百会，风府，大椎，合
谷，太冲，涌泉，十二井穴，内关，
人中。

　　操作　毫针刺，用泻法，不留
针。大椎，十二井穴三棱针点刺出
血。

2. 耳针

处方 神门，交感，脑点，心，皮质下。

操作 毫针强刺激，不留针。

3. 水针

处方 肝俞，大杼。

操作 每穴注射维生素 B_1 0.5毫升。

Infantile Convulsion

Infantile convulsion, also known as epileptic convulsion, is a disease often seen in infants. This disease may be caused by various factors or illnesses. Its main manifestations include convulsive limbs, neck rigidity, opisthotonos, or mental confusion in severe cases. It ails children mostly under the age of five. The younger the child is the higher incidence tends to be.

1. Body Acupuncture

Prescription: Baihui (DU 20), Fengfu (DU 16), Dazhui (DU 14), Hegu (LI 4), Taichong (LR 3), Yongquan (KI 1), Twelve Jing-well points, Neiguan (PC 6), Renzhong (DU 26).

Method: Apply filiform needles with reducing method but without needle retention. Dazhui (DU 14) and the twelve Jing-well points are pricked with a three-edged needle to cause bleeding.

2. Ear Acupuncture

Prescription: Shenmen, Sympathetic, Brain Stem, Heart, Subcortex.

Method: Apply filiform needles with strong stimulation but without needle retention.

3. Point Injection

Prescription: Ganshu (BL 18), Dashu (BL 11).

Method: Inject 0.5 mL of vitamin B_1 into each point.

第五节 五官科疾病

Section 5 Diseases of Eyes, Ears, Nose and Throat

麦 粒 肿

根据麦粒肿发生的部位分为两类。外麦粒肿为睫毛腺的急性化脓性炎症，表现特点为眼睑红肿，疼痛，有硬结，数天后在眼睑表面有脓疱形成。重者常有球结膜充血、水肿。内麦粒肿为睑板腺的急性化脓性炎症，其症状较外麦粒肿重。

1. 体针

处方 曲池，攒竹，合谷，承泣。

操作 毫针刺，用泻法。留针20分钟，间歇行针 3~4 次。

2. 耳针

处方 眼，目$_2$，脾，肝，耳尖。

操作　毫针强刺激，留针 20 分钟，亦可用耳穴贴敷。

3．艾灸

处方　后溪。

操作　每穴直接灸治疗 15～20 分钟，每天 1～2 次。

4．三棱针

处方　大椎。

操作　三棱针点刺出血。

| Stye |

Stye is classified into two types according to its location. External stye refers to acute suppurative inflammation of the ciliary glands. It is marked by red and swollen eyelids with pain, scleroma, and pustulation appearing several days after onset. In severe cases, congestion and edema of the bulbar conjunctiva may occur. Internal stye refers to acute suppurative inflammation of the tarsal glands with manifestations similar to but more severe than those of external stye.

1．Body Acupuncture

Prescription：Quchi（LI 11）, Cuanzhu（BL 2）, Hegu（LI 4）, Chengqi（ST 1）.

Method：Apply filiform needles with reducing method. Retain the needles for 20 minutes manipulating them 3～4 times.

2．Ear Acupuncture

Prescription：Eye, Eye 2, Spleen, Liver, Apex of Ear.

Method：Apply filiform needles with strong stimulation and retain the needles for 20 minutes, Auricular taping is also applicable

3．Moxibustion

Prescription：Houxi（SI 3）.

Method：Apply direct moxibustion to the point for 15～20 minutes once or twice a day.

4．Three-edged Needle

Prescription：Dazhui（DU 14）.

Method：Prick the point with a three edged needle to cause bleeding.

| 近　　视 |

近视是由眼屈光系统失调引起的一种病症。当平行光线经过眼屈光系统后，焦点位于视网膜之前。临床表现特点为远视力减退，近视力正常。高度近视者，近点移近眼前。常见因素为用眼不当或过度，高度近视者常与遗传有关。

1．体针

处方　睛明，肝俞，肾俞，承泣，攒竹，风池，丝竹空，翳明，合谷，光明，臂臑。

操作　眼区穴宜轻捻缓进，不捣动及大弧度捻转，出针时随即用消毒干棉球按压片刻，以防出血。承泣穴垂直进针后，针尖呈 30°，可向睛明斜刺 1 寸左右，每天 1 次。10 次 1 疗程。

2. 耳针

处方 眼，目 2，肝，肾，脾，枕，皮质下，耳尖。

操作 毫刺强刺激，留针 30 分钟；亦可用耳穴贴敷。

3. 皮肤针

处方 眼区穴位，风池。

· 操作 三棱针叩刺 10~20 分钟，每天 1 次。

4. 腕踝针

外方 十 1，双眼近视选双侧，单眼近视选患侧。

操作 毫针刺，平补平泻，留针 1 小时，每天 1 次。

Myopia

Myopia is a visual disorder caused by dysfunction of the optic dioptric system. The visual focus is formed in front of the retina when parallel light passes through the optic dioptric system. Dysfunction of this system affects the ability to focus normally. Myopia is marked by poor distance vision and normal near-range vision. The more extreme the condition the shorter the range of normal vision. A common cause of myopia is improper or overuse of the eyes although severe myopia is usually related to heredity.

1. Body Acupuncture

Prescription: Jingming (BL 1), Ganshu (BL 18), Shenshu (BL 23), Chengqi (ST 1), Cuanzhu (BL 2), Fengchi (GB 20), Sizhukong (SJ 23), Yiming (EX-HN 14), Hegu (LI 4), Guangming (GB 31), Binao (LI 14).

Method: At the points around the eye, the needle is inserted slowly with gentle twirling movement. Shaking or twisting the needle at a large amplitude is forbidden. Additionally, after withdrawal of the needle, the needle hole is pressed with a sterilized dry cotton ball immediately in order to prevent bleeding. At Chengqi (ST 1), after the needle is inserted through the skin it is pushed obliquely toward Jingming (BL 1) at an angle of 30° to the skin for 1 cun. The treatment is given once daily for ten sessions as a course.

2. Ear Acupuncture

Prescription: Eye, Eye2, Liver, Kidney, Spleen, Occiput, Subcortex, Apex of Ear.

Method: Apply filiform needles with strong stimulation and retain the needles for 30 minutes. Auricular taping is also applicable.

3. Plum-blossom Needle

Prescription: The points around the

eye, Fengchi (GB 20).

Method: Tap the points with a plum-blossom needles for $10\sim20$ minutes once a day.

4. Wrist-Ankle Puncture

Prescription: Upper 1 on the diseased side, or bilateral Upper 1 if the two eyes are diseased.

Method: Apply filiform needles with even movement method. Retain the needles for 1 hour once a day.

流行性结膜角膜炎

流行性结膜角膜炎为病毒引起的角膜部的传染性病变。流行于夏秋季。表现特点为异物感，烧灼感，眼睑水肿，结膜充血及水样分泌物。若角膜受累，则可见疼痛畏光，流泪及视力障碍。

1. 体针

处方　睛明，太阳，合谷，风池，攒竹，丝竹空，少商，臂臑。

操作　毫针眼周穴位轻刺激，留针20分钟。

2. 耳针

处方　眼，目 2，肺，肝，耳尖。

操作　毫针强刺激，留针 30 分钟；亦可用耳穴贴敷。

3. 三棱针

处方　太阳穴。

操作　三棱针点刺出血，随后拔罐。

4. 灯火灸

处方　取患侧耳背上三角窝处，对光反照，可见一条明显的小血管向耳背部分叉处。

操作　在血管上部和分叉处各取1点，以圆珠笔作一记号，用75%乙醇消毒，取灯心草蘸上植物油，点燃后迅速灼在记号上，每点各灼一下。灯心草蘸油时，一般只蘸 0.5 厘米左右，过长会使灯心草变软，且火焰过旺易烧伤皮肤，蘸的太短，会使火力不足，未碰到穴位点即减。每点灸 1 次，可闻及清脆的"啪"音，若无，应重新点灼，但一般不宜超过 3 次。注意保持皮肤清洁，当天不宜洗擦。若有小水泡不慎擦破，可涂甲紫。一般当天获效，若无效，可重新点灼 1 次。

Epidemic Keratoconjunctivitis

Epidemic keratoconjunctivitis is a communicable viral infection of the corneoconjunctival region usually occuring in the summer and autumn. It is marked by burning pain or the sensation of a foreign body in the eye, palpebral edema, conjunctival congestion, and watery secretion. If the cornea is affected pain, photophobia, lacrimation, and hypopsia may occur.

1. Body Acupuncture

Prescription: Jingming (BL 1), Taiyang (EX-HN 5), Hegu (LI 4), Fengchi (GB 20), Cuanzhu (BL 2), Sizhukong (SJ 23), Shaoshang (LU 11), Binao (LI 14).

Method: Apply filiform needles with mild stimulation around the eyes and retain the needles for 20 minutes.

2. Ear Acupuncture

Prescription: Eye, Eye2, Lung, Liver, Apex of Ear.

Method: Apply filiform needles with strong stimulation and retain the needles for 30 minutes. Auricular taping is also applicable.

3. Three-edged Needle

Prescription: Taiyang (EX-HN 5).

Method: Prick the point with a three-edged needle to cause bleeding. Then cupping is applied to the point.

4. Lampwick Moxibustion

Prescription: At the triangular fossa on the back of the auricle of the affected side, a small blood vessel and its branches may be seen obviously under light. Two points respectively superior to the vessel and at the cross are taken as the moxibustion sites.

Method: The two points are marked with a pen, and the local skin is sterilized with 75% of alcohol. Then, a rush soaked with vegetable oil is ignited and dipped accurately onto the marked spot and removed immediately. A clear crackling sound is heard. If not, the procedure is repeated but the maximum times is three. If a small blister is left broken by pushing, it is smeared with gentian violet to prevent infection. Generally, the disease is cured by one session of treatment. If it is not cured the treatment may be given once again. During the treatment period the local skin should be kept clean and not washed. Note, the portion of the rush to be soaked in the oil should be approximately 0.5 cm long because if the portion of the rush soaked in the oil is more than 0.5 cm long the rush may become too soft to apply moxibustion and the fire caused may be so strong that the skin may be burnt. As well, if the portion soaked in the oil is less than 0.5cm long, not enough fire for moxibustion may not be created.

单纯性青光眼

单纯性青光眼为青光眼的一种。其特点为早期眼压轻度增高，或在一天内一时性增高，晚期眼压持续性增高。临床症状有眼胀，视力易于疲劳，头痛，晚期视力减退。病者可有青光眼家族史。

1. 体针

处方 风池，天柱，三阴交，足三里，行间，膈俞，肝俞，肾俞。

操作 毫针刺，平补平泻，留针

30 分钟，间歇行针 3~4 次。

2. 耳针

处方　肝，肾，眼，目 1，目 2，皮质下，交感。

操作　毫针中等强度刺激，留针 20 分钟。

3. 皮肤针

处方　太阳，鱼腰，阳白，攒竹，行间，三阴交。

操作　皮肤针叩刺 20 分钟，每天 1 次。

Simple Glaucoma

Simple glaucoma, a disease of the eye, is marked by moderately or temporarily high intraocular pressure in the initial stage and continuously high intraocular pressure in the advanced stage. Manifestation include distension of the eyeballs and easily tiring vision. Headache and hypopsia may occur in the advanced stage. There may be a family history of glaucoma.

1. Body Acupuncture

Prescription: Fengchi (GB 20), Tianzhu (BL 10), Sanyinjiao (SP 6), Zusanli (ST 36), Xingjian (LR 2), Geshu (BL 17), Ganshu (BL 18), Shenshu (BL 23).

Method: Apply filiform needles with even movement method. Retain the needles for 30 minutes manipulating them 3~4 times.

2. Ear Acupuncture

Prescription: Liver, Kidney, Eye, Eye1, Eye2, Subcortex, Sympathetic.

Method: Apply filiform needles with moderate stimulation and retain the needles for 20 minutes.

3. Plum-blossom Needle

Prescription: Taiyang (EX-HN 5), Yuyao (EX-HN 4), Yangbai (GB 14), Cuanzhu (BL 2), Xingjian (LR 2), Sanyinjiao (SP 6).

Method: Apply a plum-blossom needle to tap the points for 20 minutes once a day.

急性视神经炎

本病包括视神经乳头炎和球后视神经炎两类，皆为眼科重症，预后不良。临床以发病急，视力高度下降，甚至失明为特征。本病属中医"暴盲"范畴。

1. 体针

处方　风池，瞳子髎，太冲，光明，球后。

操作　毫针刺，用泻法，留针 30 分钟，间歇行针 3~5 次。

2. 耳针

处方　目 1，目 2，肝，耳尖。

操作　毫针强刺激，留针 30 分钟。耳尖点刺出血。

3. 水针

处方 风池，肝俞，肾俞，太阳，光明。

操作 每穴注射维生素 B₁（10毫克/毫升）0.5毫升，每天1次。

Acute Optic Neuritis

Acute optic neuritis includes two types, papillitis of the optic nerve and retrobulbar neuritis, which are both severe eye diseases with poor prognosis. Clinically it is characterized by an abrupt onset, severe diminution of vision, or even total blindness. It belongs to the category of sudden blindness in traditional Chinese medicine.

1. Body Acupuncture

Prescription: Fengchi (GB 20), Tongziliao (GB 1), Taichong (LR 3), Guangming (GB 37), Qiuhou (EX-HN 7).

Method: Apply filiform needles with reducing method. Retain the needles for 30 minutes manipulating them 3~5 times.

2. Ear Acupuncture

Prescription: Eye1, Eye2, Liver, Apex of Ear.

Method: Apply filiform needles with strong stimulation and retain the needles for 30 minutes. Apex of Ear may be pricked to cause bleeding.

3. Point Injection

Prescription: Fengchi (GB 20), Ganshu (BL 18), Shenshu (BL 23), Taiyang (EX-HN 5), Guangming (GB 37).

Method: Inject 0.5 mL of vitamin B₁ (10mg/mL) into each point once a day.

视网膜色素变性

视网膜色素变性是视网膜色素上皮的原发变性，具有遗传性。临床以双眼发病，夜盲，视野缩小，晚期导致失明为特征。本病属中医"高风雀目内障"范畴。

1. 体针

处方 睛明，球后，太阳，合谷，足三里，三阴交。

操作 毫针刺，平补平泻，留针30分钟，间歇行针3~4次。

2. 耳针

处方 肝，眼，皮质下，交感。

操作 毫针中等强度刺激，留针30分钟；亦可用耳穴贴敷。

Pigmentary Degeneration of the Retina

Pigmentary degeneration of the retina refers to primary degeneration of the epithelium with heredity. Clinically it is characterized by binocular onset, night blindness, contraction of the visual field leading to blindness at the late stage. It belongs to the category of pigmentary degeneration of the retina with the pupil golden in color in traditional

Chinese medicine.

1. Body Acupuncture

Prescription: Jingming (BL 1), Qiugou (EX-HN 7), Taiyang (EX-HN 5), Hegu (LI 4), Zusanli (ST 36), Sanyinjiao (SP 6).

Method: Apply filiform needles with even movement. Retain the needles for 30 minutes manipulating them 3 ~ 4 times.

2. Ear Acupuncture

Prescription: Liver, Eye, Subcortex, Sympathetic.

Method: Apply filiform needles with moderate stimulation and retain the needles for 30 minutes. Auricular taping is also applicable.

视网膜中央动脉栓塞

视网膜中央动脉栓塞是眼科的急重疑难症，多见于老年人，中年人亦可患病。一般是单眼发病，个别亦有双眼先后发病者。该病是在动脉硬化的基础上，动脉管壁弹性降低，赘生物栓塞于动脉管腔，使视网膜缺血而失明。若失治，则致成永久性失明。本病属中医"暴盲"范畴。

1. 体针

处方　球后，睛明，太阳，风池，合谷，太冲。

操作　毫针刺，平补平泻。得气出针，不留针。

2. 耳针

处方　眼，目1，目2，肝，耳尖，交感。

操作　毫针中度强度刺激，留针20分钟。

Embolism of Central Artery of the Retina

Embolism of central artery of the retina is acute, severe and knotty eye trouble. It is most common in the old but the middle-aged may also suffer from this disease. Usually the disease occurs in one eye. In a few patients it is possible to occur successively in both eyes. The disease is the result of retinal ischemia due to the reduction of elasticity of arterial vessel wall and obstruction of the arterial lumen with emboli vegetation on the basis of arteriosclerosis, thus loss of vision occurs. If it is not treated in time permanent blindness will result. This disease belongs to the category of sudden blindness in traditional Chinese medicine.

1. Body Acupuncture

Prescription: Qiuhou (EX-HN 7), Jingming (BL 1), Taiyang (Ex-HN 5), Fengchi (GB 20), Hegu (LI 4), Taichong (LI 3).

Method: Apply filiform needles with even movement. On getting the feeling of acupuncture withdraw the inserted needle without retention of it.

2. Ear Acupuncture

Prescription: Eye, Eye1, Eye2, Liver, Apex of Ear, Sympathetic.

Method: Apply filiform needles, with moderate stimulation and retain the needles for 20 minutes.

麻痹性斜视

麻痹性斜视是以眼球偏斜并伴有复视为特征的眼病。发病突起，常单眼患病，无年龄、性别等特异性。完全性麻痹者，除复视外，眼球不能向麻痹肌作用方向转动，而被拉向拮抗肌作用的方向。不完全性麻痹者，除复视外，患眼转动受限。该病属中医"视岐"、"视　为二症"范畴。

1. 体针

处方　睛明，瞳子髎，阳白，四白，承泣，颊车，地仓，合谷，太冲，足三里，行间。

操作　毫针刺，用泻法，留针20分钟。

2. 耳针

处方　肝，眼，交感，耳尖，内分泌。

操作　毫针强刺激，留针30分钟；亦可用耳穴贴敷。

Paralytic Strabismus

Paralytic strabismus is a kind of eye disease characterized by deviation of the eye ball accompanied with double vision. The onset of the disease is sudden, often with one eye affected without age-specificity or sex-specificity. In addition to double vision, the eyeball refuses to rotate in the functional direction of the paralytic muscle in those with complete paralysis. Instead, it is drawn to the opposite direction due to an antagonistic muscle. For those with incomplete paralysis, in addition to diplopia, rotation of the diseased eye becomes limited. This disease belongs to the category of distorted vision and double vision in traditional Chinese medicine.

1. Body Acupuncture

Prescription: Jingming (BL 1), Tongziliao (GB 1), Yangbai (GB 14), Sibai (ST 4), Chengqi (ST 1), Jiache (ST 6), Dicang (ST 4), Hegu (LI 4), Taichong (LR 3), Zusanli (ST 36), Xingjian (LI 2).

Method: Apply filiform needles with reducing method and retain the needles for 20 minutes.

2. Ear Acupuncture

Prescription: Liver, Eye, Sympathetic, Apex of Ear, Endocrine.

Method: Apply filiform needles with strong stimulation and retain the needles for 30 minutes. Auricular taping is also applicable.

老年性白内障

老年性白内障是老年人常见的眼

病，系指晶状体本身逐渐老化、变性，混浊而无全身或局部其他病因者。该病为双眼发病，但两眼的发病时间、程度、速度可不同。临床以皮质性老年性白内障和核心老年性白内障为常见。此外，尚有一种囊膜性老年性白内障，多为皮质性内障成熟期或过熟期的并发症。本病属于中医"圆翳内障"、"如银内障"、"白翳黄心内障"等范畴。

1. 体针

处方　肝俞，肾俞，脾俞，太冲，足三里，合谷，瞳子髎，睛明。

操作　毫针刺，用泻法，留针30分钟，间歇行针 2~3 次。

2. 耳针

处方　肾，肝，眼，目1，目2。

操作　毫针轻刺激，留针 30 分钟；亦可用耳穴贴敷。

3. 皮肤针

处方　风池，心俞，肝俞，肾俞，眼周，三阴交。

操作　皮肤针叩刺，每次 20 分钟，每天 1 次。

Senile Cataract

Senile cataract is a common eye disease in old people. It refers to the case in which the crystalline lens itself gradually becomes aged, denatured and opaque without other systemic or local pathogenic causes. It usually occurs in two eyes but the affections of the two eyes may differ in time, degree and progressive speed. Clinically only cortical senile cataract and nuclear senile cataract are common. In addition, there exists a capsular senile cataract as a complication of mature or hypermature stage of cortical cataract. The disease belongs to the category of yuanyi neizhang, ruyin neizhang or baiyin huangxin neizhang in traditional Chinese medicine.

1. Body Acupuncture

Prescription: Ganshu (BL 18), Shenshu (BL 23), Pishu (BL 20), Taichong (LR 3), Zusanli (ST 36), Hegu (LI 4), Tongziliao (GB 1), Jingming (BL 1).

Method: Apply filiform needles with reinforcing method and retain the needles for 30 minutes, manipulating them 2~3 times.

2. Ear Acupuncture

Prescription: Kidney, Liver, Eye, Eye1, Eye2.

Method: Apply filiform needles with mild stimulation and retain the needles for 30 minutes. Auricular taping is also applicable.

3. Plum-blossom Needle

Prescription: Fengchi (GB 20), Xinshu (BL 15), Ganshu (BL 18), Shenshu (BL 23), area around the eye, Sanyinjiao (SP 6).

Method: Tap the points with a plum-blossom needle for 20 minutes once a day.

渗出性虹膜睫状体炎

渗出性虹膜睫状体炎为眼科常见病，临床以眼痛，睫状体充血，虹膜水肿及渗出，视力下降等为特征。因其发病后虹膜肿胀而有刺激性瞳孔缩小，故中医称之为"瞳神紧小症"；又因其很快产生虹膜后粘连，使瞳孔不圆整，故中医又称之为"瞳神干缺症"。

1.体针

处方 睛明，攒竹，丝竹空，瞳子髎，合谷，足三里。

操作 毫针刺，平补平泻。留针30分钟，间歇行针3～4次。

2.耳针

处方 肝，眼，目1，目2，内分泌。

操作 毫针中等强度刺激，留针30分钟；亦可用耳穴贴敷。

Exudative Iridocyclitis

Exudative Iridocyclitis is a common ophthalmic disease. It is characterized by pain of the eye, congestion of the ciliary body, edema and exudation of the iris, diminution of vision and so on. As the iris becomes swollen irritative miosis occurs after the onset. Traditional Chinese medicine gives it the name miosis because the posterior synechia soon occurs to cause the pupil to lose its normal circular outline. It has another name, pupillary metamorphosis, due to posterior synechia in traditional Chinese medicine.

1. Body Acupuncture

Prescription: Jingming (BL 1), Cuan (BL 2), Sizhukong (SJ 23), Tongziliao (GB 1), Hegu (LI 4), Zusanli (ST 36).

Method: Apply filiform needles with even movement. Retain the needles for 30 minutes manipulating them 3 ～ 4 times.

2. Ear Acupuncture

Prescription: Liver, Eye, Eye1, Eye2, Endocrine.

Method: Apply filiform needles with moderate stimulation and retain the needles for 30 minutes. Auricular taping is also applicable.

中心性视网膜炎

中心性视网膜炎为视网膜黄斑区毛细血管痉挛所致。临床表现为视力减退，或有视物变形、变小、视野正中有固定的暗影。视力检查可查出中心暗点。本病有复发倾向。

1.体针

处方 睛明，承泣，攒竹，瞳子髎，丝竹空。

操作　毫针平补平泻，留针 30
分钟，间歇行针 3~4 次。

2.耳针

处方　目 1，目 2，肝，皮质下。
操作　毫针中等强度刺激，留针
30 分钟；亦可用耳穴贴敷。

3.电针

处方　翳风，曲鬓，丝竹空。
操作　疏密波治疗 20 分钟，每
天 1 次。

Central Retinitis

Central retinitis is an eye disease
caused by spasm of the capillaries of the
macula lutea retinae. Manifestations
include hypopsia, metamorphosis, mi-
cropsia, and fixed area opaca in the
center of the visual field. Tests of visual acuity will reveal central scotoma.
The condition may recur after recovery.

1.Body Acupuncture

Prescription: Jingming (BL 1),
Chengqi (ST 1), Cuanzhu (BL 2),
Tongziliao (GB 1), Sizhukong (SJ
23).

Method: Apply filiform needles with
even movement. Retain the needles for
30 minutes manipulating them 3 ~ 4
times.

2.Ear Acupuncture

Prescription: Eye1, Eye2, Liver,
Subcortex.

Method: Apply filiform needles with
moderate   stimulation.   Retain   the
needes for 30 minutes. Auricular taping
is also applicable.

3.Electroacupuncture

Prescription: Yifeng (SJ 17),
Qubin (GB 7), Sizhukong (SJ 23).

Method: Apply sparse-dense wave
for 20 minutes once a day.

急性化脓性中耳炎

急性化脓性中耳炎是由细菌感染
引起的中耳黏膜的急性化脓性炎症。
临床以发热，耳痛，耳内流脓为主要
特征。中医称之为"实证脓耳"。

1.体针

处方　翳风，听会，听宫，耳
门，合谷，阳陵泉，行间，风池。
操作　毫针刺，用泻法。留针
20 分钟，间歇行针 3~5 次。

2.耳针

处方　内耳，外耳，三焦，内分
泌，耳尖。
操作　毫针强刺激，留针 30 分
钟。耳尖点刺出血。

Acute Suppurative Otitis Media

Acute suppurative otitis media is an
acute suppurative inflammation of the
mucous membrane in the middle ear
caused by bacterial infection. Its clinical features are fever, otalgia and o-
topyorrhea. It belongs to the category

of otopyorrhea of excess type in traditional Chinese medicine.

1. Body Acupuncture

Prescription：Yifeng（SJ 17），Tinghui（GB 2），Tinggong（SI 19），Ermen（SJ 21），Hegu（LI 4），Yanglingquan（GB 34），Xingjian（LR 2），Fengchi（GB 20）.

Method：Apply filiform needles with reducing method. Retain the needles for 20 minutes manipulating them 3～5 times.

2. Ear Acupuncture

Prescription：Internal Ear, External Ear, Sanjiao, Endocrine, Apex of Ear.

Method：Apply filiform needles with strong stimulation and retain the needles for 30 minutes. Apex of Ear may be pricked to cause bleeding.

慢性化脓性中耳炎

慢性化脓性中耳炎多由急性化脓性中耳炎治疗不当转变而来，为中耳黏膜、骨膜，乃至骨组织的慢性化脓性炎症。其临床特点是耳内长期流脓，反复不愈，听力减退，鼓膜穿孔。本病属中医"脓耳"范畴。

1. 体针

处方 翳风，足三里，阴陵泉，听会，脾俞，肾俞。

操作 毫针刺，平补平泻。留针30分钟，间歇行针3～4次。

2. 耳针

处方 内耳，外耳，三焦，胰胆，肾，内分泌，肾上腺，皮质下。

操作 毫针中等强度刺激，留针30分钟；亦可用耳穴贴敷。

Chronic Suppurative Otitis Media

Chronic suppurative otitis media is in most cases the result of inappropriate treatment of acute suppurative otitis media. It is a chronic inflammation of the mucous membrane, periost and even osseous tissue of the middle ear. The disease has the following clinical features: a long period of recurrent otopyorrea which is very difficult to cured, hypoacusis and perforation of the tympanic membrane. This disease falls into the category of nonger in traditional Chinese medicine.

1. Body Acupuncture

Prescription：Yifeng（SJ 17），Zusanli（ST 36），Yinlingquan（SP 9），Tinghui（GB 2），Pishu（BL 20），Shenshu（BL 23）.

Method：Apply filiform needles with even movement. Retain the needles for 30 minutes manipulating them 3～4 times.

2. Ear Acupuncture

Prescription：Internal Ear, External Ear, Sanjiao, Pancreas, Gallbladder, Kidney, Endocrine, Adrenal Gland,

Subcortex.

Method: Apply filiform needles with moderate stimulation and retain the needles for 30 minutes. Auricular taping is also applicable.

急性卡他性中耳炎

急性卡他性中耳炎，是指在鼓室负压下产生的中耳黏膜的非化脓性急性炎症。临床特点为耳有堵闷感，听力减退，耳鸣或耳痛，自声增强等。本病属中医"耳胀痛"、"耳聋"、"耳鸣"等范畴。

1. 体针

处方　听宫，翳风，丰隆，太冲，合谷，外关，足三里。

操作　毫针刺，用泻法。留针30分钟，间歇行针4～5次。

2. 耳针

处方　内耳，外耳，肝，内分泌，皮质下，耳尖。

操作　毫针强刺激，留针30分钟。耳尖点刺出血；亦可用耳穴贴敷。

Acute Catarrhal Otitis Media

Acute catarrhal otitis media is an acute non-suppurative inflammation in the mucous membrane of the middle ear caused by the negative pressure of the tympanic cavity. Its clinical features are feeling of fullness in the ear, hypoacusis, tinnitus or otalgia, tautophony and so on. This disease falls into the categories of distending pain in the ear, deafness or tinnitus in traditional Chinese medicine.

1. Body Acupuncture

Prescription: Tinggong (SI 19), Yifeng (SJ 17), Fenglong (ST 40), Taichong (LR 3), Hegu (LI 4), Waiguan (SJ 5), Zusanli (ST 36).

Method: Apply filiform needles with reducing method. Retain the needles for 30 minutes manipulating them 4～5 times.

2. Ear Acupuncture

Prescription: Internal Ear, External Ear, Liver, Endocrine, Subcortex, Apex of Ear.

Method: Apply filiform needles with strong stimulation and retain the needles for 30 minutes. Apex of Ear may be pricked to cause bleeding. Auricular taping is also applicable.

慢性卡他性中耳炎

慢性卡他性中耳炎是咽鼓管和中耳腔黏膜的慢性非化脓性炎症，多由于急性中耳炎治疗不当所造成。其临床特点为耳闷，重听，病程较长。本病属中医"耳闭"、"耳聋"范畴。

1. 体针

处方　翳风，耳门，听宫，太溪，听会，足三里，三阴交。

操作　毫针刺，平补平泻。留针

30 分钟，间歇行针 3～4 次。

2. 耳针

处方 内耳，外耳，肝，肾，皮质下，内分泌。

操作 毫针轻刺激，留针 30 分钟；亦可用耳穴贴敷。

Chronic Catarrhal Otitis Media

Chronic catarrhal otitis media is a chronic non-suppurative inflammation of the mucous membrane of the eustachian tube and middle ear cavity. It occurs mostly due to the inappropriate treatment of acute otitis media. Its clinical characteristics are a feeling of fullness in the ear, hard hearing and long duration. It falls into the category of ear plug or deafness in traditional Chinese medicine.

1. Body Acupuncture

Prescription: Yifeng (SJ 17), Ermen (SJ 21), Tinggong (SI 19). Taixi (KI 5), Tinghui (GB 2), Zusanli (ST 36), Sanyinjiao (SP 6).

Method: Apply filiform needles with even movement. Retain the needles for 30 minutes manipulating them 3 ～ 4 times.

2. Ear Acupuncture

Prescription: Internal Ear, External Ear, Liver, Kidney, Subcortex, Endocrine.

Method: Apply filiform needles with mild stimulation and retain the needles for 30 minutes. Auricular taping is also applicable.

耳鸣、耳聋

耳鸣表现为自觉耳内有各种不同的响声。响声重，伴眩晕易怒为实证；响声低微，伴头晕眼花，腰膝酸软为虚证。耳聋多为听力减退或丧失。针灸治疗多以神经性耳鸣、耳聋为主。

1. 体针

处方 耳门，听宫，翳风，听会，外关，中渚。

配穴 实证加丰隆，侠溪，太冲；虚证加复溜，太溪。

操作 毫针刺，实证用泻法，虚证用补法。留针 30 分钟，间歇行针 2～4 次。

2. 耳针

处方 耳，肾上腺，肝，肾，内分泌。

操作 毫针中等强度刺激，留针 30 分钟；亦可用耳穴贴敷。

3. 水针

处方 听宫，翳风，风池，听会，耳门。

操作 每穴注射 0.3～0.5 毫升维生素 B_1（共 2 毫升），每天 1 次。

Tinnitus and Deafness

Tinnitus is manifested by ringing

sound in the ears felt by the patient himself. It can be divided into two types according to differentiation of syndromes clinically: excess type and deficiency type. The excess type is characterized by strong ringing sound in the ears accompanied by dizziness and irritability. The deficiency type is characterized by low ringing sound in the ears accompanied by dizziness, soreness and weakness of the waist and knee. Deafness is manifested by failing or loss of hearing. Most tinnitus and deafness which can be treated by acupuncture and moxibustion are neural.

1. Body Acupuncture

Prescription: Ermen (SJ 21), Tinggong (SI 19), Yifeng (SJ 17), Tinghui (GB 2), Waiguan (SJ 5), Zhongzhu (SJ 3).

Supplementary points: Add Fenglong (ST 40), Xiaxi (GB 43) and Taichong (LR 3) for excess type, Fuiliu (KI 7) and Taixi (KI 3) for deficiency type.

Method: Apply filiform needles with reducing method for excess type or reinforcing method for deficiency type. Retain the needles for 20~30 minutes manipulating them 2~4 times.

2. Ear Acupuncture

Prescription: Ear, Adrenal Gland, Liver, Kidney, Endocrine.

Method: Apply filiform needles with moderate stimulation and retain the needles for 30 minutes. Auricular taping is also applicable.

3. Point Injection

Prescription: Tinggong (SI 19), Yifeng (SJ 17), Fengchi (GB 20), Tinghui (GB 2), Ermen (SJ 21).

Method: Inject 2 mL of vitamin B_1 into the points (0.3 ~ 0.5 mL each point) once a day.

梅尼埃病

梅尼埃病是由于内耳膜迷路水肿而导致的耳源性眩晕。主要表现为短暂的阵发性眩晕，因体位变动而加重。常伴有耳鸣，重听，水平眼球震颤及恶心呕吐等。本病有自愈和反复发作倾向。中医称之为"眩晕"。

1. 体针

处方　印堂，风池，听宫，太冲，百会，内关。

配穴　实证加丰隆，阴陵泉，中脘；虚证加肾俞，三阴交，太溪，足三里。

操作　毫针刺，实证用泻法，虚证用补法。留针30分钟，间歇行针2~4次。

2. 耳针

处方　肝，肾，神门，内耳，交感，肾上腺。

操作　毫针刺，平补平泻。留针

30 分钟。亦可用耳穴贴敷。

3. 艾灸

处方　百会。

操作　艾条悬灸或艾炷灸，每天
1 次，每次 15～30 分钟或 5～6 壮。

Meniere's Disease

Meniere's disease is a type of auditory vertigo caused by hydrops in the labyrinth of the ear. It is marked by transient paroxysmal episodes of vertigo, aggravated by changes of body position and usually accompanied by tinnitus, hearing loss, parallel nystagmus, nausea, vomiting, perspiration, and pale complexion. Spontaneous cure and repeated recurrence are often seen in clinical practice. Meniere's disease is classified as vertigo in traditional Chinese medicine.

1. Body Acupuncture

Prescription: Yintang (EX-HN 3), Fengchi (GB 20), Tinggong (SI 19), Taichong (LR 3), Baihui (DU 20), Neiguan (PC 6).

Supplementary points: Add Fenglong (ST 40), Yinlingquan (SP 9) and Zhongwan (RN 12) for excess type, Shenshu (BL 23), Sanyinjiao (SP 6), Taixi (KI 3), and Zusanli (ST 36) for deficiency type.

Method: Apply filiform needles with reducing method for excess type or rein-forcing method for deficiency type. Retain the needles for 30 minutes manipulating them 2～4 times.

2. Ear Acupuncture

Prescription: Liver, Kidney, Shenmen, Internal Ear, Symthetic, Adrenal Gland.

Method: Apply filiform needles with moderate stimulation and retain the needles for 30 minutes. Auricular taping is also applicable.

3. Moxibustion

Prescription: Baihui (DU 20).

Method: Suspended moxibustion is applied to the point for 15～30 minutes or moxibustion with moxa cone is applied to the point using 5～6 cones once a day.

急性鼻炎

急性鼻炎是鼻黏膜的急性感染性炎症。其临床特点是鼻内灼热，鼻塞，喷嚏，流涕，头痛，发热等。中医称之为"伤风鼻塞"。

1. 体针

处方　迎香，合谷，印堂，风池，列缺。

操作　毫针刺，用泻法。留针30 分钟，间歇行针 3～4 次。

2. 耳针

处方　内鼻，外鼻，肺，额，内分泌。

操作　毫针强刺激，留针30分钟；亦可用耳穴贴敷。

3. 艾灸

处方　迎香，合谷，印堂，足三里，大椎。

操作　每穴温和灸治疗10～15分钟，每天1次。

Acute Rhinitis

Acute rhinitis is an acute infective inflammation of the nasal mucosa. It's clinical features are a feeling of burning heat in the nose, nasal obstruction, sneezing, rhinorrhea, headache, fever, etc. It belongs to the category of stuffy nose due to the attack by exogenous wind in traditional Chinese medicine.

1. Body Acupuncture

Prescription：Yingxiang（LI 20），Hegu（LI 4），Yintang（EX-HN 2），Fengchi（GB 20），Lieque（LU 7）.

Method：Apply filiform needles with reducing method and retain the needles for 30 minutes manipulating them 3～4 times.

2. Ear Acupuncture

Prescription：Interior Nose, Exterior Nose, Lung, Forehead, Endocrine.

Method：Apply filiform needles with strong stimulation and retain the needles for 30 minutes. Auricular taping is also applicable.

3. Moxibustion

Prescription：Yingxiang（LI 20），Hegu（LI 4），Yintang（EX-HN 2），Zusanli（ST 36），Dazhui（DU 14）.

Method：Apply mild-warming moxibustion to each point for 10 ～ 15 minutes once a day.

慢性鼻炎

慢性鼻炎是鼻黏膜的慢性炎性病变。多由急性鼻炎迁延而来。本病以鼻腔窒塞为主要症状。中医称之为"鼻窒"。

1. 体针

处方　迎香，合谷，印堂，肺俞，足三里，上星，上迎香。

操作　毫针刺，用泻法。留针30分钟；间歇行针3～4次。

2. 耳针

处方　内鼻，外鼻，肺，肾上腺，额。

操作　毫针轻刺激，留针30分钟；亦可用耳穴贴敷。

3. 艾灸

处方　迎香，印堂，足三里，肺俞，内关，合谷。

操作　每穴温和灸治疗10～15分钟，每天1次。

Chronic Rhinitis

Chronic rhinitis is a chronic inflammatory change of the nasal mucosa, mainly due to the protraction of acute rhinitis. Its main symptom is nasal obstruction. This disease is called nasal obstruction in traditional Chinese medicine.

1. Body Acupuncture

Prescription: Yingxiang（LI 20）, Hegu（LI 4）, Yintang（EX-HN 2）, Feishu（BL 13）, Zusanli（ST 36）, Shangxing（DU 23）, Shangyingxiang（EX-HN 8）.

Method: Apply filiform needle with reducing method. Retain the needles for 30 minutes manipulating them 3~4 times.

2. Ear Acupuncture

Prescription: Interior Nose, Exterior Nose, Lung, Adrenal Gland, Forehead.

Method: Apply filiform needles with mild stimulation and retain the needles for 30 minutes. Auricular taping is also applicable.

3. Moxibustion

Prescription: Yintang（EX-HN 2）, Yingxiang（LI 20）, Zusanli（ST 36）, Feishu（BL 13）, Neiguan（PC 6）Hegu（LI 4）.

Method: Apply mild-warming moxibustion to each point for 10~15 minutes once a day.

过敏性鼻炎为鼻黏膜的过敏性疾病。主要表现为鼻痒，阵发性持续打喷嚏，鼻流清涕及间歇性或持续性鼻塞。病者常有其他过敏性疾病的病史或家族过敏史。中医称之为"鼻鼽"。

1. 体针

处方　列缺，合谷，迎香，印堂。

操作　毫针刺，用泻法。留针15~20分钟，间歇行针3~4次。

2. 耳针

处方　内鼻，额，肺，肾上腺。

操作　毫针强刺激，留针30分钟；亦可用耳穴贴敷。

Allergic Rhinitis

Allergic rhinitis is an allergic problem of the nasal mucosa. It is characterized by rhinocnesmus, persistent paroxysmal sneezing, dilute nasal discharge, and intermittent or persistent nasal obstruction. There is often a history of other allergic problems or a family history of allergy. It belongs to the category of "biqiu" in traditional Chinese medicine.

1. Body Acupuncture

Prescription: Lieque（LU 7）, Hegu（LI 4）, Yingxiang（LI 20）, Yintang（EX-HN 3）.

Method: Apply filiform needles with reducing method. Retain the needles for 15 ~ 20 minutes, manipulating them 3~4 times.

2. Ear Acupuncture

Prescription: Interior Nose, Forehead, Lung, Adrenal Gland.

Method: Apply filiform needles with strong stimulation and retain the needles for 30 minutes. Auricular taping is also applicable.

急性鼻窦炎

急性鼻窦炎主要包括额窦、筛小房、上额窦黏膜的急性非特异性炎症（蝶窦炎少见）。临床特点为发热、头痛、鼻塞、流脓涕等。本病属中医"鼻渊"范畴。

1. 体针

处方　百会，阳白，颧髎，太冲，血海，三阴交。

操作　毫针刺，用泻法。留针15~20分钟，间歇行针3~4次。

2. 耳针

处方　内鼻，外鼻，肺，肾上腺，内分泌，额。

操作　毫针中等强度刺激，留针30分钟；亦可用耳穴贴敷。

3. 艾灸

处方　囟会，上星，前顶，迎香。

操作　每穴温和灸治疗10~15分钟，每天1次。

4. 电针

处方　合谷，内关，内庭，足三里。

操作　每穴密波治疗1小时，每天1次。

Acute Nasosinusitis

Acute nasosinusitis is an acute nonspecific inflammation of the mucous membrane of the frontal sinus, ethmoid sinus and maxillary sinus (sphenoiditis is seldom seen). Its clinical characteristics are fever, headache, nasal obstruction and purulent nasal discharge. It belongs to the category of biyuan in traditional Chinese medicine.

1. Body Acupuncture

Prescription: Baihui (DU 20), Yangbai (GB 14), Quanliao (SI 18), Taichong (LR 3), Xuehai (SP 10), Sanyinjiao (SP 6).

Method: Apply filiform needles with reducing method. Retain the needles for 15~20 minutes manipulating them 3~4 times.

2. Ear Acupuncture

Prescription: Interior Nose, Exterior Nose, Lung, Adrenal Gland, Endocrine, Forehead.

Method: Apply filiform needles with moderate stimulation and retain the needles for 30 minutes. Auricular taping is also applicable.

3. Moxibustion

Prescription: Xinhui (DU 22), Shangxing (DU 23), Qianding (DU 21), Yingxiang (LI 20).

Method: Apply mild-warming moxibustion to each point for 10 ～ 15 minutes once a day.

4. Electroacupuncture

Prescription: Hegu (LI 4), Neiguan (PC 6), Neiting (ST 44), Zusanli (ST 36).

Method: Apply dense wave to the points for 1 hour once a day.

慢性鼻窦炎

慢性鼻窦炎由急性鼻窦炎治疗不彻底或反复发作所致，常数个鼻窦同时患病。临床特点为鼻流脓涕和鼻阻塞。本病属中医"鼻渊"范畴。

1. 体针

处方　迎香，百会，上星，足三里，合谷。

操作　毫针刺，平补平泻。留针30分钟，间歇行针3～4次。

2. 耳针

处方　内鼻，外鼻，肺，内分泌，皮质下，肾上腺。

操作　毫针轻刺激，留针30分钟；亦可用耳穴贴敷。

3. 艾灸

处方　百会，前顶，颞会，上星，足三里。

操作　每穴用温和灸治疗10～15分钟，每天1次。

Chronic Nasosinusitis

Chronic nasosinusitis, mostly caused by incomplete treatment of acute nasosinusitis or by its repeated occurences often attacks several nasal sinuses simultaneously. Its clinical features are puslike nasal discharge and nasal obstruction. It falls into the category of biyuan in traditional Chinese medicine.

1. Body Acupuncture

Prescription: Yingxiang (LI 20), Baihui (DU 20), Shangxing (DU 23), Zusanli (ST 36), Hegu (LI 4).

Method: Apply filiform needles with even movement. Retain the needles for 30 minutes manipulating them 3 ～ 4 times.

2. Ear Acupuncture

Prescription: Interior Nose, Exterior Nose, Lung, Endocrine, Subcortex, Adrenal Gland.

Method: Apply filiform needles with mild stimulation and retain the needles for 30 minutes. Auricular taping is also applicable.

3. Moxibustion

Prescription: Baihui (DU 20), Qianding (DU 21), Xinhui (DU 22), Shangxing (DU 23), Zusanli

(ST 36).

Method: Apply mild-warming moxibustion to each point for 10 ～ 15 minutes once a day.

鼻 出 血

鼻出血是临床常见症状之一，可由鼻腔疾病或全身疾病引起。鼻出血最常见部位为鼻中隔前下区黏膜，下鼻道后端的鼻－鼻咽静脉丛也是较易出血处。

1. 体针

处方　迎香，合谷，上星，少商，内庭。

操作　毫针刺，用泻法。留针30分钟，间歇行针4～5次。

2. 耳针

处方　内鼻，肾上腺，神门。

操作　毫针强刺激，留针30分钟。

3. 艾灸

处方　顖会，上星，大椎。

操作　每穴用温和灸治疗10～20分钟。

Nosebleed

Nosebleed, a common clinical symptom, can be caused by mycteric or general diseases. It is mostly seen in Kiesselbach's area. The naso-nasopharyngeal plexus at the end of the inferior nasal meatus is also an area where nosebleed is apt to occur.

1. Body Acupuncture

Prescription：Yingxiang（LI 20）, Hegu（LI 4）, Shangxing（DU 23）, Shaoshang（LU 11）, Neiting（ST 44）.

Method: Apply filiform needles with reducing method. Retain the needles for 30 minutes manipulating them 4～5 times.

2. Ear Acupuncture

Prescription: Interior Nose, Adrenal Gland, Shenmen.

Method: Apply filiform needles with strong stimulation and retain the needles for 30 minutes.

3. Moxibustion

Prescription: Xinhui（DU 22）, Shangxing（DU 23）, Dazhui（DU 14）.

Method: Apply mild-warming moxibustion to each point for 10～20 minutes.

急性扁桃体炎

急性扁桃体炎为扁桃体急性非特异性炎性病症。多发于春秋季节，以儿童和青年多见。临床表现为咽喉疼痛，吞咽时加重，恶寒、发热、头痛及周身酸痛等。可转变为慢性扁桃体炎及诱发多种病症，如中耳炎、心内膜炎、肾炎、风湿性关节炎等。因此，及时适当治疗十分必要。

1. 体针

处方 少商，合谷，颊车，尺泽，商阳，曲池。

操作 毫针刺，用泻法。留针30分钟，间歇行针3～4次。

2. 耳针

处方 扁桃体，咽喉，肺，胃，大肠，内分泌，肾上腺，耳尖。

操作 毫针强刺激，留针30分钟。耳尖可点刺出血。

3. 三棱针

处方 少商，商阳。

操作 三棱针点刺出血。

4. 拔罐

处方 大椎。

操作 快速进针2～3毫米深，不留针，再取不易传热大豆片、橘皮等置于大椎部位，上面放一小乙醇棉球，点燃后扣上火罐，留罐10～15分钟，反复做2次。

5. 水针

处方 翳风，合谷，足三里，曲池。

操作 每穴注射0.5毫升维生素B_1，每天1次。

6. 灯火灸

处方 角孙。

操作 用2寸长灯草1根，蘸清油点燃后，对准患侧角孙穴（剪去头发）快速点灸。

Acute Tonsillitis

Acute tonsillitis is an acute nonspecific inflammation of the tonsils. It occurs mainly in the spring and autumn and primarily in children and young people. Manifestations include chills, fever, headache, sore throat aggravated by swallowing, and general soreness of the body. Because acute tonsillitis may develop into chronic tonsillitis or develop accompanying complications such as otitis media, endocarditis, nephritis, and rheumatic arthritis, immediate and proper treatment is essential.

1. Body Acupuncture

Prescription: Shaoshang (LU 11), Hegu (LI 4), Jiache (ST 6), Chize (LU 5), Shangyang (LI 1), Quchi (LI 11).

Method: Apply filiform needles with reducing method and retain the needles for 30 minutes, manipulating them 3～5 times.

2. Ear Acupuncture

Prescription: Tonsil, Throat, Lung, Stomach, Large Intestine, Endocrine, Adrenal Gland, Apex of Ear.

Method: Apply filiform needles with strong stimulation and retain the needles for 30 minutes. Apex of Ear may be pricked to cause bleeding.

3. Three-edged Needle

Prescription: Shaoshang (LU 11), Shangyang (LI 1).

Method: Prick the points with a three-edged needle to cause bleeding.

4. Cupping

Prescription: Dazhui (DU 14).

Method: A needle is quickly inserted into Dazhui (DU 14) to a depth of 2~ 3 mm and withdrawn immediately. Then, a piece of soybean or tangerine skin on which a small alcohol cotton ball is placed on the point. The ball is ignited and covered with a jar for cupping and the jar is kept on the point for 10~ 15 minutes. This procedure is repeated twice at one treatment session.

5. Point Injection

Prescription: Yifeng (SJ 17), Hegu (LI 4), Zusanli (ST 36), Quchi (LI 11).

Method: Injection 0.5 mL of vitamin B_1 into each point once a day.

6. Rush-Burning Moxibustion

Prescription: Jiaosun (SJ 20).

Method: A 2 cun long segment of rush pith soaked with vegetable oil is lighted and aimed at Jiaosun (SJ 20) where the hair is cut out. It is removed quickly as soon as there is a sound of burning of the skin.

急性咽炎

急性咽炎为咽黏膜及咽黏膜下淋巴组织的急性炎症。多见于冬春季。临床以咽部干痛，灼热感为主要特点。

1. 体针

处方　少商，合谷，鱼际，列缺，内庭，廉泉。

操作　毫针刺，用泻法。留针15~20 分钟，间歇行针 3~4 次。

2. 耳针

处方　咽喉，肺，胃，内分泌，肾上腺，耳尖。

操作　毫针强刺激，留针 30 分钟。

3. 三棱针

处方　少商，商阳，鱼际。
操作　三棱针点刺出血。

4. 水针

处方　扶突，廉泉。
操作　每穴注射 10% 葡萄糖或维生素 $B_1$0.5 毫升，每天 1 次。

5. 激光疗法

处方　合谷，廉泉。
操作　每穴用氦－氖激光照射10~15 分钟，每天 1 次。

Acute Pharyngitis

Acute pharyngitis, an acute inflammation of the pharyngeal mucous membrane and the submucous lymphoid tissues, occurs mostly in winter and spring. Clinically, it has the following main characteristics: dryness and soreness as well as a sensation of burning in the throat.

1. Body Acupuncture

Prescription: Shaoshang (LU 11), Hegu (LI 4), Yuji (LU 10), Lieque (LU 7), Neiting (ST 44), Lianquan (RN 23).

Method: Apply filiform needles with reducing method. Retain the needles for 15～20 minutes manipulating them 3～4 times.

2. Ear Acupuncture

Prescription: Throat, Lung, Stomach, Endocrine, Adrenal Gland, Apex of Ear.

Method: Apply filiform needles with strong stimulation and retain the needles for 30 minutes.

3. Three-edged Needle

Prescription: Shaoshang (LU 11), Shangyang (LI 1), Yuji (LU 10).

Method: Prick the points with a three-edged needle to cause bleeding.

4. Point Injection

Prescription: Futu (LI 18), Lianquan (RN 23).

Method: Inject 0.5 mL of 10% glucose or vitamin B_1 into each point once a day.

5. Laser Therapy

Prescription: Hegu (LI 4), Lianquan (RN 23).

Method: Radiate the points with He-Ne laser beams for 10～15 minutes once a day.

慢性咽炎

慢性咽炎是咽黏膜及黏膜下淋巴样组织的慢性炎症。本病常由急性咽炎治疗不彻底或反复发作的上呼吸道感染引起，并与高粉尘环境有关。临床表现为咽痒、干痛、咳嗽、咽部异物感、堵闷感等。

1. 体针

外方 列缺，照海，然谷，合谷。

操作 毫针刺，用泻法。留针20～30分钟，间歇行针3～4次。

2. 耳针

处方 咽喉，口，肺，肾，三焦，内分泌，肾上腺，神门。

操作 毫针中等强度刺激，留针30分钟。亦可用耳穴贴敷。

3. 穴位贴敷

处方 涌泉。

操作 以吴茱萸粉醋调敷涌泉穴，每天1次。

Chronic Pharyngitis

Chronic pharyngitis, a chronic inflammation of the pharyngeal mucous membrane and submucous lymphoid tissues, is often caused by incomplete treatment of acute pharyngitis or repeated occurences of upper respiratory tract infection related to high-dust environment. Clinically it manifests itself as itching, dryness, soreness of the throat, cough, a feeling of foreign body or obstruction in the throat.

1. Body Acupuncture

Prescription: Lieque (LU 7), Zhaohai (LI 6), Rangu (KI 2), Hegu (LI 4).

Method: Apply filiform needles with reducing method. Retain the needles for 20～30 minutes manipulating them 3～4 times.

2. Ear Acupuncture

Prescription: Throat, Mouth, Lung, Kidney, Sanjiao, Endocrine, Adrenal Gland, Shenmen.

Method: Apply filiform needles with moderate stimulation and retain the needles for 30 minutes. Auricular taping is also applicable.

3. Compress on the Acupoint

Prescription: Yongquan (KI 1).

Method: Mix powder of Evodia Fruit (Fructus Evodiae) with vinegar for compress on the acupoint Yongquan (KI 1) once a day.

急性喉炎

急性喉炎是喉黏膜的急性炎症。如发于小儿则病情严重（不包括在本节内）。临床特点为声音嘶哑，或有咳嗽、发热，重者可有呼吸困难。本病属中医"暴喑"范畴。

1. 体针

处方　风池，合谷，少商，曲池，列缺。

操作　毫针刺，用泻法。留针30分钟，间歇行针3～4次。

2. 耳针

处方　咽喉，肺，扁桃体，轮1～轮6。

操作　毫针强刺激，留针30分钟。

Acute Laryngitis

Acute laryngitis is an acute inflammation of the laryngeal mucous membranes. If it occurs in infants, the condition will be a severe one (not to be discussed in this section). Its clinical characteristics are hoarseness or cough and fever as well as dyspnea in severe cases. It belongs to the category sudden loss of voice in traditional Chinese medicine.

1. Body Acupuncture

Prescription: Fengchi (GB 20), Hegu (LI 4), Shaoshang (LU 11), Quchi (LI 11), Lieque (LU 7).

Method: Apply filiform needles with

reducing method. Retain the needles for 30 minutes manipulating them 3～4 times.

2. Ear Acupuncture

Prescription: Throat, Lung, Tonsil, Helix 1～6.

Method: Apply filiform needles with strong stimulation and retain the needles for 30 minutes.

慢性喉炎

慢性喉炎是喉黏膜的慢性炎症，可波及黏膜下层及喉内肌，临床以声音不扬、嘶哑、日久不愈为主要特征。本病属中医"久暗"范畴。

1. 体针

处方　列缺，照海，太溪，鱼际，玉液。

操作　毫针刺，平补平泻，留针30分钟，间歇行针3～4次。

2. 耳针

处方　咽喉，肺，皮质下，内分泌。

操作　毫针中等强度刺激，留针30分钟；亦可用耳穴贴敷。

3. 穴位贴敷

处方　涌泉。

操作　以吴茱萸粉醋调敷涌泉穴，每天1次。

Chronic Laryngitis

Chronic laryngitis, a chronic inflam mation of the laryngeal mucous membrane, can involve submucous layer and intralaryngeal muscles. Low voice, hoarseness and long duration are its main clinical manifestations. It belongs to the category of long-time loss of voice in traditional Chinese medicine.

1. Body Acupuncture

Prescription: Lieque (LU 7), Zhaohai (KI 6), Taixi (KI 3), Yuji (LU 10), Yuye (EX-HN 13).

Method: Apply filiform needles with even movement. Retain the needles for 30 minutes manipulating them 3 ～ 4 times.

2. Ear Acupuncture

Prescription: Throat, Lung, Subcortex, Endocrine.

Method: Apply filiform needles with moderate stimulation and retain the needles for 30 minutes. Auricular taping is also applicable.

3. Compress on the Acupoint

Prescription: Yongquan (KI 1).

Method: Mix powder of Evodia Fruit (Fructus Evodiae) with vinegar for compress on the acupoint Yongquan (KI 1) once a day.

咽异感症

咽异感症，或称为癔球症，是咽部的一种功能性病变，可能因自主神经功能系统紊乱、食管和胃肠道刺激性疾病、颈椎病、代谢障碍或内分泌功能紊乱所致。多发于中年女性，表现特点为自觉咽部有肿物或异物阻塞或压迫，在吞咽唾液时出现或感觉明显，吞咽饮食无碍及咽部异物感，肿物既不能被吞下亦不能被咳出。其他症状包括精神抑郁、胸闷、食欲不振、腹胀或反酸。本病属中医"梅核气"范畴。

1. 体针

处方　天突，膻中，行间，丰隆，内关。

配穴　阴虚者加三阴交，太溪，照海；气血两虚者加关元，足三里，膈俞。

操作　毫针刺，平补平泻。留针30分钟，间歇行针3～4次。

2. 耳针

处方　咽喉，食管，肝，胸，三焦，皮质下，神门。

操作　毫针平补平泻，留针30分钟。亦可用耳穴贴敷。

3. 水针

处方　内关，合谷，廉泉。

操作　每穴注射5％葡萄糖或维生素B$_1$0.5～1毫升，隔天1次。

Pharyngeal Paraesthesia

Pharyngeal paraesthesia, also called globus hystericus, is a functional problem of the pharynx, caused by functional disturbance of the autonomic nervous system, irritative disease of the esophagus and gastrointestinal tract, cervical spondylopathy, or disturbance of the metabolism or endocrine system. It occurs mainly in adult females. It is characterized by the subjective sensation of a foreign body or mass stuck in the throat or of the throat being compressed. The sensation occurs or worsens when swallowing saliva but there is no abnormal sensation or difficulty when swallowing food. Additional symptoms may include depression, a feeling of fullness in the chest, poor appetite, abdominal distension, or acid regurgitation. It belongs to the category of plum throat in traditional Chinese medicine.

1. Body Acupuncture

Prescription: Tiantu (RN 22), Tanzhong (RN 17), Xingjian (LR 2), Fenglong (ST 40), Neiguan (PC 6).

Supplementary points: Add Sanyinjiao (SP 6), Taixi (KI 3), and Zhaohai (KI 6) for Yin deficiency, Guanyuan (RN 4), Zusanli (ST 36) and Geshu (BL 17) for deficiency of Qi and blood.

Method: Apply filiform needles with even movement method. Retain the needles for 30 minutes manipulating them 3～4 times.

2. Ear Acupuncture

Prescription: Throat, Esophagus, Liver, Chest, Sanjiao, Subcortex, Shenmen.

Method: Apply filiform needles with moderate stimulation and retain the needles for 30 minutes. Auricular taping is also applicable.

3. Point Injection

Prescription: Neiguan (PC 6), Hegu (LI 4), Lianquan (RN 23).

Method: Inject $0.5 \sim 1$ mL of 5% glucose or vitamin B_1 into each point once every other day.

复发性口腔溃疡

复发性口腔溃疡是种常见的口腔黏膜溃疡性损害。其特点为口腔黏膜反复出现圆形小溃疡，伴疼痛不适。疼痛遇冷、热、酸、甜等刺激时加重，并可影响饮食和睡眠。病情常因失眠、食欲不振或疲劳而加剧或反复发作。本病属于中医"口疮"的范畴。

1. 体针

处方 合谷，足三里，三阴交，地仓，曲池。

操作 毫针刺，平补平泻。留针20分钟，间歇行针2～4次。

2. 耳针

处方 舌，口，心，肝，三焦，内分泌，肾上腺，神门。

操作 毫针中等强度刺激，留针30分钟；亦可采用耳穴贴敷。

3. 水针

处方 牵正，曲池，颊车，手三里。

操作 每穴注射维生素 B_1 0.5毫升，隔天1次。

4. 三棱针

处方 少商，四缝。

操作 三棱针点刺出血。本法适宜于儿童。

5. 穴位贴敷

处方 涌泉。

操作 以吴茱萸粉醋调敷涌泉穴，每天1次。

Recurrent Ulcer of the Mouth

Recurrent ulcer of the mouth is the most commonly seen ulcerative condition of the mucous membrane of the mouth. It is marked by frequently recurring, painful, small, circular or oval ulcers of the mucous membrane of the mouth. The pain is aggravated by exposure of the ulcers to heat, cold, acid, or salt, and may be severe enough to affect diet and sleep. The problem may become more severe or recur more frequently in the presence of insomnia, poor diet, or overstrain. It belongs to the category of ulcer in the mouth in traditional Chinese medicine.

1. Body Acupuncture

Prescription: Hegu (LI 4), Zusanli (ST 36), Sanyinjiao (SP 6), Dicang (ST 4), Quchi (LI 11).

Method: Apply filiform needles with even movement method. Retain the needles for 20 minutes manipulating them 2～4 times.

2. Ear Acupuncture

Prescription: Tongue, Mouth, Heart, Liver, Sanjiao, Endocrine, Adrenal Gland, Shenmen.

Method: Apply filiform needles with moderate stimulation and retain the needles for 30 minutes. Auricular taping is also applicable.

3. Point Injection

Prescription: Qianzheng (EX-HN 16), Quchi (LI 11), Jiache (ST 6), Shousanli (LI 10).

Method: Inject 0.5 mL of vitamin B_1 into each point once every other day.

4. Three-edged Needle

Prescription Shaoshang (LU 11), Sifeng (EX-UE 10).

Method: Prick the points with a three-edged needle to cause bleeding. It is suitable for children.

5. Compress on the Acupoint

Prescription: Yongquan (KI 1).

Method: Mix powder of Evodia Fruit (Fructus Evodiae) with vinegar for compress on the acupoint Yongquan (KI 1) once a day.

牙　痛

牙痛是口腔疾患中常见的症状，发病原因很多，一般多因龋齿引起。牙周炎、冠周炎、急性根尖周围炎等亦引起牙痛。其临床表现为突然发作，持续时间长短不一，遇冷、热、酸、甜等刺激加剧。

1. 体针

处方　合谷，下关，颊车，太阳穴。

配穴　牙痛甚而龈肿，伴形寒身热，加外关，风池，曲池；牙痛甚而伴有口臭、便秘者加内庭，劳宫，二间，三间；牙痛隐隐，牙齿浮动，腰酸，神疲，口不臭者加太溪，行间。

操作　毫针刺，用泻法。留针20～30分钟，间歇行针3～4次。

2. 耳针

处方　颌，牙，口，三焦，肾上腺，内分泌，神门，枕。

操作　毫针强刺激，留针30分钟；亦可采用耳穴贴敷。

3. 水针

处方　下关，合谷。

操作　每穴注射维生素 B_1 1毫升，每天1次。

4. 电针

处方　合谷，下关，颊车，曲

池，太溪。

操作 采用密波治疗 20～30 分钟，每天 1 次。

5. 腕踝针

处方 上 1，上 2。

操作 消毒后，与皮肤呈 30 度角进针，进入皮下后平刺进针 1～1.4 寸，导致患者感到酸、麻、胀、痛后，留针 20～30 分钟，隔天 1 次。

6. 皮肤针

处方 颈椎，耳前区，大、小鱼际。

操作 皮肤针叩刺 20～30 分钟，每天 1 次。

Toothache

Toothache is a common ailment. It is usually due to dental caries. But periodontitis, pericoronitis and acute apical pericementitis may cause it too. In clinic it may occur suddenly lasting for an uncertain time and aggravated by stimulation of cold, heat, sweet or sour material to the tooth.

1. Body Acupuncture

Prescription: Hegu (LI 4), Xiaguan (ST 7), Jiache (ST 6), Taiyang (EX-HN 5).

Supplementary points: Add Waiguan (SJ 5), Fengchi (GB 20) and Quchi (LI 11) for severe toothache with gingival swelling accompanied by chills and fever, Neiting (ST 44), Laogong (PC 8), Erjian (LI 2) and Sanjian (LI 3) for severe toothache accompanied by foul breath and constipation, Taixi (KI 3), Xingjian (LR 2) for dull pain, loose tooth, soreness of waist, listlessness, abscence of foul breath.

Method: Apply filiform needles with reducing method. Retain the needles for 20～30 minutes manipulating them 3～4 times.

2. Ear Acupuncture

Prescription: Jaw, Teeth, Mouth, Sanjiao, Adrenal Gland, Endocrine, Shenmen, Occiput.

Method: Apply filiform needles with strong stimulation and retain the needles for 30 minutes. Auricular taping is also applicable.

3. Point Injection

Prescription: Xiaguan (ST 7), Hegu (LI 4).

Method: Inject 1 mL of vitamine B_1 into each point once a day.

4. Electroacupuncture

Prescription: Hegu (LI 4), Xiaguan (ST 7), Jiache (ST 6), Quchi (LI 11), Taixi (KI 3).

Method: Apply dense wave to the points for 20～30 minutes once a day.

5. Wrist-Ankle Acupuncture

Prescription: Upper 1, Upper 2.

Method: After routine sterilization, insert the needle into the point at an angle of 30° to the skin to the subcutaneous tissues. Then push it horizontally along the skin for 1～1.4 cun causing soreness, numbness, distension and pain to the patient. Then retain the needles at the points for 20～30 minutes once every other day.

6. Plum-blossom Needle

Prescription: Cervical vertebra, area anterior to the ear, large and small thenars.

Method: Tap the areas with a plum blossom needles for 20～30 minutes once a day.

颞下颌关节功能紊乱症

颞下颌关节功能紊乱症是口腔科的常见病症，多发于青壮年，表现特点为颞下颌关节张、闭口时发生疼痛，咀嚼、讲话时及晨起后张口疼痛尤甚。可伴有关节运动障碍及张、闭口时关节发生弹响或杂音。

1. 体针

处方　下关，颊车，合谷，翳风，颧髎。

操作　毫针刺，平补平泻。留针30分钟，间歇行针3～4次。

2. 耳针

处方　颌，面颊，牙，口，胃，大肠，三焦，神门。

操作　毫针中等强度刺激，留针30分钟。亦可采用耳穴贴敷。

Dysfunction of the Temperomandibular Joint

Dysfunction of the tempomandibular joint is a commonly seen oral problem occuring mainly in young people and adults. It is marked by pain in the temperomandibular joint when opening or closing the mouth, usually aggravated by speaking, chewing, or yawning. Articular dyskinesia may also be present with snapping or popping of the joint occuring when opening or closing the mouth.

1. Body Acupuncture

Prescription: Xiaguan (ST 7), Jiache (ST 6), Hegu (LI 4), Yifeng (SJ 17), Quanliao (SI 18).

Method: Apply filiform needles with even movement. Retain the needles for 30 minutes manipulating them 3～4 times.

2. Ear Acupuncture

Prescription: Jaw, Cheek, Teeth, Mouth, Stomach, Large Intestine, Sanjiao, Shenmen.

Method: Apply filiform needles with moderate stimulation and retain the needles for 30 minutes. Auricular taping is also applicable.

附　参考文献

1. 王一方，黄一九编．针灸气功经穴图谱．长沙：湖南科学技术出版社，1992

2. 严洁．图解中国针灸技法．长沙：湖南科学技术出版社，1992

3. 谢金华，符文彬，叶苇编著．汉英针灸治疗手册．南昌：江西科学技术出版社，1994

4. 欧明主编．汉英中医辞典．广州：广东科学技术出版社，1986

5. 吕建平，崔衍亮，史仁华编著．中国针灸．上海：上海中医学院出版社，1990

6. 许小平，陈超，张利编著．汉英对照针灸手册．北京：中国医药科技出版社

7. 姚勇主编．英汉对照简明中医学．上海：上海中医学院出版社，1993

8. 刘玉檀，俞昌正主编．针灸治疗学．北京：高等教育出版社，1991

9. 冯春祥，白兴华，杜雁编著．中国耳穴疗法．北京：科学技术文献出版社

10. 孔昭遐，屠佑生著，蔡郁，朱同生译．实用针灸学（英汉对照）．合肥：安徽科学技术出版社，1993

11. 张恩勤主编．中医临床各科（上册）．上海：上海中医药大学出版社，1990

12. 张恩勤主编．中医临床各科（下册）．上海：上海中医学院出版社，1990

13. 罗永芬主编．腧穴学．上海：上海科学技术出版社，1996

14. 王德深．针灸穴名国际标准化手册（中英对照）．北京：人民卫生出版社，1988

15. 杨长林主编．针灸治疗学．上海：上海科学技术出版社，1985

16. 上海针灸杂志编辑部编．针灸临床经验选．上海：上海中医学院出版社，1993

17. 张心曙．腕踝针．上海：上海科学技术出版社，1983

18. 焦顺发．头针．太原：山西人民出版社，1982

19. 刘冠军．针灸学．长沙：湖南科学技术出版社，1987

20. 杨占林．针刺事故预防．太原：山西科学技术出版社，1987

21. 钟梅泉．中国梅花针．北京：人民卫生出版社，1984

22. 李仲愚著．杵针治疗学．成都：四川科学技术出版社，1990

23. 封进启主编．足部反射区保建按摩．天津：天津科技翻译出版公司，1992

24. 刘冠军主编．中医针法集锦．南昌：江西科学技术出版社，1988

25. 肖少卿．中国针灸处方学．银川：宁夏人民卫生出版社，1986

26. 邱茂良主编．针灸学．上海：上

海科学技术出版社，1985

27. 帅学忠. 针灸学辞典. 长沙：湖南科学技术出版社，1997

28. 朱振华. 手针新疗法. 北京：人民军医出版社，1990

29. 彭静山. 眼针疗法. 沈阳：辽宁科学技术出版社，1990

30. 彭静山. 针灸秘验. 沈阳：辽宁科学技术出版社，1985

31. 乔志恒编著. 简易物理疗法. 北京：人民卫生出版社，1982

32. 曲祖诒编著. 中医简易外治法（修订本）. 北京：人民卫生出版社，1981

33. 于璟玲编著. 特种针具疗法. 北京：中医古籍出版社，1994

34. 张恩勤主编. 中国推拿. 上海：上海中医学院出版社，1990

35. 张恩勤主编. 中国针灸. 上海：上海中医学院出版社，1990

36. 魏遒杰. 英汉汉英中医词典. 长沙：湖南科学技术出版社，1995

37. 针灸学概要编辑小组. 中国针灸学概要. 北京：人民卫生出版社，1964

38. 王雪苔主编. 中国针灸大全. 郑州：河南科学技术出版社，1988

39. 陆寿康. 针刺手法一百种. 北京：中国医药科技出版社，1988

40. 赵振国. 指针疗法. 黑龙江人民出版社，1983

Appendix Bibliography

1. Wang Yifang, Huang Yijiu. Illustration of Channels and Points for Acupuncture and Moxibustion and Qigong (English-Chinese Edition). Changsha: Hunan Science and Technology Press, 1992

2. Yan Jie. Skill with Illustrations of Chinese Acupuncture and Moxibustion. Changsha: Hunan Science and Technology Press, 1992

3. Xie Jinhua, Fu Wenbin, Ye Wei. A Chinese-English Handbook of Acupuncture and Moxibustion. Nanchang: Jiangxi Science and Technology Press, 1994

4. Ou Ming. Chinese-English Dictionary of Traditional Chinese Medicine. Guangzhou: Guangdong Science and Technology Press, 1986

5. Lu Jianping, Cui Yanliang, Shi Renhua. Chinese Acupuncture and Moxibustion. Shanghai: Publishing House of Shanghai College of Traditional Chinese Medicine, 1990

6. Xu Xiaoping, Chen Chao, Zhang Li. A Chinese-English Acupuncture Manual. Beijing: Chinese Medical Science and Technology Press, 1990

7. Yao Yong. English-Chinese Concise Traditional Chinese Medicine. Shanghai: Publishing House of

Shanghai College of Traditional Chinese Medicine, 1993

8. Liu Yutan, Yu Chang zhen. Therapeutics of Acupuncture and Moxibustion. Beijing: Higher Education Press, 1991

9. Feng Chunxiang, Bai Xinghua, Du Yan. Chinese Auricular Therapy. Beijing: Scientific and Technical Documents Publishing House, 1994

10. Kong Zhaoxia, Tu Yousheng. A Practical Course of Acupuncture and Moxibustion. Hefei: Anhui Publishing House of Science and Technology, 1993

11. Zhang Enqin. Clinic of Traditional Chinese Medicine (1). Shanghai: Publishing House of Shanghai University of Traditional Chinese Medicine, 1990

12. Zhang Enqin. Clinic of Traditional Chinese Medicine (Ⅱ). Shanghai: Publishing House of Shanghai College of Traditional Chinese Medicine, 1990

13. Luo Yongfen. Science of Acupoints. Shanghai: Shanghai Science and Technology Press, 1996

14. Wang Deshen. Manual of International Standardization of Acupuncture (Zhenjiu) Point Names. Beijing: People's Medical Publishing House, 1988

15. Yang Changsen. Therapeutics of Acupuncture and Moxibustion. Shanghai: Shanghai Science and Technology Press, 1985

16. The Editorial Office of Shanghai Journal of Acupuncture. Selections from Clinical Experiences of Acupuncture. Shanghai: Publishing House of Shanghai College Traditional Chinese Medicine, 1993

17. Zhang Xinshu. Wrist-Ankle Acupuncture. Shanghai: Shanghai Science and Technology Press, 1983

18. Jiao Shunfa. Scalp Acupuncture. Taiyuan: Shanxi People's Publishing House, 1982

19. Liu Guanjun. Science of Acupuncture and Moxibustion. Changsha: Hunan Science and Technology Press, 1987

20. Yang Zhanlin. Prevention of Acupuncture Accidents. Taiyuan: Shanxi Science and Technology Press, 1987

21. Zhong Meiquan. Chinese Blossom Needling. Beijing: People's Medical Publishing House, 1984

22. Li Zhongyu. Therapeutic Methods of Pestle Acupuncture. Chengdu: Sichuan Science and Technology Press, 1990

23. Feng Jinqi. Foot Reflexology. Tianjin: Tianjin Science and Technology Press, 1992

24. Liu Guanjun. The Collection of Acupuncture Techniques. Nanchang: Jiangxi Science and Technology Press, 1988

25. Xiao Shaoqin. Chinese Acupuncture and Moxibustion Prescriptions. Yinchuan: Ningxia People's Health Press, 1986

26. Qiu Maolian eds. Acupuncture and Moxibustion. Shanghai: Shanghai Science and Technology Press, 1985

27. Shuai Xuezhong. Dictionary of Acupuncture and Moxibustion. Changsha: Hunan Science and Technology Press, 1997

28. Zhu Zhenhua. New Technique of Hand Acupoint Beijing: People's Army Medical Press, 1990

29. Peng Jingshan. The Eye Acupuncture. Shenyang: Liaoning Science and Technology Press, 1990

30. Peng Jingshan. The Secret Experience in Acupuncture and Moxibustion. Shengyang: Liaoning Science and Technology Press, 1985

31. Qiao Zhihong. Simple and Easy Physiotherapy. Beijing: People's Medical Publishing House, 1982

32. Qu Zuyi. Simple and Easy External Treatment of Traditional Chinese Medicine. Beijing: People's Medical Publishing House, 1981

33. Yu Jingling. Therapeutic Methods of Special Needles. Beijing: Ancient Traditional Chinese Medical Literature Press, 1994

34. Zhang Enqin. Chinese Massage. Shanghai: Publishing House of Shanghai College of Traditional Chinese Medicine, 1990

35. Zhang Enqin. Chinese Acupuncture and Moxibustion. Shanghai: Publishing House of Shanghai College of Traditional Chinese Medicine, 1990

36. Nigel Wiseman. English-Chinese, Chinese-English Dictionary of Chinese Medicine. Changsha: Hunan Science and Technology Press, 1995

37. Editorial Group of Essential of Acupuncture. Essential of Chinese Medicine. Beijing: People's Medical Publishing House, 1964

38. Wang Xuetai. Complete Works of Chinese Acupuncture and Moxibustion. Zhengzhou: Henan Science and Technology Press, 1988

39. Lu Shoukang. One Hundred Techniques of Acupuncture. Beijing: Chinese Medical Science and Technology Publishing House, 1988

40. Zhao Zhenguo. Therapeutic Methods of Acupressure. Haerbin: Heilongjiang People's Publishing House, 1983